13 March.

THE ROUGH GUIDE TO
SICILY

This eleventh
Ros Belfo

C016925544

ROUGH
GUIDES

Contents

INTRODUCTION   4

Where to go	8	Things not to miss	12
When to go	10	Tailor-made trips	20
Author picks	11		

BASICS   22

Getting there	23	Festivals	35
Getting around	25	Sports and outdoor activities	37
Accommodation	28	Culture and etiquette	38
Food and drink	31	Shopping	39
The media	34	Travel essentials	39

THE GUIDE   44

1 Palermo and around	45	6 Siracusa and the southeast	207
2 Cefalù and the Monti Madonie	87	7 Enna and the interior	251
3 The Aeolian Islands	115	8 Agrigento and the southwest	275
4 Messina, Taormina and the northeast	153	9 Trapani and the west	303
5 Catania, Etna and around	181		

CONTEXTS   358

History	359	Books	381
The Mafia in Sicily	372	Films	384
Sicilian Baroque	377	Italian	385

SMALL PRINT AND INDEX   394

Introduction to
Sicily

To say that Sicily isn't Italy is trite but true – only 3km of water separate the island of Sicily from the Italian mainland, but the historical and cultural gulf is far wider, and locals see themselves as Sicilians first and Italians second. Strategically located at the heart of the Mediterranean, the island's history is distinct from that of peninsular Italy, and some of the western world's greatest civilizations have left their mark, from ancient Greek temples and Arabic street plans to stunning Norman mosaicked cathedrals and flamboyant Spanish Baroque palaces. Sicilian dialects thrive, while many place names are derived from the Arabic that was once in wide use across the island. Markets brim with produce that speaks firmly of the south – oranges, lemons, olives, rice, almonds and peppers – and ice cream can still be found flavoured with rose and jasmine petals, a sure sign of the island's North African roots.

Moreover, the historic combination of island mentality and a wild, lawless, **mountainous interior** has fostered an "us-and-them" attitude that still defines the relationship between modern-day Sicily and Italy. The **island** was probably the most reluctantly unified of all Italian regions back in the nineteenth century, with Sicilians unsurprisingly suspicious of the intentions of the latest in a long line of rulers – Phoenicians, Greeks, Romans, Arabs, Normans, Angevins and Spanish. For many Sicilians, their place in the modern Italian state is illustrated every time they look at a map to see the island being kicked by the big boot of Italy – the perpetual football.

And Sicilians do have a point. Pockets of the island have been disfigured by bleak construction projects and unsightly industry, and despite Sicily's limited political autonomy, little has really been done to tackle the more deep-rooted problems: youth unemployment is at an all-time high, emigration of the brightest is on the rise, poverty is seemingly endemic, and there's an almost feudal attitude to business and commerce. Aid and investment pour in, but much is still siphoned off by the **Mafia**, while the

FACT FILE

- Sicily is the largest island in the Mediterranean, with extensive areas of **mountains** in the north and east, the highest being Mount Etna (3323m) – Europe's biggest active volcano. Apart from Etna's sporadic eruptions, Sicily is also prone to seismic upheavals – massive **earthquakes** destroyed the southeast from Catania to Ragusa in 1693, flattened Messina in 1908, and rocked the western part of the island in 1968.
- Sicily has a semi-autonomous status within the Italian republic, with its own **parliament** and **president**, and limited legislative powers in such areas as tourism, transport, industry and the environment. There is no **separatist movement** to speak of.
- Disregard for **regulations** long accepted in the rest of Europe is rife in Sicily, and this anarchic approach to the law manifests in myriad ways. Thanks to the local distaste for wearing **seat belts**, many garages stock a device designed to override car safety systems and save drivers the irritation of bleeping belt alerts.
- One of the most densely populated islands in the Mediterranean, Sicily's **population** is something over five million, with settlement mainly concentrated in the two cities of Palermo and Catania, on the northern and eastern coasts.
- Compared to north Italy, the **economy** has remained relatively underdeveloped. Though there are pockets of industrial activity, Sicily is mainly **agricultural**. However, the sector has suffered considerable setbacks over recent years, while local fishermen struggle with quota restrictions and competition from international mega-boats that hoover up vast shoals of tuna. These days, **tourism** plays an increasingly crucial role in the Sicilian economy.

daily arrivals during the summer months of refugees from Africa not only underline Sicily's proximity to that continent but also its vulnerability. Visitors, of course, see little of this. Mafia activity, for example – almost a byword for Sicilian life when viewed from abroad – is usually an in-house affair, with little or no consequence for travellers.

What Sicily does offer is a remarkably fresh **Mediterranean** experience. Its main resorts and famous archeological sites have attracted visitors for many years, but budget airline routes have opened up lesser-known parts of this fascinating island, while boutique accommodation and sustainable tourism projects have mushroomed in recent years. The rewards are immediate, notably the dramatic landscapes that range from pin-prick outlying islands to the volcanic heights of **Mount Etna**. Much of the island is underpopulated and, outside the few tourist zones, crowds are rare – which means plenty of opportunity to make your own personal discoveries: dazzling white- and black-sand **beaches**, sparkling coves, rolling wheat plains, upland wild-flower meadows and precarious mountain passes. Sicily was an important power base during Greek and Roman times, and its excavated **ancient cities** and temples especially are superb, standing comparison with any ruins in Greece itself. There are exquisite Arab-Norman palaces such as the Palazzo dei Normanni, as well as impressive churches and castles across the island, while the devastation wrought by the great earthquake of 1693 provided a blank slate for the building of some of the most harmonious **Baroque architecture** to be found in Europe, best seen in Noto, Ragusa and the Val di Noto.

Perhaps above all, there's a distinct way of day-to-day living that separates Sicily from the rest of Italy – an almost operatic exuberance that manifests itself in some

ICE CREAM

Eating a genuine Sicilian **ice cream** is one of the world's most indulgent gastronomic experiences, a melt-in-the-mouth sensation that suffuses your taste buds with the unadulterated essence of mandarin, almond, rose or whichever locally grown fruit, nut or flower the *gelataio* has decided is at its prime.

The art of ice-cream-making is around a thousand years old here – the **Arabs** brought with them the technique of making sherbet or *sharbat* by blending fruit syrups and flower essences with **snow** taken from Mount Etna and other mountains. It seems probable that it was a resourceful Sicilian who got the idea of making a good thing better, freezing a mixture of milk, sugar or honey, and fruit. By the sixteenth century, ices were all the rage at the trendsetting French court of Catherine de' Medici, who imported a Sicilian into her kitchen with the sole job of making ice creams, *granite* and sorbets.

The popularity of ices continued to grow and, in the eighteenth century, virtually the entire revenue of the Bishop of Catania came from selling the snow of Mount Etna – you can still visit caves used for ice storage on Etna. Years when snowfall was scant or non-existent provoked **civil unrest** during the steamy summers: in 1777 a boat rumoured to be carrying snow was attacked and its precious cargo seized by Siracusans desperate for ice cream.

Ices and ice creams were loved by rich and poor alike: at a banquet in eighteenth-century Palermo, 5000kg of snow were needed to keep the three hundred guests in constant supply of frozen refreshment, while at the other end of the scale, **street vendors** throughout the island ensured that ice cream could be enjoyed by all but the very poorest, selling it by the spoonful to those who could afford no more.

extraordinarily colourful **festivals** and celebrations. You're unlikely to forget the intensity of the Sicilian experience, whether you're shopping for swordfish in a raucous souk-like **market**, catching a concert in a dramatic open-air Greek theatre, bathing in a hidden hot spring, or island-hopping by hydrofoil across azure seas.

Where to go

Set in a wide bay at the foot of a fertile valley, the capital, **Palermo**, is an essential part of any Sicilian visit, with a vibrant, almost Middle Eastern, flavour, and featuring some of the island's finest churches, historic treasures, markets and restaurants. It gets hot and stuffy here in summer, though, which makes escapes out of the city all the more tempting, above all to the offshore island of **Ustica**, or to the extraordinary church mosaics at **Monreale**. An hour east of Palermo, meanwhile, lies one of Sicily's premier resorts, **Cefalù**, with its own fabulous church mosaics. Cefalù is also the jumping-off point for the Parco Regionale delle Madonie, whose mountains are the highest on the island after Etna.

Ferries and hydrofoils depart from Milazzo and Messina to the **Aeolians**, an enchanting chain of seven volcanic islands – including the famed Stromboli – that attract sun-worshippers, celebrities and adventurous hikers alike. Otherwise, the northeastern tip of the island is marked by the bustling city of **Messina** – crossing-point to mainland Italy – with the fashionable resort of **Taormina** to the south, the latter perhaps the single most popular holiday destination in Sicily. Further south, halfway down the Ionian coast, is dark, Baroque **Catania**, the island's second city, dominated entirely by the graceful cone of **Mount Etna**, Europe's largest and most active volcano.

The island's best concentration of historical and architectural sites is arguably in **Siracusa**, where classical ruins and stunning Baroque buildings decorate Sicily's most attractive city. In the southeast region beyond, beautiful towns like **Noto**, **Ragusa** and **Modica** were rebuilt along planned Baroque lines after the devastating 1693 earthquake, though the unique Neolithic cemeteries of **Pantalica** survived to provide one of Sicily's most atmospheric backwaters.

After the richness of the southeast towns, many find the isolated grandeur of the interior a welcome change. This is the most sparsely populated region, of rolling hills

CATACOMBS, CAVES AND HOLES IN THE GROUND

Sicily is home to some of the world's creepiest tourist destinations, in the form of its **catacombs** and **caves**, used as burial places for thousands of years and accessible to anyone with a torch and a strong nerve. The oldest, the rock-cut tombs of the great necropolis at **Pantalica**, were first used in the thirteenth century BC. Another huge swathe of tombs is on view below the Greek temples at **Agrigento**, while catacombs riddle the ground in the city of **Siracusa**. But for sheer hands-in-the-air horror, there's no beating the infamous preserved bodies that line the catacombs of Palermo's **Convento dei Cappuccini**. Bodies were placed here as late as the nineteenth century, and the locals used to pay daily visits, often standing in the adjacent niches to accustom themselves to the idea of the great ever-after.

and craggy mountains, yet it hides gems like the historic stronghold of **Enna**, the well-preserved Roman mosaics at **Piazza Armerina**, the majestic Greek excavations of **Morgantina** and the Baroque ceramics town of **Caltagirone**. Away from these few interior towns, remote roads wind back and forth, towards Palermo or Catania, through little-visited destinations like **Corleone**, whose names chime with the popular image of Sicily as a nest of Mafia intrigue.

Along the south coast, only the spectacular ancient temples of **Agrigento** and the Greek city and beach at **Eraclea Minoa** attract visitors in any numbers. Further around the coast, the up-and-coming city of **Trapani** anchors the west of the island, a great base for anyone interested in delving into the very different character of this side of Sicily. The Arabic influence is stronger here than elsewhere, especially in **Marsala** and **Mazara del Vallo**, while **Selinunte** and **Segesta** hold the island's most romantic sets of ancient ruins. It's from ports on the south and west coasts, too, that Sicily's most absorbing outlying islands are reached. On **Lampedusa**, on the **Egadi Islands** and, above all, on distant **Pantelleria**, the sea is as clean as you'll find anywhere in the Mediterranean, and you are floating on the cusp of Europe.

When to go

Sicily can be an extremely uncomfortable place to visit at the height of summer, when the dusty *scirocco* winds blow in from North Africa. In **July** and **August**, you'll roast – and you'll be in the company of tens of thousands of other tourists all jostling for space on the beaches, in the restaurants and at the archeological sites. Hotel availability is much reduced and prices will often be higher. If you want the heat but not the crowds, go in May, June or September – swimming is possible right into November.

Spring is really the optimum time to come to Sicily, and it arrives early: the almond blossom flowers at the start of February, and there are fresh strawberries in April. **Easter** is a major celebration and a good time to see traditional festivals like the events at Trapani, Erice, Scicli and Piana degli Albanesi, though again they'll all be over-subscribed with visitors.

Winter is mild by northern European standards and is a nice time to be here, at least on the coast, where the skies stay clear and life continues to be lived largely outdoors. On the other hand, the interior – especially around Enna – is very liable to get snowed under, providing skiing opportunities in the Monti Madonie or on Mount Etna, while anywhere else in the interior can be subject to blasts of wind and torrential downpours of rain.

AVERAGE MONTHLY TEMPERATURES AND RAINFALL

	Jan	Feb	Mar	Apr	May	Jun	Jul	Aug	Sep	Oct	Nov	Dec
TEMPERATURE												
max/min (°C)	14/10	15/10	16/10	18/12	21/16	25/19	28/22	28/23	26/21	22/17	19/14	16/11
RAINFALL												
mm		66	44	34	35	14	10	10	17	28	48	67	79

Author picks

Our updater, Ros Belford, has lived on Salina and explored every corner of Sicily over several decades. Here, she shares some of her top tips, favourite sights, undiscovered places and quintessential Sicilian experiences.

Unspoiled beaches Head for the wild sands of the nature reserves at Vendicari (see page 238), Marinello (see page 109) or Zingaro (see page 310), or to the long dune-fringed strands at Sampieri (see page 249) and Torre Salsa (see page 288).

Ancient places When the Greeks ruled Sicily it was the most powerful centre in the Mediterranean. Outstanding among relics from this time are the Valley of the Temples at Agrigento (see page 280), the temples of Segesta (see page 312) and Selinunte (see page 341), and the theatres of Siracusa (see page 208), Palazzolo Acreide (see page 229), Tyndaris (see page 109) and Taormina (see page 166).

Hot, hot, hot Sicily is crossed by a fault line, and has three active volcanoes – Etna (see page 198), Stromboli (see page 142) and Vulcano (see page 130). As well as visible eruptions – most reliably and regularly on Stromboli – there are other vulcanological phenomena too, from the steaming mud baths of Vulcano to emissions of underwater gases off the island of Panarea (see page 139).

Baroque and roll Sicilian Baroque reaches heights of exuberance not seen elsewhere in Italy, from the lava-stone and limestone facades of Catania (see page 182) and the palaces of Ortigia (see page 213) to the flamboyant towns of Noto (see page 233), Modica (see page 240), Scicli (see page 243) and Ragusa (see page 244).

Away from it all Come to Sicily out of season – late autumn, winter or spring – and head to the Egadi (see page 325), Aeolian (see page 116) or Pelagie (see page 294) islands for guaranteed solitude. Or find peace inland, exploring the Madonie (see page 97) or Nebrodi mountains (see page 106) or the Pantalica gorge (see page 228).

Our author recommendations don't end here. We've flagged up our favourite places – a perfectly sited hotel, an atmospheric café, a special restaurant – throughout the Guide, highlighted with the ★ symbol.

TEMPLE RUINS AT SELINUNTE

VULVANO, ONE OF THE AEOLIAN ISLANDS

20

things not to miss

It's not possible to see everything Sicily has to offer in one trip – and we don't suggest you try. What follows is a selective taste of the island's highlights – extravagant architecture, dramatic landscapes, idyllic islands and thrilling outdoor adventures. All highlights are colour-coded by chapter and have a page reference to take you straight into the Guide, where you can find out more.

1

1 MOUNT ETNA
See page 198
Climbing Europe's greatest
volcano – still very active
– is the ultimate Sicilian
adventure trip.

2 SIRACUSA
See page 208
As well as the ruins of a
magnificent ancient Greek
city, Siracusa has a Baroque
centre with plenty of places
to sit and relax.

3 SEGESTA
See page 312
Transport yourself back
in time with a visit to the
dramatic Greek temple
at Segesta.

4 EGADI ISLANDS
See page 325
The three west-coast Egadi
Islands retain a real air
of excitement, offering
boat tours, fishing trips
and excursions.

5 MONREALE
See page 74
The Duomo's delicate
cloister columns are
immaculate examples of
medieval craftsmanship.

6 VILLA ROMANA DEL CASALE
See page 264
Brightly coloured and intricate, these mosaics are unrivalled in the Roman world.

7 VALLE DEI TEMPLI, AGRIGENTO
See page 280
A stunning series of ancient Greek temples, beautifully lit up at night.

8 RISERVA NATURALE DELLO ZINGARO
See page 310
This charming nature reserve offers great walks and spectacular marine scenery.

9 LINOSA
See page 301
Get away from it all at this remote and tiny island.

10 PESCHERIA, CATANIA
See page 187
The city's vibrant fish market lives up to its top reputation.

11 CEFALÙ
See page 88
With a fabulous sandy beach and an alluring historic centre, Cefalù has it all.

12 THE AEOLIAN ISLANDS
See page 116
Go island-hopping, Sicilian-style – each of the seven Aeolians has a distinct flavour of its own.

13 SAMPIERI
See page 249
A tremendous sandy beach perfect for long strolls or swims.

14 TEATRO GRECO, TAORMINA
See page 170
Fantastically located, this ancient theatre is still in use and offers panoramic views towards Etna and down to the sea.

15 RAGUSA IBLA
See page 245
With its perfectly restored tangle of streets and some excellent restaurants and hotels, Ragusa Ibla is one of Sicily's most engaging destinations.

11

12

13

14

15

16 CAVA GRANDE DEL FIUME CASSIBILE
See page 238
Sicily's magnificent cave-riddled canyon has wonderful walks, breathtaking views and natural swimming pools for cooling off.

17 MONTI MADONIE
See page 97
The Madonie mountains offer brilliant walks, drives and views.

18 NOTO
See page 233
This totally Baroque town boasts some of Sicily's most exuberant examples of the style.

19 MONTALBANO TOUR
See page 289
Take a self-guided tour of the sites that inspired the late Andrea Camilleri's best-selling series of detective novels featuring Inspector Montalbano.

20 SCICLI
See page 243
This most alluring of UNESCO-listed Baroque towns, not only has flamboyant architecture and an ancient quarter of cave-houses, but a prestigious contemporary art scene and bags of Sicilian charm.

17

18

19

20

Tailor-made trips

These itineraries are designed to give you a taste of Sicily's manifold attractions. Our Grand Tour takes in unmissable historic towns, ancient sites and natural attractions; we've also picked out the most outstanding gastronomic experiences and the best destinations for a taste of adventure. The trips below give a flavour of what the island has to offer and what we can plan and book for you at www.roughguides.com/trips.

THE GRAND TOUR

Follow in the footsteps of illustrious travellers such as D.H. Lawrence, Jules Verne and Goethe and make a three-week Grand Tour of the island's highlights.

❶ Palermo See the glories left behind by Norman rulers, such as the vibrant mosaics of the Cappella Palatina, then visit the Galleria Regionale della Sicilia for its collection of medieval art, and head to Monreale to marvel at the mosaics in its Duomo. See page 46

❷ Cefalù Feast your eyes on exquisite mosaics in the town's cathedral, before relaxing on one of Sicily's finest sandy beaches. See page 88

❸ The Aeolian Islands Climb Stromboli, Europe's most active volcano, then wind down on the island's picture-perfect village of sparkling-white cubic houses awash with bougainvillea. See page 116

❹ Taormina Spoil yourself with a night in one of the town's many historic hotels, and take a day-trip by jeep up Mount Etna. See page 166

❺ Siracusa Spend a couple of days in historic Ortigia, enjoying masterpieces by Caravaggio and an ancient Greek temple converted into a cathedral. Devote another day to the Archeological Museum and Greek theatre. See page 208

❻ Piazza Armerina Stay the night to linger over the extensive ruins of a Roman villa, decorated with splendid mosaics. See page 262

❼ Agrigento Spend a day exploring the Valley of the Temples, including the site museum's collection of Greek black-figure pottery. Fans of crime writer Andrea Camilleri should add an extra day to see the Porto Empedocle and Agrigento locations that inspired the Montalbano novels. See page 276

❽ Ragusa Ibla Spend a day or two admiring some of Sicily's finest Baroque architecture, then splash out on a gourmet dinner before flying home from nearby Comiso. See page 245

FOODIES' SICILY

While this itinerary is really intended for inspiration, it could be done nicely in ten days, or a week if you miss out the Aeolians.

You can book these trips with Rough Guides, or we can help you create your own. Whether you're after adventure or a family-friendly holiday, we have a trip for you, with all the activities you enjoy doing and the sights you want to see. All our trips are devised by local experts who get the most out of the destination. Visit **www.roughguides.com/trips** to chat with one of our travel agents.

❶ Palermo Graze on local street food such as soft rolls stuffed with chickpea-flour fritters, or sautéed offal with ricotta and caciocavallo cheese. See page 46

❷ The Aeolian Islands Head to the island of Salina to taste malvasia wine in local *cantinas*, discover myriad uses for the bud of the caper flower, and sample what may well be the best *granitas* in Sicily. See page 116

❸ Catania Drink a fizzy seltz, made with lemon and salt or sweet fruit syrup, and sold from kiosks throughout the city centre, then visit the best fish market on the island. See page 182

❹ Etna Tour Etna's vineyards and look out for stalls selling tiny apples and pears, hazelnuts, chestnuts and Sicily's famous almonds and oranges, grown in the volcanic soil of the plains below. See page 198

❺ Bronte This town in the foothills of Etna produces the best pistachios on the island. See page 205

❻ Noto The two outstanding *gelaterias* here are famous throughout Italy – skip lunch and sample delectable cones of saffron and basil, dark chocolate and orange, or the classic jasmine or rose petal. See page 233

❼ Modica Made using a technique developed by the Aztecs and introduced to Sicily by the Spanish, Modica's chocolate is powerful, gritty-

textured stuff, and comes in flavours ranging from chilli to vanilla. See page 240

SICILY OUTDOORS

Sicily offers plenty of scope for outdoor adventures. Depending on the amount of time you have, choose a combination of destinations from this tour for an all-action trip.

❶ Ustica Dive the fabulous waters around the island of Ustica to see a submarine wonderland of plants, fish and fabulous rock formations. See page 82

❷ The Aeolian Islands Climb the active volcanoes or dive over shipwrecks and through bubbles made by emissions of volcanic gas. See page 116

❸ Mount Etna See Mount Etna by quad-bike in summer, or go cross-country or downhill skiing in the winter. See page 198

❹ Gole dell'Alcantara Wade up the river that gouges between the dramatic volcanic rocks of the Alcantara Gorge. See page 177

❺ Cava Grande Trek along this marvellous gorge to discover cave-habitations, rushing streams, swimmable pools and fabulous views. See page 238

❻ Vendicari Nature Reserve Take a hike in spring or autumn, when the salt lakes attract migratory birds such as flamingos. See page 238

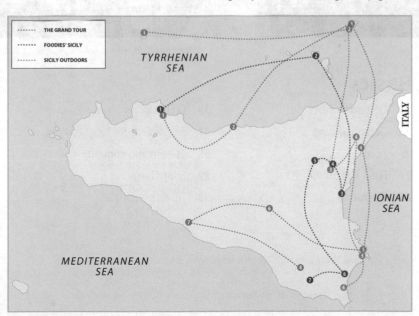

EASTER PROCESSION IN FERLA

Basics

23 Getting there

25 Getting around

28 Accommodation

31 Food and drink

34 The media

35 Festivals

37 Sports and outdoor activities

38 Culture and etiquette

39 Shopping

39 Travel essentials

Getting there

Sicily has two main airports, at Palermo in the west and Catania in the east, two smaller airports at Comiso and Trapani, and tiny domestic airports on the islands of Pantelleria and Lampedusa. There are direct flights daily to Palermo and Catania from the UK, and seasonal flights to Comiso. Catania and Palermo are well connected with many mainland Italian cities and major European hubs; Trapani and Comiso also have flights to several Italian and European destinations. There are regular flights to Lampedusa and Pantelleria from Palermo, Trapani and many Italian mainland airports. If you are travelling from the USA, Canada, Australia, New Zealand you will need to change flights at Milan, Rome or elsewhere in Europe.

If you want to see some of France or Italy en route, or are taking a vehicle, various overland combinations of **ferry**, **rail** and **road** are possible, though these will nearly always work out pricier than flying direct. European rail passes will save you some money. Finally, **package holidays** and **tours** can still be good value – from beach breaks to escorted historical or walking tours – especially if the idea of spending hours on the internet booking flights, cars and hotels is not your idea of fun.

Air fares are at their highest when demand is greatest – at Easter, Christmas and New Year, and between June and August (when the weather is hottest and the island at its busiest). UK school half term holidays also see prices rise. The **cheapest flights** from the UK and Europe are usually with budget airlines. The cheapest tickets usually have fixed dates and are non-changeable and non-refundable. Major **scheduled airlines** are usually (though not always) more expensive, so it is always worth checking on a price-comparison site.

Entry requirements

EU citizens can enter Sicily and stay as long as they like on production of a valid **passport**. Citizens of the United States, Canada, Australia and New Zealand don't need a visa, but are limited to stays of three months. Most other nationals will have to apply for a visa from an Italian embassy or consulate. Post-Brexit, UK citizens should check for any new regulations.

Legally, you're required to register with the police within eight days of entering Italy, though if you're staying at a hotel this will be done for you. Although the police in some towns have become more punctilious about this, most would still be amazed at any attempt to register yourself down at the local police station while on holiday.

ITALIAN EMBASSIES ABROAD

Australia ☎ 02 6273 3333, ⓦ ambcanberra.esteri.it
Canada ☎ 613 232 2401, ⓦ ambottawa.esteri.it
Republic of Ireland ☎ 01 660 1744, ⓦ www.ambdublino.esteri.it
New Zealand ☎ 04 473 5339, ⓦ ambwellington.esteri.it
UK ☎ 020 7312 2200, ⓦ amblondra.esteri.it
USA ☎ 202 612 4400, ⓦ ambwashingtondc.esteri.it

Flights from the UK and Ireland

There are several direct flights daily from London airports to Palermo and Catania. BA (ⓦ ba.com) flies direct to Palermo from Heathrow at least twice a week year round and to Catania from Gatwick during the summer, Alitalia routes via Rome or Milan. **From Ireland**, Ryanair (ⓦ ryanair.com) offers a direct flight from Dublin to Palermo once or twice a week depending on the time of year. **Prices** on all routes can fluctuate enormously – as usual, it's best to book well in advance for the cheapest flights, especially if you're travelling in peak seasons or during UK school holidays.

The alternative from the UK or Ireland is to fly to one of the many airports on the **Italian mainland**, and travel onwards from there. There are also flights to Sicily with the budget airlines of other countries (particularly Germany). In the end, you'll have to weigh up the extra travelling time flying via mainland Italy, or elsewhere, with the savings you might make.

Flights from the US and Canada

Alitalia (ⓦ alitalia.com) flies direct every day between the US or Canada and Italy, and their great advantage

---

A BETTER KIND OF TRAVEL

At Rough Guides we are passionately committed to travel. We believe it helps us understand the world we live in and the people we share it with – and of course tourism is vital to many developing economies. But the scale of modern tourism has also damaged some places irreparably, and climate change is accelerated by most forms of transport, especially flying. We encourage our authors to consider the carbon footprint of the journeys they make in the course of researching our guides.

is the ease of making the connecting flight to Sicily with the same airline. But several other airlines – including Delta (Ⓦdelta.com) and Air Canada (Ⓦaircanada.com) – fly to Rome or Milan, and can arrange an onward connection for you. Or you can fly to Italy with airlines like British Airways (Ⓦba.com), Air France (Ⓦairfrance.com), Lufthansa (Ⓦlufthansa.com) and Iberia (Ⓦiberia.com), which travel via their respective European hubs.

Currently round-trip **fares** from the US to Palermo or Catania, via Rome or Milan, start at around US$750, though you can pay considerably less in low season and rather more in high. From Canada, low-season fares start at around Can$1100, increasing to around Can$1500 in high season. However the lowest fares may involve several changes and stopovers. The alternative option is to pick up a discounted flight to the UK, and then fly on to Sicily with one of the European budget airlines (see page 23). It depends on how soon in advance you book, and the season, as to whether this will be a realistic way to save money. The easiest way to research the best available deals are price-comparison sites such as Ⓦskyscanner.com or Ⓦkayak.com.

Flights from Australia and New Zealand

Although there are **no direct flights** from Australia or New Zealand to Sicily, many airlines offer through-tickets with their partners via European or Asian hubs. Round-trip **fares** from the main cities in Australia start from around Aus$1600 with not a great deal of seasonal variation; from New Zealand, fares cost from NZ$2500.

Trains

It's a long journey **from the UK to Sicily** by train (2672km from London to Messina). There are no direct sleeper trains from London to Rome; it is really only worth doing if you want to take in some other Italian cities en route. The most appealing route is the following. Take the **Eurostar** service from London to Paris (from £58 return), then the **overnight Thello train from Paris to Venice** (from €35 one-way in a six-berth couchette), or the daytime TGV from Paris to Milan via Turin (from €35 one-way in a six-berth couchette). From Milan, take Trenitalia's high-speed Frecciarossa train to Bologna, Florence, Rome or Naples, perhaps stopping to sightsee en route. From Venice, Trenitalia and their rival Italotreno, run high-speed services to Bologna, Florence, Rome and Naples. From Naples or Rome

you can pick up a direct train to Messina. If you did want to do the entire journey non-stop from Paris, count on it taking at least twenty hours and costing from £69. Tickets can be booked up to 120 days before departure, and the cheapest Smart Go fares sell out quickly.

The invaluable train-travel website Ⓦ**seat61.com** tells you exactly how to book the entire journey, down to precise details about the various sleeper-train options. It also has a "Railpasses" section, which will help you decide whether or not buying a rail pass is a good idea.

Buses

It's difficult to make any case for travelling to Sicily by **bus**, especially as there's no direct service from the UK. **Eurolines** routes via Paris and Lyon, but it takes at least forty hours, depending on connections. Even with book-in-advance promotional fares (up to thirty days in advance), buses often cost as much or more than the average low-cost flight.

Car and ferry

Driving to Sicily from the UK, using the standard **cross-Channel services or Eurotunnel** (Ⓦeurotunnel.com) through the Channel Tunnel, takes at least two full days. From the France–Italy border, it's possible, with a bit of luck, to reach the Straits of Messina in a long day if you keep on the autostradas. While not a cheap option (factoring in the cross-Channel trip, tolls, overnight stops and meals), it is a good way of seeing something of France and Italy on the way.

The shortest crossing from the Italian mainland, over the Straits of Messina, is from **Villa San Giovanni by ferry** (see page 162); or, fifteen minutes further south from **Reggio di Calabria** (see page 162).

To cut the driving time in Italy, you could use one of the ferry crossings from the Italian mainland to Sicily, **from Genoa** (to Palermo, 20hr), **Salerno** (to Palermo, 12hr; or Messina, 8hr), **Civitavecchia**, near Rome (to Palermo, 12hr) or **Naples** (to Palermo, 11hr; or the Aeolian Islands from 10 hours by year-round ferry). Non-drivers could even combine a cheap flight (for example, Ryanair to Genoa) with one of these ferry crossings. The Genoa, Salerno and Naples crossing schedules are seasonal, and with several different operators, but there are daily sailings in summer and at least two or three per week throughout the year. The best places to check schedules and fares, and book tickets, are the exhaustive websites Ⓦ**directferries.co.uk** and Ⓦ**viamare.com**, which contain details about every Italian ferry service.

STAMP IT

All stations have yellow **validating machines** in which passengers must stamp any open ticket before embarking on their journey. Look out for them as you come onto the platform: if you fail to **validate your ticket** you'll be given a hefty on-the-spot fine. Note that if your ticket is booked for a specific train, validation is not necessary – but if in doubt, ask.

TOUR OPERATORS

FOOD AND DRINK

The International Kitchen US ☎ 1800 945 8606, ⓦ theinternationalkitchen.com. Four and six-night all-inclusive Sicilian culinary tours and cooking-school holidays, from US$2400, with winery and market visits included. Various themed tours, with cooking classes in Palermo, Taormina and Modica, interwoven with sightseeing.

SAILING

Nautilus Yachting UK ☎ 01/732 867 445, ⓦ nautilus-yachting. co.uk. Yacht holidays, operating out of Sant'Agata di Militello and Portorosa for the Aeolians. Prices start from £1078 for the boat for a week, though if you have no experience you can add the services of a skipper for around £1000 per week.

RAIL AND BUS CONTACTS

Eurolines ⓦ eurolines.eu.
Eurostar ⓦ eurostar.com.
Italian State Railways ⓦ trenitalia.com.
ItallaRail ⓦ italiarail.com.
Loco2 ⓦ loco2.com. Efficient, clearly laid-out international train-booking site.
Rail Europe ⓦ raileurope.com.
The Man in Seat 61 ⓦ seat61.com. Fantastic source of information and links for train-travel nerds.

Getting around

You don't have to rent a car to see Sicily's major towns and sights, but getting around by public transport is not always easy. The rail system is slow, few buses run on Sundays and route information can be frustratingly difficult to extract, even from the bus and train stations themselves. On the positive side, public transport prices are reasonable.

The "Arrival and departure" sections in this book give the full picture on transport schedules and frequencies. Note that unless specified, these refer to regular working-day schedules, ie Monday to Saturday; services are much reduced, or even non-existent, on Sundays. Note also that on the railways in particular, there are occasional gaps in the schedule, typically occurring just after the morning rush hour, when the gap between trains may be twice as long as normal.

One thing to bear in mind is that travelling by train is not the best way to see all of the island. Some stations are located a fair distance from their towns – Enna and Taormina are two notable examples (though there are bus connections) – while much of the west and centre of Sicily is only accessible by bus or car.

By train

Italian State Railways, **Ferrovie dello Stato** (**FS**), operates the trains in Sicily though a private railway, the Ferrovia Circumetnea, operates a route around the base of Mount Etna (see page 200). The FS website ⓦ **trenitalia.com** has a useful English-language version, where you can view timetables and book tickets. Trains connect all the major Sicilian towns, but are more prevalent in the east of the island than the west. On the whole they do leave on time, with the notable exception of those on the Messina–Palermo and Messina–Catania/Siracusa routes that have come from the mainland. These can be delayed by up to three hours, though around an hour late is more normal.

Of the various types of train, the most expensive are the **Intercity** (**IC**) trains that link the main cities. **Diretto** and **Inter-regionale** trains are long-distance expresses, calling only at larger stations, while the **Regionale** services (also called **Locale**), which stop at every place with a population higher than zero, are usually ones to avoid. A **seat reservation** (*prenotazione*) is obligatory on Intercity services and advisable on other services where possible, especially in summer when trains can get crowded. You can buy tickets and make reservations at any major train station, or buy online on the FS website (both regional and Intercity services) and print your own tickets. **Fares** are very reasonable – a typical journey, say Palermo to Catania, can cost as little as €13.50. Children aged 4 to 12 pay half price, while the under-4s travel free provided they do not occupy a seat. If you jump on the train without a ticket you'll pay the full fare plus a fine to the conductor. Be careful as well that the ticket you have bought is valid for the kind of train you want to take – if you have a ticket for a *regionale* and jump on an Intercity, you will be charged a supplement and possibly a fine as well.

ITALIAN TRAIN AND BUS TIMETABLE GLOSSARY

Arrivi	arrivals
Feriale	denoting a Monday-to-Saturday service; symbolized by two crossed hammers
Festivo	running on Sundays and public holidays only; symbolized by a cross
Giornaliero	daily
In Ritardo	delayed
Lavorativo	running Monday to Friday only
Partenze	departures
Periodico	seasonal
Si effetua dal… al….	operating from… to… (eg from Monday to Friday)
X	a quick way of writing per, or "for". It means the opposite of the English "ex", so, for example, "aliscafo x Salina" refers to a hydrofoil to Salina.

Unless you're visiting Sicily as part of a wider Italian or European tour, the major pan-European **rail passes** are not worth considering.

By bus

Almost anywhere you want to go will have some kind of **regional bus** (*autobus* or *pullman*) service, usually quicker than the train (especially between the major towns and cities), and generally about the same price.

Between them, four main **companies** – SAIS Trasporti (Ⓦsaistrasporti.it), SAIS Autolinee (Ⓦsaisautolinee.it), AST (Ⓦaziendasicilianatrasporti.it) and Interbus (Ⓦinterbus.it) – cover most of the island. Other companies stick to local routes. Many routes are linked to school/market requirements, which can mean a frighteningly early start, last departures in the early afternoon, and occasionally no services during school holidays, while nearly everywhere services are drastically reduced, or non-existent, on Sundays.

The local **bus station** (*autostazione*) is often in a central piazza, or outside the train station, though in some towns different bus companies have different bus terminals. **Timetables** are available on the companies' websites, and also from company offices and bus stations. You usually buy tickets on the bus, and increasingly online, something worth doing for a longer route, such as Messina to Rome, for which tickets often sell out. On most routes, it's possible to flag a bus down if you want a ride. If you want to get off, ask "*posso scendere?*"; "the next stop" is "*la prossima fermata*".

City buses usually charge a flat **fare** of €1.20–1.80, and the tickets are often valid for ninety minutes, allowing you to change services for free within that time. Invariably, you need a **ticket** before you get on, though in major cities such as Palermo, Agrigento and Messina you can often buy them from the driver for a supplement of 50 cents. Buy them in *tabacchi*, or

from the kiosks at bus stops, and then validate them in the machine in the bus. Checks are frequently made by inspectors who block both exits as they get on, though if you don't have a ticket you'll usually get off with an earful of Sicilian and be made to buy one; some inspectors might hold out for the spot fine.

By car, scooter and quad

Driving in Sicily is almost a competitive sport, and although the Sicilians aren't the world's worst drivers they don't win any safety prizes either. However, with a car you'll be able to see a lot of the island quickly, and reach the more isolated coastal and inland areas.

Most **main roads** are prefixed SS (Strada Statale) or SP (Strada Provinciale), and signposting is pretty good. On the whole these are two-lane roads with passing places on hills, though some stretches near towns and cities are dual carriageway. **Road maintenance**, however, is very patchy and even major routes can be badly potholed.

Some roads provide spectacular cross-country driving routes (see box), as do the impressive Sicilian **motorways** (autostrada), which are carried on great piers spanning the island. These link Messina–Catania–Siracusa (A18), Catania–Palermo (A19), Palermo–Trapani/Mazara del Vallo (A29) and Messina–Palermo (A20), while work continues on extending the autostradas network towards Agrigento and Gela (it has so far reached Rosolini). The Messina–Catania–Siracusa and Messina–Palermo autostradas are **toll-roads** (*pedaggio*, toll; *autostrada a pedaggio*, toll-motorway). Take a ticket as you come on, and pay on exit; the amount due is flashed up on a screen.

Rules of the road are straightforward: drive on the right; at junctions, where there's any ambiguity, give precedence to vehicles coming from the right; observe the speed limits (50km/h in built-up areas, 110km/h on country roads, 130km/h on autostradas);

and don't drink and drive. Speed cameras and traffic-calming humps are becoming more evident, but this doesn't seem to deter Sicilians from travelling at any speed they choose.

Italian **fuel prices** are roughly in line with those in the UK, with unleaded petrol (*senza piombo*) slightly cheaper than leaded (*super*). Blue lines in towns signify authorized **parking zones**, where you'll pay around €1 an hour, either in a meter or to an attendant hovering nearby. You can also often buy a *biglietto parcheggio*, a scratch card, from *tabacchi* or local bars, where you scratch off the date and time and leave it in the windscreen. However, if you've parked in a street that turns into a market by day, you'll be stuck until close of business, while if you park in a *zona di rimozione* (tow-away zone), your car will most likely not be there when you get back. Most cities also have official **car parks** and garages, charging between €10 and €15 a day. **Never leave anything visible in the car** when you leave it and always depress your aerial and tuck in the wing mirrors.

To drive in Sicily, you need a valid **driving licence** and, if you are a non-EU licence holder, an international driving permit. It's compulsory to carry your car documents and passport while you're driving, and you'll be required to present them if you're stopped by the police – not an uncommon occurrence. You are also required to carry a triangular danger sign, which will be provided with rental cars. Many car insurance policies cover taking your own car to Italy; check with your insurer when planning your trip (you'll need an international green card of insurance). You'd also be advised to take out extra cover for motoring assistance in case you break down, and **motoring organizations** like the RAC (W rac.co.uk) or the AA (W theaa.co.uk) can help. Alternatively, by dialling ☎116 you can get 24-hour assistance from the Automobile Club d'Italia (W aci.it).

Car rental

Car rental in Sicily can cost as little as €80 per week for a three-door Fiat Punto, with unlimited mileage.

It's inevitably cheaper arranged in advance through an online broker (though watch out for hidden extras). Otherwise, rental agencies – including local companies like Maggiore (W maggiore.it) – are found in the major cities and at Palermo, Catania, Trapani and Comiso airports.

It's essential to check that you have adequate **insurance cover** for a rental car. Going by the dents and scratches on almost every car on the road, you want to make sure that your liability is limited as far as possible. Ensure that all visible damage on a car is duly marked on the rental sheet. It's worth paying the extra charge to reduce the "excess" payment levied for any damage, and most rental companies these days offer a zero-excess option for an extra charge. A really brilliant way of avoiding excess charges and other mind-games the rental outfits will play as you pick up your car is to take out an annual insurance policy (from £38.99) with an outfit such as W insurance4carhire.com, which also covers windscreen and tyre damage.

Scooters, quads and mokes

Virtually everyone in Sicily – kids to grandmas – rides a **moped or scooter**, although the smaller models are not suitable for any kind of long-distance travel. They're ideal for shooting around towns, and you can rent them in Taormina, Cefalù and other holiday centres – check the Guide for details. Crash helmets are compulsory. Lampedusa and other minor islands also have **quad-bikes** and **mini-mokes** available for rent, which are great for bashing around local roads to beaches and beauty spots – just be aware that there's a high accident rate with machines like these.

Taxis

There are plenty of honest, reliable taxi drivers in Sicily, but as ever there are a few sharks; to be on the safe side, always establish a price before you set off. Although meters are supposed to be used by law, both passengers and drivers usually prefer to settle on a fee before setting out. **Fares** for long-distance

---

SICILY'S SIX BEST DRIVES

SS120, Nicosia to Polizzi Generosa Bare landscape punctuated by isolated hilltop villages, with Etna dominating the eastern horizon.

SS185, Tyrrhenian coast to Taormina Across the Peloritani mountains to Etna and the sea.

Avola to Cava Grande Winding up the mountainside to where eagles dare.

SP624 and SP5, Palermo to Piana degli Albanesi Past jagged fangs and towers of rock, with glimpses of lakes and lingering views over fertile valleys.

Trapani to Erice For the startling interplay of coast and mountain.

SS118, Agrigento to Corleone Remote western valleys and crags, rock tombs and Mafia towns.

THE SICILIAN DRIVING EXPERIENCE

If all you had to do was drive on Sicilian **motorways** – light traffic, fast travel, dramatic scenery – things would be fine. Unfortunately, you have to come off them sooner or later and drive into a town, and then all bets are off. The good news is that the swirling town **traffic** isn't as horrific as it first looks – the secret is to make it *very* clear what you're going to do, using your horn as much as your indicators and brakes. There are established **rules** of the road in force, though Sicilians, needless to say, ignore most, if not all, of them as a matter of principle. A character in Andrea Camilleri's Inspector Montalbano novels drives "like a dog on drugs", which is a pretty fair assessment of local driving skills, and if you go your entire holiday without being cut up on the inside, jumped at a junction or overtaken on a blind bend, you'll have done well.

You'll switch your satnav off the first time you encounter a Sicilian **one-way system** – installed by traffic engineers with a sense of humour – which lead you into old-town areas where the streets grow ever narrower until the point that you can't back out or turn round. It usually works out fine if you rigidly follow the one-way signs, though matters aren't helped by it being accepted local **parking** practice simply to drive your car up on the pavement, or stop where it's most convenient for the driver – this can include the middle of the street, or pausing for a chat with a mate at a major road junction. Out in the **countryside** driving is generally less of a hassle, though you do have to allow for shepherds and their sheep (and there aren't many places in Europe you can still say that about) idling around the next bend.

Pedestrians, meanwhile, deal with the general mayhem by taking a deep breath, staring straight at the drivers and strolling boldly across the road. If in doubt, follow someone old and infirm, or put out your hand policeman-like, but *never* assume that you're safe on a pedestrian crossing – they're regarded by most drivers as an invitation to play human skittles.

---

journeys are published by each city – for example, the official rate from Siracusa to Catania airport is €70, though you may be able to negotiate. A day-tour by taxi, say taking in Siracusa, Piazza Armerina and the temples of Agrigento will cost around €250.

By ferry and hydrofoil

There are **ferries** (*traghetti*) and **hydrofoils** (*aliscafi*) to the Aeolians, the Egadi and Pelagie islands, and Pantelleria and Ustica, and there's also a summer hydrofoil service from Palermo to the Aeolians. The main **operators** are Liberty Lines (Ⓦ libertylines.it), Caronte e Tourist (wcarontetourist.it), SNAV (Ⓦ snav. it) and NGI (Ⓦ ngi-spa.it); you'll find full details of services, schedules and fares in the relevant sections of the Guide. Timetables are also available online, pinned up at the dockside or available from the ferry offices and tourist offices.

You can **island-hop** year-round in the Aeolians and Egadis. Services are busy in summer, making early booking advisable, though you should always be able to get on a ferry if you just turn up. Both passenger and **car-ferry** services operate, though non-resident vehicles are banned on several islands during the summer. In fact, it's debatable how much you'll need a car on any of the islands – only Lipari, Pantelleria and Lampedusa are of any size, and in any case you can rent a vehicle there if you need to.

By plane

If you're short on time, consider flying to **Lampedusa** or **Pantelleria** from Palermo or Catania – otherwise, the alternative is an overnight ferry ride. Prices start at around €60 one-way.

Accommodation

On the whole, accommodation in Sicily is slightly cheaper than in the rest of Italy, starting at around €60 a night for a basic double or twin room (though prices can double in summer in the most popular resorts). The only accommodation cheaper than this comes in the form of the very few youth hostels and the many campsites across the island. Hotels run across the entire range, from crumbling townhouses to five-star palaces, and restored country villas to resort hotels. There's also a large number of "bed and breakfast" places and "*agriturismo*" rural properties, where the attraction is mixing with your hosts and experiencing something of Sicilian life.

In summer (usually in August) some places – especially in major resorts or on outlying islands – insist on half-board accommodation (*mezza pensione*, full board is *pensione completa*), when the price will

ACCOMMODATION PRICES

The prices quoted in this book are for the establishment's **cheapest double room in July**. In August, prices may skyrocket in major resorts, but for much of the year, however, you can expect to pay less, especially as internet booking becomes the norm (hence with prices based on availability rather than season).

Prices are for the room only, except where otherwise indicated; fancier places often include breakfast in the price – we indicate this in the listing, but check when booking.

also include lunch or dinner, and there may even be a three-night or longer minimum stay. Few single rooms are available anywhere and, in high season especially, lone travellers will often pay most of the price of a double. Sicily has hundreds of B&Bs, ranging from the basic to the boutique, and these are often better value for money than conventional hotels. **Breakfast** is often but not always included in the price – check carefully, especially if you are booking online. Breakfast will not be included if you stay in *affittacamere* ("rooms") places or apartments. Some "bed and breakfast" places will give you a voucher for breakfast at a nearby bar. Finally, note that **Airbnb** has taken off with a vengeance in Sicily – and can often offer fantastic value for money. Many B&Bs also advertise on the site.

Hotels

Sicilian **hotels** are graded with one to five stars, although with the rise in B&Bs and boutique hotels this system has become almost irrelevant, and is not by any means always displayed. Four-star hotels, plus hotels in resorts and on islands, can charge pretty much what they like, especially in August when room prices can top €300, while the dozen or so five-star hotels on the island (notably in Palermo, Taormina, Siracusa and the Aeolian Islands) charge international rates. There are plenty of bargains around on the accommodation broker sites, especially when demand is low.

Private rooms and B&Bs

Private rooms (*camere, affittacamere*) for rent are common in beach resorts and on the Aeolian and Egadi Islands. Facilities vary, but the best are clean and modern, with private bathroom and often with a kitchenette. Prices start at about €50, with variations depending on the season and location – in August in Taormina and on the Aeolians you might pay as much as €100 a night for a room. Breakfast isn't usually included, but is sometimes available for an extra charge.

Recent years have seen a huge growth in the number of "**bed and breakfasts**" (as they term themselves). Pretty much every Sicilian town now has some B&B choices, all liberally signposted as you tour around, and in many places they've taken over from the old-fashioned, family-run pensions. Many are actually little different from private rooms, with the owners either not living on the premises or not always available throughout the day – often, you have to call a mobile phone number to summon attendance. Prices start at around €30 per person per night, usually for an en-suite room in a nicely maintained building where you'll get a flavour of Sicilian home life. Some B&Bs are truly magnificent, based in remarkable Baroque *palazzi* or elegant country houses, and you can pay as much as €90 per person. The southeast particularly has lots of B&Bs, and tourist-friendly towns like Siracusa, Ragusa, Modica and Noto are awash with stylishly converted old homes.

Self-catering villas and apartments

Private **holiday apartments** and villas are available in places like Taormina, Cefalù, Siracusa and the Aeolians, and are generally rented for anything from

TOURIST TAX

The Sicilian authorities have introduced a new experimental **tourist tax** (of €1–2.50 per night depending on how luxurious your accommodation is, for a specified period, which can range from 3 to 10 nights – if you stay longer, then no further tax is charged) in recent years, levied in several cities, towns and even whole islands. It's not yet in place everywhere, but in cities such as Palermo, Siracusa and Catania, it's charged to anyone spending a night in a hotel or B&B; and in the minor islands to anyone travelling in via hydrofoil or ferry, or even on a tour boat. It remains to be seen whether the effort and cost of collecting and administering the tax will be deemed to make it worthwhile.

UNUSUAL PLACES TO STAY

Dammuso houses, Pantelleria. Native domed cube-houses, available for rent. See page 351.
Locanda Don Serafino, Ragusa. Luxury hotel in an ancient building – the best room has its shower in a cave. See page 248.
Grand Hotel Villa Igiea, Palermo. Luxury Art Nouveau seaside villa built by a tuna-canning magnate. See page 70.
Azienda Agricola Silvia Sillitti, Caltanissetta. Stay on a working organic olive, almond and wheat farm. See page 262.
La Salina Borgo di Mare, Salina. Aeolian Island chic in an old saltworks. See page 136.
Stenopus Greco, Porticello. Boutique rooms in a working fishing port near Palermo. See page 79.
Tonnara di Bonagia, Bonagia, near Trapani. Fun, family lodgings in a converted tuna-fishing village. See page 323.

---

a couple of nights to a month. Although these can be very expensive in the peak summer season – when Italian families come on holiday – real bargains can be found in May or late September, and during the winter. Good websites are ⓦhomelidays.it, ⓦcasa.it and ⓦcasavacanze.it.

Tour operators and villa companies also have self-catering **villas**, **farmhouses** and **apartments** located right across the island, usually in beautiful locations, often with swimming pools. Rates vary wildly, from €600 a week (sleeping four) to thousands for a place suitable for a house party. For an idea of what's available, contact companies like Think Sicily (ⓦthinksicily.com), Sicily Luxury Villas (ⓦsicilyluxuryvillas.com), and, of course, Airbnb.

Rural accommodation

Rural tourism has expanded significantly in Sicily in recent years, and every region now holds a choice of interesting places to stay, from **working farms** and **wine estates** to **restored palaces** and **architect-designed homes**. Accommodation is in private rooms or apartments, and many establishments also offer activities such as cooking courses, horseriding, mountain biking, walks and excursions. Hosts often speak English or French, and sometimes offer meals (or there might be a restaurant attached serving home-produced food, as is the case in many farmhouse-style places). We've recommended some of our favourites in the Guide, but many others fall within various umbrella schemes like Agriturist (ⓦagriturist.it) and Agriturismo

(ⓦagriturismo.com), whose websites have sections on Sicily, with links to the properties. Double rooms usually cost €80–120 in high season, depending on the establishment, and note that some places require a minimum stay of three nights.

Hostels, campsites and mountain huts

Hostels are rare in Sicily. Dorm beds cost €16–20 a night, depending on season, and all have some kind of self-catering facility available. Some are official IYHF hostels, others are independent backpackers' (ie no membership required), but the official ones, at least, are detailed on the Hostelling International website (ⓦhihostels.com), and if you aren't already a member of your home hostelling organization you can join upon arrival at any hostel.

There are approximately ninety officially graded **campsites** dotted around the island's coasts, on the outlying islands, and around Mount Etna. Few are open year-round; indeed, campsites generally open or close whenever they want, depending on business, but there are more details on the comprehensive website ⓦcamping.it. Many of the sites are large, family-oriented affairs, often complete with pools, bars, shops and sports facilities. Charges are usually around €7 per person per day, plus the same again for a tent and vehicle. Many campsites also have bungalows, caravans or apartments for rent (often with self-catering facilities) – demand and prices are high in summer (when a week's minimum stay might be required), but in quieter periods you can expect to pay €35–50 a night.

Staffed **mountain huts** (*rifugio*, plural *rifugi*) are available in certain magnificent locations, particularly in the Madonie and Nebrodi ranges and on Mount Etna. They're used mainly by hikers and outdoor enthusiasts, and operated by the Club Alpino Italiano (ⓦcai.it) – non-members can use them for around €20 a night, but advance reservations are essential.

ACCOMMODATION ALTERNATIVES

Airbnb ⓦairbnb.com
CouchSurfing ⓦcouchsurfing.org
HomeAway ⓦhomeaway.com

Food and drink

There's much to be said for coming to Sicily just for the eating and drinking. Often, even the most out-of-the-way village will boast somewhere you can get a good lunch, while places like Catania, Palermo, Ragusa, Trapani and Siracusa can keep a serious eater happy for days. And it's not ruinously expensive either, certainly compared to prices in the rest of mainland Italy: a full meal with local wine generally costs around €30 a head, a pizza, drink and ice cream around half that.

Contemporary Sicilian cooking leans heavily on locally produced foodstuffs and whatever can be fished out of the sea, mixed with the Italian staples of pasta, tomato sauce and fresh vegetables. Red chillies, tuna, swordfish, sardines, olives, pine nuts and capers all figure heavily, while the mild winter climate and long summers mean that fruit and vegetables are less seasonal (and much more impressive) than in northern Europe: strawberries appear in April, for example, while oranges are available right through the winter. The **menu reader** (see page 388) covers all the basics, and includes a full rundown of Sicilian specialities, some of which crop up in nearly every restaurant.

Breakfast, snacks and markets

For most Sicilians, **breakfast** (*prima colazione*) is an espresso or cappuccino, and the ubiquitous *cornetto* – a jam-, custard- or chocolate-filled croissant. Most bars and patisseries (a *pasticceria*) also offer *cannoli* (deep-fried pastry tubes filled with sweet ricotta cheese and candied fruit). The traditional summer breakfast is a *granita* (preferably almond or coffee) with a brioche. Look out also for almond milk, and freshly squeezed orange and pomegranate juices.

There are **sandwich** (panini) bars in the bigger towns, though alternatively, in most places, you can simply go into an *alimentari* (grocer's shop) and ask them to make you a sandwich from whatever they've got. Bakeries sometimes sell panini or *pane cunzato*, crusty bread rolls filled with pungent combinations such as tuna, tomato, anchovy and capers. Look out also for *impanata* or *scacce*, bread turnovers filled with combinations of potato, onion, fennel-seed and chilli sausage, broccoli and wild greens.

You'll get most of the things already mentioned, plus small pizzas, ready-prepared pasta and deep-fried, breadcrumbed balls of rice known as *arancini* (usually either *ragù*, with Bolognese sauce, peas and cheese, or *al burro*, with cheese and ham) and full hot meals in a **tavola calda** (literally, "hot table"), a sort of stand-up snack bar. In the larger cities, you'll occasionally come across an old-fashioned **focacceria** – takeaway establishments selling focaccia (an oven-baked flatbread, with a topping or filling) and other bread-based snacks. Or there's the ubiquitous **rosticceria** in every Sicilian town, a takeaway grill-house where the speciality is spit-roast chicken (*pollo allo spiedo*).

Grocers' shops (*alimentari*) and **markets** are the best places for fruit, veg and picnic food, and you'll usually be able to jazz up your picnic lunch with sweet peppers, olives, seafood salad and pickled vegetables. Some markets also sell **traditional takeaway food**, loved by Sicilians, though perhaps a challenge for some visitors – usually things like boiled artichokes, cooked octopus, raw sea urchins and mussels, and fried offal sandwiches.

Pizza

Outside its home of Naples, Sicily is the best place to eat **pizza** in Italy. It comes flat, not deep-pan, and there are some distinctively Sicilian combinations – using pecorino cheese instead of mozzarella, oregano instead of basil, and lots of anchovies, capers

---

ICE CREAM AND GRANITA

A cone (*un cono*) of famous Sicilian **ice cream** (*gelato*) – or perhaps a dollop in a brioche – is the indispensable accessory to the evening *passeggiata*. The best choice is at a **gelateria**, where the range is a tribute to the Italian imagination and flair for display. If they make their own on the premises, there'll be a sign saying "*produzione propria*"; sadly, however, this increasingly means they make the stuff from pre-packed commercial pastes and syrups. Anyhow, there's no trouble in locating the finest *gelateria* in town: it's the one that draws the crowds. And as it's hard to find decent ice cream in restaurants these days (it's mostly *confezionato*, ie mass-produced), many locals also head to the *gelateria* for dessert. **Granita** is a water-based ice made of fruit or nuts, and is eaten with a spoon – in summer it is a popular breakfast, accompanied by a brioche. Coffee, chocolate and nut *granitas* are often served with optional whipped cream.

THE ORIGINAL FUSION FOOD

Historically, **Sicilian cuisine** has been held in high regard: one of the earliest of cookbooks, the *Art of Cooking* by Mithaecus, derived from fifth-century BC Siracusa, while in medieval times Sicilian chefs were much sought after in foreign courts. As the centuries passed, the intermittent waves of immigration left their mark, from the use of prickly pears (originally imported from Mexico by the Spanish) to the North African influence evident in the western Sicilian version of couscous or in orange salads. The **Arab influence** is also apparent in the profusion of sweets – marzipan is used extensively, while *cassata*, the most Sicilian of desserts, derives from the Arabic word *quas-at*, referring to the round bowl in which it was traditionally prepared. Indeed, virtually every dish – though apparently common-or-garden Italian/Sicilian – calls upon 2500 years of cross-cultural influences, from the Greeks and Romans to the Arabs, Normans and Spanish.

and hot peppers. It's also easy to find pizzas cooked in the traditional way, in **wood-fired ovens** (*forno a legna*), so that they arrive blasted and bubbling on the surface, with a distinctive charcoal taste. The latest trends are for slow-risen and naturally yeasted doughs, and gluten-free and vegan/dairy-free options are becoming increasingly available. Because of the time it takes to set up and light the ovens, *forno a legna* pizzas are usually only served at night, except in some resorts in summer.

Restaurant meals

For a full meal, you'll have to go either to a **trattoria** or a **ristorante**. A trattoria is usually the cheaper, more basic choice, offering good home cooking (*cucina casalinga*), while a ristorante is often more upmarket (tablecloths, printed menu and uniformed waiters). In small towns and villages, the local trattoria is often open only at lunchtime, there may not be a menu, and the waiter will simply reel off a list of what's available. In tourist resorts and larger towns you'll come across hybrid establishments (a trattoria-ristorante, say, or ristorante-pizzeria) that cater to all tastes. Signs or blackboards announcing "*pranzo turistico*" or "*pranzo completo*" are advertising a limited-choice **set menu** which can be pretty good value at €15–30.

Traditionally, lunch (*pranzo*) or dinner (*cena*) starts with an **antipasto** (literally "before the meal"), at its best when you circle around a table and help yourself to a cold buffet selection. If you're moving on to pasta and the main course you'll need quite an appetite to tackle the *antipasti* as well. Otherwise, the menu starts with soup or pasta, **il primo**, and moves on to **il secondo**, the meat or fish dish. Note that fish will either be served whole (like bream or trout) or by weight (usually per 100g, *all'etto*, like swordfish and tuna), so ask to see what you're going to eat and check the price first. The second course is generally served unadorned, except for a wedge of

lemon or tomato – **contorni** (vegetables and salads) are ordered and served separately, and often there won't be much choice beyond chips and salad. If there's no menu, the verbal list of what's available can sometimes be a bit bewildering, but if you don't hear anything you recognize just ask for what you want: everywhere should have pasta with tomato or meat sauce. Dessert (**dolci**) is almost always fresh fruit, fruit salad or ice cream, though restaurants may also have a choice of cakes, tarts and puddings – unfortunately, though, many of these are mass-produced (by such brands as Ranieri), and a restaurant *tiramisù* or *cassata*, say, can be a poor substitute for the real thing.

In recent years **vegetarian** and **vegan options** started appearing in the main cities and more touristy areas, and are now taking Sicily by storm. Gluten-free pizzas and dairy-free/vegan options (including some very yummy ice creams) are also becoming more and more common. It is not just that there is increased awareness of food allergies and intolerances, but the impact of meat and dairy on the planet is being taken to heart especially among younger Sicilians.

Nearly everywhere, you'll pay a small **cover charge** per person for the bread (*pane e coperto*); **service** (*servizio*) will be added as well in many restaurants – it's usually ten percent, though fifteen or even twenty percent isn't unheard of. If service isn't charged, leaving ten percent would do, though most pizzerias and trattorias won't expect it.

Coffee, tea and soft drinks

One of the most distinctive smells in a Sicilian street is that of fresh **coffee**. The basic choice is either an espresso (or just *caffè*), a cappuccino or a latte macchiato (the equivalent to a UK or US coffee-chain latte). Milky coffees are considered a breakfast drink – no Italian would order a cappuccino or latte macchiato after a meal. Sicilians tend to drink their cappuccino or latte macchiato lukewarm – if you want yours hot, ask for it to be "ben caldo" or even "caldissimo". A longer espresso is a *caffè lungo*, a shorter one a *caffè ristretto*, and with a drop of milk it's *caffè macchiato* ("stained"), while coffee with a shot of alcohol is *caffè corretto*. In summer, you might want your coffee cold (*caffè freddo*), or try a *granita di caffè* – cold coffee with crushed ice that's usually topped with whipped cream (*senza panna*, without cream). **Tea**, too, can be drunk iced (*tè freddo*), usually mixed with lemon. Hot tea (*tè caldo*) comes with lemon (*con limone*) unless you ask for milk (*con latte*).

For a fresh **fruit juice** (usually orange, but pomegranate is becoming more widespread), squeezed at the bar, ask for a *spremuta*, while a *succo di frutta* is a bottled fruit juice. As an alternative to Coke try the home-grown Chinotto (Coke-like, but not so sweet). Also look out for the huge range of Sicilian fizzy drinks currently enjoying a renaissance – flavours like pomegranate, lemon and ginger, and green mandarin are all worth trying. Tap water (*acqua normale*) should not be drunk (it often sits in cisterns which may not be super-clean), but **mineral water** (*acqua minerale*) is cheap, either still (*senza gas, lisce* or *naturale*) or fizzy (*con gas, gassata* or *frizzante*).

Beer, wine and spirits

Beer (*birra*) – generally lager in Sicily – usually comes in 33cl (*piccolo*) or 66cl (*grande*) bottles. The Sicilian brand Messina, and the Italian Peroni and Dreher, are widely available – ask for *birra nazionale*, otherwise you'll be given a more expensive imported beer, and note that draught beer (*birra alla spina*) is usually more expensive than the bottled variety. So-called "dark beers" (*birra nera, birra rossa* or *birra scura*) are also available, which have a slightly maltier taste, and in recent years there has been a huge increase in microbreweries, making local artisan beers more and more widely available – if you are interested ⓦ lestradedellabirra.com is a font of information and enthusiasm.

Local **wine** (*vino locale*) is often served straight from the barrel in jugs. Bottled wine is more expensive, usually starting at around €10 in a modest restaurant, and from under €4 in a supermarket. The most popular aperitivo drinks are Campari and Aperol, served as spritzes, with prosecco and soda, or their non-alcoholic equivalents, Crodino (which is orange) and San Bitter (which come in red or white versions).

The most famous Sicilian **dessert wine** is marsala, made in the western town of the same name. If you're heading to the offshore islands, watch out for malvasia (from the Aeolians) and *moscato* (from Pantelleria), while around Taormina the local speciality is *vino alla mandorla*, almond wine served ice-cold. **Spirits** are known mostly by their generic names, except brandy which you should call *cognac* or ask for by name – for cheaper Italian brands, ask for *nazionale*. Look out as well for artisan gins, which are enjoying the same kind of popularity as in the UK. At some stage you should also try an **amaro** (literally "bitter"), an after-dinner drink supposed to aid digestion. The classic brand is Averna (from Caltanissetta) but there are dozens of different kinds – including the very hip and gorgeously bottled Nepéta, made with Sicilian wild mint, or Amara Rossa made with blood orange peel. Look out, too, for **rosoli**, alcohol infused with herbs or spices such as bay leaves, wild fennel, rose petal or cinnamon. Touristy gastronomic shops are full of commercial versions (often very sweet), but a few restaurants and bars make their own.

Where to drink

In most town and village **bars**, it's cheapest to drink standing up at the counter (there's often nowhere to sit anyway), in which case you pay first at the cash desk (*la cassa*), present your receipt (*scontrino*) to the bar person and give your order. It's more expensive to sit down inside than stand up (the difference in price is shown on the price list as *tavola*) and it costs up to twice the basic price if you sit at tables outside (*terrazza*). Prices are supposed to be displayed by law, but this is not always the case, so don't feel embarrassed about asking.

SICILIAN TIME

Sicily is a part of Europe where time is still a fluid concept, so giving accurate **opening hours** for bars, cafés and restaurants is difficult. In general, daytime **bars** and **cafés** open around 7.30am for breakfast and close at 8.30–9.30pm, depending on how busy they are. **Restaurants** will usually be able to feed you if you turn up at noon, but expect to be eating alone – traditional lunchtime is 1–3pm here. In the evening, most restaurants open around 8pm, and are at their busiest at around 9–9.30pm. In winter most restaurants continue serving until at least 10pm, but in summer – especially in holiday places – they will carry on for as long as there are people turning up to eat.

SICILIAN WINE

Over the past few years **Sicilian wines** have built an increasingly prestigious reputation. Indigenous grapes include **Nero d'Avola** (a hearty black cherry-plum-ish red, similar to a Syrah/Shiraz), which is well suited to the dry climate, Grillo (a fresh, zingy white), Carricante (another white, with tones of pear and melon), and the reds Frappato (light aromatic red) and Nerello Mascalese (deep cherry). Wines made of international varietals – introduced in the 1980s – including Chardonnay, Cabernet Sauvignon, Merlot and Syrah are making waves too. Boutique wineries have sprung up all over Sicily – the North side of Etna is currently the island's star wine location, and first choice for a cantina-crawl – but there are lots of interesting things going on too around Noto, Vittoria and Menfi. As for those who just want a nice, reasonably priced everyday bottle to accompany a plate of pasta, Settesoli is a reliable budget brand sold at most supermarkets, and was founded by Diego Planeta who went on to create Planeta, now one of Sicily's leading wineries. Other leading labels with mid- and high-market wines include Tasca d'Almerita, Murgo (exceptional sparkling white and rosé), Duca di Salaparuta, Nicosia, Gulfi, Donnafugata and Franchetti.

Although bars have no set **licensing hours**, outside the cities it's often difficult to find a bar open much after 9pm. Children are allowed in, and bars, like restaurants, are smoke-free (strictly enforced), though if you're drinking or eating outside it's fine to smoke. Tourist bars and cafés are open later, but they're more expensive than the typical chrome-counter-and-Gaggia-machine local joints.

Most Sicilians tend to drink when they eat, and young people especially don't make a night out of getting wasted. In recent years the **aperitivo** scene has taken Sicily (and the rest of Italy) by storm. Bars advertising aperitivo (usually between 6.30pm or 7pm and 8.30pm or 9pm) will provide a buffet or table-served nibbles which can range from simple pizza, bruschetta, miniature *arancini*, and rice, pasta or couscous salad to delectable morsels of fish, cured hams and salamis, baked aubergines, courgette fritters, fresh ricotta or other local cheeses to accompany a spritz, cocktail or glass of wine.

When young Sicilians do go out on the town, it's to a **birreria** (literally "beer shop") or something calling itself a "pub", which is actually a bar open at night. Needless to say, they're not much like English pubs, though in the various "Irish" **pubs** that are springing up in the cities and resorts, you'll be able to get a pint of Guinness and watch the big game.

The media

Many Sicilians prefer to read local newspapers rather than the national ones, even though these have local supplements. Sicilian TV is popular, too, playing to the insatiable appetite for local gossip and celebrity. For Italian news in English, go to ⓦ lifeinitaly.com.

Newspapers and magazines

The two most widely read national **newspapers** are the centre-left *La Repubblica* and authoritative and rather right-wing *Il Corriere della Sera*, both published with local Sicilian supplements. If you have a smattering of Italian, you'll get far more of a flavour of Sicily by reading one of the **regional papers**, full of news on the latest *mafioso* misdemeanours and arrests, political bickering, local gossip, transport schedules, reviews, film listings and suchlike. In Palermo, the most popular is *Il Giornale di Sicilia*; in Catania, *La Sicilia*; in Messina, *La Gazzetta del Sud*. **English newspapers** can be found in Palermo, Catania, Messina, Siracusa, Taormina and Cefalù, usually a day late, and for three times the UK cover price, so reading newspapers online is a more economic option.

TV

Much Italian **TV** is appalling, with mindless quiz shows, variety programmes and chat shows squeezed in between countless advertisements. There are three state-owned **channels** (Rai 1, 2 and 3) along with the dozen or so channels of Berlusconi's Mediaset empire. You'll also come across all kinds of tiny local channels busying themselves with the minutiae of local life, and running non-stop silent footage of scenic landscapes.

Satellite television is fairly widely distributed, and three-star hotels and above usually offer a mix of BBC World, CNN, MTV and a sport channel. Your Netflix account will work in Italy (though the choice of programmes will be slightly different. BBC iPlayer, ITV Hub and Channel 4 On Demand are not available outside the UK (unless you install a proxy VPN).

Radio

As for **radio**, the most serious RAI channel is RAI 3, while the most listened-to pop radio stations are RTL (102.5 FM) and Radio Deejay (frequency depends on where you are – check ⓦ radiodeejay. it). There are several free apps such as iRadio UK Free and BBC Sounds allow you to listen to radio stations from home, and work with 3G and 4G if you don't have wi-fi.

Festivals

There's nothing to beat arriving in a Sicilian town or village to discover that it's festival time. Many annual feast days have remained unchanged for decades, if not centuries, celebrating the life of a patron saint or some notable event lost in the mists of time. But whatever the reason for the party, you are guaranteed the time-honoured ingredients for a Sicilian knees-up – old songs and dances, a costumed procession, perhaps a traditional puppet show, special food and sweets, and noisy fireworks to finish.

Food-inspired *sagrase* (food festivals) are lower-key, but no less enjoyable affairs, usually celebrating the local speciality of a town or village (with lots of free nibbles, copious wine and the usual music and dancing). There are literally hundreds of these food festivals, and driving around Sicily, you will come across posters advertising *sagre* of wild mushrooms, ricotta, pistachios, strawberries, capers or any local produce an area is famous for.

For online information on most Sicilian festivals, visit ⓦ siciliainfesta.com

Carnevale

Carnevale (Carnival, or Mardi Gras) is celebrated in the five days immediately before the start of Lent (in practice, some time between the end of February and the end of March). Traditionally,

its significance is as the last bout of indulgence before the abstinence of Lent, which lasts for forty days and ends with Easter. Sicily's best carnival is generally judged to be at **Acireale** on the Catania coast, where flower-filled floats, parades and concerts keep the townspeople occupied for days. Most towns and villages, however, manage to put on a little bit of a show, with kids walking around in costume, and street vendors selling local carnival food – inevitably a local variation of sweetened fried bread dough.

Easter

All over the island, **Easter** week is celebrated with slow-moving processions and ostentatious displays of penitence and mourning. Particularly dramatic events take place at **Erice**, **Marsala** and **Taormina**, while at **Enna** in the interior, thousands march in silent procession behind holy statues and processional carts. It's in **Trapani**, however, that the procession of statues is raised to an art form. Just as they have been every year since the seventeenth century, the city's "Misteri" figures, portraying life-sized scenes from the Passion, are paraded through the streets on Good Friday (see page 315). There are more curious events at **Adrano**, where the *Diavolata* is a symbolic display showing the Archangel Michael defeating the Devil; while in **Modica**, the Easter Sunday celebration, known as Vasa Vasa, sees a statue of the Madonna in mourning carried through the Baroque streets as if searching for her lost Son; when she meets the resurrected Christ she kisses him ("vasa" means kiss in Sicilian) and sheds her black veil). Meanwhile, at the Albanian village of **Piana degli Albanesi**, near Palermo, the villagers retain their ancient Orthodox traditions and costumes. Other, less conventional, parades take place at **Prizzi** in the western interior, and at **San Fratello** above the Tyrrhenian coast, where masked and hooded devils taunt the processions.

THE WEIRD AND WONDERFUL

Sicily can boast some of the Mediterranean's most idiosyncratic festivals. The conquest by the Normans is echoed in August's **Palio dei Normanni** in Piazza Armerina, a medieval-costumed procession with jousting knights, while the similar **La Castellana** throngs the streets of Caccamo in September. The island's fishermen have their own rituals, such as the festive boat parade and fish-fry of **Sagra del Mare** at Sciacca. During May's **Pesce a Mare** festa at Aci Trezza, on the Catania coast, as the local tourist brochure puts it, "a fisherman pretends to be a fish and excitedly the local fishermen catch him". Unmissable, for different reasons, is the **pilgrimage** every May in the Etna foothills, when the pious run, barefoot and shirtless, up to the sanctuary at Trecastagni.

Ferragosto

The biggest island-wide celebration, bar none, is high summer's **ferragosto**, the Feast of the Assumption of the Virgin Mary. The day is actually August 15, but anywhere with a celebration of any size makes a meal of it, perhaps starting with services and parties a few days earlier, before culminating, like all *ferragosto* celebrations, with spectacular fireworks on the night of the 15th. This is a particularly good time to be in **Messina**, where the procession of the city's enormous patron giants is followed by a mad scramble when the elaborate carriage on iron skis, known as the Vara, is pulled by the faithful through the streets, with water thrown down before it to ease the way. As the night wears on, flowers are thrown to the crowds before fireworks light up the Straits of Messina late at night (see page 163).

A festival calendar

JANUARY

New Year celebrations Taormina (from Jan 1). Puppet shows, folk-singing and concerts, ending on Epiphany (Jan 6).
Epiphany (Jan 6). Orthodox procession at Piana degli Albanesi; people dress up in traditional costumes and oranges are distributed. Elsewhere the Epiphany witch Befana gives stockings of sweets to children who've been good, and coal (made of black sugar honeycomb) to those who haven't.

FEBRUARY

Sagra del Mandorlo Fiore (first/second week). The almond-blossom festival sees elaborately costumed dancers and musicians

PUBLIC HOLIDAYS

January 1 *Primo dell'anno*, New Year's Day
January 6 *Epifania*, Epiphany
Good Friday *Venerdì Santo*
Easter Monday *Pasquetta*
April 25 *Giorno della Liberazione*, Liberation Day
May 1 *Festa dei Lavoratori*, Labour Day
May 15 Festa Autonomia Regione Sicilia
June 2 *Festa della Repubblica*, Republic Day
August 15 *Ferragosto*, Assumption of the Blessed Virgin Mary
November 1 *Ognissanti*, All Saints' Day
December 8 *Immaccolata*, Immaculate Conception of the Blessed Virgin Mary
December 25 *Natale*, Christmas Day
December 26 *Santo Stefano*, St Stephen's Day

from around the world perform in the Valle dei Templi and in Agrigento town.
Festa di Sant'Agata Catania (Feb 3–5). Boisterous street events, fireworks and food stalls, and a procession of the saint's relics.
Carnevale (weekend before Lent). Carnival festivities in Palazzolo Acreide, Cefalù, Taormina, Giardini Naxos and Acireale, with processions, floats, fireworks and music.

MARCH

San Giuseppe (March 19). On the Saturday closest to San Giuseppe, horses, astonishingly decorated with flowers, follow the Holy Family through town in a candlelit procession at Scicli. On March 19 at Malfa, Salina, participants feast on pasta and *ceci* (chickpeas) cooked in huge cauldrons, along with *antipasti* and puddings made by local people, presided over by locals dressed as Mary, Joseph and Jesus. Repeated in April at Lingua, and on May 1 in Leni.
Easter (dates vary). Celebrations islandwide.

APRIL

St George's Day. There's a costumed procession and statues paraded through the streets at Ragusa Ibla (Last Sun), and another procession on the 23rd at Piana degli Albanesi.

MAY

Madonna delle Milizie Scicli (last Sat). Re-enactment of a battle between the Normans and Saracens, won by the Normans after they invoked the help of the Madonna.
Sagra del Lago Lago di Pergusa. Held throughout May, with folk events, fireworks, singing competitions and games.
International Museum Day (mid-May). Sicily's museums put on events and stay open all night to celebrate the international initiative.
Greek Drama festival Siracusa (mid-May to mid-June). Classic plays performed by international companies in the spectacular ruins of the ancient Greek theatre.
Cantine Aperte (last Sun). Wine estates all over Italy open their cellars to the public.
Festa di Sant'Alfio Trecastagni (May 9–10). Traditional high jinks including a barefoot and shirtless pilgrimage by athletic souls who run the main road linking Catania to the sanctuary at Trecastagni.
Annual World Windsurfing Festival Mondello (last week). Races, food, drink and entertainment.

JUNE

Sagra di Fragola Maletto (dates vary). This little town is famous for its strawberries, considered to be the sweetest and most intense in Sicily, and the strawberry festival here sees a weekend of processions through the streets in traditional hand-painted Sicilian carts.
International Film Festival Taormina (second/third week in June). Screenings in the Teatro Greco.

TRADITIONAL ENTERTAINMENT

Puppet theatre (*teatro dei pupi*) has been popular in Sicily since the fourteenth century. The shows are always the same, and all Sicilians know the stories, which centre on the clash between **Christianity** and **Islam**. As each strutting, stiff-legged knight, such as Orlando (Roland) and Rinaldo, is introduced, the puppeteer lists his exploits. There may be a love interest, perhaps a jousting tournament to win the hand of Charlemagne's daughter, before the main business of staged battles between the Christians and the Saracen invaders. Between bouts, Orlando may fight a crocodile, or confront monsters and magicians. Things climax with some great historical battle, like Roncesvalles, culminating in betrayal and treachery as the boys face an untimely and drawn-out death. The whole story plays out regularly in theatre shows in Acireale, and also tourist centres like Siracusa and Taormina, though it's Palermo where you can best explore the tradition (see page 58).

Sagra del Mare Sciacca (June 27–29). A statue of St Peter is paraded on a boat at sea; there's a big fish-fry and maritime-themed games at the port.

JULY

Festival of St Rosalia Palermo (July 11–15). A procession of the saint's relics, fireworks and general mayhem.
Festival of Santa Marina Santa Marina Salina, Salina (July 17). A religious procession, market, music and fireworks.
Festival of Santa Maria di Terzito Salina (July 23). Music, market and more fireworks at the sanctuary of Madonna del Terzito.
Tindari festival Tyndaris. Theatre and concerts in the ancient theatre, from the last week in July until late August
Castroreale Jazz Castroreale (late July to early Aug). The mountain village of Castroreale attracts international musicians for a series of open-air concerts.
Estate Ennese Enna (July & Aug). A series of concerts and opera in the open-air theatre at Enna's castle. Runs until end of Aug.

AUGUST

Il Palio dei Normanni Piazza Armerina (Aug 12–14). The largest of several similar events in surrounding towns, Piazza's medieval pageant commemorates Count Roger's taking of the town in the eleventh century with a processional entry into town on the 12th and a ceremonial joust on the 14th, along with costumed parades and other festivities.
Palio Ortigia Island, Siracusa (first Sun in Aug). A boat race round the island, in which the five traditional quarters of the city compete with raucous enthusiasm.
Ferragosto (Aug 12–15). Processions and fireworks throughout Sicily (see page 36); Messina has perhaps the best event.

OCTOBER

Monreale concerts A week of ecclesiastical music concerts, staged at the cathedral from the last week in October to the first week in November.

DECEMBER

Christmas week Display of eighteenth-century cribs in Acireale.

Santa Lucia Siracusa (Dec 13). Festival of St Lucy: a procession to the church of Santa Lucia.
Nativity procession Salemi (Dec 24). Procession of locals dressed as characters from the Nativity story.

Sports and outdoor activities

As a Mediterranean island, Sicily is well set up for watersports of all kinds, from scuba diving to windsurfing, while many come in the cooler months either side of summer (April, May, September and October) for the hiking. The volcanoes of Etna and Stromboli offer more adventurous excursions – probably the most emblematic Sicilian outdoor activity is the climb up Stromboli to see the nightly volcanic light show.

Watersports

The best places for **snorkelling** and **scuba diving** are the limpid waters of the offshore islands, principally Ustica, the Aeolians, Lampedusa and Pantelleria. Diving schools on each of these offer day-trips and courses for beginners and experienced divers alike. Other areas are protected as marine and natural reserves, so even at far more touristed resorts like Mazzarò (Taormina) the water is often remarkably clear. **Windsurfing** gear is available for rent at most of the major resort beaches and lidos, and **kitesurfing** is increasingly popular at places like Mozia on the west coast.

Hiking

Hiking is growing in popularity, though it's nowhere near as established as in alpine Italy. If you're keen to do a lot of walking in a short time, your best bet is to join a **walking holiday** – several tour operators now offer this as an option and the routes used have all been thoroughly tried and tested. The best walking areas are in the interior, around **Etna** in the east, and in the mountain regions of the **Monti Madonie** and **Monti Nebrodi** (between Etna and the Tyrrhenian coast), where a few marked trails have been laid out, making use of existing paths.

On the whole, though, given the paucity of information and services, unsupported hiking in interior Sicily is more for the experienced and well-equipped walker. You'd do well to get hold of *Walking in Sicily* by Gillian Price, which details 42 walks across the whole island. However, if all you're looking for is a half-day stroll or short hike you're better off sticking to the coast or outlying islands. The Aeolians and Egadis in particular offer some lovely walking, while the protected coast between Scopello and San Vito Lo Capo (north of Trapani) has an excellent network of well-maintained paths.

Outdoor pursuits

The dramatic volcanic terrain around **Mount Etna** supports a whole **outdoor activities** industry, from guided summit hikes to 4WD safaris. Local tourist offices and travel agents as far away as Siracusa and Taormina are geared up to book visitors onto trips. The small mountain towns of Nicolosi and Linguaglossa are the centres for Etna's surviving **skiing** (ski lifts keep being destroyed by eruptions), and winter sports are also available in the Monti Madonie around Piano Battaglia, where you can rent ski gear. Really, though, no one comes to Sicily just to ski. Volcanoes are a different matter, however, as few in the world are as active as Etna and **Stromboli** – the latter (the furthest flung of the Aeolian Islands) is another great base for guided crater treks (day and night), volcano-watching cruises and the like.

Finally, **horseriding and pony-trekking** are available in some areas – sometimes offered by *agriturismo* (rural tourism) properties.

Culture and etiquette

Sicilian society remains deeply conservative, though values are shifting in the big cities and in places that attract a lot of tourists. Urban Sicilians tend to dress far more smartly than their Northern European counterparts, and even in the most remote village, folk will put on their finery of an evening or for Sunday Mass. Even in holiday resorts, Sicilians would never go out for an evening drink straight from the beach, but go home to shower, and dress up first. Sicilians would rarely sport outright beachwear in a city, but in summer, shorts and strappy tops for women, and shorts (of a certain length) for men are quite normal. However, the same clothes worn on a hot day in April or October will win you stares.

Women travellers

Although Italy has a reputation for **sexual harassment** of women that is well known and well founded, there's no reason to presume that you'll encounter unwarranted intrusion at every turn. A woman travelling alone, or with another woman, can expect a certain amount of attention, including staring, horn-tooting and whistling, though bear in mind that local custom dictates that every friend and acquaintance is greeted with a toot, and that staring openly at strangers is seen as perfectly acceptable. If you follow common-sense rules, the most that you should have to deal with is the occasional clumsy attempt at a pass.

Travelling with children

Children are revered in Sicily and will be made a fuss of in the street, and welcomed and catered for in bars and restaurants. It's perfectly normal for Sicilian children to stay up until they drop, and in summer it's not unusual to see youngsters out at midnight, and not looking much the worse for it.

Pharmacies and supermarkets carry most **baby requirements**, from nappies to formula food. However, you may not see the brands you are used to at home, and don't expect there to be a full range of (or indeed any) organic food products, especially in smaller towns. Otherwise, **food** is unlikely to be a problem as long as your children eat pasta and pizza, and while specific children's menus are extremely rare, many restaurants are happy to provide a smaller version of an adult meal.

Hotels normally charge around thirty percent extra to put an additional bed or cot in the room. However, self-catering apartments, or rooms or B&Bs with the use of a kitchen, are quite common and most Sicilian resorts offer such options. Generous **discounts** apply for children at most sights and attractions, and also when travelling on trains.

> **VISITING CHURCHES, MUSEUMS AND RUINS**
> To visit churches and religious buildings you should **dress modestly**, and avoid wandering around during a service. At otherwise free **chapels, museums** and **archeological sites**, if you're shown around by a custodian or caretaker it's customary to give a small tip – say €1 each.

Shopping

Sicilian street markets provide some of the best experiences on the island – the Ballarò and Capo in Palermo, Catania's fish market and Ortigia's produce market, for example, are sights in themselves, while any market can provide inexpensive souvenirs and gifts like stove-top coffee pots or espresso cups. You'll be taken for an imbecile if you don't haggle for everything except food – ask for "*uno sconto*" (a discount).

Other day-to-day items, toiletries and basic supplies can be bought in local supermarkets. Food and drink **souvenirs** are almost endless: a bag of dried, wild oregano or salted capers from the Aeolians or Pantelliera; pistachios from Bronte; almonds from the Agrigento area; *frutta di Martorana* from Palermo; or marsala wine from Marsala.

Clothes

Taormina and Ortigia, and islands such as Panarea and Salina, have excellent **boutiques**, with clothes and shoes often sourced from niche Italian designers. All the main Italian labels and brands have outlets in Palermo, Catania and Messina, and over the last few years international high-street chains such as H&M, Zara and Mango are becoming more common; look out also for basic everyday clothes at the Italian chains Oviesse, Terranova and Motivi.

Souvenirs

Sicily has a reputation for its **ceramics**, widely available in tourist shops in the major resorts, but best sourced at the production centres, like Santo Stéfano di Camastra (Tyrrhenian coast), Sciacca (south coast) and especially Caltagirone (southern interior).

You'll also see **lace and embroidery** in gift shops in places like Palermo, Taormina and Cefalù.

Recently, small Sicilian companies such as Siculamente have begun to apply a graphic eye to Sicilian tradition, producing witty clothes and accessories that make a change from the ubiquitous *Godfather* T-shirts. There has also been an explosion in stylishly packaged local oils, pestos, conserves and liqueurs,

ideal for presents – though if you care more about contents than packaging, you'll do far better buying capers, wild oregano, olive oil and the like direct from small producers or markets.

Tourist-tat outlets usually sell gift versions of traditional Sicilian **theatre puppets** and **hand-painted carts**, along with a vast array of souvenir fridge magnets. Anywhere near Etna, you're also guaranteed to find things in shops fashioned from **lava** – from paperweights and jewellery to sculptures.

Travel essentials

Beaches

You'll have to pay for access to many of the island's better beaches (known as *lido*), with lounger, parasol and use of the showers often included in the price (usually around €10–15 per person per day). Many lidos also have other facilities like pedalo and windsurf rental, bars and restaurants, and thus make a good bet for families. Elsewhere, beaches are free, though not always clean – during the winter most look like dumps, as it's not worth anyone's while to clean them until the season starts at Easter.

Costs

Sicily isn't particularly cheap compared to other Mediterranean holiday spots, though it is usually better value than the popular tourist parts of mainland Italy. The single biggest cost is generally **accommodation**, with simple one-star hotels, private rooms and bed and breakfasts all starting at around €60 a night. A decent three-star hotel, on the other hand, will set you back up to €120. Of course, you'll pay a lot more in summer in the big tourist spots – Erice, Cefalù, Siracusa and Taormina – and more all year round on most of the offshore islands, particularly the Aeolians and Pantelleria.

Most other items are fairly inexpensive. The Sicilian staple, a pizza and a beer, costs around €12 just about everywhere, while a full **restaurant meal** can cost as little as €30 a head with wine. Of course, there are some excellent Sicilian restaurants where the bill comes in much higher, up to say €50 or €60 a head, but even

---

EMERGENCY PHONE NUMBERS

Police (Carabinieri) ☎112
Emergency services (Soccorso Pubblico di Emergenze) ☎113
Fire brigade (Vigili del Fuoco) ☎115
Road assistance (Soccorso Stradale) ☎116

---

these are remarkably good value for the quality on offer. Other snacks and drinks soon add up, especially in fancy resorts, and you should note that if you sit down in a café (rather than stand at the counter) it'll cost twice as much. **Public transport**, on the other hand, is very cheap, while even the island's showpiece museums, archeological ruins and attractions rarely cost more than €10 – and under-18s and over-65s usually get in for free.

Overall, apart from accommodation, you could reasonably expect to spend €50 a day – taking the train, eating picnics, cheap meals and pizzas, seeing the sights and so on. For a more comfortable daily experience (meals in better restaurants, plus taxis, evening drinks, concerts and the like) you're looking at €80 and upwards.

Crime and personal safety

Although Sicily is synonymous with the **Mafia**, you'll forget the association as soon as you set foot on the island. Cosa Nostra is invisible to the average tourist, and the violence that sporadically erupts is almost always an "in-house" affair. Of more immediate concern is **petty crime**, mainly in crowded streets or markets, where gangs of *scippatori*, or bag-snatchers, strike on foot or on scooters, disappearing before you've had time to react. As well as handbags, they whip wallets, tear off visible jewellery and, if they're really adroit, unstrap watches. Carry shoulder bags, as you'll see many Sicilian women do, slung across your body. It's a good idea, too, to entrust most of your money and valuables to hotel safes or management. The vast majority of petty crimes occur in Catania and Palermo, and at or on the way to and from the airports. On the whole, it's common sense to avoid badly lit areas at night, and run-down inner-city areas at all times.

If the worst happens, you'll be forced to have some dealings with the police. Most conspicuous are the **Carabinieri** – the ones with the black-and-red uniforms – who are a branch of the armed forces and organized along military lines, dealing with general crime and public disorder. They are also the butt of most of the jokes about the police, usually on the "How many Carabinieri does it take to…?" level. They share a fierce turf rivalry with the **Polizia Statale**, or state police, to whom you're supposed to report any theft

at their local HQ, the Questura. The **Polizia Urbana**, or town police, are mainly concerned with directing the traffic and punishing parking offenders. The **Guardia di Finanza**, often heavily armed and screaming ostentatiously through the cities, are responsible for investigating smuggling, tax evasion and other similar crimes, and the **Polizia Stradale** patrol the autostrada.

Electricity

The **supply** is 220V, though anything requiring 240V will work. **Plugs** have two or three round pins (and some sockets have larger holes than others); a travel adaptor plug is very useful.

Health

Sicily poses few **health problems** for visitors; the worst that's likely to happen is that you suffer from the extreme heat in summer or from an upset stomach. **Vaccinations** are not required, but you should take insect repellent and strong sun protection. The **water** is perfectly safe to drink (though bottled water tastes better). You'll find public drinking fountains in squares and city streets everywhere, though look out for "*acqua non potabile*" signs, indicating that the water is not safe to drink.

An Italian **pharmacist** (*farmacia*) is well qualified to give you advice on minor ailments, and to dispense prescriptions. There's generally one pharmacy open all night in the bigger towns and cities. A rota system is used, and you should find the address of the one currently open late/all night on any *farmacia* door or listed in the local paper.

Every town and village has a **doctor** (*médico*). To find one, ask at a pharmacy, or consult the local yellow pages (*Pagine Gialle*) under "Azienda Unità Sanitaria Locale" or "Unità Sanitaria Locale Pronto Soccorso". Out of hours (ie weekends, holidays and night-time), the local **Guardia Médica** first-aid clinic is available in most towns and, though sometimes minimally equipped, will be able to treat stings, bites, fevers and minor accidents.

In an **emergency**, dial ☎113 and ask for "*ospedale*" or "*ambulanza*". The nearest hospital will have a **Pronto Soccorso** (casualty) section, while on smaller islands, or places with no hospital, there is usually a Guardia Medica clinic.

Insurance

It's essential to take out a **travel insurance** policy to cover against theft, loss, illness or injury during your travels. A typical policy will provide cover for the loss of baggage, tickets and – up to a certain limit – cash, as well as cancellation or curtailment of your journey. Most policies exclude so-called dangerous sports, unless an extra premium is paid: in Sicily this can mean things like scuba diving, windsurfing and volcano trekking. If you need to make a claim, you should keep receipts for medicines and medical treatment, and in the event you have anything stolen, you must obtain an **official statement from the police**. This is sometimes easier said than done in Sicily, but persevere; without it, you'll not be able to claim your money back.

Internet

Free **wi-fi** access is pretty standard in B&Bs, hotels and bars.

LGBTQ travellers

Homosexuality is not illegal in Italy, and the age of consent is 16. Attitudes towards homosexuality are much more tolerant in cities and tourist resorts than in the interior. Even so, physical contact between men is fairly common in Sicily, on the level of linking arms and kissing cheeks at greetings and farewells. The main national gay organization, **ArciGay** (Ⓦ arcigay.it), has branches all over the country, including Sicily, and its English-language website is a good place to look for information. The Ⓦ gay.it website also has a wealth of information for the LGBTQ community in Italy.

Living and working in Sicily

Unemployment in Sicily is at a distressingly high level, so it is extremely unlikely that you will find a job that does not depend on your ability to speak English. All EU citizens are eligible to work and study in Italy. Work permits are pretty impossible for non-EU citizens to obtain: you must have the firm promise of a job that no Italian could do before you can even apply to the Italian embassy in your home country. Post-Brexit, UK citizens will need to check for any new regulations.

Red tape

The main bureaucratic requirements to stay legally in Italy are a *Permesso di Soggiorno* and a *codice fiscale*, respectively a piece of paper proving your right to be in the country and a tax number. Available from the *questura* (police station), a **Permesso di Soggiorno** requires you to produce a letter from your employer or place of study, or prove you have funds to maintain yourself. In reality, EU citizens can simply apply on the grounds of looking for work (*attesa di lavoro*), for which you'll need your passport and a copy of it, four passport photos, and a lot of patience. A **codice fiscale** is essential for most things in Italy including buying a transport season pass, a SIM card, opening a bank account or renting a flat. It can be obtained from the local Ufficio delle Entrate, although you can start the process online at Ⓦ www.agenziaentrate.gov.it.

Work options

One obvious option is to **teach English**, for which the demand has expanded enormously in recent years. You can do this in two ways: freelance private lessons, or through a language school. For the less reputable schools, you can get away without any qualifications, but you'll need to show a TEFL (Teaching of English as a Foreign Language) certificate for the more professional – and better-paid – establishments. For the main language schools, it's best to apply in writing before you leave (look for the ads in British newspapers), preferably before the summer. If you're looking on the spot, sift through the local English-language press and phone books and do the rounds on foot, but don't bother to try in August when everything is closed. Italian high schools are also required by law to have mother-tongue language assistants – another good source of work, though the best teaching jobs of all are with a university as a *lettore*, a job requiring fewer hours than the language schools and generally providing a fatter pay packet. Universities require English-language teachers in most faculties; write directly to enquire about positions. Strictly speaking, you could get by without any knowledge of Italian while teaching, though it obviously helps, especially when setting up private classes.

Au pairing is another option: again sift through the ads in locally produced English-language publications in Sicily's big cities in order to find openings.

Mail

Post office opening hours are usually Monday to Saturday 8.30am to 6.30pm; offices in smaller towns close on a Saturday, and everywhere else post offices close at noon on the last Saturday of the month. You can also buy **stamps** (*francobolli*) in some gift shops in tourist resorts, and in shops called *tabacchi*, recognizable by a sign displaying a white "T" on a black or blue background (these also sell cigarettes, sweets and stationery). The Italian **postal service** is among the slowest in Europe – if your letter is urgent, consider paying extra for the express service, or *posta prioritaria*.

Maps

The best large-scale **road map** of Sicily is published by the Touring Club Italiano (*Sicilia*, 1:200,000), and is available from map and travel bookshops or online retailers. Otherwise, the Automobile Club d'Italia issues a good, free 1:275,000 road map, available from the State Tourist Offices, while local tourist offices in Sicily often have free road maps of varying quality. Local tourist offices also hand out reasonable town plans and regional maps.

All national parks and nature reserves (Madonie, Nebrodi, Pellegrino, etc; see ⓦ parks.it) have walking itineraries on their websites, while the various park offices listed in the Guide can supply rudimentary hiking maps and, occasionally, English-language route guides.

Money

Italy's currency is the **euro** (€); notes are issued in denominations of 5, 10, 20, 50, 100, 200 and 500 euros, and coins in denominations of 1, 2, 5, 10, 20 and 50 cents and 1 and 2 euros. Up-to-the-minute currency **exchange rates** are displayed at ⓦ xe.com.

By far the easiest way to get money is to use your bank debit card to withdraw cash from an **ATM** (known as *bancomat* in Italy). These are found even in the smallest towns and on some of the more remote islands, as well as on arrival at the three main airports. Make sure that you have a PIN that's designed to work overseas, and check with your bank to see if you can use your debit card directly in shops and petrol stations etc, as not all systems are available in Sicily.

Chip and Pin and contactless are becoming increasingly common – but not so common that you can stop carrying any cash around. **Credit cards** can also be used for cash advances over the counter in banks and for payment in most hotels, restaurants, petrol stations and some shops. MasterCard and Visa are the most widely accepted cards.

Banking hours vary slightly from town to town, but are generally Monday to Friday 8.30am to 1.20pm and 3pm to 4pm. Outside these times you can change foreign currency at large hotels, the airports at Palermo and Catania, and some main train stations.

Opening hours

Basic opening hours for most **shops and businesses** are Monday to Saturday from 8am or 9am to around 1pm, and from around 4pm to 7pm or 8pm, though some offices work to a more standard European 9am to 5pm day. Everything, except bars and restaurants, closes on Sunday, though you might find cake shops, and fish shops in some coastal towns, open until lunchtime. Local religious holidays and festivals don't generally close down shops and businesses, but everything except bars and restaurants will be closed on the public holidays (see page 36).

Most **churches** open in the early morning (around 7am or 8am) for Mass and close around noon, opening up again at 4pm or 5pm, and closing at 7pm. More obscure ones will only open for early morning and evening services; some only open on Sunday and on religious holidays. One problem you'll face all over Sicily is that lots of churches, monasteries, convents and oratories are **closed for restoration** (*chiuso per restauro*). We've indicated the more long-term closures in the text, but even if there's scaffolding up you might be able to persuade a workman or priest/curator to show you around.

Museums are traditionally open daily from 9am to 1pm, and again for a couple of hours in the afternoon on certain days, but an increasing number now stay open all day; most close on Monday. **Archeological sites** are usually open from 9am until an hour before sunset (in practice until around 4pm from November to March, 7pm from April to October, though never bet against a custodian bunking off early on a slow day). Sites are also sometimes closed on Mondays.

Phones

To **call Sicily from abroad**, dial your international access number + 39 (Italy country code) + number.

Most **mobile phones** bought in the UK and Ireland, Australia and New Zealand, will work in Sicily, though a mobile phone bought for use in the US might not work here unless it is tri-band or supporting GSM. To make sure, check to see if your phone supports GSM 900 and GSM 1800 frequencies. There are no data roaming charges within the EU, though it is unclear what the situation will be for UK travellers post-Brexit.

Time

Sicily (and Italy) is always one hour ahead of GMT. Italy is seven hours ahead of Eastern Standard Time and ten hours ahead of Pacific Time.

Tourist information

The **Italian Government Tourist Board** (Wenit.it) has a useful website for general information, or you can contact the state tourist office organization in your own country. In Sicily, most towns, main train stations and the two principal airports have a **tourist office** (*ufficio di turismo*) or a **Pro Loco** office, usually funded by the *Comune*, overseeing cultural events and providing tourist information. However, recently, funding problems have led to the closure, or reduced opening times, of many offices in smaller centres.

Likely summer (April–Oct) tourist office **opening hours** are Monday to Friday 9am to 1pm and 4pm to 7pm, Saturday 9am to 1pm, though some offices in tourist areas open for longer. From November to March hours may be reduced.

TOURISM WEBSITES

W **bestofsicily.com** Informative site detailing history, the arts, books, food and wine, sights and travel.

W **siciliaonline.it** Some information in English, with details on everything from folklore and the weather to transport and festivals.

W **press.sicilia.it** Mostly Italian, with extracts from all sorts of articles about Sicily, plus news and reviews.

ITALIAN STATE TOURIST OFFICES

Australia & New Zealand ☎ 02 9262 1666, W italiantourism. com.au
Canada ☎ 416 925 4882, W italiantourism.com
UK ☎ 020 7408 1254, W italiantouristboard.co.uk
USA ☎ 212 245 5095, W italiantourism.com

Travellers with disabilities

Although most Sicilians are helpful enough if presented with a specific problem, the island is hardly geared towards accommodating travellers with disabilities. In the medieval city centres and old villages, few budget hotels have elevators, let alone ones capable of taking a wheelchair, and rooms have rarely been adapted for use by disabled visitors. Narrow, cobbled streets, steep inclines, chaotic driving and parking are hardly conducive to a stress-free holiday either. Crossing the street in Palermo is a major undertaking even if you're fully mobile, while Taormina, the most popular resort, poses great **accessibility challenges** for anyone in a wheelchair.

If the thought of negotiating your own way around the island proves too daunting, an **organized tour** may be the way to go. While that will cost more than planning your own trip, it means that you can request accommodation in higher-category hotels that should at least have some facilities for disabled travellers, and you'll also have someone on hand who speaks Italian to help smooth the way. Accessible Italy (W accessibleitaly.com) is an Italian organization offering tours and advice to foreigners, and though it's mainly useful for mainland Italy, you can ask for advice on travelling in Sicily. You can also contact one of the organizations in your own country dedicated to people with disabilities. Tourism For All (W tourism-forall.org.uk), for example, publishes an information pack about holidaying in Italy for disabled travellers.

Palermo
and around

46 Palermo

74 Mondello

74 Monreale

76 Bagheria and around

79 Piana degli Albanesi

80 Ficuzza

81 Corleone

82 Ustica

THE SEASIDE RESORT OF PALERMO

1 Palermo and around

Palermo, Sicily's capital, is filthy, frenetic, noisy and at times exciting – the sort of place you either love or hate. Assailed by the roar of traffic ricocheting off every wall, and the stranglehold of endless shabby concrete apartment blocks, it is not immediately evident that Palermo actually has the largest *centro storico* in Italy, a typically Sicilian fusion of foreign art, architecture, culture and lifestyle. Elegant Baroque and Norman monuments exist cheek by jowl with Arabic cupolas in narrow labyrinthine streets, while exuberant markets swamp the medieval warrens, and chic little shops are squeezed between Renaissance churches and Spanish *palazzi*. But this ancient core is grimy and unkempt; palaces, bombed in World War II, still await reconstruction; and world-class museums remain closed for decades for reasons that no one is willing to disclose.

You'll need at least three or four days to fully explore Palermo's historic sights, medieval quarters and chaotic markets; it is also a base for day-trips to the Norman cathedral of **Monreale**, the seaside resort of **Mondello**, the fishing port of **Porticello** and the fascinating Roman site at nearby **Solunto**. Those with a serious interest in Sicilian – and Mafia – history should devote half a day to the notorious Mafia capital of **Bagheria**, a deeply disturbing place, where magnificent Baroque villas are embedded in a ramshackle grid of illegal housing.

West of the city, a series of underwhelming resorts line the **Golfo di Carini**, while south of Palermo an enticing route heads to **Piana degli Albanesi**, a surviving Albanian Orthodox enclave in a stridently Catholic island, and then further into the mountains to the royal hunting lodge at **Ficuzza** and the notorious Mafia town of **Corleone**. For a real change of air, jump on a ferry or hydrofoil to the volcanic island of **Ustica**, as little as an hour and a quarter from the city, which boasts some of the most stunning diving waters in Sicily. With its good, clean swimming and lazy feel, you may end up staying longer than planned.

Palermo

In its own wide bay underneath the limestone bulk of Monte Pellegrino, and fronting the broad and fertile Conca d'Oro (Golden Shell) valley, **PALERMO** is stupendously sited. Originally a Phoenician colony, it was taken by the Carthaginians in the fifth century BC and became an important Punic bulwark against the Greek influence elsewhere on the island. It was named Panormus (All Harbour) after its obvious mercantile attractions, and it remained in Carthaginian hands until 254 BC, when the city fell to the Romans. Yet Palermo's most glorious days were still to come. In 831 AD the city was captured by the **Arabs**, under whose rule it thrived as an Islamic cultural and intellectual centre – the River Papineto that now flows beneath the city was said to speak with the Nile and abide by its tides. Two centuries later, under the Normans, the settlement continued to flower as Europe's greatest metropolis – famed for the wealth of its court, and unrivalled as a nexus of learning.

Palermo's later fortunes fluctuated with a succession of other foreign rulers, but the city always retained its pre-eminence on the island. However, Allied **bombs** during World War II destroyed much of the port area and turned large parts of the medieval town into a ramshackle demolition site – a state of affairs that is even now only partially resolved.

BARRACUDA ROAM THE WATERS NEAR USTICA

Highlights

❶ Cappella Palatina in the Palazzo dei Normanni The artistic gem of Palermo, this jewel-like chapel is entirely covered with outstanding Byzantine mosaics. See page 55

❷ Galleria Regionale della Sicilia If you only visit one Palermo museum, make it the island's finest collection of medieval art. See page 61

❸ Catacombe dei Cappuccini Contemplate mortality with a shudder at Palermo's most ghoulish site, where the mummified remains of eight thousand bodies are displayed. See page 65

❹ The Duomo at Monreale The magnificently mosaicked cathedral is a stunning testament to Sicily's eclectic Arab, Norman and Byzantine heritage. See page 75

❺ Porticello Boutique lodgings and harbourside fish restaurants make for a great day-trip from the city. See page 78

❻ A trip to Ustíca Take the ferry or hydrofoil out to the relaxed island of Ustica for a spot of hiking, diving and snorkelling. See page 82

HIGHLIGHTS ARE MARKED ON THE MAP ON PAGE 48

1

Although there are notable relics from the ninth to the twelfth centuries, it's the rebuilding of the sixteenth and seventeenth centuries that shaped the city as it appears today. Traditionally, Palermo has been a city of rich **palazzi** and **churches**, endowed by the island's ruling families and wealthy monastic orders, from the mighty Cattedrale to the nearby mosaic-decorated Cappella Palatina, tucked inside the Palazzo dei Normanni. Each old quarter features countless other fascinating churches and chapels, while enthusiasts can trace the city's Norman and Baroque heritage in a series of landmark buildings and sights. But for most visitors, what makes Palermo unique are the rollicking **markets**, traditional **street food**, backstreet **puppet theatres** and creepy **catacombs**.

The Quattro Canti

The **Quattro Canti** or "Four Corners" is the centre (if anywhere is) of the medieval town. Erected in 1611, this is not so much a piazza as a set of Baroque crossroads

1

THE MAFIA IN PALERMO

The most glaring symptom of decay in Palermo, the **Mafia problem**, is intimately connected with the welfare of the city. For years it has been openly acknowledged that a large part of the funds pouring in from Rome and the EU, ostensibly to redevelop the city centre, are unaccounted for – channelled to businessmen and politicians, or simply raked off by Mafia leaders. The subtle control exerted by the Mafia is traditionally referred to only obliquely, though it periodically erupts into the news. Traditional ground-roots Mafia activities such as demanding extortion money (*pizzo*) from local businesses, have little relevance in a world where interests are global and stakes in the billions. Where the practice of *pizzo* continues, it is in the hands of petty criminals. The refusal of many owners of shops and businesses to pay *pizzo* is nowadays more of a gesture of solidarity than a head-on confrontation with the Mafia. It is, however, worth supporting: a thriving organization, **Addiopizzo** (🔘 addiopizzo.org), coordinates the local resistance – their *consumo critico* (critical shopping) list publicizes the hundreds of enterprises now offering a *pizzo*-free Palermo experience, including restaurants, bars and B&Bs – look out for the Addiopizzo stickers in the windows of participating businesses.

that divides central Palermo into quadrants. In each concave "corner" are voluptuous tiers of statues – where, in previous centuries, the heads of convicted rebels were hung from poles. Only a few steps from here lie some of Palermo's most opulent piazzas and buildings, including several of the city's extraordinary churches.

San Giuseppe dei Teatini

Corso Vittorio Emanuele • April–Oct Mon–Sat 7.30–11am & 6–8pm, Sun 8.30am–12.30pm & 6–8pm; Nov–March Mon–Sat 7.30am–noon & 5.30–8pm • Free

Early seventeenth-century **San Giuseppe dei Teatini** is the most harmonious of the city's Baroque churches. The misleadingly simple facade conceals a wealth of detail inside, from tumbling angels holding holy water on either side of the door to the lavish side chapels and a ceiling encrusted with writhing putti. Next door, you'll find the church's former convent, which is now the main building of the **Università**. There are generally plenty of students around here, and a couple of good bars in the little piazza across from the entrance.

Museo d'Arte Contemporanea della Sicilia

Corso Vittorio Emanuele 365 • Tues–Sun 10am–7.30pm • €6 • 🕿 091 587 717, 🔘 museoartecontemporanea.it/museo_Riso/

The restored eighteenth-century Palazzo Riso is now home to the **Museo d'Arte Contemporanea della Sicilia**, with a permanent collection of Sicilian art dating back to the 1950s, as well as a programme of temporary exhibitions. Whether you want to see the collection or not, the *palazzo* is a marvellous place to escape from the hubbub of the city, with a cool bar, courtyard and arty book and gift shop.

Piazza Pretoria

Step into **Piazza Pretoria** and you're confronted by the gleaming-white nude figures of a racy sixteenth-century Florentine fountain, protected by railings to ward off excitable vandals. The piazza also holds the plaque-studded and pristine **Municipio** (city hall) and, towering above both square and fountain, the massive late sixteenth-century flank of the church of **Santa Caterina**, its entrance around the corner on Piazza Bellini.

Piazza Bellini

Piazza Bellini is largely a car park by day, with vehicles jammed together next to part of the city's old Roman wall. It's also where three of Palermo's most distinct churches –

1

Santa Caterina, **San Cataldo** and **La Martorana** – can be found. The first is Baroque, the other two medieval, and you could do far worse than to spend your first hour in the city succumbing to their charms.

Santa Caterina
Piazza Bellini • Mon–Sat 9.30am–1.30pm & 3–7pm, Sun 9.30am–1.30pm • Free

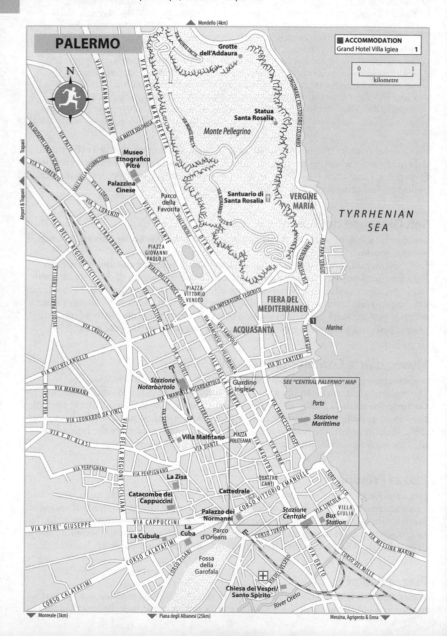

PALERMO ORIENTATION

Palermo is essentially a straightforward street-grid confused by the memory of an Eastern past and gouged by war damage. Historically, the city sat compactly around a central crossroads, the **Quattro Canti**, which is the intersection of Corso Vittorio Emanuele and Via Maqueda, two streets that date from the city's reconstruction in the sixteenth century. Parallel to Via Maqueda, and running north from Stazione Centrale, **Via Roma** was a much later addition, linking the old centre with the **modern city**. At the heart of this nineteenth-century grid of shops, apartments and office blocks are the double squares of Piazza Castelnuovo and Piazza Ruggero Séttimo – together known to Palermitans as **Piazza Politeama** – a lengthy 25- to 30-minute walk from the train station (or a quicker bus ride).

Four distinct medieval quarters lie around Quattro Canti: the **Albergheria** and **Capo** districts lie roughly west of Via Maqueda, **Vucciria** and **La Kalsa** to the east, closest to the water. In the past, the inhabitants of these quarters had their own dialects, trades, palaces and markets – even intermarriage was frowned upon. Today, the areas hold the majority of Palermo's most interesting sights and buildings, woven within a tight, undisciplined web of alleys and piazzas. Often, you'll come across tranquil gardens or chapels containing outstanding works of art, or even stabling for a goat – a world away from the din of the urban assault course outside. Beyond the old centre, on the outskirts of the modern city, are other attractions, from Palermo's best park, the **Parco della Favorita**, to the ghoulish **Catacombe dei Cappuccini monastery**, while the other quick retreat is to **Monte Pellegrino**, the mountain that looms beyond the city to the north.

Given that cars, let alone buses, can't get down many of the narrow streets in the old city centre, you'll have to **walk** around much of what is detailed in this chapter – although for certain specific sights, don't hesitate to jump on a bus, as it's no fun at all slogging up and down the long thoroughfares of the modern city.

Founded in 1566, when Palermo was still under Spanish rule, the exterior of **Santa Caterina** has a certain gravitas, while the interior demonstrates Sicilian Baroque at its most daftly exuberant, as subtle as a multicoloured wedding cake, with every centimetre of the enormous interior larded with pustular relief work, with deep reds and yellows between sculpted cherubs, Madonnas, lions and eagles. One marble panel (in the first chapel on the right) depicts Jonah about to be devoured by a rubbery-lipped whale, with a 3-D Spanish galleon surging through the waves behind them.

San Cataldo

Piazza Bellini • Daily 9am–6pm • €2.50

The little Saracenic red golf-ball domes above Piazza Bellini belong to **San Cataldo**, a squat twelfth-century chapel on a palm-planted bank above the square. Other than the crenellations around the roof it was never decorated, and in the eighteenth century the chapel was even used as a post office. It still retains an intricate geometric Byzantine-Cosmatesque pavement – inlaid with tesserae of marble, porphyry, serpentine and mosaic tesserae.

La Martorana

Piazza Bellini • Mon–Sat 9.30am–1pm & 3.30–5.30pm, often till 6.30pm in summer, Sun 9–10.30am • €2

La Martorana is one of the finest surviving buildings of the medieval city. It was paid for in 1143 by George of Antioch, King Roger's admiral, from whom it received its original name, Santa Maria dell'Ammiraglio. After the Sicilian Vespers rebellion (see page 365), the island's nobility met here to offer the Crown to Peter of Aragon, and under Spanish rule the church was passed to a convent founded by Eloisa Martorana – hence its popular name. It received its curving Baroque northern facade in 1588, but happily this doesn't detract from the great power of the **interior**; enter through the twelfth-century campanile, an original structure with ribbed arches and slender columns. The church is a popular location for Palermitan weddings, spectacular events

1

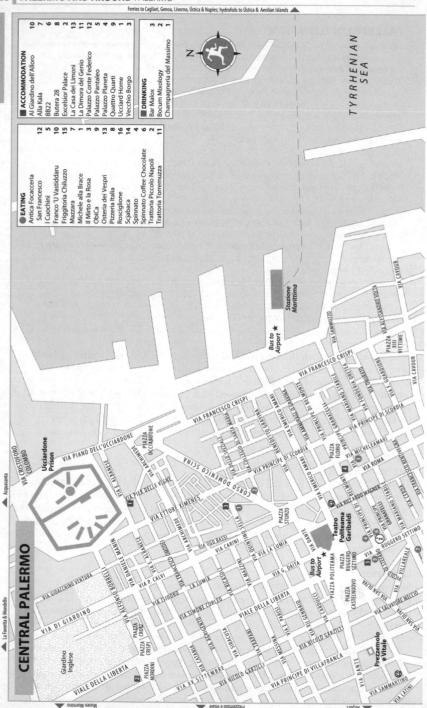

Ferries to Cagliari, Genoa, Livorno, Ústica & Naples; hydrofoils to Ústica & Aeolian Islands

CENTRAL PALERMO

● EATING	
Antica Focacceria San Francesco	12
I Cuochini	5
Franco 'U Vastiddaru	10
Friggitoria Chiluzzo	15
Mazzara	7
Michele alla Brace	3
Il Mirto e la Rosa	3
ObiCà	9
Osteria dei Vespri	13
Pizzeria Italia	8
Roscioglione	16
Scjabaca	14
Spinnato	4
Spinnato Coffee Chocolate	6
Trattoria Piccolo Napoli	2
Trattoria Torremuzza	11

■ ACCOMMODATION	
Al Giardino dell'Alloro	10
Alla Kala	7
BB22	6
Butera 28	8
Excelsior Palace	2
La Casa dei Limoni	13
La Dimora del Genio	11
Palazzo Conte Federico	12
Palazzo Pantaleo	5
Palazzo Planeta	4
Quattro Quarti	9
Ucciard Home	1
Vecchio Borgo	3

■ DRINKING	
Bar Malox	3
Bocum Mixology	2
Champagneria del Massimo	1

TYRRHENIAN SEA

N

Stazione Marittima

Bus to Airport ★

Ucciardone Prison

Giardino Inglese

Teatro Politeama Garibaldi

Bus to Airport ★

Prezzemolo e Vitale

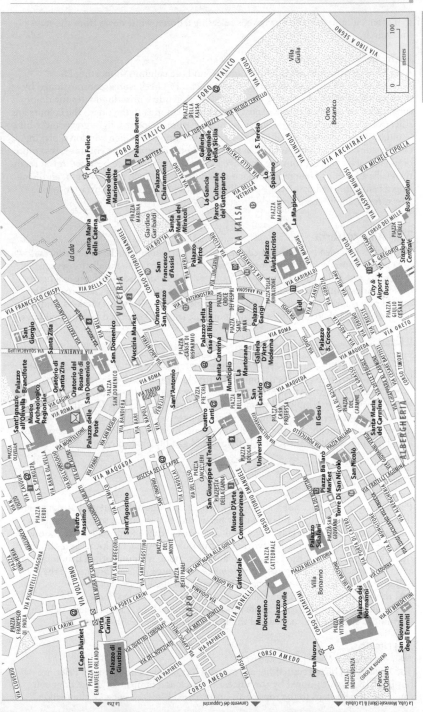

1

that often culminate in the newlyweds releasing a dozen white doves from the steps of the church.

The mosaics

A series of striking **mosaics** is laid on and around the columns supporting La Martorana's main cupola – animated twelfth-century Greek works, commissioned by the admiral himself, who was of Greek descent. A gentle Christ dominates the dome, surrounded by angels, with the Apostles and the Madonna to the sides. The colours are still strong – a golden background enlivened by azure, grape-red, light green and white – and, in the morning especially, light streams in through the high windows, picking out the admirable craftsmanship. On both sides of the steps by the entrance, two more original mosaic panels (from the destroyed Norman portico) have been set in frames on the walls: a kneeling George of Antioch dedicating the church to the Virgin, and King Roger being crowned by Christ – the diamond-studded monarch contrasted with a larger, more simple and dignified Christ.

The Albergheria

The district bounded by Via Maqueda and Corso Vittorio Emanuele, just northwest of Stazione Centrale – the **Albergheria** – can't have changed substantially for several hundred years. Although there are proud *palazzi* on Via Maqueda itself, the real heart of the quarter is in the sprawling warren of tiny streets away from the main roads. The central core is taken up by the **Ballarò**, one of Palermo's liveliest **street markets**, and there are several grand **churches** interspersed among the tall, blackened and leaning buildings.

Il Gesù

Via Ponticello • Mon–Sat 7am–noon & 4.30–6pm, Sun 7am–1pm & 5–7pm • Free

The most dramatic of the Albergheria's churches is **Il Gesù**, or **Casa Professa**, topped by a green-and-white-patterned dome. The first Jesuit foundation in Sicily, it was begun in the mid-sixteenth century and took over a hundred years to complete. It was later almost entirely rebuilt following bomb damage in World War II, and there are still signs of the devastation in the surrounding streets. The reconstruction has been impressively thorough, and the church's awesome interior, a glorious Baroque swirl of inlaid marble, majolica, intricate relief work and gaudily painted ceiling, takes some time to absorb.

Piazza Ballarò market

Mon–Sat, usually from 5am until around 1pm

Piazza Ballarò is the focus of a raucous daily fruit and vegetable **market** that starts early in the morning. Gleaming fish curl their heads and tails in the air, squashes come as long as baseball bats, and vine leaves trail decoratively down from stalls. There are some very cheap snack bars here, too, where you can sidle in among the locals and sample sliced-open sea urchins, fried artichokes and beer, along with unmarked drinking dens and gutsy snack stalls selling *pane con la milza* and *pane e panelle*. Don't leave the area without visiting *Rosciglione* (see page 72), creators of the best *cannoli* in town.

At the southern end of Piazza Ballarò, the bright majolica-tiled dome of the seventeenth-century church of **Santa Maria del Carmine** looms above Piazza del Carmine, a singular landmark amid the market stalls and rubbish-strewn alleys.

San Nicolò

Via Nasi • Usually open Tues & Sat 10.30am–12.30pm • €2.50

The **Torre di San Nicolò** started life as a watchtower in thirteenth-century Palermo, but in 1518 it was co-opted by the adjacent church as a campanile. These days you can climb the 84 steps to the top for an unsurpassed birds'-eye view of the market,

---

FRUTTA DI MARTORANA

When Palermo's religious houses were at their late medieval height, many supported themselves by turning out remarkable sculpted **confectionery** – fruit and vegetables made out of coloured almond paste. La Martorana was once famous for the quality of its almond "fruits", which were sold at the church doors, and today most Sicilian *pasticcerie* continue the tradition. In Palermo these creations are known as **frutta di Martorana**, and cake-shop windows usually display not only fruit but also fish and shellfish made out of the same sickly almond mixture. The best time to see the displays is in October, before the festival of Ognissanti (All Saints). If you want to take *frutta di Martorana* home, note that they do not need to be kept chilled.

---

teeming crowds and the city, while if there are staff around, they will help you identify surrounding landmarks.

San Giovanni degli Eremiti

Via dei Benedettini • Mon–Sat 9am–7pm, Sun 9am–1.30pm • €6

Built in 1132, the deconsecrated church of **San Giovanni degli Eremiti** – St John of the Hermits – is the most obviously Arabic of the city's Norman relics, its five ochre domes topping a small church that was built upon the remains of an earlier mosque (part of which, an adjacent empty hall, is still visible). It was especially favoured by its founder, Roger II, who granted the monks of San Giovanni 21 barrels of tuna a year, a prized commodity controlled by the Crown. A path leads up through citrus trees to the church, behind which lie some celebrated late thirteenth-century cloisters – perfect twin columns with slightly pointed arches surrounding a wilted garden.

Palazzo dei Normanni

Royal Apartments Mon, Fri & Sat 8.15am–5.40pm (last entry 5pm), Sun & hols 8.15am–1pm (last entry 12.15pm) • **Cappella Palatina** Mon–Sat 8.15am–5.40pm (last entry 5pm), Sun & hols 8.15am–9.45am & 11.15am–1pm (last entry 12.15pm) • Check the website before visiting, as parliamentary sessions often disrupt the usual opening hours • Royal Apartments and Cappella Palatina €12, Cappella Palatina only €10.30 • ☎ 091 626 2833, ⓦ federicosecondo.org

A royal palace has always occupied the high ground above medieval Palermo, and the vast length of the **Palazzo dei Normanni**, or Palazzo Reale, still dominates the western edge of the old town. Originally built by the Saracens in the ninth century, the palace was enlarged considerably by the Normans, under whom it held the most magnificent of medieval European courts. The long front was added by the Spanish in the seventeenth century, and most of the interior is now taken up by the Sicilian regional parliament (hence the security guards and limited access).

Visitors can tour the **Royal Apartments**, whose showpiece is the **Sala di Ruggero**, one of the earliest parts of the palace and richly covered with twelfth-century mosaics of hunting scenes. Other rooms, such as the **Sala del Duca di Montalto**, are used for occasional exhibitions. The highlight of the entire palace, however – and the undisputed artistic gem of central Palermo – is the beautiful **Cappella Palatina**, the private royal chapel of Roger II, built between 1132 and 1143. Its intimate interior is immediately overwhelming, with cupola, three apses and nave entirely covered in **mosaics** of outstanding quality. The oldest are those in the cupola and apses, probably completed in 1150 by Byzantine artists; those in the nave are from the hands of local craftsmen, finished twenty-odd years later and depicting Old and New Testament scenes. The colours are vivid and, as at Monreale and Cefalù, it's the powerful representation of Christ as Pantocrator that dominates the senses, bolstered here by other secondary images – Christ blessing, open book in hand, and Christ enthroned, between Peter (to whom the chapel is dedicated) and Paul. The chapel also has a delightful Arabic ceiling with richly carved wooden stalactites, a patterned marble floor

1

and an impressive marble Norman candlestick (by the pulpit), 4m high and contorted by manic carvings.

The Cattedrale

Piazza Cattedrale • **Cattedrale** Mon–Sat 7am–7pm, Sun 8am–1pm & 4–7pm; closed during services • **Area Monumentale** Mon–Sat 9am–5.30pm, Sun 10am–noon • €4, or €8 including roof tour, roof tour only €5 • ☎ 091 334 373, ⓦ cattedrale.palermo.it

As you walk down Corso Vittorio Emanuele from the Quattro Canti, there's no preparation for the sudden, huge bulk of the **Cattedrale**, an even more substantial Norman relic than the Palazzo dei Normanni. Founded in 1185 by Palermo's English archbishop Gualtiero Offamiglio (Walter of the Mill), the cathedral was intended to be his power base in the city. Yet it wasn't finished for centuries, and in any case was quickly superseded by the glories of the foundation of William II's cathedral at Monreale. Less than subtle late eighteenth-century alterations added a dome – completely out of character – and spoiled the fine lines of the tawny stone. Still, the triple-apsed eastern end (which can be seen from a side road off the Corso) and the lovely matching towers are all twelfth-century originals and, despite the fussy Catalan-Gothic facade, there's enough Norman carving and detail to give the exterior more than mere curiosity value.

The same is not true, however, of the overblown interior, which was modernized by Fuga, the Neapolitan architect responsible for the dome. Instead, the main interest inside resides in the **Area Monumentale**, where you can view the **royal tombs**, Palermo's pantheon of kings and emperors. Gathered together in two crowded chapels are the mortal remains of some of Sicily's most famous monarchs, notably Frederick II (left front) and his wife Constance (far right), Henry VI (right front) and Roger II (rear left). In a reliquary chapel to the right of the choir the remains of city patron Santa Rosalia are kept in a silver casket, while in the **treasury**, or *tesoro*, is a rare twelfth-century jewel- and pearl-encrusted skullcap and three simple, precious rings removed from the tomb of Constance of Aragon in the eighteenth century. The **crypt** is home to 23 impressive marble tombs, many of which are actually ancient sarcophagi with interesting decoration – no. 12 is a Greek sarcophagus boasting an imposing effigy by Antonello Gagini, one of a prolific dynasty of talented medieval sculptors who covered Sicily with their creations.

In summer, you can take a tour of the cathedral **roof**, reached via a spiral staircase in one of the towers, for breathtaking views of Palermo and a chance to appreciate the intricacy of the Arab-Norman architecture below.

Museo Diocesano

Via Matteo Bonello 2 • Tues–Sun 9.30am–1.30pm• €4.50 • ☎ 091 607 7303, ⓦ museodiocesanopa.it

At the western end of the cathedral, over the road, stands the **Palazzo Arcivescovile**, the one-time archbishop's palace, entered through a fifteenth-century gateway. One wing of it holds the **Museo Diocesano**, which brings together religious art from the cathedral and from city churches destroyed during World War II. There's some marvellous work here from the medieval and Renaissance periods, including a twelfth-century mosaic of the Madonna, a startling flagellation of Christ by Antonio Veneziano (1388), and a couple of lovely fifteenth-century triptychs, both showing the *Coronation of the Virgin* (one with angels blasting on trumpets).

Porta Nuova

Corso Calatafimi

Alongside the Palazzo dei Normanni, **Porta Nuovo** was Palermo's most important city gate. Erected in 1535, at the beginning of the road to Monreale, it commemorates

1

Charles V's Turkish exploits, with suitably grim, turbaned and moustachioed Moorish prisoners appearing as telamons (columns in human form) along the western side.

Il Capo

Around the back of the Cattedrale lies the **Capo** quarter, one of the oldest areas of Palermo and another maze-like web of run-down streets. The only touch of grace is in the tree-planted **Piazza del Monte**, while former grandeur is indicated by a few surviving sculpted portals in the decaying palaces. One alley, Via Porta Carini, climbs past shambolic buildings and locked, battered churches to reach the decrepit **Porta Carini** itself, one of the city's medieval gates.

These days Via Porta Carini holds one of the city's best **markets**, and the entire area is reminiscent at times of an Arab souk, though with a decidedly Sicilian choice of wares. The market extends on either side of Via Porta Carini, west to the edge of the Capo district and east, along **Via Sant'Agostino** – the closer you get to Via Maqueda, the more it's devoted to clothes and shoes rather than food.

Sant'Agostino

Via Sant'Agostino • Mon–Sat 7am–noon & 4–6pm, Sun 7am–noon • Free

Sant'Agostino was founded by the Chiaramonte and Sclafani families in the thirteenth century. Above the main door (on Via Raimondo) there's a gorgeous latticework rose window and, inside through the adjacent side door, some fine seventeenth-century stuccoes by Giacomo Serpotta. Another door leads to a quadrangle of calm sixteenth-century cloisters. Otherwise, turn the corner, and along Via Sant'Agostino, behind the market stalls, you'll came to a badly chipped, sculpted fifteenth-century doorway attributed to Domenico Gagini.

Via Roma and Via Garibaldi

If you start out from Stazione Centrale, there doesn't seem too much along modern, noisy **Via Roma** to get excited about, but many of the side streets are traditionally devoted to particular trades and commerce. Ironmongery, wedding dresses, baby clothes and ceramics all have their separate enclaves, while the pavements of narrow Via Divisi are chock-full of stacked bikes from a series of cycling shops. Via Divisi itself

---

SICILIAN PUPPET THEATRE

Sicily's most vibrant traditional entertainment is its puppet theatre, and in the engaging **Museo delle Marionette** (Mon–Sat 9am–1pm & 2.30–6.30pm; €5; ☎091 328 060, Ⓦmuseomarionettepalermo.it) you'll find the country's definitive collection of puppets and painted scenery; the museum is just down Via Butera at Piazzetta Antonio Pasqualino. The fairly wide-ranging collection also encompasses puppet figures from Rajasthan, glittering dragons from Rangoon, and the British Punch and Judy in their traditional booth, but it's the Sicilian puppets that steal the show. Best of all is to see one of the theatrical performances staged at the museum – enjoyably rowdy affairs of battles, chivalry, betrayal and shouted dialect, based around French and Sicilian history and specifically the exploits of the hero Orlando (Roland). Other backstreet **puppet theatres**, run by the same families for generations, include Figli d'Arte Cuticchio, at Via Bara all'Olivella 95, near Teatro Massimo (☎091 323 400, Ⓦfiglidartecuticchio.com) and Teatro Argento, at Via Pietro Novelli 1, off Corso Vittorio Emanuele and opposite the Cattedrale (☎349 135 3267, Ⓦpupisicilianiargento.it). Tickets at both €12. If you want your own Sicilian puppet as a souvenir, you'll find shops aplenty selling them along Via Vittorio Emanuele, Via Divisi and around Piazza Marina.

runs to **Piazza della Rivoluzione**, from where the 1848 uprising began; its marked by a surprisingly elaborate fountain. From here, **Via Garibaldi** marks the route that Garibaldi took in May 1860 when he entered the city; at Via Garibaldi 23, the immense, battered fifteenth-century **Palazzo Aiutamicristo** has retained bits of its original Catalan-Gothic structure.

Palazzo Branciforte

Largo Gae Aulenti 2 • Banco di Sicilia collection March–Oct Tues–Sun 9.30am–7.30pm, 1 Nov–28 Feb Tues–Sun 9.30am–2.30pm • €7 • ☎ 091 765 7621 • ⓦ palazzobranciforte.it

Exquisitely restored by one of the doyennes of contemporary architecture, Gae Aulenti, sixteenth-century Palazzo Branciforte once housed the city's official pawnbroker, or Monte dei Pegni. Now run by the city, it has been transformed into a very cool arts centre, with an upmarket restaurant, a cookery school run by Gambero Rosso, book shop and auditorium. The highlight, however, is the beautifully presented collection of artefacts and paintings belonging to the Banco di Sicilia's private collection. There's a wide selection of Italian majolica from the fifteenth to the eighteenth centuries, and an extensive display of Greek vases, Etruscan finds, old maps and ancient coins. Nineteenth-century paintings include the wonderful seascapes and tuna-fishing scenes of Antonino Leto.

Piazza Croce dei Vespri

North of Piazza della Rivoluzione, Via Aragona leads to Piazza Aragona, the first of a confusing jumble of squares. **Piazza Croce dei Vespri** is named for a cross erected in memory of the French who died in the 1282 Sicilian Vespers rebellion (see page 365). Dominating the square is the imposing entrance to the **Palazzo Valguarnera Gangi**, home to the ballroom where Visconti filmed the scene in *The Leopard* where Claudia Cardinale waltzes with Burt Lancaster; you may be able to get a glimpse of the interior by smooth-talking the porter.

Via Paternostro

From Corso Vittorio Emanuele, Via A. Paternostro swings right to the thirteenth-century church of **San Francesco d'Assisi** (daily 8am–noon & 4–6pm), whose well-preserved portal, picked out with a zigzag decoration, is topped by a wonderful rose. All the Baroque trappings have been stripped away to reveal a pleasing stone interior, the later side chapels showing beautifully crafted arches – the fourth on the left is one of the earliest Renaissance works on the island, sculpted by Francesco Laurana in 1468. Along Via Paternostro are lots of little artisan craft shops, most of them doubling as studios, and open from late morning until around 7pm.

Oratorio di San Lorenzo

Via Immacolatella 5 • Daily 10am–6pm • €3 • ☎ 091 611 8168

To the side of San Francesco d'Assisi, the renowned **Oratorio di San Lorenzo** contains another of Giacomo Serpotta's stuccoed masterpieces, namely intricately fashioned scenes from the lives of St Lawrence and St Francis. However, the Oratorio is best known for one of **Caravaggio**'s most dynamic and perfectly preserved canvases, *Nativity with Saints Francis and Lawrence*, which was stolen in 1969 and never recovered. While there have been several attempts to establish its whereabouts, in 2009, Mafia *pentito* (penitent) Gaspare Spatuzza claimed that in the 1980s it had been given to one of Palermo's leading Mafia families, who then hid it in a stable, where it was nibbled to shreds by rats and pigs, then burned.

1

The waterfront

From the Quattro Canti, **Corso Vittorio Emanuele** stretches east towards the waterfront, with the old city harbour of **La Cala** on its left. This thumb-shaped inlet was once the main port of Palermo, stretching as far inland as Via Roma, but the harbour was in decline from the sixteenth century, when silting caused the water to recede to its current position. With all the heavy work transferred to new docks to the northwest, La Cala's surviving small fishing fleet now plays second fiddle to the yachts of Palermo's well-heeled. The little harbour is overlooked on one side by the church of **Santa Maria della Catena**, named after the chain that used to close the harbour in the late fifteenth century. The Corso, meanwhile, ends at the Baroque **Porta Felice** gate, begun in 1582 as a counterbalance to the Porta Nuova, visible way to the southwest. From here, you can judge the extent of the late medieval city, which lay between the two gates.

The whole area beyond the Porta Felice was flattened in 1943, and has since been rebuilt as the **Foro Italico** promenade (also known as Foro Umberto I), complete with small amusement park, from where you can look back over the harbour to Monte Pellegrino. This is one of the liveliest places in the city on summer evenings, when the locals come for the *passeggiata*. A street back, on Via Butera, the seventeenth-century facade of the **Palazzo Butera** faces out over the Foro Italico. Once the home of the Branciforte family, at one time the wealthiest family in Sicily, it was gradually partitioned and sold off, and is now open only for conferences or groups of visitors, but numerous films have been shot here, including *The Talented Mr Ripley* and *The Godfather Part III*.

Piazza Marina

The large square of **Piazza Marina** encloses the tropical **Giardino Garibaldi**, famed for its enormous banyan trees. It's a popular venue for the city's elderly card-players, who gather around green baize tables at lunchtime for a game. The square itself was reclaimed from the sea in the tenth century and subsequently used for jousting tournaments and executions. It is now overlooked by the lovely Renaissance facade of Santa Maria dei Miracoli, and surrounded by pavement restaurants and *palazzi*, including the second largest of Palermo's palaces, the **Palazzo Chiaramonte**, flanking the east side of the square. Dating from the fourteenth century, the palace was a seat of the Inquisition from 1685 to 1782. Today, it is the administrative centre of the university and is only open to the public for occasional art exhibitions.

Palazzo Mirto

Via Merlo 2 • Tues–Sun 9am–6pm• €6 • ☎ 091 616 4751, ⓦ regione.sicilia.it/beniculturali/palazzomirto

Palazzo Mirto is a late eighteenth-century building that's one of the few in the city to have maintained its original furnishings, thus giving a rare insight into *palazzo* life. The exquisite ceilings, intimate Chinese Room, imposing *baldacchino* (canopy), vibrantly coloured tapestries and overblown Baroque fountain are perhaps all to be expected, but the family's more modest living quarters have also been preserved, while visitors can take in the servants' kitchen and the carriages in the stables as well.

Galleria d'Arte Moderna (GAM)

Via Sant'Anna 21 • Tues–Sun 9.30am–6.30pm • €7 • ☎ 091 843 1605, ⓦ gampalermo.it

The former Franciscan Convento di Sant'Anna has been stunningly restored and opened as the seat of the **Galleria d'Arte Moderna**. The collection of nineteenth- and twentieth-century Sicilian works here is displayed thematically (portraits, nudes, mythology, seascapes, landscapes, etc) to great effect. Its **café**, spilling into the courtyard in summer, is one of the loveliest places in the city for lunch or an aperitif. Prestigious international touring exhibitions often visit, too.

Galleria Regionale della Sicilia (Palazzo Abatellis)

Via Alloro 4 • Tues–Fri 9am–6.30pm, Sat & Sun 9am–1pm • €8 • ☎ 091 623 0011, ⓦ regione.sicilia.it/beniculturali/palazzoabatellis

1

Sicily's best collection of medieval art is displayed in the **Galleria Regionale della Sicilia**, which occupies the princely Palazzo Abatellis, a fifteenth-century building that still has echoes of its Catalan-Gothic and Renaissance origins. There are some wonderful works here, by all the major names encountered on any tour of the island, starting with the fifteenth-century sculptor **Francesco Laurana**, whose white marble bust of Eleonora d'Aragona is a calm, perfectly studied portrait. Another room is devoted to the work of the **Gagini** clan, mostly statues of the Madonna, while Antonello Gagini is responsible for a rather strident Archangel Michael, with a distinct military manner. Highlight of the ground floor, though, is a magnificent fifteenth-century **fresco**, the *Triumph of Death*, by an unknown (possibly Flemish) painter. It's a chilling study, with Death cast as a skeletal archer astride a galloping, spindly horse, trampling bodies slain by his arrows. He rides towards a group of smug and wealthy citizens, who are apparently unconcerned at his approach; meanwhile, to the left, the sick and the old plead hopelessly for oblivion.

The first floor

There are three further frescoes (thirteenth- and fourteenth-century Sicilian, and rather crude) above the steps up to the **first floor**, which is devoted to painting. The earliest works (thirteenth- to fourteenth-century) are fascinating, displaying marked Byzantine characteristics, like the fourteenth-century mosaic of the Madonna and Child, eyes and hands remarkably self-assured. For sheer accomplishment, though, look no further than the collection of works by the fifteenth-century Sicilian artist **Antonello da Messina**: three small, clever portraits of saints Gregory, Jerome and Augustine (with a rakish red hat), followed by an indisputably powerful Annunciation, a placid depiction of Mary, head and shoulders covered, right hand slightly raised in acknowledgement of the (off-picture) Archangel Gabriel.

La Kalsa

Orto Botanico Daily 9am–dusk • €5 • ⓦ ortobotanico.unipa.it

The Galleria Regionale stands at the edge of the neighbourhood of **La Kalsa** (from the Arabic *khalisa*, meaning "pure"), which is one of the oldest quarters in Palermo, originally laid out by the Saracens and heavily bombed during World War II. It's still a little on the rough side, with some unkempt squares and alleys, although the area is steadily gentrifying, with the opening of new bars, restaurants and some nice B&Bs. It is an intriguing area to stay in or explore.

To escape La Kalsa and the city noise, walk a few minutes along Via Lincoln to the eighteenth-century gardens of **Villa Giulia**. There's a children's train ride, plus bandstand, deer and ducks, while the **Orto Botanico**, next to the park, dates from 1795 and features tropical plants from all over the world.

Santa Maria dello Spasimo

Piazza Kalsa • Tues–Sun 9.30am–6pm • ☎ 091 616 1486 • Free

The former church and convent of **Santa Maria dello Spasimo** is semi-ruined and roofless – and all the more romantic for it. None other than Raphael painted *Lo Spasimo di Sicilia* for the church, installed here in 1520 (though now in the Prado in Madrid). Since then, the church has been variously used as a theatre, barracks, plague hospital and rubbish tip, but most recently it has become one of the city's most popular and atmospheric concert venues.

La Magione

Piazza Magione • Mon–Sat 9.30am–6pm, Sun 9am–1pm (winter), 9am–7pm (summer) • Donation requested

1

La Kalsa's main highlight is the lovely church of **La Magione**, standing in isolation on Piazza Magione and approached through a pretty palm-lined drive and garden. A fine example of Arab-Norman architecture, it was originally built in 1151 for the Cistercians, but given to the Teutonic knights as their headquarters by Henry VI in 1197. The **cloister** resembles that at Monreale, and boasts a rare Judaic tombstone re-carved into a basin for holy water. In the room between the cloister and the chapel, there's a **fresco** of the crucifixion and – far more interesting and rare – a plaster preparation of the fresco, opposite. It's the only example of a **fresco model** in Sicily, and its near-mathematical sketch lines show the care and detailed planning that went into the creation of such works.

La Vucciria

North of Corso Vittorio Emanuele and east of Via Roma, one of Palermo's oldest markets, **La Vucciria**, is said to be named after the French *boucherie*, for butcher's shop. Once the most renowned **market** in Palermo – and subject of one of Renato Guttuso's most famous paintings – it is now a shadow of its former self, though it still has several basic bars where the wine comes straight from the barrel and a couple of excellent little fish trattorias tucked away in the alleys (best at lunchtime).

San Domenico

Piazza San Domenico • Tues–Sat 9am–noon • Free

The northern limit of La Vucciria market is marked by the church of **San Domenico**, whose eighteenth-century facade, with its double pillars and slim towers, is lit at night to great effect. Inside, a series of tombs contains a horde of famous Sicilians – parliamentarians, poets and painters – of little interest to foreigners except to shed some light on Palermitan street-naming.

Oratorio del Rosario di San Domenico

Via dei Bambinai • April–Oct Mon–Fri 9am–6pm, Sat 9am–3pm; Nov–March Mon–Sat 9am–3pm • €6 (includes Oratorio del Rosario di Santa Zita)

Behind San Domenico is a greater treat, the sixteenth-century **Oratorio del Rosario di San Domenico**, built and still maintained by the Knights of Malta, and adorned by the acknowledged master of the art of stucco sculpture, **Giacomo Serpotta**. Born in Palermo in 1656, Serpotta devoted his entire life to decorating oratories like this – here, the figures of Justice, Strength and suchlike (resembling fashionable society ladies, who often served as models) are crowned by an accomplished altarpiece by Flemish master Anthony van Dyck.

Oratorio del Rosario di Santa Zita

Entrance on Via Valverde • April–Oct Mon–Fri 9am–6pm, Sat 9am–3pm; Nov–March Mon–Sat 9am–3pm • €6 (includes Oratorio del Rosario di San Domenico)

Stucco-seekers will find splendour aplenty behind the late sixteenth-century church of Santa Zita (or Santa Cita) on quiet Via Squarcialupo. The marvellous **Oratorio del Rosario di Santa Zita** contains some of the wildest flights of Serpotta's rococo imagination – a dazzling confusion of allegorical figures, bare-breasted women, scenes from the New Testament, putti galore and, at the centre of it all, a rendering of the Battle of Lepanto. It's a tumultuous work, depicted with loving care – notice the old men and women, or the melancholy boys perched on the ledge, and look for Serpotta's symbol on the left wall, the golden snake.

Piazza XIII Vittime

Piazza XIII Vittime is named for the five tall V-shaped steel plates that splinter out of the ground, commemorating the officials who have lost their lives in Palermo's enduring struggle with the Mafia. The installation replaces a monument commemorating thirteen citizens shot by the Bourbons in the 1860 revolt, which now stands along Via Cavour.

Museo Archeologico Regionale

Piazza Olivella 24 • Has been undergoing restoration for some years, but the ground floor is open, displaying a changing selection of exhibits Tues–Sat 9am–6pm, Sun 9am–1pm • €3 • ☎ 091 611 6806

The cloisters and surviving buildings of a sixteenth-century convent – once the property of the Sant'Ignazio all'Olivella church – now house Palermo's **Museo Archeologico Regionale**. Its magnificent collection gathers together artefacts found at all western Sicily's major Neolithic, Carthaginian, Greek and Roman settlements, but the museum has been undergoing restoration since 2009. The ground floor is now open, but the new layout unclear at the time of writing; the highlights of the collection are described below – though until the entire museums finally re-opens, only some of these exhibits may be visible.

The museum is the repository of the extraordinary finds from the Greek site of **Selinunte** on the southwest coast, gathering together the rich stone carvings that adorned the various temples (known only as Temples A–G). The oldest are single panels from the early sixth century BC, representing the gods of Delphi, the Sphinx, the rape of Europa, and Hercules and the Bull. Other reconstructed friezes are more vivid works from the fifth century BC, like Perseus beheading Medusa, while the most technically advanced tableaux are those from Temple E, portraying a lithe Hercules fighting an Amazon, the marriage of Zeus and Hera, Actaeon savaged by three ferocious dogs, and Athena and the Titan. Other Greek relics include the famous stone lion's-head waterspouts from the fifth-century BC Victory Temple at **Himera** – the fierce animal faces tempered by braided fur and a grooved tongue that channelled the water. Finds from the sites at Termini Imerese and Solunto are also here, as well as rich bronze sculptures like the naturalistic figure of an alert and genial ram (third century BC) from **Siracusa**, once one of a pair (the other was destroyed in the 1848 revolution). In addition, there's **Etruscan** funerary art, a wide range of **Neolithic** finds (including casts of the incised drawings from Addaura, on Monte Pellegrino, and Lévanzo), and a series of beautifully preserved **Roman mosaics** – the largest of which measures nearly 10m in length – excavated from Piazza della Vittoria in Palermo.

THE UCCIARDONE PRISON

A couple of blocks east of the Giardino Inglese is Palermo's notorious **Ucciardone prison**, connected by an underground passageway to the maximum-security bunker where the much-publicized *maxi processi* (maxi-trials) of Mafia suspects were held in the 1980s. At the time, the gloomy Bourbon prison was dubbed "the best-informed centre in Italy for gossip and intelligence about the operations of organized crime throughout the world", not least because it was where a good percentage of the biggest names in the Italian underworld were incarcerated. Mafia affairs were conducted here almost undisturbed, by bosses whose food was brought in from Palermo's best restaurants and who collaborated with the warders to ensure that escapes didn't happen – something that might increase security arrangements and hamper their activities. However, following the murders of Mafia investigators Falcone and Borsellino in 1992, many of the highest-risk inmates were transferred to more isolated prisons in different parts of the country.

1

The modern city

Via Maqueda assumes an increasingly modern aspect as it progresses north from Quattro Canti. Barring the bustle of activity around **Via Candelai** – a busy shopping street by day, a hubbub of cafés at night – the interesting medieval alleys are gradually replaced by the wider and more nondescript streets around Piazza Verdi.

Beyond the **Teatro Massimo** theatre, Via Maqueda becomes Via Ruggero Séttimo, which cuts through gridded shopping streets on its way to the huge double square that characterizes modern Palermo. Known as **Piazza Politeama**, it's made up of Piazza Castelnuovo to the west and Piazza Ruggero Séttimo to the east. Dominating the whole lot is Palermo's other massive theatre, the late nineteenth-century **Politeama Garibaldi**, built in overblown Pompeiian style and topped by a bronze chariot pulled by four horses. From here, broad boulevards shoot up to the shady nineteenth-century gardens of the Giardino Inglese.

Teatro Massimo

Piazza Verdi • Tours every 30min Tues–Sun from 9.30am; last tour Sun–Fri at 5.30pm, Sat at 8pm; no tours during rehearsal times • €8 • A €20 ticket gives access to the roof terraces after your guided tour with fantastic views of the city and bay. Turn up on spec or book in advance • ☎ 091 605 3267, ⓦ teatromassimo.it

Said to be the largest theatre in Italy, built on a scale to rival Europe's great opera houses, the nineteenth-century Teatro Massimo was constructed by Giovanni Battista Basile, whose Neoclassical design was possibly influenced by Charles Garnier's contemporary plans for the Paris Opera. **Tours** with an English-speaking guide show you the rich, gilded, marble **Sala Pompeiana**, where the nobility once gathered, and the domed ceiling in the six-tiered **auditorium**, constructed in the shape of a flower head, its centre and petals adorned with an allegorical portrayal of the triumph of music. Francis Ford Coppola shot the long climactic opera scene of *The Godfather Part III* here, using the theatre's sweep of steps to great effect.

Out from the centre

Highlights outside the city centre, though sadly embedded within the high-rise concrete suburbs, are the ghoulish mummies of the **Catacombe dei Cappuccini** and the UNESCO-listed Arab-Norman palace of **La Zisa**. A one-time royal Bourbon hunting ground, **Parco della Favorita** is now a public park, its charms somewhat compromised by the fact that it's crisscrossed by roads – anyone wanting to escape the city for a few hours would be better advised to head for the nature reserve of **Monte Pellegrino**.

Parco della Favorita

3km north of Piazza Politeama • **Park** No set hours • Free • **Palazzina Cinese** Tues–Sat 9am–5pm, Sun 9am–1pm • Free • Take bus #101 from Stazione Centrale to Piazza Giovanni Paolo II, then change to the #645 and ask to be dropped at the park

North of the centre lies the **Parco della Favorita**, a long, wooded expanse at the foot of Monte Pellegrino, with sports grounds and stadiums at one end, and formal gardens laid out a couple of kilometres beyond. The grounds were originally acquired in 1799 by the Bourbon king Ferdinand during his exile from Naples, and for three years he lived here in the **Palazzina Cinese**, a small but exquisite Chinese-style pavilion.

Monte Pellegrino

Santuario di Santa Rosalia Daily 7.30am–12.30pm & 2–6pm • ⓦ www.riservamontepellegrino.palermo.it • Bus #812 from Piazza Sturzo or Teatro Politeama

North of the city, and clearly visible from the port area, the massive bulk of **Monte Pellegrino** separates Palermo from the bay at Mondello. The mountain is a nature reserve, and there are marked paths across it, though for most locals Monte Pellegrino is primarily a venue for Sunday picnics and strolls. It's also a significant place of pilgrimage, the site of the shrine of the city's patron saint, St Rosalia.

LA FESTA DI SANTA ROSALIA

Next to nothing is known for sure about **Rosalia**, who was probably a member of the Norman court in the twelfth century, except that at some point she rejected her wealthy background and lived as a hermit on Monte Pellegrino. Nothing more was heard of her until the early seventeenth century, when a vision led to the discovery of her bones in a mountain cave. Pronounced sacred relics, these were carried around Palermo in procession in both 1624 and 1625, thus surviving the ravages of a terrible plague. It's a ceremony that is now re-enacted every July 15 (and also Sept 4), with a torchlight procession to the saint's sanctuary that forms part of Palermo's annual jamboree, **La Festa di Santa Rosalia** – "**U Fistinu**" in dialect. An ebullient blend of devotion and revelry, U Fistinu is the central event of the year for locals, while for tourists it's an uproarious party, perhaps the most exhilarating you'll see anywhere in Italy. The annual ritual includes both solemn processions and gaudy entertainment, with the passionate and vociferous participation of hundreds of thousands of Palermitani. The central event is a long parade through the centre of town, from the Palazzo dei Normanni along Corso Vittorio Emanuele to the seafront, headed by a candlelit statue of the saint borne aloft on the "Carro Trionfale". There are puppet re-enactments of the saint's miracles, concerts, exhibitions, and a gastronomic feast on Foro Italico, which features abundant quantities of snails, nuts, watermelons and *dolci*. The celebrations culminate in a spectacular display of fireworks over the harbour.

The half-hour ride up the mountain provides wide views over Palermo and its plain. At the very end of the road stands the **Santuario di Santa Rosalia**, part of a ramshackle collection of huts and stalls, entered through a small chapel erected over a deep cave in the hillside where the saint's bones were discovered in 1624. Inside, a bier contains a reclining golden statue of the saint, thought by Goethe to be "so natural and pleasing, that one can hardly help expecting to see the saint breathe and move". The water trickling down the walls is supposedly miraculous.

A small road to the left of the chapel leads to the clifftop promontory – a thirty-minute walk – where a more restrained statue of Santa Rosalia stares over the sprawling city. Another path, leading up from the sanctuary to the right, takes you to the top of the mountain – 600m high, and around a forty-minute walk. Elsewhere, the trails that cover Monte Pellegrino are dotted with families picnicking, while kids play on rope swings tied to the trees.

La Zisa

Piazza Guglielmo II Buono • Mon–Sat 9am–6.30pm, Sun 9am–1pm • €6 • ☎ 091 652 0269 • Bus #124 from Piazza Sturzo and Piazza Politeama stops at La Zisa • ⓦ coopculture.it/en/heritage.cfm

The palatial king's retreat of **La Zisa** – from the Arabic *al-aziz* or "magnificent" – was begun by William I in 1160, and later finished by his son William II. At one time its beautiful grounds were stocked with rare and exotic beasts, though a raid on the palace by disaffected locals in 1161 released some of the wild animals, which probably came as a bit of a shock to William's neighbours. It's now besieged by modern apartment blocks, but has been thoughtfully restored to something approaching its former glory. The centrepiece is the **Sala della Fontana**, comprising an elaborate fountain in a marble-sided chamber with glittering mosaic decoration. These are appropriate surroundings for a modest collection of Islamic art and artefacts, mostly inscribed copper bowls from periods much later than when La Zisa was constructed, and from different parts of the Mediterranean. The latticed windows afford impressive **views** over the surrounding greenery.

Catacombe dei Cappuccini

Piazza Cappuccini • April–Oct daily 9am–1pm & 3–6pm; Nov–March daily 9am–12.30pm & 3–5.30pm (closed Sun afternoon Nov–March) • €3 • ☎ 091 652 4156 • Take bus #327 from Piazza Indipendenza southwest along Via dei Cappuccini as far as Via Pindemonte, and then follow the signposts for a couple of hundred metres

1

Of all the attractions on the edge of Palermo, it's the **Catacombe dei Cappuccini** that generates the most interest among visitors. For several hundred years the Cappuccini placed its dead brothers in catacombs under the church and later, up until 1881, rich laymen and others were interred here too. Some eight thousand bodies in all were preserved by various chemical and drying processes – including dehydration, the use of vinegar and arsenic baths, and treatment with quicklime – and then placed in niches along rough-cut subterranean corridors, dressed in a suit of clothes that they had previously provided for the purpose. In different caverns reserved for men, women, the clergy, doctors, lawyers and surgeons, the bodies are pinned with an identifying tag, some decomposed beyond recognition, others complete with skin, hair and eyes, fixing you with a steely stare. Those that aren't arranged along the walls lie in stacked glass coffins, and, to say the least, it's an unnerving experience to walk among them. Times change, though, as Patrick Brydone noted in his late eighteenth-century *A Tour Through Sicily and Malta*:

Here the people of Palermo pay daily visits to their deceased friends … here they familiarize themselves with their future state, and chuse the company they would wish to keep in the other world. It is a common thing to make choice of their nich, and to try if their body fits it … and sometimes, by way of a voluntary penance, they accustom themselves to stand for hours in these niches …

Of all the skeletal bodies, saddest are the many remains of babies and young children, nothing more than spindly puppets. Follow the signs for the sealed-off cave that contains the coffin of two-year-old Rosalia Lombardo, who died in 1920. A new process, a series of injections, preserved her to the extent that she looks as though she's asleep. Perhaps fortunately, the doctor who invented the technique died before he could tell anyone how it was done.

ARRIVAL AND DEPARTURE

PALERMO

BY PLANE

Falcone Borsellino airport, also known simply as Punta Raisi (☎ 800 541 880, ⓦ gesap.it), is at Punta Raisi, 31km west of the city. **Buses** (Prestia e Comandè, ☎ 091 580 457, ⓦ prestiaecomande.it) arrive into Palermo (every 30min; 5am–midnight; 45min), and stop outside Politeama Theatre, Stazione Marittima and Stazione Centrale; tickets are €6.30 on board, €6 online, €11 return on board, or €10 via the website. For the return, departures are at 4am, 5am and then every 30min until 11pm. A taxi from the airport to the centre will cost €40–45. There are also shared taxis, which congregate close to the Prestia e Comandè stop, and charge around €6 per person. Trains from **Stazione Centrale** to the airport run approximately every 30 minutes, taking around an hour.

BUS COMPANIES

Most, but not all, services arrive and depart from the bus station at Piazza Cairoli, with direct pedestrian access to the main train station, Stazione Centrale. All companies operating from Piazza Cairoli have ticket booths, while tickets for services leaving from Via Paolo Balsamo are sold in the bar by the bus stop.

AST Piazza Cairoli ⓦ aziendasicilianatrasporti.it. For Bagheria, Castelbuono and Corleone.

Cuffaro Via Paolo Balsamo ⓦ cuffaro.info. For Agrigento.

Interbus Piazza Cairoli ⓦ interbus.it. For Catania and Siracusa.

Prestia & Comandè Stazione Centrale ⓦ prestia ecomande.it. For the airport and Piana degli Albanesi. They leave from under the trees to the right of Stazione Centrale.

Russo Piazza Cairoli ⓦ russoautoservizi.it. For Castellammare del Golfo and San Vito Lo Capo.

SAIS Piazza Cairoli ⓦ saisautolinee.it. For Caltagirone, Catania, Cefalù, Enna, Gela, Messina and Piazza Armerina.

Segesta Piazza Cairoli ⓦ segesta.it. For Alcamo, Messina, Partinico and Trapani.

Salemi Piazza Cairoli ⓦ autoservizisalemi.it. For Castelvetrano, Marsala and Mazara del Vallo.

Tarantola Via Paolo Balsamo ⓦ tarantolabus.it. For Segesta Archeological Site.

BY TRAIN

All trains arrive into Palermo at the Stazione Centrale at the southern end of Via Roma. Bus #101 runs from the station along Via Roma to Via della Libertà. It has its own priority lane, so is much faster than most of the city's other services.
Destinations Agrigento (10 daily Mon–Sat, 7 daily Sun; 2hr 10min); Bagheria (2–3 hourly; 10min); Castellammare del Golfo (5 daily; 2hr 30min–3hr 30min); Cefalù (1 hourly; 45min–1hr); Milazzo (14 daily; 2hr 30min–3hr); Messina (14 daily; 3–4hr); Termini Imerese (2–3 hourly; 25–40min).

BY BUS

The majority of country- and island-wide buses operate from the recently opened Piazza Cairoli bus station alongside the train station.
Destinations Agrigento (5 daily; 2hr 30min); Bagheria (1–2 hourly Mon–Sat; 1hr 15min); Caccamo (4 daily Mon–Sat; 1hr); Caltagirone (1 daily except Sat; 3hr); Caltanissetta (7–10 daily Mon–Sat, 5 daily Sun; 1hr 40min); Castelbuono (5 daily Mon–Sat, 1 daily Sun; 1hr 40min–2hr 30min); Castellammare del Golfo (6 daily Mon–Sat, 1–3 daily Sun; 50min); Catania (1 hourly; 2hr 40min); Cefalù (5 daily; 1hr); Corleone (1 hourly Mon–Sat; 1hr 30min); Enna (5–7 daily; 1hr 35min–1hr 50min); Gela (3–4 daily; 2hr 45min–3hr); Marsala (1 hourly; 2hr 30min); Messina (5 daily Mon–Sat; 2hr 40min); Piana degli Albanesi (6 daily Mon–Sat; 1hr); Piazza Armerina (1 hourly; 2hr 15min); San Martino delle Scale (2 daily Mon–Sat; 30min); San Vito Lo Capo (2–4 daily Mon–Sat, 1–3 daily Sun; 2–3hr); Siracusa (2–3 daily; 3hr 15min); Termini Imerese (6 daily Mon–Sat; 40min); Trapani (Segesta Archeological Site; 1–2 hourly; 2hr).

BY FERRY OR HYDROFOIL

Stazione Marittima All ferry and hydrofoil services dock at the Stazione Marittima, just off Via Francesco Crispi. A free *navetta* bus shuttles constantly between the Stazione Marittima and the port entrance (though it is only a 5min walk), from where it's a 10min walk up Via E. Amari to Piazza Castelnuovo. There is a left luggage office at the port (€3.50 per piece of luggage); it's officially open daily 7am–8pm, but they may ask you what time you want to pick up your luggage, and close for a while if things are quiet.
City transport from the port Bus #139 connects the port with Stazione Centrale, though it is rather infrequent, so it is better to walk up Via E. Amari to Piazza Politeama from where buses #101 or #102 run regularly to the train station.
Schedules The ferry and hydrofoil services detailed here refer to the period from June to Sept; expect frequencies to be greatly reduced or suspended outside these months. Ferries are run by Tirrenia (ⓦ tirrenia.it), Siremar (ⓦ siremar. it) and GNV (ⓦ gnv.it). Hydrofoils from Palermo to Ustica are run by Liberty Lines (ⓦ libertylines.it)
Ferry destinations Cagliari (Tirrenia, 1 or less weekly; 12hr); Civitavecchia (GNV, up to 3 weekly; 14hr); Genoa (GNV, 1 daily; 20hr); Naples (GNV, 1–2 daily; 11hr); Tunis (GNV, 1–2 weekly; 10hr); Ustica (Siremar, 1 daily; 2hr 20min).

GETTING AROUND

BY BUS

AMAT buses City buses run by AMAT (ⓣ 091 350 111, infoline ⓣ 848 800 817 or from a mobile ⓣ 199 240 800, ⓦ amat.pa.it) cover every corner of Palermo as well as Monreale and Mondello.
Fares and tickets There's a flat fare of €1.40 valid for 1hr 30min, or you can buy an all-day ticket for €3.50. Keep an eye out as well for little orange electric minibuses (known as the *navetta arancione*) zipping around the historic centre. When they run, the service is brilliant, and has been free. However its future is uncertain. Buy tickets for other routes from AMAT booths outside Stazione Centrale, at the southern end of Viale della Libertà, as well as in *tabacchi* and anywhere else you see the AMAT sign, or, if you forget, from the driver for a supplement of €0.40. Validate tickets in the machine at the back of the bus as you board – there has recently been a clampdown on people travelling without tickets, with spot checks carried out by plain-clothes inspectors. The main city bus rank is outside Stazione Centrale and buses run until midnight (11.30pm on Sun).

BY CAR

City driving It's far better not to drive in Palermo – you won't need a car to get around, and you can pick up a rental car on the day you leave if you plan to explore elsewhere. Driving into the city can be a bit traumatic, as directional signs are confusing and the traffic unforgiving of first-time visitors. Following signs for "Stazione Centrale" – or anything that reads "Centro" – should at least get you into the city, while Piazza Politeama is a convenient first place to get your bearings and leave your vehicle.
Parking If it is still up and running (the scheme's future is in doubt) take advantage of Palermo's park and ride and leave your car outside the centre at the Parcheggio Basile, on Via E Basile, from which free shuttles run to Piazza Independenza (bang in front of the Palazzo dei Normanni). Check whether the scheme is active on ⓦ amat.pa.it.
Finding a parking space can be a real problem, though you'll find somewhere eventually if you drive around for long enough. Metered parking costs €1 an hour (maximum 3hr) – either feed the ticket machine or buy a parking scratch card (*biglietto parcheggio*) from a nearby shop. In some areas, you will be ushered into a parking space by an unofficial attendant, who will expect a tip of a €1. It's much less hassle to use a garage, especially if you have to leave your car in Palermo's old quarter overnight: useful

1

options include L'Oasi Verde (Corso Tukory 207, southwest of Stazione Centrale), Central Garage (Piazza Giulio Césare 43, in front of Stazione Centrale), Via Guardione 81 (near Stazione Marittima, behind Via Francesco Crispi) and Via Sammartino 24 (town centre, off Via Dante). It costs around €20 per day to garage-park, usually less when arranged through a hotel.

Leaving the city Take Via Oreto (behind Stazione Centrale) for the Palermo–Messina (A19) and Palermo–Catania (A20) autostradas; Corso Vittorio Emanuele (westbound) for Monreale; and Viale della Libertà (northbound) for the airport and Trapani.

Car rental As well as the major international operators (Hertz, Avis, Budget, etc) car rental brokering sites will probably come up with several of the smaller, independent companies, all with booths at the airport. Before booking, look at other customer reviews, check carefully for hidden extras, and be sure to take note whether pick-up is from the airport itself or whether you need to take a shuttle bus to an offsite office (which can be time-consuming).

BY TAXI

Taxi companies and ranks Palermo's three taxi companies – Auto Radio Taxi (☎ 091 513 311, ⊚ autoradiotaxi.it), Radio Taxi Trinacria (☎ 255 or ☎ 091 6878, ⊚ radiotaxitrinacria. it) and Sicilia Uno (☎ 339 408 5713) – all charge the same rates. Within the city there is a flat fare of €7. There are ranks at the airport, train and bus stations, as well as at piazzas Castelnuovo, Verdi and Matteotti and at Via Roma.

BY TRAM

There are three tramlines in Palermo, two operating out of the Stazione Notarbartolo and one from outside Stazione Centrale. The historic centre is not covered at all, and unless you fancy a trip to the Forum shopping mall on Line 1 (get off at Roccella), it's unlikely you will need to use them. They are run by AMAT, and bus tickets are valid.

BY HORSE-DRAWN CARRIAGE OR APE

Taking a horse-drawn carriage (*carrozza*), is a suitably kitsch way to see the city, or you could take a tour on a Piaggio Ape, a three-wheeler pick-up. Both tout for business alongside Piazza Pretoria, outside the port and by the cathedral, and should charge around €20 per person for a tour of the city.

BY BIKE OR SCOOTER

If you're adept on two wheels, biking is not a bad option: as long as you realize the rules of the road – he who hesitates is lost, and go for the gap – weaving your way in and out of the traffic can be an exhilarating way to save time and legwork. Rent Bike, Via Giardinaccio 66, off Via Maqueda (☎ 331 750 7886) offer bicycle and scooter rental.

INFORMATION AND TOURS

Tourist offices Palermo's city-centre tourist office is at Via Principe di Belmonte 92, Mon–Fri 8.30am–2pm, 2.30–6pm, ☎ 091 585 172, ⊚ www.palermotourism.com.

Listings information For a rundown of what's on, there are several websites including ⊚ palermoweb.com, ⊚ palermoviva.it, ⊚ balarm.it and ⊚ palermotoday.it, while ⊚ visitpalermo.it is a useful source of information in English, covering everything from guided tours and wine tastings to where to stay and where to eat.

ACCOMMODATION · SEE MAPS ON PAGES 50 AND 52

Most of Palermo's traditional budget **hotels** lie on and around the southern ends of Via Maqueda and Via Roma, close to Stazione Centrale, but you'll get far more for your money in the city's **B&Bs**, many of which are charming and extremely well run. Prices tend to stay the same year-round (except out on the nearby coast, where usual summer rates apply), but advance reservations are recommended if you want to be sure of a room in a particular place (and also around the time of Palermo's annual festival, July 11–15, see page 65). The two nearest **campsites**, as well as Palermo's **youth hostel**, are at the beachside town of Sferracavallo, 16km northwest of the city or a good half an hour on the bus – convenient for beach or airport but not really for city sightseeing or nights on the town.

OLD TOWN

Al Giardino dell'Alloro Vicolo S. Carlo 8 ☎ 338 224 3541, ⊚ giardinodellalloro.it. Lovely, homely-feeling B&B in the heart of La Kalsa with books for guests to borrow, a courtyard where breakfast is served, and a living room used as an exhibition space for contemporary Sicilian artists. The rooms feature original works of art and come equipped with kettles and mugs – nice touch for winter visits. There is a small kitchen for guests' use, and more pretty rooms in the recently opened annexe. €85

Alla Kala Via Vittorio Emanuele 71 ☎ 091 743 4763, ⊚ allakala.it. An excellent, centrally located choice, this spick-and-span B&B has five stylish designer rooms and a suite with magnificent views of the sailing marina. It has a keen following among those in the know, so book in advance. €80

BB22 Palazzo Pantelleria, Largo Cavalieri di Malta 22 ☎ 091 611 1610 or ☎ 335 790 8733, ⊚ bb22.it. Faultless Milanese designer-chic (resinated cement floors, perspex chairs, walls painted in matt stone hues) combined with home comforts (free wi-fi, coffee and water) in a historic

IL CAPO MARKET

1

palazzo a few steps from the Vucciria market. Enjoy breakfast on the small roof terrace. The owners also have some marvellously chic and spacious apartments (from €160) across the square in Palazzo Moncada. **€120**

Butera 28 Via Butera 28, ☎ 00 39 333 3165432 ⓦ butera28.it. A dozen atmospheric apartments in an aristocratic palazzo on the fringes of La Kalsa, run with flair and elegance by the owners, la Duchessa Nicoletta Polo Lanza and her husband. There is everything you need in the apartments, and Nicoletta runs wonderful cooking days, that include tours of the market and lunch in the grand dining room. **€60**

Excelsior Palace Via Marchese Ugo 3 ☎ 091 7909001, ⓦ excelsior-palermo.com. Uptown Palermo hotel overlooking broad, tree-lined Viale della Libertà. Rooms are spacious and super-comfortable, breakfasts are cornucopian, and staff are attentive and friendly. There is also a fine restaurant onsite. **€180**

La Casa dei Limoni Piazza Giulio Césare 9 ☎ 334 834 3888 or 338 967 8907, ⓦ lacasadeilimoni.it. A very basic, no frills B&B right opposite the train station that's a convenient place to stay if you arrive late or have to leave early. Breakfasts are underwhelming, so better to go out to a café! **€50**

La Dimora del Genio Via Garibaldi 58 (5min walk from Stazione Centrale) ☎ 347 658 7664, ⓦ ladimora delgenio.it. Three cosy rooms in a centrally heated seventeenth-century *palazzetto*, furnished with a tasteful blend of antiques, modern furniture and original paintings. The friendly owner is a talented cook, and offers cooking courses for guests, as well as a splendid Sunday dinner for €30 a head. **€90**

Palazzo Conte Federico Via dei Biscottari 4 ☎ 091 651 1881, ⓦ contefederico.it. A magnificent (if chilly) Arabic-Norman palace built over the Punic city walls close to Ballarò market, retaining fourteenth-century frescoed ceilings and an impressive armoury. The aristocratic owners have several comfortable and practical one- and two-bedroom apartments for rent (minimum three nights stay), plus a palatial suite, and can offer cooking lessons – followed by a torchlit dinner in the defensive tower. Apartments **€100**, suite **€360**

Palazzo Planeta Via Principe di Belmonte 68 ☎ 39 0925 195 5460, ⓦ planetaestate.it. Seven spacious, airy and super-stylish apartments with full kitchens in a palazzo belonging to the Planeta family of wine makers. Wonderful mixture of contemporary and antique furniture, along with lovely Indian textiles. Great location, right off Via Roma. **€135**

Quattro Quarti Palazzo Arone di Valentino, Via Vittorio

Emanuele 376 ☎ 347 854 7209, ⓦ quattroquarti.it. A superior B&B with four smart, elegant rooms in part of a huge *palazzo* owned by the Arone di Valentino family. Guests are very well looked after, making this a great choice if you're a little nervous about finding your feet in Palermo. In the main part of the palace, there is a plush suite (€140) of rooms furnished with antiques (where Charles and Camilla have stayed). **€98**

MODERN CITY

★ **Palazzo Pantaleo** Via Ruggero Settimo 74/H ☎ 091 325 471 or ☎ 335 700 6091, ⓦ palazzopantaleo.it. This meticulously run B&B has seven huge, light, airy rooms in an eighteenth-century *palazzo*, set on a quiet square in a very safe district close to Piazza Politeama (and the airport bus-stop). Great attention to the practical details that matter to business travellers – internet access in all rooms, adaptors for charging mobile phones in all sockets – plus respect for the privacy and independence of guests. There's also a small kitchen where you can make drinks or snacks – a good choice for solo women. **€100**

Ucciard Home Via Enrico Albanese 34–36 ☎ 091 348 426, ⓦ ucciardhomehotel.com. Trendy designer hotel opposite the prison, with sixteen comfortable, stylish rooms and lovely, luxurious bathrooms. Staff are excellent, breakfasts good and deals via the website can be fantastic. **€99**

Vecchio Borgo Via Quintino Sella 1–7 ☎ 091 611 8330, ⓦ vecchioborgohotelpalermo.com. A smart and appealing hotel between the Piazza Politeama and Vecchio Borgo, one of Palermo's best little neighbourhood markets, with comfortable rooms decorated with bold printed fabrics and all amenities (including internet). The breakfast is excellent and includes home-made cakes. There's also a garage (€10 a night) and outdoor car park (free), but spaces are limited. Online deals can make it cheaper than many B&Bs. **€66.**

OUT FROM THE CENTRE

★ **Grand Hotel Villa Igiea** Via Belmonte 43 ☎ 091 631 2111, ⓦ villa-igiea.com; bus #731 or #721 from Piazza Croce, halfway along Via Liberta. This classic Art Nouveau building from 1900, originally a villa belonging to the Florio family (the people who pioneered tuna canning), was designed by Ernesto Basile and stands outside the city centre above the Acquasanta marina. It has a swimming pool overlooking the port, shady gardens, a tennis court and sweeping terraces for enjoying the most stylish aperitif in town. Give up all notions of sightseeing in favour of long lazy days by the pool. Boat trips and food tours available. **€290**

EATING

SEE MAP ON PAGE 52

You can eat fairly cheaply in Palermo, either snacking in **bars** and at **market stalls** or sitting down in one of dozens of good-value **restaurants** throughout the old town which serve *cucina casalinga* (home cooking). Pizzas and pastries, in particular, are among the best in Sicily, while fish is another local highlight – a typical Palermo speciality is *pasta con le* *sarde*, macaroni with fresh sardines, fennel, raisins and pine kernels. Traditional **street food** is enjoying something of a renaissance, and in hole-in-the-wall outlets and fancy bars alike you can try the sort of earthy snacks and fritters that the locals have eaten for decades. The other unmissable treat is **ice cream** – Palermo's best *gelaterie* (ice-cream parlours) are famed all over Italy. Restaurants tend to **close early**, especially in the central old town, where if you turn up at 10pm the waiters are likely to be packing up around you. For the most popular places, go before 8pm or be prepared to wait in line. If you are **self-catering** or **picnicking**, note that there's a chaotic branch of Lidl at Via Roma 59 (daily 8am–10pm), while the high-end gourmet supermarket chain Prezzemolo e Vitale has several branches in the smart area to the west of Viale della Libertà, most conveniently at Via Principe di Villafranca 20B and Via Noto 10 (Mon–Sat 8.30am–1.30pm & 4.30–8.30pm). They also do online orders and delivery (🖥 prezzemoloevitale.net).

CAFÉS AND SNACKS

★ **I Cuochini** Via Ruggero Settimo 68 ☎ 091 581 158. Diminutive, spick-and-span *friggitoria* – all gleaming white tiles and zinc – founded in 1826, and concealed within an arched gateway (the only sign is a small ceramic plaque). *Panzerotti* (deep-fried pastries stuffed with tomato, mozzarella and anchovy, or aubergine, courgette and cheese), *arancini* (with ragù, or with cheese and ham), *pasticcino* (a sweet pastry with minced meat), *timballini di pasta* (deep-fried pasta), *besciamelle fritte* (breadcrumbed and deep-fried bechamel) and the like – all at less than €1 a portion. Mon–Sat 8.30am–2.30pm.

Franco 'U Vastiddaru Piazza Marina. Palermitani street food such as *pane e panelle*, *arancini*, *crocchè* and *pane con la milza* – which you can eat at plastic tables on plastic plates with plastic knives and forks, on the busy corner of Piazza Marina and Via Vittorio Emanuele. Eat well for less than €10 a head, but be prepared to queue. Daily 11am until late.

★ **Friggitoria Chiluzzo** Piazza Kalsa. Stand under a canopy, drink beer from a bottle, and eat *pane e pannelle* from a paper wrapping. Fantastic. Daily morning until late.

Mazzara Via Magliocco 15 (off Via Ruggero Settimo) ☎ 091 321 443. Long-established bar-*pasticceria* where Tomasi di Lampedusa is reputed to have penned some of *The Leopard*. These days it serves light brunch and lunches – try the rare roast beef with rocket and shaved parmesan – alongside a seductive selection of pastries and ice creams. A pastry and coffee will cost around €4.50, a salad and glass of wine around €12. Tues–Sun 7am–9pm.

★ **Michele alla Brace** Piazza Borgo Vecchio. At the tiny market of Piazza Borgo Vecchio, you can't miss this huge grill (a favourite with Jamie Oliver, no less) with a couple of plastic tables and a steaming cauldron of vegetables. Buy your fish from one of the nearby stalls and bring it to Michele, who will grill it and provide you with veg, drinks and a table. Calculate on spending €5–8 a head, depending on how much you drink. Mon, Tues & Thurs–Sat lunch.

ObiCa Rinascente, Via Roma/Piazza S. Domenico ☎ 091 601 7861, 🖥 obika.com. On the top floor of the Rinascente department store, this is the Palermo branch of an exclusive chain of bars specializing in meticulously sourced *mozzarella di bufala*, which appears in exquisitely presented salads and other light dishes (from €8). A great lunchtime escape from the heat and chaos of Palermo, and a good place for an aperitivo (served daily 6.30–9pm), the drinks accompanied by a selection of mouthwatering mozzarella nibbles. Daily 9am–midnight.

PALERMO'S STREET FOOD

Street food in Palermo is pretty distinctive – apart from pizza slices and pastries there are plenty of things you may not have come across before (and a few you may not wish to encounter again). Many of the more **traditional snacks** are straight out of the market, and while chopped boiled octopus (*purpu* in Sicilian), cooked artichokes and charcoal-roast peppers and onions are at least familiar, you might be less inclined to hover at the stalls selling *pane con la milza* (*pane cu la meuza* in Sicilian) – bread rolls filled with sautéed beef spleen or tripe, which either come unadorned (*schiettu*, meaning "nubile") or topped with fresh ricotta and caciocavallo cheese (*maritatu*, "married"). Meanwhile, any old-fashioned **friggitoria** (deep-fry takeaway) – and there are still plenty in Palermo – serves up *arancini* (savoury rice balls), *pane e pannelle* (chickpea-flour fritter served in a bread roll) and *crocchè* (potato croquettes with anchovy and caciocavallo cheese). *I Cuochini* (see page 71) wins our vote for street food, but **markets** are also a great place to sample all these snacks, especially at Ballarò market (Piazza del Carmine and Piazza Ballarò), at Vecchio Borgo and along Via Sant'Agostino. The Ballarò market, in particular, has a few very basic *osterie* – wooden tables scattered between the market stalls – where you can wash down your snack with a beer or two. Anyone wanting to delve deeper into the fascinating world of Palermo street food is well advised to take one of the brilliant street food walking tours run by Streaty (🖥 streaty.com; €30 per person).

1

Rosciglione Via Gian Luca Barbieri 5 ☎091 651 2959. Watch *cannoli* being made as you eat them at this bakery (which exports worldwide) on the edge of the Ballarò market. Prices start at €3.50 for filled *cannoli*. Mon–Sat 7am–2pm & 1.30–6pm.

Spinnato Via Principe di Belmonte 107–115 ☎091 749 5104, Ⓦspinnato.it. With tables outside on a pedestrianized street, this is the perfect place for an ice cream, or an aperitivo served with an aesthetically presented cascade of roast almonds, shelled pistachios and crisps. Cornetti and pastries are less recommendable. Daily breakfast until late.

Spinnato Coffee Chocolate Via Principe di Belmonte 108 ☎0913 29 220. As the name suggests, a branch of *Spinnato* that specializes in fine chocolates along with coffees and pastries. Try hot chocolate made with *fondente* (dark) chocolate at one of the seats outside. Daily breakfast until 9pm.

RESTAURANTS

Antica Focacceria San Francesco Via A. Paternostro 58 ☎091 320 264, Ⓦafsf.it. This old-fashioned place has been in the same family for five generations. Downstairs they serve traditional Palermitani street food, such as *focaccia schietta* (focaccia with offal and caciocavallo cheese), *sfincione* (pizza with onion, tomato, caciocavallo and breadcrumbs), *crocchè* (potato croquettes) and *panelle* (chickpea-flour fritters). Upstairs you can eat full meals (try the *pasta con le sarde*). There are also several fixed-price menus: *pannelle, crocchè*, an *arancina* or slice of pizza, *cannolo* and a drink for €7.50; or the same, with pasta instead of the *arancina* or pizza for €11. If you prefer something lighter, choose from their range of salads, and in summer you can eat outside. Mon & Wed–Sun 11am–11pm.

Il Mirto e la Rosa Via Principe di Granitello 30 ☎091 324 353. One of the Palermo businesses that don't pay *pizzo* (see page 49), *Il Mirto* began life as a vegetarian restaurant, and the emphasis on vegetables remains, alongside carefully sourced local fish and meat. Signature dishes include *caponata* with pistachio-spiked couscous, and home-made *tagliolini* with a sweet, sticky tomato sauce, grilled aubergine and cheese from the Nebrodi mountains. Finish up with a decadent dessert followed by home-made cinnamon liqueur. Eating à la carte, you'll spend around €25 for three courses without wine, €30 with dessert, but there are usually several fixed-menu deals. Mon–Sat lunch & dinner.

★ **Osteria dei Vespri** Piazza Croce dei Vespri ☎091 617 1631, Ⓦosteriadeivespri.it. Palermo's best restaurant was opened by brothers Andrea and Alberto Rizzo as a hobby a decade ago and they continue to run it with passion, cooking complex meals with a loyal and intelligent use of local Sicilian ingredients. Dishes might include rabbit terrine with pistachios from Bronte, black *tagliolini* served with red mullet, ginger, red onion and fresh fava beans, or quail stuffed with prunes served on a purée of cannellini beans and celeriac. It is expensive, but well worth it – expect to pay €20 or more per course à la carte, while there are 'land' and 'sea' *degustazione* menus at €70 and a truffle menu at €90 per person, excluding wine. Or, come at lunchtime for great value fixed menus, from just €33 a head including a glass of wine. Mon–Sat lunch & dinner.

Pizzeria Italia Via Orologio 54 ☎091 589 885. Opposite Teatro Massimo and attracting large queues, this is the best place in town for light, oven-blistered pizzas (€4.50–12). Try the "Palermitana" with tomato, anchovies, onion, artichokes, caciocavallo cheese and breadcrumbs. Dinner only; closed Mon.

Scjabaca Vicolo San Carlo 42, ☎091 5976739 Relaxed, intimate little restaurant run by two sisters, serving typical Sicilian dishes such as hand-made fettuccine with sardines, fennel, raisins and pine nuts (€12), and panna cotta with a chilli jam and chocolate (€5). Daily lunch & dinner.

Trattoria Piccolo Napoli Piazzetta Mulino di Vento 4 ☎091 320 431. Lively trattoria off the Vecchio Borgo market, founded in 1951 and run by three generations of the same family. They have two boats at the fishing port of Terrasini: fish is brought in daily, and anything not eaten that day is sold on to the local market stalls. Try raw prawns, pasta with mixed seafood (€14) or what may prove to be the best *caponata* you will ever taste (€5). Mon–Sat lunch only.

★ **Trattoria Torremuzza** Via Torremuzza 17 ☎091 252 5532. Bustling, no-frills trattoria where fish is grilled on an outside brazier. Eat at streetside tables in summer, inside in winter. *Antipasti* (mussel soup, seafood salad, etc) and *primi* (pasta with broccoli, with mussels and clams, or with swordfish and aubergine) are priced at €5–7.50, except for a couple of special dishes such as spaghetti with *ricci di mare* (sea urchin) which ring in at €10. Meat *secondi* (*involtini*, charcoal-grilled sausage and the like) are around €5, while fish dishes (mixed fried or grilled fish, grilled prawns, grilled sea bream or sea bass) cost €7–10. Calamari and swordfish are frozen (but none the worse for it), the rest of the fish is fresh. The best deal of all is the fixed-priced menu at €20 a head. Wine is a dangerous €3 a litre, so lunch here could well write off your afternoon. Daily lunch & dinner.

DRINKING

After dark and over much of the city, Palermo's frenetic lifestyle stops, pedestrians flit quickly through the shadows, and the main roads are given over to speeding traffic and screaming police sirens. A lovely street for a civilized, *aperitivo al fresco* is Via dei Cassari, behind the Cala, which is lined with chic flame- or candle-lit places to eat and drink.

CENTRO STORICO MARKETS

Palermo's old quarter sometimes seems like one big market. Head to any of the three main markets of the centre – Il Capo, Vucciria and Ballarò – and you'll find an awe-inspiring abundance of fresh fish and seafood, fruit and veg, streetfood stalls, and all manner of pungent Sicilian preserves (basically if it can be preserved by sun, salt or oil it will be there). The city has several **flea markets** (*mercati delle pulci*) – with the occasional antique lurking amid the knick-knacks and curios – notably on Piazza Peranni near the cathedral, displaying chandeliers galore, and the Albergheria's Piazza San Francesco Saverio off Corso Tukory (this last on Sunday). Finally, if you want to do your bit to support the anti-mafia campaign, head to the Bottega dei Sapori on Piazza Castelnuovo, full of foods and wine created from produce grown on land confiscated from the Mafia.

For a livelier scene, head to the clutch of bars in the streets behind the **Museo Archeologico** – Via Spinuzza, Via Bara all'Olivella and Piazza Olivella – while things are grungier in the student-filled bars along and around **Via Candelai**, not far from the Quattro Canti, off Via Maqueda.

Bar Malox Piazzetta della Canna. Hidden away off an old-town alley near the Quattro Canti, this scruffy, convivial student bar has plenty of tables outside where the drinking continues till late. Tues–Sun evenings only; closed every other Sun.

Bocum Mixology Via dei Cassari 6. Decadent chic decor inside (check out the gorgeously upholstered chaises longues upstairs) and a charming candlelit terrace. Cool jazz sounds and state-of-the-art cocktails. They also do wonderful contemporary food. Wed–Mon 6pm till late.

Champagneria del Massimo Via Salvatore Spinuzza 59. Charming, retro wine bar with outdoor seating near the Teatro Massimo; along with the neighbouring bars, it's a lively spot on summer nights, and stays open till the early hours. Closed Sun.

MUSIC, CULTURE AND THE ARTS

There's always something going on in Palermo, and you can check the current cultural calendar online (see page 68) or in the daily newspaper *Il Giornale di Sicilia*. Teatro Massimo is the first choice for **classical music**, but lots of other smaller theatres and concert halls have good music programmes too. Independent **arts centres** put on a really mixed bag of concerts and events, and although there's no major venue for **live bands** (top British and American artists rarely make it further south than Naples) the *Comune* (local council) regularly stages open-air gigs in the summer, usually in city parks. Mainstream Italian-language **theatre** is less accessible to foreign visitors, but a couple of more offbeat venues are worth checking out, while **puppet theatre** is easily the best night out at the theatre in Palermo (see page 58). **Cinemas** (the main central complex is the Al Politeama Multisala at Via E Amari 160) show the latest films dubbed into Italian – it's rare to find films in their original language with subtitles.

owned by and named after a long-established world music band (check out the album *Tuareg* or the soundtrack to the film *Bagno Turco*). Regular live music and dance sessions, as well as theatre, readings, festivals and events, and a bar that's open until 1.30am. Tues–Sun evenings only.

Lo Spasimo Via dello Spasimo, La Kalsa ☎091 616 1486. The former church hosts an excellent series of classical and jazz concerts, many of them free.

Teatrino Ditirammu del Canto Popolare Via Torremuzza 6, La Kalsa ☎091 617 7865, ✆teatro ditirammu.it. An intimate venue for Sicilian folk music and traditional dance performances.

Teatro Libero Salita Partanna 4, Piazza Marina ☎091 617 4040, ✆teatroliberopalermo.it. Palermo's long-standing avant-garde theatre, with an annual festival that incorporates theatre, dance, music and performance art.

Teatro Massimo Piazza Verdi ☎091 605 3580, ✆teatro massimo.it. The concert and dance programme (classical music, opera and ballet) at Palermo's most prestigious venue runs from October to June, while in summer shows shift to the Teatro del Parco di Villa Castelnuovo for concerts and outdoor performances of ballet and operetta.

THEATRES AND LIVE MUSIC VENUES

★ **Agricantus** Via XX Settembre 82A ☎091 309 636, ✆agricantus.org. Arts centre near the Giardino Inglese,

DIRECTORY

Hospitals Ospedale Cívico, Via Carmelo Lazzaro (☎091 666 1111); Policlinica, Via Carmelo Lazzaro (☎091 655 1111). For an ambulance call ☎118.

Pharmacies All-night services can be found at Lo Cascio, Via Roma 1; Di Naro, Via Roma 207; and Farmacia Inglese,

Via Marina Stabile 177. Other chemists operate a rota system, with the address of the nearest open chemist posted on the door.

Post office Palazzo delle Poste, Via Roma 320 (Mon–Sat 8am–6.30pm).

1 Mondello

On a hot summer's day, when the city heat is oppressive, the most obvious escape from central Palermo is the 11km run to **MONDELLO**, a small seaside resort tucked under the northern bluff of Monte Pellegrino. A 2km-long sandy beach fronts the town, and there's also a tiny working harbour, on a jetty from which you can try your luck fishing, and the remnants of a medieval tower. In July and August, like most Sicilian resorts, it's a bit of a zoo, featuring tacky souvenir stalls, hot-dog and burger vans, pizza places and packed lidos. At night, there's a crush in the bars in the main square while the roads around are filled with cruising cars and preening youth. In winter it's more laidback and rarely busy, but many of the restaurants and snack stalls stay open and it's usually warm enough to swim until well past the end of the official season.

ARRIVAL AND DEPARTURE   MONDELLO

By bus To get to Mondello, take bus #806 or #833 from Piazza Politeama or Viale della Libertà – a 30min ride. The last bus back to town leaves around midnight.

By car Driving to Mondello, exit at the Tommaso Natale junction from the main road.
By taxi A taxi from Palermo costs about €35.

EATING

There's a line of **trattorias** along the seafront at Mondello – some with outdoor terraces – though the quality is patchy (have a good look at the fish on display in the fridges before you decide where to eat).
Da Calogero Via Torre 22 ☎ 091 684 1333. Right on the seafront, this is the best traditional choice in Mondello. You stand up at the window and eat freshly caught and cooked octopus (they do have chairs and tables these days, but standing is the done thing). Daily lunch & dinner.

Monreale

The major excursion from the city is to **MONREALE**, a small hill-town 8km southwest of Palermo. It commands unsurpassed views down the Conca d'Oro valley, with the capital shimmering in the distant bay, and while the panorama from the "Royal Mountain" alone is worth making the trip for, the real draw is the mighty Norman cathedral and its celebrated **mosaics**. These form one of the most extraordinary and extensive areas of Christian medieval mosaic-work in the world, and are the apex of Sicilian-Norman art. Monreale is a short drive from Palermo, but once the day-trippers leave in the late afternoon the prospect of a quiet night in town might appeal, and there are plenty of welcoming B&Bs in the medieval alleys near the cathedral.

It's hard to look beyond the Duomo, but Monreale itself is a handsome small town with a dense latticework of streets and (mostly locked) Baroque churches. For the famous view down the valley, stroll into the courtyard of the new convent (built in 1747) it's behind the cathedral cloisters to the **belvedere** (the entrance is from the other corner of Piazza Gugliemo). Come *passeggiata* time the main **Via Roma** pulses with life, and you don't have to walk very far along here to swap touristy mosaic galleries and gift shops for butchers, grocers and hardware stores.

Brief history

Monreale's cathedral owes its existence to young **King William II**'s rivalry with his powerful Palermitan archbishop, the Englishman **Walter of the Mill**. Work had started on Walter's cathedral in the centre of Palermo in 1172. Determined to quickly break the influence of his former teacher, William endowed a new monastery in his royal grounds outside the city in 1174, and its **abbey church** – the Duomo at Monreale – was thrown up in a matter of years. Monreale was made an archbishopric in 1183, two years before Walter's cathedral was finished, and this unseemly haste had two consequences. As a highly personal project, Monreale's power lasted only as long as William did: although he wanted to create a royal pantheon, he was the last king to be buried here. But the speed with which the Duomo was built ensured the splendid uniformity of its interior art – a galaxy of mosaic pictures bathed in a golden background.

The Duomo

Piazza Guglielmo II • 1 April–31 Oct Mon–Sat 8.30am–12.30pm & 2.30–4.45pm, Sun 8am–9.15am & 2.30–4.45pm, 1 Nov–31 March Mon–Sat 8.30am–12.30pm & 2.30–4.30pm, Sun 8am–9.30am & 2.30–4.30pm • €4 • ⓦ cattedralemonreale.it

Monreale's **Duomo** presides magisterially over the town centre, facing two open squares and flanked by alleys teeming with souvenir stalls and gift shops. A ticket desk provides access to the **tower and terrace** for some sweeping views, and there's a combined ticket to see the collection of reliquaries in the **treasury**. Before or after going inside, walk around the exterior to wonder at the enormous triple **apse**, a polychromatic jumble of limestone and lava, supported by slender columns and patterned by a series of interlacing arches. To see it, go through the arched alley (Arco degli Angeli) to the left of the Duomo entrance.

Bear in mind that despite the continual influx of tourists, you may not be allowed in if dressed in skimpy beach clothes.

The mosaics

The gleaming **mosaics** inside the Duomo, almost certainly executed by Greek and Byzantine craftsmen, are a magnificent achievement, thought to have been completed in just ten years. They were designed for worshippers to be able to read the Testaments straight from the walls, and eyes are drawn immediately to the all-embracing half-figure of Christ in benediction in the **central apse**. The head and shoulders alone stand almost 20m high, face full of compassion, curving arms with outstretched hands seemingly encompassing the whole beauty of the church. Underneath are an enthroned Virgin and Child, attendant angels and, below, ranks of saints – each subtly coloured and identified by name. The two **side apses** are dedicated to saints Peter (right) and Paul (left), the arches before each apse graphically displaying the martyrdom of each – respectively, an inverse crucifixion and a beheading. The **nave mosaics** then start with the Creation (above the pillars to the right of the altar) and run around the whole church, while the **aisle mosaics** depict the teachings of Jesus. Most scenes are instantly recognizable: Adam and Eve; Abraham on the point of sacrificing his son; positively jaunty Noah's ark scenes showing the ship being built, recalcitrant animals being loaded aboard and Noah's family peering out of the hatches; the Feeding of the Five Thousand; and the Creation itself, a set of glorious, simple panels portraying God filling His world with animals, water, light … and Man.

Above the two **thrones** (royal and episcopal) are more mosaics: William I receiving the crown from Christ; and the king offering the cathedral to the Virgin. Both William I and William II are buried here in side chapels, the latter resting in the white marble sarcophagus to the right of the apse.

Chiostro dei Benedettini

Enter from the corner of Piazza Guglielmo II, by the right-hand tower of the Duomo • Daily 9am–6.30pm • €6

The **Chiostro dei Benedettini**, or cloisters, is one of the undisputed highlights of the Duomo complex, an elegant arcaded quadrangle with 216 twin columns supporting slightly pointed arches – a legacy of the Arab influence in Sicilian art. No two of the carved capitals are the same: on one, armed hunters do battle with winged beasts; another has two men lifting high a casket of wine; while flowers, birds, snakes and geometric shapes dip and dance from column to column.

ARRIVAL AND DEPARTURE

MONREALE

By bus Bus #389 runs every 45 min from Palermo's Piazza dell'Indipendenza (outside the Porta Nuova, reached by bus #109 from Stazione Centrale) through the western suburbs and up the valley, and takes around twenty minutes (€1.80).

By taxi A taxi from Palermo costs around €30 each way.

By car Parking is restricted in Monreale's old town and visitors are advised to use one of the signposted car parks – there's one on Via Cappuccini, below the Duomo and belvedere (from where a pedestrian way leads up past souvenir stalls into the town) and another (Parcheggio Duomo) down Via D'Acquisto to the side of the Palazzo Communale. Parking costs €1 an hour, and it's free overnight after 8pm.

ACCOMMODATION, EATING AND DRINKING

There's only a limited number of **hotels** in town, but there are charming **B&Bs**, rooms and apartments much nearer the Duomo, especially in the tangle of alleys by the Duomo's apse. If you want to spend a few days here, Airbnb is a good bet. There are plenty of **restaurants**, though prices are generally on the high side.

Bricco & Bacco Via B. D'Acquisto 13 ☎ 091 641 7773. A definite cut above the family tourist restaurants in town, this brasserie is serious about its meat. Steaks, chops and lamb grills are €12–15. Lunch & dinner: summer Mon–Sat; winter Tues–Sun.

La Ciambra Via Sanchez 23 ☎ 091 640 9565 or ☎ 335 842 5865, ⓦ laciambra.com. A quaint, family-run B&B wedged into a plant-filled alley, with a great view of Monreale's apse. The two rooms here sleep up to four people. No credit cards. **€75**

Peppino Via B. Civiletti 12 ☎ 091 640 7770. Popular local pizzeria tucked away down a side street off Via Roma, beyond San Giuseppe church. It has a shady summer terrace, decent antipasti and crisp pizzas (€6–12) – the pizzas with buffalo mozzarella are well worth the extra. Mon & Wed–Sun noon–2pm & 7.30–10pm.

Bagheria and around

Walking around the ramshackle town of Bagheria, it is hard to believe that the Palermitan nobility of the seventeenth and eighteenth centuries chose to sit out the enervating summer heat here. The amount of concrete and lack of urban planning is down to the Mafia – Bagheria is one of their historic strongholds – and it's a surreal experience, entering the grand gates of some of the glorious Baroque country villas that have survived from the scruffy squalor of modern Bagheria. Inside the villas, it is still possible to glimpse the world described by Dacia Maraini in her memoir *Bagheria* – "the atmosphere of a summer garden enriched by lemon groves and olive trees, poised between the hills, cooled by the salt winds". Villa Palagonia is open to the public daily, and other villas may be open on request (see box page 78). If you have a full day you can also see the ancient ruins of **Solus** at Solunto and the working fishing port of **Porticello**, the latter boasting a boutique hotel and a ring of harbourside fish restaurants that might just persuade you to make a night of it.

Villa Palagonia

Via Palagonia • Daily: April–Oct 9am–1pm & 4–7pm; Nov–March 9am–1pm & 3.30–5.30pm • €5 • ☎ 091 932 088, ⓦ villapalagonia.it

Best known – or perhaps that should be most notorious – of Bagheria's Baroque villas is the **Villa Palagonia**, whose grounds boast an eccentric menagerie of statues, from grotesque gnomes, giants and gargoyles to assorted mutants. The villa was the work of Ferdinand, Prince of Palagonia, a hunchback who – in league with the architect Tommaso Napoli – took revenge on his wife's lovers by cruelly caricaturing them. Although only 64 of the original 200 statues remain, they certainly add entertainment to a wander around the garden, before you climb the stairs into the crumbling sandstone villa to view a selection of frescoed halls and the dramatic Salone degli Specchi, which is covered in mirrors and marbling.

Museo Guttuso

Via Rammacca 9 • Tues–Sat 9am–5pm • €5 • ☎ 091 943 902 • ⓦ comune.bagheria.pa.it/museo-guttuso

1

> ## BAGHERIA'S OTHER VILLAS
>
> Several of Bagheria's villas are privately owned, and only open to the public on occasion, or by special arrangement. Of these, **Villa Valguarnera** on Piazza Sturzo (ⓦvillavalguarnera.com) – whose owner, Vittoria Alliata, speaks perfect English – displays Bagheria's most sumptuous facade: pink and festooned with a royal coat of arms and Attic statues, it was designed by Tommaso Napoli. **Villa Butera**, on Corso Butera, just off the SS113, has a collection of wax figures in Carthusian apparel within its grounds. Legend has it that their creator, Ercole Branciforti, had promised the erection of a Carthusian abbey in return for the granting of a prayer, and took the crafty way out when the prayer was answered.

Some 500m from the train station along the main SS113, **Villa Cattolica** holds the **Museo Guttuso**, dedicated to Bagheria's most famous son, Renato Guttuso (1912–87), whose brilliant use of colour and striking imagery made him one of Italy's most important modern artists. His tomb, designed by his friend, the sculptor Giacomo Manzù, is in the garden.

ARRIVAL AND DEPARTURE   BAGHERIA

By bus From Palermo, buses run every half hour to Bagheria, dropping you on Corso Umberto I, from where it's a short, straight walk to Villa Palagonia.

By train Bagheria is a stop on the main line from Palermo to Cefalù. There are frequent trains, and it's a 10min walk to Villa Palagonia from the station (turn left onto Corso Butera, then left onto Via Palagonia).

By car There's free parking near Villa Palagonia, though you might find yourself sucked into the narrow streets of the old town trying to find it. Eventually you should be directed into a space by a parking attendant (tip €1 recommended).

Solus (Solunto)

Mon–Sat 9am–6.30pm, Sun 9am–2pm, last entry 1hr before closing • €4 • By train from Palermo, get off one stop beyond Bagheria (at Santa Flavia-Solunto-Porticello station), cross over the tracks and walk down the main road towards the sea; after 300m there's a signposted left turn up the hillside

Beautifully positioned on the slopes of Monte Catalfano, ancient **Solus**, a Phoenician settlement, was originally founded in the eighth century BC, resettled in the fourth century BC, and later Hellenized, finally surrendering to Rome after the First Punic War, when its name was changed to Solentum. Ruins at the **site** date mostly from the Roman period, notably the impressive remains of wealthy houses – one, with a standing column, was built on two floors, the stairs still visible, and still has a complete geometric mosaic floor. The main street leads past houses and shops to the agora itself, a piazza with nine clay-red-coloured recessed rooms at the back. Above it sit the fragmentary ruins of a theatre and a smaller odeon, deliberately sited so as to give marvellous views away to the coast. Beyond the agora are the remains of a water cistern and storage tanks – necessary, as Solentum had no natural springs. Two "pavilions" interpret the site and display many of the finds, one at the entrance (before you see the ruins) and one at the exit, though there's nothing in English.

Porticello

With views across the bay towards Cefalù and up to a line of rounded peaks on the horizon, **PORTICELLO**, 6km east of Bagheria, makes a great bolt hole from the city – Palermitani come here at weekends and in summer to eat fish and seafood at the harbourside trattorias, but the place is definitely nice enough to warrant a stay. Fishermen have been working out of the port for centuries, and an old *tonnara* (tuna fishery) is still preserved near the medieval Castello di Solanto, which guards one side of the bay. It's a real, working harbour, and Porticello's fish market is one of the most important in Sicily, with boats unloading here in the early hours before the catch is shipped across Italy and beyond. Ice-house chutes channel ice into containers for the fish, and boats and nets are still hauled under great stone arches back from the harbour to be repaired.

ARRIVAL AND DEPARTURE
PORTICELLO

By bus There is only one direct AST bus daily from Palermo to Porticello, so it's easier to take a bus to Bagheria and then

another to Porticello.

ACCOMMODATION AND EATING

★ **Stenopus Greco** ☎ 091 958 851 or ☎ 320 799 2011, ⓦ stenopusgreco.com. Imbued with real artistic flair by the charming owner Stefano, this boutique dockside hotel is a surprising find in such a working town. It's perhaps a sign of things to come, as there are also plans afoot for a new harbour and marina development for Porticello. Eight lovely

rooms are decorated in bold colours with terracotta floors and beamed ceilings, original art above the handmade beds, painted ceramics and carved Indonesian chests. Three have harbour-view balconies, others either partial harbour or town views. **€60**

Piana degli Albanesi

Less than an hour's bus ride south of the capital, **PIANA DEGLI ALBANESI** sits placidly in an upland plain above a pleasant lake. The town was founded by fifteenth-century Albanians uprooted from their homes in flight from Turkish invasions, and the six thousand inhabitants here still follow the Orthodox rite and proudly retain many of their old traditions – signs are in Albanian as well as Italian, and on Sunday mornings there are traditional Orthodox services in the three churches lining the steeply sloping main street, Via Giorgio Kastriota. At Easter, out come handsome traditional costumes – black with gold brocade on Good Friday, brightly coloured on Easter Sunday.

Museo Civico
Via Giorgio Kastriota • Fri, Sat, Sun 9.30am–12.30pm & 3.30–6.30pm, Tues, Wed, Thu 9.30am–12.30pm • Free

Rural life and local history, as well as Albanian traditions and costumes, are well covered in the fascinating little **Museo Civico**, just off Piazza Vittorio Emanuele, the small square at the top of the main street. There are reconstructions of room interiors containing anything from dental tools to cheese-making equipment as well as grainy photographs and other memorials to the infamous **massacre** at Portella della Ginestra (see box).

THE MASSACRE AT PORTELLA DELLA GINESTRA

The mountain pass 4km southwest of Piana degli Albanesi, **Portella della Ginestra**, was the scene of one of the most shocking episodes in recent Sicilian history. On May 1, 1947, when the Albanians and villagers from neighbouring San Giuseppe Jato had assembled for their customary May Day celebrations, gunfire erupted from the crags and boulders surrounding the plain, killing eleven and wounding 55, many of them children. This massacre was the work of the bandit **Salvatore Giuliano**, whose virulent anti-Communist feelings were exploited by more sinister figures high up in the political and criminal hierarchy: only two weeks previously, the people of the town, together with most other Sicilians, had voted for a Popular Front (left-wing) majority in the regional parliament. The cold-blooded killings erased at one stroke the bandit's carefully nurtured reputation as defender of the poor and friend to the oppressed. There's a car park at the pass and the site is marked by a memorial of sculpted rocks inscribed in blood-red lettering – slightly unkempt, and a haunting place still.

1

CORLEONE AND THE MAFIA

Whether by luck or with foresight, when Mario Puzo chose the name **Corleone** for his central character in *The Godfather* (published 1969), he picked a little-known place that later came to have a huge significance in Mafia circles, as the native town of many of the so-called *capo di tutti capi* (literally "boss of all the bosses"). Even before Puzo's novel, the name Corleone had a certain resonance, due to the activities of **Luciano Leggio** (also known as Liggio), leading member of the Sicilian Mafia who had a reputation as a dashing figure and was hailed for his long-running evasion of the forces ranged against him. He was, however, responsible for one of the most notorious political killings of the twentieth century, that of the trade union leader **Placido Rizzoto**, who had been trying to organize peasants into staging occupations of uncultivated Mafia-owned lands. Two years after Rizzoto's disappearance in 1948, the fire brigade hauled out his dismembered corpse from a 30m crevice near Corleone (along with sackfuls of other bodies of Mafia victims). His killers were eventually acquitted for lack of evidence, the most common end to murder charges brought against *mafiosi*. Leggio was finally imprisoned in 1974 and died in jail in 1993.

At the time of his arrest in 1993, Leggio's trusted deputy from Corleone, **Salvatore Riina**, was the most wanted man in Italy, allegedly responsible for ordering at least 150 murders, forty of which he's said to have committed himself. His capture came as a complete surprise and triggered a wave of accusations, since it became clear that for over twenty years Riina had been living in Palermo while making clandestine visits to his family in Corleone. This, it's said with some justification, could only have been the case if he had enjoyed a degree of high-level protection.

The most notable among several further members of the *corleonese* clan who have been put away since Riina's arrest is **Bernardo Provenzano**, known as "the Tractor" on account of his brutal methods and also as "the Accountant" for the way in which he increasingly blurred Mafia operations with legitimate business interests. He was finally captured in 2006, having been convicted in absentia of a string of murders, including the 1992 killings of the two anti-Mafia investigators Giovanni Falcone and Paolo Borsellino.

ARRIVAL AND DEPARTURE

PIANA DEGLI ALBANESI

By bus Prestia e Comande buses run to Piana from outside Palermo's Stazione Centrale (direction Santa Cristina; 6 daily Mon–Sat during school terms; 3 daily Mon–Sat during school holidays); the last one back leaves at around 4pm. Buses stop at the top of town, 500m from Piazza Vittorio Emanuele, at the Villa Comunale gardens (there's free parking here too). Cross the road viaduct to reach Via Kastriota and the centre of town.

Ficuzza

South of Piana degli Albanesi, a highly scenic driving route skirts the lake and then winds through rolling hills to reach the junction for **FICUZZA** after 20km. While it's really just a dead-end hamlet, it's worth visiting to see the Palazzo Reale. An information board in the piazza also shows the local waymarked **walks** (between 45 minutes and 3 hours) on mountain paths that crisscross the wooded heights of Rocca Busambra (1613m), or you can simply grab a drink or a basic meal in one of the two or three bars and trattorias in the piazza.

Palazzo Reale di Ficuzza

Usually Tues–Sun 8.30am–12.30pm, but worth phoning ahead to check • ☎ 091 846 062

Ficuzza is completely dominated by the honey-coloured stone **Palazzo Reale di Ficuzza**, set against a dramatic mountain backdrop. This stately royal palace, fronted by a grassy piazza, was once the hunting lodge of Ferdinand III. Several sections of the building, notably the hunting scenes in the Sala da Pranzo, survived destruction and burning by Mussolini's troops.

Corleone

From Ficuzza, another 20km on a quick country highway sees you in **CORLEONE**, a fairly large inland town squeezed between a couple of fortified rocks and girded by crags. It attracts a trickle of tourists, mostly on the scent of the Mafia since the town lent Mario Puzo's fictional Godfather, Don Corleone, his adopted family name. However, it is also the real-life name of Sicily's most notorious Mafia clan, and postwar Corleone was certainly a desperate place of murder and inter-family blood-letting. You wouldn't, of course, know it from the quiet streets today, and if it wasn't for the notoriety there would be no compelling reason to stop in Corleone, pleasant though the town centre is. A flurry of signs do their best to interest you in the various churches and small local museums.

CIDMA

CIDMA Via Orfanotrofio 7 • Open Mon–Fri 10am–5pm, guided tours available, though best to email or call first • ☎ 091 8452 4295, ⓦ cidmacorleone.it, ⊜ info@cidma.it • **Corleone, Come and See** ☎ 340 402 5601, ⊜ cidmacorleone@gmail.com

Off the central Piazza Garibaldi, close to the *Comune*, **CIDMA** (International Centre for the Documentation of the Mafia and the Anti-Mafia Movement) is an anti-Mafia museum where you can trace the violent history of both Corleone and the Mafia, not only through brutal photographs (taken and donated by photographer Letizia Battaglia) of the so-called "Mafia Wars", but also by examining displays of original documents used in the maxi-trials of the 1980s. It's a sobering experience, though current street names in town at least demonstrate a contemporary *corleonese* desire to make amends (Piazza Vittime della Mafia, Piazza Falcone e Borsellino, etc). And at dusk in the town gardens, when couples, teenagers and families stroll under the soaring palms and flowering oleanders, the dark dealings of earlier times seem an age away. This more enlightened view of town is the one promoted by two local women under the name "**Corleone, Come and See**" who, with a couple of days' notice, can arrange a tailor-made tour with an English-speaking guide, including a typically rustic *corleonese* lunch.

THE MAFIA TRAIL

Corleone might only be 60km from Palermo, and still in the same province, but the dry hills, rolling farmland and isolated rural outposts are far removed from the bustling capital. If you're in no hurry, consider taking the circular driving route back to Palermo which shows you a wilder side of the island, with a few Mafia connections adding a certain *frisson*. It's a quick 25km southeast over the hills on the SS118 to **Prizzi** – the name borrowed from that of a New York mob family in John Huston's 1985 black comedy *Prizzi's Honor*. On Easter Sunday here, giant statues of Christ and the Virgin Mary are taunted by masked figures representing Death and the Devil, to whom onlookers are forced to give money. Another 20km east along the SS189, the main claim of **Lercara Friddi** is as the birthplace in 1897 of the Sicilian-American gangster Lucky Luciano, whose family emigrated in 1907. While in prison in the US during World War II, Luciano was enlisted by the Americans to aid their Sicilian campaign (which was fully backed by the Mafia in its desire to end Fascist rule) and his reward when the war was over was to be freed, on the condition that he returned to Sicily. The town's main piazza was packed to welcome him home in 1946, and he repaid the adulation by opening Lercara Friddi's first cinema – apparently with a screening of the gangster movie, *Little Caesar*. A few kilometres north of Lercara, you can pick up the SS121, which winds across the entire length of Sicily from Catania to finish its run in Palermo. One final (signposted) stop is at **Bagni di Cefalà**; these eleventh-century Arab baths still flow with thermal waters which the locals use for washing clothes, and you can swim here too. Few other examples of Arab architecture in Sicily are in such good condition.

1

By bus Corleone is 60km from Palermo and there are seven buses daily (AST), taking 1hr 30min. The main bus stop is on the central Piazza Falcone e Borsellino.

ACCOMMODATION

★**Azienda Agricola Ridocco del Conte Lo Bue di Lemos** Contrada Ridocco, Campofiorito ☎091 846 1575, ⓦridocco.com. An outstanding *agriturismo* set in the gentle rolling hills above Corleone, with rooms in the main house and converted outbuildings of a typical *masseria* belonging to (and run with grace and enthusiasm by) a local aristocratic family. There are three double rooms with private bathrooms, and an independent apartment (from €90) with kitchen comprising a double, a twin and a single. There is also a small swimming pool, horseriding and pony-trekking on site, and an excellent restaurant (open to residents only) where the food is simple and delicious. Doubles **€90**

Ustica

A turtle-shaped volcanic island, 60km northwest of Palermo, **USTICA** is ideal for a few days' rest and recreation. The island's fertile nine square kilometres are just right for a ramble, and what it lacks in sandy beaches it more than makes up for in the limpid waters of a **marine reserve** that many consider to provide the best snorkelling and dive-sites in the Mediterranean. If tourism has rescued isolated Ustica, it has also been at the risk of spoiling its charms – the population of 1300 quadruples in the summer months, and you'll see the island at its best if you can avoid coming in August.

Brief history

Colonized originally by the Phoenicians, the island was known to the Greeks as **Osteodes**, or "ossuary", a reference to the remains of six thousand Carthaginians they found here, abandoned to die on the island after a rebellion. Its present name is derived from the Latin *ustum* – "burnt" – on account of its blackened, lava-like appearance. Ustica had a rough time throughout the Middle Ages, its sparse population constantly harried by **pirates** who used the island as a base. In the Bourbon period the island was commandeered as a **prison**

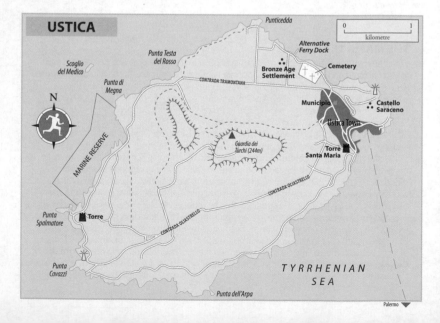

for political enemies, a role it continued to play until well into the twentieth century – Antonio Gramsci, the great theorist of the Italian Communist Party, was interned here in 1926, while Mussolini similarly exiled many other political prisoners. Only in recent decades has Ustica shaken off its chains and become a holiday destination.

Ustica town

USTICA TOWN is built on a steep slope, many of its low buildings covered in fading murals. Despite the veneer of tourism – a handful of hotels, restaurants, diving outfits and souvenir shops – it's not hard to see that life here has always been pretty tough. Most of what passes for entertainment – chatting in the open air, having a coffee in the couple of bars, impromptu games of soccer – takes place in and around the three central squares, piazzas Umberto I, della Vittoria and Vito Longo, which merge into each other, tumbling down the hill from the church.

Museo Archeologico

Largo Granguardia Tanino Russo • ☎ 333 357 4242 • Free

Ustica's museum, the **Museo Archeologico**, is a low-key affair, its collection a motley assortment of crusty anchors, shipwreck oddments and excavated Bronze Age objects. To visit, it is necessary to phone the museum guide, Tanino Russo, in advance.

Castello Saraceno

To get a sense of Ustica as an island, climb up to the remains of **Castello Saraceno**, which gives you a good view of the island's layout: from the top of the square to the right of the church, the path runs left of the fancy cross at the end of Via Calvario, an easy twenty-minute walk to an old fort pitted with cisterns to catch the precious water.

Guardia dei Turchi

From the Castello Saraceno you can see Ustica's highest point, the **Guardia dei Turchi** (244m), at the summit of a ridge that cuts the island in two, and topped by what looks like a giant golf ball – in fact a meteorological radar system. You can also climb up to the summit from the town, in about an hour or so: take Via B. Randaccio to the right of the church, turn left at the top and then take the next right, and you'll come to the Municipio, where you turn left along Via Tre Mulini for the summit – keep straight ahead on the cobbled path, cutting off to the left when you reach the stepped path.

ARRIVAL AND GETTING AROUND
USTICA TOWN

By boat Siremar (ⓦsiremar.it) ferries (one daily year-round, €15; 2hr 30min) and Liberty Line hydrofoils (€20; 1hr 15min) run to Ustica daily from Palermo (from the Stazione Marittima); summer departure times from Palermo are 7am, 8.15am, 1pm and 5.15pm, though are liable to change, during the winter services are severely cut back. There is a ticket kiosk at the harbour, open just before sailings. The island's only port is at Ustica Town, with the town centre up the flight of steps leading from the harbour.

Getting around From Piazza della Vittoria, an efficient minibus service (pay on board) plies the island's one circular road every hour or so until around 7pm.

INFORMATION AND TOURS

Online information There's no tourist office on Ustica, but you can glean some information (in English) from ⓦ ustica.org.

Bikes, boats and tours Usticamare Noleggio (☎339 218 5630, ⓦusticamare.it) has bikes from €10 per day, boats from €50–180 per day (depending on size) excluding fuel, and cars to rent, while the restaurant *Da Umberto* (ⓦusticatour.it) rents out scooters and boats and arranges tours. Boat excursions from the quay cost around €25 per person for three hours – it's best to agree a price beforehand.

ACCOMMODATION

In summer hotels fill up quickly, and in winter only a few remain open.

Ariston Via della Vittoria 5 ☎091 844 9042, ⓦustica hotels.it. A rather old-fashioned, whitewashed central

1

DIVING ON USTICA

Ustica is well set up for **divers**. The waters are protected by a natural marine reserve, divided into several zones with restrictions on where you can swim, dive and fish, and island facilities include a decompression chamber and *guardia medica* (duty doctor).

★ **Profondo Blu** (☎091 844 9609 or ☎349 672.6529, ⓦustica-diving.it), run by an Italo-Belgian couple, is the island's most organized and experienced dive-operator, arranging diving courses, holidays and accommodation in a self-contained resort with apartments outside town. It is open from May till the end of October, with prices at €490–

660 per week for an apartment sleeping two, depending on the season. Meals are also available (breakfast €5; dinner €35) and there is a very cool honesty bar in a vintage ice-cream van. There are various diving packages – a single dive costs €45; a ten-dive package €380 and a six-day open-water diver PADI course €430.

---

hotel with eleven simple, functional rooms with white walls and ceramic tiled floors, but some impressive sea views. Breakfast is included and there is a restaurant. Diving trips and scooter rental can be arranged. Sizeable reductions in winter. No credit cards. €80

Giulia Via San Francesco 16 ☎091 844 9007, ⓦgiulia hotel.com. Open year-round, with ten perfectly acceptable two-star rooms above a lovely restaurant (see below) right off the main piazza (single rooms also available). See the website for weekend packages including certain meals and excursions. No credit cards. €80

Stella Marina Residence Via Cristoforo Colombo 35 ☎091 844 8121, ⓦstellamarinaustica.it. Seventeen

smart, self-catering mini-apartments in a small complex right above the port. There's also a nice big terrace for soaking up the sun, and a small spa. Rentals range from €500–1000 per week for a two-person apartment, including breakfast, but they're available on a two-nightly basis May–July & Sept–Oct. €110

Da Umberto Piazza della Vittoria ☎091 844 9542, ⓦusticatour.it. As well as running the *Da Umberto* restaurant (see below) Gigi Tranchina rents out rooms in over twenty apartments and houses around Ustica, some with great sea views, while others are more rustic and situated in the middle of the island. Prices depend on size and quality of the accommodation. €75

EATING AND DRINKING

As well as a couple of harbourside bars, there are several places to eat on and around Ustica town's central squares, and most of the hotels have **restaurants**, often with roof terraces and sea views. The majority of restaurants not attached to hotels close during the winter. Don't neglect to visit Maria Cristina, just above the piazzas at Via Petriera 5, who sells Ustica lentils, home-made preserves, pesto, sauces, and other island treats to savour, from a tiny room in her home.

★ **Giulia** Via San Francesco 13 ☎091 844 9007. The simple trattoria attached to this hotel is the best bet on the island for genuine home cooking. Try *pennette al usticese* (with herbs, chilli, garlic, pine nuts, raisins, anchovies, capers and olives), *polpettine* (fish balls) with local capers and olives, or *totano* (a big squid) stuffed with shrimp,

tomatoes, cheese and breadcrumbs. Fish couscous is available for a minimum of two people, but book a day in advance. Expect to spend €35–40 per person for a full meal with wine. No credit cards. Daily dinner only.

Da Umberto Piazza della Vittoria ☎091 844 9542. There are tables on the terrace and a menu chiefly consisting of pasta dishes (from €9.50) and seafood main courses that depend on the day's catch (€12–16) at this popular and long-established restaurant. Try the *polpette* of fish spiked with wild fennel, spaghetti with seafood, or a soup of tiny locally grown lentils; or splash out on lobster with spaghetti or a whole fish (such as scorpion fish) cooked with capers and tomatoes (prices depend on weight). Daily lunch & dinner.

DIRECTORY

Pharmacy Piazza Umberto I, 30 ☎091 844 9382 (Mon–Sat 8.30am–1pm & 5–8.30pm). Closed Wed afternoon Nov–April.

Post office Largo Ameria off the main piazza (Mon–Fri 8am–1pm, Sat 8am–12.30pm).

Around the island

To explore the rest of Ustica you could use the minibus service that departs from Ustica town, rent a scooter or bike, or even walk – it doesn't take much more than two or three hours to walk the perimeter of the entire island. There's a path running right round the rocky coastline, with just a brief stretch along the road, and there are ample opportunities to stop for a swim or sunbathe along the northern coast. Keep straight on past the Municipio and then bear off the road to the right, down past the cemetery. The path starts at the remains of a **Bronze Age settlement** – the foundations of closely packed huts are still clearly visible. From here the path hugs the cliffs along the island's north side as far as the **Punta di Megna** (where path and road converge). There's excellent snorkelling at Punta di Megna and at the offshore rock of **Scoglio del Medico**, where the clear water is bursting with fish, sponges, weed and coral. The road then keeps to the west coast as far as the old *torre* (tower) at **Punta Spalmatore**, where you'll find some of the island's best bathing spots; try below the tower, or – below the nearby lighthouse – at **Punta Cavazzi**, where there's a *piscina naturale*, a perfect, sheltered pool of seawater that can get uncomfortably crowded in high season.

Cefalù and the Monti Madonie

88 Cefalù

95 Himera

96 Caccamo

97 Parco Regionale delle Madonie

102 Gangi

104 East of Cefalù

107 Capo d'Orlando

107 Patti

108 Tindari

110 Novara di Sicilia

110 Milazzo

RISERVA NATURALE LAGHETTI DI MARINELLO

Cefalù and the Monti Madonie

Cefalù, just an hour east of Palermo, is one of Sicily's busiest international beach resorts. Not only does it have a superb beach, an appealing historic centre, and a stupendous medieval cathedral with some of the best mosaic-work on the whole island, but on its doorstep are the Monti Madonie, a high mountain range recently added to the UNESCO list of geoparks for a geological history that spans two hundred million years. It's easy to explore the mountains by car, but you won't get far if you are using buses, as they are timed to take kids to school and back. With a car, even in just a day-trip from the coast, you'll be able to circle the high passes between Castelbuono and the twin towns of Petralia Soprana and Petralia Sottana, or visit the exquisitely restored medieval town of Gangi. Though to really get the most out of the area you need to hike, basing yourself in one of the mountain villages or towns.

There are plenty of good day-trips from Cefalù. West, en route to Palermo, lies the archeological site of Greek **Himera** and the blustery hilltop stronghold of **Caccamo**, which features what may be the best preserved of all Sicily's Norman castles. To the east (towards Messina), it's the Tyrrhenian coast that holds sway; hugged by road, rail and motorway, there are occasional eye-catching successions of cliff and cove, sandy strips and citrus groves, but for the most part these are eclipsed by monotonous tourist developments. It's worth a quick stop at the ceramics shops of **Santo Stefano di Camastra**, while from **Castel di Tusa** you can trace the sculptures of the **Fiumara d'Arte** trail. Further east, the town of **Patti** has an untouched historic centre, a lively shingle beachfront, and a convent serving some of the best – and cheapest – feasts in the region. The most beautiful sands along this stretch of the Tyrrhenian, however, lie below the clifftop sanctuary of **Tindari** at **Marinello** – a coastal nature reserve, with natural (and shifting) salt lakes. **Milazzo**, treated by most as a departure point for the Aeolian Islands, also has hidden charms – among them its recently restored Norman castle, and the coves and beaches of the **Capo di Milazzo**.

GETTING AROUND
CEFALÙ AND THE MONTI MADONIE

By bus and train A good train service makes it easy to see any of the coastal destinations from Cefalù, and buses link to some inland destinations, but timings can be tricky for day-trips, as they are designed to bring country children to school early in the morning, and return them home around 1 or 2pm.

By car A car is definitely required if you're intent on seeing much of the Madonie mountains. Driving can be slow on the SS113 coastal road, along which traffic sometimes files at a snail's pace – it's much faster on the A20 autostrada (a toll-road), which features some outstanding feats of road engineering in the form of long tunnels and soaring viaducts.

Cefalù

The finest resort on the long Tyrrhenian coast between Palermo and Messina is **CEFALÙ**, 70km from the capital, with a long sandy beach and a dramatic setting under a fearsome crag known as La Rocca. Roger II founded a mighty cathedral here in 1131 and his mosaic-filled **church** still dominates the skyline: great twin towers rear up above the flat roofs of the medieval quarter, the whole magnificent structure framed by the looming cliff behind. The shady tangle of old streets and gift shops, and nearby

CASTELBUONO

Highlights

❶ Cefalù A cathedral resplendent in Byzantine mosaics and some of the island's finest beaches. See page 88

❷ Castelbuono This charming old town is the northern gateway to the Monti Madonie, and the mountain food is both abundant and delicious. See page 97

❸ Petralia Sottana Pretty mountain town at the heart of the Parco Regionale delle Madonie, that is a great starting point for exploring. See page 100

❹ Parco Avventura Madonie Zip-wire through the trees at this climbing park in the Madonie mountains. See page 101

❺ Patti Discover the unsung charms of a friendly coastal hill-town with an unrestored historic centre, long shingle beaches, fabulous views of the Aeolians, and one of the best-value restaurants in the region. See page 107

❻ Tyndaris and Marinello Explore the Roman remains of Tyndaris, then head down to the enchanting sands of the Marinello coastal nature reserve. See page 108

❼ Milazzo Before you depart for the Aeolian Islands, take time to explore Milazzo's rambling citadel and the fishermen's stalls along the seafront. See page 110

HIGHLIGHTS ARE MARKED ON THE MAP ON PAGE 90

CEFALÙ AND THE MONTI MADONIE

HIGHLIGHTS

1. Cefalù
2. Castelbuono
3. Petralia Sottana
4. Parco Avventura Madonie
5. Patti
6. Tyndaris and Marinello
7. Milazzo

0 | 25
kilometres

N

TYRRHENIAN SEA

Palermo
Termini Imerese
Himera
Monte San Calogero (1326m)
Caccamo
Sclafani Bagni
Caltavuturo
Polizzi Generosa
Collesano
Piano Zucchi
Isnello
Munciarrati
Gratteri
Campofelice di Roccella
Gatteri
Cefalù
Santuario di Gibilmanna
Castelbuono
PARCO REGIONALE DELLE MADONIE
Pizzo Carbonara
Piano Battaglia
MONTI MADONIE
Geraci Siculo
Petralia Soprana
Petralia Sottana
Parco Avventura
Gangi
Castel di Lucio
Nicosia
Mistretta
Reitano
Motta d'Affermo
Santo Stefano di Camastra
Castel di Tusa
Halaesa
Tusa
Pettineo
San Fratello
Acquedolci
Sant'Agata di Militello
Capo d'Orlando
Naso
Floresta
Cesarò
Troina
Cerami
PARCO NATURALE DEI NEBRODI
MONTI NEBRODI
Randazzo
Maletto
PARCO DELL'ETNA
Castiglione di Sicilia
Novara di Sicilia
Patti
Tindari
Barcellona Pozzo di Gotto
Castroreale
Milazzo
Capo Milazzo

Enna & Catania
Enna, Caltanissetta & Agrigento
Etna & Catania

A19
A20
SS289
SS117
SS120
SS286
SS116

beach and promenade, are certainly touristy but also retain a real charm. Cefalù, in fact, is nowhere near as developed as Sicily's other main package resort, Taormina/ Giardini Naxos. It's busy in July and August, but never overwhelmingly so, and there's a lot to be said for making the town your base. Palermo is less than an hour away by train, there are smaller beaches and resorts on the rail line to the east, and it's an easy drive into the Monti Madonie. The sandy **beach** is one of Sicily's best, jam-packed in summer, with sheltered swimming in clear waters and marvellous views from the lungomare (promenade) over the red roofs of the town.

The cobbled old-town streets themselves are the best thing about Cefalù, dotted with hidden arches and flower-filled courtyards. The main Corso Ruggero is lined with attractive historic buildings, though most of them are now shops. The **Osterio Magno**, on the corner of Via Amendola and the Corso, is the surviving part of a medieval palace, now regularly used for art exhibitions, while the **lavatoio**, down on Via Vittorio Emanuele, is a rare relic of the Saracen occupation – a washhouse at the bottom of a curving staircase, with cold water pouring forth into basins. At the head of the Corso, a **belvedere** gives onto the old Greek walls of Cefalù, largely incorporated into the later sixteenth-century defensive bastion. A modern path has been cut into the rocks below, running in the direction of the port, and you can clamber down here to explore rock pools and sunbathe on the slabs. Further around the headland, at the **port**, is a bay full of fishing and leisure boats, and more strange rock stacks to investigate.

The Duomo

Piazza Duomo • Daily: summer 8am–6.30pm; winter 8am–5.30pm • Free • **Cloisters** • Summer Mon–Sat 10am–6pm, Sun 10am–1pm & 3–6pm; winter Mon–Fri 10am–1pm & 3–6pm • €3 • Accessed via a separate entrance down by the side of the church (walk down the main steps and turn right) • ⓦ cattedraledicefalu.com

Central to Cefalù's historic existence is its majestic **Duomo**, set back in a pretty square under the cliffs. Apocryphally, it was built in gratitude by Roger II, who found refuge at the town's safe beach in a violent storm, though it's more likely that the cathedral owed its foundation to his power struggle with Pope Innocent II. Shortly after his coronation in 1130, Roger had allied with Anacletus, the anti-pope, whose support enhanced the new king's prestige. Roger's cathedral benefited from Anacletus's readily granted exemptions and privileges, and it is at once rich and showy, from the massive, fortress-like exterior to the earliest and best preserved of all Sicilian church **mosaics**. Dating from 1148 (forty years older than those at Monreale), they are thoroughly Byzantine in concept and follow an orderly pattern: Christ Pantocrator, right hand outstretched in benediction, dominates the central apse, looking, it has to be said, rather more military than spiritual; in the vaults above him are the eight-winged heads of cherubim and seraphim; below is the Madonna flanked by archangels, then the twelve Apostles, ranked in two rows of six.

Overlooked by the sheer limestone cliff of La Rocca, and ringing with birdsong, the cloisters retain a tranquil magic that defies the centuries. Only two sides remain, of slender, engagingly mismatched pairs of columns with eroded capitals – look carefully and you can make out the once extraordinary detail of lizards, monsters and salamanders.

Museo Mandralisca

Via Mandralisca 13 • Daily: Jan–July & Sept–Dec 9am–7pm; Aug 9am–11pm, though the period of late-night opening may be extended into other summer months • €7 • ☎ 0921 421 547, ⓦ fondazionemandralisca.it

With its old ceramic-tiled floors, and cellar full of oil-pressing paraphernalia, the **Museo Mandralisca** is still recognizable as an aristocratic townhouse. The house and collection were bequeathed to the town by the nineteenth-century Baron, Enrico

2

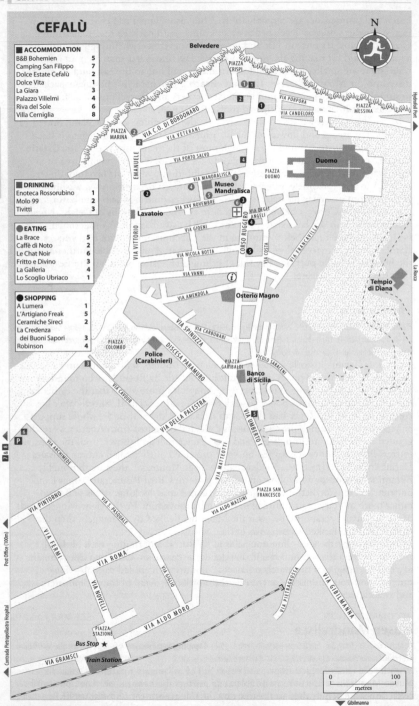

CEFALÙ

ACCOMMODATION

B&B Bohemien	5
Camping San Filippo	7
Dolce Estate Cefalù	2
Dolce Vita	1
La Giara	3
Palazzo Villelmi	4
Riva del Sole	6
Villa Cerniglia	8

DRINKING

Enoteca Rossorubino	1
Molo 99	2
Tivitti	3

EATING

La Brace	5
Caffè di Noto	2
Le Chat Noir	6
Fritto e Divino	3
La Galleria	4
Lo Scoglio Ubriaco	1

SHOPPING

A Lumera	1
L'Artigiano Freak	5
Ceramiche Sireci	2
La Credenza dei Buoni Sapori	3
Robinson	4

N

Belvedere

PIAZZA CRISPI

VIA PORPORA

VIA CANDELORO

PIAZZA MESSINA

VIA C.O. DI BORDONARO

PIAZZA MARINA

VIA VETERANI

EMANUELE

VIA PORTO SALVO

Duomo

PIAZZA DUOMO

VIA MANDRALISCA

Museo Mandralisca

Lavatoio

VIA XXV NOVEMBRE

VIA DEGLI ANGELI

CORSO RUGGERO

VIA FRANCAVILLA

VIA VITTORIO

VIA GIOENI

VIA COSTA

VIA NICOLA BOTTA

Tempio di Diana

VIA VANNI

VIA AMENDOLA

Osterio Magno

VIA CARBONARI

VIA SPINUZZA

PIAZZA COLOMBO

Police (Carabinieri)

DISCESA PARAMURO

VICOLO SARACENI

PIAZZA GARIBALDI

Banco di Sicilia

VIA CAVOUR

VIA DELLA PALESTRA

VIA UMBERTO I

VIA ARCHIMEDE

VIA MATTEOTTI

VIA PINTORNO

VIA S. PASQUALE

PIAZZA SAN FRANCESCO

VIA ALDO MAZZINI

VIA FERMI

VIA ROMA

VIA GIGLIO

VIA NOVELLI

VIA ALDO MORO

VIA PIETRAGRUSSA

VIA GIBILMANNA

PIAZZA STAZIONE

Bus Stop

Train Station

VIA GRAMSCI

La Rocca

Hydrofoil Port

Post Office (100m)

Contrada Pietrapollastra Hospital

7 & 8

P

6

Gibilmanna

0   100
metres

Piraino di Mandralisca, a passionate collector of art and archeology – along with exotic shells, stuffed birds and a taxidermy crocodile. That the Baron had a good eye is not in question – he discovered what is now one of Sicily's most famous paintings, the wry and inscrutable *Portrait of an Unknown Man* by the fifteenth-century Sicilian master **Antonello da Messina**, which was serving as a shutter on a drugs cabinet in a Lipari pharmacy. Look out, too, for the quirky ancient Greek *krater* (a large vessel used to mix wine and water dating from the fourth century BC) showing a robed tuna-fish salesman, knife in hand, disputing the price of his fish, and several delicate ceramics by the ancient Greek artist known as the Lipari painter – the distinctive pastel hues were all made from volcanic clays found on the island.

La Rocca and the Tempio di Diana

Tempio di Diana • Daily: summer 9am–6.45pm; winter closes at least an hour before sunset • €4

Towering above cathedral and town, and accessible by a stepped footpath at the side of the Banco di Sicilia in Piazza Garibaldi, is the mountain of **La Rocca**. A steep twenty-minute climb takes you to the so-called **Tempio di Diana**, a megalithic structure adapted in the fifth century BC with the addition of classical doorways; their lintels are still in place. A path continues upwards, right around the crag, through pinewoods and wild fennel, dipping in and out of a surviving stretch of medieval wall to the sketchy fortifications at the very top. You can then cut down to the temple and rejoin the path back into town, the whole walk taking a little over an hour – take water with you as it's a strenuous climb.

ARRIVAL AND DEPARTURE   CEFALÙ

By train The train station is south of the centre, 10min walk from the main old-town street, Corso Ruggero.
Destinations Messina (12 daily; 2hr 15min–3hr); Milazzo (12 daily; 1hr 40min–2hr); Palermo (12 daily; 1hr); Sant'Agata di Militello (approx 1 hourly; 1hr); Santo Stefano di Camastra-Mistretta (1 hourly; 30min).
By bus Buses pull into Piazza Stazione outside the train station.
Destinations Castelbuono (7 daily Mon–Sat, 2 daily Sun; 40min); Gangi (1 daily; 1hr 45min–2hr); Geraci (2 daily

Mon–Sat, 1 daily Sun; 1hr 25min); Palermo (3 daily Mon–Sat, 1 daily Sun; 1hr); Petralia Soprana and Sottana (1 daily Mon–Sat; 2hr).
By car There is residents-only parking throughout the old town, so the best advice is to park in the patrolled, and good value, car park, Parcheggio Dafne on Via Aldo Moro, just to the right of the train station (Oct–May €1 per hour, €12 per day, summer prices at least double). You can book ahead online, at ⓦ cefaluparking.it.

GETTING AROUND

Bike and scooter rental Scooter for Rent (Via Vittorio Emanuele 57; ☎ 338 230 9008, ⓦ scooterforrent.it), has mountain bikes (from €15/day) and scooters (€25–35/half-

day, €35–50/day).
Taxis There's a taxi rank outside the train station at Piazza Stazione (☎ 0921 422 554).

INFORMATION

Tourist information The tourist office is located at Corso Ruggero 77 (Mon–Sat 9am–8pm; ☎ 0921 421 050), where you can pick up a free town map and information about boat trips, summer concerts, theatre performances and other events.

Online information The website ⓦ cefalu.it is useful for accommodation, restaurants, outdoor activities and local services. For information (in Italian) on the Madonie mountains, try ⓦ parcodellemadonie.it, which also has details of walks, flora, fauna, events and places to eat and drink.

ACCOMMODATION   SEE MAP PAGE 92

★ **B&B Bohémien** Via Umberto I 15/C ☎ 373 714 9962, ⓦ bohemienbeb.it. Cordial, welcoming owners and four bright, stylish double rooms with original Liberty-tiled ceramic floors in a pretty stone *palazzetto* in the higher part of town, but just a few minutes walk from the Duomo and beach. The best feature is the zingy-hued common room,

which includes a very well-stocked honesty bar. **€94**
Camping San Filippo Contrada Ogliastrillo ☎ 0921 420 184, ⓦ campingsanfilippo.com. Lovely campsite, a short walk from the beach, with tent and caravan pitches under pine trees. There's a bar and minimarket, sports facilities and a children's playground. Car parking costs €6. Per person **€9**,

plus per tent €8.50

Dolce Estate Cefalù Via C.O. Bordonaro 9 ☎340 0079208, ⓦdolceestatecefalu.it. Four lovely apartments with sea views in several different houses along Via Bordonaro, and another, perched right above the rocks on Via Candelaro. All apartments sleep between 2 and 4 people. €120.

Dolce Vita Via C.O. Bordonaro 8 ☎0921 923 151, ⓦdolcevitabb.it. Right in the heart of the old town but still with the sea on one side, so rooms with a view are nice and peaceful. Two face the street, three the sea, and all are en suite and spacious (sleeping up to four), with high ceilings and restored tile floors. Best of all is the glorious terrace, a perfect haven with uninterrupted sea views, while the cheery owner can arrange boat trips, airport transfers, etc. Breakfast is taken in a bar in the cathedral piazza. Usually closed two months between Nov and Feb. €88

La Giara Via Veterani 40 ☎0921 421 562, ⓦhotellagiara.it. Three-star *La Giara* is very central, on an old-town street close to the Duomo, and has decent, if rather old-fashioned rooms with wooden fittings and a top-floor terrace with town and ocean views. Expect some noise from street-facing rooms. €77

★ **Palazzo Villelmi** Corso Ruggero 149 ☎0921 923 057 or ☎339 852 0161, ⓦpalazzovillelmi.it Stylish, elegant B&B in a beautifully restored old *palazzo* on the main street, very near the Duomo. High painted ceilings give a hint of its former grandeur, and a rooftop breakfast terrace looks right on to the cathedral. €90

Riva del Sole Lungomare G. Giardina ☎0921 421 230, ⓦrivadelsole.com. The most central seaside hotel has rooms overlooking the promenade and beach, and it's very close to the parking area. As long as you don't mind the summer noise from the bars and restaurants, it's a great location – just steps from the sand and with its own chic terrace café. Half board only in Aug, at around €100 per person. €174

Villa Cerniglia Lungomare G. Giardina ☎320 306 4275, ⓦvilla-cerniglia.cefalu.hotels-sicily.net. A selection of modern, functional rooms and apartments in a complex right on the seafront. Facilities include access to a lido for those seeking the full Sicilian beach experience. €153

EATING
SEE MAP PAGE 92

There are dozens of **restaurants** in Cefalù, though many trade on their sea view and are overpriced. Menus are broadly similar – fish and seafood is, of course, the local highlight – and the best deals are often in the form of set menus (from €20 a head). The **cafés** in Piazza del Duomo are a nice place to start the day, with breakfast in front of the cathedral.

La Brace Via XXV Novembre 10 ☎0921 423 570. A tiny place run by a Dutch mother and son, where you dine to classical music in a room formed by three stone arches. The cuisine is more varied than in many Cefalù restaurants, with European dishes such as steak tournedos or chicken liver pâté joining Sicilian dishes like swordfish *involtini*. There are lots of vegetarian options as well, such as pasta with tomato, aubergines and ricotta. Be prepared to spend around €35; booking ahead is essential. Tue–Sun dinner only; closed mid-Dec to mid-Jan.

Caffè di Noto Via Bagno Cicerone 3 ☎0921 422 654. This *gelateria* is right at the edge of the *centro storico* and the beginning of the lungomare, and has fabulous ice creams in flavours including prickly pear, mango, raspberry, pear and ricotta, and chocolate with chilli. April–Oct daily 10am–late.

★ **Le Chat Noir** Via XXV Novembre 17 ☎0921 420 697. Family-run place with an atmospheric setting in the whitewashed, plant-filled courtyard of a sixteenth-century building a short walk from the Duomo. You'll find memorable executions of homely Sicilian dishes such as aubergine *parmigiana* with salty ricotta, *pasta con le sarde*, and an orange salad spiked with chilli. Count on spending €35 for a full meal including wine if you eat fish, €25 if you opt for meat. Mon–Tues & Thurs–Sun lunch & dinner.

Fritto e Divino Via Mandralisca 6 ☎0921 423 644. Enjoy Sicilian street food and sparkling wine at one of the tables outside. There's mixed deep-fried seafood (€9), *pannelle* (€2.50), arancini (€2) and deep-fried veg (think Sicilian tempura) for €3. Daily 11.30am–3.30pm & 6.30pm until late.

La Galleria Via Mandralisca 23 ☎0921 420 211, ⓦlagalleriacefalu.it. Billed as a "literary café", and incorporating courtyard bar, exhibition space and cultural centre, *La Galleria* is also a great place for classy, contemporary Sicilian cooking – think chic, white dining room and a seasonally changing menu. Local pasta, *scialatelle* with fresh red prawns, cherry tomatoes and basil (€14), is a winner. There's a second entrance on Via XXV Novembre. Daily lunch & dinner.

Lo Scoglio Ubriaco Via C.O. Bordonaro 2–4 ☎0921 423 370. The "Drunken Rock" is a busy, traditionally touristy restaurant with a sea-facing terrace. The fish is really good though, (with plenty of mains between €9 and €13.50), and it also serves pizza (€6–10.50) in the evening. July & Aug daily lunch & dinner; Sept–June closed Tues.

DRINKING
SEE MAP PAGE 92

For sunset drinks and views, there's a line of restaurants, **bars** and *gelaterie* along the promenade by the beach, while the local *passeggiata* tends to run all the way up the main Corso Ruggero to Piazza Garibaldi and its streetside bars and ice-cream shops.

Enoteca Rossorubino Via Bordonaro 16 ☎0921 423340. Tiny wine bar that sells wine by the glass (from €4), various bruschetta (try the ricotta and truffle cream, €8 or the little crostini with anchovies, €6) and plates of local cheeses, salamis and hams (€10). Tables are outside on a pedestrianized cobbled street. March–Nov daily 11am–2pm & 5pm until late.

Molo 99 Via Piazza Marina 4–5 ☎0921 921 220. Pavement café with views over the little port which makes a nice place for a lunchtime or evening aperitivo. Campari soda (€4), cocktails (from €6). Daily 8am until late.

★ **Tivitti** Via Lungomare G. Giardina 7 ☎0921 922 642. Contemporary twist on a traditional wine bar with wines by the bottle or glass (from €5 a glass including *antipasti* nibbles), as well as excellent pizzas (€5–12), many of them using local produce and ingredients such as Madonie white truffles to great effect. There are also hamburgers using Sicilian beef served with tasty combinations of sun-dried tomatoes, local cheeses and olives. For a beach picnic, buy a bottle and cold cuts to take away. There are tables inside and out, overlooking the beach. Daily 11am–4pm, 7pm until late, often doesn't close at all in high summer.

SHOPPING

SEE MAP PAGE 92

If you're looking for more than *Godfather* T-shirts, Sicilian puppets or mass-produced cookbooks in Japanese and German, you need to dig a bit deeper in Cefalù's old town. It's worth buying sun cream or aspirin just to have a look at the beautifully carved cabinets inside the traditional Farmacia Cirincione, at Corso Ruggero 144.

A Lumera Corso Ruggero 176 ☎0921 921 801 ⓦwww.alumeracefalu.it. A good place to buy traditional Sicilian ceramics, made in nearby Santo Stefano di Camastra (see page 105). Daily, usually 10am–10pm.

L'Artigiano Freak Piazza Spinola 2. Sicilian flat caps (*coppole*) made of recycled coffee sacks, leather gloves, bags and belts, and artisan soaps. Sat only in low season, daily 9am–1pm & 4–8pm in summer.

Ceramiche Sireci Via Mandralisca 47 ☎348 651 5061. Made by the husband and wife owners at Santo Stefano di Camastra, designs on the ceramics sold here range from traditional Sicilian to more delicate and original patterns created by the owners. Mon–Sat 10am–6pm, later in summer.

La Credenza dei Buoni Sapori Via XXV Novembre 5. Good little place to buy pesto, conserves, jams, and locally grown nuts and legumes – including rare strains such as black chickpeas. Daily 9.30am–1pm & 4–8pm (later in summer).

Robinson Via Madonna degli Angeli 3 ☎339 608 2983. A treasure-trove of bric-a-brac, antiques and junk. Mon–Sat 10am–1pm & 5 8pm.

DIRECTORY

Hospital Contrada Pietrapollastra ☎0921 920 111.
Pharmacies Cirincione, Corso Ruggero 144 (Mon–Fri 9am–1pm & 4.30–8.30pm; ☎0921 421 209). There's a rota system for evening and late-opening pharmacies posted outside.

Police Carabinieri, Discesa Paramuro ☎0921 421 412.
Post office Via Vazzana 2, between Via Roma and the seafront (Mon–Fri 8am–6.30pm, Sat 8am–12.30pm).

Himera

Tues–Sat 9.30am–5.30pm, Sun 9.30am–1.30pm • €4 • There's no public transport to Himera. It's around halfway between Cefalù and Termini Imerese – take the Buonfornello exit from the autostrada and keep a keen eye out for signs once you're on the SS113 coastal road

On the coast around 20km west of Cefalù stands the site of the ancient Greek city of **HIMERA**, though the visible remains are few and it's probably one for dedicated stone-hunters only. Himera was the first Greek settlement on Sicily's northern coast, founded in 648 BC as an advance post against the Carthaginians, who controlled the west of the island. The town inevitably became a flashpoint, and in 480 BC the Carthaginian leader **Hamilcar** landed a huge force nearby. Pitted against the combined armies of Akragas (Agrigento), Gela and Syracuse, the invading force was demolished and Hamilcar himself perished – either assassinated by Greek spies before the battle, or killed when he threw himself onto the pyre afterwards, depending on whose version you read. The outcome of the battle marked a significant upheaval of the classical world – and, in the case of Sicily, a new balance of power, with the Greeks in the ascendant. But their glory was short-lived: in 409 BC Hamilcar's nephew, **Hannibal**, wreaked his revenge and razed the city to the ground, forcing the surviving citizens west to what is now Termini Imerese.

The site

Museum Same hours as site • Museum entry included in site ticket (€4)

All that's left of the important Chalcidinian settlement that once stood here is the massive **Tempio della Vittoria**, erected to commemorate the defeat of the Carthaginians – indeed, the labour was carried out by the captured Carthaginians themselves. It's a conventional Doric construction, with six columns at the front and back, and fourteen at the sides. Despite the paucity of the remains, and the proximity of the road and rail line, the solitary ruin does have a powerful appeal. It's said to stand on the very site of the 480 BC battle, and after the victory some of the rich Carthaginian spoils were pinned up inside. The acropolis lay just inland, and, though excavations have uncovered a necropolis and some smaller temples, much work remains to be done at the site. There is a good **museum**, housing some of the items dug up here (others are in museums in Termini and Palermo), including a few of the striking lion's-head waterspouts that drained the temple's roof. One strangely moving display is of the grave of a married couple, the wife curled up next to her husband, her leg resting on his.

Caccamo

Ten kilometres to the south of Termini Imerese, the small town of **CACCAMO**, set amid green hills, is worth visiting chiefly for its remarkable **castello**. Caccamo itself is not much more than an overgrown village, disturbed only by the weight of traffic along the one main street, Corso Umberto I.

Castello

Via Castello • Tues–Sun 9am–1pm & 3–7pm (depending on staffing levels) • €4 • ☎ 091 814 9252

Caccamo's **castello** is a many-splendoured thing, a chalk-white array of towers and battlements dominating the town and commanding the heights above the deep San Leonardo river valley. Built originally in the twelfth century, the castle has over 130 rooms, though only a fraction are open to the public. The highlight is the grand **Sala della Congiura**, with a fine painted wooden ceiling and walls festooned with arms, where the Sicilian barons plotted an uprising against William I ("the Bad") in 1160 – it failed and the leader was blinded, hamstrung and left to die in a Palermo prison. Other rooms hold more weapons, costumes, coats of arms and reproductions of period furniture, and a **terrace** allows you to savour the glorious views.

Chiesa Madre

Piazza del Duomo • Daily 7am–noon & 3.30–6pm • Free

Behind the castle crag sits the **Chiesa Madre**, which has reliefs around the sacristy door attributed to Francesco Laurana, the Renaissance sculptor who left his mark all over the region, particularly in Palermo. Look out, too, for the seventeenth-century **tablet** depicting St George and the Dragon over the main portal.

Chiesa delle Anime Sante del Purgatorio

Piazza del Duomo • Erratic hours, but usually Sun for services 10am–12.30pm & 4.30–7pm • Free

To the right of the Chiesa Madre as you enter the piazza, the **Chiesa delle Anime Sante del Purgatorio** is more compelling, specifically for its **catacombs**, reached down crumbling steps. Fully clothed and collapsing bodies lie in niches in the walls, topped by a row of white skulls, the remains of the town's nobility and clergy who made their last journey here between the seventeenth and mid-nineteenth centuries.

ARRIVAL AND DEPARTURE   CACCAMO

By bus Caccamo has terrible bus connections, and is only accessible from Palermo or the industrial port of Termini Imerese. Services are constantly being cut back, so see ⓦ autolineerandazzo.it for timetables before heading out. Buses arrive and depart from Via Porta Euracea on the western edge of the historic centre.

EATING

A Castellana Piazza di Caduti ☎ 091 814 8667. Right by the castle, this medieval granary is now a popular pizzeria-ristorante. Try the local goat's cheese scented with herbs and served with bresaola and rocket (€10), or *tagliatelle* *Don Mario* with burrata, anchovies, sun-dried tomatoes, cherry tomatoes, pine nuts, pistachio and raisins (€9). Great pizzas and excellent grilled meat as well. Tues–Sun lunch & dinner.

Parco Regionale delle Madonie

The Madonie mountain range and valleys south of Cefalù fall within the limits of one of Sicily's most accessible regional parks, the **Parco Regionale delle Madonie**. It's an area of beech- and pinewoods, flower-filled upland plains, craggy rocks, soft, undulating foothills, high passes and soaring peaks (including the highest mountains in Sicily after Etna). With a 200-million year geological history, the Monti Madonie has recently been added to the UNESCO list of geoparks (sites of outstanding geological interest). Villages and towns are few and far between, but a couple of places in particular make good bases for tours and walks, while several remote resort hotels and *rifugi* offer a real mountain escape. A good driving route runs from Castelbuono to Geraci Siculo and on to Petralia Soprana, before twisting back across the mountains to the ski and hiking area of Piano Battàglia – though note that warm winters make the likelihood of decent snow increasingly unreliable – and round again to Castelbuono. You could do this in a day (about a 90km, 3hr, drive), but spending at least one night in the mountains would give you time for a walk, a country picnic or two and endless stunning views.

Northern gateway to the Madonie park (pronounced Mad-on-*ee*-eh) is the attractive town of **Castelbuono**, 20km southeast of Cefalù, while right across the mountains on the south side is the smaller settlement of **Petralia Soprana**. Mountain trails are becoming better signposted since the UNESCO citation, and a walking map should be available from the park office in Petralia Sottana by the time you read this.

GETTING AROUND   PARCO REGIONALE DELLE MADONIE

By car You'll need a car to get around the Madonie mountains, particularly as accommodation outside the towns is extremely limited and fairly remote. **By bus** Buses (ⓦ saistrasporti.it) run between Cefalù and Castelbuono (7 daily Mon–Sat, 2 daily Sun; 45min).

Castelbuono

CASTELBUONO – self-styled "capital" of the Monti Madonie – doesn't actually feel much like a mountain town at all, but it is a pretty place that makes a good day-trip from Cefalù, even if you plan to go no further and higher into the Madonie park. It owes its origins to the Ventimiglia family, who made the town something of a thriving cultural centre in the fifteenth century, and their seat was the squat **Castello Ventimiglia** that's visible for many kilometres around.

Castelbuono's main street, **Via Umberto I**, is closed to traffic for much of the day. Like the rest of town, it makes for an enjoyable stroll, with a maze of cobbled streets on either side opening on to occasional churches and shady piazzas. For three days every June, the streets are laid with amazing floral designs and pictures during the **Infiorata Castelbuonese**. The eye-catching freestanding "Venus and Cupid" **fountain** on Via Umberto I is a good thirst-quencher on a hot day, while if you stroll around for any length of time you'll also probably come across Castelbuono's **eco-donkeys** – the town

2

EXPLORING THE PARCO REGIONALE DELLE MADONIE

Though largely in Italian, there's useful information on the several **park websites**, W parks.
it, W parcodellemadonie.it, and at W madonie.it. There is also a **park information office** in
Petralia Sottana at Corso Paolo Agliata, 16 (**☎** 0921 680 201, W parcodellemadonie.it) where you
should be able to pick up maps and other information, and a PDF of a walking map can be
downloaded for free from W caisicilia.it. Popular hikes, such as the easy ascent of the Madonie's
highest mountain, Punta Carbonara, are simple to follow, but if you are not an experienced
trail-finder it might be sensible to hire the services of a guide.

A good point of contact for guided walks, rock climbing, mountain biking, snow-shoe
trekking and Nordic Walking is Vincenzo Scavuzzi (W ariaterra.com) who also rents out
equipment, including mountain and electric bikes.

RECOMMENDED WALKS

Some local **tour operators** organize hikes, pony treks and other mountain activities, which
offer another great way of getting to grips with the Madonie – check the websites above for
details of what is on offer during your stay.
From the Rifugio Crispi to Piano Porno along Sentiero #1 An easy one-hour circular
walk taking in an ancient mountain oak forest.
From Piano Battaglia to the summit of Pizzo Carbonara Straightforward and easy to
follow, it takes three or four hours to complete this circuit. Make the ascent on Sentiero #1,
before Sentiero #2a and #2b. Walk down along Sentiero #2.
From Portella Ferrone outside Petralia Soprana to Piano Catarineci Fantastic, varied
walk along Sentiero #10, with views right across the Madonie to the Aeolian Islands.

---

has replaced its rubbish trucks with a unique door-to-door donkey collection service
for household waste and recycling.

Matrice Vecchia
Piazza Margherita • Daily 11am–1pm & 5–7pm • Crypt €0.50

From the restored gateway and enclosed castle piazza, a charming tree-lined street
runs down to central Piazza Margherita, where terrace cafés overlook the fourteenth-
century **Matrice Vecchia**, fronted by a pretty loggia. If it's open, you can pay to descend
well-worn steps into the **crypt** to view a series of remarkably well-preserved sixteenth-
century frescoes of the Passion of Christ.

ARRIVAL AND DEPARTURE   CASTELBUONO

Destinations Cefalù (7 daily Mon–Sat, 1–2 daily Sun; 40min);
Gangi (1 daily; 1hr–1hr 20min); Geraci (2 daily Mon–Sat, 1
daily Sun; 45min); Palermo (3 daily Mon–Sat; 1hr 45min).
By car If you're staying in Cefalù consider leaving the car
and taking the bus, as parking can be tricky; otherwise,

park where you can in the modern periphery and walk
into the *centro storico*. Traffic loops through town on a
convoluted one-way system, and it has to be said that initial
impressions of Castelbuono by car are not good; it's much
nicer once you're on foot.

ACCOMMODATION

4 Cannola Via Dafni 7 **☎** 0921 671 490 or **☎** 333 242
1018, W bb-4cannola.it. The town's most central B&B
has clean, plain rooms in a restored house just behind the
Venus fountain (also known as the Quattro Cannola or Four
Spouts) on the main street. €60
★ **Azienda Agrituristica Bergi** Contrada Bergi
☎ 0921 672 045, W agriturismobergi.com. A laidback
organic estate in a gorgeous valley, 3km southeast of town
on the SS286 Geraci Siculo road, with spacious, country-
style one- and two-room units set around landscaped
gardens and a pool. It's a working farm of orchards and

olives – home-made preserves and fruit from the trees are
served at breakfast, while a good four-course dinner (€25,
or included in the €75 half-board per person rate) uses more
of their produce. €87
Relais Santa Anastasia Contrada Santa Anastasia
☎ 0921 672 233, W abbaziasantanastasia.com. For a
sumptuous stay, try this rather grand restored twelfth-
century abbey 8km outside town, with honeyed stone
walls, elegant rooms in deep colours, and a glorious outdoor
pool. Rates can be high, but contact them for special deals,
especially out of season. Dinner in the lovely restaurant is

€40 per person, with the dishes based around local produce and home-grown vegetables – and there are vegetarian and vegan menus. €185
Rifugio Francesco Crispi Piano Semprià ☎0921 672 279, 🖥rifugio-crispi.it. The nearest mountain refuge to

Castelbuono is at 1300m above sea level, and a good two hours' strenuous walk away in the Milocca forest. It's open all year, providing basic accommodation in double, triple and quad rooms. Breakfast and dinner are included. €50 per person

EATING

A line of appealing **cafés** and **restaurants** with outdoor terraces lies between the castle and Piazza Margherita, while yet more places are hidden away in the surrounding alleys. Pork, beef and especially wild mushrooms are typical menu items in this mountain region.
Antico Baglio Piazza Ten. Schicchi 3 ☎0921 679 512. It's a couple of hundred metres off the beaten track, but this restored old *baglio* (warehouse) has both a cool interior and shady outdoor deck, where you can sample hearty home-made pasta with a sausage-meat and mushroom *ragù* (pasta dishes from €7–9, main dishes from €9–16). At night there are pizzas too. Follow the signs from Piazza Matteotti at the end of Via Umberto I. Tues–Sun lunch & dinner.
Fiasconaro Piazza Margherita 10 ☎0921 671 231. Known throughout Italy for its gourmet panettone and other goodies made with locally grown pistachio *and* manna (the latter unique to the area), this is a must for foodies. Enjoying a home-made ice cream or a dish of strawberry *granita* at a seat here in the charming old-town

square takes some beating on a hot day. Thurs–Tue 9am–1pm & 3.15–8pm.
★ **Nangalarruni** Via delle Confraternite 5 ☎0921 671 428. The best place in town for serious mountain cuisine, this upmarket rustic tavern does marvellous things with wild mushrooms. They appear in soups, sauces and pasta dishes and, with pork and beef to follow, finishing with a shot of the sweet local *digestivo*, Elisir di Fontana, is definitely a good idea. Dishes start at €8, and there are three tasting menus at €24, €26 and (if you are seriously hungry) €30. It's just down Via Umberto I from Piazza Margherita, second alley on the right. Daily lunch & dinner; closed Wed in low season.
Palazzaccio Via Umberto I, 23 ☎0921676289. Set on Castelbuono's main street, this restaurant serves good, hearty food for the dedicated carnivore. A huge fixed-price dinner (€35) includes mixed *antipasti* (great veal carpaccio), home-made pasta *primo*, and pork stewed slowly in wine usually features for the main course. If they have the chocolate *crostata*, go for it. Tues–Sun lunch & dinner.

Geraci Siculo

For an initial taste of the mountains, make the thirty-minute drive from Castelbuono up the winding SS286 to **GERACI SICULO**, 20km away. If ever a town was buttoned up tight against the threat of winter, it's this one, with its packed houses lining streets so narrow that laundry is strung across from balcony to balcony. At the highest point, up back-breaking cobbled alleys, the scant, restored ruins of a castle and an ancient chapel stand amid wild flowers and scented pines. Amazing 360-degree panoramas unfold, while back down the valley Castelbuono and its own mighty castle are easily seen. The road south of town climbs even higher before dropping down to the SS120 Gangi–Petralia road, from where you can pick up the route into the central park region.

EXPLORING GOLE DI TIBERIO

A fabulous karst gorge about a 45min drive from Castelbuono, the Gole di Tiberio (May to Oct; free) makes a great day out in the summer months. The entrance to the gorge is just beyond the little hamlet of Tiberio – walk down the five hundred steps from the picnic and barbecue area or take the shuttle (€2 per person). Once there, you can splash around alone, or, more fun, take a *gommone* (a RIB or "rigid inflatable boat", €10) 400m along the river to a natural pool. Ariaterra (🖥ariaterra.com) also organize water-trekking (walking down the river, in the water).

GETTING THERE

Signposted off the SP60 From Castelbuono, take the SS286 to Finale di Pollina, then the SP52 heading towards San Mauro Castelverde and Gangi. At the junction for Borrello, bear right towards Gangi, and then after 1.5km take the narrow road on the right, signposted Gole di Tiberio.

2

By bus There is a bus to Geraci a couple of times a day from Cefalù via Castelbuono, which then runs on to Gangi, but the town really doesn't merit the hours of time you'll have on your hands between one bus and the next. Realistically, Geraci is only a coffee stop for drivers.

Piano Zucchi and Piano Battaglia

The heart of the Madonie lies southwest of Castelbuono, in the upland slopes and valleys below the two peaks of Pizzo Antenna Grande (or Pizzo della Principessa, 1977m) and Pizzo Carbonara (1979m). These are the highest of Sicily's mountains after Etna, with a winter ski business based at the two resort areas of Piano Zucchi and Piano Battaglia – though "resort" is pushing it, since there are no villages here and only very limited facilities. Outside winter time, it's an enjoyable drive up into the high mountains, with plenty of places to park up, take a walk through the alpine meadows and have a picnic.

There's nothing much at all at **Piano Zucchi** (1100m), save a little mountain chapel, a children's playground and views of peaks to all sides. **Piano Battaglia**, sited at 1600m (ⓦpianobattaglia.it), is a rather nicer area for picnics under the beech trees, as well as being the departure point for the easy ascent of Pizzo Carbonara.

By car From Castelbuono, drive 9km west to Munciarrati (also known as Mongerati), between Collesano and Isnello, where there's a turn-off up into the mountains. Piano Zucchi is 17km from the junction, with Piano Battaglia 7km further on again. From Piano Battaglia, it's another 20km, or half-hour drive, over the tops and down to the Petralia towns.

EATING

Lo Scoiattolo Località Piano Battaglia ☎ 349 643 9987. Tiny mountain trattoria with a hut where you can watch ricotta being made. The menu is unpretentious and simple, with dishes such as pasta with mushrooms, and grilled sausages. Call before you go to make sure that they're open. Opening times weather dependent.

Petralia Soprana and Petralia Sottana

The southern edge of the Madonie range is marked by the twin towns of Petralia, which lie on opposite sides of a hill. There are some wonderful views, as you might imagine, from the upper town of **PETRALIA SOPRANA**, which sits at an altitude of

---

A TASTE OF HEAVEN

And when the dew that lay was gone up, behold, upon the face of the wilderness there lay a small round thing, as small as the hoar frost on the ground. And when the children of Israel saw it, they said one to another, It is manna: for they wist not what it was. And Moses said unto them, This is the bread which the Lord hath given you to eat. This is the thing which the Lord hath commanded, Gather of it every man according to his eating.   Exodus 16:14–16

Famous for the sustenance it gave Moses and the Israelites, **manna** is the sap of the south European flowering ash (*Fraxinus ornus*), cultivated uniquely in several plantations around Castelbuono. The sap is obtained by making incisions with a knife in the trunks of the trees between July and September. The liquid sap is at first bitter, but it sweetens as it solidifies on the trunk. As well as being a mild laxative and purgative, it is also a cough sedative, an expectorant, a sweetener, and can be used as an eyewash and for softening boils – and, according to locals in Castelbuono, it can even bring the dead back to life.

Chewy and tasting like a mixture of honey and maple syrup, manna is put to rather more pleasant use by the *pasticcerie* of Castelbuono, most notably *Fiasconaro* (see page 99), who use it in their unforgettably delicious panettone, nougat and ice cream.

nearly 1150m. This was the birthplace of the craftsman Fra Umile da Petralia (1580–1639), whose wooden crosses are found in churches all over southern Italy. From the edge of the village you get a long view over the Madonie and Nebrodi mountains, as well as an occasional sight of Etna.

However, it's the lower town 3km away, **PETRALIA SOTTANA**, that acts as the mountain base for the region. Clinging to the hillside, it's an evocative place with one long main street, Corso Paolo Agliata, which is lined with weathered medieval churches, small piazzas and shuttered houses, culminating in the usual castle ruins.

2

Parco Avventura

April–June, Sept & Oct Sat & Sun 10am–6pm; July & Aug daily 10am–8pm • Picnic area €2, adventure course €18 adults, €11 children • ☎ 091 748 7186, ⓦ parcoavventuramadonie.it

For a fabulous day out in the trees above town you can drive to the **Parco Avventura**, 3km beyond Petralia Sottana on the Piano Battaglia road, where as well as picnic areas and marked trails there's a thrilling **high-rope adventure course** through the pines – booking is a good idea in summer and at weekends (especially Sundays).

INFORMATION

Tourist information The tourist office is in Petralia Sottana at Corso Paolo Agliata 100 (daily 8.30am–2pm & 3–8pm; ☎ 0921 641 811, ⓦ petraliavisit.it). The Ente Parco delle Madonie office, at Corso Paolo Agliata 16 (officially daily 8am–2pm, but erratic in reality; ☎ 0921 684 011, ⓦ parcodellemadonie.it), should be able to tell you about hiking, skiing and escorted excursions.

ACCOMMODATION AND EATING

★ **La Locanda di Cadì** A Fuoco Lento Borgo Cipampini, Petralia Soprana ☎ 338 289 0100, ⓦ lalocandadicadi. it. Run with passion and incredible attention to detail, this authentic country inn is really quite special, located in a minuscule medieval *borgo* outside Petralia Soprana. It's best known as a place to eat, with mains based on whatever is in season at the time – every ingredient is meticulously sourced or picked from the garden. The quality free-range chickens and Madonie lamb are fragrantly stuffed and oven-roasted, and a full meal will be €25–30. There are simple rooms as well, each with their own log burner, and staying here is an unforgettable experience. **€80**

★ **Trattoria Da Salvatore** Piazza S. Michele 3 ☎ 0921 680169. This trattoria has been here since anyone can remember, serving traditional mountain food. The mixed *antipasto* is abundant (and a lunch in itself), featuring grilled zucchini, peppers and aubergines, *caponata*, wild mushrooms (depending on the season), spicy tomatoes, fresh ricotta and local cheeses and salamis. There are also divine frittatas – with ricotta, wild fennel and other wild greens – while in spring, there is a delicious pasta with the season's first peas, fava beans, artichokes and wild fennel, with or without a dollop of ricotta. After a brisk mountain walk, the soups of beans and lentils are perfect – look out for soup made with rare *fagioli badda*, grown in nearby Polizzi Generosa. Main courses (if you can manage them) include grilled meats, and in the evening there are pizzas. A full meal can be had for less than €25 a head. Wed–Mon lunch, Sat & Sun lunch & dinner.

Polizzi Generosa

A twenty-minute drive west of the Petralias, the small town of **POLIZZI GENEROSA** is another possible Madonie base. Mountain views aside, the grand old **Chiesa Matrice** contains the area's greatest work of art, a triptych of the Madonna and Child flanked by saints. Attributed to a mysterious fifteenth-century Fleming known only as the "Maître au Feuillage brodé", it's reckoned to be his finest achievement. If you happen to be in the area around Easter, don't miss the Via Crucis procession – the costumes were designed and donated by Dolce and Gabbana, a gift to his home town from Domenico Dolce.

ARRIVAL AND DEPARTURE

By bus Polizzi Generosa is connected to Palermo by very infrequent buses (2 daily; 1hr 20min; ⓦ saistrasporti.it).

ACCOMMODATION AND EATING

Giardino Donna Lavia Contrada Donna Lavia ☏0921 551 104, ⊚www.giardinodonnalavia.com. Set within a former Jesuit monastery, this is the perfect location for a country holiday, with five rooms and a suite with its own terrace in a tower. The restaurant (dinner daily; €25) is exceptional, with locally sourced meats, home-grown vegetables and pulses, and freshly picked wild greens and herbs. Try the home-made tagliatelle with a tasty purée of *fagioli badda* (a dramatic-looking violet and white bean unique to Polizzi), wild borage and wild fennel. In season, there are lots of wild mushrooms, and a fabulous roast suckling pig. Doubles **€66**, suite **€100**.

Santa Venera Contrada Santa Venera ☏0921 649 421, ⊚santavenera.com. It's worth making the trip to hole up in this place, run by the same family behind *U Bagghiu* and located 7km north of Polizzi Generosa, towards the Scillato autostrada junction. A comfortable farmhouse *agriturismo*, it's surrounded by vineyards and orchards, with seven en-suite rooms, a swimming pool and good views in all directions. You can eat in the restaurant here (daily, dinner only) for €15–25, and there's a half-board deal for €50 per person. **€70**

The Sicilian House Palazzo Notar Nicchi, Via Notar Nicchi ⊚thesicilianhouse.com. A traditional Sicilian townhouse right in the heart of Polizzi Generosa that has been marvellously and luxuriously restyled to a contemporary design by an Australian-Sicilian family. It can be rented as two separate apartments, or as a whole (for large parties – there are six bedrooms in all). Stunning roof terrace, six balconies and every little luxury you can think of. Minimum stay of two nights for either the one- or three-bedroom options, or three nights for the entire house. Contact the owner via the website directly for prices.

U Bagghiu Via Gagliardo 3 ☏0921 551 111. Serves a great pasta speciality, *penne al Bagghiu* (cheesy penne with tomato and garlic), along with hearty mountain dishes featuring lots of wild boar and mushrooms, and pizzas in the evening. Pasta from €7. Mon & Wed–Sun lunch & dinner.

Gangi

Thanks largely to the dynamism and determination of its mayor – who made international headlines in 2015 by offering houses for sale for €1 – the medieval hill-town of **GANGI** has been thoroughly restored, and has become the Madonie's liveliest, most picturesque and most tourist-friendly town. Its cobbled streets and stone houses have been exquisitely restored, the centre has been pedestrianized, and tourist routes to the most picturesque sights and corners are marked with pretty ceramic plaques. Though there may be no great sights, it is a wonderful place to wander, and there are several nice places to eat and stay. All in all, Gangi makes a fabulous base for exploring the Madonie. Summer sees a rapidly evolving series of festivals and processions (⊚comune.gangi.pa.it). If you are interested in finding out about the €1 deal in Gangi and other Italian and Sicilian villages, check out ⊚casea1euro.it, the only catch being that you have to restore your purchase within four years.

GANGI INFORMATION

Ufficio Turistico Corso Umberto I (Tues–Sun 9am–1pm & 3.30–7.30pm; ☏0921 501471). Useful little office that has lots of information on Gangi and the surrounding area. If you fancy a commentary to accompany your wanderings, you can rent an audioguide (English, Spanish and Italian).

By car Look for a place to park along the belvedere as you drive up the hill into town. If you have no luck, there is free parking for an hour if you have a time-slot disc in your car (most hired cars have them), outside the church of San Paolo at the beginning of Corso Umberto.

ACCOMMODATION, EATING AND SHOPPING

Antichi Sapori delle Madonie Corso Umberto I, 5 ☏0921 689 570. First stop for a picnic – pizza slices, focaccia, fabulous *pane di casa* (traditional rustic bread) along with a good choice of local hams, salamis and cheeses. Sandwiches made to order. Daily in season 9am–8pm, reduced hours in winter.

BB Casa e Putia Via Giuseppe Fedele Vitale 113–115 ☏333 147 6972, ⊚casaeputia.it. Small, perfectly formed B&B with two en-suite bedrooms and a kitchen – which means that families or small groups will have the apartment all to themselves. The helpful owners have a little shop selling artisan souvenirs. **€50**

La Capra Canta Corso G F Vitale 122 ☏380 310 2903. Remarkable shop where the young Fabrizio Fazio makes traditional drums (*tamburo*) out of donkey skin – if he agrees to demonstrate you are in for an unforgettable treat. Daily 10am–1pm & 4–8pm (longer hours in summer).

Trattoria Sant'Anna Corso Umberto 1, 42 ☎0921 602 422. Gangi's most popular place to eat, with a fantastic panoramic terrace. There's local bread, traditional dishes like *maccu* (broad bean soup with wild fennel) and good hearty pasta dishes such as the handmade pasta with chilli and fennel-seed spiked sausage and fresh ricotta. Best enjoyed with a glass or two of local red wine (€3 for a quarter litre). You can eat very well for less than €20 a head. Mon, Tues & Thurs–Sun lunch & dinner.

Sperlinga

SPERLINGA owes its name to the numerous cave dwellings (from the Latin *spelunca*, cave), some hundreds of years old, that pit the sandstone slopes below the town. Several are still inhabited, looped up to the electricity grid and furnished with mod cons such as microwaves and fridges. To arrange a visit call Grotta Solidale per La Vita ☎349 6669.

The castello

Daily 9am–7.30pm (closes earlier in winter) • €5

Fused seamlessly to a sheer crag erupting in the centre of town like something out of Gormenghast, gleamingly polished by wind and rain, the Castello di Sperlinga is indubitably the most formidable castle in Sicily. Sperlinga was the only town in Sicily to open its doors to the Angevins, bloodily expelled from other Sicilian towns during the thirteenth-century Vespers rebellion: barricading themselves inside the castle, the French held out for a year before surrendering. Recently reopened after a serious landslide, it's an amazing place, with worn steps carved straight into the rock, leading through a vertical labyrinth of caves and fortifications.

ARRIVAL AND DEPARTURE   **SPERLINGA**

By bus There is one daily bus to Sperlinga from Enna, run by SAIS (⊛saisautolinee) and departing Mon–Sat during school termtime only from Enna's bus terminal, via Calascibetta, leaving at 2.10pm. The return is the following day at 6.20am. If you need to stay, there's not much in the way of accommodation – just a couple of places on ⊛airbnb.

East of Cefalù

To the east of Cefalù, the Tyrrhenian coast is traced by rail, road and motorway, and is pretty built up for the most part. There are several resorts tucked along the narrow strip of land between the Nebrodi mountains and the sea, and though most of them are not worth going out of your way for – or indeed getting off your bus or train – there are several spots, ranging from an unusual **art hotel** to the bustling ceramics town of **Santo Stefano di Camastra**, where those travelling by car might want to take a break for a stroll around.

Castel di Tusa

Some 25km east of Cefalù, the coastal village of **CASTEL DI TUSA** features the remnants of a defensive castle and some good rocky beaches. In recent years, however, the place has become rather better known for its modern art, thanks to the efforts of **Antonio Presti** (born in Messina in 1957), who in the late 1980s and early 1990s invited artists from around the world to create a group of large-scale sculptures along the *fiumara* (river bed) and valley of the Tusa River, which flows down from the Nebrodi mountains just east of the village. After a protracted legal battle with the authorities, the sculptures were formally inaugurated as the **Fiumara d'Arte** sculpture park in 2006. You can pick up a brochure and map from Presti's other venture, the equally arresting *L'Atelier Sul Mare* "**art hotel**" (see page 105), at Via Cesare Battisti 4, which itself has become something of a tourist attraction: non-guests can be shown

2

A TOUR OF THE FIUMARA D'ARTE

All the structures and sculptures along the **Fiumara d'Arte** lie south of Castel di Tusa, and seeing the lot entails a 50km round trip by car through some magnificent countryside. Follow the signposts and you can't go far wrong, starting at the turn off the SS113 for Pettineo, a couple of kilometres east of Castel di Tusa (Santo Stefano/Messina direction). One of the earliest commissions – *La Materia Poteva Non Esserci*, resembling two giant hands joined in prayer – comes almost immediately into view, standing right under the motorway viaduct. It's 6km further up the valley to **Pettineo** itself, a gorgeous little village with the shards of a ruined castle at its highest point and a couple of bars in the old centre for refreshment. More signs then direct you another 6km up the nearby mountain to the precariously located village of **Motta d'Affermo** for *Energia Mediterranea* – a graceful concrete curving wave in mottled blue astride a dusty hilltop. Beyond lies the dramatic clifftop pyramid that is *38° Parallelo* (also known as *La Piramide*), after which you backtrack to Pettineo. There's a further cluster of works a twisting 10km south of Pettineo, in the environs of the striking hilltop hamlet of **Castel di Lucio**, from where you can either return the way you came, back to the coast, or continue on to Mistretta, which offers an alternative way back down to Santo Stefano di Camastra (or on over the mountains to Nicosia).

around the rooms and grounds on guided tours (see the website ⓦ ateliersulmare.com for details).

Halaesa

Daily 9am–1hr before sunset • Free

Just 3km up the road from Castel di Tusa, on the way to the village of Tusa, are the sparse ruins of **Halaesa**, a fifth-century BC Sikel settlement that enjoyed some success under Rome. The name derives from the Greek *alaomal*, meaning to wander aimlessly, and refers to the original settlers here, the peripatetic Alesini, who had tried settling just about everywhere else. You can make out the chequered layout of the streets, remains of the agora, and – at the highest point – the foundations of two third-century BC temples, with lofty views down over the Tusa valley.

ACCOMMODATION	CASTEL DI TUSA
★ **L'Atelier Sul Mare** Via Cesare Battisti 4 ☏ 0921 334 295, ⓦ ateliersulmare.com. Just metres from the sea, many of the rooms here have been given the designer-art treatment by individual artists: one is adorned with Arabic and Italian poetry and sports a mammoth window looking	onto the sea, with a shower that works like a car wash, while another is bathed in a red glow at night. Other rooms are more conventionally styled, though still with original artworks and furnishings. **€120**

Santo Stefano di Camastra

Cefalù aside, quite the nicest stop along the Tyrrhenian coast is **SANTO STEFANO DI CAMASTRA**, reached by train or via a quick drive along the SS113. It's actually much the better for being split in two – beach and harbour below (where the train station is) and town high above, the latter forming a handsome old grid on a panoramic shelf of land. A steep cobbled path connects the two. Santo Stefano is renowned for its colourful **ceramic work** and the road through town is lined with shops selling platters, plates, cups, jugs, statues, household goods and decorative pottery. Off the main road, the old town is kept largely free of traffic and there's a small public garden, a belvedere with sea views and a pedestrianized main street, **Via Vittorio Emanuele**, of shops, cafés, boutiques and grocery stores. It's certainly touristy, but all very charming, while in the signposted **Museo della Ceramica** (Via Palazzo 1; Fri–Sun 10am–1pm & 3–6pm, possibly longer hours in summer; free; ☏ 0921 331 110), in the handsome Palazzo Trabia, you can admire the best historic examples of the local pottery.

By train Santo Stefano is on the train line between   approximately once hourly.
Palermo and Messina, with regional services only stopping

Mistretta

Six buses run daily between Santo Stefano di Camastra railway station and Mistretta

From Santo Stefano, a high viaduct flies off 16km inland to one of the biggest of the nearby hill-villages, **MISTRETTA**. The handsome old centre of eighteenth- and nineteenth-century buildings and cobbled alleys is largely unspoiled by modern construction: wrought-iron balconies and flower boxes overlook the long main street and the seventeenth-century cathedral has the hoary look of a medieval monument, while the population is largely composed of brown-suited pensioners milling around their veterans' associations. There's not much else to it, save some old-fashioned barbers' shops, the public gardens, and castle ruins atop a small hill, but it makes a nice quiet place to stay away from the coast.

Sant'Agata di Militello

SANT'AGATA DI MILITELLO, 28km east of Santo Stefano, is a small Tyrrhenian resort that's moribund for most of the year. In truth, it can hardly be called attractive, though its very long pebbled **beach** and calm sea are popular with holidaying Italian families, who pack the town's apartments for a few weeks each summer. There's a **fishing harbour** at one end, a palm-studded **promenade**, and a gridded town centre set back up the hillside, while a restored **castle** (daily 8.30am–12.30pm & 4–8pm; €2) speaks of more illustrious times.

By bus There are hourly buses along the coast from Santo Stefano di Camastra to Sant'Agata.
Destinations San Fratello (6 daily; 20min); San Marco d'Alunzio (4 daily; 20min).
By train Sant'Agata is a stop on the coast train line between

Palermo and Messina for regional trains (approximately 1 hourly). The station is a 10min walk east of the town centre.
By car Follow the "porto" signs and drive in along the seafront, where there's plenty of free parking.

San Fratello

Fifteen kilometres up in the hills from Sant'Agata, the large village of **SAN FRATELLO** was once populated by a Lombard colony, introduced to Sicily by Roger II's queen, Adelaide di Monferrato. On the Thursday and Friday of Holy Week, before Easter, the town puts on the **Festa dei Giudei** (Feast of the Jews) – a unique carnival-type celebration when locals dress up in red devils' costumes, complete with black

---

THE MONTI NEBRODI

The **Monti Nebrodi** – a sparsely populated expanse of high forest and rocky peaks – covers a huge wedge of land between Santo Stefano di Camastra and Mistretta in the west and Randazzo and the Etna foothills in the east. Much of the mountain range is protected as the **Parco Naturale dei Nebrodi**, though it's difficult to get a good impression of the whole by car since few roads connect the scattered villages within the park and even the towns on the periphery are minor attractions for the most part. However, adventurous hikers can follow any number of trails through the hills and valleys – there are some detailed on the useful **park website**, Ⓦ parcodeinebrodi.it – while there is a road up to the highest peak, **Monte Soro** (1847m), between San Fratello and Cesarò (SS289), from which extensive views reach to the Aeolian Islands to the north and Etna to the southeast.

tongues and horses' tails (a reminder of their traditional trade of horse-raising), to the cacophonic accompaniment of trumpets, bells and drums. Needless to say, the ecclesiastical authorities take a dim view of these proceedings, but have to make do with having the Easter Sunday church congregations in suitably contrite and sober mood. For a panoramic picnic spot, head for the Norman church of **Santi Alfio, Filadelfio e Cirino**, which is isolated on top of a hill outside the village (follow the rough track from the cemetery). The church is dedicated to three brothers horribly martyred by the Romans: the first had his tongue torn out, the second was burnt alive, and the third was hurled into a pot of boiling tar.

2

Capo d'Orlando

Some 17km northeast of Sant'Agata, occupying a headland where Aragonese king Frederick II suffered a historic defeat at the hands of a group of rebellious barons in 1299, **CAPO D'ORLANDO** is now a slick Sicilian holiday town surrounded by good rocky and sandy beaches. If you're sufficiently charmed by the **swimming**, which is best on its eastern side (around the San Gregorio area), you might well want to stay. The town has plenty of restaurants, bars and *birrerias*, and a choice of discos in summer.

ARRIVAL AND INFORMATION

CAPO D'ORLANDO

By train Capo d'Orlando is a stop for regional trains running between Palermo and Messina (around 1 hourly); the station is a 10min walk from the town centre and beach.
Tours From Capo d'Orlando there are daily excursions,

weather permitting, to the Aeolian Islands between June and September, with departures generally at around 10am, returning at around 9pm: there are masses of people operating boats– all are advertised around town.

ACCOMMODATION

Hotel Faro Via Libertà 7 📞0941 902 466, 🌐nuovo hotelfaro.com. This 1960s-style hotel has spacious rooms and balconies fronting the beach. Turn right out of the

station and walk along Via Crispi, head for the sea at Piazza Matteotti, and it's a few blocks to the right. €75

Patti

With its views out to the Aeolian Islands, a crumbling hilltop historic centre, and a general – and infectious – sense of wellbeing, **PATTI** is an engaging little place, with more charm than many of the centres on this coast. At the top of the semi-restored upper town, the **Cattedrale** has a powerful *Madonna* by Antonello de Saliba and, in the right transept, the tomb of **Adelasia**, much-loved first wife of Roger I, with the date of her death inscribed at the bottom, 1118. After your visit, you could take one of the frequent buses that depart from outside the hospital just below the old centre to **Patti Marina**, where there's a long, fine pebble beach.

ARRIVAL AND DEPARTURE

PATTI

By train Patti's station (known as Patti–San Piero Patti) is on the main coastal train line between Palermo and Messina, and is located in the lower town, but connected by regular buses to the upper town; for the *centro storico* get off

at Piazza Marconi (the stop after the hospital).
By bus There's one daily bus here from Messina and one from Milazzo (both Mon–Sat). Buses arrive and depart from Piazza Marconi at the foot of the *centro storico*.

ACCOMMODATION AND EATING

BB Casa Rubes Via Magretti 127 📞0941 21 64, 📱347 527 5001, 🌐casarubes.it. An oasis: a picturesque, relaxed B&B in a beautifully converted townhouse in the heart of the old town. Highlights include the flower-filled

terrace where breakfast is served at a long table. Gracious, welcoming owners. €60
Sacra Famiglia Via Dante Alighieri 1 📞0941 241 622, 🌐sacrafamiglia.it. A spruce, modern convent perched

atop the old town, with functional rooms and a fabulous, unpretentious restaurant (daily lunch & dinner), where the crowds flock in for the *antipasto* feast (€15), a seemingly endless series of tasty morsels eaten on a terrace looking out to the Aeolian Islands. There are other great fixed-menu deals as well, but make sure you arrive hungry. Open Easter to late Aug. **€70**

Tindari

Now famous throughout Sicily as the location of a much-revered black Madonna, **Tindari** began life in 396 BC as **Tyndaris**, an outpost of Siracusa. Built and fortified as a defence against Carthaginian attacks along this coast, it was one of the last Greek settlements in Sicily. Almost impregnable thanks to its commanding height, the town continued to prosper under Rome, when it was given special privileges in return for its loyalty.

Santuario di Tindari

Mon–Sat 6.45am–12.30pm & 2.30–7pm, Sun 6.45am–12.45pm & 2.30–8pm; closes 1hr earlier in winter • Free • ⓦ santuariotindari.it

Climbing the hill to the site, the first thing you see, glistening from its clifftop position, is the **Santuario di Tindari**, a lavishly kitsch temple erected in the 1960s to house the much-revered *Madonna Nera*, or Black Madonna. A plaque underneath this Byzantine

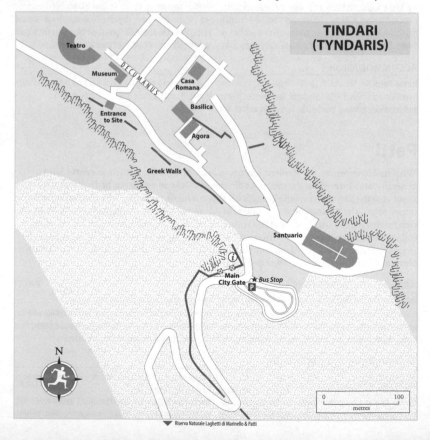

2

ANCIENT THEATRE AT TINDARI

Each year from late May until mid-June, **classical dramas** are staged in the ancient theatre at Tyndaris on alternate evenings, and between late July and late August there is also a season of theatre and **concerts** here. Performances normally start at 9pm, and **tickets** cost around €20. Ask at the ticket office by the entrance to the archeological site or contact the **box office** directly (☎ 0941 240 912, ⌨ teatrodeiduemari.net) for details. You can also pick up a programme from the Tindari tourist office.

---

icon proclaims *Nigra sum, sed hermosa* ("I am black, but beautiful"), a reference to the esteem in which she has been held for a thousand years since the icon appeared from the east to perform a series of miracles. Pilgrims throng to the sanctuary to pay their respects, especially around the Black Madonna's feast day on September 8. There's a great view from the top, overlooking a long tongue of white sand and the Marinello lagoons below.

Tyndaris archeological site

Daily 9am until 2hr before sunset • €6 includes museum entry

The archeological site of **Tyndaris** lies at the end of a path that starts in front of the sanctuario. Most of the visible remains are Roman, including some houses and shops along the main street, the decumanus – one of them (probably a caldarium, or bathhouse) with traces of plumbing still surviving – and an impressive **basilica** at the eastern end. The basilica would have been the entrance to the agora lying beyond (now covered by tourist shops). It was restored in the 1950s, using modern materials, though it still has a certain grandeur. You can just about make out the manner of its construction, which bridged Greek and Roman building techniques, and was designed in such a way that the central gallery could be shut off at either end and used for public meetings, with the market traffic diverted along the side passages.

The decumanus has streets running off it, and at the bottom of one is the **Casa Romana**, a Roman house in good condition, with mosaic floors. At the other end of the main street, the **teatro**, cut into the hill, boasts a superb view over the sea, as far as the distant Milazzo promontory. A part of the stage remains from the original third-century BC Greek edifice, but most of the rest is Roman, dating from the Imperial Age when the theatre was converted for use as a gladiatorial arena. Later, it was partly dismantled to furnish stone for the **city walls** that once surrounded the settlement, of which a good portion remain. You'll have seen some of them on the road up, including the ancient city's **main gate**, built to the same "pincer" design as the one at the Euryalus castle outside Siracusa.

The **museum** contains some of the best finds from the excavations, including a massive stone head of Augustus. There's also a reconstruction of the theatre's scenebuilding, and eighteenth-century watercolours showing how the basilica once looked.

Riserva Naturale Laghetti di Marinello

Directly below Tindari and west of Oliveri lies one of Sicily's most entrancing **beaches**, forming part of the **Riserva Naturale Laghetti di Marinello**, where saltwater lagoons, sand dunes and dramatic rocky cliffs provide a sanctuary for migratory birds. The lagoons, fine sand and clean water are irresistible, and there are bars and a campsite, but precious little shade on the beach.

ARRIVAL AND INFORMATION   **TINDARI**

By bus Frequent buses from Patti (3–6 daily; 15min) stop in the car park over 1km from the sanctuary, from where minibuses shuttle every 10min or so up to the foot of the church (return tickets €0.80). The car park charges €1/hr.

Buses depart Patti at 6.55am, 8.20am and 11.30am and there is an additional bus at 1.30pm on schooldays (mid-June to Sept also 2.45pm & 6pm). **By train** The closest train station to Tindari is Oliveri-Tindari, a good 3km (uphill) walk.

Tourist information Tindari has a tourist office right next to the site on Via Teatro Greco (Mon–Fri 9am–1pm; ☎ 0941 369 184, ✆ pattitindari.com).

ACCOMMODATION

Marinello Località Marinello ☎ 0941 313 000, ✆ www. villaggiomarinello.it. Perfectly located for the Laghetti di Marinello, this well-equipped campsite is at the bottom of the cliffs holding the Tindari sanctuary, within steps of the sandy beach and with bungalows and mini-apartments (both €70) rentable by the week. Camping/tent €9, plus €9 per person

Novara di Sicilia

Branching inland into the mountains at the nondescript village of San Biaggio, the SS185 to Giardini-Naxos (see page 176) is the only road connecting the Tyrrhenian and Ionian coasts. One of the most dramatic routes on the island, the road climbs gently into the hills through some handsome countryside to **NOVARA DI SICILIA**, whose main street is dotted with bars and shops that sell the strong local sheep's cheese, *maiorchina*.

The dense woods above the village, with expansive views over the sea, are a favourite spot for locals, who come out here on a Sunday armed with picnic hampers and portable stoves, though there are enough shady nooks and glades to find your own space. Soon after Novara, the road climbs to 1270m before descending, in sight of Etna's dramatic slopes, to Francavilla (see page 177) and Castiglione (see page 178).

EATING   NOVARA DI SICILIA

La Pineta Via Nazionale ☎ 0941 650 522. A traditional trattoria, with no menu, where you can sample the local ricotta, deep-fried *crespelle* (little pancakes) stuffed with fresh vegetables, and home-made pasta with simple sauces – tomato, tomato and fennel-spiked sausage, or pistachio pesto. A starter and pasta with a glass or so of wine should cost about €15 a head. Tues–Sun lunch & dinner.

Milazzo

If it weren't for the industry besieging **MILAZZO**, it wouldn't be a bad-looking place. A long plane- and palm-tree-lined promenade looks across the sparkling sea, while behind the town a rambling old castle caps Milazzo's ancient acropolis. Most people, though, are put off by the unsightly oil refinery that occasionally produces a yellow smog overhead, and only stop long enough to get out again, taking the first ferry or hydrofoil to the Aeolian Islands (see page 116), for which Milazzo is the major embarkation point.

Historically, the site's strategic importance made it one of the most fought-over towns in Sicily. The Greeks arrived in 716 BC, after which the town was contested by successive armies, from the Carthaginians to the Aragonese. It even became a base for the British during the Napoleonic Wars, while fifty years later Garibaldi won a victory here that set the seal on his conquest of Sicily.

If you're in a hurry, Milazzo is easy enough to handle. You could be on an outward-bound ferry or hydrofoil within an hour of arriving. But there's enough in and around town to make it an enjoyable overnight stop, before or after your Aeolian trip, ranging from a great **castle** to the surprisingly gorgeous **Capo Milazzo**, where there's a beguiling cove and sand and quartz beaches.

The lower town

Milazzo's **lower town** has a nice, brisk feel. It is not really a place to sightsee, more a place to go for a stroll, coffee or aperitivo while you wait for your ferry or hydrofoil.

Given the inflated prices on the islands, anyone self-catering is well advised to do their food shopping here before setting off. There is a daily morning **market** behind the post office on Via G. Medici. If you have time to kill, the best thing to do on a sunny day is to walk along the shore, passing little booths and tables where fishermen sell their daily catch. Carry on long enough along the promenade towards the Capo (around 20min), and you'll reach a small sandy beach with refreshments.

Duomo Nuovo

If you fancy a touch of sightseeing, drop by the silver-domed **Duomo Nuovo**, which has some Renaissance paintings in the apse: four panels of saints Peter, Paul, Rocco and Thomas Aquinas; between the last of these, there's an *Adoration of the Child* by Antonello de Saliba, and an *Annunciation* by Andrea Giuffrè above that.

The citadel

The **Borgo**, Milazzo's old hilltop **citadel**, dominates the town. Here, the views open out over bay and plain, while the higher you climb, the older and more decrepit the buildings become – some churches and *palazzi* on the approach to the castle are little more than precariously balanced shells. To appreciate the citadel's size, walk round to the north side, where the formidable defences erected by the Spanish still stand almost in their entirety. The massive walls are magnificent, and pierced by a suitably imposing tunnelled gateway.

Also within the citadel's walls are the **Duomo Antico**, its Byzantine fragments, a central Norman keep, the old Sala del Parlamento, and the remains of the Palazzo dei Giurati, later used as a prison. Outside the walls, opposite the castle's entrance, is the Dominican **Chiesa del Rosario**, formerly a seat of the Inquisition.

The castello

Via del Castello • 1 May–30 Sept Tues–Sun 9am–1.30pm & 4.30–8.30pm, 1 Oct–30 April Tues–Sun 9am–6pm, though note that staffing levels can cause opening hours to change at short notice so call ☎ 090 922 1291 to be sure • €6

The **castello** itself is steeped in military history: built by Frederick II in the thirteenth century on the site of the Greek acropolis and on top of Arab foundations, it was enlarged by Charles V, and restored by the Spanish in the seventeenth century. Restored again in the last five years, excellent information boards in English and Italian recount the history of the site, which retains the pile holes made by Bronze Age huts, and a newly excavated medieval quarter with a complex system of cisterns.

Capo Milazzo

Bus #6 runs to the cape, departing from the stop to the left as you leave the hydrofoil dock

Some 6km north of Milazzo, the thin **Capo Milazzo** promontory is the focus of most summertime activity. There

2

are plenty of good little **beaches** here, but the loveliest spot to swim and snorkel is right at the tip of the cape, where the road ends and a path leads down to a natural sea-pool known as the **Piscina di Venere**, or pool of Venus. From here, a path runs along the west coast to a longer sand and shingle beach, which is rarely busy, even in the summer.

ARRIVAL AND DEPARTURE
MILAZZO

By train Trains running on the main Palermo–Messina line stop at Milazzo. The train station is a good 3km south of the centre. Local buses are scheduled to run into town via the port every 30min or so during the day, but the service is not entirely reliable. Buy tickets (€1.20) aboard, or take a taxi (☎ 340 628 7546) for around €10. There are usually a few enterprising locals offering an unofficial taxi service in dodgy-looking cars. These are best avoided.

By bus Buses (including the Giuntabus service from Messina, whose timings are organized to tie in with hydrofoil

arrivals and departures) stop on the portside car park – turn right as you disembark from the hydrofoil.

Destinations Messina (approximately hourly; 50min).

By ferry and hydrofoil Milazzo is the main departure point for ferries and hydrofoils to the Aeolian Islands. All hydrofoils now depart from the new departure terminal at the north end of Via dei Mille, right by the Giuntabus stop. Details of ferry and hydrofoil services are given in Chapter 3 (see page 120).

INFORMATION AND TOURS

Boat tours During the summer there are daily boat excursions to the Aeolians from Milazzo, usually sailing from Milazzo at 8.15am or 9am, stopping at two or three of the islands, and returning at around 6pm. Tickets are €35–60,

(€80 if you want to include the ascent of Stromboli) and the trips are run by Tar.Nav, Via dei Mille 17 and 43 (☎ 090 922 3617 or ☎ 340 070 7285, ⓦ minicrociere.tarnav.it).

ACCOMMODATION
SEE MAP PAGE 111

★ **Cassisi** Via Cassisi 5 ☎ 090 922 9099, ⓦ cassisihotel. com. Elegant, minimalist, family-run hotel, with a deft touch of oriental style. The buffet breakfast is abundant, with local salamis and cheeses, typical pastries and biscuits, and lots of fresh fruit. A 5min walk from the port, and close to the main shopping area. **€110**

Giardino di Sicilia Via Santa Maria Maggiore 29 ☎ 090 922 2191. Five simple rooms with en-suite facilities, belonging to one of Milazzo's most appealing restaurants. The location is perfect for those who want to discover the hidden delights of the town: right at the foot of the Borgo, a few steps from the seafront, and a short walk to the first beach of Capo Milazzo. **€60**

Locanda del Bagatto Via M. Regis 11 ☎ 090 922 4212, ⓦ locandadelbagatto.com Sexy, chic, modern rooms above Milazzo's best restaurant – just the place to cheer yourself up if your hydrofoil to the Aeolians has been cancelled. Comfy beds, chromatic showers, minibars and over-life-sized photos on the walls. **€100**

Orchidea Via Nino Bixio ☎ 090 928 8004, ⓦ beb orchidea.it. Clean, functional B&B in a modern *palazzo*, overlooking the port and sandwiched between Via XX Luglio and Via Nino Bixio. The rooms won't win any design awards,

but they are clean, serviceable and four have sea views, plus there's a kitchen for guests' use. There are also two family suites with a twin room, double room and bathroom. Signposted from the port. Doubles **€74**

★ **Petit** Via dei Mille 37 ☎ 090 928 6784, ⓦ petithotel. it. Eco-architectural hotel in a nineteenth-century building on the seafront that uses eco-friendly materials and cleaning methods. Staff go out of their way to be helpful, and breakfasts include cured meats, cheese, organic yoghurt, eggs and jams, and home-made cakes. **€87**

Solaris Via Colonnello Berte 70 ☎ 333 605 0091, ⓦ bed andbreakfast.milazzo.info. Bright and welcoming B&B a block from the port, with five cheerfully decorated rooms with a/c and fridges. All the rooms have balconies and one has a small covered terrace. **€70**

Il Vicolo Via Salemi 14 ☎ 349 504 6851, ⓦ ilvicolobeb. it. Located in a quiet side street on the Ponente (eastern) side of town, 30m from the beach and just a 5min walk from the port, this B&B has three spick-and-span rooms with en-suite bathrooms, and a fourth with a separate bathroom. All have use of a fully equipped kitchen, and there's a courtyard for outside dining. Facilities include a washing machine, and the use of bikes. **€80**

EATING
SEE MAP PAGE 111

There's a small range of **restaurants and trattorias** in Milazzo's centre; those furthest from the port tend to do the best food. The town's *passeggiata* is one of the liveliest in Sicily, with baby buggies, scooters and cars clogging up Lungomare Garibaldi, and a swarm of couples and families

dropping in for ice cream at the **bars** along the way, most of which stay open late in summer. There are plenty of "pubs" dotted around the Borgo, too, open every evening in summer and at weekends in winter.

La Casalinga Via R. D'Amico 13 ☎ 090 922 2697. Local

favourite for fish, where the speciality is spaghetti *polpa di granchi* (with crab sauce). First courses are €9–10, mains €7–16. It's worth booking in advance. Mon–Sat lunch & dinner, Sun lunch only.

Giardino di Sicilia Via Santa Maria Maggiore 29 ☎ 090 922 2191, ⓦ giardinidisicilia.net. Amiable family-run restaurant and pizzeria, with a summer garden courtyard, serving what may be one of the best pizzas (from €4.50) you ever eat – their crisp, tasty feather-light bases the result of dough fermented for 48 hours and a man who knows how to get the best out of a *forno a legna*. The emphasis on quality ingredients is evident right across the menu, making even simple *pepata di cozze* (peppered mussels; €9) an unforgettable experience. Daily lunch & dinner.

Osteria Il Bagatto Via M. Regis 11 ☎ 090 922 4212. You can sample local salamis and cheeses as well as more substantial dishes (€10–16) at this chic wine bar and restaurant. Try the *tagliata* of seared, thinly sliced rare beef (€16). There's a great selection of wines and a cool, laidback ambience, with some tables outside. Mon–Sat from 6pm for aperitivo & dinner.

★ **Pescheria Caravello** Via S. Paolino Milazzo ☎ 340 9181215/090 928 3627. Fantastic find – a family-run fishmongers with a few plastic tables for customers eating in. Choose fresh fish from the counter and have it cooked as you wish or select one of the dishes of the day. The wine is good and cheap and it's full of in-the-know locals and business people entertaining. Mon–Sat lunch only.

Lo Spizzico Via dei Mille s/n. This café does the best takeaway *arancini* hereabouts, including versions filled with aubergine or spinach and mozzarella. Perfect for taking on a ferry journey. Open daily.

The Aeolian Islands

122 Lipari

130 Vulcano

133 Salina

139 Panarea

142 Stromboli

145 Filicudi

149 Alicudi

LIPARI

The Aeolian Islands

The Aeolian Islands, or Isole Eolie, are a mysterious apparition when glimpsed from Sicily's northern coast. Sometimes it's clear enough to pick out the individual white houses on their rocky shores; at other times they're murky, misty and only half-visible. D.H. Lawrence, on his way to Palermo by train in bad weather, was clearly not in the best of moods when he wrote that they resembled "…heaps of shadow deposited like rubbish heaps in the universal greyness". The sleepy calm that seems to envelop this archipelago masks a more dramatic existence: two of the islands are still volcanically active, and all are buffeted alternately by ferocious storms in winter and a deluge of tourists in summer. But their unique charm has survived more or less intact, fuelled by the myths associated with their elemental and unpredictable power.

Closest island to the mainland is the day-tripper magnet of **Vulcano**, with its mud baths, hot springs, black-sand beaches and smoking main crater. Across the channel lies the main island, **Lipari**, which is the hub of the ferry and hydrofoil system. It also has the widest choice of accommodation and restaurants, and is the only island with any kind of life outside the main summer season. Of the central group of islands, **Panarea** is the smallest and most elite, and in August the conspicuously rich float in to commune with nature from their multimillion-euro yachts and villas, overlaying the gentle lapping of the waves with a cacophony of extremely loud music. Though the regular fireworks of its volcano bring droves of trekkers to **Stromboli**, this island too attracts its share of fashionistas – Domenico Dolce and Stefano Gabbana bought a house here – and the town is full of whitewashed Aeolian houses transformed into idyllic villas. Twin-peaked **Salina** springs perhaps the best surprise – the second largest island, it attracts a less flamboyant crowd and, being unusually fertile, remains green year-round, making walking in its mountains pleasant at all times. **Filicudi**, long favoured by the trendy left, has something of a radical-chic feel, though it is all very understated and relaxed; wandering its mule tracks, it's not hard to get a taste of what life in the archipelago was like twenty – or even a hundred – years ago. If this is what you are looking for, make the effort to get out to distant **Alicudi**, an uncompromising kind of place and, some would say, the hardest to like.

Individual identity aside, each Aeolian island is embraced by water of a limpid quality rarely found along the coast of Sicily. Most of the beaches are pebble – sandy stretches are sparse, and tend to be ash-black – but **boat tours** (available at every Aeolian harbour) provide access to any number of secluded coves, hidden caves and quiet snorkelling and scuba-diving waters.

Brief history

The first historic settlers exploited the volcanic resources of the Aeolians, above all the abundance of **obsidian**, a hard glass-like rock that can be worked to produce a fine cutting edge, and was traded far and wide, accruing enormous wealth to the archipelago. The islands were drawn more closely into the Greek ambit by the arrival, around 580 BC, of **refugees** from the wars between Segesta and Selinus (Selinunte). Those Greeks based at the fortified citadel of Lipari later allied themselves with Carthage, which made Lipari its base during the First Punic War. For its pains, Greek Lipari was destroyed by the Romans in 251 BC and the islands became part of the

Highlights

❶ **Upper town, Lipari** The ancient citadel, high above two harbours, shelters the island's magnificent archeological museum. See page 123

❷ **Lingua, Salina** With its traffic-free piazza and promenade overlooking protected pebble beaches, this relaxed little village is the perfect destination for families with children. See page 135

❸ **Panarea snorkelling** Snorkel in sparkling waters above bubbling fumaroles and Roman remains, and explore the craggy uninhabited offshore islets. See page 140

❹ **The ascent of Stromboli** Don't miss a guided climb up one of the world's most active volcanoes. See page 142

❺ **Zucco Grande, Filicudi** This remote village, abandoned to emigration, makes a great target for a hike along the mule tracks of Filicudi. See page 147

❻ **A sojourn in Alicudi** Few places in Europe are more remote than Alicudi. For an experience of true isolation, join its population of eighty in low season. See page 149

HIGHLIGHTS ARE MARKED ON THE MAP ON PAGE 118

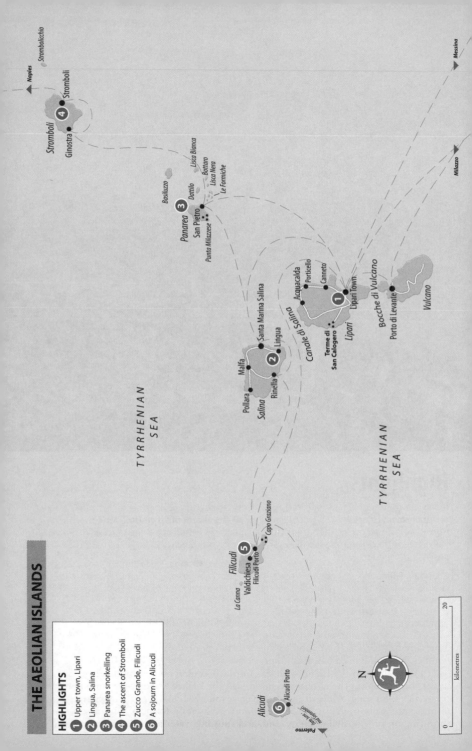

THE AEOLIAN ISLANDS

HIGHLIGHTS

1. Upper town, Lipari
2. Lingua, Salina
3. Panarea snorkelling
4. The ascent of Stromboli
5. Zucco Grande, Filicudi
6. A sojourn in Alicudi

Strombolicchio

→ *Naples*
Stromboli
Stromboli
4
Ginostra

Basiluzzo
Panarea **3** *Dattilo*
San Pietro *Liska Bianca*
Punta Milazzese *Bottaro*
Lisca Nera
Le Formiche

→ *Messina*

Milazzo

Acquacalda
Porticello
Canneto
1 **Lipari Town**
Lipari
Bocche di Vulcano
Canale di Salina
Terme di San Calogero
Porto di Levante
Vulcano

Salina
Pollara
Malfa
Santa Marina Salina
Lingua
Rinella

T Y R R H E N I A N S E A

T Y R R H E N I A N S E A

La Canna
Filicudi **5**
Valdichiesa
Filicudi Porto
Capo Graziano

Alicudi **6**
Alicudi Porto

→ *Palermo*

N

0   20
kilometres

VISITING THE AEOLIANS

Aeolian food is among the most distinctive in Italy, fish of course providing the mainstay but with the traditional crops of capers, olives and mountain herbs flavouring most dishes, while the malvasia grapes provide one of Sicily's more ancient wines. Other foods (as well as much of the water on some islands) have to be imported, so restaurants tend towards the expensive, as do hotels and B&Bs. If you book well in advance, there are some great privately owned villas and apartments up for grabs – ⓦairbnb.co.uk has recently taken off on the islands, so is the best first port of call. **Accommodation rates** in the Aeolians fluctuate a lot more than in other parts of Sicily, and consequently the offers available online can be fantastic – think seriously about booking six or more months in advance to get the best deals. Prices for August quoted on hotel websites – and the ones you would pay if you turned up on spec – are often at least double those charged in low season, and sometimes rates can as much as triple. For example, a hotel charging €200 for a double room with breakfast in August would probably cost €60 in early spring and late autumn; €80 in May or October; €100 in June or September; and €120 in July. Many places also insist on half board (*mezza pensione*, ie dinner, bed and breakfast) and multi-night stays in high season. It's wise to book ahead if you plan on visiting at this time – but, thankfully, August is arguably the least appealing month for non-Italians to visit, with the heat and crowds making it hard to get a sense of the true identities of the islands.

Ferries and **hydrofoils** ply between the islands year-round – their arrival is often the high point of the day in a place like Alicudi, which has a permanent population of around eighty. Services are reduced out of season (basically Oct–May), but you should still be able to reach most islands daily. Indeed, visiting outside **peak season** is highly recommended, since there's a refreshing absence of other tourists, and accommodation rates plummet accordingly. However, be warned that many hotels and restaurants close their doors for the entire **winter** – at this time of year, Airbnb is your best bet. And bear in mind that if the weather turns, you're in danger of being stuck – the archipelago is frequently lashed by **storms** between October and March. Even in summer high winds and storms can strike, and heavy seas can mean the cancellation of ferry and hydrofoil services to both the mainland and the other islands. If this happens, there's no alternative but to sit and wait the storm out.

There are **ATM**s on all the islands except Alicudi. **Power cuts** are commonplace – caused by storms in winter, and in August by over-demand – so a torch is a good idea, especially in winter. Don't be surprised if hotels ask you to be sparing with the water, as it's imported by tanker.

Roman province of Sicily, paying hefty taxes on exports of obsidian. The islands subsequently changed hands several times before being abandoned to the frequent attacks of wide-ranging North African **pirates**, culminating in a terrible slaughter that took place in 1544 at the hands of Khair ed-Din, or Barbarossa, who consigned all the survivors of the massacre – a figure estimated to have been as high as 10,000 – to slavery.

Political prisoners, emigration and Il Postino

Italian unification saw the islands used as a **prison** for political exiles, a role that continued right up to World War II, with the Fascists exiling their political opponents to Lipari. The last political detainee to be held here was, ironically, Mussolini's own daughter, Edda Ciano, in 1946. By the 1950s **emigration**, especially to Australia, had reduced the Aeolian population to a mere handful of families, when the release of **Rossellini**'s *Stromboli: Terra di Dio* (1949) and the story of his affair on the island with star Ingrid Bergman put the archipelago under the spotlight. The curious began to visit the islands, many of them buying properties for a song, while other film-makers followed, many of them pioneers in underwater photography. Today's economy is based on **tourism**, with hotels sprouting on previously barren ground, and running water and electricity installed

AEOLIAN LEGENDS

Volcanoes have always been identified with the mouths of hell, and Roman legend has it that Jupiter's son, **Vulcan**, had his workshop in the Aeolians. Vulcano is named after this god of fire and metalworking, while according to ancient Greek mythology, Lipari takes its name from Liparus, whose daughter Ciane married **Aeolus**, ruler of the winds and master of navigation; Aeolus, in turn, lent his name to the whole archipelago. These winds were kept in a cave, and were presented to Odysseus in a bag to facilitate his journey back home to Ithaca. Unfortunately, just as Ithaca came into sight, Odysseus nodded off, and his curious crew, thinking that the bag contained gold and silver, opened the bag and blew his ship straight back to the Aeolians.

(almost) everywhere. Nonetheless, enough primitive splendour has remained for the islands to continue to attract film crews, and Michael Radford's *Il Postino* (1994), filmed on Salina, and Nanni Moretti's *Caro Diario* (1994) still draw tourists in their droves.

GETTING TO THE AEOLIAN ISLANDS

BY FERRY AND HYDROFOIL

Essentials The main embarkation point is Milazzo, from where ferries (*navi* or *traghetti*) and hydrofoils (*aliscafi*) depart year-round (weather permitting), with more frequent departures during high season (June–Sept). There is also a twice-weekly year-round ferry service from Naples, and a daily year-round service from Messina. In summer there is one daily hydrofoil connection with Palermo and Naples, and in 2016 a new route from Vibo Valentia in Calabria was introduced, although whether or not this service continues remains to be seen. Car-carrying ferries take roughly twice as long to most destinations as the hydrofoils, but are around sixty percent cheaper. Hydrofoils tend to be prone to cancellation in bad weather, particularly out to the more distant islands, and the low-season ferry to Naples is subject to frequent cancellations.

Ferry and hydrofoil operators Hydrofoils are all run by Liberty Lines, except for the Naples route which is run by SNAV (℗ snav.it). Ferries from Milazzo are run by Siremar (℗ siremar.it) and NGI (℗ ngi-spa.it).

Tickets Tickets are sold online and at the companies' harbourside offices before departure; up-to-date schedules are also available online. In July and August, and at the beginning and end of public holidays, you might need to buy tickets in advance (for which there is a surcharge); otherwise, services are rarely full.

Fares One-way high-season fares from Milazzo are around €16 by hydrofoil or €10 by ferry to Lipari; €18/€12 to Salina; €21/14 to Stromboli; and €28/16 to Alicudi. Hydrofoils from Messina to Lipari cost around €23, while from Palermo you'll pay around €26 to Alicudi, €38 to Lipari and €54 to Stromboli. Transporting a car on the car ferry starts at around €30 one-way (Milazzo to Lipari), while on all services children under 4 go free and under-12s go half-price. If you have more than one large suitcase you may be charged an extra €2 on the hydrofoils.

DEPARTURES FROM MILAZZO

Getting to Milazzo Milazzo (see page 110) is 50min from Messina by bus (℗ giuntabustrasporti.com); arrivals are timed to coordinate with hydrofoils, and drop you right by the hydrofoil dock. Be sure to take a bus that goes via the autostrada; if not, the journey time is 1hr 30min. There are also minibus shuttle services run by Garage delle Isole between the port and Catania airport, costing €25 per head – book in advance (℗ 090 928 8585). There is also a direct bus to and from Catania airport at least twice daily from April to October (℗ www.giuntabus.com). Trains are not as convenient, as Milazzo station is on the edge of town and the buses to the port infrequent. Taxis are rare outside the main summer season, though plenty of dodgy guys in beat-up cars offer an unofficial taxi service. If you need to book an official taxi call Francesco (℗ 347 189 3440): it should cost around €15 to the station.

Ferry destinations (June–Sept) Alicudi (7 weekly; 6hr); Filicudi (7 weekly; 5hr); Ginostra (Stromboli) (4 weekly; 5hr 20min); Lipari (5–8 daily; 2hr–2hr 30min); Naples (2 weekly; 17hr); Panarea (4 weekly; 4hr 20min); Rinella (Salina) (8 weekly; 3hr 30min); Santa Marina Salina (4–5 daily; 3hr–3hr 30min); Stromboli (6 weekly; 5hr 50min–6hr 40min); Vulcano (5–8 daily; 1hr 30min–2hr).

Ferry destinations (Oct–May) Alicudi (6 weekly; 6hr–6hr 30min); Filicudi (6 weekly; 5hr 10min); Ginostra (3 weekly; 5hr 45min); Lipari (3–5 daily; 2hr–2hr 30min); Naples (2 weekly; 17hr 30min); Panarea (4 weekly; 4hr 10min–5hr); Rinella (6 weekly; 3hr 45min); Santa Marina Salina (2–4 daily; 3hr–3hr 30min); Stromboli (5 weekly; 5hr 45min–7hr); Vulcano (3–5 daily; 1hr 30min–2hr).

Hydrofoil destinations (June to mid-Sept) Alicudi (2 daily; 2hr 35hr–3hr 15min); Filicudi (2 daily; 2hr 20min–

2hr 35min); Ginostra (4 daily; 1hr 20min–2hr 30min); Lipari (16 daily; 1hr); Palermo (1 daily; 5hr 15min–6hr); Panarea (8 daily; 1hr 15min–2hr); Rinella (7 daily; 1hr 35min–1hr 40min); Santa Marina Salina (13 daily; 1hr 25min); Stromboli (8 daily; 1hr 5min–2hr 50min); Vulcano (15 daily; 40min).

Hydrofoil destinations (mid-Sept to May) Alicudi (1 daily; 2hr 35min); Filicudi (1 daily; 2hr); Ginostra (2 daily; 1hr 20min–2hr 30min); Lipari (12 daily; 1hr); Panarea (4 daily; 1hr 40min–2hr 5min); Rinella (8 daily; 1hr 40min–2hr 20min); Santa Marina Salina (12 daily; 1hr 20min–2hr); Stromboli (4 daily; 1hr 5min–2hr 45min); Vulcano (12 daily; 45min).

DEPARTURES FROM MESSINA

Getting to Messina Departures from Messina (see page 156) are more convenient if you're coming directly from Catania airport out of season. The port is a 7min walk from the train station, where buses also stop. Liberty Lines runs hydrofoils out to the islands all year (at least once daily even in winter).

Hydrofoil destinations (June–Sept) Lipari (5 daily 2hr 35min); Panarea (3 daily; 2hr–2hr 50min); Rinella, Salina (2 daily 2hr 20min–3hr); Santa Marina Salina (4 daily 2hr 10min–2hr 45min); Stromboli (3 daily 1hr 25min–3hr 30min); Vulcano (5 daily 2hr 30min–3hr 20min).

DEPARTURES FROM NAPLES

By ferry The most direct way to get to the islands from central Italy is by ferry, run by Siremar, from Naples, with departures twice weekly (Tues & Fri) throughout the year at 8pm (weather permitting); ferries return to Naples on Mon and Thurs. If you're heading to or departing from Salina, note that ferries alternate between using the ports of Rinella and Santa Marina Salina, though in winter the choice of port will depend on weather conditions.

Between June and September, SNAV (ⓦsnav.it) run a hydrofoil from Naples, calling at Stromboli, Panarea, Salina, Vulcano and Lipari. It is well worth booking in advance via the website – as an example, tickets from Naples to Salina can vary between €60 and €110 depending on availability.

Ferry destinations Filicudi (1 weekly; 13hr 15min); Ginostra (2 weekly; 10hr 20min); Lipari (2 weekly; 13hr 30min–15hr 30min); Milazzo (2 weekly; 16–18hr); Panarea (2 weekly; 11hr 15min); Rinella (1 weekly; 14hr 20min); Santa Marina Salina (1 weekly; 12hr 30min); Stromboli (2 weekly; 9hr 40min); Vulcano (2 weekly; 14hr 15min–16hr 10min).

By hydrofoil Lipari (7hr); Panarea (5hr); Salina (5hr 30min); Stromboli (4hr 30min); Vulcano (6hr 10min).

GETTING AROUND

Inter-island ferries and hydrofoils Travelling between the Aeolians is easy, as ferries and hydrofoils link all the islands. In winter, services are reduced, and in rough weather may be cancelled altogether, particularly on the routes out to Alicudi, Filicudi and Stromboli. Ferries can sail in stormier conditions than hydrofoils, but even these are cancelled on occasion. However, as long as your schedule is not too tight, travelling around the islands out of season is perfectly feasible – especially if you base yourself on Lipari, Salina or Vulcano, taking side trips to remoter islands when conditions permit. A reliable source for weather forecasts is ⓦwindfinder.com.

DRIVING IN THE AEOLIANS

In a measure designed to cut down on the density of tourist traffic on the islands, **cars** are banned from Stromboli, Panarea and Alicudi. In July and August, cars belonging to non-residents can disembark from ferries to Lipari, Vulcano and Filicudi only if drivers can prove they are staying on the island for at least a week, whether in a hotel or in private accommodation. Ferry companies will ask for proof of a hotel booking before issuing tickets to those wanting to take their own car.

However, it's easy enough to manage without your own transport. Lipari and Salina have a good **bus** network, while you can **rent bicycles**, **mopeds** and **scooters** on all the main islands, or simply walk around the smaller ones.

If you need to leave a car in Milazzo, you can do so at one of several **garages**, the most convenient of which are listed below; expect to pay around €15 per day. Some offer a shuttle service to the port.

GARAGES

Central Garage Via Cumbo Borgia 60 ☎090 928 2472. By the Duomo Nuovo, 5min from the port.
Garage delle Isole Via San Paolino 66 ☎090 928 8585. About 10min walk from the port, just off the SP68B.

Mil Nautica Via Acquaviole 49 ☎090 928 1912. South of the port, on the road to the train station.
Ullo Via Nino 40 ☎090 928 3309. Signposted up Via Minniti from the port.

Lipari

LIPARI is the busiest, biggest and most diverse island in the Aeolian archipelago, with a long history of settlement and trade. The main town – also called Lipari – is a thriving little port, dominated by impressive castle walls that surround an upper citadel housing the bulk of the archeological remains and a terrific **museum**. Historically, it has always been Lipari that has guided the development of the Aeolians. In classical times, after obsidian had been superseded by metals, the island's prosperity was based on its sulphur baths and thermal waters, while its alum, too, was much prized, and was found more abundantly here than anywhere else in Italy.

The road that circles the island from town takes in several much smaller villages, some good beaches and excellent views out to the neighbouring islands, though development

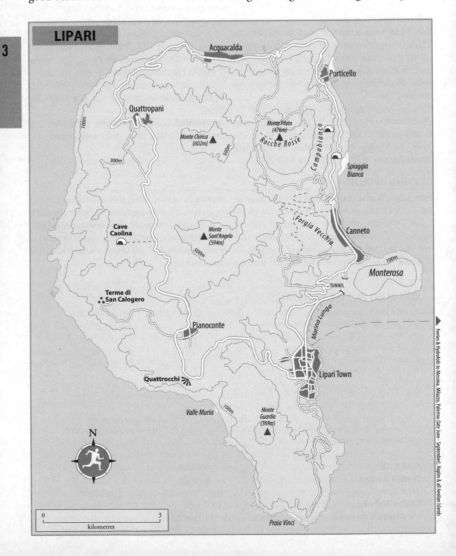

TOP 5 VOLCANIC THINGS TO DO

If you – or your kids – are into volcanoes, check out the best volcanic activities on the islands, as follows:

Stromboli Take a guided hike at sunset and see eruptions explode against the night sky (see page 145).

Vulcano Wallow in the sulphurous mud baths then swim over fumaroles offshore (see page 130).

Panarea Snorkel over the columns of volcanic bubbles (see page 140).

Lipari Collect pumice and obsidian from Spiaggia Bianca (see page 129).

Salina Relax at the thermal spa at the *Signum Hotel*, Salina (see page 137).

---

has not been carefully controlled. While parts of the island are beautiful and unspoiled, getting there inevitably means passing through villages cluttered with brassy holiday houses, or with rusting machinery and ghostly abandoned factories – relics of the island's now defunct pumice-mining industry, and the reason why huge chunks of the mountains on the east coast are missing – but under the auspices of UNESCO this mining has now been banned, and today the economy is firmly based on tourism.

3

Lipari Town

LIPARI TOWN is split into upper and lower sections. Virtually everything of historic interest lies in the upper town, or **citadel**, protected by the sturdy walls of the castle, while all the shops and services are in the lower town, mostly along and off the attractive, colourful main **Corso Vittorio Emanuele**, with the town's two **harbours** at either end. The most impressive approach from lower to upper town is from Via Garibaldi, from which long steps cut straight up through the thick defensive walls, emerging right outside the Duomo.

Most of what remains of Lipari's formidable **citadel** is sixteenth-century Spanish in style, though it incorporates fragments of earlier medieval and even Greek buildings. Until the eighteenth century, this upper zone was the site of Lipari Town itself, which explains the presence of the island's most important church, the **Duomo**, along with the dilapidated ruins of several other Baroque churches. Scattered in between are the excavations of superimposed layers of occupation, from the Neolithic to the Roman age, a continuous record covering almost two thousand years and a unique sequence that has allowed archeologists to date other Mediterranean cultures.

Parco Archeologico
Via Castello • Mon–Sat 9am–dusk • Free

At the southern end of the citadel walls, the **Parco Archeologico** has some Greek and Roman tombs on display, as well as a modern amphitheatre. It also makes a good place to lay out a picnic and enjoy the views over the rooftops and Marina Corta.

Museo Archeologico Regionale Eoliano
Via Castello 2 • Mon–Sat 9am–7.30pm, Sun 9am–1.30pm • €6 • ☎ 090 988 0174, ⓦ www.regione.sicilia.it/beniculturali/museolipari/pagina.asp

All the finds from the Parco Archeologico are displayed in Lipari's superb **Museo Archeologico Regionale Eoliano**, which is housed in various buildings on either side of the Duomo. Despite the official opening hours, most of the sections are usually only accessible in the mornings – only the **Sezione Classica** tends to keep the full opening times.

Sezione Classica

The **Sezione Classica** holds classical and Hellenic material retrieved from various necropoli, and includes re-creations of both a **Bronze Age burial ground** and of the **Lipari necropolis** (eleventh century BC), where bodies were either buried in a crouching position in large, plump jars or cremated and placed in bucket-shaped jars (situlae). Most eye-catching of all are the towering banks of **amphorae**, each 1m or so high, dredged from shipwrecks under Capo Graziano (Filicudi), many still encrusted with barnacles. There are also shelves of **vases** decorated in polychrome pastel hues – showing sacrifices, bathing scenes, mythical encounters and

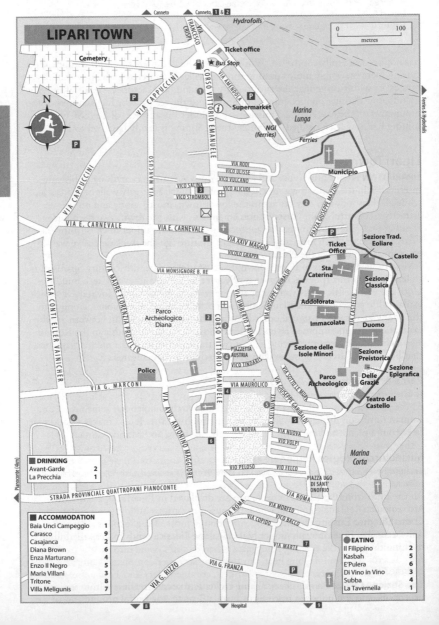

LIPARI TOWN

Canneto
Canneto, **1** & **2**
Hydrofoils
Ticket office
★ Bus Stop
Cemetery

N

Marina
Lunga

Supermarket

NGI
(ferries)

Ferries

Municipio

VIA RODI
VICO ULISSE
VICO VULCANO
VICO ALICUDI

VICO SALINA
3
VICO STROMBOL

VIA E. CARNEVALE
VIA E. CARNEVALE

1

VIA XXIV MAGGIO

VICOLO GRAPPA

Ticket
Office

Seziore Trad.
Eoliare

Castello

Sta.
Caterina

Sezione
Classica

VIA MONSIGNORE B. RE

Addolorata

Parco
Archeologico
Diana

2

Immacolata

Duomo

3

PIAZZETTA
AUSTRIA

Sezione delle
Isole Minori

Sezione
Preistorica

Sezione
Epigrafica

VICO TINDARIS

4

Police

Parco
Archeologico

Delle
Grazie

VIA MAUROLICO

Teatro del
Castello

4

5

VIA NUOVA
VICO VOLPI

6

VIA NUOVA

5

Marina
Corta

VIO PELOSO
VICO FELCO

■ DRINKING
Avant-Garde   **2**
La Precchia   **1**

STRADA PROVINCIALE QUATTROPANI PIANOCONTE

PIAZZA UGO
DI SANT'
ONOFRIO

VIA ROMA

VIA ROMA
VIA MORFEO
VICO BACCO

■ ACCOMMODATION
Baia Unci Campeggio   1
Carasco   9
Casajanca   2
Diana Brown   6
Enza Marturano   4
Enzo Il Negro   5
Maria Villani   3
Tritone   8
Villa Meligunis   7

VIA COPIDO

VIA MARTE

7

VIA G. FRANZA

VIA G. RIZZO

● EATING
Il Filippino   2
Kasbah   5
E'Pulera   6
Di Vino in Vino   3
Subba   4
La Tavernella   1

8   Hospital   **9**

0 ——— 100
metres

Ferries & Hydrofoils

Pianoconte (4km)

BOAT EXCURSIONS FROM LIPARI

Tour operators all over town offer **boat excursions**, usually from Easter to October, both around Lipari and to the other islands, which offer an easy way to do some sightseeing without bothering about bus timetables and hydrofoil schedules. The boats mostly run from Marina Corta, but agencies are prominent at the main port too. Universally recommended is Da Massimo, Via Maurolico 2 (☎ 090 981 3086, ⓦ damassimo.it), where there will be someone who can speak English, and where boats are clean, well maintained, and have freshwater showers and canopies. Prices are pitched roughly the same everywhere, from €15 for a Lipari and Vulcano tour, €30 for Lipari and Salina, and from €35 from Lipari to Panarea and Stromboli. Da Massimo also work with the excellent Magmatrek (see page 145) for boat trips to Stromboli which include a night ascent of the volcano (€80). If you want to rent a **gommone** (rubber boat) and putter around yourself, expect to pay around €100 per day for a 5m-long boat with shower and canopy and space for six people. Most operators also run **beach shuttles** in summer to good beaches on Lipari that are otherwise tricky to reach, like Praia Vinci.

ceremonies – with many identified as those of an individual known as the Lipari painter (300–270 BC) and his pupils and rough contemporaries. Other poignant **funerary goods** include toy vases and statuettes from the grave of a young girl, and delicate clay figurines of working women using mortar and pestle or washing children in a little bath.

The Sezione Classica, however, is best known for the oldest and most complete range of Greek **theatrical masks** in existence. Many are models, found in fourth-century BC graves, and cover the gamut of Greek theatrical life from the tragedies of Sophocles and Euripides to satyr plays and comedies. One room has a collection of small terracottas grouped in theatrical scenes, while there are also statuettes representing actual dancers and actors – nothing less than early Greek pin-ups of the period's top stars.

Sezione Preistorica

Set in the seventeenth-century bishop's palace, the **Sezione Preistorica** traces the early exploitation of **obsidian**, which was made into blades and exported all over the western Mediterranean – glass cases contain mounds of shards, worked flints, adzes (axes) and knives. Meanwhile, the **pottery** finds from ancient burial sites allowed archeologists to follow the development of the various Aeolian cultures, as burial techniques became gradually more sophisticated and grave goods more elaborate – as in the lid of a mid-sixth-century BC bothros, or sacred repository of votive articles, embellished with a reclining lion.

The rest of the museum

Other museum sections cover subjects as diverse as vulcanology and Aeolian traditions and customs, while the **Sezione Epigrafica** contains a little garden of tombs and engraved stones, and a room packed with more inscribed Greek and Roman tombstones and stelae. Unless you're really keen, though, there are diminishing returns to be had from soldiering on to the bitter end.

Corso Vittorio Emanuele

The **Corso Vittorio Emanuele** runs the length of the lower town – it is closed to traffic in summer during the evening *passeggiata*, when its cafés come into their own. Most of the gift shops are found along here, but tourism has never completely dominated life in Lipari, so among the carved obsidian trinkets, coral jewellery and Etna postcards there are still shops selling screwdrivers, fishing tackle and goldfish, along with a very useful supermarket and some great bakeries.

DIVING OFF LIPARI

The most spectacular dives in the Aeolians are off Panarea, Stromboli and Filicudi, all accessible on day-trips from Lipari. Closer at hand, the most interesting dives are along the rocky west coast. Many of the larger hotels can put you in touch with a **diving school**, or contact Diving Centre La Gorgonia (Salita S. Giuseppe, Marina Corta ☎090 981 2616 or ☎335 571 7567, ☻lagorgoniadiving.it). Single dives start at €40 (€60 including equipment); three dives from €110 (€150 including equipment), and night dives from €50. The PADI open-water diver course is €500, and the scuba-diver course €280.

Marina Corta

Overlooked by parasol-shaded cafés and pastel-facaded *palazzi*, the little harbour of **Marina Corta** is the departure point for most boat excursions. There's a beguiling and very photogenic little **chapel** right on the water (which is sometimes open for art exhibitions), while beyond the pavement cafés, steps climb up from the south side of the port into the narrow alleys and courtyards of the old **fishing quarter**.

ARRIVAL AND DEPARTURE
LIPARI TOWN

By ferry and hydrofoil Ferries and hydrofoils dock to either side of Marina Lunga (sometimes called Porto Sottomonastero), at the north end of town. The services detailed below are year-round; schedules increase during the summer months.

Ferry and hydrofoil companies Dockside offices sell tickets and post timetables. For hydrofoils, the Liberty Lines ticket office (☎090 981 2448 or ☎328 031 8861) is just up from the gangways leading from the hydrofoils. For ferry tickets, Siremar (☎090 981 1312) have an office on the other side of the port, while NGI (☎090 981 1955) sell tickets from a kiosk in the port car park.

Ferry destinations Alicudi (2–3 weekly; 4hr); Filicudi (2–3 weekly; 3hr); Ginostra (2–3 weekly; 3hr); Milazzo (5 daily; 2hr); Naples (2 weekly; 15hr); Panarea (2–3 weekly; 2hr); Santa Marina Salina (5 daily; 1hr); Stromboli (2–3 weekly; 3hr 40min); Vulcano (5 daily; 30min).

Hydrofoil destinations Alicudi (1 daily; 1hr 45min); Filicudi (2 daily; 1hr); Ginostra (1 daily; 1hr 30min); Messina (1 daily; 1hr 25min); Milazzo (14 daily; 1hr); Palermo (1 daily in summer; 4hr); Panarea (2 daily; 1hr); Rinella (9 daily; 30min–1hr); Santa Marina Salina (13 daily; 20–40min); Stromboli (2 daily; 1hr 45min); Vulcano (15 daily; 10min).

INFORMATION

Tourist information The tourist office, at Via Maurolico 7 (Mon–Fri 9am–1.30pm, ☎090 988 0095), can advise on accommodation, boat excursions and current events.

GETTING AROUND

By bus From Lipari Town, buses operated by Urso Guglielmo (☎090 981 1262, ☻ursobus.com) run in two directions around the island: clockwise to Quattropani, and anticlockwise to Canneto, Porticello and Acquacalda. Services depart approximately every hour (every 15–30min in summer for Canneto, less often on all routes on Sun and outside July and Aug); nowhere is more than a 30min ride away. The bus stop is at Marina Lunga, opposite the petrol station and close to the quayside ticket agency. Current timetables are posted at the kiosk window; you can buy tickets on board or from the kiosk. Ticket prices vary from €1.30 to €2.50 depending on your destination, and return tickets always work out cheaper.

By car, bike and scooter Rental agencies line the dockside at Marina Lunga (the ferry and hydrofoil port), and you'll have to leave your passport, credit card or a hefty deposit as security. Bikes cost from €10/day, scooters €15–20/day, and small cars from around €40/day for most of the year, with prices skyrocketing in August.

ACCOMMODATION
SEE MAP PAGE 124

There's quite a **range** of accommodation in Lipari Town – but if you want to be right on a beach, you might prefer to be based in Canneto (see page 129).

Carasco Porto delle Genti ☎090 981 1605, ☻carasco. org. Superbly located three-star hotel, with its own terraces, rocky cove, good pool and sparkling views. There's a wide range of rooms, though not all standard rooms look out onto the sea. It's out of the centre, but not too far from Portinente beach and the Marina Corta. Closed Nov–March. **€156**

★ **Diana Brown** Vico Himera 3 ☎090 981 2584 or ☎338 640 7572, ☻dianabrown.it. Run by a jovial South

African and her Sicilian husband, this is a really friendly and well-organized B&B, located in a tiny lane parallel to Corso Vittorio Emanuele. Seven smart rooms have a/c, heating, fridges and kettles, while another five also have small kitchenettes, and there's a great roof terrace where you eat breakfast. There's a book exchange and laundry service available, while Diana and her family know plenty about the island, and can advise about walks and boat tours. Breakfast is €5, though it's not available in Aug. **€90**

Enza Marturano Via Maurolico 35 ☎ 368 322 4997, ⓦ enzamarturano.it. Four bright, modern rooms with a/c, cooking facilities and views, ranged around a communal lounge, with a terrace overlooking the Corso. No credit cards. **€60**

Enzo Il Negro Via Garibaldi 29 ☎ 090 981 3163, ⓦ enzo ilnegro.com. "Enzo the black" takes its name from the bronzed owner's local nickname. Just up from Marina Corta, its eight rooms, all with a/c and fridge, share one of the best private roof terraces in town. **€90**

Maria Villani Via Salina 27 ☎ 090 981 2784. Nice little B&B with a shady roof terrace on a plant-filled, pedestrian-only alleyway off the main Corso Vittorio Emanuele. There are five rooms, two of which have cooking facilities, one with a private terrace. All guests have the use of a fridge, either in their room or in the corridor outside. **€80**

Tritone Via Mendolita ☎ 090 981 1595, ⓦ eolie experience.it. This superior five-star on the southern edge of the town centre is the best of the resort-style hotels. It is set away from the town bustle amid quiet gardens, and extremely competitively priced. There's a good pool, a lovely spa, a superb restaurant, and rooms all have a balcony or terrace. **€124**

★ **Villa Meligunis** Via Marte 7 ☎ 090 981 2426, ⓦ villameligunis.it. A converted *palazzo*, this elegant central four-star has excellent views of the citadel and sea from its rooftop restaurant, which sports a pool alongside. Rooms are tastefully turned out, many with sea views and balconies; there is also a beautifully restored eighteenth-century annexe with studio apartments. Apartments **€80**, doubles **€140**

EATING SEE MAP PAGE 124

There's a fair choice of **restaurants** in Lipari Town, though many close between October and March. Prices are on the high side, but a couple of the restaurants rank among the best in the archipelago.

★ **Il Filippino** Piazza Municipio ☎ 090 981 1002, ⓦ filippino.it. This stupendous fish restaurant – Lipari's best, and in business since 1910 – really knows its stuff. It's in the upper town and has a shaded outdoor terrace where you can eat classy Aeolian specialities like borlotti bean, sardine and fennel soup, *risotto nero* (coloured with squid ink), grouper-stuffed *ravioloni* and local fish in a *ghiotta* sauce (tomatoes, onions, celery, capers and olives). Choose carefully and you might get away with €50 a head, though you could easily spend €80 plus – and more if you give any serious thought to the impressive wine list. Daily lunch & dinner; closed Mon Oct, Nov & Jan–March; closed mid-Nov to Dec.

★ **Kasbah** Vico Selinunte 45 ☎ 090 981 1075, ⓦ kasbahlipari.it. Chic but unpretentious restaurant with minimalist decor and a beautiful garden; the Anglo-Aeolian owner will advise on the best ways to sample the fresh fish. *Antipasti* (from €9) and *primi* (from €11) make creative use of local ingredients and all are beautifully presented – try the kamut tortellini stuffed with artichokes and scattered with peas and clams, or spaghetti (made from wheat grown on land confiscated from the Mafia) served with aubergines, tuna, mozzarella and breadcrumbs. They also make their own bread and the island's best pizza (€6–910), using stone-ground flour. Daily dinner only; Oct–March closed Wed.

E'Pulera Via Diana ☎ 090 981 1158, ⓦ pulera.it. A romantic courtyard-garden restaurant specializing in classic Aeolian food: swordfish *involtini*, caper salads, home-made pasta with wild fennel and prawns, almond biscuits and malvasia wine. The super cuisine is well worth the highish prices, and it stays open till late (kitchen closes at midnight).

STONE SOUP AND OTHER ISLAND DISHES

Aeolian cuisine is based solely around what can be caught or cultivated on the islands. Fresh fish, salted anchovies, tomatoes, pulses and capers dominate, with meat appearing only occasionally – just thirty years ago, beef came to the island of Salina weekly in the form of a cow who was thrown into the sea from the Saturday ferry, to swim to shore, where the butcher was waiting with his knife. Bread was baked once a month, in huge ovens, 30 or 50kgs at a time, then baked again until it was hard, so that it would last. A sure sign that times could be extremely tough is a recipe for stone soup, cooked at times when there were no fish. The recipe calls for tomatoes, garlic, wild fennel and volcanic pebbles, preferably with lots of tiny bubble holes, which need to be taken straight from the sea. The ingredients are cooked together for an hour or so, with the idea that the pebbles give the soup a flavour of the sea.

3

3

Expect to pay €50 plus per head excluding wine. Daily dinner only; closed Oct–March.

Di Vino in Vino Corso Vittorio Emanuele 102 ☏334 110 8455. This classy enoteca has a well-researched range of wines, along with hams and cheeses from the Nebrodi mountains (tasters of which appear with your glass of wine at aperitivo time). They also serve a choice of salads, bruschetta and toasted sandwiches. Daily 9am–late; closes early in winter, and for most of Feb.

★**Subba** Corso Vittorio Emanuele 92 ☏090 981 1352. Open since 1930, this is the island's best and most traditional café, with a nice shaded terrace at the rear in the square. Try a *Lulu*, a cloud of *crema*-filled choux pastry, or the delectable pistachio- and almond-studded *eoliana* ice cream. Mon & Wed–Sun 7.30am–8.30pm, closes later in summer.

La Tavernella Corso Vittorio Emanuele 271 ☏360 268 512. On the main Corso just round the corner from the port, this little *tavola calda* is perfectly located for a snack while you wait for a ferry or hydrofoil. Great spinach frittata, and a daily choice of *pasta al forno* and other hot dishes. Daily 8am–10pm.

DRINKING

SEE MAP PAGE 124

Bars along the Corso fill up from early evening onwards, as the *passeggiata* swings into action. Alternatively, for a drink with a sea view, head down to the Marina Corta where a line of tables belonging to late-opening bars spills out across the harbourfront.

Avant-Garde Corso Vittorio Emanuele 135 ☏090 988 0505. You get a huge plate of nibbles here at evening aperitivo time, and there are tables outside (along with a rowdy TV), plus DJs and live jazz on most summer evenings. Daily 7am–late; closed mid-Jan to mid-Feb.

La Precchia Corso Vittorio Emanuele 191 ☏090 981 1303. A cosy spot in winter for a glass of wine or any of a vast range of hot chocolates, from white chocolate to dark chocolate with chilli, chocolate and hazelnut or chocolate and orange – a treat if you've done the night trip to Stromboli. Not a bad place for breakfast, too. Daily 7am–late.

ENTERTAINMENT

Theatre and live music Every summer (June–Sept), Lipari's council sponsors several theatre performances and concerts, including some spectacularly sited events at the Teatro del Castello, the modern Greek-style theatre up at the citadel's Parco Archeologico. Ask at the tourist office for details.

Festivals There are annual processions in town at Carnevale (Feb/March) and at Easter, but Lipari's main festival, dedicated to the island's patron, St Bartholomew, takes place over three days around August 24.

DIRECTORY

Banks and exchange There are plenty of ATMs down the main Corso, and you can exchange cash at the post office and some travel agencies. It's best to make sure you have enough cash before you set off island-hopping, as other island ATMs do occasionally run out of money.

Hospital Ospedale Civile, Via Sant'Anna ☏090 98 851. For emergencies or an ambulance, call ☏118. The hospital also has a walk-in 24hr first-aid service on ☏090 988 5267.

Left luggage The hydrofoil ticket office at Marina Lunga has a small left-luggage facility (daily from 8.30am until the last hydrofoil departs; €5 for 12hr).

Pharmacies Cincotta, Via Garibaldi 60 (☏090 981 1472); Internazionale, Corso Vittorio Emanuele 28 (☏090 981 1583); Sparacino, Corso Vittorio Emanuele 95 (☏090 981 1392). Pharmacies open late according to a rota system, detailed on the front doors of the shops.

Police Carabinieri, Via Madre Florenzia Profilio, near Via G. Marconi ☏090 981 1333.

Post office Corso Vittorio Emanuele 207 (Mon–Fri 8.20am–7pm, Sat 8.20am–12.35pm).

Around the island

It's well worth taking time to explore the rest of Lipari. Buses (see page 126) from town are frequent enough to enable getting around the whole island in a single day, and it's also possible to scoot or drive around Lipari's winding roads in a couple of hours flat, stopping at places like Monte Guardia, Quattrocchi, Quattropani and Monterosa for some stunning views out across the archipelago. With its mountains tumbling straight into the sea, the island's **west coast** is perhaps the more alluring, largely undeveloped and with some lovely **walks**, especially between the **Terme di San Calogero** and the **Caolina quarries**. Exploring the **east coast** offers a chance to see the relics of Lipari's pumice and obsidian mining industries. It may not be the idyllic Aeolian island scenery of your dreams, but if industrial archeology holds any appeal, a few hours here – with a camera at the ready – is a must. Bring mask and snorkel to explore the extraordinary deep-blue waters of **Porticello**, with their bed of white pumice sand.

Canneto

It's around 3km north from Lipari Town to the nearest village, **Canneto**, a shabby resort set on a wide bay on the other side of the headland. A long stony beach fronts the village, which has a rather abandoned feel outside summer when most businesses are closed, although this may be preferable to the gaudiness and noise when they are open. For more secluded swimming, head to the Spiaggia Bianca, signposted from the northern end of town, along a stepped path that runs up, around and down to the **Spiaggia Bianca**, an expansive sand-and-pebble beach that is worth the effort to reach. Refreshments and parasols are available here in summer.

ACCOMMODATION   **CANNETO SEE PAGE 124**

Baia Unci Campeggio Via Marina Garibaldi s/n, Località Canneto ☎ 090 981 1909, ⓦ campingbaiaunci. it. The island's only campsite is across from the long beach at Canneto, and has one-bedroom bungalows available, as well as tent pitches and its own bar and restaurant. Camping prices include water and parking space. No credit cards. Closed Oct–March. Camping €10 for one person, **€18**

for two people including two-person tent; bungalows **€60**

Casajanca Marina Garibaldi 109, Canneto ☎ 090 988 0222, ⓦ casajanca.it. If you don't mind being out at Canneto, you might prefer this boutique-style place to the resort hotels in town. It's a charming townhouse hotel, three-star standard, 20m back from the beachfront promenade, with ten stylish rooms and personal service. **€150**

Campobianco and Monte Pilato

North of Canneto at **Campobianco**, pumice workings have left huge white scars on the hillside. For 2–3km all around, the ground looks as if it's had a dusting of talcum powder, while years of accumulation of pumice sediment on the sea bed have turned the water a piercing aquamarine colour. Above Campobianco, a path leads up the slopes of **Monte Pilato** (476m), which was thrown up in the eruption from which all the pumice originally came. The last explosion occurred in around 700 AD, leading to the virtual abandonment of Lipari Town and creating the obsidian flows of Rocche Rosse and Forgia Vecchia, both of which can be climbed. Although it's overgrown with vegetation, you can still make out the outline of the crater at the top, and you may come across the blue-black veins of obsidian.

Porticello

From the bus stop above the stony beach at **Porticello**, a road (and a quicker, more direct path) winds down to a small bay, which sunbathers share with the forlorn Heath Robinson-style pumice-work machinery that connects the white hillside with the pier. After storms, this is ripe hunting ground for hunks of obsidian, which are washed up on the strand. There's no shade here, and the pebble beach soon reaches scalding temperatures. A couple of vans sell cool drinks and snacks in the summer.

Quattrocchi

Three kilometres west of Lipari Town is **Quattrocchi**, a noted viewpoint over Vulcano and the spiky *faraglioni* rocks, which puncture the sea between the two islands. The curious name (meaning "Four Eyes") is said to derive from the fact that newly wedded couples traditionally come here to be photographed, so gracing every shot with two pairs of eyes.

San Calogero

A couple of kilometres beyond Quattrocchi, just before the fragmented village of Pianoconte, a side road slinks off down to the old Roman thermal baths at **San**

Calogero. It's a particularly pleasant route to follow on foot, across a valley and skirting some impressive cliffs, with the baths hidden behind a long-disused spa hotel: there's usually an unofficial guide to show you around and allow you a dip, if you dare, in the scummy 57°C Roman pool.

Cave Caolina

For a really great coastal hike, head another two kilometres along the road to the junction marked **Cave Caolina**. This is a quarry of multicoloured clays used as pigments by the ancient Greek artist responsible for the polychrome painted vases in Lipari's museum, known simply as "the Lipari painter". From here an easy-to-follow path leads down through the quarry, and back to San Calogero, passing sulphurous fumaroles, a hot spring, and a couple of places where you can scramble down the cliffs for a swim.

3 Vulcano

Closest of the Aeolians to the Sicilian mainland, and just across the narrow channel from Lipari, **VULCANO** is the usual first port of call for ferry and hydrofoil services from Milazzo, and as such suffers the bulk of the archipelago's day-trippers. As on more distant Stromboli, volcanic action defines the island, with the main crater hanging menacingly over its northern tip and constant vapour trails issuing from its flanks. It's a very old volcano, in the last, smoking, phase of its life, and you often don't even have to disembark to experience its other apparent trait – the disconcerting sulphurous, rotten-egg smell that pervades the island's entire inhabited area when the wind comes from behind the mountain.

The **volcano** was threatening enough to dissuade anyone from living here before the eighteenth century, since when there have been some hasty evacuations – subterranean activity is still monitored round the clock, as Vulcano is felt to be more potentially dangerous than the constantly active Stromboli. In the nineteenth century a Scot called Stevenson bought the island to exploit the sulphur and alum reserves, but all his work was engulfed by the next major **eruption**. Although the volcano's last gasp of activity occurred between 1886 and 1890, its presence gives Vulcano an almost primeval essence. Everything here is an assault on the senses, the outlandish saffron of the earth searing the eyes, as violent as the intense red and orange of the iron and aluminium sulphates that leak out of the ground in the summer, to be washed away with the first autumn rains.

However, none of the summer trippers and B-list celebs bronzing themselves on Vulcano's **black-sand beaches** or wandering the main village, Porto di Levante, are discouraged, while many others come to dip themselves in the sulphurous **mud baths**. That said, even if the lingering smell doesn't put you off, accommodation is overpriced, while restaurants tend to command exorbitant prices for barely edible food. Bear in mind that you can climb the crater, and cycle or bus across the island and back, all on a day-trip from the far pleasanter Lipari, just a ten-minute hydrofoil ride away.

Porto di Levante

Porto di Levante has the flimsy feel of a hastily erected film set, consisting of a couple of ramshackle streets lined with whitewashed cubes that house restaurants, bars and lots of tacky souvenir shops. If you need provisions, you'll find a small supermarket tucked into an alley at the end of the main street.

ARRIVAL AND DEPARTURE

By ferry and hydrofoil Ferries and hydrofoils dock at Porto di Levante, the main harbour; ticket offices are located near the dock. All ferries, and virtually all hydrofoils, stopping at Lipari also call at Vulcano. The services detailed below are year-round; schedules increase during the summer months.

Ferry departures Alicudi (2–3 weekly; 3hr 30min); Filicudi (2–3 weekly; 2hr 30min); Ginostra (2–3 weekly; 2hr 30min); Lipari (5 daily; 35min); Milazzo (5 daily; 1hr 30min); Naples (2 weekly; 15hr 30min); Panarea (2–3 weekly; 1hr 30min); Santa Marina Salina (5 daily; 1hr 30min); Stromboli (2–3 weekly; 3hr).

Hydrofoil departures Alicudi (1 daily; 1hr 45min); Filicudi (1 daily; 1hr 15min); Ginostra (1 daily; 1hr 15min); Lipari (15 daily; 10min); Messina (1 daily; 1hr 45min); Milazzo (14 daily; 40min); Palermo (1 daily in summer; 4hr 20min); Panarea (2 daily; 50min); Rinella (9 daily; 1hr); Santa Marina Salina (13 daily; 40min); Stromboli (2 daily; 1hr 30min).

GETTING AROUND

By bus From the Porto di Levante dockside, buses run year-round to Piano (Mon–Sat 7–8 daily; 10min), and in summer to Gelso (mid-June to mid-Sept Mon–Sat 3 daily; 20min).

By bike and scooter Da Paolo (☎090 985 2112) and Sprint (☎090 985 2208), in the centre of the village on the main Strada Comunale Porto Levante, rent out mountain bikes (€7/day) and scooters (€15/day).

Boat tours The boat trips (around €15 per person) offered at the Porto di Levante in summer visit the caves and bays on the island's west side.

3

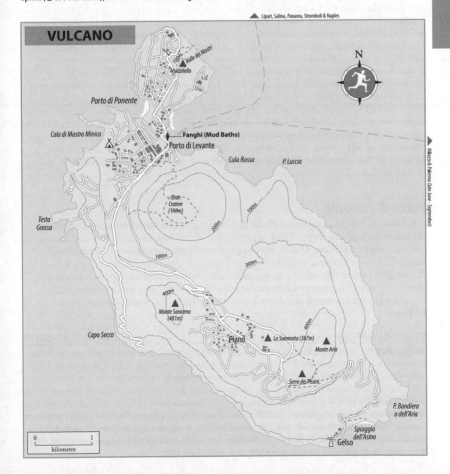

▲ Lipari, Salina, Panarea, Stromboli & Naples

VULCANO

100m — ▲ Valle dei Mostri
▲ Vulcanello

Porto di Ponente

Cala di Mastro Minico
Ⓐ ━ Fanghi (Mud Baths)
Porto di Levante

Cala Rossa   P. Luccia

Gran
Cratere
(386m)

Testa
Grossa   200m   100m

100m   300m

400m
▲ Monte Saraceno
(481m)   400m

Capo Secco   Piano   ▲ La Sommata (387m)
▲ Monte Aria

Serra dei Pisani

P. Bandiera
o dell'Aria

Spiaggia
dell'Asino
Gelso

0 ────────── 1
kilometre

Milazzo & Palermo (late June – September)

The fanghi

Via Porto Levante s/n • Easter–Oct daily 7am–9pm; Nov–Easter open 24h • Easter–Oct €3; Nov–Easter free.

Located directly to the north of Porto di Levante, a brief walk between the multicoloured rock pinnacles, are the famed **fanghi** or **mud baths**, more exactly one pool containing a thick yellow soup of foul-smelling sulphurous mud, in which people flop belly-up, caking every centimetre of their bodies with the stuff. The smell is indescribable, and the degree of radioactivity makes it inadvisable to immerse yourself for any length of time, and unsuitable for young children or pregnant women. Don't wear your favourite costume, avoid contact with the eyes (it stings mightily) and remove contact lenses as well as any silver or leather jewellery, which will be ruined just by coming into contact with the sand hereabouts. When you've had enough, hobble over to rinse yourself off in the nearby sea, where natural hot-water springs bubble up. Note that outside of the summer season, you can just walk in and wallow for free.

3

The Gran Cratere

Daily daylight hours • Small charge in summer • Follow the road immediately to the left of Porto di Levante dock for 500m or so until you're directed off the road to the left and up the slope to the crater

Vulcano's main crater, the **Gran Cratere**, is just to the south of Porto di Levante. It takes an hour to walk up to the crater, and it's a toughish climb, on a slithery path that's totally exposed to the sun – do it early or late in the day in the summer months, and wear strong shoes. The only vegetation consists of a few hardy gorse bushes on the lower slopes, nibbled at by goats whose bells echo across the scree. The first part of the path ascends a virtually black sand dune before reaching the harder volcanic crust, where it runs above the rivulets caused by previous eruptions. Reaching a ledge with views over all the other Aeolian Islands, you look down into the vast **crater** itself, where vapour emissions – acrid and yellow – billow from the surrounding surfaces. Follow the crater in an anticlockwise direction, so you are going downhill rather than up through the clouds of sulphurous emissions on the northern rim, where nerves are not exactly steadied by the admonitory notices at the start of the climb reading "Do not sit down, do not lie down".

Porto di Ponente

A narrow neck of land separates Porto di Levante from **Porto di Ponente**, a fifteen-minute walk past the *fanghi*. Here, a perfect arc of fine black sand lines a bay looking onto the towering pillars of rock that rise out of the channel between Vulcano and Lipari. There are a couple of seafront cafés here, and some large hotels set back from the sands. From the beach, the only road heads north through the trees to **Vulcanello**, thrown up out of the sea in a famous eruption in 183 BC, and joined to the main island by another flurry of activity a few centuries later. The walk takes less than an hour.

ACCOMMODATION   PORTO DI PONENTE

★**Eden Park** Via Porto Ponente 10 ☎090 985 2120, ⓦisolavulcano.it. This holiday village, set in its own grounds on the south side of the bay and slightly inland, is by far the island's best budget option. Campers can pitch tents on real grass, or even bivouac on the lawn, while there are also single-room apartments with terrace, shower and kitchen, and "economic" double rooms with two bunk beds and a shared bathroom. Note that prices double for ten days on either side of the *ferragosto* (Aug 10–20). Breakfast is available, and campers pay extra for showers. No credit cards. Closed Dec–Feb. Camping/person €15, doubles €50, apartments €60

Orsa Maggiore Via Porto Ponente 4 ☎090 985 2018, ⓦorsamaggiorehotel.com. It's a few hundred metres from the black-sand beach, but this small hotel does have a very nice pool, surrounded with chic decking, terrace and gardens. Prices are raised by €40/night overnight for ten days on either side of the *ferragosto* (Aug 10–20). Closed Nov–March. €100

Gelso

At the far south of Vulcano, 15km from Porto di Levante, the coastal hamlet of **Gelso** is named for the mulberries that grow here, along with capers. There's a tiny patch of black sand (with a seasonal trattoria, *Da Pina*), and a better beach at **Spiaggia dell'Asino**, a larger cove accessible from a steep path which you'll have passed on your way into Gelso. This is a great spot for a swim, with a little summer café for cold drinks, and umbrellas and deckchairs available.

Salina

The ancient name of **SALINA** was Didyme, or "twin", referring to the two volcanic cones that give the island its distinctive shape. Both volcanoes are long extinct, but their past eruptions, combined with plenty of ground water – unique in the Aeolians – have endowed Salina with the most **fertile** soil of all the islands. The slopes are verdant, the island's tree cover contrasts strongly with the denuded crags of its neighbours, and both capers and malvasia grapevines – classic Aeolian staples – are vigorously cultivated. The island's central position in the archipelago makes it a good alternative base to Lipari for exploring the others, while Salina itself has a network of **hiking trails**, some good **beaches** and several distinct **villages**. Tourism here is fairly sophisticated, with some charming boutique-style accommodation and excellent restaurants, especially in the main port, **Santa Marina Salina**, and in the town of **Malfa**. It's quieter and more relaxed than Lipari or Vulcano and still very much part of the ebb and flow of traditional Aeolian life, which makes it many people's favourite island.

There are two **ports** on Salina: Santa Marina Salina in the east and smaller **Rinella** on the south coast. Not all ferry and hydrofoil services call at both ports, so it's essential to check timetables carefully.

Santa Marina Salina

On the east coast, **Santa Marina Salina** is Salina's main port and the location of most of the island's services. A village of whitewashed Aeolian houses and elegant townhouses

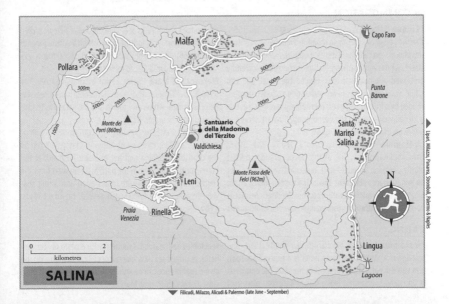

built in the nineteenth century by those who made their fortunes with malvasia wine, it's a relaxed place, with a couple of pebble beaches. A long lungomare reaches north from the harbour, running from the town **beach** to the more secluded **Punta Barone**, backed by the relics of an ancient Roman fish farm. Running parallel to the water but one block back, the narrow pedestrianized main street, **Via Risorgimento**, holds chic boutiques that mingle with grocery shops, fruit shops, butchers and bakery. A couple of the gift shops sell a decent map of the islands.

ARRIVAL AND INFORMATION   SANTA MARINA SALINA

By ferry and hydrofoil The Liberty Lines/NGI (☎090 984 3003 and ☎340 902 8559) ticket office is close to the dock on the waterfront piazza, usually open 30min before sailings. The services detailed below are year-round; schedules increase during the summer months.

Hydrofoil destinations Alicudi (1 daily; 1hr 15min); Filicudi (1 daily; 40min); Ginostra (1 daily; 45min); Lipari (14 daily; 20min); Messina (1 daily; 2hr 35min); Milazzo (10 daily; 1hr 20min); Palermo (1 daily in summer; 3hr 25min); Panarea (1 daily; 20min); Rinella (9 daily; 10min); Stromboli (1 daily; 1 hr); Vulcano (10 daily; 40min).

Ferry destinations Alicudi (2–3 weekly; 3hr 30min); Filicudi (2–3 weekly; 2hr 30min); Ginostra (2–3 weekly; 2hr 30min); Lipari (5 daily; 1hr); Milazzo (5 daily; 3–4hr); Naples (1 weekly; 13hr 30min); Panarea (2–3 weekly; 1hr 30min); Stromboli (2–3 weekly; 3hr); Vulcano (5 daily; 1hr 30min).

Tourist information There is a seasonal tourist information point in Santa Marina Salina (usually July & Aug daily 9am–1pm & 4–8pm) just up the hill from the piazza, on Via Cristoforo Colombo, below *Bar La Vela*.

Services Santa Maria has a clinic with emergency doctors and ambulance, a pharmacy, a post office, and a bank with ATM.

GETTING AROUND

By bus The bus stop for Lingua is just beyond the main seafront piazza; buses to Malfa, Rinella and Pollara stop on the other side of the piazza, right by the port. Buses cover all points on the island; departures to all destinations are roughly every 1hr 30min, hourly in summer, and you pay on board. In winter you may have a lengthy wait in Malfa, the island hub, for an onward connection to Pollara or to Leni and Rinella.

By car, bike and moped Nino Bongiorno, Via Risorgimento

222 (☎090 9843 409, ⓦrentbongiorno.it), at the beginning of the road to Lingua, rents cars, bikes and mopeds.

Boat tours Booths in the piazza by the port sell tickets for half-day cruises around the island from Easter to October (€35 per person), as well as day-trips further afield to Panarea and Stromboli, Filicudi and Alicudi, and Lipari and Vulcano (from €40 per person depending on the itinerary), all with plenty of chances for swimming and sightseeing stops.

ACCOMMODATION

I Cinque Balconi Via Risorgimento 38 ☎090 094 3508, ⓦicinquebalconi.it. Simple rooms in a nineteenth-century townhouse on Santa Marina's pedestrianized shopping street, whose most striking feature is the subtle, carefully preserved original floor tiles. Behind the hotel, you can while away afternoons in an enchanting secluded garden, shaded by citrus and fig trees. There are eight rooms, several with sea views, and in the evenings aperitivi are served at tables on the street outside. **€150**

★**Mamma Santina** Via Sanità ☎090 984 3054, ⓦmammasantina.it. The affable Mario presides over a highly personal, boutique-style restaurant-with-rooms, set on wide terraces above the town. The sixteen rooms are in bright seaside colours, with gorgeous Mediterranean tile floors and big bathrooms with walk-in showers, while guests

can lounge in hammocks or around the pool. Call to be picked up from the port, or follow the signposts off Via Risorgimento (after no. 66) – it's a 12min walk, with the last 300m up a very steep hill. Closed mid-Dec to mid-March. **€170**

Mercanti di Mare Piazza Santa Marina 7 ☎090 984 3536, ⓦhotelmercantidimare.it. Harbourfront three-star hotel with nine white, airy rooms and an attractive terrace overlooking the water. **€150**

Da Sabina Via Risorgimento 5/C ☎090 984 3134 or ☎333 272 6025, ⓦwww.bbsalina.it. Classy B&B run by the charismatic Sabina and her ex-baker husband, at the far end of the village from the port, a 10min walk from the centre. Three smart en-suite rooms open onto a big sea-view terrace, where breakfast is served. No credit cards. **€100**

EATING

★**Mamma Santina** Via Sanità ☎090 984 3054. The restaurant at *Mamma Santina* hotel is a marvellous spot, and you can eat outside for most of the year. The emphasis is on island specialities, like a grilled *antipasto* platter of

vegetables and seafood, spaghetti with a pesto of fourteen herbs, or grilled sea bass (pasta from €12, fish from €15). Be aware that service can be very slow. Daily lunch & dinner; closed mid-Dec to mid-March.

WALKING ON SALINA

There are well-maintained, waymarked **hiking trails** right across Salina, in particular to the heights of Monte Fossa delle Felci and the sanctuary of Madonna del Terzito. It's great walking country, since most of the island has been zealously protected: wild flowers are much in evidence, and hunting and shooting are banned, which helps keep the bird numbers high.

For a good day out on the tops, first take the bus to the sanctuary – all buses except those between Malfa and Pollara pass right by. **Madonna del Terzito** is set in the saddle between the two peaks of Salina, with fine views over the sea. A signposted track leads up to the summit of **Monte Fossa delle Felci** (962m), the archipelago's highest peak. It's a steady climb through forest and mountain parkland, which takes the best part of two hours – only in the latter stages does it become tougher, with a final 100m clamber over rocks to reach the stone cairn and simple wooden cross at the top, from where the views are magnificent.

You can come back the same way to the sanctuary and catch the return bus, but signposts point out alternative approaches and **descents** to Malfa, Lingua or Santa Marina. However, not all the tracks are clear; they can be very steep, and soil erosion and the crumbling volcanic underlay can make getting a grip a tricky business, so if you are not an experienced walker, it's best to stick to the main track. Count on another two hours back down, whichever descent you follow.

3

Nni Lausta Via Risorgimento 188 ☎ 090 984 3486. Cool bar-restaurant whose New York-trained owner-chef gives local dishes an adventurous twist – try raw tuna dressed with wild fennel and capers, or crispy fishcakes made from the day's catch. A full meal will cost at least €45 without wine, or you could just have a drink at the bar (until 2am) – €5 will buy you a glass of decent Salina wine, with *crostini* and home-made dips, pestos and salsas – sit on the little stools and tables on the street outside and watch life pass by. Daily lunch & dinner; closed Nov–March.

Porto Bello Via Lungomare 2 ☎ 090 984 3125. Set right above the harbour, and with a terrace looking out to the lights of Lipari, this reliable and long-standing restaurant serves excellent local *antipasti* and is a good choice if you want to splash out. It's worth trying the *pasta al fuoco*, with cherry tomatoes, chilli and grated oven-baked ricotta, or

the raw prawns with a yoghurt salsa. Main courses include standards such as deep-fried squid, but this is a place to go for the catch of the day (priced by weight). If they have *scorfano* (scorpion fish), ask to have it hard-fried, otherwise owner Teodoro or his son Dario will recommend a fish and cooking method that suits. A four-course meal will cost at least €50 without wine. Daily lunch & dinner; closed winter.

La Vela Via Risorgimento 135 ☎ 090 984 3541. Great hazelnut pastries, along with traditional biscuits featuring lots of almonds, pistachios and a sticky *cedro* (citrus) jam, while *cannoli* are filled to order. There's also a decent range of savoury snacks such as *arancini* and pizza, all best enjoyed on the terrace overlooking the sea. Daily: summer 7.30am–late; winter 7.30am–1pm & 4–8pm.

DRINKING

Le Papagayo Piazza Santa Marina ☎ 333 141 0974. Minuscule bar owned by a local sculptor, with a terrace that spills out onto Santa Marina's seafront piazza. Good music, generous cocktails and a laidback vibe – this is the kind of place where spontaneous parties erupt. Olives, *crostini* and local cheeses to accompany drinks at aperitivo time. Daily from spring through autumn, usually 6pm–late, though may close in rain storms.

Porto Bello Sea Lounge Via Lungomare 2 ☎ 090 984 3125. With its whitewashed walls and white-resin floors, sea terrace, chilled soundtrack and driftwood decor, this is Santa Marina's most chic hangout, though service can be lackadaisical at times. Cocktails are served with an array of snacks. If you're lucky there will be tuna carpaccio, a delectable aubergine *parmigiana*, *crostini* with *caponata*, and courgette-flower fritters. Daily Easter to October 6.30pm–late.

Lingua

Three kilometres to the south of Santa Marina, **Lingua** is a prettier base, and its traffic-free waterfront makes it ideal if travelling with young children. It's connected to Santa Marina by bus, though the undulating road makes a fine forty-minute stroll, weaving around the coves in between the two settlements. Lingua itself is not much more than a seafront promenade and a narrow beach, backed by a tiny cluster of hotels and trattorias facing the shore of Lipari. At the end of the road is the **salt lagoon** from which Salina takes its name, and a car park where locals used to gather after bumper anchovy catches to salt fish en masse. Overlooking the lake, two typical Aeolian houses have been converted into museums: a small **ethnographic museum** (the Museo Etnografico; May–Oct Tues–Sun 9am–1pm & 3–6pm; free) holds examples of rustic art and island culture, mainly kitchen utensils and mill equipment, much of it fashioned from lava rock, while the **Museo Archeologico** (May–Oct Tues–Sun 9am–6pm; free) has finds from Bronze Age and Roman Salina.

ACCOMMODATION
LINGUA

A Cannata Via Umberto I ☎090 984 3161 or ☎339 575 4240, ⓦacannata.it. Set a few metres back from the sea near the church, there are simple rooms here above a decent restaurant, and they also have several apartments of various sizes and styles to rent around the village, starting from around €600 a week in mid-season (€350 in low). Doubles €160

Il Delfino Via Marina Garibaldi 5 ☎090 984 3024, ⓦildelfinosalina.it. Smart rooms with marvellous terraces and views, set back from Lingua's lungomare; and older rooms opening directly onto it, which are a good bet if you have children. €130

La Salina Borgo di Mare Via Manzoni ☎090 984 3441, ⓦlasalinahotel.com. This impressive four-star hotel is set in the restored buildings of the old saltworks, by Lingua's lagoon. The lovely rooms are individually furnished, and most have sea views and private terraces, while public areas are enhanced by traditional tiles and stonework. There's good swimming from below the hotel, with sunbeds set out on the rocks. No restaurant, but you can eat at nearby *Il Gambero* on a half-board basis (an extra €30 per person). €110

EATING AND DRINKING

★ **Da Alfredo** Piazza Marina Garibaldi ☎090 984 3075. Right on the seafront piazza, this little café is famous throughout Italy for its fresh fruit *granitas* – summer yachties and boat-trippers queue up for a taste. The other speciality is *pane cunzato*, a huge round of grilled bread piled with various combinations of home-cured tuna, capers, tomatoes, baked ricotta and olives (€10–16). Daily 8am till last customer leaves; closed Dec–Easter.

Il Delfino Via Marina Garibaldi 5 ☎090 9843 024, ⓦildelfinosalina.it. Lovely restaurant, with tables on the lungomare, well known for its *antipasto* buffet (arrive around 8pm to make the most of it). The signature dish is the stuffed calamari braised with onions and malvasia wine (€16), but check out daily specials as well. Daily lunch & dinner; closed Dec–Easter.

Franco Manca Piazza Marina Garibaldi 3 ☎090 9843 070. Giuseppe Mascoli, founder of the burgeoning UK pizza chain, spends his holidays in Salina, hence the Lingua outpost! The trademark scorched pizzas, topped with high-quality ingredients – along with sensationally speedy service – have made it a true winner. June–Sept, noon–late.

Il Gambero Piazza Marina Garibaldi ☎090 984 3049. This restaurant serves excellent fish – try the mixed fish *antipasto* (€16) and *involtini di pesce spada* (rolls of swordfish wrapped around cheese, herbs and breadcrumbs and grilled; €16) – as well as pizza and *pane cunzato*, and all-day snacks and aperitivo in summer. Look out as well for good-deal set menus. Daily lunch & dinner; closed Dec–Easter.

Malfa

Six kilometres from Santa Marina, reached along Salina's sole, tortuous coast road, **Malfa** is the island's biggest village, spilling down from the gentle, neatly cultivated vineyards on the lower slopes of Monte Fossa. At the centre of the village is the main church and a large **piazza** with views out to sea, inlaid with a *rosa dei venti* or compass rose, which names the eight prevailing Mediterranean winds.

A devilishly twisting road runs down from here to the **port**, across which cuts a more direct series of paths and steps. A little further along, by the *Punta Scario* hotel, steps lead down to Malfa's boulder **beach**, Punta Scario, picturesquely backed by vertiginous cliffs. In summer there is an appealing little beach bar here selling cold drinks, sandwiches and *pane cunzato*, as well as renting out mattresses, lilos and umbrellas.

INFORMATION AND GETTING AROUND
MALFA

By bus The bus stops on the main road by the bank, then down in the village by the main piazza, and again a few hundred metres below, directly above the path that leads down to Punta Scario beach.

Tourist information In summer there is usually a little information office somewhere along Malfa's main street.

Boat tours There are booths in the main piazza with information on boat tours around the island and to other islands. If you're confident enough to putter about yourself, you can rent a small *gommone* (rubber dinghy) in the port for a day or half-day (from €40 per half-day, excluding petrol).

ACCOMMODATION

Capo Faro ☎ 090 984 4330, ⓦ capofaro.it. Some 3km east of Malfa, scattered among the lush vineyards of the Tasca d'Almerita malvasia wine estate, the sophisticated, contemporary rooms here occupy seven Aeolian-style houses and a former lighthouse. Facilities are top-notch, from magnificent pool to classy bar and restaurant, and you can tour the vineyards or have a wine-tasting on request. No children under 12. **€515**

★ **Signum** Via Scalo 15 ☎ 090 984 4222, ⓦ hotel signum.it. Style and luxury deftly balanced with friendly and relaxed service – island hotels don't come much better than this. Thirty comfortable rooms display a seamless blend of antique furniture and contemporary style and have either terraces or balconies, sea or garden views. Night swimming in the splendid infinity pool and catching sight of Stromboli's eruptions across the water takes some beating, and the exquisite outdoor spa is also not to be missed. **€280**

EATING AND DRINKING

A Lumeredda Via San Lorenzo ☎ 090 984 4130. Hidden down one of Malfa's myriad flower-lined alleyways, this is exactly what an island restaurant should be – relaxed and unpretentious with wooden tables on a simple, shady terrace. Come for a deftly cooked crispy-edged pizza (from €5), and a carafe of house wine or a beer, and for once you won't break the bank. The pasta is also splendid – especially the chilli-spiked linguine with clams. Daily lunch & dinner; closed Dec–Easter.

Maracaibo Punta Scario beach. Beach hut with a shady, flower-filled covered terrace serving a couple of kinds of fresh fruit *granitas* (usually lemon and watermelon), plus salads (€4.50–6) and sandwiches (€3.50–4.50) that make copious use of local ingredients such as capers, sun-dried tomatoes and tuna. Daily mid-morning till sunset; closed winter.

Ravesi Via Roma 6 ☎ 090 984 4385, ⓦ hotelravesi. it. Good drinks and a help-yourself buffet of nibbles are served in the candlelit garden of this elegant hotel – a must for aperitivo junkies. In mid-Aug there's a programme of aperitivo-hour concerts. Daily 7–9pm; closed winter.

★ **Signum** Via Scalo 15 ☎ 090 984 4222, ⓦ hotel signum.it. Italy's youngest Michelin-starred chef, Martina Caruso, and enthusiastic, attentive staff plus great cooking ensure dinner at *Signum* is always special: candlelit and subdued, but refreshingly relaxed. Martina's cooking style is fresh, light and nuanced – but never over-complicated – and fresh fish takes first place. Hotel guests have priority, but it is worth phoning early to get on the waiting list. Easter–Oct daily lunch & dinner.

Pollara

Just above Malfa, a minor road (served by several buses a day) snakes off west before hairpinning down to secluded **POLLARA**, raised on a cliff above the sea – the ledge of a crater, most of which is now submerged by the sea. Scenes from Michael Radford's 1994 film *Il Postino* were shot in a house here and down on the narrow beach at the base of cliffs below the village, but film pilgrims and the many boat tours that pitch up here have caused severe erosion over the years, and the beach is closed. You can swim instead from ramps in front of the so-called *balate*, caves in which fishermen traditionally kept their boats and equipment; or clamber and splash along the rocky coast to more private swimming spots. In summer two resourceful locals rent out kayaks, lilos, mattresses and sun umbrellas at the ramps.

ACCOMMODATION AND EATING   POLLARA

★ **Al Cappero** Pollara Via Chiesa 38 ☎ 090 984 3968. Simple, family-run place, with something of a Greek taverna feel, this is one of the best-value places to eat on the island. Be sure to arrive in time to watch the sun sink over the isles of Filicudi and Alicudi. *Frittelle di zucchine* (deep-fried courgette fritters) or other daily nibbles come free, after which you can choose from two or three pasta dishes of the day (€7.50–10), inevitably including one dressed with a pesto made from their own capers. Fish (€9–12) comes grilled or fried, but the signature dish is a tasty *coniglio in agrodolce* (€12), rabbit stewed in a typical Sicilian sweet-sour sauce. Wines from €12. Daily lunch & dinner.

La Locanda del Postino Via Picone 10 Pollara ☎ 090 984 3958, ⓦ lalocandadelpostino.it. A great choice if you want to turn your back on the world and enjoy spectacular sunsets. The best rooms are no. 7 and no. 10, with large, private terraces (terraces of other rooms are divided by potted plants and are pleasant but lack privacy). Discounts are available for longer stays. Dinner is €35 per person à la carte with water and house wine included. Specialities include linguine with local wild fennel, anchovies, pine nuts, raisins and toasted breadcrumbs, with set dishes costing around €15, and fresh fish priced by the kilo. You could also come for an aperitivo with snacks – timed to coincide with sunset. Restaurant daily lunch & dinner; closed Nov–Easter. **€120**

L'Oasi Piazza Sant'Onofrio. Set in an immobile caravan, Pollara's only bar offers home-made lemon and watermelon *granitas*, along with wine, beer, soft drinks, ice cream and, plus salads making good use of local capers and tomatoes. It is also a nice place to come and watch the sunset over an aperitivo. There is a shady terrace – position yourself at the back, and you can keep an eye on the hairpin road for the arrival of the bus – it takes at least 5min for the bus to make its way down to the village: plenty of time to finish your drink. Daily 9.30am–9.30pm; closed winter.

Valdichiesa and Leni

In the saddle between Salina's two mountains, between malvasia vineyards and smallholdings of fruit trees and vegetables, **Valdichiesa** is lush, cool and green all year. Dominated by the twin-towered church of Santa Maria del Terzito, this sparse scattering of whitewashed houses is the starting point for the easiest ascent of Monte Fossa, the trailhead kicking off from directly behind the church. There is also a paved track below the church running down to the port and beach of Rinella, via the village of Leni. There are no shops or bars, making it the most peaceful place to stay on the island – even in high summer. The silence is shattered just once a year, on July 21–22, when the festival of **Madonna del Terzito** is celebrated with the usual music, market, fireworks and dancing.

Leni, a couple of kilometres beyond, spills along a ridge above Rinella. Though not quite as away-from-it-all as Valdichiesa, it has an appealingly sleepy feel, and fantastic views over to Lipari and Vulcano.

ACCOMMODATION AND EATING   VALDICHIESA

Agriturismo Galletta Via Ruvoli 7 ☎ 333 367 1706. The restaurant of this simple *agriturismo* offers a gutsy taste of traditional Aeolian life, and is surrounded by vineyards, vegetable gardens and fruit trees. There are six simple rooms with en-suite bathrooms, and a kids' playground, but it's best as a place to eat (daily lunch & dinner). The owners keep island traditions alive, preserving fruit and veg, making wine and, in summer, cooking up tomato sauce on their terrace in huge cauldrons. Pasta dishes kick off at €6 for a simple spaghetti with cherry tomatoes, and you'll pay €8–10 for pasta with home-made caper pesto, or with swordfish, capers, tomatoes, olives, aubergine, pine nuts and wild mint. The outstanding choice is the grilled lamb seasoned with local herbs (€12), though there are fish dishes as well, including stuffed *calamaretti* (€12). Follow it with a salad, and wind up with a home-made liqueur of wild fennel, wild mint or apple and rose petal (€3). Book in advance in low season. **€80**

Rinella

On the island's south coast, 15km from Santa Marina, the tiny port of **RINELLA** consists of a cluster of houses, a sandy **beach** and a quay at the very bottom of a steep and winding road. It has clear water, and the beach is popular, so it receives a fair number of visitors in summer, though it's otherwise rather remote in feel. To escape the crowds, take the path from behind the former campsite (recognizable by several half-constructed concrete structures) to the stone boulder beach of **Praia Venezia**. The walk takes about twenty minutes, and there is a bar en route in the summer.

ARRIVAL AND DEPARTURE   RINELLA

By ferry and hydrofoil Rinella is Salina's second port, and the first stop on the island if you are arriving from Palermo, Filicudi or Alicudi. The ticket office is on the dock, right by the bus stop (☎ 090 980 9170 and ☎ 327 412 3089).

Buses call here several times a day, but don't always coincide with ferries and hydrofoils, so unless you have accommodation in Rinella, it's far better to disembark at Santa Marina. Note that the services detailed below are year-round; schedules increase during the summer months. Ferry destinations Alicudi (1 daily; 2hr 20min); Filicudi (1–2 daily; 1hr 10min); Ginostra (1 daily; 2hr); Lipari (1–2 daily; 1hr 40min); Milazzo (1–2 daily; 1hr 35min–2hr); Naples (1 weekly; 13hr 30min); Panarea (1 daily; 1hr 15min); Santa Maria Salina (6 daily; 10min); Stromboli (1 daily; 4hr); Vulcano (1–2 daily; 2hr 20min).

Hydrofoil destinations Alicudi (2 daily; 1hr); Filicudi (2 daily; 25min); Ginostra (1 daily; 2hr 45min); Lipari (10 daily; 25min); Messina (1 daily; 2hr 20min); Milazzo (7 daily; 1hr 40min); Panarea (1 daily; 2hr 20min); Santa Marina Salina (6 daily; 10min); Stromboli (1 daily; 3hr); Vulcano (8 daily; 25min–1hr).

ACCOMMODATION

L'Ariana Via Rotabile ☎ 090 980 9075, ⊛ hotelariana. it. A hotel above the port to the left, occupying an old villa with a frill of terracotta busts around its roof. The interior doesn't quite live up to expectations – and high-season rates are not worth paying – but the location is unbeatable, and it's just a couple of minutes' walk from the sandy beach. **€100**

EATING AND DRINKING

Da Marco Via Rotabile ☎ 090 980 9120. Just up the road from L'Ariana, this excellent pizzeria offers some inspired inventions alongside all the usual suspects from about €6. Easter–Nov daily lunch & dinner; limited opening in winter.

Le Tre Pietre Via Rotabile 72 ☎ 090 980 9081. Friendly, unpretentious restaurant and pizzeria; the TV is always on, and it serves up a nice line in fresh fish. *Antipasti* include simple island staples such as anchovies with capers (€6), while among the spaghetti dishes (€7–10), there are several with an authentic Aeolian feel – try the *finochietto*, dressed with a pesto of wild fennel. The fish menu depends on the day's catch, but the island speciality of *polpette di totano* (deep-fried patties of flying squid) is a regular feature. March–Nov daily lunch & dinner.

★ **Papero Al Glicine** Via Strada Provinciale 16, ☎ 090 980 9161. A lovely bar run by three engaging siblings in an Aeolian house looking out to sea. There is a shady courtyard downstairs, and a large courtyard up a flight of steps, where there is often live music at aperitivo hour. A great place for breakfast (try the fig *granita*), and there's a great *tavola calda* of home-cooked food at lunchtime (fantastic oven-baked pasta, and vegetable gratins). Cocktails are fantastic. Open daily 8am until late.

Panarea

Only 3km by 1.5km, **PANAREA** is the smallest, loveliest and, sadly, the most painfully stylish and ridiculously expensive of the Aeolians: in summer, its harbours, hotels and villas overflow with an international crowd of designers, models, pop stars, actors, royalty and their lackeys. In low season, however, the island is an utter delight. Come in spring or autumn and you'll find accommodation prices relatively sane and beaches and bays uncrowded, while the weather should be cool enough to follow the path that hugs the entire length of Panarea's fractured **coastline**, one of the most stunning anywhere in Italy.

Cars are banned, and the only transport is by Vespa or electric golf car. Panarea's couple of hundred year-round inhabitants live in three linked hamlets on the eastern side of the island, **Iditella**, **San Pietro** and **Drauto**, with the boats docking at San Pietro.

3

BOAT TOURS AND DIVES AROUND PANAREA

The islets and rocks off Panarea make for a great day out. You can either go on a **tour** (from around €25 per person) – there'll be plenty of time for swimming – or **rent your own boat** (from €100 for a half-day excluding fuel). Check out the seafront kiosks at San Pietro or look for the signs advertising "*Noleggio barche*" (boat rental) in nearly every bar, shop and restaurant.

The nearest of the islets to Panarea, **Dattilo**, points a jagged, pyramidal finger skyward and has a minuscule beach. There's better swimming at **Lisca Bianca**, the stark setting of Antonioni's 1960 film *L'Avventura*, where the tranquil water is sheltered by **Bottaro** opposite. Just offshore, submarine fumaroles, created during the last major eruption of Stromboli in 2002, send columns of bubbles rising to the surface – a great snorkelling experience – though check before leaving if access is permitted, as gas emissions can occasionally be dangerous. Nearby Lisca Nera and Le Formiche (The Ants) are mere wrinkles on the sea surface, albeit a constant hazard to shipping. The largest islet is **Basiluzzo**, which retains the remains of a Roman fort and port (the latter now submerged) but is currently only used for caper cultivation.

There are some great **dives** too: take a day out with Amphibia (☎ 335 613 8529, ⓦ amphibia. it) to see what appears to be a submarine snowstorm – the water is full of blobs of a weird white bacteria that grows on sulphur and has the consistency of egg white. You can also dive the remains of a British cargo ship deliberately sunk during the Depression as an insurance scam – for the past fifteen years it has been inhabited by a giant fish (about 80kg). Amphibia also offers introductory and PADI diving courses, plus **snorkelling** and **children's activities**.

San Pietro and Iditella

The core of Panarea's settlement is **San Pietro**, tucked onto gentle terraces and backed by gnarled outcrops of rock. It's here that you'll find most of the accommodation, restaurants and facilities, while just to the north, passing through **Iditella**, you'll see evidence of volcanic activity in the steaming gas emissions (fumarole) on the sand-and-pebble beach below here, the **Spiaggia Fumarole**, also known as Calcara.

ARRIVAL AND DEPARTURE SAN PIETRO AND IDITELLA

By ferry and hydrofoil All boats dock at San Pietro harbour, where you'll find the ticket office (☎ 090 983 344 and ☎ 340 902 4537). The services detailed below are year-round; schedules increase during the summer months.
Ferry destinations Ginostra (2 weekly; 1hr 40min); Lipari (2 weekly; 1hr); Milazzo (2 weekly; 3hr 40min); Naples (2 weekly; 12hr 15min); Stromboli (2 weekly; 1hr); Vulcano (2 weekly; 1hr 40min).
Hydrofoil destinations Ginostra (2 daily; 25min); Lipari (4 daily; 50min); Milazzo (4 daily; 1hr 40min); Rinella (1 daily; 35min); Santa Marina Salina (2 daily; 25min); Stromboli (2 daily; 35min); Vulcano (4 daily; 1hr 20min).

INFORMATION

Services San Pietro has a pharmacy, an ATM and a summer-only police post and Guardia Medica, while in the warren of alleys behind the harbour is a little supermarket, two or three *alimentari* and a bakery. The little electric buggies down at the harbour act as taxis. However, all the hotels provide a free pick-up service.

ACCOMMODATION

Lisca Bianca Via Lani, San Pietro ☎ 090 983 004, ⓦ liscabianca.it. This typical Aeolian building – covered wide terraces, blue shutters, white walls – has some gorgeous views, with stylish rooms overlooking either the sea or the bougainvillea-clad gardens and port. You can see Stromboli from the breakfast terrace, and the bar is one of the best on the island. Closed Nov–March. **€400**
Quartara Via San Pietro, San Pietro ☎ 090 983 027, ⓦ quartarahotel.com. Very classy four-star boutique hotel run by a cheerful family, whose thirteen fashionable rooms have elegant wood furniture and stone floors. A terrace jacuzzi out the back overlooks the port and there's a well-regarded restaurant. Closed Nov–March. **€300**
Raya Via San Pietro, San Pietro ☎ 090 983 013, ⓦ hotelraya.it. Opened in the 1960s, this is the hotel that put Panarea on the party map, and it remains the hippest, sexiest and most expensive hotel in Sicily – even though the owner's refusal to install televisions and telephones means that it has only two stars. It's built entirely of natural materials, and the food is organic; though its claim to be a

simple retreat for nature lovers seems a little disingenuous when the place is crawling with party animals. Rooms (whitewashed walls, teak furniture, hand-batiked textiles, citronella candles) are built into the hillside above the village, with great views to the sea over groves of olives, hibiscus and bougainvillea; there are also some cheaper rooms in town above their boutique of the same name (€250). **€400**

EATING AND DRINKING

Da Adelina Via Comunale Mare, San Pietro 28 ☎090 983 246. Intimate candlelit restaurant with a romantic roof terrace overlooking Panarea's port. It's relaxing and unpretentious, with a simple menu of seasonal dishes such as *moscardini* (tiny octopus cooked with tomato, capers, wild fennel and chilli; €15) appearing alongside year-round dishes like *pennette adelina*, pasta dressed with anchovies, aubergine, capers, olives, mint and basil (€11). For the main course opt for the fish of the day, either fried or grilled (around €20). Wonderful afternoon cooking lessons can also be arranged, followed by eating what you have created – you learn to fillet fish, make marvellous sauces and marinades, all the time entertained by stories about the cuisine and traditions of the islands (ⓦadelina-panarea. com). Daily lunch & dinner; closed Nov–Feb.

Da Francesco Via San Pietro, San Pietro ☎090 983 023, ⓦwww.dafrancescopanarea.com. This place overlooks the harbour and is pretty good value for pasta (around €12), including the signature dish "*disgraziata*", with peppers, chilli, capers, olives, aubergine, tomatoes and baked ricotta, plus fish from €18. Daily lunch & dinner; closed Dec–Feb.

Da Paolino Via Iditella 75, Iditella ☎090 983 008. A 10min walk north of the port heading towards Iditella, this family-run restaurant has a terrace with fine views of Stromboli. You'll spend quite a bit if you eat three courses, but you can have a very unpretentious meal of pasta, salad and a glass of wine here for around €30 – try the *mille baci* pasta with greens; and the fish is whatever the family has caught that day. Daily lunch & dinner; closed Nov–March.

Drauto and Zimmari beach

South of San Pietro through the tangle of lanes, a gentle thirty-minute stroll above the coast leads to the mainly stone beach below **Drauto**. Just beyond here, the path descends to **Zimmari**, a popular, dark-gold sandy beach – the only one on the island – overlooked by a seasonal (and expensive) bar-trattoria. Steps at the far end of the beach climb up and across to the headland of **Punta Milazzese**, passing the trailhead of a waymarked path (look for the signposts) that wends into Panarea's interior, passing below the island's highest peak, the craggy **Punta del Corvo** (421m), before descending back to San Pietro – a hike of two to three hours on a path that is easy to follow.

ACCOMMODATION   DRAUTO

Albergo Girasole Via Drauto ☎090 983 018 or ☎328 861 8595, ⓦhotelgirasole-panarea.it. Family-run hotel with bright, pretty rooms out on the way to the sandy beach at Zimmari. Great place to stay in low season, but even this part of the island is chock-full in August, the skinny road buzzing with electric cars and *motorini* (motorbikes). **€156**

Villaggio Preistorico

Beautifully situated on a craggy headland above Zimmari, atop Punta Milazzese and overlooking two rocky inlets, the **Villaggio Preistorico** is the archipelago's best-preserved Bronze Age village. The 23 huts here were discovered in 1948, and the oval outlines of their foundation walls are easily visible. The site is thought to have been inhabited since the fourteenth century BC, and pottery found here (displayed in Museo Eoliano, see page 123) shows a distinct Minoan influence – fascinating evidence of a historical link between the Aeolians and Crete that goes some way towards corroborating the legends of contact between the two in ancient times.

Cala Junco

Steps descend from Punta Milazzese to **Cala Junco**, a superb cove whose aquamarine water, scattered stone outcrops and surrounding coves and caves make it a popular spot for snorkelling.

Stromboli

The most spectacular of all the Aeolian Islands, **STROMBOLI** is little more than a volcanic cone thrust out of the sea. It's very much alive and kicking, throwing up showers of sparks and flaring rock from the craters every twenty minutes or so, while a handful of more serious **eruptions** over the last century have caused major lava flows. That of 1930 led to serious damage to many homes and sparked a spate of emigration from the island, while threatening eruptions in 2002 and 2003 spewed volcanic rock into the sea, spawning a tsunami and ejecting rocks onto rooftops. In 2007, two new craters opened on the summit, creating new lava streams into the sea, and in July 2010 fiery boulders set the mountain alight, though the fire was swiftly extinguished. Periods of intense activity continue to come and go – sometimes a flow of lava is visible from afar, slowly sliding down the northwest side of the volcano into the sea, at other times, clouds of volcanic gases glow pink.

Amazingly, perhaps, people have chosen to live here for centuries, reassured that, historically, the main lava flows have been confined to the channel of the Sciara del Fuoco, down the western side of the island. This leaves the eastern parishes of San Vincenzo, San Bartolo and Piscità (often grouped together simply as **Stromboli village**), and the solitary southern community of **Ginostra**, to lead something of a charmed life, their white terraced houses adorned with bougainvillea, plumbago and wisteria, remote from the fury of the craters above. The island's permanent population numbers perhaps five hundred, plumbing is often rudimentary, and access sometimes restricted because of winter storms, but despite this, Stromboli has become a chic resort, attracting an eclectic moneyed crowd that ranges from fashionistas to hip intellectuals, a mix leavened with a generous dose of holidaying families and hardy mountain types. Its black-sand **beaches** are overlooked by attractive terraced hotels, while thrill-seekers come from all over the world to climb one of the planet's most accessible volcanoes.

GETTING AROUND

By taxi Stromboli has no public transport – indeed the only transport on the island is by three-wheeler pick-up (the Ape, or bee, known as a *lapa* in Sicilian dialect), motorbike or electric car – so if your hotel is any distance from the port you may need a taxi. Though unofficial *lapas* may offer their services, the only official taxis are the electric golf carts; but as these take ten hours to charge for every two hours' driving, demand quite often outstrips supply.

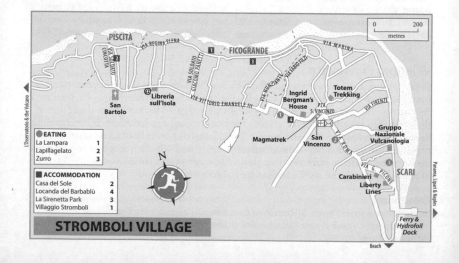

STROMBOLI VILLAGE

EATING
La Lampara — 1
Lapillagelato — 2
Zurro — 3

ACCOMMODATION
Casa del Sole — 2
Locanda del Barbablù — 4
La Sirenetta Park — 3
Villaggio Stromboli — 1

STROMBOLI BOAT TOURS

The main daytime boat tour from Stromboli is the **round-island excursion** (2hr 30min; around €35 per person), calling at Ginostra and Stromboli's extraordinary basalt offspring, Strombolicchio. You usually get half an hour to scramble around Ginostra, which is plenty of time to see it, while at Strombolicchio there's swimming and a two-hundred-step climb up the battlemented rock to the lighthouse on its top.

At night, the stock-in-trade is the cruise to see the **Sciara del Fuoco** (1hr 30min; around €30 per person), the lava channel rising sheer out of incredible deep-blue seawater. Boats aren't allowed to dock on the shoreline, since it's too unpredictably dangerous, but through the gloom you'll see orange and red flashes from the crater above.

You can book tours at any of the stands by Stromboli village harbour (prices are broadly similar on all the boats), where you can also charter a boat for longer tours or rent your own.

As a precaution, ask your hotel at the time of booking if they have, or can organize, transport for you. Of the official taxis, Sabbia Nera (☎ 090 986 399), based near the port, are reliable and friendly. In high season, consider booking one in advance to meet you on arrival.

3

Stromboli village

The main settlement of **Stromboli** spreads for a distance of around 2km between the lower slopes of the volcano and the island's beaches. It's an utterly straightforward layout of two largely parallel roads and steep, interconnecting alleys, though the profusion of local place names keeps visitors on their toes. From the scruffy quayside area known as **Scari**, the lower coastal road (Via Marina and Via Regina Elena) runs around to the main beach of **Ficogrande**, a long black stretch overlooked by several hotels. Further on is **Piscità**, around 25 minutes' walk from the port, with the island's most beautiful and secluded ashy beach at its far end. There's also a sand-and-stone stretch south of Scari, past the fishing boats, and if you clamber over the rocks at the end of this beach, there's a further sweep of lava stone that attracts a fair bit of nude sunbathing.

Pottering around Stromboli village as you go about your daily business is one of the great pleasures of being on the island. The other road from the quayside, Via Vittorio Emanuele III, cuts up into what could loosely be described as "the village", where, turning into Via Roma, it runs as far as the church of **San Vincenzo**, whose square offers glorious views of the Strombolicchio basalt stack. Beyond Piazza San Vincenzo, it's another fifteen minutes' or so walk to the second church of **San Bartolo**, above Piscità, just beyond which starts the path to the crater. Once you've got this far, you've seen all that Stromboli village has to offer. The only "sight",• apart from the churches, is the house in which **Ingrid Bergman** lived with Roberto Rossellini in the spring of 1949, while making the film *Stromboli: Terra di Dio*. A plaque records these bare facts on the pink building, just after San Vincenzo church, on the right.

ARRIVAL AND INFORMATION   STROMBOLI VILLAGE

By ferry and hydrofoil Several ferry and hydrofoil services from Lipari call first at Ginostra, though the main port is Stromboli village. The ticket office is right by the port (☎ 090 986 003 and ☎ 340 902 8012) and is open just before sailings. The services detailed below are year-round; schedules increase during the summer months.
Ferry destinations Lipari (2 weekly; 1hr 45min); Milazzo (2 weekly; 3hr); Naples (2 weekly; 11hr); Panarea (2 weekly; 25min); Vulcano (2 weekly; 2hr).

Hydrofoil destinations Ginostra (1 daily; 10min); Lipari (4 daily; 1hr 20min); Milazzo (4 daily; 2hr 30min); Panarea (4 daily; 25min); Vulcano (4 daily; 1hr 30min).
Information Libreria sull'Isola bookshop on Via Vittorio Emanuele (June–Sept daily 10am–1pm & 5–8pm, much later in summer; ☎ 090 986 5755), and several other shops in town, sell a good map of Stromboli showing local hiking trails.
Services There's internet access at the Libreria sull'Isola bookshop.

ACCOMMODATION
SEE MAP PAGE 142

Casa del Sole Via Soldato Cincotta, Piscità ☎090 986 300, ⓦcasadelsolestromboli.it. A cheapie in an old building within metres of the sea. Accommodation is pretty flexible, whether you want an off-season single or multi-bedded room in summer. Shared kitchen facilities are available, and there's a sun terrace. No credit cards. Doubles €65

Locanda del Barbablù Via Vittorio Emanuele 17 ☎090 986 118, ⓦbarbablu.it. This old Aeolian house provides some of the most charming boutique accommodation on Stromboli, with five antique rooms, four-poster beds and original tile floors in a period townhouse. There's a nice shady courtyard – a fine place for a lazy afternoon drink. Closed Nov–Feb. €120

La Sirenetta Park Via Marina 33, Ficogrande ☎090 986 025, ⓦlasirenettahotel.it. Four-star hotel set opposite the black sands of Ficogrande, with a decent-sized outdoor pool, a summer nightclub and access to watersports facilities. The room rates drop considerably outside summer and at the beginning or end of the season you can stay for around €120. Closed Nov–March. €185

Villaggio Stromboli Via Regina Elena ☎090 986 018, ⓦvillaggiostromboli.it. With simple rooms jutting up against the breaking waves, this pleasant, quiet place offers one of the island's nicest seaside stays; it also has a good terrace restaurant (guests only) where you can gaze out over the water. €140

EATING
SEE MAP PAGE 142

La Lampara Via Vittorio Emanuele ☎090 986 009. Dine on pizza, pasta and grilled meat and fish on the large raised terrace under a pergola of climbing vines among huge pots of basil and rosemary. Pizza from €6.50. Daily dinner; closed Nov–March.

Lapillagelato Via Roma s/n ☎333 320 8966. Artisan ice cream made with natural ingredients and no hydrogenated fats, added colours or preservatives. Try the fig, the vanilla with caramel or the dark chocolate with cinnamon. Daily 3.30–11pm; closed winter.

Zurro Via Marina s/n ☎090 986 283. Not exactly romantic, with its startlingly bright lights and sliding aluminium framed windows, but you eat well at *Zurro*. It's named for its bearded, piratical-looking chef, a one-time fisherman who shocked his mates by tampering with traditional recipes, but opened a restaurant nevertheless. Try razor-thin slices of raw aubergine, flecked with chilli flakes and served with balsamic-dressed rocket and parmesan; *spaghetti alla strombolana*, with cherry tomatoes, anchovies, mint, chilli and garlic (€15), or *pietre di mare*, black ravioli stuffed with *ricciola* (amberjack) and dressed with capers, cherry tomatoes and basil (€15). The chocolate cake is a must. Daily dinner; closed Nov–Feb.

Ginostra

Without seeing its name on boat timetables, you might not even be aware of the existence of **Ginostra**, the hamlet on the southwest side of Stromboli. From the minuscule harbour, zigzag steps climb into a cluster of typical white Aeolian houses on terraces. It's a refreshingly simple place: donkeys are tethered to posts outside homes; ancient exterior stone ovens lie idle; and cultivated hedges and volcanic stone walls snake up the hillside. Hydrofoils run to and from Stromboli village in summer, though a boat tour is a more realistic way to see Ginostra (unless you fancy actually staying here at the one small hotel). A century ago, there was also a maintained path that skirted the shore back to Stromboli, but assault by the elements has done for most of it. However, following the coast anticlockwise, you don't need to go very far to find spots where you can swim off the rocks.

ARRIVAL AND DEPARTURE
GINOSTRA

By ferry and hydrofoil Weather permitting, a couple of hydrofoils run to and from Stromboli village per day in summer (once daily in winter), weather permitting of course, continuing to Panarea, Santa Marina Salina, Lipari, Vulcano and Milazzo. There is also a ferry to the same places daily except Saturday. The twice weekly ferry to Naples stops at Ginostra. The ticket office (☎090 981 3161 and ☎334 200 8283) opens just before sailings.

Ferry destinations Lipari (3 weekly; 3hr); Milazzo (3 weekly; 5hr 25min); Naples (2 weekly; 12hr); Panarea (3 weekly; 45min); Santa Marina Salina (weekly; 2hr); Stromboli (1 weekly; 30min); Vulcano (3 weekly; 3hr 45min).

Hydrofoil destinations Lipari (2 daily; 1hr 15min–3hr 15min); Milazzo (3 daily; 2hr 15min–4hr 25min); Panarea (1 daily; 30min–2hr 20min); Santa Marina Salina (1 daily; 3hr 35min); Stromboli (2 daily; 10min); Vulcano (3 daily; 1hr 15min–3hr 35min).

CLIMBING STROMBOLI'S VOLCANO

Climbing Stromboli's **volcano** is big business, and while you can freely walk along the trails below 400m, you have to be accompanied by a licensed guide to go any higher. Numbers at the crater are also limited, so it's essential to reserve a place on an **organized excursion** (about €30, including the local council's marvellously named 'volcano access tax'; see below) as soon as you can – calling on the day is usually fine for most of the year, but advance booking is advised in high summer – and be prepared for the trip to be postponed because of poor weather or other climatic or geological reasons. You need to be in decent health, have proper hiking boots and clothes (you can rent these in the village), and carry plenty of water and sun protection. Guides usually supply helmets.

If you want to see eruptions without the effort or expense of climbing to the summit, follow the track a few minutes' walk beyond San Bartolo church at the far end of Piscità, climbing to the first orientation point, *L'Osservatorio*, a bar-pizzeria (closed in winter) which has a wide terrace and a view of the volcano. Beyond, you'll see the frighteningly sheer **Sciara del Fuoco** lava outflow plunging directly into the sea. This is a huge blistered sheet down which thousands of years' worth of volcanic detritus has poured, scarring and pock-marking the hillside. Menacing little puffs of steam dance up from folds in the bare slope, where absolutely nothing grows.

THE CLIMB

Most excursions leave in the late afternoon, taking around five or six hours – this lets you catch the amazing sunsets and gives you around an hour or so at the top, watching the fireworks. The **ascent** takes three hours, and you are expected to go at a fair whack; at first, it's no different from walking up any mountain, then suddenly all vegetation stops, giving way to black ash strewn with small jagged boulders spewed out by the volcano. Once at the top, all you see at first are clouds of white steam – then suddenly there will be a resounding clash, the clouds glow red, and spouts of fire shoot up into the air, the glowing boulders drawing tracks of red light across the night sky. The **descent** takes around two hours – for the most part trudging down a steep slope of lava sand.

GUIDES, EQUIPMENT AND INFORMATION

Gruppo Nazionale Vulcanologia Via Marina ☎090 986 708, ⓦgnv.ingv.it. Located near the harbour, the national vulcanology organization has an office with useful background information on the volcano. It's open most days and shows a video about Stromboli, while the national website has photos, technical information and some scary seismograph readings from previous eruptions.
★ **Magmatrek** Via Vittorio Emanuele, just off the piazza ☎090 986 5768, ⓦmagmatrek.it. Local climbing guru Zazà and his colleagues run daily volcano treks throughout the year. Guides are knowledgeable and experienced and in constant contact with the vulcanological centre.
Totem Trekking Piazza San Vincenzo 4 ☎090 986 5752. Useful little shop that sells and rents out hiking equipment and accessories.

ACCOMMODATION AND EATING

Petrusa ☎090 981 2305 or 334 2036757, ⓦginos traincontro.it. This place has three large rooms with their own terraces, sharing a bathroom, and you can eat at their bar-restaurant, *L'Incontro* (July & Aug daily lunch & dinner), which has fairly high prices (everything has to be shipped in) but is pretty good. No credit cards. Closed Oct to April. **€80**

Filicudi

The larger of the Aeolians' two most westerly islands, **FILICUDI** is a fascinating place, the contours of its sheer slopes traced with steep stone terraces and crisscrossed by stone mule tracks. It's an island best explored on foot – which is just as well, as there's no public transport. The tarmac road that connects Filicudi's small settlements gives a false impression of the island, making villages seem far apart even if they're just a few

FILICUDI BY BOAT

To explore the island's uninhabited northern and western coasts you'll need to **rent a boat**. The highly recommended I Delfini at Pecorini Mare (☎090 988 9077 or ☎340 148 4645, ✆idelfinifilicudi.com) rent traditional gozzi (wooden boats) for people with and without nautical licenses (€100/day), rubber dinghies (€120/day), kayaks (€15/day), and offer boat tours around the island (€25/person; minimum 4 people). In summer, there's usually someone at Filicudi Porto or Pecorini Mare touting for custom, and any hotel, shop or restaurant can point you in the right direction. The main sights include the fine natural arch of **Punta Perciato** and the nearby **Grotta del Bue Marino** ("Seal Grotto" – there aren't any), a wide rocky cavity 37m long by 30m wide, its walls of reddish lava barely visible in the pitch black of the interior. Near the island's northwest coast, the startling **Canna**, a rugged obelisk 85m tall, is the most impressive of all the *faraglioni* of the Aeolian Islands.

3

minutes' walk from each other – at least if you're fit. Most of the tracks are pretty steep, following and cutting up and down between the ancient terraces carved into slopes of maquis and prickly pear.

Climb away from the port, up the flight of steps opposite the jetty, and you're in another world. The well-kept **paths** are lined with volcanic boulders interspersed with great flowering cacti, whose pustular blooms erupt upon elephant-ear leaves. You can clamber down to pebble **beaches** and swim in deserted coves; make your way along the terraced headlands to phenomenal **viewpoints**, or hire a little wooden boat (see box) for the day and snorkel around splintered offshore rocks and hidden sea caves.

Filicudi's sheer slopes are all painstakingly lined with stone **terracing**, a reminder that before mass emigration in the 1950s and 1960s there was a great deal of agricultural activity here. Many terraces were subsequently abandoned, and cultivation is now down to a few vines and olives, but they do serve to reduce soil erosion. Today, there are only 250 or so permanent island residents, and while this number swells perhaps

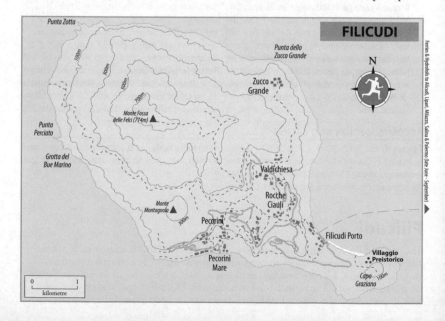

tenfold in August with visitors – a coterie of left-wing villa owners (including former Rome mayor Francesco Rutelli), and returned *emigranti* – Filicudi is still a long way from being overdeveloped.

GETTING AROUND   FILICUDI

By taxi There is no public transport on Filicudi. There's usually a minibus taxi (*bus navetta*) waiting at the harbour, which will take you where you want to go on the island. It costs €12 to Pecorini Mare, less per head if there's a group of you. If it's not there, call D&G Servizio Navetta (☎ 347 757

5916 or ☎ 347 517 1825).

By car and scooter There's scooter rental (about €25/day, but more in mid-August) at the port and from I Delfini at Pecorini Mare (☎ 090 988 9077or ☎ 340 148 4645), who also rent cars (from €40/day).

Filicudi Porto

Filicudi's main settlement is **Filicudi Porto**, a functional place with a few colour-trimmed whitewashed cubes containing a couple of shops, hotels, basic services and two or three bar-restaurants, with terraces overlooking the water and Salina in the distance. Staying here won't really allow you to appreciate the magic of the island, however, so unless you have an early-morning ferry or hydrofoil, it's far better to base yourself elsewhere.

ARRIVAL AND INFORMATION   FILICUDI PORTO

By ferry and hydrofoil Filicudi Porto is an hour by hydrofoil from Lipari, and three hours from Palermo. The Liberty Lines office (☎ 090 988 9975 and ☎ 327 882 7777) is on the dockside, open before departures. Although there is one weekly ferry from Naples to Filicudi, there are no direct services back to Naples from here – you'll need to connect to another ferry at Rinella or Santa Marina Salina. The services detailed below are year-round; schedules increase during the summer months.
Ferry destinations Alicudi (1 daily; 1hr 10min); Lipari (daily; 2hr 50min); Milazzo (1 daily; 5hr); Rinella (1 daily;

1hr); Santa Marina Salina (1 daily; 1hr 50min); Vulcano (1 daily; 3hr 20min).
Hydrofoil destinations Lipari (2 daily; 1hr); Rinella (2 daily; 30min); Santa Marina Salina (2 daily; 45min), Palermo (1 daily in summer, 2hr 30min).
Services The one-street port has a pharmacy (limited opening), general store and ATM. One of the bar-restaurants here, *Da Nino sul Mare* (see below), also sells ice cream, postcards, newspapers and beautifully designed island maps (€5) showing Filicudi's footpaths.

ACCOMMODATION AND EATING

Da Nino sul Mare ☎ 090 988 9984. The seafront terrace of this bar, *pasticceria* and newsagent is the focal point of life in the port. Come for breakfast, a lunchtime snack or aperitivo at sunset. April–Oct daily 7.30am–midnight.
Phenicusa ☎ 090 988 9946, ⓦ hotelphenicusa.com. The only hotel right by the village harbour opens for just

four months a year – it's a traditional three-star, with reasonable rooms, though not all have sea views (and you pay a supplement for those that do). Breakfast is served on the sun-soaked terrace, and the decent restaurant has the same sea and harbour views. Half board is required in Aug. Closed Oct–May. **€65**

FILICUDI'S ABANDONED VILLAGE

There are plenty of good **walks** along the ancient mule tracks of Filicudi: one of the nicest is out to the abandoned village of **Zucco Grande**. From the port, walk up to *La Canna* hotel (see page 148), following the well-kept stone mule track that begins from a point almost opposite the hydrofoil and ferry dock, then continue until you meet a tarmacked road. The path continues on the other side of the road, heading towards the settlement of Valdichiesa. After about twenty minutes, the path forks, and you'll see the first of several signs to Zucco Grande. This path is well marked, following the contours through a spiky terrain of gorse, lentisk, prickly pear and euphorbia. Another twenty minutes brings you to the village, abandoned forty years ago when its last inhabitants left for Australia. A couple of pioneering souls have bought ruins here, which are being renovated.

Capo Graziano

Signposted off the main road from Filicudi Porto, it's a pleasant twenty-minute walk along a steep stone path to **Capo Graziano**. Here, on a grassy plateau, high above the harbour, are the remains of a dozen or so oval **prehistoric huts**, dating from the eighteenth to the thirteenth century BC. The site is always open, and though there's not much to see, it's a good place from which to watch the comings and goings at the harbour below, and there are several rocky places to swim from on the south side of the cape.

Rocche Ciauli

Filicudi's magic begins to make itself felt in the little whitewashed village of **Rocche Ciauli**, above the port and accessible by road or up a stiff stepped path from the quayside. There's not a lot to the village – just a hotel, a few houses and a huge bar/ *pensione*/pizzeria/disco, but if you're not bothered about having the sea on your doorstep, it's a lovely place to spend a few lazy days.

3

ACCOMMODATION AND EATING   ROCCHE CIAULI

★ **La Canna** Via Rosa 43 ☎ 090 988 9956, ⓦ lacanna hotel.it. Bright rooms with tiled bathrooms, which open onto spacious terraces with a magnificent view over the bay below. There's a small pool (summer only), and the restaurant here (daily lunch & dinner, closed winter) is excellent – home-made pasta, fresh fish, local caper salads and plenty of home-produced wine and fruit. In summer, half board (€25/30) is obligatory in rooms with a sea view, but the food is so good, we'd recommend that anyway. It's a stiff climb up the steps from the port; call ahead and they'll pick you up from the dock. **€140**

Villa La Rosa Via Rosa 24 ☎ 090 988 9965, ⓦ villalarosa. it. Open all year, *Villa La Rosa* is, inevitably, the social hub of

Filicudi, where locals gather to watch sports matches, play pool or ping pong, eat a pizza, buy a loaf of bread (they make their own) or boogie the night away. There is even a rudimentary selection of groceries (pasta, tinned tomatoes, eggs, oil and the like). Cook Adelaide Rando produces some great dishes (and has written a book on Filicudari cuisine). Try the lasagne with fresh tuna and wild fennel; the herbed rabbit; swordfish wrapped in lemon leaves; or the prickly pear pudding. Expect to pay around €25 a head for a full meal – or go for the half-board option (€70 per person). The restaurant opens daily for lunch and dinner; call ahead out of season. There are also rooms in a couple of houses nearby. **€100**

Pecorini Mare

About 6km from Filicudi Porto, at the foot of a narrow switchback road below the hamlet of **Pecorini** (no more than a few houses grouped around a church), is the little harbour of **Pecorini Mare**, a mere scrap of a fishing hamlet with a small dockside, a Carabinieri post, a "saloon" selling drinks and *gelati*, a fine trattoria (see below), a marvellous grocery shop with fresh fruit and veg and genuine local produce (bottled tuna, anchovies, honey, capers, almonds and various conserves), and a stylish **lido** (€15 per person per day). It's a gorgeous, end-of-the-road place,

---

TO PECORINI MARE BY MULE TRACK

It is a long, twisty drive by road from Filicudi Porto to Pecorini Mare, but by **mule track** it's a mere 3km. From the port, go up the steps by the Postamat bank machine at the far end of the waterfront (not the path by the Bancomat, which leads straight up to La Canna) and follow the cobbled track until you come to a fork. The right fork leads to *Villa La Rosa* (see above), but for Pecorini Mare bear left until you hit the tarmacked road. Head right along the road; at the first bend there is an electricity cabin – a little dirt path from here leads down to a good swimming spot, while the main, cobbled mule track heads right towards Pecorini, following a terrace. Keep on along this track until you come to a white house, from where a track heads uphill to Valdichiesa; the path to Pecorini Mare squeezes past the wall of the white house, before descending to the village.

with a long pebble beach backed by fishermen's houses and holiday homes, and perfectly clear water. In the evenings take a slow stroll up the hill (preferably with a bottle of wine) and out to the clifftop belvedere above to watch the sun set over the offshore rock known as La Canna, the Italian slang for joint (which may clue you in to the mindset of Filicudi's first wave of tourists back in the 1970s).

ACCOMMODATION AND EATING   PECORINI MARE

Saloon ☎ 347 047 4914. The quayside below the *Saloon* is the social hub of Pecorini Mare, and on a summer evening folk gather outside in their hundreds for a sundowner. It has been going since the 1950s, and little has changed: inside there's a fridge, a kitchen and a table where you pay your bill. Early June to mid-Sept daily 10.30am–2pm & 5–11pm.

★ **La Sirena** ☎ 090 988 9997, ⓦ pensionelasirena. it. An oasis you won't want to leave, this inn is run with relaxed cosmopolitan flair by a Milanese art-gallery owner and sits right on the Pecorini Mare seafront, with fishing boats drawn up alongside. Rooms have little waterfront

balconies, and there's a couple right on the beach itself. Out on the shaded terrace is the island's most relaxed restaurant (daily lunch & dinner). It gets very busy in Aug, but at most times of the year all you can hear is the sound of lapping water as you tuck into exquisite dishes like spaghetti with almond sauce, orange-scented *involtini* of swordfish and (if they have it) an unforgettable Sicilian-style tuna hamburger spiked with fennel seeds, raisins and almonds. Expect to pay around €40 a head for three courses without wine. Closed Oct–Easter. They also run the cool (though expensive) lido, set on the rocks at the edge of the village. **€180**

Alicudi

One of the most remote spots in Europe, two and a half hours from the mainland by hydrofoil, or five by ferry, the island forms a perfect cone, a mere Mediterranean pimple, and its precipitous shores are pierced by numerous caves. Up the sheer slope behind the only settlement, terraced smallholdings and white houses cling on for dear life, decorated with tumbling banks of flowers. Indeed, Alicudi's ancient name of Ericusa was the word for the heather that still stains its slopes purple in spring. Its rocky isolation was formerly exploited by the Italian government, who used the island as a prison for convicted Mafiosi, but now it's virtually abandoned by all but a few farmers and fishermen. It's this solitude, of course, that attracts tourists; not many, it's true, but enough for there to be some semblance of facilities in the village to cater for visitors. Electricity arrived at the start of the 1990s, so now there's television and internet, too. There are two general stores, plenty of fancy boat hardware and even a car or two parked at the dock (though, since there are no navigable roads, it's not clear whether this is bravado or forward planning on behalf of the owners). You have to walk to reach anywhere and the network of volcanic stone-built paths behind the village is extremely steep and tough – all heavy fetching and carrying is still done by donkey or mule, whose indignant brays echo across the port all day.

Once you disembark at **Alicudi Porto**, things to do are limited. The most exhausting option is the hike up past the castle ruins to the island peak of **Filo dell'Arpa** (675m). The path runs up through the village houses from the port and there's a proper stone-built track most

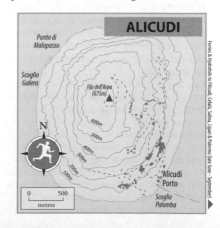

> ## HIKING ON ALICUDI
>
> Most of Alicudi's **hiking** is up stepped tracks that seem to have been designed with giants in mind, so be prepared for a good deal of calf-work. If you don't fancy hauling yourself to the top of the island (675m; 2hr), you'll still get plenty of exercise climbing up to the church of **San Bartolomeo**, where controversy rages over the removal of a statue of the saint to a more easily accessible church lower down the hill (it is said that since the statue was moved, the island has had bad luck). Otherwise, follow the path north out of the port behind the church of the Carmine from where it's an easy walk to the narrow stony beach of **Bazzina**, with a couple of smallholdings behind it.

of the way. Unfortunately, the track looks as though it was created by a malevolent giant emptying a bag of boulders from the top and letting them fall where they will. There's absolutely no shade, and the ascent takes at least two hours, though the magnificent views make it worthwhile.

Otherwise, you could opt for the gentler option of clambering over the rocky **shore** to the south of the port. The path soon peters out beyond the island's only hotel and the power station, but the rocks offer a sure foothold as they get larger the further you venture. The water is crystal clear and the only sounds are the echoed mutters of offshore fishermen, the scrabbling of little black crabs in rock pools, and the lap of waves.

ARRIVAL AND INFORMATION ALICUDI

By ferry and hydrofoil Ferries and hydrofoils arrive at the only port, Alicudi Porto. Set in the cave-like dwellings to the left of the dock is the ticket office (☎ 090 914 8353 and ☎ 328 655 9228). Even in summer, when hydrofoil services increase to a maximum of four daily, it's usually necessary to change at Lipari if you're travelling on to Vulcano, Milazzo, Panarea or Stromboli. In summer there's also one hydrofoil daily to Palermo. Unless specified, the services detailed below are year-round; schedules increase during the summer months.

Ferry destinations Filicudi (4–5 weekly; 1hr); Lipari (4–5 weekly; 4hr); Milazzo (4–5 weekly; 6hr 15min); Rinella (4–5 weekly; 2hr 10min); Santa Marina Salina (4–5 weekly; 2hr 50min); Vulcano (4–5 weekly; 4hr 40min).

Hydrofoil destinations Filicudi (2 daily; 25min); Lipari (2 daily; 1hr 35min); Palermo (1 daily in summer, 2hr); Rinella (2 daily; 55min); Santa Marina Salina (2 daily; 1hr 10min).

Services Alicudi has just two little grocery stores, both near the port. Supplies of fresh fruit and vegetables are limited at the best of times, so you'd do well to bring what you need with you. Self-catering carnivores should also bring a coolbox of fresh meat, as there is no butcher.

ACCOMMODATION AND EATING

Ericusa Hotel Alicudi Porto ☎ 090 988 9902, ⓦ alicudi hotel.it. A modern twelve-room hotel of little architectural charm, a 5min walk south of the port along the shore. Compensating are sea views, spacious terraces and a restaurant. Closed Oct–May. Offers half board only; rates are per person. **€130**

Casa Mulino Alicudi Porto ☎ 090 988 9681, ⓦ alicudi casamulino.it. Small apartments with cooking facilities and terraces sleeping two, four or six people. Three-night minimum stay. **€85**

Da Rosina Alla Mimosa Via Vallone 3 ☎ 090 988 9937 or ☎ 368 361 6511, ⓦ rosina-barbuto.it. Named after a huge mimosa tree that was uprooted by a recent tornado, the glassed-in terrace of this *agriturismo* (decorated with abundant artificial flowers) is the best place to eat in Alicudi – though you will need to call ahead. Virtually everything is produced or – in the case of rabbit and fish –

caught by the family: a raisiny rough red wine, good olive oil, fruit, vegetables and meat (cows and sheep are grazed way up the mountain, goats and rabbits run wild, chickens are free-range). In autumn there are wild mushrooms, and from autumn to spring wild pickings such as fennel and borage. Menus are set (€25 per head); a typical dinner would include an *antipasto* of grilled vegetables or frittata (with ricotta and borage if you're lucky), pasta, grilled meat or fish, salad and fruit. There are also a handful of simple rooms to rent. No credit cards. Closed Oct–March, though open on request at other times. Breakfast €10 extra. **€60**

Signore Silvio Taranto Via Regina Elena s/n ☎ 090 988 9922. It's well worth calling in on Signore Taranto, who lives up the hill behind the ticket office (anyone can point you in the right direction). He cooks dinner on request – spaghetti, fresh fish, salad, fruit and wine – for around €25 a head, served on his bougainvillea-covered terrace in the company of whoever else happens to turn up, which in summer will include other tourists, in winter a motley array of builders, technicians, doctors and others who come to the island to work. Daily dinner only.

3

Messina, Taormina and the northeast

156 Messina

164 The road to Punta del Faro

165 Savoca and around

166 Forza d'Agrò

166 Taormina

175 Around Taormina

177 The Alcantara valley

TEATRO GRECO, TAORMINA

Messina, Taormina and the northeast

Lying between the Tyrrhenian and Ionian seas, and divided from mainland Italy by the Straits of Messina, northeastern Sicily is not the most immediately appealing part of the island. Messina itself was destroyed by the worst earthquake ever to hit western Europe in 1908, and the remote, forgotten villages of the Peloritani mountains that form the area's backbone are subject to frequent floods and landslides. Jerry-built housing – both rural and within Messina – contribute to the danger of natural hazards. It is not unusual to read reports of great sections of mountain villages being swept away by flood or landslide, and were a serious earthquake to hit Messina again, the result could be devastating, as the new city was built on the rubble of the old. There is just one exception. Perched on a crag festooned with magenta bougainvillea, and with its dramatic backdrop of mountains and narrow coastal strip, this strange corner of Sicily includes the island's most renowned resort, Taormina. Once the decadent retreat of D.H. Lawrence and Oscar Wilde, Taormina is now the most-visited tourist town on the entire island, and its ancient Greek theatre, grand hotels and engaging small-town charm captivate most visitors.

With railway and motorway running along the narrow strip of land between the Peloritani mountains and the Ionian sea, the coast is for the most part underwhelming, with long grey beaches of fine quartz shingle, and an almost unbroken ribbon of shoddy beach towns. None are very appealing – far better to base yourself at Taormina, whose local beaches are all a short ride below town, including the extensive sands that line the curving bay at the more down-to-earth international resort of Giardini-Naxos.

If you are looking for the Sicily conjured by the *Godfather* films, the dour villages of **Savoca** and **Forza d'Agrò** are worth a visit – not only were most of the Sicilian scenes shot here, but you can take in the area's most gruesome attraction – the mummified bodies on display in Savoca's Cappuccini monastery. Further south, beyond Taormina, the **Alcantara valley**, with its spectacular gorge, is the best target hereabouts for those seeking outdoor adventure; while beguiling, unspoiled **Castiglione di Sicilia** is the hill-town most likely to pull at the heartstrings of those yearning to begin a new life in rural Sicily.

GETTING AROUND
MESSINA, TAORMINA AND THE NORTHEAST

By bus Fast buses are the most convenient link heading west between Messina and Milazzo, the main port for the Aeolian Islands. Travelling south down the coast, local buses get snarled up in the succession of towns and villages along the coast – an excruciatingly slow ride passing pretty much nowhere you would want to stop (or even see). Far better to take one of the fast buses (look for a sign saying via autostrada in the bus window).

By train The line traces the shoreline all the way from Messina to Taormina allowing sparkling views across to Calabria on a clear day.

By road The toll autostradas (the A18 south and A20 west) are the fastest way to get around the northeast, plunging through some fairly dramatic scenery as they cruise above the sea.

VARA AT MESSINA *FERRAGOSTO*

Highlights

❶ Messina by night Climb the Via Panoramica to the floodlit sanctuary of Cristo Re for magical views over the lights of the city and the Straits to mainland Italy. See page 160

❷ Ferragosto in Messina On August 15 the Vara, an opulent silver scaffolding mounted on iron skis showing the Madonna ascending to heaven, is hauled through the streets of Messina's historic centre. See page 163

❸ Casa Cuseni, Taormina Taormina's remarkable heritage as a retreat for the bohemian and marginalised comes to life in this extraordinary house – which includes what may be art history's first depiction of a gay family. See page 170

❹ Teatro Greco, Taormina The island's most dramatically sited classical theatre makes a superb summer venue for concerts, films, opera and classical Greek dramas. See page 170

❺ Cultural Tour of Taormina Tour Taormina in a vintage-style Piaggio pick-up, hearing the stories of the bohemian antics of writers, artists, film stars and philosophers. See page 171

❻ The Gole dell'Alcantara Wade through chalky green water between extraordinary lava rock formations in the deep gorge of the Alcantara River. See page 177

❼ Castiglione di Sicilia Clustered below a castle, this mellow medieval village has a gentle pace of life and great views of Etna. See page 178

HIGHLIGHTS ARE MARKED ON THE MAP ON PAGE 156

Messina

MESSINA may well be your first sight of Sicily, and – from the ferry – it's a dramatic one, the glittering town spread up the hillside beyond the sickle-shaped harbour. Sadly, the image is shattered almost as soon as you step into the city, bombed and shaken to a shadow of its former self by a series of devastating earthquakes. Allied bombing raids in 1943 didn't help, undoing much of the post-earthquake restoration. Messina is one of Sicily's major ports, and the city is at its most atmospheric down by the **harbour**, with its combination of constant activity and compelling vistas over the Straits. Sicily's deepest natural harbour is a port of call for freighters and cruisers of all descriptions, as well as for frequent NATO warships. But the greatest traffic consists of ferries, endlessly plying back and forth, which are Sicily's chief link with the mainland.

Today, the remodelled city guards against future natural disasters, with wide streets and low, reinforced concrete buildings. Few people hang around for long, but if you do need to stay overnight, Messina has a couple of worthwhile sights – the reconstructed Norman **Duomo** and the **Museo Regionale**, home to some of Sicily's best fifteenth- to seventeenth-century art. It's also a good place to be on the feast of the Assumption, or **ferragosto** (Aug 15), when a towering carriage, the Vara – an elaborate column supporting dozens of papier-mâché putti and angels, topped by the figure of Christ – is hauled through the city centre, followed by a firework display on the seafront.

If you're here in summer, you'll notice the passage of tall-masted *felucche*, or **swordfish boats**, patrolling the narrow channel, attracted to these rich waters from many kilometres up and down the Italian coast; you can enjoy their catch the same day in the city. Messina's wide remodelled boulevards, the best of them lined with trees and Liberty or Art Nouveau style *palazzi*, have a certain bourgeois grace, but much of the

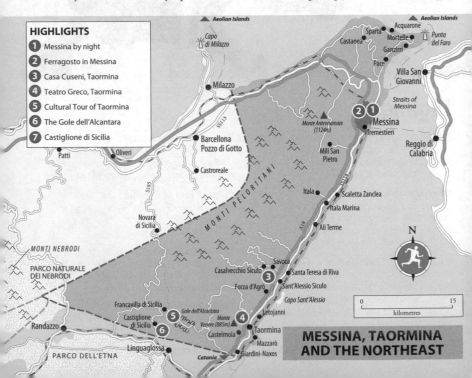

HIGHLIGHTS

1. Messina by night
2. Ferragosto in Messina
3. Casa Cuseni, Taormina
4. Teatro Greco, Taormina
5. Cultural Tour of Taormina
6. The Gole dell'Alcantara
7. Castiglione di Sicilia

MESSINA, TAORMINA AND THE NORTHEAST

THE TRIALS AND TRIBULATIONS OF MESSINA

Messina straddles a faultline which has been responsible for several centuries of catastrophic **earthquakes**. The most devastating ones on record occurred in 1783 and 1908; on the latter occasion the shore sank by half a metre overnight and at least 84,000 Sicilians lost their lives – although as records were destroyed in the earthquake, the figure could be far higher. Few families were untouched by the quake, and almost everyone you meet will have some earthquake story – of miraculous escapes, or of people driven insane by the loss of loved ones and their city – passed down from grand- or great-grandparents. The 1908 earthquake destroyed virtually every building in town (98 percent according to the contemporary seismologist Giuseppe Mercalli), leaving the site of the former city covered by an estimated one million cubic metres of rubble. Several thousand corpses were retrieved and buried, but the majority were never recovered. When the new city was built, its ground level was 2m higher than before.

As if that wasn't enough, the few surviving buildings, along with everything that had been painstakingly reconstructed in the wake of the earthquake, were subsequently the target of **Allied bombardments**, when Messina achieved the dubious distinction of being the most intensely bombed Italian city during World War II.

city centre is given over to charmless buildings, more or less anti-seismic, depending on the honesty of whoever was responsible for their construction.

The Duomo

Piazza del Duomo • Daily 9am–12.30pm & 4–7pm • Free, but campanile €4 or €6 including Treasury

Messina's most important monument, the **Duomo**, epitomizes the city's determination to re-create itself from the ashes of its last disaster. It's the reconstruction of a twelfth-century cathedral erected by Roger II, one of a series of great Norman churches that included the sumptuous cathedrals of Palermo and Cefalù. Formerly, the building dominated medieval Messina, and was the venue for Archbishop Palmer's marriage of Richard the Lionheart's sister Joan to the Norman-Sicilian king, William II. Devastated by the earthquake in 1908, it was rebuilt in the years following World War I, only to fall victim to a firebomb in 1943 that reduced it once more to rubble. What you see today is mostly a faithful copy, which took years to complete, with few elements remaining of the original fabric.

The Romanesque facade is its best aspect, the lower part mostly authentic and dominated by a richly decorated, late Gothic **central portal**, extravagantly pointed and flanked by two smaller contemporary doors. Almost everything in the undeniably grand **interior** is a reproduction, from the marble floor to the elaborately painted wooden ceiling. Two rows of sturdy columns line the nave, topped by carved capitals faithfully copied from originals, some of which survive in the Museo Regionale. The **mosaic work** in the three grand apses holds most interest, though it pales into insignificance beside the island's other examples of the genre, and only the mosaic on the left – of the Virgin Mary with St Lucy – is original. All the same, try to find someone to switch on the lights, as the mosaics then take on a majesty that's entirely lost in the gloom that normally shrouds the cathedral's interior. Little else here predates the twentieth century, apart from some salvaged tombs, most handsome of which is that of Archbishop de Tabiatis from 1333, on the right of the altar and heavily graffitied.

The tesoro

Aug daily 9.30am–1pm, rest of the year usually open for a couple of hours in the morning Mon–Sat 9.30am–1pm • €4, or €6 including campanile

The Duomo's **tesoro** (treasury) holds precious reliquaries, highlight of which is the *Manta d'Oro*, a holy adornment designed to "dress" an icon of the Madonna and Child on special occasions, festooned with jewellery donated by aristocrats and royalty. In a similar decorative vein is the Stendardo banner, designed to be carried in sacred processions and encrusted with brooches, rings, chains, necklaces and even watches.

Fontana di Orione

Piazza del Duomo

In front of the cathedral, the graceful **Fontana di Orione** was daintily carved in the mid-sixteenth century by Montorsoli, a Florentine pupil of Michelangelo. The fountain depicts Orion, the city's mythical founder, surmounting a collection of cherubs, nymphs and giants, and surrounded by four figures (representing the rivers Nile,

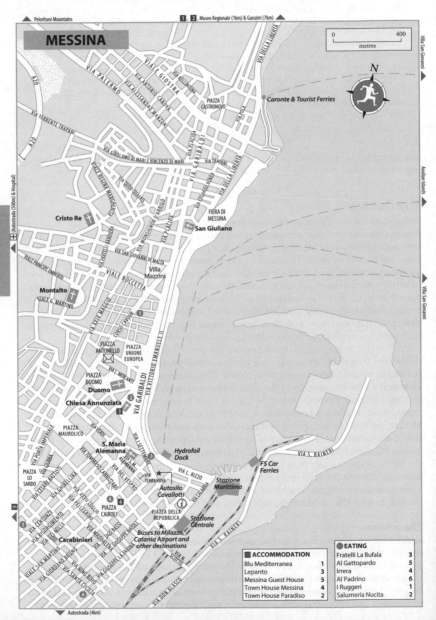

▣ ACCOMMODATION	
Blu Mediterranea	1
Lepanto	3
Messina Guest House	5
Town House Messina	4
Town House Paradiso	2

● EATING	
Fratelli La Bufala	3
Al Gattopardo	5
Irrera	4
Al Padrino	6
I Ruggeri	1
Salumeria Nucita	2

MESSINA'S ROARING CAMPANILE

The Duomo's detached **campanile**, or belltower, claims to be the largest astronomical clock in the world, and puts on its best show at noon every day, when a bronze lion (Messina's ancient emblem) unleashes a mighty roar over the city – quite alarming if you're not expecting it. On the side facing the cathedral two dials show the phases of the planets and the seasons, while above them a globe shows the phases of the moon. The elaborate panoply of moving gilt figures facing the piazza, activated on the hour, half-hour and quarter-hour, ranges from representations of the days of the week and the four Ages of Man to Dina and Clarenza, two semi-legendary women who saved the city from a night attack by the Angevins during the Wars of the Vespers.

You can climb to the top of the tower to enjoy a great **view** of the piazza and city (Jan, Feb closed; March Sun 11am–1pm, April daily 11am–1pm, May Mon–Fri & Sun 10am–1pm & 3.30–5pm, Sat 10.30–1pm, June and July daily 10am–1pm, Tues 9.30am–3.30pm, Aug daily 10am–1pm, Tues 9.30am–4pm, Sept daily 10am–1pm, Tues 9.30am–3.30pm, Oct daily 10am–1pm, Tues 9.30am–3.30pm).

Ebro, Camaro and Tiber) reclining along the balustrade. The upper part was carefully restored after earthquake damage in 1908.

Chiesa Annunziata dei Catalani

Via Garibaldi 111 • Usually Mon–Sat 9.30–11.30am, but often closed; call to check • ☎ 090 675 175

Just back from the Duomo, the truncated section of the twelfth-century **Chiesa Annunziata dei Catalani** squats two metres below the current pavement level of the city (see page 157), and is Messina's only surviving example of an Arab-Norman church. The blind arcading around the apses and the Byzantine-style cupola are the perfect antidote to the ugly cement **facade** surrounding its three portals, and the **interior** is suitably simple, with the transept and apse true to their original construction. In front, a martial statue by the sculptor Andrea Calamecca (Calamech) stands half-hidden under the trees, depicting a proud Don Giovanni of Austria, victor of the Battle of Lepanto – the victorious Christian fleet sailed from Messina in 1535.

Museo Regionale

Via della Libertà 465 • Tues–Sat 9am 7pm (last entry 6.30pm) • €8 • ☎ 090 361 292, ⟨w⟩ blt.ly/museoregionale • Iram #28 to the terminus, Annunziata, or a 45min walk out of town along Via della Libertà; the museum lies on the left, immediately after the Regina Margherita hospital

Messina's **Museo Regionale** is a repository for some of the city's greatest works of art, many of them carefully rescued from earthquake rubble, and includes what is perhaps Sicily's finest collection of Renaissance and Baroque art including an ethereal statue of the Madonna and Child, attributed to Francesco Laurana, and a collection of mainly ecclesiastical silverware, an art at which Messina once excelled.

The collection

There is also some lovely Byzantine work, larded with a helping of Gothic, well evident in a fourteenth-century triptych of the *Madonna with Child between Saints Agatha and Bartholomew*, and a remarkably modern-looking wooden crucifix from the fifteenth century, with a sinuous, tragic Christ. The museum's most famous exhibit, the *St Gregory* polyptych, by Sicily's greatest native artist, **Antonello da Messina**, demonstrates a masterful synthesis of Flemish and Italian Renaissance styles that's an illuminating example of the various influences that reached the port of Messina in the fifteenth century. Striking a very different note is a sixteenth-century statue of *Scilla*, the classical Scylla who terrorized sailors from the Calabrian coast (as described in Homer's *Odyssey*), an alarming spectacle, with contorted face and eyes awash with

MESSINA BY NIGHT

Messina can be particularly beautiful by **night**, especially from the high **Via Panoramica** – from here, with the city at your feet, there's a great view across the Straits to mainland Italy. Via Panoramica changes its name along its route west of the centre from Viale Gaetano Martino to Viale Principe Umberto and Viale Regina Margherita. From the centre, the closest sections of this route, reached on foot, are the Viale Principe Umberto and Viale Regina Margherita stretch, where there are bars and pizzerias around two floodlit sanctuaries (Cristo Re and Montalto) and plenty of scope for pleasant evening strolling.

expression. Sculpted by Montorsoli in 1557, it once formed part of a monumental fountain showing Neptune in the act of calming the seas by chaining up Scylla and her partner in crime, Charybdis. You can see a copy on Piazza Unità d'Italia, overlooking the seafront. Also unmissable are a couple of large shadowy canvases by **Caravaggio**, commissioned by the city in 1609, when he was on the run from the Knights of Malta – a chilling *Raising of Lazarus* and a glowing *Adoration of the Shepherds*.

ARRIVAL AND DEPARTURE

MESSINA

BY TRAIN

Note that for routes to destinations on the Italian mainland there can be a vast difference in time and ticket price depending on which route or type of train you select. Some routes from Messina Centrale include a change of trains at Messina Marittima. If this is the case (all changes are clearly shown if you are booking online) save time by getting on the train at Messina Marittima rather than Messina Centrale – the two stations are contiguous, and you can walk from one to the other in about 8min, simply by following platform 1.

Train stations Arriving by train, disembark at Stazione Centrale, Piazza della Repubblica (unless you're coming on the train ferry from the mainland, in which case you might as well get off at the Stazione Marittima) even if you're changing trains, as it takes a good hour to reassemble trains from the ferry – and walk 100m on to the Stazione Centrale, along platform 1. If arriving from elsewhere in Sicily, with a hydrofoil or ferry to catch, get off at Stazione Centrale and simply walk along the same platform to the Stazione Marittima. The hydrofoil dock is straight across the road from the station entrance. Allow 10min on foot if you have luggage. On no account take a taxi from outside the station – drivers will attempt to charge €15.

Destinations Catania (approximately 1 hourly; 1hr 30min–2hr); Cefalù (almost 1 hourly; 2–3hr); Milazzo (almost 1 hourly; 20–35min); Naples (8 daily; 4–6hr); Rome (7 daily; 5hr 46min–9hr 16min); Palermo (10 daily; 2hr 50min–4hr 20min); Taormina (1–2 hourly; 40min–1hr 10min).

BY BUS

Most local and long-distance buses arrive and depart from Piazza della Republica.

Destinations from Piazza della Republica Catania (11–19 daily Mon–Sat, 8 daily Sun; 1hr 35min–1hr 50min); Catania

airport (9–15 daily Mon–Sat, 8 daily Sun; 1hr 20min–1hr 50min); Giardini-Naxos (8–9 daily Mon–Sat; 45min–2hr); Milazzo (fast service 1 hourly Mon–Sat, 3 daily Sun; 50min); Naples (1 daily; 7hr); Novara di Sicilia (1 daily; 2hr 45min); Palermo (4–8 daily Mon–Sat, 4 daily Sun; 2hr 40min); Patti (1–2 hourly Mon–Sat; 1hr–1hr 20min); Rome (2 daily; 9hr–9hr 20min); Taormina (5–8 daily Mon–Sat, 2 daily Sun; 1hr 45min).

Destinations from Autosilo Cavallotti, Via 1 Settembre Capo d'Orlando (14 daily Mon–Fri, 7 daily Sat); Forza d'Agrò (1 daily Mon–Sat; 1hr 15min); Patti (11 daily Mon–Fri, 6 daily Sat); Santa Teresa di Riva (12 daily Mon–Sat; 1hr).

BY FERRY

Arrivals and tickets Ferries from Villa San Giovanni dock at the Stazione Marittima, apart from Caronte & Tourist ferries which pull in further up, adjacent to Via della Libertà (10min walk north along the harbour). All tickets across the Straits are on sale at the respective terminals (see page 163).

Destinations Salerno (Caronte & Tourist Tues–Sun 1 daily; 9hr); Villa San Giovanni (Bluvia 1–2 hourly, Caronte & Tourist every 20min or every 40min–1hr at night; 20–30min).

BY HYDROFOIL

Arrivals and tickets Hydrofoils (from the Aeolian Islands and Calabria) dock at the terminal in the port area signposted "aliscafi". If you're driving, follow the signposts from the autostrada. There is one hydrofoil daily to the Aeolian Islands throughout the year, and several daily in summer (mid-June to mid-Sept). Hydrofoils (currently ⓦ bluferries.it) to Villa San Giovanni run several times a day throughout the year. Tickets are on sale from company booths at the hydrofoil terminal. Timetables and online booking are available at ⓦ libertylines.it, ⓦ bluferries.it and ⓦ ntacalabria.it.

Destinations Lipari (5 daily June to mid-Sept, 1 daily mid-Sept to May; 1hr 20min–3hr 25min); Panarea (3 daily June to mid-Sept; 2hr 5min); Santa Marina Salina (4 daily June to mid-Sept, 1 daily mid-Sept to May; 2hr–2hr 45min); Stromboli (3 daily June to mid-Sept; 1hr 25min); Villa San Giovanni (14 daily; 20min); Vulcano (3 daily June to mid-Sept, 1 daily mid-Sept to May; 1hr 20min–2hr 50min).

BY CAR
Getting to the centre Driving into Messina, leave the autostrada at the Boccetta exit for the centre and ferries (which are fairly well signposted).

Car rental Avis, Via Garibaldi 231 (☎ 090 679 150, ⓦ avis. co.uk); Maggiore, Via Vittorio Emanuele II 75 (☎ 090 675 476, ⓦ maggiore.it); Sicilcar, Via Garibaldi 187 (☎ 090 46 942, ⓦ sicilcar.net).

BY PLANE
Reggio di Calabria Airport Geographically, Messina's nearest airport is on the mainland outside Reggio di Calabria, on the other side of the Straits (☎ 0965 640 517, ⓦ sogas.it). There's a year-round bus service linking the airport with Reggio's port.

Catania airport With its regular bus links, it is usually far easier to fly into Catania.

GETTING AROUND

By tram You can walk easily from the station or harbour to the centre of town, but to venture anywhere further, take the city's single tram line (#28), running between Annunziata in the north (for the Museo Regionale) to Gazzi in the south, with departures from Piazza della Repubblica, Piazza Cairoli and Piazza Municipio every 10min (30min on Sun).

By bus Useful routes include the #79 to Ganzirri, and the #81/ (81 *barrato*) to Ganzirri and Mortelle, which you can pick up at the Autosilo Cavallotti on Via 1 Settembre.

Bus and tram tickets All city buses and trams are run by ATM (☎ 090 228 5263, ⓦ atm.messina.it), with tickets (€1.20 for 1 journey, €1.25 valid 1h 30min; €1.70 valid 2 journeys per day, or €2.60 all day) available at *tabacchi* and from Autosilo Cavallotti on Via 1 Settembre, the terminal for most services. Tickets can be bought on board for €1.50.

Taxis Ranks at Piazza Cairoli, Piazza della Repubblica, outside Stazione Centrale, and at the Caronte & Tourist terminal; there's also a 24hr Radio Taxi Jolli (☎ 090 6505). Don't pay more than €10 for a journey within the city centre, €15 to the outskirts, and establish a price up front.

INFORMATION

Tourist information The local tourist office is just outside Stazione Centrale on Piazza della Repubblica (Mon & Wed 9am–1pm & 2–5pm, Tues & Thurs 9am–1pm & 3–5pm, Fri 9am–1pm; ☎ 090 772 3701), where English is spoken.

Tours Messina City Sightseeing's Hop On Hop Off open-top red bus takes you around the main sights, as well as out to Ganzirri and Punto Faro, with recorded commentary (April–Nov; €15).

ACCOMMODATION

SEE MAP PAGE 158

Blu Mediterranea Viale Libertà 341 ☎ 090 914 8777, ⓦ blumediterraneobb.com. Three vibrant, pristine rooms in an apartment a little out of town, overlooking the Straits. Though there are no views from the rooms, there is a pleasant inner courtyard (with shower) and Messina's nearest lido is a 10min walk away. There is a tram stop right outside, so whizzing in and out of the centre is easy. **€70**

Lepanto Via Lepanto 7 ☎ 090 669 528, ⓦ bedand breakfastlepantomessina.com. Five rooms in a Liberty *palazzo* overlooking the Catalana church, close to the

---

MESSINA BUS COMPANIES

Most buses depart from Piazza della Repubblica, right outside the Stazione Centrale, where each company has a ticket office. If a ticket office is closed, tickets will be sold on board the buses.

AST ⓦ aziendasicilianatrasporti.it. Departing from Piazza della Repubblica for Novara di Sicilia and Patti.

Giuntabus ⓦ giuntabustrasporti.com. Departing from Piazza della Repubblica for Milazzo.

Interbus ⓦ interbus.it. Departing from Piazza della Repubblica for the coast south to Letojanni and Taormina.

Jonica ⓦ insicilia.com. Departing Autosilo Cavallotti for Forza d'Agrò, Itala, Santa Teresa di Riva and Savoca.

SAIS Autolinee Freephone ⓦ saisautolinee.it. Departing from Piazza della Repubblica for Palermo, Catania and Catania airport, also regular connections to Umbria, Marche, Tuscany, Bologna, Genoa, Venice and Milan.

SAIS Trasporti ⓦ saistrasporti.it. Departing from Piazza della Repubblica for Puglia, Naples and Rome.

TAI/Magistro ⓦ costruzionesitiweb.eu/magistro. Departing from Autosilo Cavallotti on Via 1 Settembre, for Capo d'Orlando and Patti.

4

CROSSING THE STRAITS FROM THE MAINLAND

Crossing the **Straits of Messina** is arguably the most evocative entry into Sicily. The main embarkation point is **Villa San Giovanni**, but you can also travel by hydrofoil from **Reggio di Calabria**, 12km further south towards the tip of Italy's boot.

Caronte & Tourist also operates a ferry service direct to Messina **from Salerno**, leaving once daily all year and taking nine hours; fares are from around €40 for foot passengers, more for an armchair or berth, and from €80 with a car.

TRAVELLING FROM VILLA SAN GIOVANNI

From **Villa San Giovanni** there are two **ferry** services, the state-railway-run Bluvia (☎ 090 678 6478, ⊛ rfi.it) and the private firm Caronte & Tourist (☎ 800 627 414, ⊛ carontetourist.it), and one hydrofoil (*aliscafo*) service run by Bluvia.

Drivers should follow signs from the Villa San Giovanni autostrada exit, a straightforward run with ferry ticket offices clearly marked. The most frequent service is operated by Caronte & Tourist, which has two ticket kiosks en route to the port; the second one, past the railway, can be a bit of a scramble, with nowhere to park. The FS/Bluvia ticket office lies across the square from here, with plenty of parking space. **Tickets** are €38 for a car one-way, or a day-return including driver and four passengers; returns valid for ninety days cost €75 (including driver and four passengers), three-day returns €44 (including driver and four passengers). The queue for boarding involves an average wait of around fifteen minutes – even in the peak times of August and rush hour, it's rarely more than 25 minutes.

Travelling **by train**, you might want to stay on if you're crossing at night (though you'll probably be woken by the clanking din as the train is loaded onto the Bluvia ferry), but by day it's quicker to leave the train at Villa San Giovanni station and skip the shuttling operation, boarding an earlier ferry by foot. In this case, follow the signs from the platform and descend to sea level, where there are ticket offices for Bluvia ferries (one-way tickets €2.50). Overhead signs tell you which bay leads to the first departure, or follow everyone else.

Journey time for crossings is twenty to forty minutes by ferry; hydrofoils take twenty minutes. On ferries, a bar on board serves snacks (including some good *arancini*), coffee and refreshments. Drivers might as well leave their vehicles, though look sharp as the ferry approaches Messina, as disembarkation is a rushed affair.

Duomo, so an excellent location for anyone coming to Messina for a touch of sightseeing. Rooms are comfortable and traditionally furnished, and breakfast is served on site. **€68**

Messina Guest House Via Reitano Spadafora 1 ☎ 090 958 6266, ⊛ guesthousemessina.it. Smart, stylish B&B occupying the first floor of an apartment on the boulevard-like Corso Europa. Rooms are soundproofed, with custom-made contemporary dark-wood fittings and furniture contrasting with creamy upholstery and soft furnishings, and there are prints on the walls by local artist Felice Canonico, a pupil of Guttuso. Bathrooms are spacious, with fabulous showers. **€80**

Town House Messina Via Giordano Bruno 66 ☎ 090 293 6097, ⊛ townhousemessina.it. Bijou B&B just off Piazza Cairoli, with gently minimalist rooms decorated in shades of white, grey and mink, lovely bathrooms (including one with an exposed glass shower) and a changing selection of contemporary art on the walls. The word is out, so it can be difficult to get a room. All rooms have free wi-fi. **€90**

Town House Paradiso Via Consolare Pompea 189 ☎ 320 633 5212, ⊛ townhousemessinaparadiso.it. Four charming rooms in a pretty Liberty-era villa right beside the Straits, owned by the same people who created the wonderful *Town House Messina*. There's not a more peaceful or romantic place to stay in Messina. **€90**

EATING
SEE MAP PAGE 158

Messina has several fairly grotty inexpensive **places to eat around the port and station**, though you should head away from the port for a more relaxed and civilized atmosphere. If you're here in early summer, make a point of sampling the local **swordfish**; May and June are the height of swordfish season. The city is also renowned for its pastries and biscuits, and there's a cluster of classy **pasticcerie** on Piazza Cairoli. For those who are self-catering, Oviesse is a convenient supermarket on Piazza Cairoli (daily 9am–1pm & 4–8pm).

Fratelli La Bufala Corso Vittorio Emanuele 1 ☎ 090 662 513, ⊛ fratellilabufala.eu. A branch of the superior Neapolitan pizza chain committed to using no hydrogenated fats, glutamates or GM ingredients. Handy for the hydrofoil dock, it serves up great pizza (with buffalo mozzarella, of course) along with buffalo-meat *secondi* and Campanian wines. Pizza and a glass of wine for two will be less than €20. Daily lunch & dinner.

★ **Al Gattopardo** Via Santa Cecilia 184 ☎ 090 673 076. With tables outside on a pretty tree-lined avenue overlooked by an exuberant Liberty-era *palazzo*, *Al Gattopardo* is a Messinese institution. The pizzas are some of the best in town (try the Messinese with escarole, mozzarella, anchovies and black pepper; €8), but there are other tempting choices such as raw prawns (€12), *zuppa di cozze* (mussel soup; €9), and a delicious lemon risotto with prawns and *cernia* (grouper; €12.50). Meat is carefully sourced too, and even includes steaks of Irish Angus (€16). Daily lunch & dinner.

Irrera Piazza Cairoli 12 ☎ 090 673 823, ✉ irrera.it. Founded in 1910, this historic *pasticceria* makes typical Sicilian biscuits, cakes, pastries, *cornetti* and *cannoli*, while slick service during lunch (good sandwiches) and at aperitivo hour make this a popular spot throughout the day. Daily 8am–8.30pm.

Al Padrino Via S. Cecilia 54–56 ☎ 090 292 1000. This bare, frill-free neighbourhood *trattoria* specializes in traditional Sicilian dishes, such as *maccu*, *melanzane al Padrino* (aubergines stuffed with fresh pasta and ricotta) and *pasta con legumi riposata* (pasta with beans, left to rest a while after cooking so that broth thickens and flavour develops), both €6–8. A three-course meal with house wine should cost under €25. Mon–Sat lunch & dinner.

I Ruggeri Via Pozzoleone 21 ☎ 090 343 938. Wonderful place in the heart of Messina where local produce and traditions are creatively interwoven with contemporary tastes – there are even some marvellous oriental fusion dishes, a rare thing indeed in Sicily. The raw fish tartares are spectacular – try the tuna and shrimp – and pasta dishes include spaghetti with *neonati* (whitebait), and *trofie* (short, thin twists of pasta) with clams – both are delicious. With carefully sourced and deftly cooked meat as well as fish on the *secondi* menu, it can be hard to choose. Expect to pay around €35 per person for a full meal, excluding wine. Open Mon–Fri lunch & dinner, Sat dinner only, Sun lunch only.

Salumeria Nucita Via Garibaldi 125 ☎ 090 657 243. Tasty panini and other cold snacks are on offer at this *alimentari*. Mon–Wed & Sat 9am–1pm & 4–8pm, Thurs 9am–1pm.

ENTERTAINMENT

Exhibitions and classical concerts take place near the port at the church of Santa Maria Alemanna (Via I Settembre), while free **concerts** are staged in Piazza del Duomo in July and August. July and Aug also see free **film screenings** (usually at 8.30pm), usually in the Villa Mazzini public gardens near the hydrofoil dock, or nearby next to the church of San Giuliano off Via della Libertà, around the Fiera di Messina – though venues may change. If films are showing, arrive early, as these events tend to get crowded. Ask at the tourist office for details of all of the above events.

DIRECTORY

Hospital Ospedale Policlinico, Via Consolare Valeria 1 (☎ 090 2211); take the tram to the Bonino terminus. For emergencies call ☎ 113.

Pharmacy There's an all-night service on a rotating basis: consult any pharmacy window to find out current *farmacie notturne*.

Police Carabinieri, Via dei Mille (☎ 112 or ☎ 090 771 332); *questura* (police headquarters), Via Placida 2, near Villa Mazzini (☎ 113 or ☎ 090 3661).

Post office Main office at Corso Cavour 138, behind Piazza Duomo (Jan–July & Sept–Dec Mon–Fri 8.20am–7.05pm, Sat 8am–12.35pm.

FERRAGOSTO

If you're in Messina in midsummer, you might catch the festivals around the Feast of the Assumption, or **ferragosto**. Although all the villages on both sides of the Straits hold festivals around this time, with some pretty spectacular fireworks lighting up the sky on any one night, Messina's festivities are grander, beginning around August 12, when two plaster **giganti** (giants) are wheeled around town, and finally stationed near the port opposite the Municipio. These are said to be Messina's two founders, Mata and Grifone, one a white female, the other a burly Moor, and both mounted on huge steeds. On *ferragosto* itself, August 15, another towering carriage, the **Vara**, is hauled through the city centre. It's an elaborate column supporting dozens of papier-mâché cherubs and angels, culminating in the figure of Christ stretching out his right arm to launch Mary on her way to heaven. This unwieldy construction, which sits on iron skis, is towed on long ropes, pulled by hundreds of penitents – semi-naked if they're men, all in white if they're women – with water chucked down to ease its progress, and cheered on by thousands of people along the way. The whole thing is a sweaty and frenetic performance, finishing up at Piazza del Duomo, where flowers are thrown out to the crowds, many of whom risk being crushed in the mad scramble to gather these luck-bearing charms. Late at night, one of Sicily's best **firework displays** is held on the seafront near Via della Libertà.

The road to Punta del Faro

Several coastal destinations are less than thirty minutes from the centre of Messina by bus or car. If you're driving, you might wish to follow the high-level **Via Panoramica** north rather than the congested coastal road. You can enjoy the fresh fish and shellfish at **Ganzirri**, where gaudy lakeside fish restaurants provide some relief from the city. Beyond is the little resort of **Punta del Faro**, dominated by its lighthouse, while lidos line the coast at **Mortelle**, whose beaches, bars and pizzerias are where the city's bronzed youth come to relax.

Ganzirri

Wedged between a salt lake (where mussels are farmed) and the sea, 10km north of central Messina, is the ramshackle fishing village of **GANZIRRI**. Messinese flock here in summer to eat fresh shellfish, swordfish or whatever else has been hauled in that day by the many boats operating on the lake and in the Straits. It's a pleasant spot for a meal, though prices can be high and quality variable. Bear in mind too that traffic can be hell in the summer – whether you get here by bus or car, expect to spend quite some time in jams. Most of the **trattorias** are squeezed in between the lake and sea, and you can eat outside at nearly all of them.

ARRIVAL AND DEPARTURE

GANZIRRI

By bus Buses #79, #80 and #81 run regularly to Ganzirri from Messina, taking between 20min and 1hr, depending on traffic.

EATING

La Sirena di Mancuso At Via Lago Grande 96 ☏ 090 391 268. No frills place, with lake views from its covered veranda. It's no temple of gastronomy, so go for something simple, like a plate of Ganzirri mussels 'impepata' (with black pepper). Mon, Tues & Thurs–Sun lunch & dinner.

Punta del Faro

Punta del Faro (also called Capo Peloro) is the very tip of Sicily, the nearest point to mainland Italy, and on summer evenings it's the venue for open-air **free films**. The lighthouse here (the *faro*) is dwarfed by one of the two towering electric pylons that flank either side of the Straits. No longer in use (Sicily is now tethered to the mainland electricity grid by underwater cables), the pylons remain a much-loved landmark, decked out with multicoloured lights each Christmas. Here, too, was the whirlpool where the legendary **Charybdis** once posed a threat to sailors – along with the rock of Scylla on the opposite shore – still remembered in the locality's name of Cariddi.

ON THE *GODFATHER* TRAIL

Many scenes from Francis Ford Coppola's **Godfather** movies were filmed in Savoca and Forza d'Agrò, both forbidding little villages fused to jagged peaks with beetling views down to the sea below. Corleone, the actual setting of Mario Puzo's novel, was not deemed sufficiently picturesque. Fans of the film are spoilt for choice when it comes to **guided tours** of locations: key stopoffs are **Bar Vitelli** in Savoca, which displays a collection of photographs taken during the filming of *The Godfather II* – the table where Michael Corleone sat to ask the *padrone* for the hand of his delightful daughter Apollonia is still in situ. You can also see the Chiesa Madre in the piazza, where they married on screen. The best tours continue to the crows' nest village of **Forza d'Agrò**, perched on a spur of the Peloritani mountains high above the sea (see page 166), which featured in the third *Godfather* movie.

For a tour run by enthusiastic, well-informed English-speaking guides contact Sicily Travel (☏ 360 397 930, ⓦ sicilytourguides.net/Godfather_tour.htm).

Savoca and around

Around 30km south of Messina, the small resort of Santa Teresa di Riva is the jumping-off point for the evocatively situated villages of **SAVOCA** – a must for fans of *The Godfather* – and **Casalvecchio Siculo**. Savoca sits at the end of a winding 4km run up from the coast, its houses and three churches perched on the cliffsides in clumps, and with a tattered castle (originally Saracen) topping the pile. Two pincer-like streets, Via San Michele and Via Chiesa Madre, reach around to their respective churches, the grandest being the square-towered thirteenth-century **Chiesa Madre**. Seated on a tiny ridge between two opposing hills, it's a fine vantage point from which to look down the valley to the sea and across the surrounding hills. Spare a glance, too, at the house next door, lovingly restored and displaying a fifteenth-century stone-arched double window; one of many in the village that have had a facelift as outsiders move in to snap up run-down cottages as second homes. These days, Savoca lies within the Taormina commuter belt and most of the people who live here work elsewhere. That's to its advantage: during the day the streets and hillside alleys are refreshingly empty, and the medieval atmosphere still intact.

Cappuccini monastery

April 1–Oct 31 daily 9.30am–7.30pm; Nov 1–March 31 Tues–Sun 9.30am–5pm • Donations requested

Signs in Savoca point you to the **Cappuccini monastery (Convento dei Cappuccini)**, whose **catacombs** contain a spooky selection of mummies. These are the remains of local lawyers, doctors and the clergy: two hundred to three hundred years old, they stand in niches dressed in their eighteenth-century finery, the skulls of less complete colleagues lining the walls above. An added grotesque touch is the green paint with which the bodies have been daubed, the work of vandals and hard to remove without damaging the cadavers. Ask the custodian and you'll probably be shown the church **treasury** as well, which holds a small collection of liturgical books and seventeenth- and eighteenth-century Bibles.

Casalvecchio Siculo

The only road beyond Savoca along the ridge runs 2km to **CASALVECCHIO SICULO**, which has even better views of the valley from its terraces. There's not much to detain you here, except the quiet village atmosphere, but walk through Casalvecchio and, after about 500m, a rough (signposted) road drops away to the left, snaking down into a lush, citrus-planted valley. It's about a twenty-minute hike to the Norman monastery of **Santi Pietro e Paolo**, gloriously situated on a high bank above the river. Built in the twelfth century, its battlemented facade and double domes are visible from a distance through the lemon groves. Though considered Sicily's best example of Basilian architecture, the church betrays a strong Arabic influence, particularly in the polychromatic patterns of the exterior. If it's locked, there should be someone around in one of the adjacent buildings with a key.

From the church, either head back up to the main road and wait for the return bus to pass, or continue downhill for a longer **walk**, beyond the monastery to the River Agrò. It's about another hour's tramp, alongside the wide (and mostly dry) riverbed to Rina, back towards the sea. The main (SS114) coastal road is signposted from Rina, and in another twenty minutes, through a small tunnel, you're back in Santa Teresa di Riva, on the Messina–Catania bus route.

ARRIVAL AND DEPARTURE   **SAVOCA AND AROUND**

By bus Jonica buses (Mon–Sat only) connect Messina with Santa Teresa di Riva, from where there are six connections daily to Savoca. From Taormina, take an Interbus service to Santa Teresa Riva and change there for Savoca and Casalvecchio.

Forza d'Agrò

The nicest spot on the coast south of Messina is the **Capo Sant'Alessio**, where a pinnacle cliff supports a sturdy castle; you can climb up to it, but you can't get in. Four kilometres inland of here, atop a corkscrew road, is **FORZA D'AGRÒ**. Like so many Sicilian villages, it's a breezy place defiantly crumbling all around its mostly elderly inhabitants, and with little left of the Norman **castello** that crowns it. A memorable clamber will take you up to the top: the streets become ever more perilous, and the stone cottages increasingly neglected and held together by rotting spars of wood. The lower parts of the village are better maintained, but not much – shops are tucked into tiny cottage interiors, and a couple of churches are locked and decrepit.

Still, this is close enough to Taormina to attract tour buses, which deposit their passengers in the village square, where there are a couple of bars to help idle the time away.

ARRIVAL AND DEPARTURE FORZA D'AGRÒ

By bus Four daily Interbus services run to Forza d'Agrò from Taormina.

ACCOMMODATION AND EATING

O Dammuseddu Via Heros Cuzari 2 ☎ 0942 98 030. The perfect hill-town restaurant. Go for the abundant house *antipasto*, then follow with a wild mushroom dish, or some herby grilled meat. Expect to spend around €25 for a meal with house wine. Daily lunch & dinner.

Villa Souvenir Viale delle Rimembranze ☎ 0942 721 078. If you're tempted to overnight in Forza d'Agrò, the small and simple *Villa Souvenir* hotel is a reasonable option. It also has a decent restaurant, with half-board deals (from €45) available on request. Doubles **€65**

Taormina

TAORMINA, dominating two grand, sweeping bays from high on Monte Tauro, is Sicily's best-known and classiest resort. Although it has no beach of its own – they are all sited quite a way below town – the outstanding remains of the classical **Teatro Greco** and the sheer beauty of the town's site, framed by a distant Etna, amply compensate. Beloved of writers, artists and celebrities across the decades, it's an expensive place, but the air of exclusivity at least is only skin-deep – at heart, what was once a small hill-village still can't seem to believe its good luck. Much of its late medieval character remains intact, with the one main traffic-free street presenting an unbroken line of aged *palazzi*, flower-decked alleys and intimate piazzas. The downside is that most of the time, and particularly between June and September and at New Year and Easter, Taormina simply seethes as the narrow alleys are filled shoulder-to-shoulder with tourists. Things get a little quieter in winter, and this is also the time when the views of Etna – snowcapped to boot – are incomparably clearer, while the spring brings flamboyant hillside displays of flowering plants and shrubs. Entering Taormina's old centre from Porta Messina, you'll find yourself immediately on the town's axis, Corso Umberto I, magnificently heralded by the turreted **Palazzo Corvaja**.

Palazzo Corvaja

Corso Umberto I · **Museo Siciliano di Arti e Tradizioni Popolari** Tues–Sun 10am–1pm & 4–8pm · €3 · ☎ 0942 610 274

Palazzo Corvaja began life back in the tenth century as a defensive tower built by the Arabs. The tower still forms the body of the *palazzo*, while in the courtyard, Arab-style ogival windows harmonize perfectly with Gothic elements such as a staircase crowned by a Romeo-and-Juliet-style balcony.

ISOLA BELLA

Within Palazzo Corvaja is the chamber where the so-called Sicilian "parliament"– actually a group of Aragonese nobles – met in 1410 to choose the next king. It now houses the tourist office (see page 172) and the engaging **Museo Siciliano di Arti e Tradizioni Popolari**, a collection of quirky folkloric items ranging from painted Sicilian carts to cork-and-wax Nativity scenes. One of the highlights is the 25 panel paintings of the 1860s showing people being saved by miraculous

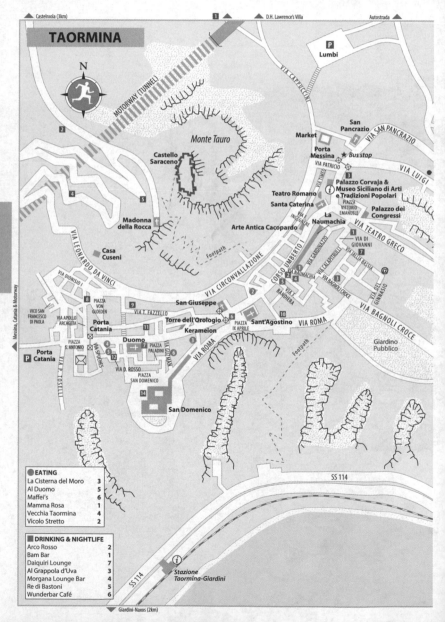

TAORMINA

EATING
La Cisterna del Moro	3
Al Duomo	5
Maffei's	6
Mamma Rosa	1
Vecchia Taormina	4
Vicolo Stretto	2

DRINKING & NIGHTLIFE
Arco Rosso	2
Bam Bar	1
Daiquiri Lounge	7
Al Grappola d'Uva	3
Morgana Lounge Bar	4
Re di Bastoni	5
Wunderbar Café	6

intervention from such terrible fates as falling onto a stove or being attacked by cats.

Santa Caterina

Corso Umberto 1 • Daily 9am–8pm (closes earlier in winter) • Free

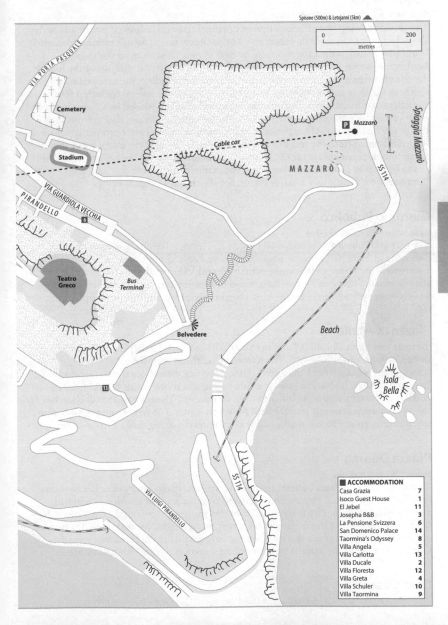

ACCOMMODATION	
Casa Grazia	7
Isoco Guest House	1
El Jebel	11
Josepha B&B	3
La Pensione Svizzera	6
San Domenico Palace	14
Taormina's Odyssey	8
Villa Angela	5
Villa Carlotta	13
Villa Ducale	2
Villa Floresta	12
Villa Greta	4
Villa Schuler	10
Villa Taormina	9

Opposite Palazzo Corvaja, the church of **Santa Caterina** was built almost on top of a small, brick-built odeon, known as the **Teatro Romano** (originally used for musical recitations): peer down at it through the railings around the back, and then enter the church to take a closer look at bits of the theatre exposed in the floor of the nave.

Teatro Greco

Via del Teatro Greco • Daily 9am until 1hr before sunset • €10

The crowds flowing from Piazza Vittorio Emanuele past an unbroken parade of tourist shops will point you towards Taormina's **Teatro Greco**, one of Sicily's unmissable sights – and best visited in the early morning or near closing time to avoid the throngs. Nothing, however, can detract from the site's natural beauty. Carved out of the hillside, the theatre offers a complete panorama of the Sicilian coastline, the mountains of southern Calabria across the water and of Etna – a glorious natural backdrop for the audiences of classical times. Despite its name, and though founded by Greeks in the third century BC, the existing remains are almost entirely Roman, dating from the end of the first century AD, a period when Taormina enjoyed great prosperity under Imperial Roman rule. The reconstruction completely changed the character of the theatre, though not always for the better – the arched apertures, niches and columns of the impressive Roman scene-building, for example, must have obscured the views of Etna that were presumably a major reason for the theatre's original siting.

Giardino Pubblico

Via Bagnoli Croce • Daily dawn–dusk • Free

The **Giardino Pubblico** were endowed by a Scot, Florence Trevelyan, who settled in Taormina in 1899 having been "invited" to leave England in the wake of a romantic liaison with the Prince of Wales, the future Edward VII. She also contributed the curious *apiari* ("beehives") – pavilions, variously resembling rustic log cabins and stone- or brick-built pagodas, which now hold caged birds, plants and a children's play area.

Piazza IX Aprile

Tourists and locals all collide bang in the middle of Corso Umberto I at **Piazza IX Aprile**, Taormina's "balcony". The restored twelfth-century Torre dell'Orologio (clocktower) straddles the Corso here, while sweeping views from the terrace overlook Etna and the bay. It's hard to resist the lure of a café seat here – just be warned that you'll be presented with a big bill, even for an espresso. There are two small churches in the square: squat fifteenth-century **Sant'Agostino** is now a library, while **San Giuseppe**'s seventeenth-century facade is adorned with plaques depicting skulls and crossbones.

Piazza Duomo

Duomo Daily 8.30am–8pm • Free

Taormina's intimate **Piazza Duomo**, set on a quirky slant, makes it very clear just how small-scale Taormina was until fairly recently. Entered via an arch in the clocktower, and with a pretty seventeenth-century fountain in its centre, the square contains the battlemented **Duomo**, originally built in the thirteenth century, though much restored since. The interior is simple – the pink marble columns along the nave are thought to have come from the Greek theatre, while the beamed wooden ceiling is decorated with Arab-Gothic motifs.

Casa Cuseni

Via Leonardo da Vinci 5–7 ☎ 0942 28725, ⓦ casacuseni.it. Guided tours daily at 11.30am, reserve in advance • €15

A CULTURAL TOUR OF TAORMINA

As part of the Taobuk International Book Festival (see page 174) a fascinating itinerary has been created, with 21 sites – ranging from houses to hotels to a former casino and the railway station – connected with artists, writers, photographers, film-stars and film-makers who have visited, lived, worked or been inspired by Taormina. Perhaps the most interesting is D.H. Lawrence, who lived in Taormina for three years in the 1920s and wrote many of his short stories and essays here, including much of *Lady Chatterley's Lover*, which was supposed to have been inspired by the exploits of an Englishwoman living in Taormina who had fallen for a local farmer. Lawrence wasn't always enamoured of the town; in a letter of December 1921 he described Corso Umberto as "one long parade of junk shops … things dearer than ever, more faked, food tiresome as it always was. If only Etna would send down 60,000,000 tons of boiling lava over the place and cauterise it away." Oscar Wilde, still raw from his break-up with Bosey, was rather more enthusiastic, calling the town 'a paradise of lovers', an opinion the German artist Wilhelm Von Gloeden clearly agreed with – he turned his attention to the town's beautiful boys, photographing them in homoerotic scenes inspired by Classical art.

Outside every site on the trail is a plaque, in English and Italian, full of offbeat anecdotes. Maps are not easy to get hold of, but if you start at Casa Cuseni, then walk along the Circonvallazione, Via Pirandello, Via Bagnoli Croce, Via Roma and then up Corso Umberto and off to the Greek Theatre, you will pass most of the sights.

Casa Cuseni (Robert Kitson, Frank Brangwyn, Ezra Pound, Bertrand Russell, Henry Faulkner, Tennessee Williams, Roald Dahl, Greta Garbo, Giacomo Ballà)

Hotel San Domenico (Monica Vitti, Jean Reno, Luc Besson, Roberto Benigni, Rudyard Kipling, John Steinbeck)

Von Gloeden's Studio (a garage behind the San Domenico, where the infamous gay photographer worked)

Hotel Victoria (Oscar Wilde)

Fontana Vecchia (D.H. Lawrence, Peggy Guggenheim, Truman Capote, Christian Dior)

4

In 1897, Robert Kitson, an artist and architect from Leeds, arrived in Taormina and fell in love immediately with what was then simply a small medieval hill-town surrounded by walls in an extraordinary location. Kitson was gay, homosexuality was a crime in the UK (Oscar Wilde had recently been imprisoned) and in Sicily, living on the margins of society, he found a freedom he could never dream of in England. He bought a mountainside of orange and almond trees and, with his friend the artist Frank Brangwyn, he designed and built Casa Cuseni. When Kitson died, the house was inherited by his niece, Daphne Phelps, who managed to hang on to it by turning it into a guesthouse for the artists, writers and philosophers – ranging from Bertrand Russell and Picasso to Roald Dahl and Greta Garbo – who formed part of her circle. Phelps wrote engagingly about the house, its visitors and the experience of living in Taormina in the immediate post war years in her book, *A House in Sicily*.

Casa Cuseni can still be visited (and it still runs as a B&B). Evocative guided tours include the dining room, frescoed by Brangwyn with what is probably the first depiction in art of a gay family – Kitson and his partner adopted a child after the Messina earthquake of 1908 – along with works of art (including a Picasso) donated by artists to Phelps, and a wonderful library where you can see the desk where Dahl wrote *Charlie and the Chocolate Factory*, and hear tales of how he would read every evening to then housekeeper's young daughter.

ARRIVAL AND DEPARTURE | TAORMINA

By train One of Italy's most attractive stations, in Sicilian-Gothic style with Art Nouveau decoration, Taormina-Giardini train station is way below town, on the water's edge. To get up to town, you either need to take a taxi (€20) or catch one of the Interbus services leaving once or twice hourly (fewer on Sun) from outside the station; buy your ticket from the driver.

Destinations Catania (1–2 hourly; 45min–1hr); Messina (1–2 hourly; 40min–1hr); Siracusa (4–7 daily; 2hr–2hr 30min).

A WALK TO THE CASTELLO SARACENO

It's well worth taking a walk up above Taormina to the clifftop chapel of **Madonna della Rocca** and the remains of the town's tumbledown medieval **Castello Saraceno**. There are glorious views over Teatro Greco and the town towards the coast, and a couple of restaurants and cafés here that are perfect for a sundowner. Buses taking just a few minutes run up the winding road once or twice hourly from town, but it's more evocative to walk up – there's a steep processional path to the chapel (signposted "Castel Taormina/Via Crucis") from Via Circonvallazione, starting just past the Q8 petrol station, and taking around twenty minutes.

By bus Most buses stop in Taormina's bus station on Via Luigi Pirandello. Buses to the Alcantara and Randazzo leave from outside the train station, while local bus services depart hourly from Piazza San Pancrazio up to Madonna della Rocca (for the castle) and Castelmola, and down to the beach at Spisone/Letojanni.

Destinations Castelmola (1 hourly Mon–Sat, 9 daily Sun; 15min); Castiglione di Sicilia (2 daily Mon–Sat; 1hr 20min); Catania (1 hourly Mon–Sat, 12 daily Sun; 1hr 10min–1hr 50min); Catania airport (1 hourly Mon–Sat, 11 daily Sun; 1hr 25min); Forza d'Agrò (2 daily; 40min); Francavilla di Sicilia (3 daily Mon–Sat, 1 daily Sun; 1hr); Giardini-Naxos (1–2 hourly Mon–Sat, every 1–2hr Sun; 15min); Gole dell'Alcantara (4 daily Mon–Sat, 1 daily Sun; 1hr); Messina (6–7 daily Mon–Sat, 2 daily Sun; 55min–1hr 45min); Santa Teresa di Riva (8–9 daily Mon–Sat, 3 daily Sun; 35min).

By cable car The *funivia* to Mazzarò departs from Via Luigi Pirandello, between Porta Messina and the bus terminal.

GETTING AROUND

By taxi There are ranks at the train station (though there are not always taxis present, so best to book one to meet you on arrival in advance), at Porta Catania (☎0942 628 090), in Piazza San Pancrazio and in Piazza Vittorio Emanuele (☎0942 23 000).

Car and scooter rental Supply can outstrip demand in Taormina, and for car rental, you'll get better prices booking through a broker site online in advance, such as ⓦholidayautos. co.uk. California, Via Bagnoli Croce, 86 (☎0942 23 760, ⓦcaliforniarentcar.com) will book you a scooter in advance.

INFORMATION AND TOURS

Tourist information There's a small tourist office (Mon–Fri 9am–2pm; ☎0942 52 189) in the train station, and another inside Palazzo Corvaja, off Piazza Vittorio Emanuele (Mon–Fri 8.30am–2pm & 3.30–7pm; ☎0942 23 243).

Tours Top of the town tours are the Taormina Cult tours in gorgeous cream vintage-style Piaggio Apes, taking you around the sites on the literary tour (see page 171) but with enthusiastic and knowledgeable guides that know how to bring history to life. If you are using Taormina as a base to explore Sicily, there are **tours** to Etna, the Alcantara gorge and Siracusa, or further afield to places like the Valley of the Temples and Piazza Armerina. The tourist office and hotels have flyers.

ACCOMMODATION SEE MAP PAGE 168

Nowhere in Sicily can match Taormina for its range of gorgeously sited places to stay (many of them elegant old villas) with sweeping views of sea and mountain. Although there are excellent deals to be had online if you **book in advance**, prices can be steep if you arrive on spec. Drivers should enquire whether their hotel has parking facilities, as otherwise cars have to be left in one of the car parks (see box).

HOTELS

Isoco Guest House Via Salita Branco 2 ☎0942 23 679, ⓦisoco.it. The five rooms in this small boutique hotel are quirkily themed around such artists as Botticelli and Keith Haring, and each has its own entrance, a/c, safe and minibar, with a private bathroom across the corridor. Amazing breakfasts are served round a large table in the shady garden, where there's also a hot tub, while the roof terrace has sunbeds and views extending north up the coast as far as Calabria. Free wi-fi. No credit cards. Closed Dec–Feb. **€132**

El Jebel Salita Palazzo Ciampoli ☎0942 625 494, ⓦhoteljebel.com. A shrine to conspicuous consumption, with nine suites occupying three floors of a dandified fifteenth-century *palazzo* up from the main corso. Inside it's all very Hollywood-Dubai: lavish bathrooms caked in treacly, liquorice-veined marble, gold taps, claw-foot baths and enough mirrors to make narcissists feel right at home. The rooms themselves are more subdued, spacious and very comfortable. Service is slick, and waiter-served breakfasts exceptional. Expect to feel exceedingly (but discreetly) pampered, especially at the spa. **€340**

La Pensione Svizzera Via Luigi Pirandello 26 ☎0942 23 790, ⓦpensionesvizzera.com. Just up from the bus terminal and cable-car station, this comfortable hotel has lovely views from its spacious rooms (with prices increasing by €5–10 for a sea view), 24hr bar service, free wi-fi throughout and a shuttle to a private beach. Great value for money. €121

San Domenico Palace Piazza San Domenico 5 ☎0942 613 111, ⊛san-domenico-palace.com. One of the most celebrated hotels in Italy, this "palace" is housed in a fifteenth-century convent with gorgeous formal gardens, unsurpassable views and a Michelin-starred restaurant. As this book went to press, it was undergoing a major renovation – check the website for updates.

★**Villa Angela** Via Leonardo da Vinci ☎0942 27 038, ⊛hotelvillaangela.com. Ever wondered what rock stars do in their spare time? Jim Kerr of Simple Minds, a devotee of Taormina, plumped for opening a four-star boutique hotel, high on the Castelmola road above town. It's a swish, contemporary take on a traditional villa, with terrific views from soaring picture windows, a pool and a terrace restaurant. The staff are especially friendly. It's a steep walk from Taormina itself, but there's an efficient shuttle to town and beach, and a bus stop directly outside. €282

Villa Carlotta Via Luigi Pirandello 81 ☎0942 626 058, ⊛hotelvillacarlottataormina.com. Splendidly sited above the sea among abundant subtropical vegetation – the roof garden has views of Mount Etna and the sea (very romantic and candlelit at night), and a terraced garden with a small pool is set among citrus and olive trees, bougainvillea and mint, and lies between the walls of an old chapel and the remains of a Romano-Byzantine cemetery. There's a comfortable, homely sitting room with books, games and snooze-inducing sofas, and all the stylish rooms except one have bathtubs. The website has a useful calendar showing the best prices by the day – a great way of picking up a bargain. €250

★**Villa Ducale** Via Leonardo da Vinci, 60 ☎0942 28153, ⊛villaducale.com. Luxurious enclave with a relaxed vibe set on narrow terraces high above Taormina with sumptuous rooms, stunning views, a pretty pool, outstanding Sicilian food and a wizard cocktail creator. A series of steep stepways and paths cut down to Taormina, though there is also a free shuttle service. €309

Villa Schuler Piazzetta Bastione ☎0942 23 481, ⊛hotelvillaschuler.com. This lovely old hotel has been in the same family of German émigrés for a century, and retains the feel of an elegant family-run *pensione* (they take no tour groups). Decor retains a quiet vintage feel, without being overstated, there are great views from its rooms and terrace, and a beautiful garden behind. €256

Villa Taormina Via Tommaso Fazzello 39 ☎0942 620 072, ⊛hotelvillataormina.com. A superior four-star that oozes old-fashioned charm – and with only eight antique-filled rooms, the feel is more private house party than hotel. It's also blessedly quiet, off the main drag, and with a terrace that has a hot tub and excellent views. Parking and beach shuttle available. Closed Nov–Feb. €300

B&BS AND HOSTEL

Casa Grazia Via Iallia Bassia 20 ☎0942 24 776. You won't find accommodation much cheaper than this in the centre, nor with such positively mothering management. Most of the basic but clean rooms have fridges, private bathrooms and balconies – the best ones are at the top, with use of a panoramic terrace. No breakfast. Free wi-fi. No credit cards. €60

Josepha B&B Vico Zecca 31 ☎0942 628 871 or ☎348 844 2971. Set in a little courtyard, through a hacked-out archway immediately inside the Porta Messina, this has two doubles and two singles, sharing two bathrooms. There's also a kitchen, a terrace and laundry facilities for guests. It's pretty flexible, since families or groups can rent all or part of the building. Breakfast is taken at a nearby bar. No credit cards. €70

Taormina's Odyssey Via Paternò di Biscari 13 ☎0942 24 533 or ☎349 810 7733, ⊛taorminaodyssey.com. Near Porta Catania, this homely and comfortable place is more of a B&B than a hostel, with four double rooms (some with bunk beds; €48) and two dorms. All rooms have a/c and TV, and there's a kitchen and even a terrace. It is understandably popular, so book well ahead. Dorms €20–24, doubles €60

Villa Floresta Via Damiano Rosso 1 ☎0942 620 184 or ☎331 708 0115, ⊛villafloresta.it. Pleasant, family-run B&B in a nineteenth-century *palazzo*, tucked into a courtyard with a crumbling fifteenth-century staircase behind Piazza del Duomo. Most rooms have balconies, with a choice between a view of the sea or the Duomo. €75

PARKING IN TAORMINA

Unless there's parking at your hotel, drivers will have to use one of the long-stay **car parks** signposted on the approaches to Taormina, notably outside Porta Catania at the southwestern end of town or at the Lumbi car park northeast of the centre; Lumbi car park is further from the centre, and is a lengthy walk up steps to Via Cappuccini, though a free **minibus service** (*bus navetta*) shuttles from Piazza San Pancrazio (just below Porta Messina) to and from the Lumbi car park and saves you the 10min climb. Alternatively, park near the coast at Mazzarò, and take the cable car up to town. **Sample tariffs** are €1 for 1 hour, €5 for 2 hours, €14 for 24 hours, €26 for 48 hours but are higher at all car parks over the Easter weekend and throughout August.

4

Villa Greta Via Leonardo da Vinci 41 ☎0942 28 286, ⓦvillagreta.it. A 15min walk out of town on the road up to Castelmola, this family-run place has superb balcony views, as well as a dining room with home cooking. In winter, there's tea with complimentary home-made cakes and biscuits. €93

EATING

SEE MAP PAGE 168

Eating out in Taormina can be very expensive, though there are plenty of places offering competitively priced set menus. While there are lots of **restaurants**, menus are standard across the board, although a few at the top end stand out as special. Because of the demand, **pizzas** are widely available here at lunchtime too (unlike most other places in Sicily).

La Cisterna del Moro Via Bonifacio 1 ☎0942 23 001. An all-day pizza joint – they are thin-based and crisp – though with the low lights and a bougainvillea-draped terrace it's also a romantic spot for local couples on a night out. Pizzas €6.50–12. Daily noon–midnight; closed Nov.

Al Duomo Vico Ebrei 11 ☎0942 625 656. Pleasant restaurant with a commitment to local ingredients and local dishes such as spaghetti with squid ink and ricotta, seafood spaghetti and a risotto with citrus-spiked red prawns. There are good meat dishes too, featuring locally sourced black pig and game. Count on spending at least €45 a head for three courses without wine. There's a delightful terrace above the Duomo square and a simple, pretty interior. Daily lunch & dinner; closed Mon Nov–March.

Maffei's Via San Domenico de Guzman 1 ☎0942 24 055, ⓦristorantemaffeis.com. If you want one really memorable fish meal, this formal restaurant is the place. From sea bass to lobster, the day's specials are written on the board, while oysters, sea urchins, pastas and carpaccios are offered as appetizers. English-speaking staff guide you through the menu, and all you can hear on the bougainvillea-covered terrace is the gentle clatter of cutlery and contented murmurs. It's small, so book ahead in the evening, and expect to spend at least €40 a head without wine. Daily lunch & dinner.

Mamma Rosa Via Naumachia 10 ☎0942 24 361. This does a roaring trade in *forno a legna* pizzas (€6.50–10), served at tables that down the stepped alley. There's also a full menu, though you'll easily pay €30 a head for a couple of courses and glass of wine. Daily lunch & dinner; closed Tues Nov–Feb.

Vecchia Taormina Vico Ebrei 3 ☎0942 625 589. Bustling pizzeria with a stack of olive wood outside the door for the fire, and tables outside in a sheltered courtyard. Pizzas (from €7.50) are light, crispy and blisteringly hot, and ingredients are rigorously sourced (they use traditional Sicilian varieties of flour like *tumilia* and *russello*) and are also available at lunchtime. Daily lunch & dinner.

Vicolo Stretto Vicolo Stretto 6 ☎0942 625 554. Reached up the skinniest of alleys off the Corso, by Piazza IX Aprile, this is a chic place to try "real Sicilian cuisine", from pasta with swordfish and mint to beef in a Nero d'Avola wine sauce; mains are €16–22, and fish is sold by weight (from around €6 per 100g). There's a small terrace for eating *al fresco*. Daily lunch & dinner.

DRINKING AND NIGHTLIFE

SEE MAP PAGE 168

Taormina's **cafés** and **bars** are particularly pricey. Barring a few chic retreats, Taormina's drinking scene isn't especially exclusive, with people milling around the streets all night in summer, hopping from bar to bar until the small hours. There's also a fairly discreet gay scene, mostly centred on the stylish bars around Piazza Paladini, and a buzzing evening *passeggiata* along the Corso.

Arco Rosso Via Naumachia 7 ☎335 582 1830. This proper little old-fashioned bar is quite a rarity. Tucked down steps just off the Corso, it sells wine by the glass or bottle and doesn't charge the earth for it. Scrumptious bruschetta and sandwiches too. Mon, Tues & Thurs–Sun

---

TAORMINA'S FESTIVALS

Taormina stages **festivals** and parades at Christmas and Carnevale, but summer is the best time for cultural events. Best known is the **Taormina FilmFest** (ⓦtaorminafilmfest. it), which runs for a week every June, previewing new movies from around the world in their original versions on a big screen at the Teatro Greco (tickets €9–14). However, the international book festival **TaoBuk** (ⓦtaobuk), founded in 2016 and attracting guests such as Ian McEwan, Orhan Pamuk, Jhumpa Lahiri and Elizabeth Strout, is rapidly becoming a must in the literary calendar. It also runs in June, following on from the film festival. Between June and September, **Taormina Arte** (ⓦgotaormina.com) features a varied theatre, music and dance programme, from rock bands and symphony orchestras to classical dramas, held either at the spectacular Teatro Greco or the Palazzo dei Congressi in Piazza Vittorio Emanuele. **Tickets** for all Taormina Arte events are available online or at the Palazzo dei Congressi, Piazza Vittorio Emanuele.

SHOPPING IN TAORMINA

Corso Umberto I is the place to go if you want to track down a Gucci bag, coral necklace or a genuine Baroque candelabra. Of course, you can also pick up mass-produced ceramic dishes, Sicilian puppets, model Etnas and AC Milan football shirts. The bulk of the out-and-out tourist gift shops are up Via Teatro Greco on the way to the theatre, but for quirkier boutiques and souvenirs, delve into the side alleys and stepped streets off the Corso.

Among the glitz and glamour a couple of really special shops are worth seeking out. The **ceramic workshop** at Kerameion, Corso Umberto I 198 (daily 9am–1pm & 3–8pm; closed Sun Jan–March, Nov & Dec; ☎ 339 207 9032, ⊕ kerameion.com) creates tiles, plates, vases and espresso cups, among other items, with exquisitely subtle shades, gorgeous glazes and beguiling designs.

There's a daily indoor **market** (Mon–Sat) for fruit and veg off Via Cappuccini, and a weekly **Wednesday market** for household items, above town at Parcheggio von Gloeden, off Via Leonardo da Vinci; both are morning affairs, open till around 1.30pm. The Punto SMA supermarket (Mon–Sat 9am–1pm & 4–8pm) is outside Porta Catania (and to the right) on Via Apollo Arcageta.

noon–midnight.

Bam Bar Via Di Giovanni 45 ☎ 0942 24 355. Popular spot for ice cream and *granitas*, which come in a lip-smacking range of flavours – recommended choices include watermelon, coffee with almond, and nutella. The owner will show you photos of all the celebrities who have dropped by, and the interior is a delight. Daily 7am–late, closed Mon except in high summer.

Daiquiri Lounge Piazza Duomo ☎ 0942 625 703. Specializing (as you might guess) in daiquiris, this pleasant, perfectly located bar makes a great place for an aperitivo (served with a generous selection of nibbles) or an after-dinner drink. Daily 6pm–late.

Al Grappola d'Uva Via Bagnoli Croce 6–8 ☎ 0942 625 874. Friendly, unpretentious wine bar – a good place to sample Etna wines with olives and local cheeses (€5 including nibbles). There are also several little tables

outside in a narrow little alley. Daily 11am–late.

Morgana Lounge Bar Scesa Morgana 4 ☎ 0942 620 056. International party place off Corso Umberto I, for serious cocktail consumption. Violet velvet inside, a cool outdoor space, and nightly DJ sets. Daily 8pm–late.

Re di Bastoni Corso Umberto I ☎ 0942 23 037. Funky, Bohemian pub that is quite alternative for Taormina, and attracts a lively crowd. Daily, 11.30am–late; closed Mon in winter.

Wunderbar Café Piazza IX Aprile ☎ 0942 625 302. Once the haunt of Garbo and Fassbinder, this remains Taormina's favoured spot for the see-and-be-seen brigade, with outdoor seats beneath the clocktower and a determinedly elitist pricing policy. The piano is wheeled out every night for ivory-tinkling beneath the stars. Go for an Aperol spritz, and sip it slowly as you people-watch. Daily 9am–midnight.

4

DIRECTORY

Hospital Ospedale San Vincenzo, in Via Crocefisso, Contrada Sirina, south of Porta Catania (☎ 0942 5791; for emergencies ☎ 0942 5791).

Pharmacy British Pharmacy, Corso Umberto I, 152, corner of Piazza IX Aprile (June–Sept daily 8.30am–9.30pm, Oct–May Mon–Fri 8.30am–1pm & 3.30–8pm; ☎ 0942 625 735);

outside these hours pharmacies operate according to a rota system, indicated on pharmacy doors.

Police Carabinieri, Piazza Vittorio Emanuele 4 (☎ 0942 23 232 or ☎ 112).

Post office Piazza Sant'Antonio, outside Porta Catania (Mon–Fri 8.20am–7.05pm, Sat 8.20am–12.35pm).

Around Taormina

Taormina is overlooked by the lofty mountain village of **Castelmola**, which is visited for the superb views in all directions, and an easy trip from town. The **coastline** below Taormina, north and south, is immensely appealing – a mixture of grottoes, rocky coves and good sand beaches – although much of it is either sectioned off as private lidos (which you have to pay to use; prices vary from around €10 to €20 or more a day) or simply gets very packed in summer. Easiest to reach, by bus or cable car, are the small, stony stretches around **Mazzarò**. For decent expanses of sand you'll have to travel to **Giardini-Naxos**, a 5km, fifteen-minute bus ride south of Taormina. Cheaper and less pretentious than Taormina, it's very much a separate town, with its own holiday trade and nightlife.

Castelmola

Some 5km above Taormina, the tiny hill-village of **CASTELMOLA** seems to sprout out of the severe crag beneath it, with just a jumble of precipitous alleys to explore and the remnants of a long-demolished castle. Hardly surprisingly, it is entirely given over to tourism, with souvenir shops and up to a dozen bars and restaurants flanking the cobbles.

Above Castelmola, intrepid hikers can embark on the roughly two-hour climb to the top of **Monte Vénere** (885m), the highest peak hereabouts. The **walk down** from Castelmola is much easier than the ascent, and the views are better, too; it's an easy fifteen minutes to Madonna della Rocca, thirty minutes to town.

ARRIVAL AND DEPARTURE CASTELMOLA

By car Drivers should park in the car park at the end of the road from Taormina before entering the village.

By bus Hourly buses from Taormina (15min) stop 200m below the main square.

DRINKING

CASTELMOLA

Bar San Giorgio Piazza Sant'Antonio ☎0942 28 228. This bar in the main square is the doyen of Castelmola, purveying drinks and views for decades, as the old newspaper cuttings in the corner attest. Try a glass of *vino alla mandorla* (almond wine) here, the sweet local brew. Daily, usually 8am–11pm, but later in summer.

Bar Turrisi Piazza Duomo ☎0942 28 181. The decor here is dedicated to the phallus in all its manifestations, and without the slightest hint of irony. Nice views from the terrace – but probably best not to take the kids. Daily, usually 10am–midnight, but later at weekends and throughout the summer.

Mazzarò

The closest beaches to Taormina are the scintillating pebbled coves at **MAZZARÒ**, which you can reach by cable car (*funivia*). Of the two beaches, the southernmost is usually the most packed, fronting its much-photographed islet, the **Isola Bella**, now protected as a marine-life sanctuary. The waters are remarkably clear, and you can rent boats, plus snorkelling and scuba gear down here.

ARRIVAL AND DEPARTURE

MAZZARÒ

Cable car The *funivia* service from Taormina (Mon 8.45am– 8pm, Tues–Sun 8am–8pm, until 1am daily in summer; €3, weekly pass €30) arrives right behind the beach. If it is closed for maintenance, it is replaced with a bus.

Spisone

A little further north from Mazzarò are the beach bars and restaurants at **SPISONE**, which you can either walk to from Mazzarò (10min) or directly down from Taormina (around 30min); take the path from below the cemetery, off Via Guardiola Vecchia.

ARRIVAL AND DEPARTURE

SPISONE

By bus The Linea Beach Bus runs year round from Piazza San Pancrazio and Parcheggio Lumbi (7 daily; €1.10).

Giardini-Naxos

The best sand beaches close to Taormina are those at **GIARDINI-NAXOS**, south of town, where a long strip of sand curves around the wide bay, backed by a busy promenade of bars, cafés, restaurants and hotels. It's much more of a resort in the Italian style than

Taormina – packed and noisy until late September each year, and then largely drawing up the shutters until the following spring. Half of the beach is free ("*spiaggia libera*"), although the better sands further around the bay towards the cape are partitioned off as private lidos, complete with sun-loungers, shades, watersports gear, bars and restaurants.

Greek colony excavations

Daily 9am until 1hr before sunset • €4

Significantly, Giardini-Naxos bay was the site of the first **Greek colony** in Sicily. As an obvious stop for ships sailing between Greece and southern Italy, there was a settlement here by 734 BC, named **Naxos** after the Greek island from which the colonists came, though it was never very important. The **excavations** on the site of the ancient settlement lie right on the cape, Capo Schisò, with the entrance by *La Sirena* restaurant, overlooking the harbour. The remains are disappointingly sketchy, though they stretch across a large area of the cape and it's pleasant to stroll through the olive and lemon groves around the site. There's scarcely any interpretation of what you're seeing – scant foundations of a large, gridded town and a long stretch of ancient, lava-built city wall – and the small museum on site that houses some of the finds doesn't really help either.

ARRIVAL AND DEPARTURE　　　　　　　　　　　　　　　GIARDINI-NAXOS

Giardini-Naxos shares a train station with Taormina. Head left out of the station and you'll hit the promenade in less than five minutes.

The Alcantara valley

Around 2400 BC, an eruption of the Monte Moia volcano, at the head of the **Alcantara valley**, smothered the river and filled the valley with lava. Over four millennia, the Alcantara river has carved its way through the deposits of slick grey basalt, forming a magnificent gorge, the **Gole dell'Alcantara**, and scooping the rock into all manner of strange, sculptural formations. It is a lovely drive from Taormina, some 20km to the east, through gentle hills covered with citrus groves, olive trees and wild flowers, and there are a couple of beguiling towns to visit, namely **Francavilla** and, more notably, **Castiglione di Sicilia**. The road through the valley runs over and alongside the river, and the various bridges are a reminder that the name, Alcantara, is a corruption of the Arabic word for bridge.

Francavilla di Sicilia

If you want to escape the crowds at the Alcantara gorge, continue another 4km to the largely modern town of **Francavilla di Sicilia**. Set alongside the river and overlooked by the few surviving walls of its toothy old hillside **castle**, this was the site of one of the bloodiest battles fought in Sicily, when the Austrian army (given logistical support by the British) engaged with the Spanish in 1719, to no obvious result apart from the loss of some 8000 lives. There's a path up to the ruins, and although much of the town is newly built there's a fair amount of interest in the couple of old central streets. From below the castle a well-marked path winds down to the river at **La Gurne**, through groves of citrus and nut trees. Here you'll find a series of waterfalls and natural round ponds where you can swim without the crowds.

Convento dei Cappuccini

Easter–Oct daily 11am–1pm & 3.30pm–sunset; in winter call ahead as hours vary • €2.50 • ☎ 0942 981 017 or ☎ 338 941 8324

VISITING THE ALCANTARA GORGE

There are numerous tours to the **Alcantara gorge** on offer in Taormina, but you can do the trip yourself easily enough, as four buses a day (one on Sunday) run out this way from Taormina's bus terminal. It's an hour's ride to the main entrance to the **Gole dell'Alcantara**, where there's a car park, bar and restaurant. The gorge is protected nationally as the Parco Fluviale dell'Alcantara (Ⓦ parcoalcantara.it), but the Sicilian affection for Byzantine bureaucracy has resulted in access (daily 9am–sunset) being controlled by the office at the main entrance. Here you pay €10 (€13 in August) to descend in a lift to the bottom and to follow a geological and botanical itinerary extending for 1.5km above the river. There's a 3-D video installation explaining how the gorge was formed, and you can rent waders and wetsuits in summer in order to slosh along the river (it's always icy) through pools and into the main gorge. Gole Alcantara (Ⓣ 0942 985 010, Ⓦ golealcantara.it) organizes **river-trekking** and **body-rafting expeditions** (€30 and €40 respectively) which you can book online. There are also guided quad excursions in the Alcantara valley from the main entrance (Ⓣ 339 879 2940, Ⓦ siciliaquad.com), though the bikes alone can be rented by the hour for far less. There's a free public entrance, 200m beyond the main entrance (Francavilla direction), though it's 200 steps down and back. Note that the last bus back to Taormina leaves at 6.15pm.

Taking the signposted right turn as you approach Francavilla di Sicilia, you might drop in to the **Convento dei Cappuccini** that peers over town and river, where a modest little **museum** shows how the monks – now reduced to two – passed their time in baking, brewing and crafting. You can also inspect the herbarium and buy some of their honey, perfumes or almond- or lemon-flavoured liqueurs. If you want to be sure they are home (hours can be a bit erratic), give them a ring first.

Castiglione di Sicilia

The nicest place to stay (and eat) in the Alcantara valley is **Castiglione di Sicilia**. Fused to a hilltop high above the valley, the town's lovely weather-eroded houses with pantiled roofs cluster below the remains of its castle. Numerous church spires and the lofty, ruined rock-built castle make an inviting target as you approach up the switchback road, and it's easy to spend a couple of hours just wandering the quiet streets of this old mountain settlement. You can meander up as far as a small piazza at the top of town – with fabulous views of Etna – where there's a flight of steps leading up to the shattered castle, or **Fortezza Greca** (always open), supposedly founded in the fifth century BC by Greek exiles from nearby Naxos and offering grand panoramic views.

Just outside Castiglione in the valley below (and signposted from town) is a perfectly restored Byzantine chapel known as **La Cuba** for its perfect symmetry. Behind La Cuba, a path leads to the river where there are little waterfalls and pools.

ACCOMMODATION AND EATING — CASTIGLIONE DI SICILIA

Alcantara Formaggi Via Federico II Ⓣ 0942 984 268. A small, artisan cheesemakers where the Camiglia family produce and sell a range of traditional and inventive cheeses, mostly made of local sheep's milk. Mon–Sat 8am–1pm & 4.30–6pm.

Belvedere d'Alcantara Ⓣ 0942 984 037. A short walk beyond the piazza, and well signposted all over town, this simple restaurant has a rooftop terrace that takes full advantage of the soaring views, as well as a €20 tourist menu and pizzas in the evening. Tues–Sun, lunch & dinner.

★ **Hotel Federico II** Via Maggiore Baracca 2 Ⓣ 0942 980 368, Ⓦ hotelfedericosecondo.com. A chic, smart and very reasonably priced little hotel with an excellent restaurant just off the main piazza. The restaurant, *Sine Tempore* (daily lunch & dinner; closed Wed if there are no hotel guests), serves local produce to great effect in simple, tasty dishes, and has fantastic value fixed menus at €18 and

€25 including Etna rosso wine. The mixed *antipasto* is a great way of trying lots of local goodies, while to follow there is *tagliatelle Federico Secondo* (with porcini mushrooms, courgettes and pancetta) or handmade ravioli dressed with pistachios from Bronte. If you're lucky there will be fresh ricotta warm from the local cheesemaker at lunchtime and breakfast. Half board an extra €15 per person. €80

4

Catania, Etna and around

182 Catania

196 Catania's beach resorts

196 Acireale

197 Lentini and around

198 Mount Etna

MIGHTY ETNA

5 Catania, Etna and around

Bang in the middle of the Ionian coast, with Mount Etna looming high above it, Catania is Sicily's second-largest city, a major airport, port and transport hub and a thriving commercial centre. Within the periphery of shabby apartment blocks and edgy urban wasteland is a vibrant city, its small historic centre full of jaunty Baroque buildings of black lava and creamy white limestone built in the wake of the 1693 earthquake that wrecked the whole region. There's an iconic fish market, plenty of restaurants, an easy-going drinking and nightlife scene, and just enough historical sights to pique your interest without being overwhelming.

Along the jagged volcanic coast to the north of Catania, a string of small resort-villages run up to the little Baroque town of **Acireale**, while to the south the main driving route to Ragusa and Enna crosses the fertile plain of the **Piana di Catania**. This rich agricultural region was known to the Greeks as the Laestrygonian Fields after the mythical Homeric monsters, the Laestrygonians, a race of cannibals who devoured several of Odysseus's crew. It's a pretty enough ride, but there is little worth stopping for, unless you happen to be an archeological buff, in which case the ugly town of Lentini, once a Greek colony, may appeal.

There's absolutely no mistaking the single biggest draw in the province, namely **Mount Etna**, Europe's highest volcano, whose foothills start a few kilometres north of Catania. It's still highly active and its massive presence dominates the whole of this part of the coast, with every town and village in the neighbourhood built at least partly from the lava that it periodically ejects. A road and a small single-track railway, the **Ferrovia Circumetnea**, circumnavigate the lower slopes, passing through a series of hardy towns, such as **Randazzo**, almost foolishly situated in the shadow of the volcano and surrounded by swirls of black volcanic rock. Meanwhile, higher villages and ski stations like **Nicolosi** and the **Rifugio Sapienza** are the base for escorted tours and ascents to the **summit craters**. If you're Etna-bound by public transport you'll have to leave from Catania itself – if you have a car, you could base yourself in one of the prettier towns and villages to the north.

Catania

First impressions don't say much at all for **CATANIA** – there's heavy industry here, a big port and depressing suburbs, while the traffic-choked city centre is largely constructed from suffocating, black-grey volcanic stone. Indeed, the influence of Etna is pervasive, with the main thoroughfare named after the volcano, which looms threateningly just to the north. Yet Catania is not a bad place for a brief stay – if you are arriving or leaving from the airport and want to see Etna as well, you might want to stay for a couple of nights. It is first and foremost a commercial city, with two of the island's best **markets**, while if you look beyond the darkened shadows of the buildings you'll detect some of the most distinct Baroque architecture in Sicily – more restrained than elsewhere and making great play with the contrast between black lava stone and creamy white limestone. A large student population enlivens the centre, and the thronged piazzas and bars make for exuberant evening promenades. In early February Catania devotes itself to celebrating the festival of its patron, **Saint Agatha**, with a passion and intensity diminished not a jot by the fact that this is Sicily's most outward-looking, contemporary and international city.

CARNEVALE FUN IN ACIREALE

Highlights

❶ Pescheria, Catania Scoop the flesh from a sea urchin as you stand at a stall, or have spaghetti and clams for lunch on a table laid with newsprint in a bustling seafood trattoria – Catania's raucous fish market is Sicily's best. See page 187

❷ Teatro Massimo Bellini, Catania Experience a night at the opera with the music of Catania's most famous native son. See page 195

❸ Carnevale Acireale's Carnevale is one of the best, liveliest and most exuberant in Italy, celebrated with five days of riotous fancy-dress parades. See page 197

❹ The Linguaglossa drive For spectacular views, and amazing close-ups of fields of lava, drive the circular route from Linguaglossa via remote Rifugio Cutelli. See page 200

❺ The ascent of Etna The smoking cone of Etna dominates much of eastern Sicily, and invites an ascent of its blackened upper slopes, not least for the awesome views. See page 201

❻ The Pistachios of Bronte Europe's finest pistachios come from exquisitely tended orchards outside Bronte, best sampled in the town's ice creams, pestos and pastries. See page 205

HIGHLIGHTS ARE MARKED ON THE MAP ON PAGE 184

5

Catania is a major **transport terminus**, with buses (from the central bus station and the airport) to just about every major destination on the island. The train service is less comprehensive, though the lines south to Siracusa and north to Taormina and Messina are useful. You could see the whole of central Catania in a busy day's strolling. Most of the sights are confined within a small area, centred on **Piazza del Duomo** and the cathedral, from where the wide main avenue, **Via Etnea**, steams off to the north up to the city's **Bellini gardens**. The **Pescheria** (fish market) and **castle** lie to the south, and the landmark **Teatro Bellini** to the east. Much of this entire area, sections of Via Etnea included, is closed to traffic, so walking around is quite enjoyable, especially at night when certain areas transform into bar and café zones.

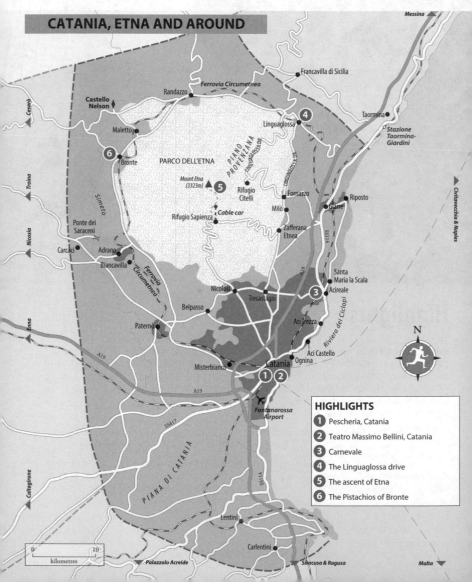

CATANIA, ETNA AND AROUND

HIGHLIGHTS

1. Pescheria, Catania
2. Teatro Massimo Bellini, Catania
3. Carnevale
4. The Linguaglossa drive
5. The ascent of Etna
6. The Pistachios of Bronte

THE FESTA DI SANT'AGATA

Catania's biggest annual festival, the **Festa di Sant'Agata**, takes place each year between February 3 and 5. It's a 500-year-old celebration of the life and death of the virtuous Agatha, born in the city around 230 AD and destined for dreadful tortures after spurning the unwelcome advances of the Roman praetor, Quintianus, in 252 AD: prison, whipping, mutilation and burning followed. The three days of the festival see hundreds of thousands of people processing through the streets following a silver, bejewelled reliquary that holds the relics of the saint. There's also a procession of decorated candlesticks, up to 6m high, carried for hours at a time by groups representing different trades. On the morning of February 5, the saint's relics are carried back into the Duomo, where they remain until the following year. Meanwhile, there are fireworks, food stalls, special services and concerts throughout the *festa*.

Brief history

Some of the island's first **Greek colonists**, probably Chalcedonians from Naxos, settled the site as early as 729 BC, becoming so influential that their laws were eventually adopted by all the Ionian colonies of Magna Graecia. Later, the city was among the first to fall to the **Romans**, under whom it prospered greatly. Unusually for Sicily, Catania's surviving ancient relics are all Roman (albeit lava-encrusted, after successive historic eruptions). In the early Christian period Catania witnessed the martyrdom of **Agatha**, who, having rejected the improper advances of the praetor, Quintianus, was put to death in 252 AD. She was later canonized (becoming the patron saint of Catania), and it was her miraculous intervention that reputedly saved the city from complete volcanic destruction in the seventeenth century. Even with the saint's protection, Catania has had its fair share of disasters: Etna erupted in 1669, engulfing the city in lava, while the **great earthquake** of 1693 devastated the whole of southeastern Sicily. The eighteenth-century Sicilian architect **Giovanni Battista Vaccarini** was largely responsible for the rebuilding, deftly employing black lava stone, white limestone and mauve-like mink stucco to emphasize the geometry of grand palaces and imposing churches. The result is far more restrained and cerebral than elsewhere on the island, a version of Baroque that teeters on the brink of Neoclassical sobriety.

Piazza del Duomo

Piazza del Duomo is one of Sicily's most elegant Baroque piazzas, rebuilt completely in the first half of the eighteenth century by the Palermo-born Giovanni Battista Vaccarini, who was made Catania's municipal architect in 1730. With the majestic cathedral as his starting point, he produced a dramatic open space – kept traffic-free today – softened by the addition of a central fountain, no less than a **lava elephant** supporting an Egyptian obelisk on its back. The elephant has been the city's symbol since at least the thirteenth century, a talismanic protection against Etna eruptions, and this one also features an inscription, *Agatina MSSHDEPL* – an acronym for the snappy slogan, "The mind of St Agatha is sane and spontaneous, honouring God and liberating the city".

The Duomo

Piazza Duomo • Mon–Sat 7am–noon & 4–7pm, Sun 7.30am–12.30pm & 4.30–7pm • Free

Agatha is the dedicatee of Vaccarini's grandest project, the **Duomo**, which flanks the eastern side of the piazza. The original cathedral here was founded in the eleventh century, and was itself built on the site of a complex of Roman baths, but of this medieval church only the beautifully crafted apses survived the 1693 earthquake; you can see them through the gate at Via Vittorio Emanuele II 159. Vaccarini added an imposing Baroque facade, on which he tagged granite columns filched from Catania's Roman amphitheatre, while the interior is adorned with a rich series of chapels. The

5

Cappella di Sant'Agata is to the right of the choir, and is the repository of the relics that are paraded through the city on the saint's festival days. Next to it, entered through a fine sixteenth-century doorway, is the **Cappella della Madonna** which holds a Roman sarcophagus containing the ashes of the Aragonese kings – Frederick II, Frederick III and the child-king Louis, who died of the plague at the age of 16 in 1355. The tomb of the composer **Bellini**, a native of the city, is set in the floor before the second

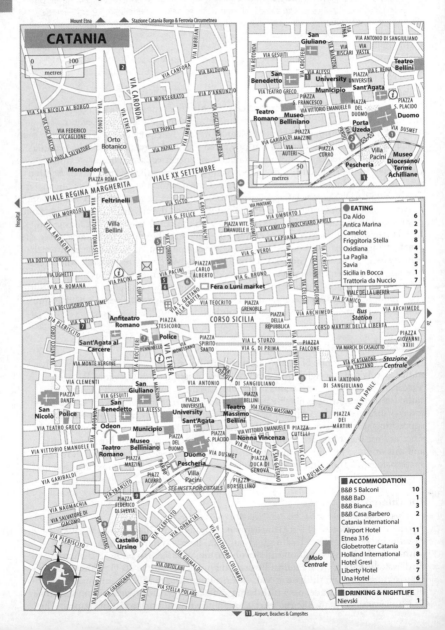

● EATING

Da Aldo	6
Antica Marina	2
Camelot	9
Friggitoria Stella	8
Oxidiana	4
La Paglia	3
Savia	5
Sicilia in Bocca	1
Trattoria da Nuccio	7

■ ACCOMMODATION

B&B 5 Balconi	10
B&B BaD	1
B&B Bianca	3
B&B Casa Barbero	2
Catania International Airport Hotel	11
Etnea 316	4
Globetrotter Catania	9
Holland International	8
Hotel Gresi	5
Liberty Hotel	7
Una Hotel	6

■ DRINKING & NIGHTLIFE

Nievski	1

> ## PRAWNS IN THE PESCHERIA
>
> You'll commonly find three kinds of freshly caught, wild prawn at Sicilian fish markets: the prized, and extremely tasty red prawn, or **gambero rosso** (Aristaeomorpha foliacea), is at its best simply poached (or raw); the less expensive, but still delicious, pink **gambero rosa** (Parapenaeus longirostris), which is tastiest quickly fried in the shell; and the big striped prawn, or **mazzancolle** (Penaeus Kerathurus), which is basically a Mediterranean tiger prawn – fantastic simply poached for a few minutes, but wonderful in a pasta dish as well. Look out for tagliatelle with *mazzancolle*, courgettes, and pesto made from pistachios from the town of Bronte in the foothills of Etna. Not only does it taste extraordinary, but the contrast of pink and green colours in the dish looks incredible.

column on the right as you enter, inscribed with a couple of bars from his opera, *La Sonnambula* (The Sleepwalker) Ah! non credea mirarti Sì presto estinto, o fiore (I did not believe you would fade so soon, oh flower).

Museo Diocesano and the Terme Achilliane

Piazza Duomo • Mon–Fri 9am–2pm, Tues & Thurs also 3–6pm, Sat 9am–1pm • Museum €7, Terme Achilliane €5, joint ticket €10 • ☎ 095 281 636, ⓦ museodiocesanocatania.com

To the right of the Duomo, the **Museo Diocesano** is home to the cathedral's collection of religious art and silverware, with items dating back to the fourteenth century, including pieces recovered from the pre-1693 cathedral. Beautifully presented as the museum is, most people will find that the highlight is the panoramic terrace with magnificent views over the cathedral and city to the sea and Mount Etna.

Below ground are the remains of the **Terme Achilliane**, Catania's Imperial Roman baths, which form part of the museum. They're perhaps not quite as alluring as they were in the days of eighteenth-century French traveller Jean Houel, who, discovering a hall covered with stuccoes of Cupids, vines, grapes and animals, concluded that it must have been a Temple to Bacchus. Delightful as the idea of a temple devoted to the most decadent of Greek gods might be, it was actually a Roman baths complex – you can still see the form of the frigidarium. Originally stretching right across the piazza as far as the Pescheria (where remains of the caldarium were discovered), water was provided by the River Amenano, which still flows below the city.

The Pescheria

Piazza Pardo and Piazza Alonzo de Benedetto • Mon–Sat, from around 7am–2pm

Catania's best-known food and fish market, the **Pescheria**, is reached from the back of Piazza del Duomo by nipping down the steps behind a gushing marble fountain. This takes you right into the main part of the fish market, where fishmongers shout across slabs and buckets full of twitching fish, eels, crabs and shellfish. Brandishing wicked-looking knives, the stallholders slice off swordfish steaks to order, while others shuck oysters, mussels and sea urchins for browsing customers. The side alleys off the fish market are dense with fruit, vegetable and dried goods and herb stalls – it's great for buying things like salted capers, sun-dried tomatoes and bags of wild oregano – as well as cheese counters and bloody butchers' tables.

Via Vittorio Emanuele II

On the other side of the Duomo, across busy Via Vittorio Emanuele II, the church of **Sant'Agata** is another of Vaccarini's works, though the lighter, pale grey Rococo interior postdates his death. A little further up the street, at no. 140, there's the minor curiosity that was the home of Catanese erotic poet and philosopher **Domenico Tempio** (1750–1821). It's now desperately neglected, though you can still make out the raunchy

5

figures of men and women playing with themselves, which support the balcony above the blackened doorway.

Teatro Romano

Via Vittorio Emanuele II 260 • Daily 9am–6.30pm • €6

The **Teatro Romano**, built in the second century AD, is an intimate little theatre, which preserves much of the Roman seating and an underground passageway. A small antiquarium here displays finds from the site. The smaller **Odeon**, adjacent, was used for music and poetry recitations. Today the Teatro Romano is still occasionally used as a super-atmospheric venue for opera, film and music.

Castello Ursino and the Museo Civico

Museo Civico Daily 9am–7pm • €6 (not including temporary exhibitions) • ☎ 095 345 830

Beyond the Pescheria, Via Plebiscito winds through a dilapidated though appealingly neighbourly quarter to Piazza Federico di Svevia, dominated by the **Castello Ursino**, once the proud fortress of Frederick II. Originally, the castle stood on a rocky cliff above the sea, but the 1669 eruption of Etna resulted in this entire area becoming landlocked, and left just the keep standing. The castle still presents a formidable appearance, and now houses the **Museo Civico**, part of whose ground floor is taken up with temporary exhibitions, while permanent exhibits include retrieved mosaic fragments, stone inscriptions, elegant painted Greek amphorae and terracotta statuettes. Upstairs, the **Pinacoteca** (art gallery) holds mainly religious art from the seventeenth century.

Via Crociferi

The best place to appreciate the eighteenth-century rebuilding of Catania is along its most handsome street, **Via Crociferi**, where the wealthy religious authorities and private citizens competed with each other to construct dazzling houses, palaces and churches. They were building using the very bones of the Roman and medieval city; the arcaded **Piazza Mazzini** (straddling Via Garibaldi) was constructed from 32 columns that originally formed part of a Roman basilica.

Via Crociferi begins to the north of Piazza San Francesco, running under an imposing Baroque arch that announces the start of a series of arresting religious and secular buildings, little changed since the eighteenth century. Amble up the narrow street and you can peer into the courtyards of the *palazzi* (one holds a miniature plantation of banana trees) and poke around the churches. About halfway up on the right, the finest of these, **San Giuliano** (usually open only for services), has a facade by Vaccarini and an echoing elliptical interior.

Museo Belliniano

Piazza San Francesco d'Assisi 3 • Mon–Sat 9am–7pm, Sun 9am–1pm) • €5 • ☎ 095 715 0535

At the bottom of Via Crociferi, opposite San Francesco church, the house where the composer Vincenzo Bellini was born in 1801 is now open as the **Museo Belliniano**, displaying photographs, original scores, his death mask and other memorabilia. Born into a musical family, Bellini supposedly composed his first work at the age of 6, and later studied in Naples, where he produced his first opera in 1825. Ten more operas followed during the next decade – his first big success was *Il Pirata* (1827) – with Bellini living largely in Milan until his early death in Paris, aged only 33. His body was transported back to his native Sicily to be buried, and Catania subsequently did her favourite son proud, with the airport, a piazza, the city's main theatre and a park all named after him, as well as the ultimate accolade – a pasta dish, *spaghetti alla Norma*, cooked with tomato and aubergine and named after Bellini's famous 1831 opera.

San Nicolò

Piazza Dante • Mon–Sat 9am–1pm • Free

Opposite the peculiar crescent-shaped Piazza Dante looms the unfinished facade of **San Nicolò**, studded by six enormous, lopped columns. It was conceived on a ridiculously grand scale, and the work was ultimately curtailed by earthquake damage and soaring costs. What's left is a stark 105m-long **interior**, virtually undecorated save for the sculpted choir stalls and a meridian line etched in marble across the floor of the transept, embellished with zodiacal signs. Its organ, Sicily's largest, was destroyed in the nineteenth century before being restored in 2004, and is occasionally used for concerts (some have been posted online).

The church is part of an adjoining **Benedictine convent**, with equally impressive dimensions – it's the second-largest convent in Europe after Mafra in Portugal. Through a gate to the left of the church lie the remains of some **Roman walls**, and, behind, the massive conventual buildings. These are now used by the university's language and literature faculties, but you should be able to stroll in for a look around the once grand cloistered courtyards.

Via Etnea and around

The main city thoroughfare, **Via Etnea**, runs north from Piazza del Duomo and out of the city. Following its full length would eventually lead you right to the foothills of Mount Etna – and from the street's northern end there are photogenic views of the peak in the distance.

Piazza dell'Università holds some outdoor cafés and the main building of the **University**, founded by the Aragonese kings in the fifteenth century, while the tangled streets off to the east form the heart of the student nightlife zone, converging eventually on the restored Piazza Bellini, which is overlooked by the flagship **Teatro Massimo Bellini** (see page 195), built in 1890.

Anfiteatro Romano

Piazza Stesicoro • Thurs only 9am–1pm & 2.30–6pm • Free

Halfway up Via Etnea, **Piazza Stesicoro** marks the modern centre of Catania, with its western side almost entirely occupied by the sunken black remains of the **Anfiteatro Romano**, built from lava blocks in the second or third century AD. Much is still concealed under the surrounding buildings, but a diagram shows the original dimensions of the theatre, which could hold sixteen thousand spectators – it's quite evident that the section you can walk through represents only one tiny excavated corner.

Sant'Agata al Carcere

Piazza Santo Carcere • No set hours • Free

Behind the Anfiteatro Romano is the twelfth-century church of **Sant'Agata al Carcere**, built on the site of the prison where St Agatha was confined before her martyrdom at the hands of the Romans. When it's open (hours are sporadic), a custodian will let you into the third-century **crypt** and show you the chapel's medieval stone doorway, which is topped by evil, grinning, sculpted heads and ape-like creatures.

Fera o Luni market

Piazza Carlo Alberto • Mon–Sat usually around 7am–2pm

Off the east side of Via Etnea, at Piazza Stesicoro, the stalls are out from early in the morning, ranged up Via San Gaetano alla Grotta, and heralding the city's rambunctious **Fera o Luni market** (literally "the Monday market" in Sicilian, though it is now held every day except Sunday), which is centred on the broad Piazza Carlo Alberto. As well as fruit, vegetables and fish, all kinds of clothes (new and secondhand),

5

shoes, accessories and household goods are sold here, from tat piled high on a wooden cart to cut-price designer labels (or copies thereof), all accompanied by the constant patter and haggling of cheery traders. The market is a great spot for souvenir-hunting, even more so on Sundays when an **antiques fair** takes over the space.

Villa Bellini

The interesting stretch of Via Etnea finishes at the **Villa Bellini**, just beyond the post office, a large, ornamental public garden that provides a welcome touch of greenery. The stand-up drinks bar here is where the local police hang out, whiling away time between meal breaks; rather touching photos of the regulars are pinned up, posing stiffly in uniform on horseback or motorbikes.

Le Ciminiere: Zo

Piazzale Chinicci · **Museo del Cinema** Tues–Sun 9am–4pm · €4 · ☎ 095 401 1928 · **Museo Storico dello Sbarco in Sicilia 1943** Tues–Sun 9am–4.45pm · €4 · ☎ 095 401 1929, ⓦ zoculture.it

In the east of the city near Stazione Centrale, Catania's former sulphur works, Le Ciminiere, has been transformed into a cultural centre known as **Zo**. The original red-brick chimneys and lava-block walls have been wrapped in a contemporary glass-and-steel frame, while inside are theatre and performance spaces and a café-restaurant. It's an interesting place to visit even if you don't come for an exhibition or event, and it holds two museums as well: the **Museo del Cinema**, which focuses on the history of film in Sicily, and the **Museo Storico dello Sbarco in Sicilia 1943**, or the Museum of the Allied Invasion of Sicily. The latter is a winner with kids, who get to walk through a replica of a typical Sicilian village piazza, take cover in an air-raid shelter as the siren sounds, and emerge at all-clear into a bombed version of the same piazza.

ARRIVAL AND DEPARTURE   **CATANIA**

BY PLANE

Fontanarossa airport From the airport, 5km south of the city, the cheapest way into the centre is the Alibus #457 (every 20min, daily 5.30am–midnight; €4), departing from right outside, which runs to the central Piazza Stesicoro (on Via Etnea) and to Stazione Centrale in around 20min (longer in heavy traffic). Most regional express buses (to Siracusa, Taormina, Ragusa, Agrigento, Enna, Messina and Palermo) also stop at the airport, and from April to October you can get a direct bus from the airport to Milazzo (for the Aeolian Islands). A taxi ride to the centre costs around €20.

BY TRAIN

Stazione Centrale Trains pull in at Stazione Centrale in Piazza Giovanni XXIII, just east of the centre. It's easy to jump on a city bus outside to reach Piazza del Duomo or Via Etnea (see page 189), or to take a taxi (around €10). Otherwise, it's a 20min walk to the Duomo. For information and timetables see ⓦ trenitalia.com. For Circumetnea services, note that there is a reduced service in July and August, and no trains on Sundays and holidays in winter.

Mainline destinations Acireale (1–2 hourly; 10 15min); Caltagirone (2 daily Mon–Sat; 1hr 50min); Caltanissetta (11 daily; 2hr); Enna (11 daily Mon–Sat, 3 daily Sun;

1hr–1hr 20min); Giarre-Riposto (1–2 hourly; 20–30min); Lentini (11 daily Mon–Sat, 5 daily Sun; 20min); Messina (approximately hourly; 1hr 20min–2hr 10min); Palermo (7 daily; 2hr 50–3hr); Siracusa (11 daily Mon–Sat, 6 daily Sun; 1hr 30min); Taormina (1–2 hourly; 45min).

Stazione Catania Borgo The other city station, Stazione Catania Borgo on Via Caronda, off the northern end of Via Etnea, is for trains on the Ferrovia Circumetnea, the round-Etna line (☎095 541 250, ⓦ circumetnea.it; see page 200); it's connected by metro with Stazione Centrale. A taxi to the centre from here is around €12.

Circumetnea destinations Bronte (11 daily; 1hr 30min); Maletto (11 daily; 1hr 45min); Randazzo (11 daily; 2hr). Note that if line improvement works are taking place, parts of the route may be substituted by buses.

BY BUS

Virtually all long-distance buses stop at the **airport** as well as at the bus station – a far easier place to change buses if you are not intending to spend time in the city. The city bus station is a grotty 5min walk from the train station, up Viale della Libertà, on Via Archimede, and the ticket offices are currently inconveniently located on the other side of Viale della Libertà, so buy them before going into the station.

5

CATANIA CITY TOURS

To see a lot of Catania in a short time and without too much walking, join one of the **bus tours** operated by Katane Live (☎095 354 704, ⓦkatanelive.com), which offers a hop-on, hop-off service (daily 9am–7pm; €5, plus €2 for audioguide; tickets sold on board or online) around the centre, taking in Via Etnea, Piazza del Duomo and Villa Bellini, with additional stops at the train station, Piazza Stesicoro and Piazza Verga, among other places. There is also a nice hop-on, hop-off Sea Tour, which will take you to Acitrezza, Acicastello and other beaches (€15; leaving at 11am, 2pm, 4pm and 6pm). If you are travelling with kids, they will doubtless like the **Trenino Turistico** (☎095 820 4281), a mini-train on wheels, which leaves from Piazza Duomo and performs a wide 35min circuit of the centre including Via Vittorio Emanuele II, Via Etnea and Via Crociferi (€5).

Services are much reduced on Sundays. If you arrive by bus, there is no need to stay on until Viale della Libertà – the Piazza Borsellino stop is much more convenient for the historic centre: just cross the little park full of old guys playing cards, duck through the arches, and you are at the Pescheria (fish market).

Bus companies The major companies have terminals around Stazione Centrale, including: AST, Via L. Sturzo 230 (☎840 000 323 or ☎095 723 0535, ⓦazienda sicilianatrasporti.it) for services within Catania province, including Etna; Interbus, Via d'Amico 187 (☎095 530 396, ⓦinterbus.it) for Acireale, Caltagirone, Giardini-Naxos, Messina, Nicosia, Noto, Piazza Armerina, Ragusa, Siracusa and Taormina; SAIS Autolinee, Via d'Amico 181 (☎095 536 168, ⓦsaisautolinee.it) to Palermo, Messina, Enna and Caltanissetta; SAIS Trasporti, Via d'Amico 213 (☎095 536 201, ⓦsaistrasporti.it) to Messina, Agrigento, Caltanissetta and mainland destinations.

Destinations Acireale (4 daily; 50min); Agrigento (approximately hourly; 2hr 50min); Caltagirone (4 daily; 1hr 30min); Enna (7 daily; 1hr 30min); Giardini-Naxos (1 hourly; 1hr); Lentini (1–2 hourly; 1hr–1hr 15min); Messina (1–2 hourly; 1hr 35min); Milazzo (1–2 daily April–June & Oct, 4 daily July–Sept; 1hr 50min); Palermo (1 hourly Mon–Sat, 9 daily Sun; 2hr 30min); Nicolosi (1 hourly; 40min); Nicosia (3 daily; 2hr); Noto (6 daily; 1hr 35min); Piazza Armerina (6 daily; 1hr 40min); Ragusa (1 hourly; 2hr); *Rifugio Sapienza* (1 daily; 2hr); Rome (2–3 daily; 11hr); Siracusa (approximately hourly; 1hr 20min); Taormina (at least hourly; 1hr 40min).

BY FERRY

To Malta The historic fast-ferry service to Malta no longer departs from Catania – instead there is a coach transfer to the port of Pozzallo, near Modica. Services to Malta run once weekly in winter, around four times a week in spring and daily in summer (☎095 703 1211, ⓦvirtuferries.com).

To Naples TTT Lines (☎081 575 2192) run a daily ferry from Catania to Salerno, which takes 12hr. The port is along Via VI Aprile, a 5min walk southwest of the train station, and is also served by a stop on the Metropolitana (Stazione Porto). The TTT Lines website does not always work – instead, book through a broker site such as ⓦaferry.co.uk.

Destinations Salerno (1 daily; 12hr); Valletta, Malta (1–7 weekly; 4hr 15min including coach transfer to Pozzallo).

GETTING AROUND

By bus AMT city buses (☎800 018 696 or ☎095 751 9111, ⓦamt.ct.it) have terminals at Stazione Centrale and Piazza Borsellino, where there's a stop for the airport. Central pick-up points are Piazza del Duomo and Piazza Stesicorot. Tickets (€1) are valid for any number of journeys within 1hr 30min and are available from *tabacchi*, the newsagents inside Stazione Centrale or the booth outside the station. The same outlets also sell a *biglietto giornaliero* (€2.50), valid for one day's unlimited travel on all local AMT bus routes.

By metro The city's metro system (run by the same folk who run the Circumetnea line) operates every 15min (7am–8.30pm) on a limited route running from the main Stazione Centrale (beyond Platform 11) south to Catania Porto and north and northwest to Catania Borgo, the terminal for the Stazione Circumetnea on Via Caronda. Buy the special "biglietto integrato" (€1.20) which is valid for 2hr on both bus and metro and must be punched at machines before boarding the train.

By car Driving into Catania isn't too difficult (just follow signs for "centro" for Via Etnea), but driving around the city is a different matter thanks to chaotic traffic, the fiendish one-way system and the utter impossibility of parking. Some hotels have their own parking or arrangements with nearby garages, but as you really don't need to drive in Catania, the best advice if you're renting a car is to do so on the day you leave the city, and to consider picking it up from the airport, which is connected by frequent local buses with the centre.

Car rental All agencies have outlets at the airport (opposite the bus stops outside arrivals) and in the city, though, given Catania's disorienting one-way system, the airport is a far easier place to pick up a car than the city centre.

By taxi There are taxi ranks at Stazione Centrale, Piazza del Duomo and Via Etnea (Piazza Stesicoro); call ☎095 330 966 or ☎095 338 282 for 24-hour service. Taxis are metered – most journeys within the centre shouldn't cost more than €10.

INFORMATION

Tourist office There are InfoPoints run by the city council at Via Vittorio Emanuele 172, near the Duomo, and at the airport (both open Mon–Sat 8.15am–7pm, Sun 8.30am–1.30pm; ☎ 800 841 042, ⓦ www.comune.catania.it.

Listings information For what's on, check out ⓦ cataniatoday.it or check out the Catania editions of daily newspapers *Giornale di Sicilia*, *La Sicilia* and the *Gazzetta del Sud*.

ACCOMMODATION

SEE MAP PAGE 186

Catania's **hotels** have raised their game in recent years, with grubby old *pensioni* replaced by some lovely B&Bs and a few stylish boutique places. It's always wise to reserve in advance, especially in July and August and during the Sant'Agata celebrations, with prices usually determined by availability, resulting in some excellent deals on websites.

HOTELS AND B&BS

★ **B&B 5 Balconi** Via del Plebiscito 133 ☎ 338 727 2701, ⓦ 5balconi.it. This clean, relaxed B&B has artistically decorated rooms with vintage furnishings and plenty of personality; and, as the name implies, five balconies. The young Anglo-Sicilian couple who run it are full of local tips. Bathrooms are shared, and there's a/c. It's on a busy road, but noise intrusion is minimal. Breakfast includes traditional Catanese pastries. No credit cards. €60

B&B BaD Via C. Colombo 24 ☎ 095 346 903, ⓦ bad catania.com. Four vibrant rooms and an apartment (€100) with cooking facilities and a terrace with a view of Etna, all set in a funky, self-styled B&B with 1960s and 1970s furniture and walls covered with psychedelic geometries and optical illusions. It's conveniently located behind the Pescheria and Piazza del Duomo. Doubles €67

B&B Bianca Via S. Tomaselli 43 ☎ 095 989 0989, ⓦ biancabb.com. B&B behind the Giardino Bellini, where the young, friendly owners make sure that guests are well informed about what's going on in Catania. There are two rooms, at present with shared bathroom. The communal area is a cheerful place to hang out and chat, with white walls and fittings, scarlet chairs, and a tangerine sofa where you can flop and watch a DVD. €74

★ **B&B Casa Barbero** Via Caronda 209 ☎ 095 820 6301, ⓦ casabarbero.com. Contemporary colours and design in a beautifully restored Liberty-era *palazzo* with six quiet rooms set around a courtyard. Breakfast is served either in the courtyard, or in the elaborately stuccoed and frescoed dining room, at tables elegantly laid with Japanese-style ceramics and modern pewter. Bikes for guests' use (free but €100 deposit). €86

Catania International Airport Hotel Via San Giuseppe La Rena 94 ☎ 095 723 4555, ⓦ cataniainternational airporthotel.com. Ten minutes' walk from the terminal, this is convenient, new and comfortable, and has a restaurant. Perfect if you arrive late or have an early departure. €95

Etnea 316 Via Etnea 316 ☎ 095 250 3076, ⓦ hotel etnea316catania.com. Real care has gone into the maintenance of this charming old B&B, where ten spruced-up rooms retain their original tile floors and lofty proportions. There's a pretty lounge and breakfast room, and a calm air envelops all. €67

Globetrotter Catania Vicolo della Lanterna 14, ☎ 095 093 3021 or ☎ 333 577 9854, ⓦ globetrottercatania. com. Bright, friendly, homely-feeling B&B, where all rooms have private bathrooms and guests breakfast together at a communal table – so a great choice if you want to hook up with other travellers. It is set in a little alleyway, and there are tables outside – perfect for a quiet read or evening drink. They have their own expert Etna guides, and are brilliant at helping you organize trips around Sicily that will take you off the beaten tourist track. Daniele, one of the owners, runs one-day cooking courses, which include a trip around the Pescheria. They also have several apartments around the historic centre, usually rented by the room. €72

Holland International Via Vittorio Emanuele 8 ☎ 095 533 605, ⓦ hollandintrooms.it. Old-fashioned *pensione*, convenient for the station and charging competitive prices for rooms on the first floor of an old *palazzo* with vaulted frescoed ceilings. Rooms come with and without bathrooms and all have tea- and coffee-making facilities. The friendly Dutch owner speaks English. €61

CATANIA'S STREET FOOD

The Catanese do a lot of eating on the hoof, from grazing on raw mussels and sea urchins in the Pescheria to eating ice cream as they parade up Via Etnea during the evening *passeggiata*. February's Festa di Sant'Agata sees food stalls selling traditional **nougat** (*torrone*) and confections of **marzipan and sweet ricotta** (including little cakes with a cherry on top, known as *Minne di Sant'Agata*, or Saint Agatha's boobs), while during summer kiosks offer that thirst-quenching Catania speciality, soda water and crushed lemon, served with or without salt (*seltz e limone con/senza sale*). In autumn the **roast-chestnut** vendors are out in force, and around San Martino's Day (November 11) it's the time for **crispelle** – fritters of flour, water, yeast and ricotta or anchovies.

5

SHOPPING IN CATANIA

Via Etnea is the central spine of the city and its major shopping street, with department and chain stores, designer labels, boutiques and brands. Off here, just before the Villa Bellini, **Via Pacini** is devoted to cheap clothes, shoes, underwear and accessories, along with purveyors of spices and other exotic goodies (ranging from Heinz baked beans and Marmite to fresh lemongrass and *kecap manis* sauce).

Across Piazza del Duomo, in the arches under the Porta Uzeda gateway, there are two or three well-stocked Sicilian souvenir stores, for puppets, postcards, ceramics, painted carts and almond wine. And around the back of the Duomo, in the old Palazzo Biscari at Piazza San Placido 7, look for the historic main branch of the now ubiquitous **Nonna Vincenza** (Mon–Sat 8am–9pm, Sun 8am–2pm; ☎095 715 1844), the most traditional place in the city to buy artisan sweets in gorgeous packaging.

As for **books**, Feltrinelli, Via Etnea 283-7 (Mon–Sat 10.30am–1.30pm & 4.30–8.30pm; ☎095 352 9001), has a good range of English books; and there is a branch of Mondadori at Piazza Roma 18 (Mon–Sat 9am–8pm; ☎095 716 9610).

Hotel Gresi Via Pacini 28 ☎095 322 709, ⓦgresihotel.com. Traditional hotel, with a pleasantly old-fashioned atmosphere, where spacious rooms with frescoed ceilings offer exactly what you'd expect of a three-star hotel – charmless veneer furniture, plain furnishings, phones, fridges and a/c. Handy location between Via Etnea and the bustling Piazza Carlo Alberto market. **€64**

Liberty Hotel Via San Vito 40 ☎095 311 651, ⓦliberty hotel.it. Intimate and romantic hotel in an early twentieth-century *palazzo*, a 10min walk from Via Etnea. Decorated in a carefully researched Liberty style, the hotel has a calm atmosphere and a trellis-shaded courtyard, and is an ideal place to recuperate after a long journey. There are good-value discounts and packages, including trips to Etna via the website. There's no restaurant, but a local pizzeria will deliver to the hotel. **€131**

Una Hotel Via Etnea 218 ☎095 250 5111, ⓦunahotels.it. Chic designer hotel belonging to a national chain, whose decor reflects the dominant black and white of the city's Baroque architecture (and of snowcapped Etna): floors of Etna lava and Comiso limestone; beds laid with cream cotton and black velvet; and Baroque-style chairs sprayed gold and upholstered in black. Facilities include a roof terrace and restaurant-bar with spectacular views of Etna, and a gym with steam bath. **€132**

EATING

SEE MAP PAGE 186

Catania's streets teem until late, especially in summer. **Restaurants** are pretty good value, thanks to the presence of so many students. If you're self-catering, note that the nearest big supermarket is Punto SMA, Corso Sicilia 50 (Mon–Sat 8.30am–8.30pm, Sun 8.30am–1.30pm; ☎095 326 099).

★ **Da Aldo** Piazza G. Sciuti 2 ☎095 311 158. The best choice near the Fera o Luni market, this is an amiable first-floor lunchtime grill-house where bustling waiters reel off the daily specials (*pasta alla Norma*, stuffed squid or a simple grilled sea bass or steak). It's great value; less than €20 for a full meal including house wine. From Piazza Carlo Alberto, take the first left off Via Pacini, down Via al Carmine. No credit cards. Mon–Sat lunch only.

Antica Marina Via Pardo 29 ☎095 348 197. Trattoria bang in the heart of the fish market where you can eat reasonably priced fresh fish. Go for one of the set menus, ranging in price from €25 to €65. Daily except Wed lunch & dinner.

Camelot Piazza Federico di Svevia 75 ☎095 723 2103. Lively, cheap and cheerful place where you can feast for a song on Sicilian *antipasti* (€5), a huge range of panini (€3) or barbecued sausages and meat (from €3 per (large) sausage), pasta (from €5) and drink local wine from plastic cups. Daily for dinner only.

Friggitoria Stella Via Monsignor Ventimiglia 66 ☎095 535 002. A great place to try *crispelle* and other traditional fried snacks, this backstreet establishment off Via Giovanni di Prima has been going for years. Tues–Sun 5pm–late; closed in summer.

Oxidiana Via Conte Ruggero 4/A ☎095 532 585, ⓦoxidiana.it. Scores of different sushi, including California rolls, along with *tataki*, tempura, stir-fries and a marvellous sesame-crusted tuna (best in May and June, the height of the tuna season). There are vegetarian options and lots of gluten-free dishes, plus fabulous cocktails and over sixty different rums for the trying. A great place, and they deliver too (daily 6.30–8.30pm only). Daily dinner only.

La Paglia Via Pardo 23 ☎095 346 838. Basic trattoria (wipe-clean tablecloths, panel-board walls) for a reasonably priced fish-market lunch – when the *signora* runs out of something at lunchtime she just bellows through the kitchen window at the stallholders for more. *Antipasti* cost €5–10, pasta dishes such as spaghetti and clams are €7–10, and the vast majority of the fish mains are €10. The house wine is the kind that you can run your car on.

Mon–Sat lunch & dinner.

Savia Via Etnea 302 ☎ 095 322 335. Opposite the main entrance to the Villa Bellini, this is the city's most notable *pasticceria*, open since 1897 and always busy with folk digging into savoury *arancini*, ricotta-stuffed *cannoli*, real *cassata* and the like, all for around €2 apiece. Tues–Sun 7am–8pm.

Sicilia in Bocca Via Dusmet 35 ☎ 095 250 0208. One of the nicest places in town to sit outside, this is pizzeria one side, restaurant the other (though in practice you can mix and match menus), sharing a shaded terrace. It's set in the old arched sea wall (through Porta Uzeda from Piazza del Duomo and turn left), and service is friendly and English-speaking. Pizzas are €6–10, pasta dishes €8–12, mains €12–20. Mon–Fri dinner only, Sat & Sun lunch & dinner.

Trattoria da Nuccio Via Penninello 34–38, ☎ 095 322 461. On a side street just a short walk uphill from Via Etnea, this little fish trattoria is a good choice if you want a little more peace and refinement than you'll find in the fish market eateries. The fragrantly herbed steamed mussels are to die for, there's a lovely pasta dish with lemon, prawns and pine nuts, and the *fritto misto* is a great way to sample some of the tiny fish so beloved of Sicilians, along with crisp calamari, and *polpette*, traditional Sicilian fishcakes. Expect to pay around €30 a head for a full dinner excluding wine. Tues–Sat lunch & dinner, Sun lunch only.

DRINKING AND NIGHTLIFE

SEE MAP PAGE 186

Catania's student population makes sure there is some lively **nightlife**. The whole ambience is helped by the fact that the *Comune* closes old-town streets and squares to traffic (the so-called *café concerto*) and bars spill tables outside until the small hours. Of the outdoor **cafés**, those in Piazza del Duomo and Piazza dell'Università have the best views, while the cooler studenty **bars** are found around Piazza Bellini (particularly down Via Teatro Massimo, in Via Rapisardi and in adjacent piazzas Ogninella and Scammacca). In summer, there are open-air venues for **dancing** until the early hours along the coast on the outskirts of town – ask around and look for posters and flyers for the latest spots.

Nievski Via Alessi 15–17 ☎ 095 313 792. They love Che Guevara in this *"pub-trattoria alternativo"*, where you can come for a plate of organic food, a Fair Trade coffee or a beer. There's internet access, all kinds of concerts and events, and more goatees and ponytails than you can shake a stick at. It's on the Alessi steps up to Via Crociferi. Tues–Sat noon–late, and Sun eve.

ENTERTAINMENT

While the Bellini theatre is the traditional centre of opera, music and ballet, Catania's new focus for **culture and the arts** is the Zo centre (see page 190). Summer is the best time for **concerts and events**, from open-air jazz in the Villa Bellini gardens to classical concerts in churches and theatres across the city. To find out what's on, check the **listings information** in several local publications (see page 193).

Teatro Massimo Bellini Via Perrotta 12 ☎ 095 730 6111 or ☎ 095 715 0921, ⊛ teatromassimobellini.it. Facing Piazza Bellini, Catania's impressive opera house has a concert season that runs from Oct until May, which includes classical music and ballet as well as opera.

Zo Viale Africa ☎ 095 533 871, ⊛ zoculture.it. Catania's centre for contemporary arts (see page 190) is the place for cutting-edge theatre, electronic and world music, experimental art shows, off-the-wall installations and offbeat festivals. It's a 2min walk from Stazione Centrale.

DIRECTORY

Hospital Ospedale Garibaldi, Piazza S. Maria di Gesù 7 ☎ 095 759 111.

Pharmacies Caltabiano, Piazza Stesicoro 36 (☎ 095 327 647); Croce Rossa, Via Etnea 274 (☎ 095 327 232); Europa, Corso Italia 111 (☎ 095 383 536); Cutelli, Via Vittorio Emanuele II 54 (☎ 095 531 400). All open daily 8.30am–1pm & 5–8pm; late openings are indicated by a rota posted on the shop windows.

Police In emergencies call ☎ 112. Otherwise, the Carabinieri are at Via Teatro Greco 111 (☎ 095 326 666); questura (police HQ) is at Piazza S. Nicolella (☎ 095 736 7111).

Post office The main post office is close to the Villa Bellini at Via Etnea 215 (Mon–Fri 8.20am–7.05pm, Sat 8.20am–12.35pm).

THE SCOGLI DEI CICLOPI

Aci Castello, 10km north up the coast from Catania, marks the beginning of the so-called Riviera dei Ciclopi, named after the jagged points of the **Scogli dei Ciclopi** that rise from the sea just beyond town. Homer wrote that the blinded Polyphemus slung these rocks (broken from Etna) at Odysseus and his men as they escaped from the Cyclops in their ships. The largest of the three main sharp-edged islets – also known as *faraglioni* – sticks some 60m into the sky.

5

Catania's beach resorts

The main sandy beaches (known simply as the Playa) lie south of Catania, on the wide **Golfo di Catania** (Viale Kennedy), but it's actually the coast north of the city that's the most popular **resort area**. The lava streams from Etna have reached the sea many times over the centuries, turning the coastline into an attractive mix of contorted black rocks and sheer coves, excellent for swimming. Consequently, what was once a series of small fishing villages is now a fair-sized strip of hotels, lidos and restaurants, idle in the winter but swarming in summer with day-trippers. Incidentally, the prefix "Aci", given to a number of settlements here, derives from the local River Aci, said to have appeared following the death of the herdsman Acis at the hands of the giant, one-eyed Polyphemus, jealous that the nymph Galatea had fallen in love with him. According to Ovid, the distraught Galatea turned Acis' blood into the river (which is, disappointingly, no longer identifiable).

The first stop on trains heading north along the coast is **OGNINA,** a small suburb on the northern outskirts of Catania, built on lava cliffs formed in the fifteenth century. It has a few restaurants overlooking the little harbour, as well as a campsite (see below). Continue up the coast, and, 9km from Catania, you'll reach **ACI CASTELLO**, which is a striking place, its castle rising high above the sea in splinters from a volcanic rock crag. The base of the rebel Roger di Lauria in 1297, it's remarkably well preserved, despite many threatening eruptions and the destruction wrought by Frederick II of Aragon, who took the castle from Roger by erecting a wooden siege engine adjacent. The ragged coastline to the north is popular for sunbathing and swimming and, in summer, a wooden boardwalk is built over the lava rocks (you pay a small fee to use the changing rooms and showers).

You could always walk the couple of kilometres north along the rough coast from Aci Castello to **ACI TREZZA**, the fishing village at the heart of nineteenth-century Sicilian novelist Giovanni Verga's masterpiece *I Malavoglia*. It is a pleasant resort, with bars, *gelaterie* and seafood restaurants ranged along the lungomare.

ARRIVAL AND DEPARTURE

CATANIA'S BEACH RESORTS

By bus AMT bus #534 runs approximately hourly from Catania's Piazza Borsellino to Aci Castello and Aci Trezza, or take the Katane Live hop-on, hop-off bus from Piazza Duomo (see page 192). The beaches of the Golfo di Catania are reached by taking summer bus #D (approximately hourly June–Sept) from Piazza Borsellino.

ACCOMMODATION

Camping Jonio Via Villini a Mare 2 ☎095 491139, ⓦ campingjonio.com. Campsite with fixed tents, tent pitches and bungalows perched on the lava cliffs in the residential suburb of Ognina. Pitches €8, pitches with fixed two-person tent €15, bungalows (sleeping three) €55.

Acireale

ACIREALE, 16km north of Catania, has a marvellous site, high above the rocky shore and the surrounding lemon groves. It's a location best appreciated from the public gardens at the northern end of town, from where you can look right back along the Riviera dei Ciclopi. Known since Roman times as a spa centre (the thermal baths are still heavily used), Acireale is also another striking example of Sicilian Baroque town planning. This is the fourth successive town on the site, rebuilt directly over the old lava streams after the 1693 earthquake, and, as in Catania, it relies on grand buildings, a handsome central square and Duomo, and some long thoroughfares for its effect.

Santa Maria la Scala

The pleasantest place to while away a few hours in Acireale – especially over lunch – is the tiny hamlet of **Santa Maria la Scala**, 2km below town, huddled around a minuscule harbour full of painted fishing boats, where three or four trattorias overlook the bay. To get here on foot, go down Via Romeo (to the side of the Municipio), across the busy main road and then down the steep rural path to the water.

ARRIVAL AND DEPARTURE ACIREALE

By bus Buses to Acireale from Catania stop outside the public gardens or near the Duomo.

By train Trains run regularly (1–2 hourly) between Acireale and Catania. The train station is well to the south of town, near the thermal baths, and a long walk into the centre along Via Vittorio Emanuele II.

Lentini and around

Thirty minutes or so south of Catania by road, **LENTINI** has a long pedigree that puts it among the earliest of the Greek settlements in Sicily, and the first of all the inland colonies. Established in 729 BC as a daughter city of Naxos, Lentini (Leontinoi) flourished as a commercial centre for two hundred and fifty years, before being colonized by the expansionist Hippocrates of Gela in 476 BC. Eventually, the city was absorbed by Syracuse, sharing its disasters but never its prosperity. It was Leontinoi's struggle to assert its independence, by allying itself with Athens, that provided the pretext for the great Athenian expedition against Syracuse in 415 BC. Another attempt – this time an alliance with the Carthaginians during the Second Punic War – resulted in the Romans beheading two thousand of its citizens, a measure that horrified the whole island, as no doubt it was intended to do. By the time Cicero got round to describing the city, Lentini was "wretched and empty", though it continued as a small-scale agricultural centre for some time, until the great earthquake of 1693 completely demolished it.

Noisy, sprawling, modern Lentini has little to recommend it, and the extensive remains of the ancient city are a few kilometres out of town and easier to reach from the upper town of **CARLENTINI**, which itself has a fairly pleasant central square with a few bars. Some finds from ancient Lentini are on display in the **Museo Archeologico** (Tues–Sun 9am–6pm; €4), at Piazza Studi, east of central Carlentini off Via Piave. However, the best artefacts have been appropriated by the museums at Catania and Siracusa.

Leontinoi

The site is a 20min walk south of Carlentini; most Lentini buses also stop on the outskirts of Carlentini, closer to the Zona Archeologica, as do local buses from Lentini's train station, from where the site is a 5min walk • Daily 9am–1pm • Free

The **Zona Archeologica** is spread over the two hills of San Mauro and Metapiccola. The first of these is the more interesting, holding the ancient town's **acropolis**, the substantial remains of a vast **necropolis** nearby and the pincer-style south gate, part of a well-conserved system of fortifications that surrounded the town. Together, the hills make for a couple of hours' rambling, while a dirt road to the side of the main entrance climbs around the perimeter fence to allow views over the whole site and down to Lentini in the valley below.

ACIREALE DRESSES UP

Acireale is known throughout Italy for its celebrations during **Carnevale** (Feb/March), when it hosts one of Sicily's best festivals, with extraordinarily elaborate flower-decked floats and fancy-dress parades clogging the streets for five noisy days. The town also has a long tradition of Sicilian **puppet theatre**, with regular shows performed in summer by its surviving theatre companies, like that of Turi Grasso at Via Nazionale 195 (☏ 095 764 8035, ⊛ operadeipupi.com), which also has a small **museum** at the theatre (summer Wed, Sat & Sun 9am–noon & 6–9pm; winter Wed, Sat & Sun 9am–noon & 3–6pm; free).

5

> ### SNOW, ICE AND THE BISHOP
>
> Even in winter, the **snow** on Etna's southern side tends to lie only in patches, partly melted by the heat of the rocks. On the northern side, however, hollows in the ground are filled year-round with snow. From here, the **ice** used to be cut, covered with ash and then transported to the rest of the island, the mainland and even Malta, for refrigeration purposes – a peculiar export that constituted the main source of revenue for the Bishop of Catania, who owned the land until comparatively recently.

ARRIVAL AND DEPARTURE   LENTINI

By train Most trains between Catania and Siracusa stop at Lentini. Buses for Carlentini leave hourly from outside the station.
By bus Buses from Catania run to Lentini approximately half-hourly taking around an hour, and many also stop in Carlentini – ask your driver and he will let you off at the stop closest to the archeological zone.

EATING

Navarria Via Conte Alaimo 8 ☎095 941 045. For a snack in Lentini, seek out this fabulous *pasticceria* (anyone can point the way), where pastries and *granitas* are really superb. Tues–Sun 7am–9.30pm.

Mount Etna

One of the largest volcanoes in the world, **Mount Etna** (3323m) dominates much of Sicily's eastern landscape, its smoking summit an omnipresent feature for travellers in the area. The main crater is gradually becoming more explosive and more dangerous, with recent eruptions far eclipsing those of the preceding decade (see page 204). Despite the risk, the volcano remains a remarkable draw, though the unpredictability of eruptions – they may be expected, but cannot be pinpointed to a precise time – means that it's often impossible to get close to the main crater.

Etna was just one of the places that the Greeks and Romans thought to be the forge of Hephaestus/Vulcan (the god of fire), a fitting description of the blustering and sparking emitted from the main crater. The philosopher Empedocles studied the volcano closely, living in an observatory near the summit. This terrifying existence was dramatized by Matthew Arnold in his *Empedocles on Etna*:

Alone! –
On this charr'd, blacken'd melancholy waste,
Crown'd by the awful peak, Etna's great mouth.

Certainly, it all proved too much for Empedocles, who in 433 BC jumped into the main crater in an attempt to prove that the gases emitted would support his body weight. They didn't.

The higher reaches of Etna resemble a lunar landscape, the ground underfoot alternately black, grey or red depending on the age of the lava. The most recent stuff lies in great folds; below, the red roofs and green fields of the lower hills stretch away to the sea. You'll not be in any danger, provided you stay within the limit that is currently deemed safe to reach. Note that **ascending the volcano** is only possible between about May and October; the rest of the time, it's swathed in snow. For obvious reasons, access to the upper reaches of Etna, around the craters, is strictly controlled – current volcanic activity and weather conditions will dictate how far up you'll be able to go.

However you go, at whatever time of year, take warm clothes, good shoes or boots and glasses to keep the flying grit out of your eyes. You can **rent boots and jackets** cheaply from the Etna Sud cable-car station. Food up the mountain is poor and overpriced, so you might want to bring a picnic.

5

Approaches to Etna

A ring of villages circles the lower slopes of Etna, including the ski centres of **Linguaglossa** (on the Circumetnea rail route) and **Nicolosi**, which hold the bulk of the accommodation, restaurants and tour facilities. The two main approaches to the summit are from north and south. Some of the best scenery is on the north side (signposted "**Etna Nord**"), and if you have your own transport, the circular road that leads up from Linguaglossa to Piano Provenzana, and then to the *Rifugio Cutelli*, is highly recommended – though the road beyond **Piano Provenzana** is strictly controlled in snowy weather, and even with a 4WD you may be strongly encouraged to leave your vehicle and take an organized jeep trip. From the south side ("**Etna Sud**"), beyond Nicolosi, the chief departure point is the mountain refuge-hotel of **Rifugio Sapienza**, connected by daily bus from Catania.

If you're short on time, the easiest way to see the volcano and climb its slopes is by **organized tour**. 4WD minibuses and guided hikes operate out of Piano Provenzana and *Rifugio Sapienza*, though many tourists simply book an all-day tour via their hotel or B&B in places like Taormina, Giardini-Naxos, Catania and Siracusa. If you're pushed for time or unable to ascend higher due to adverse conditions, you'll have to make do with the glimpses of Etna's peak and hinterland from the **Ferrovia Circumetnea** (see box).

Etna Nord

If you have a car, head to **LINGUAGLOSSA** and drive through the town following the brown signs to **Etna Nord**. There are several picnic places with barbecues along the road, and buying some quality local meat before you leave Linguaglossa is probably the only reason to stop in town.

The road up the mountain from Linguaglossa is at its most spectacular in winter, when the peak of Etna is covered in snow. As you drive along, look out for ungainly lumps of solidified lava colonized with lichen protruding through the undergrowth. Beyond **Rifugio Ragabo** (1425m), follow the sign for **Piano Provenzana**. Today, the scorched skeletons of trees still protrude eerily from a vast river of solidified lava, dating back to an eruption in 2002. Head back to the main road and continue until you come to a side road marked **Rifugio Citelli** (1750m). On a clear day the views stretch across the Nebrodi mountains, to Taormina, and over the Ionian Sea, to the Aspromonte mountains in Calabria. The Refugio isn't always staffed, but when it is, basic food is available, as are treks up the volcano (snow shoes are provided during winter). The

---

THE FERROVIA CIRCUMETNEA

Although there's nothing to beat an ascent of Etna, you can experience something of the majesty of the volcano along the route of the **Ferrovia Circumetnea**, or Circumetnea railway (☎ 095 541 250, ⊛ circumetnea.it). This is a private line, 110km long, starting in Catania and circling the base of Etna as far as Riposto on the Ionian coast, 30km north of Catania. It's a marvellous ride, running through fertile vegetation – citrus plantations, vines and nut trees – and past the strewn lava of recent eruptions, with endless views of the summit en route. If you don't have time to do the whole circuit, note that some of the best views of Etna are between Adrano and Bronte, as the railway line climbs ever closer to the lava flows.

You can easily do the whole round trip in a day from Catania, although the medieval town of Randazzo also makes an interesting overnight stop. The Circumetnea ends its run 20km southeast of Linguaglossa at Riposto, where you switch to the mainline station Giarre-Riposto for frequent trains south to Catania (or north to Giardini-Naxos).

Circumetnea trains depart from Stazione Catania Borgo, on Via Caronda in Catania. They take two hours to Randazzo, three to Linguaglossa and three and a half to Riposto (no Sunday service; timetables available on the website), and **tickets** cost €7.90 one-way, €13 return. Note that frequently sections of the line are under repair – not least because of eruptions! In this case a replacement bus service operates.

THE ASCENT OF ETNA FROM RIFUGIO SAPIENZA

The easiest way to ascend Etna is by the **Funivia dell'Etna** (☎095 914 141, ☯funiviaetna.com) **cable car** from the *Rifugio Sapienza*, essentially an Alpine-style hostel/restaurant with a huge car park and numerous trashy souvenir shops and snack bars. It is also the closest place to the summit served by bus from Catania. From here the cable car (daily: summer 9am–5.30pm; winter 9am–3.30pm; €24 one-way, €30 return) lurches up the barren slope of the volcano to a ridge known as Monte Montagnola, taking ten to fifteen minutes. Volcanic activity levels will affect how far you can explore once you are up there – either independently or by 4WD minibus.

On foot You can walk all the way up from the *Rifugio Sapienza* but it will take around four hours, and is a dull trudge up slopes of lava. You are better off taking the cable car to Monte Montagnola and walking from there. Once at the top, paths are clearly marked, though not signposted, giving various views of the three central craters and Valle di Bove.

By 4WD minibus These leave from the top of the cable-car station (April–Oct daily 9am–5pm, weather permitting) and the total journey, including cable car, minibus and guide, takes around two hours thirty minutes (€65/person). When the wind is up, or conditions are otherwise difficult, the entire journey is undertaken from *Rifugio Sapienza* by minibus.

descent takes you through a black moonscape of lava and back along the foothills of Etna to Linguaglossa.

ACCOMMODATION AND EATING   ETNA NORD

Rifugio Ragabo Pineta Bosco Ragabo ☎095 647 841, ☯ragabo.it. Simple, cosy pine-wood *rifugio*-hotel, high up on Etna near Linguaglossa, which makes a perfect base for an active mountain holiday – winter or summer – with cosy doubles and family rooms and a pleasant restaurant, serving hearty mountain food, that is open to all. Half and full board are available (€50/€70 per person); otherwise rates include breakfast. Closed Nov. Bed and breakfast **€70**

Etna Sud

More built-up and touristy than the north slope, **Etna Sud** offers the easiest approach to the volcano via public transport, with buses connecting Catania with the *Rifugio Sapienza* (see below), which is at the foot of the cable car to the summit and at the end of the negotiable road up the south side of Etna. The ride up Etna to the *rifugio* throws up some truly bizarre scenery: the green foothills give way to wooded slopes, then to bare, black-and-grey seas of volcanic debris, spotted with the hardy endemic plants – yellow-green *spino santo* and Etna violets – that are the only things to grow on the heights of the volcano. The most recent lava streams lie to the right of the road, where you'll also see earlier spent craters, grass-covered on the lower reaches and no more than black pimples further up.

ARRIVAL AND DEPARTURE   ETNA SUD

By bus One or two buses a day, depending on the time of year, head from Catania to *Rifugio Sapienza*, the mountain refuge-hotel that marks the end of the negotiable road up the south side of Etna. The year-round service leaves from Piazza Giovanni XXIII, outside Catania's Stazione Centrale, daily at 8.15am, with a stop at Nicolosi; an additional summer service (mid-June to mid-Sept) leaves daily at 11.20am, and necessitates a change at Nicolosi. Altogether, it's a two-hour journey; tickets cost €6.60 return. (You can, of course, catch the bus at Nicolosi, from where departures to the refuge are at 9.15am and – in summer – 12.30pm, an hour-long trip.) The return bus from *Rifugio Sapienza* leaves for Catania at 4.30pm.

ACCOMMODATION

Hotel Corsaro ☎095 914 122, ☯hotelcorsaro.it. Ski-lodge-type place popular with tour groups, advertising itself as Etna's highest lodging. It has a restaurant and offers half-board deals (€70 per person). **€79.**

Rifugio Sapienza ☎095 915 321, ☯rifugiosapienza. com. At 1400m below the summit, this is the cheapest place on the south side of Etna to spend the night, so it's always wise to ring ahead and book. Its modern rooms have clean lines and en-suite bathrooms, and there's a restaurant (excursions can also be arranged from here). **€69**

5

Nicolosi and around

The tidy little resort of **NICOLOSI** (698m), which had a narrow escape in the 2002 eruption, is a popular winter ski centre and the most useful base in the foothills on the south side of the volcano. With several hotels and some good places to eat, it also has decent bus connections from Catania. It gets pretty busy around here, even in summer, with some lovely walking possibilities in the area. Best of these, certainly if you're going no further, is the hike up to the **Monti Rossi** craters, around an hour each way. Formed in the eruption of 1669, they're the most important of the secondary craters that litter the slopes of the volcano.

Five kilometres or so east of Nicolosi is **Trecastagni**, is worth a look for its main church, the Chiesa Madre, a fine Renaissance building probably designed by Antonello Gagini, and for the marvellous views over the coast from its elevated position. Frankly, though, you're hardly likely to come here for just these; better, if you're driving, to look upon Trecastagni as a coffee-stop.

ARRIVAL   NICOLOSI

By bus Nicolosi is the last main bus stop before the steeper   slopes begin; AST buses run hourly from Catania, taking 40min.

ACCOMMODATION AND EATING

Camping Etna Via Goethe ☎ 095 914 309. Nice campsite in a shady pine wood with a pool (summer only) signposted from town just past the hotels. Open all year. Tent pitch plus two people **€20**
Al Centro Storico Via Garibaldi 26 ☎ 095 910 735 or ☎ 348 266 4310, ⌨ alcentrostorico.it. A good, central B&B with antique-style touches, along with fridges and TV,

just off Piazza Vittorio Emanuele. **€60**
Nero di Cenere Via Garibaldi 64 ☎ 095 791 8513. Wine bar and restaurant serving taster plates of local cheeses and salami, along with pastas and various vegetarian dishes, which you can enjoy al fresco on the terrace. Mon 4pm–midnight, Tue–Sun noon–3.30pm & 4.30pm–midnight.

Zafferana Etnea

The most appealing of the villages on Etna's southeastern side, **ZAFFERANA ETNEA** is surrounded by vineyards and citrus groves, and is renowned for its honey, the smell of which lingers in the air. Although lava has reached its surroundings on several occasions (most recently winter 2018), the centre has remained untouched, and it retains an eighteenth-century air in its buildings and churches, making it a pleasant stop, perhaps for a coffee in the bar on the corner of the elegant central piazza.

Zafferana has acquired a reputation as a low-key hill resort, and the population of around seven thousand practically doubles at weekends and holidays as the trippers arrive. Certainly, there's some good walking to be done in the green hills behind the village, and if you fancy

---

ETNA NORD BY ORGANIZED TOUR

If you don't have your own vehicle, you can join an **organized hike** to the summit from Linguaglossa or the ski centre of Piano Provenzana – contact Guide Etna Nord for details (Via Roma 93, Linguaglossa; ☎ 095 777 4502 or ☎ 348 012 5167, ⌨ guidetnanord.com). Solo expeditions are not encouraged. From Piano Provenzana, there are **tours** aboard 4WD minibuses operated by STAR (daily May–Oct, weather permitting; ☎ 095 371 333 or ☎ 347 495 7091). There are several itineraries (though these can change without warning if the volcano is active!) but in general the early-morning and early-evening tours are the best – Etna at dawn or sunset is a spectacular sight – but do need booking. The minibuses don't run to a fixed timetable; they simply take off when full, and the operation is a more low-key affair than on the southern side.

Katane Live in Catania (see page 192) have also added an Etna tour to their portfolio (€30), leaving from Piazza Duomo at 11am, with brief stops at Nicolosi, *Rifugio Sapienza* (1hr stop) and Zafferana Etnea. For a more intense Etna experience, opt for a jeep tour with Geo Etna Explorer (☎ 349 610 9957, ⌨ geoetnaexplorer.com) where you get to visit a spectacular basalt quarry, "pahoehoe" and "aa" lavas, the Bove Valley, a house surrounded by lava, and a volcanic cave, using helmets and lights (€5). The cost is from €59 for a half-day, and includes pick-up from your hotel.

THE WINES OF ETNA

Thanks to mineral-rich volcanic soil, an extremely low yield and a varied climate (temperatures can range from 30°C to 0°C in a single day), the **vineyards** on Etna's foothills have the potential to produce some of Italy's most interesting **wines**. They were also some of the only vineyards in Europe to survive the phylloxera epidemic of the late nineteenth century – the virus couldn't pass through volcanic powder, sand or snow. The richness and complexity of the grapes grown here has led several producers to rebel against the trend of ageing wines in *barriques* (small oak barrels), preferring instead to use stainless-steel vats or even ceramic amphorae, so that there is nothing to interfere with the natural taste of the grape. At the vanguard of this movement are the highly talented Tuscan wine-producer **Andrea Franchetti**, whose Etna vineyards produce the international award-winning Passopisciaro (☏ 366 358 9926, ⊛ passopisciaro.com); and eccentric Belgian **Frank Cornelissen** (⊛ frankcornelissen.it), who spurns the use of sulphates in wines such as Magma and MunJebel, which now enjoy a cult following (especially in Japan) for their extreme unpredictability. You can get a free tour of these vineyards by appointment.

a longer stay there's a choice of **hotels**, all north of the centre. A road from Zafferana Etnea winds directly up the mountain to *Rifugio Sapienza* (see page 201), a drive of around 45 minutes, while a lower road leads 15km north past various old lava flows to Linguaglossa.

ARRIVAL AND DEPARTURE ZAFFERANA ETNEA

By bus Buses run hourly Mon–Sat (4 daily Sun) from Catania to Zafferana Etnea, taking 1hr 15min.

ACCOMMODATION

Monaci delle Terre Nere Stunning eco-minimalism on a former wine estate, with a super-cool lava stone edged swimming pool, and a restaurant where much of the produce is home-grown. They even make their own syrups for the cocktails. Attention to every detail, and a zen-like atmosphere combine to make this one of Sicily's finest hotel experiences, just as it should be for the price. **€500**

Primavera dell'Etna Via Cassone 86 ☏ 095 708 2348, ⊛ hotel-primavera.it. Large, well-equipped hotel, if a bit shabby at the seams. It's more popular with Italians than foreigners, with fabulous views of Etna and the sea from its terraces, and lovely grounds with a tennis court and solarium. Rooms can be a bit old-fashioned, but the location is great, staff friendly and there is a restaurant too, serving local food, with half-board deals should you so wish. **€90**

Milò and around

Five kilometres or so north of Zafferana, **Milò** offers impressive views of the Valle del Bove above. Maps show a road from Milò that climbs northwest, up the volcano to the *Rifugio Citelli* (see page 200) and back towards Linguaglossa, but frequent landslides often make this route impassable. You should be able to get some of the way up though, for more striking views of the summit and the coastline below.

Etna Adventure

Parco Sbargaglio, Via Acque del Vescovo • Daily 10am–sunset; sometimes closed weekends mid-Sept to mid-June, call ahead to check • From €18 for adults, €10–14 for children depending on age and height • ☏ 329 918 8187, ⊛ etnaadventure.it

If you've kids in tow, you may get no further than **Etna Adventure**, just outside Milò on the road to Linguaglossa. An excellent adventure park, it has challenging Tarzan-like obstacle courses slung among the trees for adults and children (from age 2 and up). They also organize all manner of activities on and around Etna, including snow-shoe trekking, whitewater rafting, potholing and jeep tours.

Randazzo

Great rivers of volcanic rubble clutter the slopes on all sides of **RANDAZZO**, the closest town to the summit of Etna, just 15km away as the crow flies. Walls belonging to

5

MOUNT ETNA'S ERUPTIONS

Of the scores of recorded **eruptions** of Etna since the one in 475 BC described by Pindar, some have been disastrously spectacular: in 1169, 1329 and 1381 the lava reached the sea, while in **1669**, the worst year, parts of Catania were wrecked and its castle was surrounded by molten rock.

The Circumetnea railway line is repeatedly ruptured by lava flows, the towns of the foothills were threatened, and roads and farms destroyed – an eruption in **1971**, ironically enough, destroyed the observatory that was supposed to give warning of such an event, and in **1979** nine tourists were killed by an explosion on the edge of the main crater. During the **1992** eruption, which engulfed the outskirts of Zafferana Etnea, the American navy joined Italian forces in an attempt to stem the lava flow by dropping reinforced concrete blocks (so-called "Beirut-busters", usually used to defend military camps) from helicopters into the fissures.

In **2001**, military helicopters were out again in force, this time water-bombing forest fires and blazing orchards. Regarded as the most complex in the last three hundred years, the 2001 eruption spewed forth from six vents on Etna's northern and southeastern sides and sent vast, fiery fountains of lava to the skies. Drivers found the roads blocked and air passengers were forced to divert to other island airports, while Catania suffered a rain of black ash day and night. Luckily there were no fatalities; the cluster of buildings around *Rifugio Sapienza* narrowly escaped and the lava flow petered out 4km short of Nicolosi, though the upper cable-car station was destroyed and the hut that held the monitoring live-cam incinerated (somehow the equipment was saved).

Triggered by an earthquake, the eruption of **2002** saw lava streams pouring down both north and south flanks, destroying restaurants, hotels and a cable car in the ski resort of Piano Provenzana, and threatening the villages of Nicolosi and Linguaglossa below. Emergency teams, however, succeeded in diverting the flow, and a major catastrophe was averted. Some local villagers, on the other hand, preferred to place their faith in parading statues of the Virgin Mary before the volcano, although the devout were far outnumbered by the flocks of sightseers who made excursions as close as they dared, until curtailed by the authorities.

More eruptions followed in **2006**, **2007** and **2008**, the last accompanied by minor local earthquakes and continuing at a low intensity for some six months, making it the longest of the eruptions in the twenty-first century. A significant eruption of ash also occurred in **2010**, producing an ash plume that rose to a height of 800m above the crater.

In late **2013**, Etna began erupting again, with most of the activity centred around the southeast crater. Pulsating lava fountains reached 600m in height, and explosions of giant magma bubbles ejected liquid lava for hundreds of meters, destroying the Torre del Filosofo and entering the Valle del Bove. There were also some pretty spectacular explosions in **2018–19**, with lava fragments raining on the town of Giardini-Naxos, and glowing lava visible from as far away as Siracusa. Anyone intending to visit Etna is advised to consult the regularly updated English-language **website** ⓦ volcanodiscovery.com for an update on current conditions.

former orchards or vineyards are occasionally visible through the black debris. Despite its dangerous proximity, the town has never been engulfed, though an eruption in 1981 came perilously close – as you can see from the jagged frills of lava around its periphery. Randazzo has not escaped entirely unscathed, however: as one of the main forward positions of the German forces during their defence of Sicily in 1943, the town was heavily bombed, and most of the lava-built churches and palaces you'll see here, originally dating from the wealthy thirteenth- to sixteenth-century era, are the result of meticulous restoration. The result is a handsome old centre, with enough to occupy a half-day's exploration – and Randazzo is easily the best place to break your Circumetnea trip if you fancy a night in the sticks.

In medieval times, three churches took turns to act as Randazzo's cathedral, a sop to the three parishes in town whose inhabitants were of Greek, Latin and Lombard origin. The largest, **Santa Maria**, on the main Via Umberto I, is the modern-day holder of the title, a severe Catalan-Gothic structure with a fine carved portal with vine decoration. Further up the road, facing a small square, the blackened tower that forms part of the old city walls is all that survives of Randazzo's Castello Svevo, which did duty as a prison from around 1500 until 1973.

Museo Vagliasindi

Via Castello 1 • Tues–Sun 10am–1pm & 3–6pm • €4 • ☎ 095 799 0064

Museo Vagliasindi holds a good collection of objects from a nearby Greek necropolis, including wine jugs in the form of women's heads, and a vessel in the shape of a spunky little rat. Downstairs you'll find ranks of dangling Sicilian puppets, variously sporting armour, a velvet cloak or a deer-stalker cap – typically for eastern Sicily, they are taller than the puppets you may have seen in Palermo. The tower was once a prison, and you can still see the minuscule cells where inmates once rotted. The museum's other rooms display agricultural tools and other rustic items.

ARRIVAL AND INFORMATION

RANDAZZO

By Circumetnea train Arriving on the Circumetnea, walk straight up Via Vittorio Veneto to reach the central Piazza Loreto, with the medieval town further on, down Via Umberto I.
Destinations Catania (up to 7 daily Mon–Sat; 2hr 20min); Linguaglossa (4 daily Mon–Sat; 35min); Riposto (4 daily Mon–Sat; 1hr 10min).

By bus The bus station is a couple of blocks back from Piazza Loreto off Via Vittorio Veneto. There are frequent connections with Catania (1–2 hourly Mon–Sat; 1hr 45min), and limited services (early morning and lunchtime) to several other places you might want to visit, such as Bronte, Castiglione di Sicilia and Gole Alcantara. There's also a morning bus (leaving at 8am) to Taormina.

ACCOMMODATION AND EATING

Ai Tre Parchi Bed and Bike Via Tagliamento 49 ☎ 095 799 1631 or ☎ 329 897 0901, ⓦ aitreparchibb.it. Basic place offering B&B rooms and self-catering apartments (from €120), plus bike rental and local bike tours. To reach Via Tagliamento, turn left off Via Vittorio Veneto from the station. Doubles **€55**
Da Antonio Via Pietro Nenni 8 ☎ 095 799 2534. Best place in town for typical local dishes and pizzas (€6–10); the house *antipasto* is really good, too. The restaurant is a few hundred metres from Piazza Loreto – walk down the Linguaglossa road, past the petrol stations, and it's up a side

road on the right. Tues–Sun lunch & dinner.
San Giorgio e Il Drago Piazza San Giorgio 28 ☎ 095 923 972. Lovely, cosy trattoria housed in a nineteenth-century wine cellar, run by Samantha and Daniele Anzalone, with seasonal food cooked by their two mothers. In spring, there's the chance to eat home-made pasta with wild asparagus; in autumn, look out for dishes using porcini mushrooms collected from the woods of Etna; and in winter, sausage fried with wild greens. Expect to pay around €35 per head for a full meal with a glass of wine. Mon & Wed–Sun dinner only.

Bronte

A small, unassuming town with a noble past, **BRONTE** lies thirty minutes' drive southwest of Randazzo along the SS284. It was founded by Charles V in 1535, and many echoes of its original layout survive, particularly in the numerous battlemented campaniles that top its ageing churches. The town gave its name both to the dukedom bestowed upon Lord Nelson (granted by King Ferdinand in gratitude for British help in repressing the Neapolitan revolution of 1799) and to Yorkshire's trio of novelists, the Brontë sisters, whose father, the Rev Patrick Prunty, harboured such an obsession for Nelson that he changed his name to Brontë (and added an umlaut). Otherwise, Bronte's sole claim to fame these days is as the centre of Italy's **pistachio** production (see box).

BRONTE'S PISTACHIOS

The mineral-rich volcanic soil of Bronte produces what are considered to be the best **pistachios** in Italy, grown in the exquisitely tended orchards that stretch around the town. In fact, Sicily is the only place in Italy where the pistachio tree grows, and Bronte itself is responsible for eighty-five percent of the country's production – though the nuts are only harvested in the early autumn of odd-numbered years. Pistachios are widely used in Sicilian pasta and dishes, most deliciously (and aesthetically) partnered with shrimps or fresh tuna, while, not surprisingly, there is no shortage of places where you can sample the striking violet-and-green nut in town – and indeed throughout Sicily. Take home a jar of pistachio pesto, or a box of pistachio biscuits, or taste either in situ at one of the cafés lining Bronte's main corso, such as *Conti Gallenti*, Corso Umberto 1 (daily 6am–10pm; ☎ 095 691 165), an unassuming little place that has changed little since the 1970s, and is famous for its pistachio *arancini* and ice cream.

Siracusa and the southeast

208 Siracusa

228 Pantalica

229 Palazzolo Acreide

233 Noto

236 South of Noto

239 Ispica and the Cava d'Ispica

240 Modica

243 Scicli

244 Ragusa

248 Around Ragusa

TEATRO GRECO, SIRACUSA

Siracusa and the southeast

6

Sicily's southeast is one of the island's most alluring regions, and in Siracusa it boasts a city whose long and glorious history outshines all others on the island. Siracusa was once the most important city in the Western world, and although today it is simply a provincial capital, it remains the most compelling destination in this part of the island. Not only is it charged with historical resonance, but it has one of the most beautiful historic centres in Italy – a photogenic tangle of medieval streets and Baroque palaces, set on the tiny island of Ortigia. Whether you have a car, or are getting around by public transport, it is the most obvious base for visiting the region's many other highlights – it is a great place to return to, with several swimming spots, and a civilized bar and restaurant scene.

Inland, Sicily's southeast is characterized by the rough and wild **Monti Iblei**, riven by spectacular ravines, or *cave*, (pronounced "cah-ve"), which are riddled with rock-cut tombs that prove occupation of the area as far back as the thirteenth century BC. The most renowned is **Pantalica**, northwest of Siracusa, Sicily's greatest necropolis, while at the **Cava Grande del Fiume Cassibile**, near Avola, you can peer into the distant depths of Sicily's own "Grand Canyon". Greek colonists appropriated many early Neolithic sites, such as **Akrai**, just outside the small town of **Palazzolo Acreide**. Several other, much smaller, archeological sites lie strung along the coast, many neglected, but legacy nonetheless of the first colonizations of the island.

However dramatic the natural scenery, it's the built environment that most defines the southeast. **Earthquakes** have repeatedly afflicted the area, none as destructive as that of January 11, 1693, which devastated the entire region. This catastrophe did, however, have one lasting effect: where there were ruins, a confident new generation of architects raised planned towns, displaying a noble, vivacious Baroque style that endures today. **Noto** and **Ragusa Ibla** have some of the most spectacular Baroque cityscapes, while nearby **Modica** and **Scicli** hold Baroque centres of varying refinement. Local authorities have slowly awoken to the tourist potential hereabouts: the southeast holds more B&Bs than any other region of Sicily, many housed in restored Baroque mansions, while tours and activities are increasingly available, from mountain biking to gorge-walking.

The **coast** is a mixed bag, virtually off-limits north of Siracusa thanks to the petrochemical industry that disfigures the **Golfo di Augusta**. To the south, sandy beaches have spawned small-scale summer resorts of modest villas and apartments aimed squarely at a local clientele. None has much architectural charm; they are empty most of the year and heaving in July and August, but the beaches are good. The most interesting stretch of coastline is to the south of Noto, from **Avola** to Sicily's southern cape, **Capo delle Correnti**, in between which lie assorted pristine beaches, old tuna-fishing villages and market-garden towns, with the undisputed highlight being the lagoons, paths and bird hides of the **Riserva Naturale di Vendicari**. West of the Capo, there is no shortage of long sandy beaches, such as Marina di Ragusa, but the finest is at **Sampieri**, a modest little resort which still retains a core of cobbled streets lined with cubic fishermen's houses.

Siracusa

More than any other Sicilian city, **SIRACUSA** (ancient Syracuse) has a past that is central not just to the island's history, but to that of the entire Mediterranean. Its

FLAMINGOS AT RISERVA NATURALE DI VENDICARI

Highlights

❶ Ortigia, Siracusa Surrounded by the sea, Sicily's most graceful *centro storico* is studded with Baroque palaces and churches – and has a great café scene and little swimming places to boot. See page 213

❷ Siracusa's Teatro Greco Classical dramas are still staged in the theatre where Aeschylus attended performances of his own plays. See page 222

❸ Noto The apotheosis of Baroque town planning, Noto offers glorious vistas at every turn, from extravagantly balconied *palazzi* to soaring church facades. See page 233

❹ Cava Grande del Fiume Cassibile Eagles soar high above the Cassibile River canyon,

while a track leads down to secluded swimming spots. See page 238

❺ Riserva Naturale di Vendicari Have a swim and see the pink flamingos fly at this idyllic coastal nature reserve. See page 238

❻ Chocolate-tasting, Modica Sample the goods at Sicily's oldest chocolate manufacturer. See page 240

❼ Ragusa Ibla Spend the night in Ragusa's chic Baroque old town. See page 245

❽ Sampieri beach Follow in the footsteps of Inspector Montalbano and the artists of the Gruppo di Scicli with a walk on the southeast's most beautiful beach. See page 249

HIGHLIGHTS ARE MARKED ON THE MAP ON PAGE 210

greatest splendour belongs to antiquity. Syracuse established its ascendancy over other Sicilian cities for more than five hundred years, and at its height was the supreme power in Europe, home to at least three times its present population. Its central position on the major trade routes ensured that even after its heyday the port continued to wield influence and preserve its prestige. All this is reflected in a staggering diversity of monuments, spanning the Hellenic, early Christian, medieval, Renaissance and Baroque eras – the styles are often shoulder-to-shoulder, sometimes in the same building. It's one of the most enjoyable cities in Sicily, with a fascinating old island centre, and superb archeological zone (now surrounded by the modern town).

Ortigia is the heart and soul of Siracusa, a predominantly medieval and Baroque web of mansions and palaces, surrounded by the sea, and home to most of the city's best B&Bs, hotels, cafés and restaurants. And for a quick escape from the city, buses run all year to the Plemmirio coastal nature reserve, to local beaches, and to the bridge across the **Fiume Ciane** (Ciane River) from which you can take a boat trip.

Brief history

The **ancient city** grew around Ortigia, an easily defensible offshore island with fresh springs, natural harbour, and access to extensive trade routes. Though Corinthian colonists arrived here in 733 BC, apparently at the behest of the Delphic oracle, it wasn't until the start of the fifth century BC that the city's political position was boosted by an alliance with Greeks at Akragas (Agrigento) and Gela. With the transfer of Gela's tyrant, **Gelon**, to Syracuse and the crushing victory of their combined forces over the Carthaginians at Himera in 480 BC, the stage was set for the beginning of the city's long supremacy. The grandest surviving monuments are from this period, and more often than not were built by slaves provided from the many battles won by Syracuse's bellicose dictators.

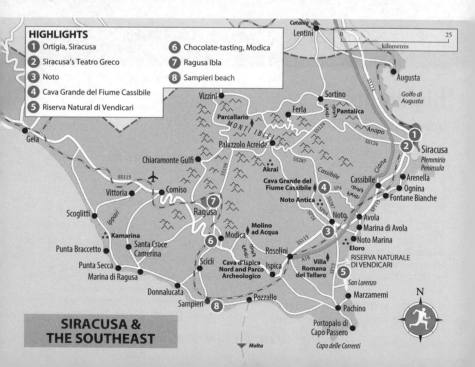

HIGHLIGHTS

1. Ortigia, Siracusa
2. Siracusa's Teatro Greco
3. Noto
4. Cava Grande del Fiume Cassibile
5. Riserva Natural di Vendicari
6. Chocolate-tasting, Modica
7. Ragusa Ibla
8. Sampieri beach

SIRACUSA & THE SOUTHEAST

The colony rebels

Inevitably, the city's ambitions provoked the intervention of Athens, which dispatched one of the greatest fleets ever seen in the ancient world. This **Great Expedition** was scuppered in 413 BC by a mixture of poor leadership and astute defence: "to the victors the most brilliant of successes, to the vanquished the most calamitous of defeats", commented the historian Thucydides. But Syracuse earned the condemnation of the Hellenic world for its seven-year incarceration of the vanquished Athenians – in appalling conditions – in the city's notorious quarries.

Tyrants, dramatists and philosophers

Throughout this period Syracuse was in a state of constant tension between a few overweening but extremely capable rulers, and sporadic convulsions of democracy. Occasionally the tyrants displayed a yearning for cultural respectability that sat uncomfortably beside their vaulting ambition. **Hieron I** (478–466 BC), for instance, described by the historian Diodorus as "an utter stranger to sincerity and nobility of character", invited many of the luminaries of the age to his court, including **Pindar**, and **Aeschylus** – who possibly witnessed the production of his last plays, *Prometheus Bound* and *Prometheus Released*, in the city's theatre. **Dionysius the Elder** (405–367 BC) – "cruel, vindictive and a profane plunderer of temples" and responsible for the first of the **Euryalus** forts – comically harboured literary ambitions to the extent of regularly entering his poems in the annual Olympic Games. His works were consistently rejected, until the Athenians judged it politic to give him the prize, whereupon his delirious celebrations were enough to provoke the seizure that killed him. His son **Dionysius II** (367–343 BC) dallied with the "philosopher-king" theories of his tutor **Plato** until megalomania turned his head and Plato fled in dismay. Dionysius himself, recorded Plutarch, spent the end of his life in exile "loitering about the fish market, or sitting in a perfumer's shop drinking the diluted wine of the taverns, or squabbling in the streets with common women".

Rarely, the rulers themselves initiated democratic reforms – men such as **Timoleon** (343–337 BC), who arrived from Corinth to inject new life into all the Sicilian cities, and **Hieron II**, who preserved Syracuse's independence from the assertions of Rome by a novel policy of conciliation, abandoning expansion in favour of preserving the status quo. His long reign (265–215 BC) saw the construction of such monuments as the **Ara di Ierone II**, and the enlargement of the **Teatro Greco** to more or less its existing proportions.

The end of the glory days

Following the death of Hieron II, Syracuse, along with practically every other Sicilian city, sided with Carthage against Rome in the Second Punic War. For two years the city was besieged by the Romans, who had to contend with all the ingenious contrivances devised for its defence by **Archimedes**, though Syracuse eventually fell in 211 BC, an event that sent shockwaves rippling around the classical world. The city was ransacked, and Archimedes himself – the last of the great Hellenic thinkers – was hacked to death, despite the injunctions of the Roman general Marcellus.

Syracuse languished under Roman rule, though its trading role still made it the most prominent Sicilian city, and it became a notable centre of early Christianity, as attested by its extensive **catacombs**. The city briefly became the capital of the Byzantine Empire when Constans moved his court here in 663 AD, but otherwise Syracuse was eclipsed by events outside its control and played no active part against all the successive waves of Arab, Norman and other medieval conquerors. The 1693 **earthquake** laid low much of the city, but provided the impetus for some of its Baroque masterpieces, notably the creations of the great Siculo-Spanish architect **Giovanni Vermexio**, who contributed an imposing facade to the Duomo, itself adapted from the bones of an early Greek temple and later Norman cathedral – and thus a building that encapsulates perfectly the polyglot character of modern Siracusa.

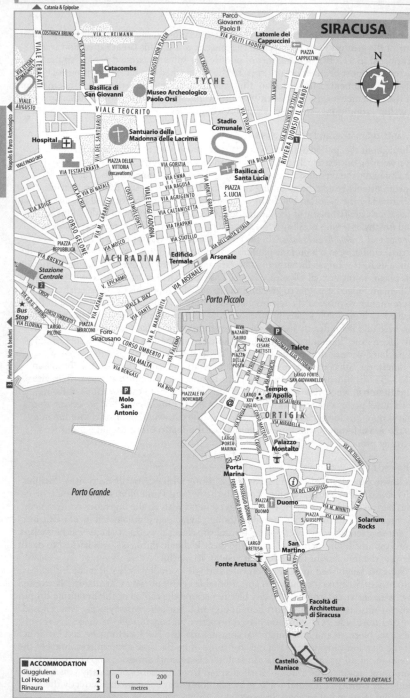

Catania & Epipolae

SIRACUSA

N

Parco Giovanni Paolo II

VIA COSTANZA BRUNO
VIA C. REIMANN
VIA POLITI LAUDIEN
Latomie dei Cappuccini
PIAZZA CAPPUCCINI

VIA SAN SEBASTIANO
VIA AUGUSTO VON PLATEN
VIA PADOVA

VIALE TERACATI
VIA ETTORE ROMAGNOLI
Catacombs
Basilica di San Giovanni
Museo Archeologico Paolo Orsi

TYCHE

VIALE AUGUSTO

VIALE TEOCRITO

VIA TORINO

Stadio Comunale

VIA DEL SANTUARIO

RIVIERA DIONSIO IL GRANDE

VIA DELL'UNITÀ D'ITALIA

6

Hospital
Santuario della Madonna delle Lacrime

VIALE PAOLO ORSI

VIA TESTAFERRATA
PIAZZA DELLA VITTORIA (excavations)
VIA GORIZIA
VIA ENNA
VIA RAGUSA
VIA AGRIGENTO
VIA CALTANISETTA
VIA TRAPANI
VIA STATELLO

VIA BIGNAMI
Basilica di Santa Lucia
PIAZZA S. LUCIA

VIA MONTE GRAPPA
VIA FILOGETTA
VIA DELL'UNITÀ D'ITALIA

VIA ADIGE
VIA ARCHIA
VIA DI NATALE
VIA M. CARBELLI
CORSO GELONE
CORSO TIMOLEONTE
VIALE LUIGI CADORNA

PIAZZA REPUBBLICA
VIA BRENTA
VIA MOSCO
ACHRADINA
Edificio Termale
Arsenale

Stazione Centrale
V. EPICARMO
VIA ARSENALE

Porto Piccolo

VIA V.T. CRISPI
CORSO UMBERTO
VIA S.C. RUBINO
VIA CATANIA
VIALE A. DIAZ
VIA DANTE
VIA R. MARGHERITA

Bus Stop
VIA ELORINA
LARGO PICONE
PIAZZA MARCONI
Foro Siracusano
CORSO UMBERTO I
VIA MALTA
VIA BENGASI
VIA RODI
VIA R. PALERMO

RIVA NAZARIO SAURO
PIAZZA DELLA POSTA
PIAZZA CESARE BATTISTI
P
LUNGOMARE ELIO VITTORINI
Talete

Molo San Antonio
PIAZZALE IV NOVEMBRE
@
LARGO XXV LUGLIO
Tempio di Apollo
VIA RESALIBERA
VIA SAVOIA
VIA TEOLO
VIA BENEDETTO
LARGO FORTE SAN GIOVANNELLO

Porto Grande

LARGO PORTA MARINA
VIA CAVOUR
VIA MAESTRANZA
ORTIGIA
VIA MIRABELLA
Palazzo Montalto
VIA DE TOLOMEI

Porta Marina
PASSEGGIO ADORNO
FORO VITTORIO EMANUELE II
PIAZZA DEL DUOMO
Duomo
VIA DEL CROCIFISSO
i
VIA M. MINNITI
PIAZZA S. GIUSEPPE
VIA LARGA
VIA NIZZA
Solarium Rocks

LARGO ARETUSA
San Martino
Fonte Aretusa
LUNGOMARE ORTIGIA
VIA SALOMONE
VIA G. MARCANTE ORTIGIA

Facoltà di Architettura di Siracusa

Castello Maniace

SEE "ORTIGIA" MAP FOR DETAILS

Neapolis & Parco Archeologico

Plemmirio, Noto & beaches

■ ACCOMMODATION	
Giuggiulena	1
Lol Hostel	2
Rinaura	3

0 ——— 200
metres

Ortigia

The ancient nucleus of Siracusa, **Ortigia** best conserves the city's essential spirit, with the artistic vestiges of over 2500 years of history concentrated in a space barely 500m across and 1km in length – and all within an easy stroll through quiet streets and alleys. Although parts of Ortigia were badly neglected in the past, the 21st century has seen wholesale restoration, and its tangled streets are now peppered with bijou hotels, B&Bs, bars, restaurants and boutiques.

You can **swim and sunbathe** from Ortigia off Largo della Gancia, where there are rocks, wooden decks and handy nearby bars; from a little beach below the end of Via Roma; or from a paying beach below the Talete car park, where sunloungers and parasols are available.

6

Tempio di Apollo

Largo XXV Luglio

Siracusa announces its long history immediately across the narrow ribbon of water that severs the island from the mainland. The **Tempio di Apollo** is thought to have been the first of the great Doric temples built in Sicily (seventh- or early sixth-century BC) and, though not much survives apart from a couple of columns and part of the south wall of its cella, it's a dignified old ruin. A **scale model** in Siracusa's archeological museum (see page 219) shows you what it looked like in its heyday – the arched window in the wall dates from a Norman church that incorporated part of the temple into its structure. To help you make sense of what remains here, imagine the entrance with a double row of six columns, topped by a pediment at the eastern (far) end, and seventeen columns along each side. Visiting in the eighteenth century, the French writer Vivant Denon reported finding one of the columns embedded in the wall of a bedroom in a house on the adjacent Via Resalibera, part of it hacked away by the owner to make more room.

Ortigia market

Via de Benedictis • Mon–Sat from 7am until around 2pm

Ortigia's weekday **market** spreads along Via de Benedictis, running north of the temple of Apollo towards the sea. One of the best stalls is run by Claudio Romano, who sells the wild herbs he collects near Pantalica, and fresh ricotta, while several stalls sell ready cut fruits, and a couple sell oysters to eat on your feet, washed down with a cup of fizz. At the far end is a cluster of unofficial stalls where locals sell fish, sea urchins and whatever wild vegetables are in season. On Sundays there is a **farmers' market** (8am–1pm) in the Renaissance-style courtyard of the nineteenth-century Antico Mercato, which backs onto Via de Benedictis, but has its entrance on parallel Via Trento.

Piazza Archimede

Lined with Fascist-era *palazzi* housing clothes and shoe shops, Corso Matteotti leads uphill from Largo XXV Luglio to **Piazza Archimede**, its centrepiece a twentieth-century **fountain** depicting the nymph Arethusa (the symbol of Ortigia) at the moment of her transformation into a spring. The square is surrounded by restored medieval *palazzi*, while down the skinny Via Montalto you can admire the facade of the **Palazzo Montalto**, which is graced by immaculate double- and triple-arched windows, and a star of David cut into the stonework. This is one of the few buildings in this style to have survived the 1693 earthquake – an inscription dates its construction to 1397.

Piazza del Duomo

Ortigia's most impressive architecture belongs to its Baroque period, and nowhere does this reach such heights as in Sicily's loveliest square, the **Piazza del Duomo**. It's been gloriously restored, and the traffic kept out, so that the encircling seventeenth- and eighteenth-century buildings are now seen at their best from the pavement cafés, notably the **Municipio** (corner of Via Minerva), Duomo, Palazzo Borgia del Casale (now owned by Dolce and Gabbana) and the **Palazzo Beneventano**.

6

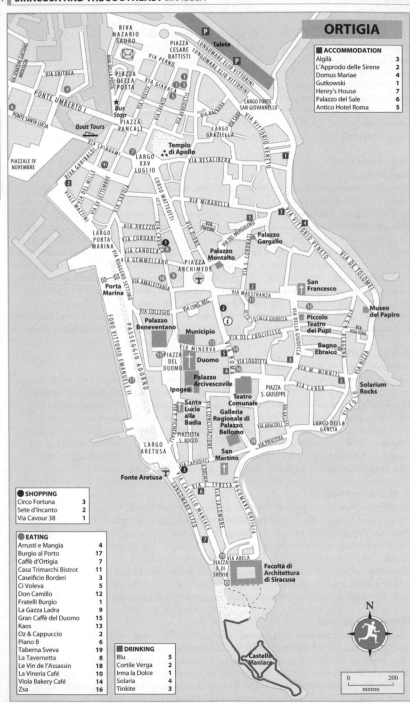

ORTIGIA

ACCOMMODATION

Algilà	3
L'Approdo delle Sirene	2
Domus Mariae	4
Gutkowski	1
Henry's House	7
Palazzo del Sale	6
Antico Hotel Roma	5

SHOPPING

Circo Fortuna	3
Sete d'Incanto	2
Via Cavour 38	1

EATING

Arrusti e Mangia	4
Burgio al Porto	17
Caffè d'Ortigia	7
Casa Trimarchi Bistrot	11
Caseificio Borderi	3
Ci Voleva	5
Don Camillo	12
Fratelli Burgio	1
La Gazza Ladra	9
Gran Caffè del Duomo	15
Kaos	13
Oz & Cappuccio	2
Piano B	6
Taberna Sveva	19
La Tavernetta	8
Le Vin de l'Assassin	18
La Vineria Café	10
Viola Bakery Café	14
Zsa	16

DRINKING

Blu	5
Cortile Verga	2
Irma la Dolce	1
Solaria	4
Tinkite	3

N

0   200
metres

> **GOING UNDERGROUND**
>
> An entrance on the Piazza Duomo in the Palazzo Arcivescovile, next to the cathedral, leads down into the **Ipogeo di Piazza Duomo**. This series of underground tunnels and water cisterns, dating back centuries, was used by the *Siracusani* as an air-raid shelter during the heavy Allied bombing of 1943. You can follow one of the tunnels right the way under the piazza, to emerge by the harbour on the Foro Vittorio Emanuele II, close to the Fonte Aretusa. Staffing shortages mean that it is not always open, but when it is, entrance is €5, and the experience well worth it. At the time of writing there were plans afoot to open a permanent exhibition devoted to Caravaggio's exploits in Sicily, provisionally titled The Caravaggio Experience.

6

The Duomo

Piazza Duomo • Usually daily 8am–7pm; may close earlier, and at lunchtime in winter • €2

The great age of Siracusa's **Duomo** is first glimpsed from around the side in Via Minerva, where stout Doric columns (part of an earlier Greek temple) form the very skeleton of the structure. The site was already sacred when the Greeks started work on an Ionic temple to Athena here in about 530 BC, though this was abandoned when a new temple was begun in thanksgiving for the victory over the Carthaginians at Himera. The extravagant decoration that adorned this building spread its fame throughout the ancient world, and tantalizing details of it have come down to us through **Cicero**, who visited Syracuse in the first century BC and listed the temple's former contents as part of his prosecution of the Roman praetor and villain Verres, who appeared to have walked off with a good proportion of them – part of the booty he plundered from many Sicilian temples. The doors were of ivory and gold, and its walls painted with military scenes and portraits of various of Syracuse's tyrants – claimed to be the earliest examples of portraiture in European art. On the temple's roof stood a tall statue of the warrior-goddess Athena carrying a golden shield which, catching the sun's rays, served as a beacon for sailors out at sea.

Although all this rich decoration has vanished, the main body of the temple was saved further despoliation thanks to its conversion into a Christian church, which was elevated to cathedral status in 640 AD. A more drastic overhaul was carried out after the 1693 earthquake, when the Norman facade collapsed and was replaced by the present formidable Baroque front, with statues by Marabitti. This is in sharp contrast to the more muted **interior**, in which it's the frame of the ancient temple that is still prevalent. The aisles are formed by the massive Doric columns, while the cella walls were hacked through to make the present arched nave. Along the **north aisle**, the distorted pillars give some inkling of how close the entire structure came to toppling when the seventeenth-century earthquake hit Siracusa. The Duomo's **south aisle** shows more characteristic Baroque effusion in the series of richly ornate chapels, though the first one (nearest the main door, on the right) – actually the baptistery – is from an earlier age. Enlivened by some twelfth-century arabesque mosaics, it contains a Norman font that was cut from a block still marked with a Greek inscription, and is supported by seven bronze lions.

Santa Lucia alla Badia and Caravaggio's Burial of Santa Lucia

Piazza Duomo • Tues–Sun 11am–2pm • Free

With its twisted barley-sugar columns, intricate wrought-iron balcony, and stone as delicately worked as silver, the facade of **Santa Lucia alla Badia** is one of Ortigia's prettiest, and for several years now has been home to Siracusa's sole Caravaggio canvas. The original church, built by Queen Isabella of Castille on the site where it was thought Santa Lucia had been raped, was completely destroyed in the 1693 earthquake. Dedicated to Siracusa's much-loved patron saint, it was the focus of celebrations for the **miracle of Santa Lucia** in May. The mother superior clearly understood the resonance of this site for the people of Siracusa, and immediately after the earthquake requested that a shack be erected among the rubble, as a temporary church.

6

THE MIRACLE OF SANTA LUCIA

In the mid-seventeenth century, Sicily was suffering from **famine**. Under Spanish rule, the island was in a parlous state: rural areas were neglected by the aristocracy and fleeced by farm managers known as *gabelloti*, and urban centres were riven with poverty. In Palermo these conditions gave rise to a riot; in Siracusa, in May 1646, people gathered instead in the cathedral to pray to **Santa Lucia**. As they were praying, a dove flew into the Duomo, shortly followed by the news that a ship laden with grain had arrived in the harbour. According to tradition, people were so hungry that there was no time to grind the wheat into flour, so they ate the grains boiled in a kind of porridge, known as **cuccia**. These days *cuccia* has been vastly improved – the wheat berries are served mixed with sweetened ricotta, candied fruit and chocolate; while Santa Lucia is still celebrated with processions and fireworks on her feast day, December 13, and in May, when quails are released in Piazza Duomo to record the miraculous news-bearing dove.

Her request was denied, so that work could start on the new church straight away. The building was supposed to be completed within two years – another sign of how important this church was felt to be for Siracusa – although in the end, it wasn't finished until 1703. The nuns – belonging to a closed Cistercian Order – returned, and there are still poignant indications of what life was like for them here, notably the oval *parlatorio* (to the left as you enter), with grills set in the wall so that nuns could talk to their families without being seen.

The Burial of Santa Lucia

Santa Lucia alla Badia is currently home of one of Siracusa's most prized works of art, *The Burial of Santa Lucia* by **Caravaggio**. Having escaped from prison in Malta, Caravaggio arrived in the city in October 1608 and received an immediate commission to have a painting of Santa Lucia ready for her festival on December 13. Some scholars think the fact that the upper two-thirds of the canvas are taken up by a bare wall may have more to do with lack of time than aesthetics, for as Caravaggio was painting it, he was in fear of his life, pursued, it's thought, by the Knights of Malta.

The canvas was designed not for this church, but for the church of Santa Lucia across in the Borgata, scene of the saint's martyrdom, and home of her tomb (if not her body, which has been in Venice since the time of the Crusades). Bathed in shafts of sunlight, dwarfed by stark, scorched bare plaster walls, two mighty gravediggers brace themselves to lower the corpse of the saint into her tomb, watched by a bishop and mourners. One tradition is that the bearded gravedigger to the left is a portrait of Alof de Wignacourt, Grand Master of the Knights of Malta – and that painting him in this role was Caravaggio's way of taking revenge on the man who had had him imprisoned. Paranoid and persecuted, Caravaggio slept fully dressed and fully armed while painting the work, and fled from Siracusa as soon as it was finished, not even waiting for the painting to be unveiled at the feast of Santa Lucia.

Fonte Aretusa

Largo Aretusa

Down from the Duomo towards the seafront, the freshwater spring known as the **Fonte Aretusa** is probably the next most photographed part of Ortigia. Planted with papyrus, and filled with bream below the water and ducks above, it's a compulsory stop on the evening *passeggiata*. It's ringed by cafés, while the terrace above offers sweeping views across the bay. The **spring** was mentioned in the original Delphic directions that brought the first Greek settlers here, and the number of myths with which it's associated underlines the strong sentimental links that continued to bind the colonists to their motherland. This was where the nymph Arethusa rose after swimming across from the Peloponnese, having been metamorphosed into a spring by the goddess Artemis to escape the attentions of the predatory river-god Alpheus; all in vain, though, for the determined

NOTO, A BAROQUE GEM

Alpheus pursued her here to mingle with her in a watery form. Other legends declared that the spring's water would stain red at the time of the annual sacrifices at the sanctuary of Olympia, and that a cup thrown into the river there would rise here in Ortigia.

Porto Marina

The promenade runs both ways from the Fonte Aretusa, south towards the castle and north along the tree-lined Foro Vittorio Emanuele II (also known as Foro Italico) to **Porta Marina**, a fifteenth-century gateway surmounted by a curlicued Spanish heraldic device. The vast, still pool of the **Porto Grande** spreads out beyond, and is dotted with fishing boats, liners and tankers, and the odd millionaire's yacht.

Galleria Regionale di Palazzo Bellomo

Via Capodieci 14–16 • Tues–Sat 9am–7pm, Sun 2–7pm • €8 • ☎ 0931 69 511

Siracusa's tradition of architectural hybridism is again apparent in the **Palazzo Bellomo**, with a courtyard that features thirteenth-century arcading and a Spanish-style stairway leading up to the loggia. The palace is the home of the city's **Galleria Regionale di Palazzo Bellomo**, whose most treasured exhibit is an *Annunciazione* by Antonello da Messina, painted for a church in Palazzolo Acreide, in which the Hyblaean mountains are visible through the windows behind the angel and the Madonna. Early Christian **sculpture** and a fine collection of **altarpieces** and **icons** are also fascinating evidence of the enduring Byzantine and Gothic influence in Sicily. As late as the sixteenth century, while the rest of Italy was swept by the Renaissance, Siracusa's artists were still painting heavily stylized Byzantine or Gothic works.

San Martino

Via San Martino • Usually open Sun morning only

The church of **San Martino** is among Siracusa's oldest. Originally a sixth-century basilica, it was rebuilt in the fourteenth century and smartened up with a good-looking rose window and Gothic doorway. It's not often open (it's used by the local scout group), but the dusky **interior** is a treat – plain stone columns leading to a tiny mosaic half-apse with a fifteenth-century triptych to the right of the choir.

Castello Maniace

Via del Castello Maniace • Opening hours variable, but in theory Mon 2.30–7.30pm, Tues–Sat 8.30am–1.45pm • €4 • ☎ 0931 464 420

The dangling southern limb of Ortigia is entirely taken up by the parade grounds and buildings of the stout **Castello Maniace**, a defensive bulwark erected around 1239 by Frederick II, but named after George Maniakes, the Byzantine admiral who briefly reconquered Syracuse from the Arabs in 1038. Now that the military has moved out, the barrack buildings are used by the university's archeological department, while visitors are allowed to enter through the imposing main gate and wander the echoing halls, chambers and defensive ramparts. Restoration work continues to shore up the neglected castle interior – one of the rooms displays a copy of the famous bronze ram statue, known as *L'Ariete*, a pair of which once guarded the castle gates. The original is now in Palermo's archeological museum.

Museo del Papiro

Via Nizza • May–Sept Tues–Sat 10.30am–6pm, Sun 10.30am–2pm; Oct–April Tues–Sun 9.30am–2pm • €5 • ☎ 0931 22 100, ⓦ museodelpapiro.it

Walking along the beautiful lungomare, you reach the sensitively restored ex Convento di Sant'Agostino, whose serene rooms now house a fascinating collection of papyrus, ancient and modern. There are fragments of papyrus from Pompeii, carbonized by the eruption of Vesuvius, papyrus boats from Ethiopia and Chad, and even a pair of papyrus sandals. Ever since papyrus was introduced to Siracusa in the reign of Hieron II – it still grows in abundance at the source of the River Ciane – there's been a thriving industry here, and gift shops on Ortigia are awash with it.

SWIMMING IN SIRACUSA

Every summer, towards the end of June, the local *Comune* erects wooden swimming platforms on the Solarium rocks on the eastern coast of Ortigia, and at several points along the cycle track that runs across the cliffs north of the modern city from Piazza Cappuccini. Access is free, and the platforms remain until the end of September – sometimes later. There is also a free beach, Cala Rossa, at the end of Via Roma (below the Royal Maniace hotel), and a couple of seasonal lidos with bars, Nettuno on the east coast, Zefiro on the west, both of which charge from €20 a day for sunlounger and umbrella. If you prefer a long, sandy beach, head to Arenella (a 40min ride on bus #23, via Plemmirio). For a wild rocky coast with several secluded swimming spots, ask the driver to let you off at the "bivio Punta della Mola". From here, a side road leads down to a sheltered cove with two tiny, sandy beaches. It is also the starting point for the cliff path that traces its way across the Plemmirio peninsula to the Murro del Porco lighthouse – the walk should take about 1hr 30min.

6

Mainland Siracusa

Modern development in the mainland quarters of Siracusa makes it difficult to picture the ancient city that Plutarch wept over when he heard of its fall to the Romans. Much of the new building dates from after World War II, when Siracusa was bombed twice over – once by the Allies, then, after its capture, by the Luftwaffe in 1943. But even so, some extraordinary relics survive, notably the **Greek theatre** in the archeological park and the unsurpassed **archeological museum**. There are also underground **catacombs**. Regular city buses run to all these places, departing from Riva della Posta on Ortigia, or you can walk to the museum, catacombs or archeological park in under half an hour from Ortigia.

Basilica di Santa Lucia

Piazza Santa Lucia • Daily 7am–noon & 3–7pm • Free • **Catacombs** Guided tours have to be booked in advance through the cultural association Kairos (Ⓦ kairos-web.com) • €8 • ☎ 0931 64 694, Ⓦ kairos-web.com

At the northern end of the huge Piazza Santa Lucia, the church of **Santa Lucia**, built in 1629, supposedly marks the spot where St Lucy, Siracusa's patron saint, was martyred in 304 AD. Within is a fine wooden ceiling, but you don't need to enter to admire its Norman tower or, from the piazza outside, Giovanni Vermexio's octagonal chapel of **San Sepolcro**, where the mortal remains of St Lucy were originally preserved before being carried off to Constantinople by the Byzantine admiral Maniakes in 1038, and later shipped to Venice as part of the spoils plundered by the Venetian "crusaders" in 1204.

If you're interested in **catacombs**, you can book onto a guided tour of the labyrinthine complex below the church, which is full of the tombs of those who wanted to be buried close to the sight rendered holy by Santa Lucia's death.

Museo Archeologico Paolo Orsi

Via Teocrito 66 • Tues–Sat 9am–6pm, Sun 9am–1pm; last entry 1hr before closing • €8, combined ticket with Parco Archeologico or Palazzo Bellomo €13.50 • ☎ 0931 489 511

If you have any interest at all in the archeological finds made in this extraordinary city, then all roads lead to Siracusa's **Museo Archeologico Paolo Orsi**. It was purpose-built for Sicily's most wide-ranging collection of antiquities, and it's certainly worth seeing, though there are caveats. Finding your way around can be extremely confusing, with notes in English either non-existent or mind-numbingly detailed and academic, and to cap it all, sections are sometimes closed as continuing renovations attempt to address its organizational shortcomings. That said, the collection is amazing. The museum is basically split into four sections: prehistoric (section A); items from Syracuse, Megara Hyblaea and the Chalcidinian colonies (B); finds from Gela, Agrigento, Syracuse's subcolonies and the indigenous Sikel centres (C); and Greek and Roman Siracusa (D).

6

Section D

It's **section D** that's the easiest to understand, where Siracusa in the **Greek and Roman age** is laid bare in an extraordinary series of tomb finds and public statues, none more celebrated than the statue of **Venus Anadiomene**, also known as *Landolina* after the archeologist who discovered her in 1804. *Anadiomene* means "rising from the sea", which describes her coy pose: with her left hand she holds a robe, while studs show where her broken-off right arm came across to hide her breasts. Probably Roman-made in the first century AD, from a Greek model, the headless statue has always evoked extreme responses, alternately exalting the delicacy and naturalism of the carving, and condemning her knowing sensual attitude that symbolized the decline of the vigorous classical age and the birth of a new decadence. By the statue's feet, the dolphin, Aphrodite's emblem, is the only sign that this was a goddess. Of the tomb finds, pride of place is given to the superb **Sarcofago di Adelfia**, a finely worked fourth-century marble tomb found in the catacombs below San Giovanni. It held the wife of a Roman official, the couple prominently depicted and surrounded by reliefs of scenes from the Old and New Testaments.

Section B

Section B goes some way towards putting many of the finds into context, showing where excavations occurred in the city, and even reconstructing useful models of the fallen temples. Among the earlier Hellenic pieces, the museum has some excellent **kouroi** – toned, muscular youths, one of which (from Lentini) is one of the most outstanding fragments still extant from the Archaic age of Greek art – around 500 BC. A striking image from the colony of Megara Hyblaea dates from the same period: a **mother/goddess suckling twins**, its absorbed roundness expressing a tender harmony as close to earth and fertility rites as the *Venus Landolina* is to the cult of sensuality.

Basilica di San Giovanni catacombs

Piazza San Giovanni • Nov–Feb Tues–Sat 9.30am–12.30pm & 2.30–4.30pm; March–June daily 9.30am–12.30pm & 2.30–5.30pm; July & Aug daily 10am–1pm & 2.30–6pm; Sept & Oct daily 9.30–12.30 & 2.30–5pm • Tours depart every 30min • €8 • ☎ 0931 64 694, ⊛ kairos-web.com

Close to the Museo Archeologico, below the ruined **Basilica di San Giovanni** off Via San Sebastiano, lies the most extensive series of catacombs in the city, their presence explained by the Roman prohibition on Christian burial within the city limits (Siracusa having by then shrunk back to its original core of Ortigia). Fronted by a triple arch, most of the church was toppled in the 1693 earthquake and the nave is now open to the sky, but you can still admire the seventh-century apse and a medieval rose window. San Giovanni was once the city's cathedral, and was built over the crypt of St Marcian, first bishop of Siracusa, who was flogged to death in 254.

The tours take you down into the **crypt** to see Marcian's tomb, the remnants of some Byzantine frescoes, and an altar that marks the spot where St Paul is supposed to have preached, when he stopped in the city as a prisoner on his way to Rome. Then you're led into the **catacombs** themselves, labyrinthine warrens hewn out of the rock, though often following the course of underground aqueducts, disused since Greek times. Numerous side passages lead off from the main gallery (decumanus maximus), often culminating in *rotonde*, round caverns used for prayer; other passages are forbiddingly dark and closed off to the public. Entire families were interred in the thousands of niches hollowed out of these walls and floors, anxious for burial close to the tomb of St Marcian. Most of the treasures buried with the bodies have been pillaged, though the robbers overlooked one – an ornate Roman-era sarcophagus unearthed from just below the floor in 1872 and now on show in the archeological museum.

Parco Archeologico della Neapolis

Viale Paradiso • Daily 8.30am–7.30pm (last entry at 6pm) (may be earlier Nov–April) • €10 or €13.30 with Museo Archeologico or Palazzo Bellomo • ☎ 0931 66 206 • The electric minibus line #2 from Molo Sant'Antonio and Corso Umberto (the stop is just after the main bridge to Ortigia) calls at the Parco Archeologico car park although it is so unreliable that unless you see one coming, it is probably a waste of time to wait.

Siracusa's **Parco Archeologico** encompasses the classical city district that was Neapolis. This contained most of the ancient city's social and religious amenities – theatres, altars and sanctuaries – and was thus never inhabited, though these days it's in danger of disappearing under the sheer weight of visitors. The **ticket office** is hidden beyond a street market of souvenir stalls and ice-cream stands, which cater to the busloads of tourists that arrive every few minutes in the summer.

Anfiteatro Romano

As you enter the Parco Archeologico, a path to the left leads down to the **Anfiteatro Romano**, a large elliptical arena built in the third century AD to satisfy the growing lust for circus games. The rectangular **tank** in the centre of the arena is too small to have been used for aquatic displays, and is more likely to have been for draining the blood and gore spilled in the course of the combats. But not before the spectators had had their fill: at the end of the contests the infirm, ill and disabled would attempt to suck warm blood from the bodies and take the livers from the animals, in the belief that this would speed their recovery.

Ara di Ierone II
No public access

On the main path into the Parco Archeologico, past the turn-off to the Anfiteatro Romano, is the ruined base of the **Ara di Ierone II**, a 200m-long altar erected by Hieron II in the second half of the third century BC. It commemorated the achievements of Timoleon, who liberated the city from tyranny and decline, and was the biggest construction of its kind in all Magna Graecia. It was also the venue for some serious sacrificing: Diodorus records that 450 bulls were led up the ramps at either end of the altar to be slaughtered in the annual feast.

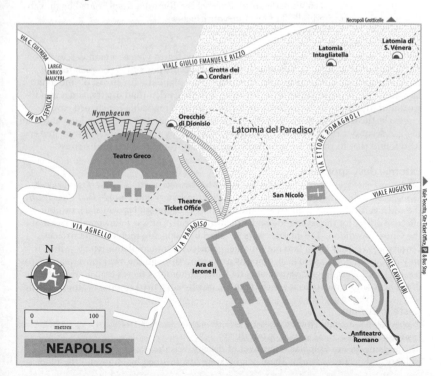

6

HEAR HEAR

The **Orecchio di Dionisio** owes its name to the painter **Caravaggio**, who was taken to visit the cave during a visit to Siracusa in October 1608. Said to have been used as a prison by the ancient Greek tyrant, Dionysus, the cave's natural acoustics amplified every sound, and from their base above a crack at the apex, sentries could eavesdrop on the prisoners hundreds of metres below. Having just escaped from prison and fled to Siracusa, Caravaggio was deeply disturbed by this ingenious quirk. He noted that the cave amplified sound in the same way as the human ear – which led recent biographer Andrew Graham Dixon to speculate that Caravaggio saw the "speaking cave" as an image of his own contracting world, where every movement was monitored by spies, every remark overheard by eavesdroppers.

Teatro Greco

You may be asked to show your ticket again at the office at the foot of the steps leading up to the **Teatro Greco**, Siracusa's most spectacular monument. One of the largest and best-preserved Greek auditoriums anywhere, its site has been home to a theatre since at least the fifth century BC, though it was frequently added to at different periods. Hieron II expanded it to accommodate 15,000 people, in nine sections of 59 rows (of which 42 remain). The **inscriptions** around the top of the middle gangway on the west side of the theatre – faint but still visible – date from the third century BC, giving the names of the ruler and his family, with Zeus Olympios in the middle. Most of the alterations carried out by the Romans were made to adapt the arena for gladiatorial combat, and they also installed some marble-faced seats for privileged spectators, while the seventeenth row was removed, possibly to segregate the classes. The high terrace above the theatre contains the **Nymphaeum**, a large artificial grotto (fed by water from an ancient aqueduct) where a number of statues were found. To the left of here, the overgrown **Via dei Sepolcri** (Street of the Tombs) is deeply rutted by the carts that plied to and fro, and is flanked by more votive niches.

Latomia del Paradiso

From the ticket office at the foot of the steps to the Teatro Greco, a path descends to the largest of Siracusa's huge *latomie* (pits or quarries), from which the rock for the city's multifarious monuments was excavated. Now planted with citrus, oleander and bay trees, the so-called **Latomia del Paradiso** is more garden than quarry, and a steady stream of tour parties troops down mainly to see the remarkable ear-shaped cavern known as the **Orecchio di Dionisio** (Ear of Dionysius), which is over 60m long and 20m high. A second cave, the **Grotta dei Cordari**, was used by the ancient city's rope makers, who found that its damp air prevented rope strands from breaking under stress.

Latomie dei Cappuccini

Largo Latomie 3 • Opening hours variable, but in theory Thurs, Fri, Sat & Sun 10am–6pm • €5 • ☎ 329 241 7142 • ⓦ secretsiracusa.it

Gouged out of the hillside below the Cappuccini monastery and *Grand Hotel Villa Politi*, the wide, vertically walled quarries of the **Latomie dei Cappuccini** provided a harsh but effective prison for the seven thousand Athenian prisoners of war following the fiasco of the Great Expedition. The quarries were acquired by Capuchin monks in the sixteenth century, who turned them into both market garden and contemplative retreat, which is why the cavern floors are so lush. Sinuous paths wind through the overgrown quarries, past natural rock pillars, huge caverns and early Christian tombs – there's even a cavern-theatre down here, sometimes used for performances, usually advertised by posters around town.

Castello Eurialo

Epipolae • No fixed hours at the time of writing so call before setting out • A 20min ride on bus #11 or #25 to the village of Belvedere, from Corso Gelone and outside the Parco Archeologico • ☎ 0931 711 773

The outlying area of **Epipolae**, 7km west of the city, was the site of ancient Siracusa's military and defensive works. These heights were first fortified by Dionysius the Elder in about 400 BC, and subsequently modified and extended over a couple of centuries. What remains today consists of a great wall, which marked the city's western limit, and the **Castello Eurialo**, just before the village on the right. This is the major extant Greek fortification in the Mediterranean, most of it dating from Hieron II's time, when Archimedes, as his General of Ordnance, must have been actively involved in its renovation. Despite the effort and ingenuity that went into making this site impregnable, the castle has no very glorious history: ignored altogether by the attacking Carthaginians, it surrendered without a fight to the Roman forces of Marcellus in 212 BC.

Assailants had to cope with three defensive **trenches**, designed to keep the new artillery of the time at bay, as well as siege engines and battering rams. The first of the trenches (approached from the west, where you come in) lay just within range of catapults mounted on the five towers of the castle's keep, while in the trench below the keep you can see the high piers supporting the drawbridge that once crossed it. Long galleries burrow beneath the walls into the keep, serving as supply and escape routes, and also enabling the defenders to clear out by night the material thrown in by attackers during the day.

Epipolae gate

Behind the keep is a long, wedge-shaped fortification, to the north of which is the main gateway to the western quarter of the city. This, the **Epipolae gate**, was built indented from the walls, allowing the defenders to shower attackers with missiles, and is reminiscent of the main gate at Tyndaris, a city that shared the same architects. The longest of the underground passages surfaces here, stretching 180m from the defensive trenches. From the gate, you can stroll along Dionysius's extensive walls, looking down over the oil refineries and tankers off the coast north of the city, and back over Siracusa itself, with Ortigia clearly visible pointing out into the sea.

ARRIVAL AND DEPARTURE	SIRACUSA

By train Siracusa is at the beginning of two train lines: the main line running up to Catania, Taormina and Messina, and a little branch line to Gela via Noto, Sampieri, Scicli, Modica, Ragusa and several other small Baroque towns. The city's train station is on the mainland at the end of Via Francesco Crispi. You can walk from here to Ortigia in around 20min, and there's a taxi rank outside the station. Taxis cost €10 to anywhere within Ortigia or central Siracusa.

Destinations Catania (12 daily; 1hr 15min); Lentini (12 daily; 45min); Messina (11 daily; 2hr 25min–3hr); Modica (4 daily Mon–Sat; 1hr 45min); Noto (8 daily Mon–Sat; 30min); Ragusa (3 daily Mon–Sat; 2hr 20min–2hr 30min); Sampieri (3 daily Mon–Sat; 1hr 20min); Scicli (3 daily Mon–Sat; 1hr 25min).

By bus All regional buses stop across the road from the train station, on the parallel streets Corso Umberto I and Via Rubino. AST (☏ 0931 462 711, ⊚ aziendasicilianatrasporti. it) has services to and from Noto, Ispica, Modica, Noto, Palazzolo Acreide and Ragusa; while Interbus (☏ 0931 66 710, ⊚ interbus.it) runs to Avola, Catania, Catania airport,

THE FIUME CIANE

Just southwest of Siracusa, the source of the **Fiume Ciane** (Ciane River) forms a pool said to have been created by the tears of the nymph Cyane when her mistress Persephone was abducted into the underworld by Hades. The pool and the riverbanks are overgrown by thickets of papyrus, apparently the gift of Ptolemy Philadelphus of Egypt to Hieron II, making this the only place outside North Africa where the plant grows wild. **Boat cruises** operate between early March and November from the bridge over the Ciane, a 5km signposted drive from Siracusa on the SS115; you can also take bus #21, #22 or #23 from Via Rubino. There are daily departures in good weather through spring, summer and autumn between 10am and 6pm, with tickets costing €10 per person (minimum 3 people); call ☏ 346 159 9635 or ☏ 368 729 6040 for information. As well as the river, you'll also see the scant but evocative remains of the **Olympieion**, or Tempio di Giove Olimpico, a Doric temple built in the first half of the sixth century BC. The hillock that the ruin stands on, a vital strategic point in classical times, was often occupied by Siracusa's enemies when the city was under attack. The pestilential air of the Lysimelia marshes below saved the day on more than one occasion, infecting the hostile armies with malaria.

6

PARKING IN SIRACUSA

Siracusa's drivers are as undisciplined as any in Sicily, but nevertheless drivers will find the city a breeze after Palermo and Catania. Ortigia is completely closed to traffic (except for residents) at certain times during the week, and from 4pm on Saturdays and 11am on Sundays – a traffic signal at the foot of Corso Matteotti indicates whether access is permitted or not. Cameras are installed, so if you ignore the lights, a fine will arrive. At times when access is not permitted, you can cross the Via Malta bridge, turn left and go directly to the Talete car park (€0.50 for the first hour, €1 for subsequent hours). Even when access to Ortigia is permitted, there are virtually no non-resident parking spaces.

As in the rest of Italy, **parking** is free for everyone on the **white lines**. For streets with **blue lines**, payment is required during times specified on signs; on Riva Nazario Sauro, fees are charged all day, every day, but everywhere else in the city, you pay only Mon–Fri 9am–1pm & 4–8pm. Parking tickets are sold at tobacconists and newsagents, and cost €0.60 per hour.

Noto, Pachino and Palermo. Services are much reduced on Sundays, so check websites before planning a trip, especially if you have a flight to catch.
Destinations Avola (5 daily; 40min); Catania (roughly hourly; 1hr 25min); Catania airport (roughly hourly; 1hr 15min); Ferla (1 daily Mon–Sat; 1hr 35min); Ispica (1 daily, 1hr 40min); Modica (8 daily Mon–Sat, 3 daily Sun; 1hr 45min–3hr); Noto (5 daily Mon–Sat, 4 daily Sun; 55min); Pachino (4 daily Mon–Sat; 1hr 20min); Palazzolo Acreide (around 1 hourly Mon–Sat; 2 daily Sun; 1hr 10min–2hr 15min); Palermo (2 daily; 3hr 20min); Ragusa (4 daily; 2hr 15min–3hr).

GETTING AROUND

By bus Siracusa's bus service is the worst in Sicily, and you are strongly recommended to walk. City buses are run by AST (☎ 0931 462 711, ⓦ aziendasicilianatrasporti. it) and depart from Piazza Pancali in Ortigia. All services run on circular routes. Tickets cost €1.20 for 120min, and, hard to believe as it is, are only on sale at the newsagent/ tobacconist at the railway station. Scarcely more reliable (though with no fixed timetable, they run on circular routes and timings depend on traffic and staffing levels) are the electric minibuses run by Siracusa D'Amare, which operates three routes, with stops at many major tourist sites (ⓦ siracusadamare.it).
Line #1 does a circuit of Ortigia, starting and finishing at the Molo Sant'Antonio; Line #2 also starts at Molo Sant'Antonio, and has stops at Santa Lucia, the San Giovanni Catacombs, the Museo Archeologico Paolo Orsi, and the Zona Archeologico; Line #3 runs from Molo Sant'Antonio along to the Latomie dei Cappuccini. Every bus stop has the stopping points along the route marked clearly, so it is easy to use. Tickets (€0.50) are bought on board and last for 90min.
The most useful (and reliable) AST routes are those to the beaches (#21 and #22 to Fontane Bianche, and #23 which runs through Plemmirio to Arenella). They all run on a circular route, which means that it takes 45min to get to Arenella, but only 10min to get back. This also means that if you get off the #23 in Isola or Plemmirio, to return to Siracusa you need to pick up a later bus and continue the journey out to Arenella before swinging back to town.
By taxi There are ranks in Piazza Pancali (☎ 0931 60 980) and at the train station (☎ 0931 69 722).

INFORMATION AND TOURS

Tourist information For maps, accommodation, details of performances in the Greek theatre, and other information, head for the tourist office (Info Point), inside the provincial offices at Via Roma 31 on Ortigia (Mon–Sat 8am–8pm, Sun 9.15am–6.45pm; ☎ 0931 462 946 or ☎ 800 055 500, ⓦ provsr.it).
Boat trips Ortigia Tours (☎ 368 317 0711, ⓦ ortigiatour. com) offers daily cruises around the city's harbours and nearby coastline. Boats leave from near the bridge on Ortigia (from 9am in summer, 10am in winter, weather permitting), and trips last an hour or so; tickets are €10 per person (minimum 4 people). In summer, a kiosk on the quayside provides tickets and information.

ACCOMMODATION
SEE MAPS PAGES 212 AND 214

Siracusa has a lot of **accommodation**, much of it in the old town on Ortigia, which is by far the best place to stay, with scores of **B&Bs** in the backstreets and a cluster of four-star **hotels** on the waterfront. Note that in high summer and during the theatre season (May–June), it's wise to book in advance. Unless your chosen establishment has private parking, it's best to leave the car overnight in the Talete garage (see box). The cheapest beds are at the **hostel** by the train station; **camping** is available at a very basic site outside the city or at a much better equipped site down the coast towards Avola. For **apartment rentals** contact ⓦ lacasadellefate.it.

HOTELS AND B&BS

Algilà Via Vittorio Veneto 93 ☎ 0931 465 186, ⓦ algila. it. A very appealing hotel occupying two lovely historic *palazzo* on the eastern seafront of Ortigia, with all the comforts of a four-star, plus friendly, helpful staff. Styled by Siracusa-born theatre director Manuel Giliberti, the design has a Maghreb feel, with Tunisian tiles in the bathrooms, kilims on the floors, watercolours of sun-scorched palms and North African piazzas, and a tiny decorative courtyard with fountain. **€215**

L'Approdo delle Sirene Riva Garibaldi 15 ☎ 0931 24 857, ⓦ apprododellesirene.com. A smart B&B in a tastefully renovated waterfront *palazzo* overlooking the channel between Ortigia and the mainland. Owned and run by a charming mother-and-son team: Fiora runs cookery courses in her apartment next door and Friedrich owns the pizzeria *Piano B*. Great home-made breakfasts with abundant fresh fruit are served on a terrace overlooking the sea. Facilities include mini-laptops in rooms, free wi-fi and bikes for guests' use. **€97**

Domus Mariae Via Vittorio Veneto 76 ☎ 0931 24 858, ⓦ www.sistemia.it/domusmariae. Occupying a former religious school, this three-star hotel is still owned and run by an order of nuns. Half of the rooms have views to the sea and all are efficiently maintained, if a little plain. There's a fitness centre, a roof terrace, parking and, of course, a chapel. They have expanded across the road, transforming another convent into a hotel and spa. **€112**

★ **Giuggiulena** Via Pitagora da Reggio 35 ☎ 0931 468 142, ⓦ giuggiulena.it. Chic but friendly and relaxed B&B in a clifftop villa, on the eastern seafront of Siracusa and ideal for families. Flooded with light from floor-to-ceiling windows, the main living/eating area has a glass cube suspended above the ocean and a bookcase stuffed with English paperbacks. All rooms have balconies overlooking the sea, and you can swim off rocks or forage in rock pools (the hotel has a supply of chairs, mats and beach shoes), yet Ortigia is just a 15min walk away. There is also a self-catering apartment with terrace. Breakfasts are abundant and delicious, and eaten on a balcony overhanging the sea. **€135**

★ **Gutkowski** Lungomare Vittorini 26 ☎ 0931 465 861, ⓦ guthotel.it. Chic simplicity and intelligent design make this hotel overlooking the sea on the eastern edge of Ortigia a good, restful choice. It's worth booking in advance to secure one of the rooms with private terrace. Great breakfasts, with freshly squeezed orange juice and, in summer, home-made almond *granita*. There is also a little

wine bar, and private dinners can be arranged for four or more guests. **€110**

Henry's House Via del Castello Maniace 68 ☎ 0931 21 361, ⓦ hotelhenryshouse.com. A wonderful, bijou hotel overlooking the serene waters of the Porto Grande, *Henry's House* sports a gorgeous terrace awash with flowers and voluptuous Baroque interiors furnished with antiques – imagine *The Leopard* remade by the Downton Abbey team. Perfect for a romantic escape or honeymoon. Breakfasts and aperitivi on the terrace are unforgettable. **€168**

★ **Palazzo del Sale** Via S. Teresa 25 ☎ 0931 69 558, ⓦ palazzodelsale.it. A stylish, relaxed B&B in a nineteenth-century salt merchant's home and warehouse on a quiet street behind Piazza del Duomo. It has six spacious rooms with wooden floors, architect-designed beds, and intriguing touches such as mirrors framed with driftwood, and lamps with palm-bark shades. Breakfasts are superb, and service is unfussy and friendly. Free wi-fi – though the hefty stone walls mean that the signal can be weak – and a PC for guests' use. **€140**

Antico Hotel Roma Via Roma 66 ☎ 0931 465 626, ⓦ algila.it. A serene, four-star oasis in the old centre, the chic *Roma* offers spacious, contemporary rooms with wood-block floors and excellent bathrooms. Staff are charming, breakfast is an extensive buffet spread, there's great food in the Monzu restaurant, and there is a charming candlelit pavement terrace ideal for time-wasting and people watching. Excellent deals online, even in high season. **€183**

HOSTELS AND CAMPSITES

Lol Hostel Via Francesco Crispi 92 ☎ 0931 465 088, ⓦ lolhostel.com. This smart, modern youth hostel in a converted old *palazzo* is just a few steps down from the train station, with dorms holding up to ten beds, as well as private singles and doubles, all air-conditioned and with en-suite bathrooms. Reception is 24hr, no membership is required. There's internet access and the cheapest bike rental in town, plus use of a kitchen. Dorms **€20**, doubles **€37.50** per person

Rinaura Località Rinaura ☎ 0931 721 224, ⓦ camping rinaura.it. Some 4km south of Siracusa, this is a lovely simple campsite – a couple of fields, a farm shop, kids play area and a new swimming pool. The washing facilities are fine, though, and there are electric hook-ups, as well as self-catering bungalows. They also run a shuttle bus to and from Siracusa. Camping/person **€8**, plus per tent **€6**, bungalows **€55**

EATING

SEE MAP PAGE 214

Ortigia holds the city's best array of **cafés** and **restaurants**, most within a short walk of each other. Prices are on the high side for Sicily, though there are few nicer places in Sicily to sit outside in a medieval street or courtyard while the evening away.

CAFÉS

Burgio al Porto Foro Vittorio Emanuele II 6 ☎ 0931 60 069. The inimitable Burgio brothers' latest enterprise is an open-air bar on the traffic-free marina with uninterrupted views over the Porto Grande. Aperitivo time doesn't get much better than this – a fine glass of wine and a platter of gourmet hams, cheeses and salads (from €12) – while you watch some of the best sunsets in Sicily. Daily Easter–Oct from lunchtime until late.

Caffè d'Ortigia Largo XXV Luglio ☎349 628 9674. Opposite the Temple of Apollo, on bustling Largo XXV Luglio, this is not only a great spot for people-watching, but has friendly staff and great *cornetti* filled with fresh ricotta. Daily 6am–9pm.

Casa Trimarchi Bistrot Via del Labirinto 1 ☎0931 156 7471. Wonderful little place owned by a Sicilian estate, selling delightfully wonky organic fruit and veg from its farm, and using the rest to fine effect in its kitchen. This is good honest food at its very best, proof that simplicity wins out when produce is top notch. Antipasti are all on display on the counter – typical Sicilian larder dishes such as *caponata*, octopus salad, marinated anchovies. There is also a tempting choice of typical Sicilian pasta dishes (some using the home-made pestos that are also on sale). Meat eaters should not miss the chance to sample the *bracciole* – little parcels of skewered beef or chicken stuffed with melted cheese and fried in breadcrumbs. You won't find better anywhere. Open Thurs–Tues for lunch and dinner.

Caseificio Borderi Via De Benedictis 6 ☎329 985 2500. An Ortigia institution, this theatrical family of cheesemakers produce their own ricotta, tricotta (baked ricotta with a pleasant custardy texture and sweet-savoury caramel crust) and mozzarella daily, as well as *provola* (smoked – with almond shells – and unsmoked) and pecorino spiked with pistachio. They also stock some excellent artisan cheeses from the Ragusa area, and three Sicilian DOP cheeses. Nothing is wasted – cheese whey is fed to the Borderi's pigs, who are eventually made into salami and sausages. Join the queue for one of the gigantic, custom-made sandwiches (€4–6.50) – watching Andrea make them is part of the shop's theatre – then sit at one of the tables and enjoy the spectacle of the market. Mon–Sat 7am–3pm.

★ **Fratelli Burgio** Piazza Cesare Battisti 4 ☎0931 60 069 A mecca for foodies, this deli-café in the heart of the market is the place to come for a lunch of artisan, DOP and Slow Food Presidio cheeses and cured meats from all over Italy, beautifully served with a tantalizing array of miniature salads and condiments on wooden platters – best savoured with a glass of chilled white wine (from €15 per platter). As for special things to take home, look out for speck matured in myrtleberry grappa, a prosciutto crudo of *suino nero* (black pig) from the Nebrodi mountains, handmade salami from Trentino's Val di Non and a blue buffalo-milk cheese from Piemonte. Mon–Sat 7am–2.30pm.

Gran Caffè del Duomo Piazza del Duomo 18 ☎0931 21 584. Right in front of the cathedral, this is the place to sit and watch life pass by over a lazy breakfast or aperitif – staff are friendly and attentive, and prices are very reasonable, with local municipal workers stopping by for a coffee on

their morning rounds. Try the *cornetti* filled to order with fresh ricotta. Summer daily 8am–late; Sept–June closed Mon.

Viola Bakery Café Via Roma 43 ☎331 861 8415. A contemporary urban look, and free, reliable wi-fi have made *Viola* popular with locals and travellers alike. The food is good, too – nice, light *cornetti*, and at lunchtime there are salads, focaccia and *scacce* (a kind of bread pie stuffed with combinations of vegetables, cheeses and ham), all priced at €5 and under. Daily 7.30am–9pm.

RESTAURANTS

★ **Arrusti e Mangia** Ronco Cristina 3 ☎333 644 0847. Hidden in a dead end behind Corso Umberto, just across the bridge from Ortigia, this is a very simple place, run and owned by butcher Ciccio and his childhood friend Mauro. It offers a fixed-price set menu (€18) of *antipasti*, charcoal-grilled meats and wine. It is always full. Thurs–Sat 8pm–midnight, Sun 1–3pm.

Ci Voleva Via Trento 14 ☎339 120 5261. Just some tables out on the pavement in a side street off the market, but this little place does the best *spaghetti alla siracusana* (spaghetti with anchovies, capers, tomato, currants and crispy breadcrumbs) you may ever taste (€10). They also do a fab plate of roast tiger prawns (€12). Great service too. Daily 9am–midnight (closes 4pm Sun).

Don Camillo Via della Maestranza 96 ☎0931 67 133, ⓦ ristorantedoncamillosiracusa.it. If locals want to impress visitors, they bring them to this refined restaurant in the fifteenth-century vaults of a former convent. The fish is fantastically fresh, and the menu emphasizes unusual Sicilian specialities, such as pasta with tuna, mint and tomatoes; or a whole fish baked inside a crust of golden bread. It also has Siracusa's finest wine cellar. Prices are high, but the various tasting menus are highly recommended: a five-course fish menu is €55, an eight-course fish menu €70, a six-course meat menu €50, and there is a four-course vegetarian menu for €35. All exclude wine. Mon–Sat lunch & dinner; closed part of Feb, July & Aug.

La Gazza Ladra Via Cavour 8 ☎340 060 2428. Most restaurants around Via Cavour are very similar, but the "thieving magpie" tries to do things a little differently. A friendly, family-run *osteria*, it has just eight tables and concentrates on authentic Sicilian cuisine with a home-style touch, using staple ingredients like courgettes, aubergines, tuna, capers, olives, mint and oregano to great effect in *antipasto* platters and pasta dishes. Mains of the day (mostly fish) are chalked on the board. A meal will cost around €20, or you can just drop in for a salad, panino and a drink. Tues–Sat dinner only; closed July & Aug.

Kaos Piazza Minerva 7 ☎338 612 9831. The pizza (from €6.50) here is astonishingly light, with a crisp crunch and not a hint of sogginess – even when piled with a rich tangle of juicy Mediterranean vegetables. With tables outside, on

6

a pedestrianized piazza looking on to the ancient Greek columns embedded in the Duomo wall, this really is very hard to beat. Daily from 7.30pm.

Oz & Cappuccio Via Giaracà 8 (no phone). Joint venture between a musician from Berlin and the son of the market's biggest fishmongers. There's no booking, and no frills, just spanking fresh fish served in biodegradable cardboard boxes at little tables. Wine made by Oz on his vineyard outside Siracusa goes down a treat too. Try the super-crispy mixed fried fish (squid, anchovies and prawns), or the tuna burger. Expect to queue, but pass the time while you are waiting with a glass of Oz's rosé.

Piano B Via Cairoli 18 (off Via Malta, across the bridge from Ortigia) ☎ 0931 66 851. Fantastic light pizza made of slow-risen dough (from €6), fine quality burgers cooked over charcoal (€11) and traditional Roman dishes (a homage to the owner's mother) such as *carciofi alla giudia* (deep-fried artichokes), *fiori di zucca fritti* (deep-fried courgette flowers) and *baccalà in pastella* (battered salt cod). Tues–Sun 7.30pm–late.

Taberna Sveva Piazza Federico di Svevia 12 ☎ 0931 24 663. Reasonably priced, for Ortigia, and a wonderful atmospheric terrace just outside the gates of Castello Maniace. Fish and seafood are the thing here. The mixed seafood pasta is memorable, and portions are generous – and the avuncular waiters really don't mind you sharing courses. Pasta around €10, mains from €12. Thurs–Tues lunch & dinner.

La Tavernetta Via Cavour 44 ☎ 0931 66 385. Quintessential trattoria, family-run with passion, and packed every evening. Opt for the catch of the day: perhaps *spaghetti matallotta*

(€13.50), where the fish is cooked with cherry tomatoes, capers, olives and oregano, or cooked to order in white wine, with seafood or with a zingy lemon sauce. In summer they put a few tables out on the street. Fri–Wed lunch & dinner.

Le Vin de l'Assassin Via Roma 115 ☎ 333 288 4189. Relaxed, romantic and contemporary, with menu chalked up on blackboards, this small French bistro welcomes couples, groups of friends, and families with children. The standard of the cooking can vary; safe bets are the French onion soup (€9.50), honey-roast duck breast (€13.50) and lobster (€16), and save room for dessert. Tues–Sat 7.30pm–midnight, Sun noon–3pm & 7.30pm–midnight.

La Vineria Café Via Cavour 9 ☎ 0931 185 6049. A stylish, but relaxed fusion of café, wine bar and restaurant, using carefully sourced ingredients in unusual ways. Look for ravioli with Puglian burrata, prawn carpaccio with ginger, or Sicilian pork marinated in Hyblaean honey and peppercorns. *Primi* start at €10, and you can expect to pay around €40 per head for dinner, although there are some excellent set lunch deals, including a superior kids' menu. Daily lunch & dinner. Evening drinks from around 6pm.

★ **Zsa** Via Roma 73 ☎ 0931 22 204. Good pizza – the dough is made with a light touch, and comes blistered from the wood oven, and the quality ingredients on top are abundant. They kick off at €4.50, but for a bit more you can feast on a *vegetariana*, laden with succulent grilled vegetables laced with radicchio, or a *stufata*, scattered with chilli and fennel-seed-scented sausages and potatoes. In summer, there is pizza at lunchtime, too, though the choice of seafood pasta might divert you. Take-away available. Tues–Sat lunch & dinner.

DRINKING

SEE MAP PAGE 214

Ortigia has excellent **bars** – from Italian-style pubs to cocktail joints – and most of the late-night action is concentrated on the streets and alleys near the Fonte Aretusa, particularly around Piazzetta San Rocco and along Lungomare Alfeo.

Blu Via Nizza 50 ☎ 0931 445 052. Don't leave Ortigia without tasting a seasonal fresh-fruit prosecco or daiquiri at *Blu*. It's also one of the few places where you can sit outside and watch the open sea. Owner Seby plays a laidback and eclectic range of music, and serves full meals featuring fresh fish (try pasta with tuna, capers and pistachio for €13). During the day there are fresh fruit *gremolatas* and *pane cunzato* (Sicilian-style bruschetta) to eat on the terrace or on the swimming rocks across the road. April–Oct daily 11am–late; Nov–March Mon–Sat 6.30pm–late.

Cortile Verga Via Maestranze 33, ☎ 333 168 3212. Candle-lit cocktail and wine bar occupying a secluded courtyard. Decent wines, some very innovative cocktails, this is the perfect place to come when you need to escape from the summer crowds packing Ortigia's streets. Daily from 5.30pm till late.

Irma la Dolce Via dei Mergulensi 39 ☎ 348 597 5369. Set on a quiet piazza, this is a lovely, chilled, shabby-chic café-

bar off the tourist track. There are home-made cakes, a range of teas, and some very delicious cocktails. Usually open all day from 8am until late, but depends on the weather.

Solaria Via Roma 86 ☎ 0931 463 007. Friendly young owners have given new life to a traditional enoteca, which sells wine by the bottle or the glass, with or without nibbles or a light meal. Sit inside at long wooden tables, or outside and watch life pass by on Via Roma. Plates of cheeses, hams and olives start from €5, *crostini* with pâtés and pestos are €4, local sausages €8 and a *parmigiano di melanzane* €5. Wines from €3.50 per glass. Mon–Sat 11.30am–2.30pm & 6pm to around midnight.

Tinkite Via della Giudecca 61–63 ☎ 348 597 5369. In the heart of the Giudecca, *Tinkite* attracts a rather hip crowd, and with gas-heaters and blankets, it's one of the few places in Ortigia where you can sit outside comfortably in cold weather. Help yourself from the buffet of snacks to accompany your drink. If you're not in the mood for alcohol, choose from the huge choice of speciality teas (served with little biscuits), hot chocolate, and, of course, coffee. Daily: April–Oct 9.30am–1.30pm & 7–11pm; Nov–March 8.30am–1pm & 5–10pm; closed Wed am year round.

SHOPPING SEE MAP PAGE 214

Circo Fortuna Via Capodieci 10, Fonte Aretusa ☎ 347 216 3374, ⓦ circofortuna.it. Caroline Van Riet creates quirky and original ceramics that will make you think of Ortigia and smile when you get back home. Mon–Sat 10am–1pm & 5–7pm.

Sete d'Incanto Via Roma 27 ☎ 333 594 4518, ⓦ silk inortigia.wordpress.com. Owner-artist Hélène Moreau

produces hand-painted silk scarves and wall-hangings inspired by Ortigia's architectural forms and natural elements. Mon–Sat 11am–2pm & 6–8.30pm.

Via Cavour 38. Head here for carefully sourced clothes and shoes to die for by niche designers. Mon–Wed & Fri–Sun 1pm–8pm.

ENTERTAINMENT

Siracusa is one of the easiest places to catch a traditional Sicilian **puppet theatre** performance, though the best-known cultural entertainments on offer are the open-air classical **Greek dramas** performed in the Teatro Greco. Focusing on contemporary music and performance art, the **Ortigia Festival** in September has lapsed, though may be revived.

Istituto Nazionale del Dramma Antico (INDA) Palazzo Greco, Corso Matteotti 29 ☎ 800 542 644 or ☎ 0931 487 200, ⓦ indafondazione.org. Classical Greek drama is performed each year (May & June, usually Tues–Sun at 6.45pm) at the Teatro Greco in the Parco Archeologico. It's a real spectacle, though performances are in Italian only. Tickets range from €30 (standing) to €80, but are cheaper

Mon–Thurs, with €15 last-minute tickets available for some performances. Get details on the INDA website or from the INDA box office on Corso Matteotti.

Piccolo Teatro dei Pupi Via della Giudecca 17 ☎ 0931 465 540 or ☎ 328 532 6600, ⓦ pupari.com. Traditional puppet shows by the Vaccaro-Mauceri family, Siracusa's pre-eminent puppeteers, are held every evening March–Oct Mon–Sat (twice daily in Aug) in their thriving theatre. You can check up-to-date schedules on the website; behind-the-scenes tours and special shows take place throughout the year, and they also run a small museum (Mon–Sat, 11am–1pm & 2–7pm; €3). Tickets theatre only €9, theatre plus museum €10.50.

DIRECTORY

Hospital Ospedale Umberto I, Via Testaferrata, near Madonna delle Lacrime church (☎ 0931 724 111); for the 24hr accident and emergency service call ☎ 0931 724 285.

Internet There's free wi-fi in many central bars.

Pharmacies Gibiino, Via Roma 81 (☎ 0931 65 760). Outside normal working hours, pharmacies open on a rota system that's posted outside, and is also available at

ⓦ www.comune.siracusa.it.

Police For police, call ☎ 0931 495 111; call ☎ 112 in an emergency. There's a Carabinieri post in Piazza San Giuseppe, Ortigia (☎ 0931 441 344).

Post office The main post office is at Piazza delle Poste 15, Ortigia (Mon–Fri 8.20am–7.05pm, Sat 8.20am–12.35pm).

Pantalica

40km northwest of Siracusa • Always open • Free

PANTALICA, Sicily's greatest **necropolis**, lies in the folds of the Monti Iblei. Here, in the deep gorge of the River Anapo, you can follow tracks past several thousand tombs hollowed out of the valley sides at five separate locations. Several skeletons were found in each tomb, suggesting that a few thousand people once lived in what is now largely a craggy wilderness. It's an extraordinary location, designated a UNESCO World Heritage Site, but it's virtually impossible to get to Pantalica by public transport; by car, the approaches are from the small towns of **Sortino** or **Ferla**, at either end of the gorge, with parking at various points near both places; the northern necropolis, approached via Sortino, makes the most dramatic introduction to the area.

The site was first used between the thirteenth and the tenth centuries BC by Sikel refugees from the coast. After the eighth century BC, it is thought to have been the location of the city of **Hybla**, whose king invited Megarian Greeks to colonize Megara Hyblaea; remains from this era are visible, but all pale into insignificance in contrast with the five thousand or so tombs hewn out of the gorge below. In some were found the traces of several separate skeletons, probably of the same family, while others show evidence of habitation – though much later, when the Syracusans themselves were forced to flee inland from barbarian incursions. The atmosphere is primeval and almost sinister – for Vincent Cronin, even something terrifying: "Here is Sicily of the stone age, intent on nothing higher than the taking of food and the burial of its dead." For Cronin, the free play of nature in this ravine embodied Sicily's own particular contribution to the man-made wonders bestowed later by the island's conquerors, and as such – symbolized by a honeycomb he came across in one of the caves – the object of the quest described in his book, *The Golden Honeycomb* (1954).

The site

6

The most obvious place to begin is the parking area at the entrance to the **northern necropolis**, 6km from Sortino (follow the signs). A rocky path leads around a plateau, then down to the river and up the other side. You'll soon see the **tombs**, first just dotting the walls of the valley in clusters and finally puncturing the whole vertical cliff face – this last view is about 1km, or a thirty-minute walk, from the parking area. There are superb views from the higher reaches, and the path and rock-cut steps remain good all the way.

Back on the road, you can head west to Ferla, another 9km beyond. Look out for the parking area (clearly signposted) that gives access to the foundations of the so-called **Anaktoron**, or prince's palace. It was long assumed to be a building from Bronze Age Hybla, but many archeologists now think it may simply be an old farmhouse, which says a great deal about how little Sicilian vernacular architecture has changed over the millennia. The road continues to the **southern necropolis**, where more rock tombs are visible.

A lower road from Ferla descends through the little village of Cassaro to the bottom of the gorge where there is another parking area by a disused railway station. From here you can stroll easily along the gorge, following the river and the line of the old railway. It's a lovely walk, and there are a couple of places where it is possible to swim – even if the park authorities don't encourage it. If you are heading straight to this side of the gorge, it is easier to approach from the Palazzolo Acreide side – take SS124 from Siracusa towards Palazzolo, turning off along the SP45 marked Cassaro and Ferla. The entrance and car park are at the very bottom of the hill.

Palazzolo Acreide

Set on a hill some 40km west of Siracusa, **PALAZZOLO ACREIDE** is a fine provincial town, with some wonderful Baroque and Liberty architecture, a tumbledown castle, some fascinating museums, and, on its fringes, the remains of the ancient city of **Akrai**, featuring a perfect miniature Greek theatre, and Europe's only surviving statues from the ancient matriarchal cult of Cybele. Add to this great food (it has Slow Food recognition for its sausages), civilised streetlife, and any number of labyrinthine alleyways to explore at leisure, and you might well decide to make it a base for exploring the region if you have your own transport.

Palazzolo's main square, **Piazza del Popolo**, is the heart of the Baroque town, dominated by the handsome church of San Sebastiano and the gleaming town hall. From here lanes radiate down past opulent facades, hidden courtyards and gargoyled balconies, eventually leading to a trio of fine Baroque **churches**, the Chiesa Madre, San Paolo and the Annunziata. Everything you will want to see is within walking distance of the centre, and everything is well signposted. It is quite a slog up the hill to Akrai, especially in the height of summer – if you don't fancy walking, take advantage of the Comune's free minibus.

Casa-Museo di Antonino Uccello

Via Machiavelli 19 • Mon–Sat 9am–7pm, Sun 2.30–7pm • €2 • ☎ 0931 881 499, ⓦ casamuseo.it

Tucked away in a rambling house in the old centre of town is the **Casa-Museo di Antonino Uccello**. The fruit of one man's thirty-year obsession to preserve the traditions of rural

Sicily, it constitutes an important documentation of folk art, showing trousseaux, kitchen implements, carved wooden saddles, ceramics, an olive press, puppets, reconstructions of houses and stables, some wonderful painted panels taken from traditional *carrozze* (carriages) and anything else judged by Uccello to be in danger of extinction. Don't miss the extraordinary man's nightgown with a convenient slit for night-time tumbles.

Palazzo Rizzarelli-Spadaro

Via Spadaro 2, entrance Via Roma 234 • Guided tours daily 10am–5pm • €10 • ☏ 3336098126 • ⓦ http://museo.letradizioninobiliari.com

By way of total contrast to Uccello's Casa-Museo, this sky-blue Baroque *palazzo* has been restored as a museum and exhibition space in which the aristocratic owner, Augusta Zabert Colombo's private family collection of fashion, textiles, photos and an eclectic array of domestic items are used to give compelling – often moving – insights into the everyday life of minor royalty and nobility. The collection reflects the fact that Colombo's true passion is for the textile arts, which she brings to life, not only opening the eyes of visitors to the intricacies of the work, but conjuring up the context in which generations of privileged – but often desperately bored and unhappy – women filled up the tedium of their days.

Akrai

Daily 8.30am–7.30pm (or one hour before sunset in winter) • €5 • A 20min walk up from Palazzolo Acreide town centre, or you can park close to the entrance.

The first inland colony of Siracusa, ancient **Akrai** thrived during the peace and security that characterized Hieron II's reign during the third century BC. It declined under the Romans, but later re-emerged as an important early Christian centre (as shown by the number of rock-cut tombs in the area), only to be eventually destroyed by the Arabs.

Many remains give little impression of their former grandeur. You'll have a job identifying the excavated Roman **Tempio di Persefone**, above the Greek theatre, an unusually round chamber that was formerly covered by a cupola. Equally fragmentary is the much older **Tempio di Afrodite**, sixth or fifth century BC, lying at the head of

what was the agora. From here you can look straight down into one of the two quarries from which the stone to build the city was taken. Later they were converted into Christian burial chambers, and in the first of them, the **Intagliata**, you can plainly see the recesses in the walls: some of them catacombs, others areas of worship, the rest simply rude dwellings cut in the Byzantine era. The narrower, deeper quarry below it, the **Intagliatella**, holds more votive niches and a relief cut from the rock face, over 2m long, that combines a typically Greek scene – heroes banqueting – with a Roman one of heroes offering sacrifice. It's thought to date from the first century BC.

Teatro Greco

Of the visible remains, the most complete is the small **Teatro Greco**, built towards the end of Hieron's reign. A perfect semicircle, the theatre held six hundred people and retains traces of its scene-building. Behind the theatre to the right is a small **senate house**, or bouleuterion, a rectangular construction that was originally covered. Beyond lies a 200m stretch of decumanus that once connected the two gates of the city. In the second two weeks of May, the theatre hosts an **international youth festival of Classical drama**, attracting school and university student theatre groups from all over Europe (ⓦwww.festivaldeigiovanipalazzolo.it).

Santoni

The sculptures are signposted a 15min walk from the main Akrai site

Comprising twelve rock-cut sculptures (carved no later than the third century BC), the **Santoni** represent the fertility goddess Cybele, a predominantly eastern deity whose origins are steeped in mystery. There's no other example of so rich a complex relating to her worship, and the local name tagged to these sculptures – *santoni*, or "great saints" – suggests that the awe attached to them survived until relatively recently. For the past couple of years the area has been officially closed, though locals think nothing of clambering over the wall to see the deities, their faces vandalised, it is said, by a local shepherd fed up of people disturbing his flock. Restoration of the site, with the idea of assuring full access, is due to take place in 2020.

Mulino ad Acqua Santa Lucia

Valle dei Mulini • To visit call ☏ 3388505712 • €3

The fast-running river below Palazzolo is lined with old watermills – indeed Palazzolo still supplies much of the province with flour, although the old watermills have been replaced by a modern factory. Most of the mills have been abandoned, but the Molino Santa Lucia has been lovingly restored as a working museum. In common with all mills in Sicily, the waterwheel is horizontal rather than vertical – and operated by funnelling water from the stream through a narrow tube to maximise pressure – a method for running a mill with shallow waters introduced to the island by the Arabs. Visits include the chance to see the wheel operating, and to watch grain being ground to flour. If there's a group of you, book ahead and you can combine a visit with a bread-making workshop (€30 total for up to ten people) in the shade of a riverside tree.

Parcallario

Bosco di Santa Maria, Buccheri • June–Sept daily 10am–sunset; Oct–March weekends or by appointment 10am–sunset, but always call first • from €10 depending on routes chosen • ☏ 333 921 8145, ⓦ parcallario.it • No public transport

Half an hour's drive northwest of Palazzolo on the Vizzini–Caltagirone road (the SS124), set in cool, shady woods outside the little village of Buccheri, the well-run **Parcallario** adventure park offers the opportunity to head up into the tree canopies. There are currently six routes of varying difficulty, with rope-walks, zip wires and swinging wooden bridges, as well as courses for young children, with and without equipment. There are also barbecues (Buccheri and Palazzolo are famous for their butchers), picnic tables and a small bar selling freshly grilled sausage sandwiches and powerful local red wine.

Buscemi and the Museo Diffuso

Corso Vittorio Emanuele 25, Buscemi • ☎ 0931 878528 • Daily 9am–1pm, other times by prior arrangement • €5 • ⓦ museobuscemi.org

Back in the late 1980s a group of young men and women from Palazzolo and Buscemi, noting that the kind of rural crafts memorialised in Uccello's Casa-Museo had died out or were dying out, decided to do what they could to preserve as many traditions as they could. With virtually no budget, but with a lot of work, passion and dedication, they began to rent and restore old crafts workshops in the little village of Buscemi, and to persuade the last of the craftsmen – carpenters, pan-menders, cobblers, weavers, shoemakers – to bequeath their equipment to them. The result is an evocative series of exquisitely presented workshops scattered around Buscemi, often with the photograph of the last craftsman to work there hanging on the wall. Guides, who often knew the craftsmen, bring the old ways to life with some colourful anecdotes. Perhaps most extraordinary of all is the insight into a culture where nothing was ever thrown away – they even found a way to mend broken plates by stitching the pieces together with wire and sealing the cracks with carob pulp.

ARRIVAL
PALAZZOLO ACREIDE

By bus AST buses to and from Siracusa, Catania, Buscemi and Buccheri pull up on Viale Alighieri on the fringe of Palazzolo's historic centre. Tickets are sold at the nearby pasta shop, Antico Pastificio Puglisi, Viale Alighieri 1.

ACCOMMODATION
SEE MAP PAGE 230

B&B Del Corso Via Ortocotogno 11 ☎ 339 732 8523, ⓦ bebdelcorsopalazzolo.it. Chic contemporary restoration of a narrow three-storey townhouse just off the main corso. There is one room on each floor, connected by a spiral wooden staircase. The first floor room has a balcony, the second floor room a terrace, and all have slick bathrooms with rain showers, mini-fridges and wi-fi. **€60**

Dimora di Catullo Via Carlo Alberto 42/44 ☎ 327 291 8860, ⓦ dimoradicatullo.it. Superior chic B&B with a secluded fruit-tree-shaded walled garden with pool tucked away in the heart of the old town. There are three immaculately restored rooms and an elegant living room,

all furnished with a pleasing mixture of antiques and contemporary pieces. You can also rent the entire structure as a single holiday villa, naturally including the kitchen. **€170**

Fattoria Giannavi Contrada Giannavi ☎ 0931 881 776, ⓦ fattoriagiannavi.it. A farm with rooms, pool and a restaurant serving home-grown, home-cooked food, with good deals if you stay on a full- or half-board basis. The atmosphere is lovely, and it's set high on a bluff with extensive views, 8km from Palazzolo on the Giarratana/Ragusa road (10min drive). **€70**

EATING AND DRINKING
SEE MAP PAGE 230

Corsino 7 Via Nazionale 7 ☎ 0931 882572. Directly across the road from Pasticceria Corsini, this very cool shop and takeaway lifts the art of gluten-free baking to unsuspected levels of gloriousness. Indeed the gluten-free *arancini* are even better than their conventionally breadcrumbed cousins. There are marvellous cakes, and a dazzling array of exquisitely presented dried fruits and nuts, roasted, candied, salted, spiced or coated with chocolate. They also sell some lovely local ceramics, a range of books and, best of all, a range of excellent thermo water bottles. Wed–Mon 9am–1pm & 4.30–8pm.

Pasticceria Corsino Via Nazionale 2 ☎ 0931 875533. All you could ever ask of a *pasticceria*. Divine cakes and pastries, home-made ice creams and *granitas* featuring local ingredients, and a nice line in inventive *arancini* (try mushroom and speck, sardine with fennel and raisin, or

squash with walnut). There are seats outside, and plenty of seating in a large room at the back. Prices are very reasonable – and if you come at cocktail time an Aperol Spritz will set you back a mere €3.50. Wed–Mon 5.30am–late.

Soccorso Via del Soccorso 7 ☎ 389 7908000. Minimalist architect-designed cocktail bar hidden in the heart of a labyrinth of cobbled streets right next to a tiny chapel left open for prayer. There are tables on the rickety sloped cobbles outside, and drinks are a very reasonably priced. Open daily evenings only.

Spiga d'Oro Via Roma 82 ☎ 0931 875350. You really shouldn't leave town without sampling a *scacce* from the town's best bakery. Looking like Cornish pasties, but made from bread dough rather than pastry, fillings include potato and onion, spiced cauliflower, broccoli and sausage. And if you happen to arrive in the evenings, as the focaccia is taken out of the oven, you may be lucky enough to be given a slice drizzled with olive oil, salt and oregano, to eat as you queue. Mon–Sat around 5.30am–2.30pm & 5–7.30pm.

Trattoria del Gallo Via Roma 228 ☎ 0931 881334. A true rarity. A simple, traditional trattoria, with no written menu – just a handful of hand-made pasta dishes and a choice of three or four locally sourced meat dishes daily. Examples are ricotta-stuffed ravioli served with a melting, tomatoey pork *ragù*, aubergine-stuffed ricotta with tomato sauce and gratings of oven-baked ricotta, a generous mixed grill (sausages, pork chop and beef), lamb roasted with potatoes, or, best of all pork hock oven baked for six to eight hours with potato. Portions are huge, and for most people one pasta dish and one meat dish between two will be more than adequate. If you do go the whole hog, expect to pay €30 per person plus wine (bottles from €12). Open Thurs–Tues for dinner only.

Noto

Some 32km southwest of Siracusa, the exquisite town of **NOTO** represents the apogee of the wholesale renovation that took place following the cataclysmic earthquake of 1693, a monument to the achievement of a few architects and planners whose vision coincided with the golden age of Baroque architecture. Although a town called Noto, or Netum, had existed in this area for centuries, what you see today is in effect a "New Town", conceived as a triumphant symbol of renewal. The fragile Iblean limestone used in its construction was grievously damaged by modern pollution, but years of restoration work have gradually shaken off the grime and most of the harmonious buildings have regained their original honey-hued facades. With its traffic-free, old-town streets, particularly charming as the lights come on at dusk, and some characterful B&B accommodation, this is one of the island's essential stopovers.

Brief history

Noto was flattened by the earthquake on January 11, 1693, and a week later its rebuilding was entrusted to a Sicilian-Spanish aristocrat, **Giuseppe Lanza, Duke of Camastra**, on the strength of his work at the town of Santo Stefano di Camastra, on the Tyrrhenian coast. Lanza visited the ruins, saw nothing but *"un monton de piedras abandonadas"* (a mountain of forsaken rocks), and quickly decided to start afresh, on a new site 16km to the south. In fact, the ruins weren't abandoned; the city's battered population was already improvising a shantytown, and even held a referendum when

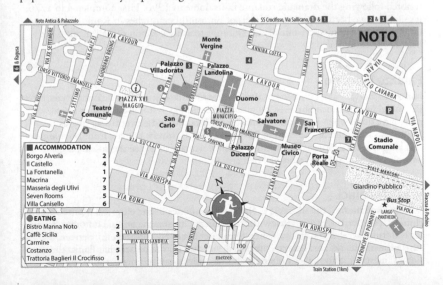

Lanza's intentions became known, rejecting the call to relocate their city. But partly motivated by the prestige of the undertaking, partly by the need to refurbish the area's defences, Lanza ignored the local feeling, even pulling down their new constructions and the old town's remaining church.

With the help of the Flemish military engineer Carlos de Grunemburg, Lanza devised a revolutionary new **plan**, based on two gridded sections that were to be almost completely separated from each other – a lower area for the political and religious establishment, the upper town for the people. The best **architects** were to be used: Vincenzo Sinatra, Paolo Labisi and the master craftsman Rosario Gagliardi – not innovators, but men whose enthusiasm and experience enabled them to concoct a graceful synthesis of the latest architectural skills and forms. Their collaboration was so complete that it's still difficult to ascribe some buildings to any one person. Within an astonishingly short time the work was completed: a new city, planned with the accent on symmetry and visual harmony, from its simple street plan to the lissom figures adorning its buildings. It's easily the most successful post-earthquake creation, and, for a time, in the mid-nineteenth century, the new Noto replaced Siracusa as the region's provincial capital.

Porta Reale

From the public gardens on the eastern side of town, the centre of Noto is approached through the monumental **Porta Reale**, built in 1838 and topped by the three symbols of the town's allegiance to the Bourbon monarchy: a dog, a tower and a pelican (respectively, loyalty, strength and sacrifice). The main **Corso Vittorio Emanuele**, running from here through the heart of the lower, patricians' quarter, is lined with some of Sicily's most captivating buildings. Now the traffic's kept out you can stand back and admire them at will, while floodlights, many set into the pavement, show them off to glorious effect at night.

The Duomo

Piazza del Municipio • Usually daily 10am–1pm & 3–8pm, but may close earlier in winter, or for special services • Free

Midway along Corso Vittorio Emanuele, **Piazza del Municipio** forms the dramatic centrepiece of the town's design, with the imposing twin-towered **Duomo** magnificently restored following the dramatic collapse of its dome in 1996. First completed in 1776, it's said to have been inspired by models of Borromini's churches in Rome – the story of its reconstruction, and some of the Duomo's treasures, are on display around the back of the cathedral.

Palazzo Ducezio

Piazza del Municipio • Opening hours vary, and the Hall of the Mirrors is sometimes closed for civic events; check with the tourist office • €4

Piazza del Municipio is bordered by gleaming buildings restored to look as they must have done when first built. Opposite the Duomo and currently serving as the Municipio (town hall), the **Palazzo Ducezio** presents a lovely, convex front of columns and long stone balconies. The **interior** is well worth a visit to see the so-called Hall of Mirrors, with its splendid trompe l'oeil ceiling.

Via C. Nicolaci

West of the Duomo, the steep **Via C. Nicolaci** culminates in the elliptical **Monte Vergine** church. It's a perfectly framed view that's enhanced during the annual **Infiorata** flower festival (third weekend of May), when flower petals are laid up the entire street in a swirl of intricate designs. **Palazzo Nicolaci di Villadorata**, the palace that flanks the west side of the street, also makes rather an unusual, not to say eccentric, sight. Onto a

6

AMONG THE RUINS OF NOTO ANTICA

Until finally abandoned in 1693, the original town of Noto had several times been a significant historical stronghold: one of the few Sicilian towns to resist the looting of the Roman praetor Verres, it was also the last bastion of Arab Sicily before the Norman conquest of the island. Only sparse remnants of the old town survive, but **Noto Antica** makes a fascinating side trip nonetheless. It's 16km northwest of Noto, signposted from the western end of the Corso in town (there's no bus) – the turn-off to the site is also that for the convent of Santa Maria delle Scale, with Noto Antica another 5km past the convent. You park outside the surviving gate of the **castle** (occupied from the eleventh to the seventeenth century), where renovation work has rebuilt some of the circular tower. Early Christian **catacombs** honeycomb the rock beneath the tumbled walls that line the valley cliff. An unsurfaced country lane pushes on through the castle gate past the now-puzzling, completely overgrown remains of an **abandoned city** – square-cut stone blocks, shattered arches, bramble-covered courtyards and crumbling walls. A side path leads to the keep of the castle, once used as a prison – peer through the (usually locked) metal grille-gate to see the carved graffiti of seventeenth-century prisoners. Behind the castle, a path runs along the edge of the gorge – the second stile along the path leads into the valley below, Cava Carosello, where there are the remains of tanneries and watermills, and lovely pools for river swimming.

---

strictly classical front six extravagant balconies were grafted, supported by the last word in sculpted buttresses – griffins, galloping horses and bald and bearded figures with fat-cheeked cherubs at their bellies. The *palazzo* is sometimes open for guided visits – ask at the tourist office.

ARRIVAL AND INFORMATION   NOTO

By bus All buses stop at the Giardino Pubblico at the eastern end of town, close to the Porta Reale.
Destinations Avola (1–2 hourly; 15min); Eloro (2–4 daily Mon–Sat; 20min); Ispica (8 daily Mon–Sat, 6 daily Sun; 45min); Siracusa (5 daily Mon–Sat, 4 daily Sun; 55min).
By train The train station is a good 10–15min walk away down Via Principe di Piemonte, has no facilities – not even a bench – and is often unstaffed. If you have luggage, you may need a taxi (☎ 0931 838 713 or ☎ 338 945 8206).
Destinations Ragusa (1 daily Mon–Sat; 1hr 40min); Siracusa (8 daily Mon–Sat; 35min).

By car Traffic through town is all one-way and while it's easy enough to drive in (follow "centro" signs) or out (destinations are all well signposted), finding a particular spot while driving can be difficult. The best advice is to park first (there's a free waste-ground car park behind the stadium, among others) and get your bearings. Many hotels and B&Bs are signposted through town as well.
Tourist information There's a tourist office (Info Point) at Corso Vittorio Emanuele 135 ☎ 339 481 6218 (Sept–June daily 10am–7pm; July & Aug daily 10am–midnight; Ⓦ notoinforma.it).

ACCOMMODATION   SEE MAP PAGE 233

Il Castello Via Fratelli Bandiera 2 Ⓦ ostellodinoto.it. Youth hostel in a converted *palazzo* in the upper part of town with wonderful views, small dormitories and double, triple and family rooms (with private facilities). It's accessible from the centre in a few minutes up signposted steps from Via Cavour, behind the Duomo. You might want to pay extra for a room with a view over the town. Dorms **€22**, doubles **€80**
La Fontanella Via Rosolino Pilo 3 ☎ 0931 894 735, Ⓦ albergolafontanella.it. Thirteen rooms in a restored nineteenth-century *palazzo* on a busy road on the northern edge of Noto Alta. It's a three-star place, and the only hotel (as opposed to B&B) within walking distance of the centre (10min), but there's no restaurant. It's cheaper than most of the B&Bs, though lacks some of their charm. Parking is, for once, easy around here. **€75**
Macrina Vico Grillo, cnr Via Fabrizi ☎ 0931 837 202,

Ⓦ b-bmacrina.com. A family-run B&B in a neighbourly street, with three spacious and airy rooms, each with its own terrace. There's also a huge walled garden with a couple of swings plus use of a barbecue, making this a good choice if you have kids. The small breakfast terrace is useful if you want to rustle up a snack or aperitivo. **€80**
★ **Seven Rooms** Via Cavour 53 ☎ 0931 835575, Ⓦ villadorata.it. Seven heavenly rooms in a wing of Palazzo Nicolaci, Noto's landmark Baroque palace. Décor is all subtle monochromes and beguiling textures, rooms come with everything you might need, from Nespresso machines, artisan teas and an inspired mini bar, to a divine array of toiletries made on their country estate. For anyone seeking boutique exclusivity there is really nothing to beat this place in Sicily. Breakfast, served at a communal table, adds to the feel of being in a private home. **€225**

6

NOTO ANTICA

Borgo Alveria Contrada Noto Antica ☎0931 810 003, ⓦborgoalveria.com. Stylish *agriturismo* set enticingly close to the evocative ruins of Noto Antica – perfect for anyone wanting to get completely away from it all. Lavastone floors, exposed sandstone walls and high dark-wood ceilings act as a foil to contemporary designer furniture and fittings – the suite comes with a Japanese bath and waterfall shower. There is a pool surrounded by olive groves, and the only drawback is the lack of restaurant. **€130**

Masseria degli Ulivi 12km north of Noto, SS287 ☎0931 813 019, ⓦmasseriadegliulivi.com. This estate deep in the countryside has been beautifully restored using traditional materials. Simple rooms a decent restaurant (try the home-made pasta with sausage *ragù*), plus a spa area and a huge outdoor pool surrounded by olive trees. Closed Dec–March. **€150**

Villa Canisello Via Cesare Pavese 1 ☎0931 835 793, ⓦvillacanisello.it. An old farmhouse on the western outskirts of town in a quiet residential suburb; rooms open onto a patio or terrace, and there's parking. Signs lead you right there from the western end of the Corso – it seems like a bit of a slog, but it's actually only a 10min walk to the centre. Closed Nov–Easter. **€80**

EATING

SEE MAP PAGE 233

There is a good range of restaurants in Noto, most of them along, or just off, the main Corso. The cafés on the Corso come into their own during the evening *passeggiata*, while the local authorities put on a full range of **concerts** and **events** throughout the year, from religious processions at Easter to summer music festivals – get details from the tourist office.

Bistro Manna Noto Via Rocco Pirri 19 ☎0931 836 051. A stylish new addition to the Noto fine-dining scene – housed in the wine cellars of magnificent Palazzo Nicolosi – which have been given a minimalist makeover. Food is seasonal and locally sourced and the menu short – try the *linguine con gamberi e pomodorini di pachino*, and the delicious suckling pig, and wind up with a *semifreddo* of the famous local almonds. They have a choice and informed wine list. Expect to pay around €45 a head for a full meal. Mon, Wed, Thurs & Fri dinner only, Sat & Sun lunch & dinner.

Caffè Sicilia Corso Vittorio Emanuele 125. You really shouldn't leave Noto without sampling the ice creams at its rival prize-winning *gelaterie*, *Costanzo* and *Sicilia*. This is the more radical of the two, with flavours such as lemon and saffron, and even basil. It is also a good choice for an evening aperitivo. Tues–Sun 8am–late.

★ **Carmine** Via Ducezio 1 ☎0931 838 705. Locals flock to this trattoria for a good meal at low cost, and it's certainly pretty remarkable value, with rustic *antipasto* and pasta dishes for around €7, grilled fish from around €12, and a mixed grill at €13.50. It perfectly defines the phrase "cheap and cheerful", though the downsides are that it's too brightly lit, the house wine is challenging, to say the least, and the interconnected rooms get very busy. Daily lunch & dinner; closed Mon Sept–June.

Costanzo Via Silvio Spaventa 7–11. A well-known *pasticceria* and *gelateria*, known for producing what may be the best ice cream in Italy (the other contender is *Sicilia*) in flavours such as mandarin, ricotta, jasmine and rose (depending on the season), as well as sweets and pastries, including dreamy *cassata*. The almond milk is joyous. It is also a good place to come for an evening aperitivo. Mon–Tues & Thurs–Sun lunch & dinner.

Trattoria Baglieri Il Crocifisso Via Principe Umberto 46 ☎0931 571 151. Nationally recognized super-chic trattoria using seasonal local ingredients in ways that make the taste buds zing: spaghetti with white prawns and Siracusan lemon, rabbit with orange blossom honey, wild greens, celery, carrot and peppers, tuna in a pistachio and sesame crust. There is a €45 tasting menu; otherwise expect to pay between €50 and €60 a head without wine. Thurs 7.30–10.15pm, Fri–Tues 12.30–2.30pm & 7.30–10.15pm.

South of Noto

South of Noto lies the most undeveloped stretch of coast on the east side of the island, sheltering excellent sandy beaches – like **Noto Marina** and **Eloro** – and the extensive **Vendicari** nature reserve. Minor roads run all the way south to the Capo delle Correnti, the southernmost point of Sicily, while in between, the old restored fishing villages of **Marzamemi** and **Portopalo di Capo Passero** serve as small-scale summer resorts. There are several good rural **accommodation** options in the area; you'll need a car, as public transport is practically non-existent.

Noto Marina and Eloro

Buses, operated by Caruso (☎ 0931 836 23), run from Noto to Noto Marina

6

CAVA GRANDE DEL FIUME CASSIBILE

A spectacular winding route northwest of the ramshackle agricultural town of Avola climbs past the Convento di Avola Vecchia to the magnificent gorge and nature reserve of the **Cava Grande del Fiume Cassibile**. There's parking by a sensational viewpoint over the Cassibile River gorge, which really is quite Grand Canyon-esque, with sheer rock walls visible across the divide, birds of prey circling, and the river glistening far below. The very steep path that leads down to the bottom of the valley is closed at times of high fire risk, and you need to be properly shod, fit enough to climb back out, and to carry plenty of water. The round trip requires a good three hours, plus any time you spend splashing in the natural swimming pools or following the footpath alongside the river, which runs for most of the gorge's 11km length. If you don't fancy going right down to the bottom, follow the gentler path that hugs the canyon walls, branching off to the left about halfway down the steps. At the top, at the parking area, you can get a drink or a meal from a rustic tavern, the *Trattoria Cava Grande* (June–Sept Tues–Sun lunch & dinner; Oct–May Sat & Sun lunch only).

Cava Grande is not accessible on public transport. It's a 15km drive from Avola, or you can also approach from Noto up the SS287, past the turn-off for Noto Antica.

Noto's local beach, 5km southeast at **NOTO MARINA** (also called Lido di Noto), is fine for a swim and a bite to eat (in summer at least). You can walk from here (though it's easier to drive) just south to the seaside ruins of Helorus, or **Eloro** (no regular hours because of staffing levels, but the fences have fallen down in places along the coast, so you can just walk in), a Syracusan colony founded in the seventh century BC at the mouth of the Tellaro River. It's all a bit ramshackle, and the few remains are quite difficult to make head or tail of, but its position right above the shore is very attractive. The broad expanse of sand below offers good swimming, but direct access is tricky from the site: a road to the south, across the river, leads directly to the **beach**.

The Riserva Naturale di Vendicari

Daily: April–Oct 7am–8pm; Nov–March 7am–6.30pm • Free, parking €3 • ☎ 0931 67 450, ⓦ vendicari.net

Some 10km south of Noto is the magical **Riserva Naturale di Vendicari**, an enchanting landscape of marshes, lagoons, dunes and saltpans. There's parking at the entrance, but no other facilities. Numerous waterbirds can be seen from the hides, including herons, cranes, black storks and even pelicans, though the more than three hundred flamingos can be elusive at times, while sandy tracks and boardwalks fan out north and south through the marshland, leading to some splendid sand crescents. The reserve takes its name from the brick tower, the Torre Vendicari, which looms over a part-restored *tonnara* (tuna-fishing village) by one of the beaches. Its internal courtyards and sandstone pillars gleam brightly against a turquoise sea. Another good beach, signposted **San Lorenzo**, lies just a short drive further south of the reserve, down the main Pachino road, and has very clear water and a small summer lido.

ACCOMMODATION

RISERVA NATURALE DI VENDICARI

Agriturismo Cala Mosche Riserva Naturale l'Oasi di Vendicari ☎ 347 858 7319. This *agriturismo*, with six rooms and a restaurant, is set right inside the reserve (take the Cala Mosche entrance), within walking distance of the beaches. Ideal for families. **€65**

Il Roveto Contrada Roveto-Vendicari ☎ 338 742 6343, ⓦ roveto.it. This beautifully restored old farmhouse is signposted at the Riserva Naturale turn-off on the SP19 Pachino road. The five self-contained apartments with kitchen sleep either two, four or six people, and you're only

800m from the pristine Torre Vendicari beach. Three-night minimum stay. **€90**

Terre di Vendicari Contrada Vaddeddi ☎ 346 359 3845, ⓦ terredivendicari.it. Minimalist chic in a country hotel at the heart of the Vendicari nature reserve, with views out to sea over its olive and lemon groves. Rooms are cool and stylish, with freestanding Philippe Starck baths and abundant bathtime products. Fabulous swimming pool, too. **€200**

Villa Romana del Tellaro

Contrada Vaddeddi · Daily 9am–7pm · €6 · ☎ 0931 573 883, ⓦ villaromanadeltellaro.com

In 1971, the remains of the **Villa Romana del Tellaro**, an Imperial-era Roman country villa dating back to the fourth century AD, were discovered on land above the River Tellaro, about 2km inland from Vendicari. Though on a smaller scale than the Villa Romana del Casale (see page 264), Tellaro has some fantastic **mosaics**, including scenes from the *Odyssey*, and a wonderfully realized wild-animal hunting scene in which people and animals are shown wading through water. There is a magnificent tiger, too – suggesting that these mosaics, like those at Casale, were the work of North African craftsmen.

6

Marzamemi

MARZAMEMI, prettily set around a crescent harbour backed by the port's old *tonnara*, is still renowned for its tuna dishes, and is home to a **film festival** in late July (ⓦ cinemadifrontiera.it), showing international contemporary and vintage films in open-air venues. Behind the shell of a church and *palazzo*, the restored *tonnara* square shelters bars and restaurants that come into their own in high summer, when tourists descend on the village in droves. There are two beaches, one to the left and one to the right of the *tonnara*.

EATING	**MARZAMEMI**

La Cialoma Piazza Regina Margherita 23 ☎ 0931 841 772. An immediately appealing, cosy restaurant run by a family of women, occupying one of the diminutive buildings of the *tonnara* complex and specializing not just in tuna, but in several local varieties of *pesce azzurre* – literally blue fish, actually oily fish such as anchovies, sardines, and the local *cappone* (mahi-mahi) – served in hearty and tasty traditional dishes with a light, creative touch. Daily lunch & dinner; closed Nov & Tues Dec–Feb.

Ristorante Campisi Via Marzamemi, 12b ☎ 346 942 0323, ⓦ ristorantecampisi.com. Campisi are Sicily's most famous producers of top-notch bottled tuna, anchovies, tomatoes, pestos and multitudinous fishy delights, and Marzamemi is their base. Shop in their warehouse first, then sit on the lovely blue and white terrace overlooking the bay for an innovative lunch of hand-made *busiate* pasta with tuna *bottarga*, cherry tomatoes, hazelnuts and a little scatter of bitter Modica chocolate, or gnocchi with pistacchio, garum (based on the salty-fishy Roman condiment and utterly addictive) and datterino tomatoes. Choose carefully and you can have two courses plus a desert for under €30 excluding wine. Open daily for lunch and dinner late May–30 Sept; Easter–May & Oct open lunch only, but call ahead to check.

Portopalo di Capo Passero

Eight kilometres south of Marzamemi down the rugged coastal road, **PORTOPALO DI CAPO PASSERO** is another low-key summer resort. You might be able to persuade someone to row you over to the little islet that lies just offshore, complete with a seventeenth-century castle. Otherwise, follow the minor cape road out to the southeastern point of **Isola delle Correnti** (the tiny islet just off the cape, linked to it at low tide). You're on the southernmost tip of Sicily here, with nothing between you and Africa.

Ispica and the Cava d'Ispica

Inland from the cape at **ISPICA**, 18km southeast of Modica, human settlement can be traced back four thousand years, to the cave dwellings and tombs carved out of the wide gorge of the **Cava d'Ispica**. These were later used by generations of Sikels, Greeks and early Christians to bury their dead, while during medieval times, a strong fortified castle, town and churches were built on the rocky bluff above the southern section of the gorge. Then, in 1693, disaster struck, as the great quake levelled thousands of years of habitation in one swift blow. A new town was rebuilt on the neighbouring hill, which is where modern Ispica thrives today, a rather sprawling place set around a central kernel of restored squares and Baroque churches, including the rather special elliptical **Piazza Santa Maria Maggiore**.

Parco Archeologico della Forza

Daily 9am–1 hour before sunset • Free • ☎ 0932 951 133 • You can walk here from the centre of Ispica: follow signs to Rosolini, and at the foot of the town the road forks – the left fork is marked Parco Archeologico della Forza, where there's a car park

Ispica lies at the head of its dramatic limestone **gorge, the Cava d'Ispica**, some 13km long and honeycombed with rock-cut tombs and dwellings. The area nearest to Ispica, designated as the **Parco Archeologico della Forza**, has a well-marked path taking you past the broken remains of palaces and churches and into the southern section of the gorge itself, where caves were used as houses, storerooms, stables, workshops and cemeteries, right up until 1693. The nearest water supply was the river at the bottom of the gorge, reached by 3300 steps, no less. A separate path from the parking area leads to the church of **Santa Maria La Cava**, cut into the rock and dating back to the very earliest days of Christianity in Sicily – some medieval frescoes can be seen inside.

In the week before Christmas, **tableaux vivants** are staged in the caves of the Parco della Forza, with locals dressed up as peasants, reviving old traditions such as making ricotta and shoeing horses.

Cava d'Ispica Nord

April–Oct daily 9am–1hr before sunset; Nov–March Mon–Sat 9am–1.30pm • €4

The Ispica gorge actually runs for 13km northwest towards Modica, with rock-cut dwellings and tombs lining the entire route. It's possible to walk through the gorge, starting either at Ispica or at the northern section, the **Cava d'Ispica Nord**, which is around 7km east of Modica (and very clearly, indeed almost obsessively, signposted).

From the Cava d'Ispica Nord entrance (where there's a café), a landscaped **path** descends into the gorge, where towering fronds of bamboo and wild fennel grow amid the fig, pomegranate and walnut trees. There are some truly astonishing **catacombs** immediately below the site entrance, while the path meanders back through the site past tombs and dwellings cut into the cliff face. The route through the gorge starts on the other side of the road from the entrance, running under the road bridge.

Molino ad Acqua

Via Cava d'Ispica 89, Modica • Daily 9am–7pm • €4.50, reductions for groups or large families • ☎ 0932 771048, ⓦ cavallodispica.it

Heading to Cava d'Ispica Nord from either Modica or Ispica, you may like to make a stop at the fascinating working watermill of **Molino ad Acqua** – just follow the many signs. Here you can watch the mill – set on the horizontal, rather than the vertical, so that it could still work when water levels were low – grinding wheat into flour, and visit the cave-house (with bed, laundry and kitchen) where members of the family who ran it lived until the 1950s.

Modica

The small but busy town of **MODICA**, 17km northwest of Ispica and 18km south of Ragusa, is enjoying a new lease of life as a select tourist destination, based again on its remarkable late Baroque heritage. A powerful medieval base of the Chiaramonte family, and later the Cabreras, it was once far more important than Ragusa itself, though ironically, following the reconstruction after 1693 (which has earned it UNESCO World Heritage status) it never regained its erstwhile prestige. There's really not much to see to Modica – a night would do it full justice – but it is an enjoyable place to visit. There's interest enough in simply strolling the Corso and window-shopping in the boutiques, fancy shoe shops, enotecas and gourmet delis.

Corso Umberto I

Modica's upper and lower towns are divided by the long main drag of **Corso Umberto I** – which originally was a river until a flood of 1902 prompted the authorities to cover it over. The Corso is flanked by a run of handsome *palazzi*, whose balconies are buttressed by gargoyles, twisted heads and beasts, while its churches make grandiose Baroque statements of intent. That of **San Pietro**, for example, has a wide flight of steps framing the life-sized statues of the Twelve Apostles.

6

Modica Alta

The warren-like upper town of **Modica Alta** holds some genius in the shape of the magnificent eighteenth-century facade of **San Giorgio**, a worthy rival to the church of the same name in Ragusa Ibla. It's thought that architect Rosario Gagliardi was responsible for this, too: the elliptical facade is topped by his trademark, a belfry, while the approach is characteristically daring – twin flights of stairs zigzag up across the upper town's hairpins, ending in a terrace before the church. From here, and from the tight streets above San Giorgio, you can look back over the grey-tiled roofs and balconies of the town, built up two sides of a narrow valley. There are more views from the remains of the **castle** and its clocktower, which perches on a rocky spur above the main part of town.

ARRIVAL AND INFORMATION

MODICA

By bus Regional buses drop you right in Modica's centre on Corso Umberto I.

Destinations Catania (9 daily Mon–Sat, 4 daily Sun; 2hr 10min); Catania airport (9 daily Mon–Sat, 4 daily Sun; 1hr 55min); Ispica (9 daily Mon–Sat, 1 daily Sun; 30min–1hr 10min); Noto (hourly Mon–Sat, 5 daily Sun; 1hr 25min); Ragusa (1–2 hourly Mon–Sat, 4 daily Sun; 25min–1hr); Scicli (1–2 hourly Mon–Sat, 4 daily Sun; 30–40min); Siracusa (10 daily Mon–Sat, 4 daily Sun; 2hr–2hr 40min).

By train The train station is a good 10min walk away from the town centre.

Destinations Noto (3 Mon–Sat; 1hr 15min); Ragusa (8 Mon–Sat; 15min); Scicli (3 Mon–Sat; 20min); Siracusa (4 Mon–Sat; 1hr 45min).

By car Drivers can park on the street, but in most central areas you need to buy a parking voucher (from *tabacchi*) to put in your window (€0.75/hr, half-day €2.40; charges apply Mon–Sat 9am–1pm & 4–8pm). Note also that if you're going to the Cava d'Ispica, you can drive directly to the northern section closest to Modica (there's a brown sign at the ornamental fountain) – you don't need to take the main road to Ispica itself.

Tourist information The tourist office is at Corso Umberto I, 141 (Mon–Sat 8am–1.30pm & 3–7pm; ☎ 346 655 8227).

ACCOMMODATION

★**Casa Talia** Via Exaudinos 1 ☎ 0932 752 075, ⓦ casatalia.it. Occupying a cluster of restored houses in what was once Modica's Jewish ghetto, *Casa Talia* is far removed from the city-centre bustle, yet just a 5min walk down a series of steps and alleyways from the main Corso. A garden planted with fruit trees adds to the feeling of seclusion. Rooms, designed by the architect owners who live on-site, are stylish and practical, and breakfasts are excellent (freshly squeezed juices, home-made cakes, jams and breads), served in a nook-and-crannied whitewashed room occupying what were once caves used as a cistern and stables. **€160**

L'Orangerie Vico de Naro 5 ☎ 0932 754 703 or ☎ 347 067 4698, ⓦ lorangerie.it. Tranquil, refined B&B with three huge suites (with kitchens) and four spacious rooms, in a *palazzo* with frescoed ceilings and private flower-filled terraces. Doubles **€70**, suites **€140**

Palazzo Il Cavaliere Corso Umberto I 259 ☎ 0932 947 219, ⓦ palazzoilcavaliere.it. A down-to-earth aristocratic family run their eighteenth-century palace as a B&B. The setting is splendid and authentic – original Caltagirone tiled floors, frescoed ceilings and antique furniture, and three of the eight rooms open on to a courtyard. **€60**

Palazzo Failla Via Blandini 5 ☎ 0932 941 059, ⓦ palazzofailla.it. Reborn as a comfortable four-star hotel, this handsome upper-town palace by the Santa Teresa church retains its intimate, aristocratic feel. The seven rooms are elegant and traditional, with tiled floors, high frescoed ceilings and antique beds. There are also three contemporary minimalist rooms in an annexe across the road by the trattoria *La Locanda del Colonnello*. Excellent advance and last-minute deals. **€70**

I Tetti di Siciliando Via Cannata 24 ☎ 0932 942 843, ⓦ siciliando.it. A simple, friendly, budget hotel, popular with backpackers and cyclists and set in the tangle of historic streets above Corso Umberto I. Rooms are pretty basic, but it's very reasonably priced and sociable. The owners are very helpful; they have rental bikes (€15/day) and can help organize bike tours of the surrounding area.

6

THE CITY OF CHOCOLATE

If you associate chocolate-making with Alpine Switzerland and the chocolatiers of Paris, think again. The vibrant Baroque town of **Modica** in Sicily's deep south is the unexpected harbinger of a tradition of **chocolate-making** that has its roots in Aztec America.

In the sixteenth century, as Spanish conquistadores were colonizing the New World, they came across many new foods, among them a concoction of cacao beans, known as xocolatl. It was eaten either as it was, or as a drink, mixed with water. "A cup of this miraculous beverage gives every soldier the strength to march for an entire day," the conquistador Hernán Cortés reported to Emperor Charles V. He had discovered Europe's first energy drink. By the sixteenth century the first cases of chocolate addiction had been reported.

In seventeenth-century Europe, chocolate became all the rage and cacao beans became big business. Looking for a suitable place to cultivate cacao and produce chocolate closer to home, the Spanish settled on Modica. Not only did its climate resemble that of South America, but there were plentiful supplies of lava stone, which meant that the beans could be ground in authentic Aztec style. Modica became rich, and the Modican aristocracy notorious for their decadent extravagance, dining on dishes such as hare cooked in chocolate, and 'mpanatigghi, a pastry filled with minced meat, chocolate and spices, a delight that you can still sample on Modica's high street today.

Modica's ladies took to drinking **hot chocolate** in church during Mass, claiming it prevented them from fainting. Their priest was not impressed, complaining that the practice violated the law of fasting. He was, so Modicans claim, despatched with a mug of poisoned chocolate. To prevent further chocolate-fuelled disputes, in 1662, the Archbishop of Siracusa decided to consult the Pope. "Liquidum non frangit jejunum," was his reply. Liquids do not break a fast. The chocolate drinkers had won.

By the eighteenth century, the Spanish Empire had vanished, but Modica's love of chocolate remained. Chocolate vendors known as ciucculattari pushed colourful carts through the wealthiest quarters of town. On board was a charcoal brazier, lava-stone pestle and mortar, and supplies of roasted cocoa beans, sugar, vanilla, cinnamon, and spices. Chocolate was made to order on the spot. They ground the beans, mixed them with sugar and spices to taste, then heated the powder until the cocoa butter had melted. The molten chocolate was poured into a tin mold, and left until it hardened.

Anyone inspired by Modica's history to try their hand at chocolate-making themselves can do so (by booking in advance) at Casa Cio Mod (⊛ ciomod.com). If you don't have time for that, seek out Sicily's **oldest chocolate manufacturer**, the **Antica Dolceria Bonajuto**, up an alley at Corso Umberto I, 159 (daily 9am–8pm; ☎ 0932 941 225, ⊛ bonajuto.it), which has been making the stuff since 1880. The shop's a beauty, filled with old display cabinets, and you can sample from dainty little tasting dishes on the counter before you buy.

Look for the sign opposite the Agip petrol station towards the top of the Corso (where you'll have to park), and follow the steps up around the passageway for the signposted "bed, bike and breakfast". **€40**

EATING AND DRINKING

La Locanda del Colonnello Via Blandini 5 ☎ 0932 941 059. The restaurant belonging to Palazzo Failla is one of the city's best, with an innovative and ambitious young chef. For antipasto try the smoked soft-yolked egg with gently braised artichoke, fava beans and wild asparagus, and for a primo try the local cavatelli pasta with caciocavallo cheese, black pepper, saffron and asparagus. Modica is famous for its rare breed beef – try the steak crusted with hazelnuts and served with a salad of tiny wild flowers. Mon &Wed –Sun lunch & dinner.

Osteria dei Sapori Perduti Corso Umberto 1, 228–30 ☎ 0932 944 247. Right on the Corso, offering reasonably priced rustic dishes with a strong emphasis on beans and pulses. The abundant mixed antipasto (€7.50) is a good way to start, and enough for two people, followed by lolli con le fave (handmade pasta with fava bean purée) or pasta with broth and meatballs. Primi start at €7. The menu is in Sicilian, but translations are available, and it's marvellous value – you can walk away with a full stomach for €10–15. Mon & Wed–Sun lunch & dinner.

Taverna Nicastro Via S. Antonino 30 ☎ 0932 945 884. For traditional meat (and especially pork) dishes, try this delightfully old-fashioned and very reasonably priced trattoria with tables outside on a flight of steps in Modica Alta. Specialities include sausages and salamis made on the premises, good hearty legume dishes, and classic Modican fare such as ricotta ravioli with a sauce of tomato, pancetta, sausage and pork. Secondi highlights include rabbit with potato, olives, tomato and pork, and lamb stewed with tomato, capers, cherry tomatoes and onion. You could eat a four-course meal (including a *cannolo*, or a lemon, cinnamon or almond jelly) for under €20, while house wine is €4 per litre.

Nicastro is signposted from outside San Giorgio, but it's quite a walk, and you will probably still have to stop several people to ask the way before you find it. Tues–Sat dinner only.

Scicli

Ten kilometres south of Modica, **SCICLI** is dramatically pitched against the bottom of a knobbly limestone bluff. Like southeast Sicily's other Baroque towns, it has seen quite a restoration in recent years, most strikingly on the main **Piazza Italia** and the pedestrianized **Via Mormina Penna**.

Around Piazza Italia

Just off Piazza Italia is one of Scicli's Baroque showpieces, the **Palazzo Beneventano**, which sports spectacularly grotesque grinning faces with lolling tongues and bald heads, tucked under the balconies and clinging to the walls. Beyond the *palazzo*, the voluptuously curvy Baroque church of **San Bartolomeo** stands embraced by the towering limestone gorge. Walking on, you'll find yourself in the honeycomb of the old town, clamped to the sides of the gorge, with dwellings at times almost indistinguishable from the natural caves. Although it has a fair number of abandoned houses, the area is by no means deserted, and several of the buildings are now undergoing restoration.

Via Mormino Penna

Via Mormino Penna is Scicli's showpiece, a scenographer's dream of a street. It's lined with exuberant and painstakingly restored Baroque churches and *palazzi*, including the Municipio fronted by the marvellous sculptural staircase that features in every episode of Inspector Montalbano, as the location of the police HQ. Other highlights include a filigree wrought-iron bandstand, a historic pharmacy, discovered a few years ago to have retained its stock, untouched, since it closed in the 1970s, and the church of **San Giovanni** (daily 10am–10pm), which houses the astonishing Cristo di Burgos, a painting of Christ wearing what appears to be a white calf-length dirndl skirt. Dating back to the seventeenth century, the painting originated in the Spanish city of Burgos, where representing Christ in a skirt (actually his death shroud) was normal, and was given to the city by a Spanish nobleman.

San Matteo

Continuing up the stepped path above Palazzo Beneventano, you can enjoy grand views over Scicli from the terrace of the abandoned church of **San Matteo**. Just below the church, a further stepped path (signposted "Chiesa S. Lucia") leads to the remains of another church; at the top of the ridge here, you're standing right above a series of abandoned **cave dwellings** that litter the hills around, and were used from Neolithic times until fairly recently. From the vantage point you can make out bricked-up entrances, caves and doorways in the tree-dotted cliffs below.

ARRIVAL AND INFORMATION   SCICLI

By car Scicli is an easy stop by car en route to or from Modica or Ragusa.

By bus Regional buses from Modica and Ragusa drop you in the centre on Piazza Italia.

By train Scicli is a stop on the Siracusa–Gela train line. The train station is a 15min walk from the centre, along Corso Mazzini.

ACCOMMODATION

Conte Ruggero Piazza Italia 24 ☎ 0932 931 840, ⓦ conteruggero.it. A smart old B&B in a restored palace on the main square, fine for a night or two. The spacious rooms have a/c, and some have minibars and balconies. **€80**

6

IL GRUPPO DI SCICLI

Sampieri beach, down the road from Scicli, is the spiritual home of a group of artists known as the **Gruppo di Scicli**. For over thirty years they met here every morning, to walk together on the strand before starting work. They walk less often now – the oldest members of the Gruppo are over 80 and the younger ones live away in Modica or Catania – but they still come down for a stroll occasionally.

Since its beginnings in the 1980s, the Gruppo di Scicli has shrunk and grown and shrunk again, accommodating and adapting, like an extended family. At present it has nine members. Operating outside the mainstream of contemporary art, the Gruppo has no manifesto or ideology. The artists were brought together by their shared approaches to painting, sculpture, light and landscape and, not least, in how they wanted to live.

Having exhibited widely – in group and solo shows – all over Italy, 2012 saw the first Gruppo di Scicli exhibition abroad, at the Bernaducci Meisel Gallery in New York. In Scicli, their works can be seen on the walls of the *Hotel Novecento*, and often at the **QUAM art gallery**, Via Mormino Penna 79 (Tues–Sat 10am–1pm & 4.30–8pm, Sun & hols 5.30–8.30pm; ☎0932 931 154, ⓦtecnicamista.it), which occupies the vaulted space of a monastery refectory. If it's open (hours vary), poke your head in too at the cosy Brancati Associazione Cuturale, also on Via Mormino Penna, which was founded by members of the group back in the 1980s.

★ **Novecento** Via Duprè 11 ☎0932 843 817, ⓦhotel 900.it. Occupying a Baroque *palazzo* in the heart of town, this stylish hotel has fully equipped rooms with architect-designed beds and arty, sumptuous bathrooms with Bisazza mosaic tiles. The tone is contemporary and cultured, and staff are friendly and helpful. €80

Scicli Albergo Diffuso Reception at Via Mormino Penna 15 ☎0932 185 555, ⓦsciclialbergodiffuso.it. A great idea, this – accommodation on a B&B or self-catering basis in one of eleven restored houses scattered around the historic town centre, ranging from a Baroque *palazzo* to a pretty town house with garden. Two-person apartments €70

EATING AND DRINKING

Baqqala Piazzetta Ficili ☎0932 931 028. On the steps above Palazzo Beneventano, this shabby-chic *osteria* has lunchtime snacks and fuller meals in the evening (most dishes €8–14). But it's most fun for a drink at night, when you can lounge on the divans outside, soaking up the mellow soundtrack. Tues–Sun lunch & dinner.

Nivera Via Mormino Penna 14, ☎393 838 3833. The focus is on fresh, seasonal and local ingredients, and there is a choice between ice cream, sorbet and *granita*. The Sicilian nut flavours, using hazelnuts from Mount Etna, Avola almonds and Bronte pistachios are particularly good, but then, so too are the fruit flavours. Daily 10am till 11pm (earlier in low season, later in high summer).

Don Tabaré Via Aleardi, 16/A, ☎349 242 8333. Set on a charming piazzetta overlooking the river channel, this serves exquisitely made cocktails and designer *arancini* created by several of Sicily's leading chefs. A very sophisticated choice for an aperitivo. Tues–Sun 10am–11pm.

Le Gioie Via Aleardi 5, ☎340 547 9265. Spartan place with outdoor tables run by a father and son, serving simple traditional dishes such as mussels with beans, beans with wild greens, and grilled calamari. If you choose carefully and stick to a couple of courses and a glass house wine you can spend less than €20 a head. Daily for lunch and dinner.

Satra Via Duca degli Abruzzi 1 ☎0932 842 148. In the vaulted cellars of a former convent, this restaurant has a seasonally changing menu featuring sophisticated and innovative dishes, as well as some more traditional offerings. Alongside handmade spaghetti with a cream of toasted almonds and tuna *bottarga* or smoked macaroni with ricotta, lemon zest and seared *alalunga*, you'll find fish couscous and a fabulous version of *pasta alla Norma*, with local *cavati* pasta, oven-baked ricotta, tomato sauce and aubergine. Choose carefully and you could eat for under €50. Mon & Wed–Sun dinner only.

Ragusa

A Baroque town laid out on a grid system over a mountain plateau, **RAGUSA** has two very distinct identities. The 1693 earthquake destroyed many towns and cities that were then rebuilt in a different form, but the unique effect on Ragusa was to split the city in two. The old town of **Ragusa Ibla**, on a jut of land above its valley, was comprehensively flattened, and within a few years a new town on a grid plan emerged on the higher ridge to the west, known simply as Ragusa (or **Ragusa Superiore**). However, Ibla was stubbornly rebuilt by its inhabitants, following the old medieval street layout. Rivalry between the two was commonplace until 1926, when both towns were nominally reunited.

Ragusa Ibla

The original lower town of **Ragusa Ibla** is totally beguiling, its appealing, stepped alleys and dead-end courtyards a delight to wander around. Over the past decade or so, Ibla (spurred on by EU funding) has undergone a renaissance, with the renovation of historic buildings and the opening of some stylish hotels and restaurants. Something of a magnet for Americans and northern Europeans tired of the charms of Tuscany and Puglia, Ibla is, however, something of a charmed and slightly unreal museum town, with just two thousand inhabitants and little in the way of everyday Sicilian life. It is, however, undeniably gorgeous, and wandering along its limestone pavements, past the grand facades of golden palaces and town houses, is like walking onto a film set. What's more, Ibla is virtually traffic-free, and certainly makes for a very agreeable night or two's stay.

San Giorgio
Piazza del Duomo • 10am–noon & 4–7pm • Enter up the steps to the left-hand side

The central focus of Ragusa Ibla is the sloping **Piazza del Duomo**, split by six palms, which ends in impressive wrought-iron fencing, beyond which broad steps lead to the church of **San Giorgio**. A masterpiece of Sicilian Baroque, it's the work of Rosario Gagliardi – one of Noto's chief architects – and took nearly forty years to complete. Its three-tiered facade, with sets of triple columns climbing up the wedding-cake exterior to a balconied belfry, is an imaginative work, though typically not matched inside. As with Gagliardi's other projects, all the beauty is in the immediacy of the powerful exterior. The architect gets another credit for the elegant rounded facade and bulging balconies of **San Giuseppe** in Piazza Pola, 200m below San Giorgio.

MONTALBANO COUNTRY

When it came to filming the **Inspector Montalbano TV series**, director Alberto Sironi decided to re-create Camilleri's Sicily in the province of **Ragusa**. Free of the aggressive development that has ruined many urban centres, the towns of the Ragusana remained a part of Sicily where old values and ways of life still held good. And it looked good, too: crumbling Baroque architecture; a sunbaked landscape with a geometry of dry limestone walls; and a coastline with endless sandy beaches, Swabian towers, scuffed lighthouses and evocative industrial architecture.

"Camilleri described Montalbano's house as being on a beach," said Sironi, "a sandy beach. Once we had chosen the house, everything else grew from there."

Montalbano's TV beach house is in **Punta Secca**, a modest seaside hamlet in the *Comune* of Santa Croce Camarina, full of little holiday houses. The house, now known as the **Casa di Montalbano**, operates as a B&B (ⓦlacasadimontalbano.com; from €90). **Montelusa**, the provincial capital, is a digital montage of several Ragusana towns. Its Piazza Duomo is that of Ragusa Ibla, as is the evocative Neoclassical Circolo di Conversazione, while the spectacular road bridge spanning the gorge is to be found in Ragusa Superiore. Montelusa's main street is Via Mormino Penna, in **Scicli**, a tiny provincial town that also provides the TV series' police station (Scicli's town hall, or Municipio), and several *palazzi* and churches, most strikingly San Bartolomeo, sited at the foot of beetling limestone cliffs.

To search out other crime scenes, head to the **Grotta delle Trabacche**, outside Ragusa, where a network of underground tunnels and caves conceals the tomb of two lovers in *The Terracotta Dog*, and to the ruins of the nineteenth-century brickworks, the Fornace Penna, stunningly sited at the head of the beach at Sampieri, near Scicli, a favourite hangout in the TV series of Montelusa lowlife.

The Giardini Ibleo and around

The main **Corso XXV Aprile** runs down the hill through the restored heart of town, past stores selling designer sunglasses, "slow food" gourmet delis, galleries and wine bars. At the foot of town, the **Giardino Ibleo** public garden is a favourite spot for an evening stroll and a drink in the nearby cafés. You can enjoy dramatic views from the very edge of the spur on which the town is built, while the violet-strewn flowerbeds set off the remains of three small churches, abandoned in the grounds. To the right of the garden's entrance stands the **Portale San Giorgio**, a surviving Gothic church portal whose badly worn stone centrepiece depicts a skeletal St George killing the dragon.

Ragusa Superiore

If you're driving – in which case you can head straight to Ibla – you might not visit the upper town of **Ragusa Superiore** at all, though that's where most of the city's shops and services are located. It's built on a grid plan, slipping off to right and left on either side of the sloping Corso Italia, just off which stands the sombre Duomo, completed in 1774. Although Baroque Ragusa has its share of good-looking buildings (like the few grand *palazzi* on Corso Italia), most of the architects' efforts seem to have been devoted to keeping the streets as straight as possible, and the town's most striking vistas are where this right-angled order is interrupted by a deep gorge, exposing the bare rock on which the city was built.

If you're walking back down to Ibla, you could make a stop on the terrace by the restored fifteenth-century church of **Santa Maria della Scala** (which features the remains of an unusual exterior pulpit). A mighty view lies beyond – of the weather-beaten roofs of Ragusa Ibla straddling the outcrop of rock, rising to the prominent dome of San Giorgio. From the church terrace, steps descend beneath the winding road to another church, the **Chiesa del Purgatorio**, from where winding alleys climb back into the heart of Ragusa Ibla.

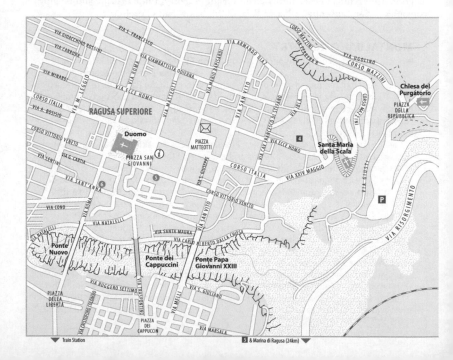

ARRIVAL AND INFORMATION

By train The station is just off Piazza del Popolo in Ragusa Superiore, a short walk from Ponte Nuovo and Via Roma.
Destinations Comiso (7 daily Mon–Sat; 30min); Ispica (3 daily Mon–Sat; 1hr–1hr 36min); Modica (8 daily Mon–Sat; 20min); Noto (3 daily Mon–Sat; 1hr 30min); Scicli (3 daily; 35min); Siracusa (3 daily Mon–Sat; 2hr).

By bus Buses stop next to the train station.
Destinations Catania airport/Catania (hourly; 1hr 45min/2hr); Chiaramonte Gulfi (5 daily Mon–Sat; 50min); Ispica (5 daily Mon–Sat, 1 daily Sun; 55min–1hr 40min);

RAGUSA

Marina di Ragusa (hourly; 1hr); Modica (1–2 hourly Mon–Sat, 3 daily Sun; 30min–1hr 10min); Noto (6 daily Mon–Sat, 4 daily Sun; 1hr 45min–2hr 15min); Palermo (4 daily Mon–Sat, 2 daily Sun; 4hr); Scicli (9 daily Mon–Sat; 1hr–1hr 50min); Siracusa (6 daily Mon–Sat, 2 daily Sun; 2hr 45min).

By car Follow the signs to Ragusa Ibla, where there's a capacious car park below Piazza della Repubblica.

Tourist information Piazza Repubblica, Ragusa Ibla (☏ 366 874 2621; Mon–Fri 9am–7pm, Easter–Oct & Dec also open Sat & Sun 9am–2pm).

6

GETTING AROUND

By bus City buses are run by AST. Bus #11 (every 30–60min; buy tickets in advance from any *tabacchi*) plies between the upper and lower towns ending in Ibla outside the Giardino Ibleo.

On foot If you're based in the upper town, the best advice

is to walk down to the lower town – less fatiguing and you can enjoy the magnificent view – and catch the bus back. The walk down to Ibla takes about half an hour, along Corso Italia and the narrow Via XXIV Maggio.

ACCOMMODATION

SEE MAP PAGE 246

It's infinitely preferable to stay the night in Ibla than in Superiore, where you can stroll the traffic-free streets in the evening and hop from bar to trattoria. Ibla has more than two dozen **B&Bs** alone, as well as a handful of small, stylish **hotels** – all signposted – and most can find you a parking space outside or nearby. There's a similar number of B&Bs in the upper town, as well as a few largely colourless, business-type hotels.

Il Barocco Via Santa Maria la Nuova 1, Ragusa Ibla

☏ 0932 663 105, ✉ ilbarocco.it. A very charming old-town hotel set around a bright courtyard – the rooms are in traditional style, with tile floors and oak furniture, but it's a modern place, all very tasteful and understated. **€90**

Eremo della Giubiliana Contrada Giubiliana ☏ 0932 669 119, ✉ eremodellagiubiliana.it. Some 7.5km south of Ragusa on the Marina di Ragusa road, this five-star country property is housed in the restored buildings of

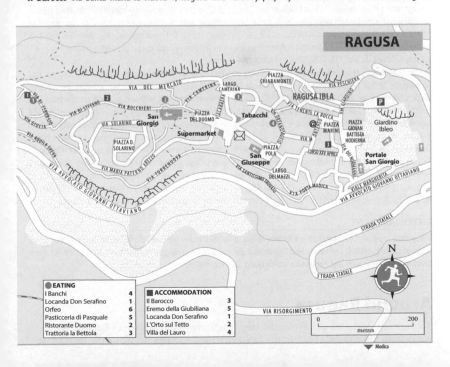

● EATING		■ ACCOMMODATION	
I Banchi	4	Il Barocco	3
Locanda Don Serafino	1	Eremo della Giubiliana	5
Orfeo	6	Locanda Don Serafino	1
Pasticceria di Pasquale	5	L'Orto sul Tetto	2
Ristorante Duomo	2	Villa del Lauro	4
Trattoria la Bettola	3		

a feudal estate and hermitage dating back to the twelfth century. Rooms (converted from monks' cells), suites and self-contained estate cottages all feature traditional Sicilian furnishings, the grounds are ravishing, and you can dine on their own organically grown food. It's no surprise to find it also has its own airstrip and private beach, plus pool, nature trails and all sorts of tours and activities available. **€150**

★ **Locanda Don Serafino** Via XI Febbraio 15, Ragusa Ibla ☎0932 220 065, ⊕locandadonserafino.it. Beautifully set within the hefty stone walls of a row of carefully restored Baroque cottages. The reception area is tucked under exposed limestone vaults and paved with chocolate-brown *pietra pece* (a kind of limestone suffused with petroleum). Rooms combine rustic stone vaults (and in one case a Gothic arch that survived the earthquake) with boxy, cream, leather furniture. The most unusual is the room in what was once the stables, with its shower inside a cave. **€120**

L'Orto sul Tetto Via Tenente Distefano 56, Ragusa Ibla ☎0932 247 785 or ☎338 478 0484, ⊕lortosultetto.it. A short walk from the Duomo, this warm, friendly place, run by a mother and son, has three serene bedrooms. Breakfasts are served on a roof terrace full of plants and include pastries fresh from the bakery. **€75**

Villa del Lauro Via Ecce Homo, Ragusa Superiore ☎0932 655 177, ⊕villadellauro.it. Minimalist style within the exposed limestone walls of an eighteenth-century *palazzo* in the historic part of Ragusa Superiore. It's an excellent choice in summer, when you can while away afternoons in the serene, stylish garden with swimming pool. **€94**

EATING

SEE MAP PAGE 246

Good **restaurants** are easy to find in Ibla, while a few cafés put out tables in Superiore's Piazza del Duomo – as night falls, and the lights come on, it's not too much of an exaggeration to suggest that this is the prettiest square in Sicily.

I Banchi Via Orfanotrofio 39 ☎0932 655 000, ⊕ibanchi ragusa.it. Styled as a "basilica of taste" by its creator, Ciccio Sultano of *Duomo*. At the root of it all is their fantastic home-made bread and pasta, along with meticulously sourced deli produce – all on sale. Then there's café-style service for traditional (but exceptional) street food and pastries; and a more sophisticated set lunch for €30. There are also special events, worth looking out for on the *I Banchi* Facebook page. 8.30am–11pm; closed Thurs.

Locanda Don Serafino Via Avvocato G. Ottaviano 13, Ragusa Ibla ☎0932 248 778. This stylish and costly cave-like restaurant, with two Michelin stars, is lit as deftly as an exclusive fashion boutique, and is a natural Mecca for foodies. Six-course evening tasting menus kick off at €120, but the three-course lunch menu (€55) is a fantastic way to experience some of Italy's finest cooking, without breaking the bank. Mon & Wed–Sun lunch & dinner.

Orfeo Via Sant'Anna 117, Ragusa Superiore ☎0932 621 035. Worth seeking out for traditional dishes like broad-bean soup, stuffed sardines or the local speciality of *cavati ragusana* (fresh pasta with a pork *ragù*). Count on €20–25 for a full meal excluding drinks. Mon–Sat lunch & dinner.

Pasticceria di Pasquale Corso Vittorio Veneto 104, Ragusa Superiore ☎0932 624 635, ⊕pasticceriadi pasquale.com. The best ice cream in town, plus utterly divine pastries and cakes. Just downhill from the Duomo of San Giovanni. Tues–Sun 7am–9pm.

Ristorante Duomo Via Capitano Bocchieri 31, Ragusa Ibla ☎0932 651 265. Meticulously sourced Sicilian ingredients reworked to stunning effect, in what is arguably Sicily's greatest restaurant. Put yourself in the hands of the double-Michelin-starred chef Ciccio Sultano, and opt for one of the great value lunchtime menus (€45 for three courses without wine, €59 for three courses with two glasses of wine). April–Oct Mon dinner only, Tues–Sat lunch & dinner; Nov–March Tues–Sat lunch & dinner, Sun lunch only.

Trattoria la Bettola Largo Kamarina, Ragusa Ibla ☎0932 653 377. A rarity in Ibla: a simple, inexpensive, family-run trattoria with red-and-white tablecloths that has been around for thirty years. *Antipasti* cost €5 and include deep-fried and breadcrumbed morsels of local cheeses, aubergine *polpette* and a lemon-scented *tortino* of courgettes. *Primi* (all €7.50) include tagliatelle with cream and saffron, *secondi* (€7–10) feature *maiale ubriaco*, pork braised in wine and wild herbs, in winter, and pork chops with citrus in summer. There is horsemeat as well, if you feel like going totally local. Tues–Sun lunch & dinner.

ENTERTAINMENT

The annual entertainment highlight is **L'Estate Iblea**, a series of concerts, recitals and events held throughout the town between late June and September, culminating in a spectacular fireworks display down at the nearby resort of Marina di Ragusa; ask at the tourist office for more information.

Around Ragusa

To the south and west of Ragusa, the largely unsung Baroque town of **Comiso**, the views from **Chiaramonte Gulfi** or the low-key resorts and beaches along the local **coast**

> **COMISO AIRPORT**
>
> If you are hiring a car (public transport links are poor) Comiso airport is a good gateway to the region. There can be some fantastic deals on flights, and with a car, you could easily explore the Ragusa area in a long weekend from the UK.

can fill another day's touring, but these are all mere sideshows compared with Ragusa itself. By public transport, to be frank, it's barely worth the trouble to visit any of the places covered below.

6

Chiaramonte Gulfi

Twenty kilometres north of Ragusa, the little town of **CHIARAMONTE GULFI** merits a visit largely for its far-reaching **views**. This is one of several places dubbed the "balcony of Sicily" and, though hazy in summer, the panorama (west towards Gela and north to Etna) embraces dun-coloured farmland interspersed with solitary villages – a still, silent scene, but for the occasional dog's bark or the whine of a Vespa.

Sampieri

There's more to the province of Ragusa than its feted Baroque towns. Head down to the coast from Modica or Scicli and you'll strike the magnificent beach of **Sampieri**, a stunning 2km sweep of sand running between the dramatic Gothic ruins of an abandoned brick factory (which fans of Montalbano will recognize). Sampieri **village**, a small and pleasantly low-key local resort, retains a core of traditional cubic fishermen's houses, built of the same gleaming limestone as the cobbles on the streets. In summer a couple of small lidos open on the beach, but for the rest of the year it's a marvellous place to spend a few days if you want to do nothing but swim and take long beach walks.

ACCOMMODATION   SAMPIERI

If you want to rent a **house** or **apartment** in Sampieri, you'll find that the Abitare Solemare agency (☎ 334 633 4423, ⓦ abitaresolemare.it) has the widest choice, with high-season prices starting at €500 per week for two people – and low-season prices around half that.

Marina di Ragusa

Southwest of Ragusa, it's a straight 24km run down to the coast, and the start of the so-called "riviera", which extends as far as Gela. The small resort of **MARINA DI RAGUSA** is a typical Sicilian mix of private lidos and apartments, and bars and restaurants that really only do business for four or five months of the year. A coastal road westwards offers access to more beaches near Punta Secca (of Montalbano fame) and beyond to the desolate remains of ancient **Kamarina** (also spelt Camerina), a Syracusan colony founded in 599 BC. It lies on a headland overlooking beaches on either side, and has a small **Museo Archeologico** (due to re-open following restoration early 2020). Behind the antiquarium is all that's left of a fifth-century BC Tempio di Atena, surrounded by the rubble of city walls and the various ruins of the Hellenistic-Roman city.

Enna and the interior

254 Enna

258 Northeast of Enna

260 Caltanissetta

262 Piazza Armerina

264 Villa Romana del Casale

268 Around Piazza Armerina

270 Caltagirone

PIAZZA ARMERINA

Enna and the interior

… for the last five hours all they had set eyes on were bare hillsides flaming yellow under the sun … They had passed through crazed-looking villages washed in palest blue; crossed dry beds of torrents over fantastic bridges; skirted sheer precipices which no sage and broom could temper. Never a tree, never a drop of water; just sun and dust.
Giuseppe Tomasi di Lampedusa, *The Leopard*

In Sicily's vast and mountainous interior – thoroughly depleted by mass emigration – you can truly begin to get off the tourist trail. Outside just three or four decent-sized towns, bunched together almost in the centre of the island, are mile upon mile of rolling hills, green and lush in winter and spring, burnt dry and yellow during the long summer months. The extensive cornfields have been a feature of the Sicilian landscape since Greek times – but the rolling hills are mostly silent and empty, punctuated only by occasional moribund towns and villages wrapped around easily defensible heights. Even crossing through the centre via the Catania–Palermo motorway gives a powerful flavour of rural Sicily. However, travelling slowly through this land has its rewards, not least the fascinating glimpses of a way of life that has all but disappeared in the rest of the island. This is true not just of the countryside, but of the cities too – perhaps manifested most intensely during religious festivals, such as Easter. Indeed, one of the most evocative times to visit the area is Holy Week, which sees costumed processions in Caltagirone, Troina, Caltanissetta and, most striking of all, Enna.

Symbol of the entire interior is the blustery mountain settlement of **Enna**, a provincial capital easy to reach from both Catania and Palermo. It's a historic place, with a mighty castle and some even mightier views. The motorway may be fast and fantastic, but to really get a sense of life here, you need to get onto the minor roads and take things slowly, through the mountain towns and villages on the fringes of the Nebrodi and Madonie mountains. Travelling through these off-the-beaten-track places is more about sitting in a café watching small-town life unfold, than sightseeing. The largest town in the region is actually **Caltanissetta**, gateway to the south coast and the deep west, though it's also the most disappointing and is devoid of much charm. The historic sites of the interior are all in the southeast, especially the single biggest draw: the lavish Roman mosaics at the **Villa Romana del Casale**. This lies just outside the enjoyable Baroque town of **Piazza Armerina**, which could also be your base for seeing the extensive and unsung Greek ruins of **Morgantina** and the fabulous and largely undiscovered collection of the Archeological Museum in **Aidone**. Further south, ceramic-studded **Caltagirone** makes a handy departure point for the Baroque towns of the southeast.

GETTING AROUND ENNA AND THE INTERIOR

By car The interior's main roads at least are pretty good and distances not too large, and with a car you could pick any of the towns and use it as a base for seeing the rest of the region. Minor roads can be narrow and potholed – with hold-ups caused by tractors and sheep – fine for leisurely exploring, but not much good for getting from A to B quickly. **By bus** Enna, Caltanissetta and Piazza Armerina are the only towns with frequent bus connections to the rest of Sicily, so if you're relying on public transport, you're pretty much limited to these places plus a side trip from Piazza Armerina to Aidone and Morgantina. It's more difficult to travel north and west into the mountains by bus, though there are services out of Enna along the two major routes, the SS120 and SS121.

Highlights

❶ **Enna** Spend the night high up in the hill-town of Enna and watch the sun set from its spectacular terraces, or visit on Good Friday to see thousands take part in traditional processions. See page 254

❷ **Piazza Armerina** The old Baroque town of Piazza Armerina is an undiscovered gem, its highlight the church of San Giovanni Evangelista, dubbed the Sistine Chapel of Sicily. See page 262

❸ **Villa Romana del Casale** The extraordinary mosaics in this ancient Roman villa, created by artists from North Africa, are unmatched anywhere in Italy. See page 264

❹ **Museo Archeologico, Aidone** See the incredible ancient Greek sculptures and silverware recently returned to Sicily after a protracted legal battle. See page 268

❺ **Morgantina** A little-known Greek archeological site in gorgeous rural surroundings. See page 268

❻ **La Scala, Caltagirone** In a town famed for its ceramics, these 142 steps are adorned with beautiful patterned tiles. See page 270

HIGHLIGHTS ARE MARKED ON THE MAP ON PAGE 254

Enna

From a bulging V-shaped ridge almost 1000m up, **ENNA** lords it over the surrounding hills of central Sicily. One of the most ancient towns on the island, Enna has only ever had one function: Livy described it as "inexpugnabilis", and, for obvious strategic reasons, the town was a magnet for successive hostile armies, who in turn besieged and fortified it. The Arabs, for example, spent twenty years trying to gain entrance to Enna before eventually, in 859, resorting to crawling in through the sewers. The approach to this doughty mountain stronghold is still formidable, the road climbing slowly out of the valley and looping across the solid crag to the summit and the town.

Enna remains a medieval hill-town at heart, with a tightly packed centre of narrow streets, small squares and hemmed-in churches, where occasional gaps through the buildings reveal swirling drops down into the valleys below. Most of Enna's churches – even the ones in use – have cracked facades and weeds growing out of improbable places, but there are some that catch the eye, like fourteenth-century **San Giovanni** (behind the much larger San Giuseppe, on Piazza Coppola), which has a Catalan-Gothic facade and a tower crowned by a little cupola. When all is said and done, apart from the **castle**, the all-encompassing **views**, and the usual desultory pleasures of provincial town life (like the little street market on

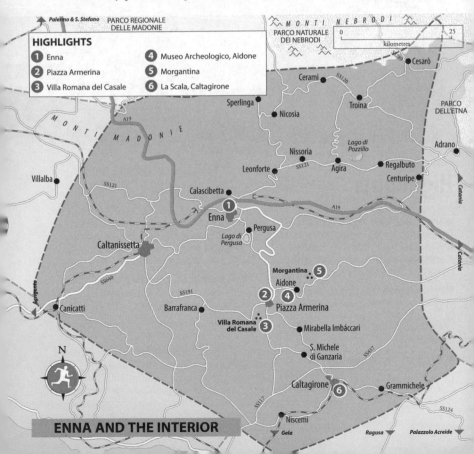

HIGHLIGHTS

1. Enna
2. Piazza Armerina
3. Villa Romana del Casale
4. Museo Archeologico, Aidone
5. Morgantina
6. La Scala, Caltagirone

ENNA AND THE INTERIOR

LAGO DI PERGUSA

The **Lago di Pergusa** was the site of Hades' abduction of Persephone to the underworld. The story has it that Persephone, surrounded by nymphs, was gathering flowers on the lush banks of the lake when Hades emerged from a chasm beneath the water and spirited her away. Demeter searched in vain for her daughter, and her grief at the loss of Persephone prevented the corn from growing. To settle the matter, Zeus ruled that Persephone should spend half the year as queen of the underworld, and live for the other six months in Sicily with her mother as one of the island's goddesses. In her gratitude, Demeter, as goddess of grain and agriculture, made the corn grow again – a powerful symbol in a traditionally fertile land. Interestingly, in the original myth, it is the summer months when Persephone is with Hades – not the winter months, as in the northern European versions.

These days, the Pergusa road is choc-a-bloc with apartments, hotels and holiday developments, while the lake is encircled by a motor-racing track. It's hard now, despite the pleasant wooded banks beyond the water, to imagine a less romantic spot. Mary Taylor Simeti's journal, *On Persephone's Island*, labels the Lago di Pergusa "a brilliant example of the Sicilians' best efforts to ruin their landscape".

There's really no point coming to the lake for any glimpse of the truth behind the legend, though it does make a possible base near Enna, especially if you fancy a retreat with Moleskine and pencil to ★ *La Casa del Poeta* at Contrada da Parasporino, 1km from Lago di Pergusa (Ⓣ 329 627 4918 or Ⓣ 328 657 2731, Ⓦ lacasadelpoeta.it; €85), a nineteenth-century villa, where you're invited to immerse yourself in literature from their library or write in their "writing room". Those suffering from writer's block can seek inspiration as they lounge by the pool. There are also half- and full-board deals with meals at the family's farm, Masseria Bannata (see page 264), a ten-minute drive away.

Piazza Coppola), there's little to keep you here more than a night. However, that night is very definitely worth it – with some stupendous vantage points from which to watch the sun set, summer evenings here must count among the most enjoyable in Sicily. Come in winter and you should expect snow, the wind blowing hard through the streets, and the white slopes beyond blending with the anaemic stone buildings.

Castello di Lombardia

Via Nino Savarese • Daily: Nov–Feb 10am–5pm, March & April 10am–6pm, May–Oct 10am–8pm • Free (although there are constantly discussions about introducing an entrance fee)

Despite numerous wars and attacks over the years, most of Enna's medieval remains are in good condition. Dominating the easternmost spur of town is the thirteenth-century **Castello di Lombardia**, built by Frederick II who, according to some sources, spent his summers here. There's a huge area inside enclosed by the walls, split into various courtyards, while six surviving towers (out of an original twenty) provide lookouts. Climb the tallest, **Torre Pisana**, for some great views of Enna, the rugged countryside in all directions, and across to Mount Etna.

Rocca di Cerere

Via Nino Savarese • Free access (no gates)

Up above Enna's castle is the **Rocca di Cerere**, an exposed outcrop where some scattered foundations are presumed to be the remnants of a temple erected by Gelon in 480 BC. Enna was the centre of the Greek cult of **Demeter**, the fertility goddess (her Roman counterpart was Ceres, hence the rock's name), and the most famous of the myths associated with the goddess – the carrying off of her daughter, Persephone, to the underworld – is supposed to have taken place just a few kilometres away, at Lago di Pergusa (see box).

The Duomo

Piazza Duomo • Daily 9.30am–1pm & 3.30–8pm (closes earlier in low season)

Enna's **Duomo** fronts a shady little square, which has been rebuilt several times since its foundation in 1307. It's not much to look at from the outside, but the sixteenth-century interior is a different story, with every surface covered in ornamentation. Look closely at the bottom of the huge supporting dark-grey columns, the bases of which are carved with snarling heads with human hands and snake bodies.

Piazza Vittorio Emanuele

The western extremity of Via Roma is marked by the sloping, rectangular **Piazza Vittorio Emanuele**, focal point of the evening *passeggiata*. Off here, a long cliff-edge promenade looks out to the little rust-coloured town of Calascibetta over the valley. The plain, high wall of the church of **San Francesco**, which flanks the piazza, has a massive sixteenth-century tower, previously part of the old town's system of watchtowers that linked the castle with all of Enna's churches.

Torre di Federico II

Via Torre di Federico • Daily: March, Sept & Oct 9am–6pm; Nov, Dec, Jan & Feb 9am–5pm; April to end Aug 9am–8pm • Free (but there are discussions about introducing an entrance fee)

An octagonal watchtower, 24m high, the **Torre di Federico II** is linked by a (now hidden) underground passage to the castle. Built in the thirteenth century by Frederick II, it now stands in isolation amid the **Giardino Pubblico** in the largely modern south of the town. Several local historians believe that it occupies the very centrepoint of Sicily – and to have been built over a site used by the ancient Sikels as an astronomical observatory. You can climb to the top of the tower for great views.

Calascibetta

6km from Enna • Buses every two hours from the terminal but only two on Sunday

The small town that you can see from Enna's terraces, hugging a lower hill to the north across the valley, is **Calascibetta**, and it hints at what Enna would be like without the

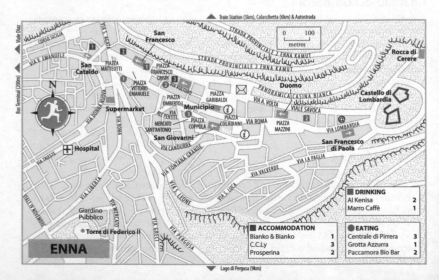

tower blocks. Once a Saracen town, it was fortified by Count Roger in his successful attempt to take Enna in 1087, and the tangled streets seem straight from that age. The tightly packed red-stone buildings perch above a sheer drop on the eastern side, rising to the restored Chiesa Madre at the very top.

ARRIVAL AND DEPARTURE ENNA

By bus The terminal is on Viale Diaz, just outside the old centre and a 10min walk from Piazza Vittorio Emanuele. All bus companies are at the bus terminal: SAIS (☎ 0935 500 902, ⓦ saisautolinee.it) covers Calascibetta, Caltanissetta, Catania, Catania airport, Gangi, Messina, Palermo, Pergusa, Piazza Armerina and Sperlinga; Interbus (☎ 0935 22 460, ⓦ interbus.it) covers Catania and Leonforte; and ISEA (☎ 095 464 101, ⓦ iseaviaggi.it) Nicosia and Troina.
Destinations Calascibetta (8 daily Mon–Sat; 30min); Caltagirone (2 daily Mon–Fri, 1 daily Sun; 1hr 25min); Caltanissetta (2 daily Mon–Fri, 1 daily Sun; 55min); Catania (5–8 daily Mon–Sat, 2 daily Sun; 1hr 15min); Gangi (1 daily, Mon–Fri; 2hr); Leonforte (6 daily Mon–FRI, 2 daily Sat; 35–45min); NIcosia (1 daily Mon–Sat; 1hr 30min); Palermo (5 daily Mon–Sat, 4 daily Sun; 1hr 35min); Pergusa

(5–10 daily Mon–Fri, 2 daily Sat, 1 daily Sun; 20min); Piazza Armerina (8 daily Mon–Fri, 4 daily Sat, 1 daily Sun; 30min), Sperlinga (1 daily Mon–Fri; 1hr 35min), Troina (1 daily Mon–Sat; 2hr 30min).
By train The train station is 5km north of town: a local bus (SAIS) runs around 6 times daily to the Viale Diaz terminal and back (less frequently on Sun); a taxi costs around €15.
Destinations Caltanissetta (10 daily Mon–Sat, 5 daily Sun; 35min); Catania (10 daily Mon–Sat, 5 daily Sun; 1hr–1hr 20min); Palermo (6 daily Mon–Sat, 3 daily Sun; 1hr 45min).
By car The narrow streets of Enna can cause extreme congestion, and you really don't want to drive around more than you have to. There's a car park just off Viale Diaz, by the Cappuccini cemetery and near the bus terminal (look for the blue "P" sign).

GETTING AROUND

By bus Everywhere in Enna itself can be reached very easily on foot.
By taxi Ranks can be found on Viale Diaz, near the bus

terminal, and at Piazza Vittorio Emanuele; alternatively, call ☎ 0935 500 905.

INFORMATION

Tourist information You can pick up a good town map and accommodation details at the tourist office (Info Point) at Via Roma 413 (Mon, Tues & Thurs–Sat 8.30am–1.30pm, Wed 8.30am–7pm; ☎ 0935 528 288), or at the larger office on Piazza Colaianni (Mon–Fri 8am–2pm, plus Wed 2.45–

6.15pm; ☎ 0935 500 875, ⓦ regione.sicilia.it/turismo/web_turismo/), off Via Roma next to the *Grande Albergo Sicilia*.
Online information There's information on Enna at ⓦ turismoenna.it, but only in Italian.

ACCOMMODATION SEE MAP PAGE 256

★ **Bianko & Bianko** Via Longo 15 ☎ 331 329 4288 or ☎ 327 159 8426, ⓦ biankoebianko.it. An effortlessly cool and uncluttered B&B in a nineteenth-century townhouse, with three spacious, light-filled rooms in stylish white. It's handy for the old town, just to the right of the steps of San Cataldo church at the bottom of Via Vittorio Emanuele. There's no staff on the premises (you have to call first), and breakfast is taken at the bar around the corner. €60
★ **C.C.Ly** Via Vulturo 3 ☎ 0935 072 257, ⓦ ccly-hostel. com. Clean, bright doubles, triples and quads in a beautifully

restored old stone building with lovely views. Free wi-fi and use of kitchen, plus lots of info about the area and what to see. €65
Prosperina Piazza Scelfo 108, cnr Via Sant'Agata ☎ 333 299 1957, ⓦ bbenna.it. A tall townhouse B&B right in the historic centre, with seven polished rooms perched on top of one another and reached by a lift. They sleep from one to four (including a good family room, with separate bunk beds), and there's a dining room and little covered terrace area for breakfast. Doubles €55

EATING SEE MAP PAGE 256

There's only a limited choice of restaurants in the old part of Enna, but enough for a night or two.
Centrale di Pirrera Piazza VI Dicembre 9 ☎ 0935 500 963. Attracts a largely local crowd, and has a shady terrace off the main street. The *antipasti* table is impressive, and there are several fixed-price menus (€16–25, including wine and fruit). Mon–Sat lunch & dinner, Sun lunch only;

closed Sat in winter.
★ **Grotta Azzurra** Via Colaianni 1 ☎ 0935 24 328. Run by the charming Giuseppe and Maria, this tiny, no-frills basement trattoria has changed little since it was opened in the 1960s serves the cheapest meals in town: from €3.50 for *primi* and €5.50 or €6 for *secondi*. It's nothing fancy (baked pasta, simple grills and roasts, omelettes, and fruit for

7

dessert), and the home-brewed wine could fuel a mission to Mars, but it's a real taste of the past. It's at the very bottom of Via Roma, past Piazza Vittorio Emanuele and down an alley on the left (there's a sign). No credit cards. Daily lunch & dinner; closed Sat in winter.

Paccamora Bio Bar Piazza Vittorio Emanuele 21 ☎ 0935 182 4786. A trendy organic bar, a great place for a tisane, smoothie, drink or light meal; daily specials are

chalked on a board. As you might expect, spelt, quinoa barley and pulses are prominent, but the food is not exclusively vegetarian, and the deft use of local ingredients (wild fennel, and local cheeses and hams) results in dishes that are both delicious and virtuous. Try the *orzotto* with cauliflower and *scamorza* cheese, or the scrummy chickpea burger. All mains cost around €8. There is sometimes live music in the evenings. Mon–Sat roughly 8am–11.45pm.

DRINKING
SEE MAP PAGE 256

The cafés and bars around Piazza Vittorio Emanuele fill up during the evening, while during the *passeggiata* dawdling locals hold up the traffic all along Via Roma.

Al Kenisa Via Roma 481 ☎ 0935 500 972, ☻alkenisa. blogspot.co.uk. This old church has been stripped bare and revamped as a cultural centre and café. There are warm stone walls, art exhibitions and books inside, and Arab-style lounging outside on the cobbles at low tables and

cushions. Check the blogspot page for events. Tues–Sun 6pm–midnight.

Marro Caffè Piazza Vittorio Emanuele 22 ☎ 0935 502 836. *Marro Caffè*'s outdoor deck is the best perch on the main square. When you get tired of people-watching, you can look at the song lyrics that are pasted on the back of every chair. Tues–Sun 7.30am–8pm.

DIRECTORY

Emergencies Ambulance ☎ 118; police ☎ 113.
Hospital Ospedale Umberto I, Contrada Ferrante in Enna Bassa, on the road to Pergusa (☎ 0935 516 111).
Pharmacies Librizzi, Piazza Vittorio Emanuele 20 (☎ 0935 500 908); Farmacia del Centro, Via Roma 315 (☎ 0935 500

650). Both open Mon–Sat 8.30am–1pm & 4.30–8pm, and a late-opening rota is posted in all pharmacy windows.
Police Questura at Via San Giuseppe 4 (☎ 0935 522 111).
Post office Via A. Volta, off Piazza Garibaldi (Mon–Fri 8am–6.30pm, Sat 8am–12.30pm).

Northeast of Enna

There's a great driving route northeast of Enna, along the minor **SS121** which runs all the way to Adrano and the Etna foothills. It's rolling countryside for the most part, punctuated by a succession of viewpoints and sleepy little towns and villages such as **Leonforte** and **Cesarò**, and with an occasional coffee and a stretch of the legs the route can occupy half a day. The road is in a bit of a state, with the surface breaking up here and there, though it's perfectly drivable with care. Buses come this way too, though with services timetabled to take local kids to school in Enna, you might find yourself spending longer than you'd want in many of the towns – generally you can expect to have to leave Enna after school finishes for the day around 2pm, and then to return the next day at the crack of dawn.

Forty kilometres north of Enna, the small hill-town of **Nicosia** is the main stop on the trans-mountain **SS120**, which cuts across some of the remoter stretches of the Sicilian interior. It's hardly a major destination in its own right, though onward routes from Nicosia are all dramatic, especially north over the Madonie mountains to Gangi, Mistretta and the Tyrrhenian coast (see Chapter 2) and east along the SS120 through a bare landscape dominated ever more dramatically by the giant silhouette of Etna. Again, the road isn't in great condition, with slips and wash-outs common, but it's no problem if you heed the signs and drive carefully.

Leonforte

Some 20km from Enna along the SS121, **LEONFORTE** is typical of the small towns hereabouts, with its roots firmly in the seventeenth century and an attractive central square that sprouts bars in profusion. Other than the impressive Duomo and the domineering Palazzo Baronale, Leonforte's most noteworthy sight is **La Granfonte**, overlooking the hills on the edge of town. Built in 1651, it's not so much a fountain as a row of 24 waterspouts set in a sculpted facade of carvings and inscriptions. Once you've filled your water bottle, it's time to move on, unless you fancy stocking up on the lentils for which the town is famous.

Nicosia

Sitting under looming crags, **NICOSIA** is a medieval mass of cracked *palazzi* topped by the remains of a Norman castle. Traffic all funnels up to the chatter-filled Piazza Garibaldi, the site of Nicosia's lovely old cathedral, **San Nicola**, a stately construction with a fourteenth-century facade and belltower, and a handsome sculpted Gothic portal. To the side of the cathedral (left side, as you face the church), Via Francesco Salamone rises steeply to the former Saracen district of the town, a jumble of streets occupying one of the four hills on which Nicosia is built.

Santa Maria Maggiore
Via Francesco Salamone

Founded in 1267 but rebuilt after an eighteenth-century landslide, **Santa Maria Maggiore** has the bells from its campanile piled up outside – they fell down after another earthquake and the sound of them is now electrically reproduced. Inside, amid "No Spitting" notices, you'll find an impressive marble polyptych by Antonello Gagini and a throne used by Charles V when he passed through here in 1535, on the way back from his Tunisian crusade. The views from outside encompass the town's other three promontories, on the highest of which sits the ruined castle.

ARRIVAL AND DEPARTURE | **NICOSIA**

By bus Buses drop you a few minutes' walk below Piazza Garibaldi. Although you could head to Gangi and the Madonie mountains from here, services are scant and timed for school kids and workers, which can mean a 5.30am start. Destinations Catania airport/Catania (4 daily Mon–Sat, 1 daily Sun; 2hr/2hr 10min); Enna (1 daily Mon–Sat; 1hr 30min); Gangi (3 daily Mon–Fri; 40min); Leonforte (4 daily Mon–Sat, 1 daily Sun; 40min); Petralia Soprana (1 daily Mon–Sat; 1hr 10min); Petralia Sottana (1 daily Mon–Sat, 2 daily Sun; 1hr 20min); Polizzi Generosa (2 daily; 2hr); Sperlinga (3 daily Mon–Sat; 15min).

By car There are several signposted parking areas as you drive into the centre.

ACCOMMODATION

Baglio San Pietro Contrada San Pietro ☎0935 640 529 or ☎335 876 7396, ⓦbagliosanpietro.com. Some 1km west of Nicosia and signposted off the Sperlinga road, this is a restored farm estate, originally dating from the seventeenth century. The comfortable rooms here make a good base for visiting the area, as the farm has its own restaurant, pool and gardens. **€65**

Troina

From a distance, **TROINA** appears like a thimble perched on a hill, 1120m high. A twisting 30km ride from Nicosia, the town has long played a strategic role in the various wars and power struggles that have wracked Sicily, initially coming to prominence during the reconquest of Sicily from the Arabs, when it became one of the first cities to be taken by the Normans. Count Roger withstood a siege here (see box page 260) in 1061 that nearly put paid to his Sicilian adventures, a victory he commemorated by founding the monastery of **San Basilio**, now in ruins. The top of town features an eleventh-century **cathedral** with an adjacent fifteenth-century **church** dedicated to San Giorgio (notice the relief of George and the Dragon above the door under the cupola). The wide piazza-terrace in front has a simply magnificent Etna view, while beyond stretches the main street. It's laid out along a high ridge, and it makes for an atmospheric stroll down a narrow thoroughfare between noble mansions, with a steep drop to either side.

THE SIEGE OF TROINA

In the summer of 1061, **Count Roger** marched his troops across the mountains from Messina, holing up in Troina, the highest place around. There he posted soldiers, and left his wife, **Judith**, while he went on to try to seize Nicosia from the Arabs. Unfortunately, Troina had a large population of Byzantine Greeks, who hated the Normans even more than they hated the Arabs, and one night they attempted to kidnap Judith, which resulted in rioting on the streets. Roger rushed back and, in the face of a united Arab and Byzantine attack, took refuge in Troina's **fortress**. Roger and Judith spent four months of a freezing winter in the castle, with no fuel, and just one cloak between them, which they used as a blanket at night. One particularly freezing evening, Roger's and Judith's troops, starving and frozen, hearing the Arabs and Byzantines partying on wine in the town below, could stand no more, crept out over the snow and slaughtered them, finally bringing the siege to an end.

Cesarò

7

CESARÒ stands under fearsome crags at the crossroads of the SS120 and the SS289, the road that runs north across the Nebrodi mountains to the coast at Sant'Agata di Militello (see Chapter 2). On a clear day there are remarkable views over to Etna as you approach town, though the hemmed-in streets of Cesarò itself give no hint of the grandeur of its setting – for a panorama, you must climb or drive up to the mammoth bronze statue of Jesus, the **Cristo Signore della Montagna**, in the cemetery above town.

ARRIVAL AND DEPARTURE
CESARÒ

Cuts in bus services mean that it is now only feasible to visit Cesarò if you have your own transport.

ACCOMMODATION AND EATING

Hotel Fratelli Mazzurco S.S. 120 Via Conceria ☎ 095 773 2100. The *Mazzurco* not only has decent rooms but a restaurant (Aug daily lunch & dinner; rest of the year closed Thurs), specializing in local produce (namely home-made pasta, wild mushrooms, pork and pistachios). Portions are huge, so make sure you are very hungry before ordering the fixed-price menu at €30. There's a garden courtyard for *al fresco* meals and some scintillating views from the front of the hotel. **€60**

★ **Lo Scudiero di San Teodoro** Contrada Fondachello, San Teodoro, nr Cesarò ☎ 3208748058, ⓦ loscudiero.it.

This is a really great *agriturismo* set in a remote, romantic valley just outside Cesarò, in between the Nebrodi mountains and Mount Etna. There's a swimming pool, fantastic views of Etna, and the owners can organize excursions by bike, quad-bike, jeep, foot or horseback in the Nebrodi, up Etna and into the Alcantara gorge. The food is lovely, making great use of local produce, including the famous Nebrodi *suino nero* (black pig), along with artisan cheeses, wild vegetables and local olive oil and wine. B&B **€70**, half board **€55** per person.

Caltanissetta

With twice as many inhabitants as Enna, the provincial capital of **CALTANISSETTA** (35km to the southwest) is easily the largest town in the interior, though little else about it is remarkable. Moreover, its sprawling modern suburbs give way suddenly to rolling empty fields beyond – the town is very much the last gasp before the almost ghostly rural expanses of Sicily's western interior.

The largely traffic-choked centre breathes a sigh of relief around the prettily restored **Piazza Garibaldi**, with its splashing fountain, handsome Duomo and the wedding-cake confection that is the church of San Sebastiano. The churches may well be locked but they form a pleasing ensemble, while the nearby sandstone and salmon-pink **Sant'Agata**, at the other end of Corso Umberto I, is equally easy on the eye. You can also take a spin around the imposing walls of the seventeenth-century **Palazzo Moncada** two blocks to the north of Piazza Garibaldi, an aristocratic mansion belonging to one of Sicily's great feudal dynasties. Down behind the Duomo (follow Via Pugliese

Giannone and Via San Domenico), it's less than ten minutes' walk to one of the island's stranger castle ruins, the **Castello di Pietrarossa**, improbably balanced on an outcrop of rock. It's off-limits and looks like it should have fallen down years ago, though it's finally getting some belated attention as restoration work continues on the adjacent church and monastery.

Museo Archeologico

Via di Santo Spirito • Daily 9am–1pm & 3.30–7pm; closed last Mon of month • €4 • ☎ 0934 567 062 • Take a bus from the train station (direction Villaggio Santa Barbara), and ask to get off near the museum; the stop is about 300m from the museum; if driving, follow the brown "Museo Archeologico" signs from town, though it's easy to get lost

Located 3km north of the centre, the **Museo Archeologico** is a vast circular bunker straight out of the Thunderbirds school of architecture, and contains some of Sicily's earliest finds (from the Bronze Age to the fourth century BC), including treasures like an unusual votive clay model of a temple. It's all beautifully presented, with clear English notes throughout, and there's unlikely to be another soul around save the attendants.

Santo Spirito

Alongside the Museo Archeologico, the restored twelfth-century abbey church of **Santo Spirito** was founded by Count Roger and – a rare thing in Sicily – is purely Norman in form. The plain structure is only enlivened by three tiny apses at the back, though the interior has a fifteenth-century fresco over the central apse and a twelfth-century font. If the church is locked, you can try ringing at the door on the right (home of the parish priest).

ARRIVAL AND DEPARTURE   CALTANISSETTA

By bus Caltanissetta's bus station is at Piazza Roma, outside the train station, about a 10min walk from Piazza Garibaldi.
Destinations Agrigento (almost hourly Mon–Sat, 10 daily Sun; 1hr 35min); Catania (almost hourly Mon–Sat, 10 daily Sun; 1hr 35min); Enna (4–6 daily Mon–Sat, 2 daily Sun;

50min); Palermo (6–9 daily Mon–Sat, 5 daily Sun; 1hr 40min); Piazza Armerina (4 Mon–Fri, 1 Sat & Sun; 1 hr).
By train Although buses are usually faster and more frequent, Caltanissetta has reasonable train connections with Enna, Palermo, Catania and Agrigento (though avoid services

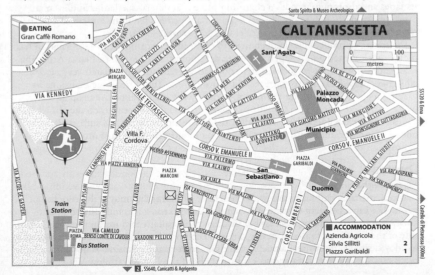

with lots of changes). If you're heading to Enna it's easier to take the bus, as the town's train station is a long way out from the centre. Going the other way, the railway line meanders northwest, ultimately to Palermo, through empty upland plains, one of the most desert-like of Sicilian journeys.

Destinations Agrigento (5 daily Mon–Sat, 2 daily Sun; 1hr 25min–2hr 50min); Catania (10 daily Mon–Sat; 1hr 40min–2hr); Enna (10 daily Mon–Sat, 5 daily Sun; 30–45min); Palermo (10 daily; 1hr 40min–3hr 30min).

By car Note that there is no entry to Piazza Garibaldi or surrounding streets between 5pm and 8.30pm, while the evening *passeggiata* is in progress, and there is resident-only parking in the *centro storico*. It's not usually difficult to find free street parking outside the centre (white lines).

ACCOMMODATION   SEE MAP PAGE 261

★ **Azienda Agricola Silvia Sillitti** ☎ 0934 930 733 or ☎ 338 763 4601, ⊕ sillitti.it. Some 12km out of town off the SS640 Agrigento road, this wonderful *agriturismo* is set on a working organic farm of olive and almond groves, wheat fields and vegetable plots. There are rustic rooms in three apartments, expansive terraces with views on all sides, hammocks in the shade, and a sparkling swimming pool. Silvia is a charming host who prepares excellent Sicilian dinners (vegetarian on request, and all food intolerances catered for; €25). She also runs fantastic cooking courses, using produce from the estate (which

guests can pick themselves). A five-hour course, in which you prepare your own dinner, costs €80 per person for a minimum of two people, but there are also cooking classes on Sicilian bread and pizza using ancient grains, also grown on the estate (see their Facebook page for up-to-date details). Two-person apartment €90

Piazza Garibaldi Piazza Garibaldi 11 ☎ 0934 680 510 or ☎ 340 379 5803, ⊕ piazzagaribaldi11.it. A first-class B&B in a restored palace opposite the Duomo, with colourful bedrooms sporting murals of Sicilian rural landscapes. €50

EATING   SEE MAP PAGE 261

Gran Caffè Romano Corso Umberto I 147 ☎ 0934 21 402. The best café in town, with an 8m-long counter full of almond *mandorle* biscuits (the local speciality), *cannoli*

and other treats, and chunky leather sofas outside on the pavement. Daily 8am–8pm.

Piazza Armerina

The small town of **PIAZZA ARMERINA** lies amid thickly forested hills. A quiet, unassuming place, it is mainly seventeenth- and eighteenth-century in appearance, with a skyline pierced by towers and houses that huddle together under the joint protection of a decrepit castle and pristine cathedral. Despite the dense traffic that fills its lanes and thoroughfares, it's a charming place that deserves a detour and even an overnight stop, though many visitors bypass it altogether, given the enticement of the mosaics at the nearby Villa Romana del Casale (see page 264).

The town's central core is small enough to cover in a morning's stroll. Restoration has pretty much started and stopped in **Piazza del Duomo**, but the rest of Piazza Armerina is an endearing jumble of cobbled steps and faded grandeur, dilapidated yet graceful churches and *palazzi*, narrow streets and skinny alleys. There are noble mansions in varying stages of decay along **Via Monte**, formerly the medieval town's main street, while down Via Floresta (to the side of Palazzo Trigona) you soon reach the closed and tumbledown **castello**, built at the end of the fourteenth century and surrounded by once-rich *palazzi*, now with broken windows and tattered wooden shutters.

Duomo

Daily 8am–noon & 4–7pm

Piazza Armerina's best views are from the terrace of **Piazza Duomo**, at the very top of town. The town's elegant seventeenth-century **Duomo** has a marvellously cool, blue-and-white stuccoed interior accessible through the small green door on the Via Cavour side of the building. Across from the cathedral campanile, and its blind Catalan-Gothic windows, stands the spruce facade of the eighteenth-century **Palazzo Trigona**, its simple brick exterior crowned by a spread-eagle plaque.

San Giovanni Evangelista

Via Umberto I 98 ☎ 333 474 4351 • The church is open 7–8am daily

The absolute highlight of the town, however, is the scruffy-looking church of San Giovanni Evangelista, dubbed the Sistine Chapel of Sicily by art critic Vittorio Sgarbi, for its dazzlingly frescoed Baroque ceiling featuring brilliantly hued visions of St John the Evangelist by the Dutch artist Guglielmo Borremans (1670–1744). Unable to get funding for the restoration, the church priest, Monsignor Antonino Scarcione, took out a bank loan and paid for it himself.

Castellina

The **Castellina** quarter, off Via Mazzini, is a fascinating area to explore, with its steep residential alleys dropping down to the **Porta Castellina**, a surviving part of the medieval town wall – with a rough arch hacked through it for traffic access. From pretty **Piazza Garibaldi**, Via Mazzini, Via Garibaldi and Via Umberto I are the main

7

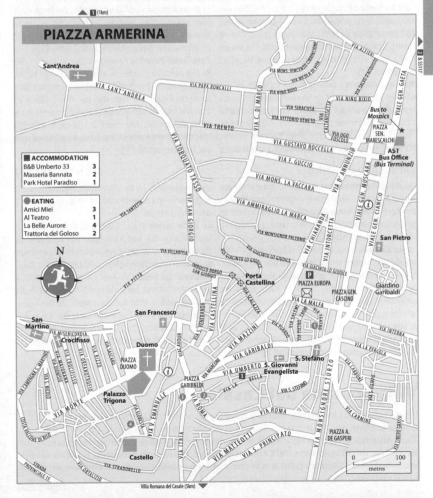

old-town shopping streets, all leading eventually to the large twin squares that separate old town from new, with the **Giardino Garibaldi** gardens beyond.

ARRIVAL AND INFORMATION

By bus Buses drop you off at Piazza Senatore Marescalchi, a large square on the main road in the lower, modern town, a 15min walk from the old centre. For bus information and tickets to Aidone, Caltagirone, Catania and elsewhere, ask in the *Bar della Stazione* in Piazza Senatore Marescalchi, or the AST office next door.

Destinations Aidone (almost hourly Mon–Sat, 2 daily Sun; 15min); Caltagirone (5 daily Mon–Sat; 1hr–1hr 30min); Catania (6 daily Mon–Sat, 1 daily Sun; 1hr 40min); Enna (3–6 daily; 30min); Palermo (5 daily Mon–Sat, 1 daily Sun; 2hr 15min).

PIAZZA ARMERINA

By car There's metered on-street parking in the lower town, but you can get closer to the sights by following the signs for "centro" and then "Duomo". The narrow streets may seem challenging, but a fairly sensible one-way system runs along Via Mazzini to Piazza Garibaldi and then dog-legs up Via Cavour to the Duomo – there's a fair amount of metered parking on the way, and free parking in Piazza Duomo itself.

Tourist information There's a tourist office at Viale Generale Muscarà 47 (Mon–Fri 8am–2pm; ☎0935 680 201).

ACCOMMODATION

SEE MAP PAGE 263

B&B Umberto 33 Via Umberto 33 ☎0935 683 344 or ☎340 558 6002, ⓦumberto33.com. A centrally located B&B on one of the old town's main shopping and strolling streets, with three handsome en-suite rooms. The owners have a lovely wine and local produce shop, and breakfasts are delicious. **€45**

Masseria Bannata Contrada Bannata (SS117 bis km 41) ☎328 2988448, ⓦagriturismobannata.it. Lovely rooms and an apartment (sleeps four; €190) in a traditional *masseria* of golden stone a short drive from Piazza Armerina. There is also a good restaurant where the menu includes traditional, rustic, as well as the more refined, dishes favoured

by the local aristocracy, while breakfast features home-made cakes and biscuits and local cheeses. Ricotta tastings can be arranged as well. Half board an extra €25 (vegetarian) €28 (carnivorous) per person excluding wine. Doubles **€100**

Park Hotel Paradiso Contrada Ramaldo ☎0935 680 841, ⓦparkhotelparadiso.it. It's out of the historic centre, 1km beyond the church of Sant'Andrea (signposted from town), but if you want a resort-style stay this is the place. It's a modern four-star with echoing public spaces aimed at the convention-and-wedding market, but the rooms are pretty spacious and well equipped, and there's a pool, sauna, gym and formal restaurant. **€90**

EATING AND DRINKING

SEE MAP PAGE 263

The old-town **restaurants** have the most atmosphere and are handy for the B&Bs. The liveliest cafés and bars, though, are those around **Piazza Generale Cascino**, in front of the Garibaldi gardens. This is where to come at *passeggiata* time for a stroll, an ice cream or a beer.

★ **Amici Miei** Largo Capodarso 5 ☎0935 683 541. "My friends" has charming terrace seating outside and a rustic, brick-walled dining room, plus a menu that's especially good for hearty bean soups and the like. Pastas and mains are €7.50–12, or there are also really good pizzas (€4.50–8) at night. Daily lunch & dinner; closed Thurs in winter.

Al Teatro Via del Teatro 6 ☎0935 85 662. It takes a bit of finding (easiest from the end of Via Garibaldi), but it's worth it for the terrace tables with nice views over the old theatre

and town rooftops. Try the home-made *pappardelle*, or one of the thirty-odd different types of pizza. Daily lunch & dinner; closed Wed.

La Belle Aurore Piazza Castello 5, ☎0935 686 333. Candlelit artsy club with a bohemian vibe right opposite the castle. Live music sometimes. Perfect for an aperitivo or after dinner drink. Opening hours are variable.

Trattoria del Goloso Via Garao 4 ☎0935 685 693. A good-value trattoria (most dishes €7–10) just off Piazza Garibaldi, with a little outdoor terrace. Try the home-made pasta (for a treat look out for pasta dishes featuring pistachios) and follow up with deftly herbed, grilled, local lamb. Daily lunch & dinner; closed Wed eve in winter.

Villa Romana del Casale

Daily: April–Oct 9am–7pm; Nov–March 9am–5pm; Fri-Sun July & Aug open until 11.30, last entry 1hr before closing • €10 • ⓦvillaromanadelcasale.it

Built on terraces in a sparsely inhabited neighbourhood 5km southwest of Piazza Armerina, the **Villa Romana del Casale** dates from the early fourth century AD and remained in use right up until it was covered by a mudslide in the twelfth century. It

was then hidden from view for seven hundred years until excavations began in 1950, revealing multicoloured mosaic floors that are unique in the entire Roman world for their quality and extent. A roof and walls were added to indicate the original size and shape of the villa, and the mosaics are now protected from the elements, with walkways leading through the various rooms and chambers. It's an essential visit on any trip to Sicily, but the continuous stream of coach parties and tour groups hardly makes for a relaxing trip. If you can, it's best to come at lunchtime in order to avoid the crowds – to see everything, you'll need a couple of hours.

The site

Conflicting theories surround the function of the **villa**, but the most convincing explanation of its deeply rural location is that it was an occasional retreat and hunting lodge. That theory is supported by the many mosaics of animals and birds, including two specific hunting scenes. It's also immediately clear from the extent of the remains that the villa complex belonged to an important owner, possibly **Maximianus Herculeus**, co-emperor with Diocletian between 286 and 305 AD. There are four

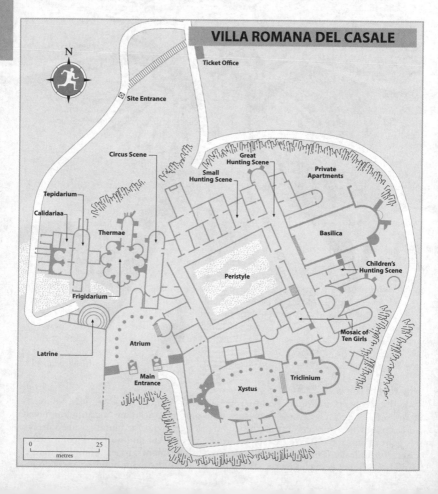

separate groups of buildings, built on different levels of the hillside and connected by passageways, doors and courtyards. Nearly all of what you see would have been occupied by the family for which it was built – slaves' housing and other outbuildings are still to be excavated properly.

While there are other splendid Roman villas in Italy, none has anything like the extraordinary interior decoration of the Villa Casale. The floors of almost the entire building are covered with bright **mosaics** of excellent quality, stylistically belonging to an early fourth-century Roman-African school, which explains many of the more exotic scenes and animals portrayed. Their design also contains several hints as to their period and patron, though given their extent they're likely to have taken fifty or sixty years to complete.

The main building

The villa's **main entrance** gives one of the best impressions of its former grandeur, with the approach leading through the remains of a columned arch into a wide courtyard. Today's site entrance, though, is through the adjacent **thermae** (or baths): a typical arrangement of dressing/massage rooms and plunge-baths around an octagonal **frigidarium**, its central mosaic a marine scene of sea nymphs, tritons, and little cherubs rowing boats and spearing fish. A walkway leads out of the baths and into the villa proper, to the massive central courtyard or **peristyle**. This is where guests would have been received, and the vestibule displays a fragmented mosaic depicting a formal welcome by an attendant holding an olive branch. The corridor around the four sides of the courtyard is covered with a series of animal-head medallions: snarling tigers, yapping dogs and unicorns. Just off here, a balcony looks down upon one of the most vivid pictures, a boisterous circus scene showing a chariot race. Starting in the top right-hand corner, the variously coloured chariots rush off, overtaking and crashing at the turns, until finally there's victory for the green faction. The next room's mosaic shows a family attended by slaves on their way to the baths. Period detail – footwear, hairstyles and clothes – helped archeologists to date the rest of the mosaics.

Small rooms beyond, on either side of the peristyle, reveal only fragmentary geometric patterns, although one displays a **small hunting scene**, an episodic adventure that ends with a peaceful picnic in the centre. Another room contains what is the villa's most famous image, a two-tiered scene of **ten girls**, realistically muscular figures in Roman "bikinis", taking part in various gymnastic and athletic activities. One of the girls, sporting a laurel wreath and a palm frond, is clearly the winner of the competition.

The great hunting scene

The peristyle is separated from the private apartments and public halls beyond by a long, covered corridor, which contains the best of the villa's mosaic works. The **great hunting scene** sets armed and shield-bearing hunters against a panoply of wild animals, on sea and land. Along the entire 60m length of the mosaic, tigers, ostriches, elephants and even a rhino, destined for the games back in Rome, are pictured being trapped, bundled up and down gangplanks and into cages. The caped figure overseeing the operation is probably Maximianus himself. Much of the scene is set in Africa, Maximianus's main responsibility in the Imperial Tetrarchy, while an ivy-leaf symbol on the costume of the attendant to his right is that of his personal legion, the Herculiani.

The rest of the site

Family apartments and public halls beyond the great hunting scene are nearly all on a grand scale. A large courtyard, the **xystus**, gives onto the **triclinium**, a dining room with three apses, whose mosaics feature the labours of Hercules. One bloody scene portrays his fight against the giants, all struck by arrows, who writhe and wail with contorted faces. A path leads around the back to the **private apartments**, based around a large basilica, with mosaics echoing the spectacular scenes of the main building: a **children's** circus, where the small chariots are drawn by colourful birds, and a **children's hunt**, the tiny tots being chased and pecked by the hares and peacocks they're supposed to snare.

ARRIVAL AND DEPARTURE	VILLA ROMANA DEL CASALE

By bus From Piazza Armerina, a bus (May–Sept) leaves Piazza Senatore Marescalchi for the Villa Romana on the hour between 9am and noon, and between 3pm and 6pm, with a stop at Piazza Generale Cascino; it's a half-hour ride, and the return service is on the half-hour, starting at 9.30am.

By taxi A taxi from Piazza Generale Cascino in Piazza Armerina costs €10 each way.

ACCOMMODATION AND EATING

Trattoria La Ruota Contrada Paratore ☏ 0935 680 542. In an attractive rustic setting a little way up the road from the Villa Romana, this handsome former watermill offers shaded outdoor seating and excellent regional food, from home-made pasta to local sausage, lamb and rabbit (mains from €10). The best place to eat near the mosaics. Daily lunch only.

7

Around Piazza Armerina

The extraordinary remains of the Greek city of **Morgantina**, which was at its height in the fourth century BC, lie 15km northeast of Piazza Armerina. That it's not better known is a shame, but also a boon as your visit will be mercifully free of the tourist shenanigans associated with the famous Casale mosaics. Unfortunately, buses from Piazza Armerina only run as far as the pretty village of **Aidone** (site of Morgantina's museum), with the archeological site itself another 5km beyond.

Museo Archeologico Aidone

Aidone • Daily 9am–6.30pm • €6, or €10 with Morgantina • ☏ 0935 87 307 • Buses for Aidone leave from Piazza Senatore Marescalchi in Piazza Armerina 2–6 times daily

With its quiet central square and thoroughly laidback air, **AIDONE** is a charming little spot. There are a couple of agreeable bars on the square and a crumbling church, but the true reason for a visit is the **Museo Archeologico**, impressively housed in a former Capuchin monastery on Largo Torres Trupia – it's signposted, right at the top of the village. It makes an indispensable adjunct to seeing the Morgantina archeological site, since it's here that you'll find everything that was removed from the ancient city – from ceramics, statuettes and busts to coins, candleholders and domestic artefacts. Aerial photos and plans also provide a useful idea of the layout of the site. The highlights, however, are the objects recently returned to Sicily from America, after years of legal battles: the exquisite **Morgantina Venus** (now known as the Dea di Morgantina, as it's thought she is, in fact, Demeter); the so-called **Eupolemo Silver**, fifteen pieces of tableware dating from the third century BC; and the acroliths of Demeter and Persephone, the heads, hands and feet of sixth-century BC **statues** of the goddess Demeter, and her daughter Persephone, or Kore (see box).

Morgantina

Daily 10am–5pm, usually later in summer, depending on staff availability • €6, or €10 including Museo Archeologico at Aidone

Five kilometres northeast of Aidone, at the end of a long cobbled lane, the **site of Morgantina** occupies two quiet hillsides with gorgeous views of the valley below. The car park is just under the east hill, and it's around a 500m walk down to the main entrance and ticket office, where you're given a brochure and map: all the signs on the site are in Italian and English.

After its demise in around 211 BC, the city became buried and forgotten for almost two thousand years, and even after the site's discovery it wasn't identified as Morgantina

THE RETURN OF THE GODDESSES

When Greeks began to arrive in Sicily during the eighth century BC, attracted by the island's legendary fertility, their cults of **gods and goddesses** found fecund ground among the local inhabitants, who lived side by side with the Greeks in provincial towns such as Morgantina. Over time, indigenous fertility cults of death and rebirth centred on the annual cycle of harvests became intertwined with the Greek fertility cult focusing on the goddess **Demeter** and her daughter, **Persephone**, who was abducted by Hades and taken to the underworld. According to the myth, the summer months (when nothing grows in Sicily) occur when Persephone is in the underworld; then, at the beginning of autumn, when the seeds of the old crop are scattered, she returns to earth to be reunited with Demeter. (Interestingly, when the myth is retold in English, Persephone is absent from the earth in winter, and returns in spring, the myth having to be adapted to the exigencies of climate.) That Morgantina, in the agricultural interior of Sicily, where survival depended on the vagaries of the weather, should have been home to an immense temple to Demeter and Persephone, is thus no surprise.

In the summer of 1979, rumours began to circulate in Aidone about the secret discovery of several **marble sculptures**. They had been found, the story went, by illegal excavators, sponsored by the Mafia and working close to the site of Morgantina, a few kilometres away. A short while later, legal excavations revealed the foundations of a vast sanctuary at Morgantina dedicated to fertility goddess, Demeter. But there was no sign of any statues. A few years later, word spread among the New York art world of the acquisition, by an anonymous collector, of several elements of ancient Greek statuary. Then in 1986, hitherto unknown fragments of ancient Greek statues were exhibited at the **Paul Getty Museum** in Malibu, on loan from a private and still anonymous collector. American archeologist Malcolm Bell, director of the legal excavations at Morgantina, was able to establish that the pieces had been **stolen** from Morgantina.

In 1988 Enna's Public Prosecutor, Silvio Raffiotta, established that the pieces had been sold to multimillionaire **Maurice Tempelsman**, last husband of Jackie Onassis, via London art dealer Robin Symes. The Italian Ministry of Culture attempted to negotiate for the statues' return to Sicily, but with no result. In 2002, however, Tempelsman donated the sculptures to the Bayly Art Museum of the University of Virginia, on three conditions: the donation had to receive no publicity, the donor had to remain anonymous, and the sculptures could not be returned to Italy for five years.

In early 2008, the university finally succumbed to pressure and agreed to return the statues to their rightful home, and in late 2009 the **acroliths of Demeter and Persephone** were put on public display in Aidone's museum for the first time, "dressed" by innovative fashion designer Marella Ferrara. The exhibition marked the beginning of a series of **restitutions** to Sicily of antique objects scavenged from the site of Morgantina and sold to the Metropolitan Museum New York and Paul Getty. **Eupolemo silverware** arrived in January 2010, followed in 2011 by the most important of all Morgantina antiquities: the so-called **Morgantina Venus**, a superb example of late fifth-century BC sculpture, showing a mighty goddess, with her drapery blown against her muscular, almost masculine, body.

7

until 1957. To date, only a fraction of the city has been excavated, but the finds have shed much light on the island's pre-Hellenic Sikel population, who inhabited central Sicily from the ninth century BC. In the sixth century BC, Chalcidian Greeks settled here and lived in harmony alongside the Sikels until the city became the centre of a revolt led by the Sikel leader Ducetius, who destroyed it in the mid-fifth century BC. Swiftly rebuilt on a grid plan with walled and towered defences, Morgantina reached its apogee in the fourth and third centuries BC under the protection of Syracuse, and many of the surviving buildings date from this period. A couple of hundred years later the city was in decline, and was soon abandoned altogether.

The agora and the teatro

Heading left into the site from the main entrance leads you directly to Morgantina's most distinctive ruin, the **agora**, which is bounded by three stepped sides that served as seats for public meetings. The small **teatro** to its right was built in the third century BC, but reconstructed in Roman times. Concerts, Greek plays and modern drama are sometimes held here in the summer – you can get more information from the tourist offices in Enna (see page 257) or Piazza Armerina (see page 264).

The santuario and Fornace Grande

Other buildings here include a fourth-century BC **santuario** of Demeter and Kore, while on the level ground behind the agora is a granary and square slaughterhouse, beyond which stretches the 100m-long **east stoa**. A great kiln, the **Fornace Grande**, is one of the biggest ancient kilns ever excavated, and probably produced heavy-duty roof tiles, massive storage jars and the like. Further up the hillside in the residential quarter stand the ruins of some Hellenic **houses**, with two mosaic floors. One, the "House of Ganymede", has an illustration of the youth Ganymede being carried away to Olympus by Zeus's eagle to become the cupbearer of the gods.

The west hill

There's an awful lot more of the site to explore, though in summer the heat might dissuade you. A path leads up to excavations on the **west hill**, which, though less revealing, include the fairly substantial remains of houses, roads and walls in what was another large residential area. In recent years, the remains of a second temple and a spring and aqueduct have also been unearthed.

Caltagirone

Around 35km southeast of Piazza Armerina, **CALTAGIRONE** is a curious place. One of the most ancient of Sicilian towns, it was settled well before the arrival of the Greeks, and has an Arabic name (from *kalat*, "castle" and *gerun*, "caves"), yet an overwhelmingly Baroque aspect, dating from the dramatic rebuilding after the 1693 earthquake that flattened the area. The Arabs, though, had one extraordinary and lasting influence on the town, introducing local **ceramic craftsmen** to the glazed polychromatic colours – in particular, blues and yellows – that subsequently became typically Sicilian in execution. Until the great earthquake, the town supported a population of around 20,000, of whom perhaps five percent were actively engaged in the tiled decoration of churches and public buildings. The Baroque rebuilding saw a further burst of creative construction, while later, during the nineteenth century, came the principal period of ceramic figurative work. Caltagirone's traditional industry is still flourishing, with scores of ceramicists displaying work at galleries across the town, while public buildings, churches, house balconies and gardens all feature ceramics in every nook and cranny – not to mention the famous tiled steps of **La Scala**, Caltagirone's pride and joy. The old centre is small and easy to see in half a day, but there's an upbeat air here (and plenty of shopping opportunities) that makes a night an enjoyable prospect.

La Scala

The emblem of Caltagirone is undoubtedly the 142 steps of **La Scala**, which cuts right up one of the town's three hills to the sorely neglected church of Santa Maria del Monte at the top. The staircase was originally conceived at the turn of the seventeenth century as a road between the church (then the cathedral) and the town centre below; the steps were added once it was clear that the incline was too steep. The risers in between each step are covered with hand-painted ceramic patterns, added in the 1950s, no two the same. Having puffed your way up, your reward is the magnificent **view** down across town to the distinctive spire of the Sicilian Baroque church of San Francesco all'Immacolata, with the plain stretching away into the distance beyond. At night the steps are lit, and couples and families spread out on them, chatting away. In May, there are floral decorations laid up the entire length, while on July 24 and 25 every year La Scala is lit by thousands of coloured paper lamps as part of the celebrations for the feast of St James (San Giacomo).

Piazza Municipio

The main square of the old town is **Piazza Municipio**, where the sturdy seventeenth-century **Corte Capitaniale**, decorated by the Gagini family, is used for temporary art exhibitions. Named after the locally born mayor, reformer and anti-Fascist Luigi Sturzo (1871–1959), modern **Galleria Luigi Sturzo** is another exhibition venue.

Museo Civico al Carcere Borbonico

Carcere Borbonico, Via Roma 10 • Tues–Sun 9.30am–1.30pm, plus Tues & Fri–Sun also 3.30–6.30pm • Free • ☎ 0933 41 812

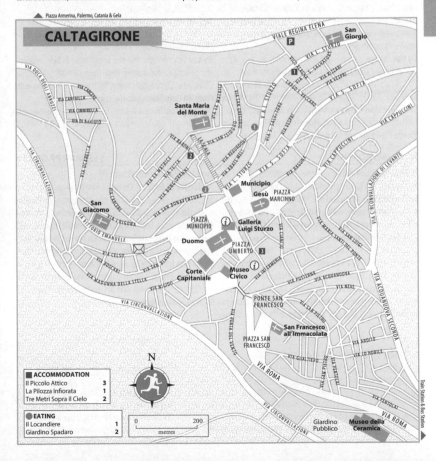

Located off Piazza Umberto, the square building with grilled windows and spike-studded metal doors that was a Bourbon prison in the eighteenth century now houses the **Museo Civico**. There's nothing essential to see inside, just the usual mildly intriguing collection of local curios, folklore items and architectural fragments, plus paintings by the Vaccaro family, who renovated the cathedral in the nineteenth century.

Museo Regionale della Ceramica and the Giardino Pubblico

Via Roma • Daily 9am–6.30pm • €4 • ☎ 0933 58 418

The road to the newer town crosses the **Ponte San Francesco** – studded with ceramic flowers and emblems – and then runs down towards the large **Giardino Pubblico** (a 10min walk), where you'll find the last word on the five-thousand-year-old tradition of local ceramics in the **Museo della Ceramica**. The gardens themselves are worth a whirl in any case, the centrepiece being a wonderful Art Nouveau bandstand, overlooked by a couple of kiosk cafés. This is one of several elegant examples in Caltagirone of the "Liberty" style – you'll also pass the Art Nouveau theatre outside the main entrance to the gardens.

ARRIVAL AND INFORMATION

CALTAGIRONE

Apart from a frequent service to Catania, Caltagirone is possibly the worst connected town of any real interest to travellers in the whole of Sicily. Patience and planning are required to move anywhere.

By bus The bus station is in the lower town, 2km below the old centre and connected to it by half-hourly local bus.
Destinations Catania/Catania Airport (5 daily Mon–Sat, 1 daily Sun; 1hr 15/30min); Enna (3 daily Mon–Fri, 1 daily Sun; 1hr 25min); Grammichele (5 daily Mon–Sat; 45min); Palermo (1 daily at 4.40am Mon–Fri & 4.40pm Sun; 2hr 45min) Piazza Armerina (1 daily Mon–Sat; 1hr–1hr 30min);

Ragusa (2 daily Mon–Sat; 2hr).

By train The train station is adjacent to the bus station.
Destinations Catania (2 daily Mon–Sat; 1hr 40min); Grammichele (2 daily; 15–20min).

By car Driving right into the upper town is best avoided, and parking is easiest at the large free space off Viale Regina Elena, near San Giorgio church, from where it's a 5min walk down Via Luigi Sturzo into the centre.

Information There is a tourist office at Corte Capitaniale, Via Duomo 15 (Mon–Sat 9am–6.30pm; ☎ 335 579 5945).

ACCOMMODATION

SEE MAP PAGE 271

Il Piccolo Attico Via Infermeria 82 ☎ 0933 21 588 or ☎ 320 077 3315, ⓦ ilpiccoloattico.it. One large double room with a bathroom, and one attic apartment composed of two double rooms, with great views on all sides, taking in Etna. Generous breakfasts on lovely local ceramics. **€60**

La Pilozza Infiorata Via San Salvatore 97 ☎ 0933 22 162 or ☎ 339 735 2861, ⓦ lapilozzainfiorata.com. A rather fancy B&B in a restored "Liberty"-style *palazzo* with six individually styled en-suite rooms, three with cooking facilities. There's no view to speak of – the house is tucked into an old-town street – but the rooms are spacious and comfortable, and there's a small terrace. Double without

breakfast **€58**, with breakfast **€68**

★ **Tre Metri Sopra il Cielo** Via Bongiovanni 72 ☎ 0933 193 5106 or ☎ 392 213 3228, ⓦ bbtremetrisoprailcielo. it. Caltagirone's friendliest B&B is this perfectly situated place right on La Scala steps, near the top. Helpful owner Gaetano has three simple rooms in his charming house (you may have to share a bathroom, depending on numbers), but he can also find space in up to half a dozen other rooms in adjacent buildings. Everyone gets to take breakfast on the top-floor terrace, which has a stupendous view over the town and surrounding hills. **€72**

THE CITY OF CERAMICS

All the way up La Scala staircase, and in the alleys on either side, are ceramicists' **workshops and galleries**, though you'll also find shops and showrooms all over town. Some are huge warehouses, others just a room in an old house, selling copies of traditional designs or original work – plates, vases, jars, figurines – from just a few euros to a few thousand. The other Caltagirone specialities are sculpted terracotta **whistles** and **presepi**, or Nativity crib scenes; again, you can find examples in shops and galleries all across town.

A GEOMETRIC DIVERSION

Just fifteen minutes east of Caltagirone by train, twenty by car (via the Ragusa road), **Grammichele** ranks among the strangest and most ambitious of the new towns built after the 1693 earthquake that flattened much of this land. At its heart is a hexagonal design centred on an imposing central piazza with six radial streets, each bisected by secondary piazzas. The shape is no longer entirely perfect, due to a surfeit of new building around the edges of town, but it makes for an intriguing couple of hours' stroll, with all the streets in each segment corresponding exactly to their neighbours in dimension and appearance. It's disconcertingly easy to lose your bearings and, despite the grand design, Grammichele remains a predominantly rural-looking, old-fashioned town. Piazza Carafa, the main square, has a handful of *circoli*, or clubs, where most of the town's over-60s gather, while a café has ringside seats for all the comings and goings.

EATING AND DRINKING　　　　　　　　　　　　　　　　SEE MAP PAGE 271

Il Locandiere Via Luigi Sturzo 55 ☎ 0933 58 292. A tastefully restored old restaurant that's primarily a fish place, though there are good vegetarian *antipasti* and pastas. The menu depends on what's available. Mains are €10–16. May be closed Sun if they run out of fish. Mon–Sat lunch & dinner, Sun lunch only.

Giardino Spadaro Via San Giuseppe 5 ☎ 0933 21 331. A simple garden bar just up an alley off the bottom of La Scala, which is cool and shady by day, often thronged in the evening when the music is turned up. Mon & Wed–Sun 8am–8pm.

7

Agrigento and the southwest

276 Agrigento and the Valle dei Templi

286 Around Agrigento

288 Licata

290 North of Agrigento

294 The Pelagie Islands

SCALA DEI TURCHI BEACH

Agrigento and the southwest

Set on a ridge below the town of Agrigento, the golden Doric temples of the Valle dei Templi are Sicily's prime tourist destination. Throughout the year, charabancs disgorge their hordes here, but only a fraction of visitors see anything else of this area. This is a shame, as this part of Sicily has its own fascination, especially for fans of Inspector Montalbano. The fictional detective's creator, Andrea Camilleri, was born in Porto Empedocle, and wove instantly recognizable elements of both his home town and Agrigento into his detective novels and other writings. You could spend a happy day or so in the southwest just searching out the authentic Montalbano locations – which are very different from the romanticized locations of the TV series.

This is a part of Sicily that will appeal to realists, not romantics, a land where decaying 1970s apartment buildings encircle crumbling historic centres; of dusty roads running through sleepy, shabby villages; and of abandoned settlements at the top of parched hills. The long south coast, from **Licata** to **Sciacca**, is sparsely developed, its marvellous sandy beaches and low-key Mediterranean ports and resorts barely known to Italians, let alone tourists. But there's good swimming in clean waters, and on the coast to either side of Agrigento, isolated sandy **beaches** – packed with locals on summer weekends – warrant the occasional trip off the busy SS115 main road. One of the best beaches lies just below the Hellenic site of **Eraclea Minoa**, to the north of Agrigento, while the port of **Licata**, to the south, offers a few old-town diversions to go with its sand and sea. Of the other coastal towns, **Sciacca** is perhaps the most enjoyable, a fishing port and summer resort with amazing clifftop views, and a good base for detours into the tall and craggy mountains that back this part of the coast. Those seeking Sicily's romantic side could take the midnight ferry from **Porto Empedocle** to the remote island of **Linosa**, closer to Africa than Europe, while its neighbour, the larger island of **Lampedusa** (with its own airport), has fantastic beaches and a lively summer season that continues despite the deepening migrant crisis.

GETTING AROUND **AGRIGENTO AND THE SOUTHWEST**

By public transport Agrigento is connected by bus with most major Sicilian cities, and as ever, buses are usually far quicker than trains. However, as many buses are timed to bring kids to school in the towns in the early mornings, and return them at 2pm, you may end up spending nights in one-horse villages if you rely on them. Catania airport is a 3hr journey by bus, around 2hr if you're driving, Comiso airport is much closer, but a 2hr drive nevertheless. Regular trains and buses link the coastal towns and villages, though services to the inland towns are less frequent.

Agrigento and the Valle dei Templi

No one comes to **AGRIGENTO** for the town, though its worn medieval streets and buildings soak up the thousands of tourists who come every year to marvel at the **Valle dei Templi**. The Doric temples of **Akragas**, Pindar's "most beautiful city of mortals", strung along a ridge facing the sea a couple of kilometres below town, are the most captivating of Sicilian Greek remains, unique outside Greece. This is a big and very beautiful site, and it is a shame to see it (as most tourists do) in a single day. Take it easy, with time to sit around and relax among the ruins or in the shade of a tree, and you'll enjoy it all the more. And if your visit coincides with the summer night-time opening of the three main temples, you're in for a truly magical experience.

TEMPIO DELLA CONCORDIA, AGRIGENTO

Highlights

❶ Valle dei Templi, Agrigento Take a walk through ancient Akragas, with its sandstone Greek temples dramatically sited between town and sea. See page 280

❷ Torre Salsa Several kilometres of unspoilt sands, backed by cliffs of crystalline selenite and a nature reserve – sheer bliss. See page 288

❸ Montalbano tour, Porto Empedocle Take a tour of the places that inspired Andrea Camilleri, creator of Inspector Montalbano, and discover aspects of Sicily few tourists ever see. See page 289

❹ Eraclea Minoa A superb sandy beach overlooked by the impressive remains of a Greek city. See page 291

❺ Sciacca With a labyrinthine Arabic upper town and spas that have been offering cures since antiquity, this vital, salty Mediterranean port town is a fascinating place to visit. See page 292

❻ Isola dei Conigli, Lampedusa Paddle or swim across to this idyllic desert-island nature reserve, with its pristine white sands and crystal-clear blue waters. See page 297

❼ Linosa Six hours by ferry from Porto Empedocle, Sicily's most remote island is completely unspoilt, with only the briefest of tourist seasons. See page 301

HIGHLIGHTS ARE MARKED ON THE MAP ON PAGE 278

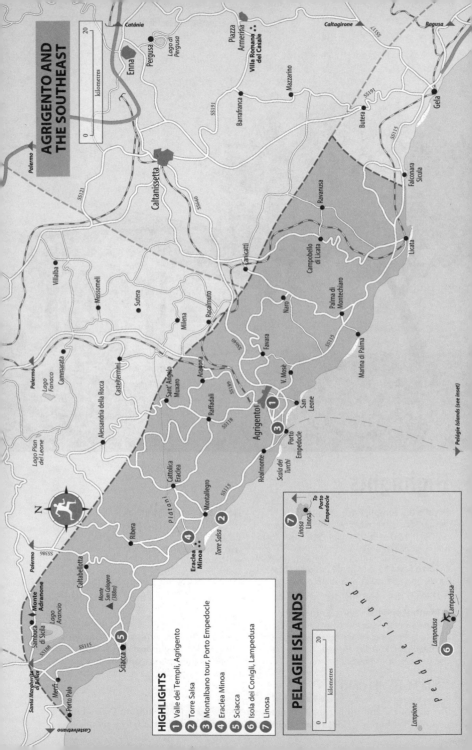

AGRIGENTO AND THE SOUTHEAST

HIGHLIGHTS

1. Valle dei Templi, Agrigento
2. Torre Salsa
3. Montalbano tour, Porto Empedocle
4. Eraclea Minoa
5. Sciacca
6. Isola dei Conigli, Lampedusa
7. Linosa

PELAGIE ISLANDS

Pelagie Islands

Lampedusa

Linosa

Lampione

To Porto Empedocle

PIRANDELLO AND THE BELLS

Pirandello (see page 286) spent much of his boyhood in a house overlooking Piazza Jose Maria Escriva and the church of **San Pietro**. The story goes that Pirandello's father, a supporter of Garibaldi and a committed anti-clericist, was so incensed by the racket of the **bells** chiming, that he took a rifle and shot at them. These days, the church is usually closed, but the piazza is a nice place to sit, with views down to the sea.

Agrigento

AGRIGENTO retains a historical core of a certain charm, with a fascinating little museum, and after visiting the temples you may well want to have a little wander.

Via Atenea and Rabato

Agrigento's main shopping street, the semi-pedestrianized **Via Atenea** is pleasant enough, with a tangle of steep, narrow side streets harbouring ramshackle *palazzi* and minuscule *cortili* (courtyards). At the far end of Via Atenea is Piazza Sinatra, beyond which is the **Rabato** district, the old Arab quarter, scene of a landslide in 1966 that destroyed much of the historic centre and left 7500 homeless. Although there's a handful of B&Bs in Rabato, full-blown gentrification is dragging its heels.

Santo Spirito
Piazza Santo Spirito • If closed, ring the bell at Piazza Santo Spirito 8

The **Santo Spirito** church and its adjoining convent began life as part of a grand Norman palace belonging to the Chiaramonte family, and were bequeathed to the Cistercian order in the thirteenth century by a widowed baron mourning the death of his young wife. There is usually a young nun about to show you around the **interior**, where florid early eighteenth-century monochrome stuccoes by Serpotta sprawl across the walls and domed trompe l'oeil ceiling.

Back on Piazza Santo Spirito, if you ring the bell at no. 8 and ask for "*dolci di mandorla*", a nun will bring you a tray of almond cakes, which are expensive, chewy, and worth the experience. If you are lucky there will also be sweet couscous (*cuscus dolce*), made to a recipe the nuns inherited – along with seven Tunisian servants – back in the thirteenth century.

Museo Civico Santo Spirito
Piazza Santo Spirito • Mon–Sat 9am–noon • €2.50 • ☎ 0922 590371

An enticing muddle of Romanesque, Byzantine, Norman, Gothic and Spanish building styles and motifs, with a cloister sliced in half to give the nuns (who live in a modern convent overlooking it) a private garden, the restored remains of the Chiaramonte family's Norman palace now house the **Museo Civico**. The friendly, well-informed custodian will take you to see a chapterhouse with a zigzag Gothic arch, and the tower, with beautiful faded Byzantine frescoes – the holes in the painted saints were created when American soldiers, billeted here during World War II, drilled holes to hang up their kit. The most enticing part of the museum, however, is the **Ethno-anthropological section**, crammed onto the top floor. Created in the 1990s with everyday objects donated by ordinary Agrigentini, it's a fascinating collection, with items ranging from an exam-busting ammunition belt (with cheat-notes instead of ammo), recipe notes, an old-fashioned ice-cream maker and a clothes drier fuelled by almond shells. Don't miss the marvellous **views** of the temples across the fields from the museum windows.

Santa Maria dei Greci
Via Santa Maria dei Greci • Key from the guardian at Via Santa Maria dei Greci 15

The narrowest and steepest of Agrigento's streets spread up the hill from Piazza Duomo, passing the church of **Santa Maria dei Greci**, which was built over a Greek temple of

8

the fifth century BC. The flattened columns can be seen in the nave, and through glass panels set into the floor, while outside, visible from an underground tunnel in the flower-filled courtyard, the stylobate and column stumps are incorporated into the church's foundations. Inside are the remains of Byzantine frescoes. Just up from here, Via Duomo leads past a line of decrepit *palazzi* to the massive **Duomo**, set on a terrace at the top of the hill and fronting a spacious, if slightly forlorn, piazza. After being closed for years of restoration it should be open by the time you read this.

The Valle dei Templi

The astonishingly well-preserved temples of the **Valle dei Templi** are the most captivating of Sicily's Greek remains. Magnificently strung along a fertile ridge high above the coast, **Akragas** was one of Sicily's richest and most powerful Greek cities – visitors reported that people had ivory furniture, abundant silver and gold, and even made elaborate tombs for their pets. Silver, gold and ivory may have gone, but the sandstone temples are stunning, and the site itself is beautiful too – especially when

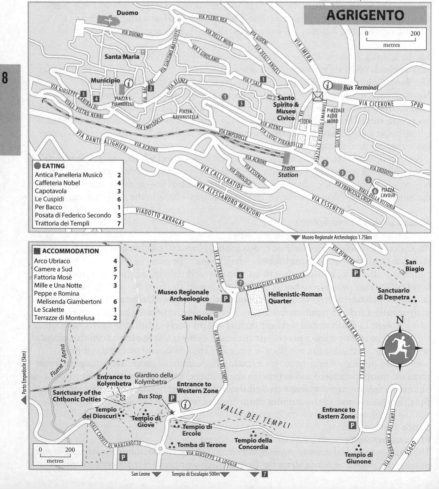

EATING

Antica Panelleria Musicò	2
Caffeteria Nobel	4
Capotavola	3
Le Cuspidi	6
Per Bacco	1
Posata di Federico Secondo	5
Trattoria dei Templi	7

ACCOMMODATION

Arco Ubriaco	4
Camere a Sud	5
Fattoria Mosè	7
Mille e Una Notte	3
Peppe e Romina Melisenda Giambertoni	6
Le Scalette	1
Terrazze di Montelusa	2

VISITING THE VALLE DEI TEMPLI

The Valle dei Templi is open daily 8.30am–7pm (ⓦparcovalledeitempli.it). An €10 **entry fee** covers both the eastern and western sites, though not the Giardino della Kolymbetra (see page 283); there's also a €13.50 **combined ticket** covering the temples and the archeological museum, and a €15 ticket including these two plus the wonderful Giardino di Kolymbetra (see page 283). Tickets can be bought online (to print or pick up at the site) via the above website or (for a booking fee) from ⓦtiqets.com (who also do smartphone tickets).

The easiest way to **get to the temples** is by bus; **buses** #1, #1/, #2, #2/ and #3/ leave every 20min or so from Piazza Rosselli in Agrigento (also stopping outside the train station), and drop off at the museum or at the main car park in between the eastern and western sites. **Taxis** charge about €15 from the city centre to the eastern entrance or museum. If you're coming **by car**, you'll find car parks clearly signposted.

The Giunone, Concordia and Ercole temples are also open for **evening sessions** (July, Aug & Sept Mon–Fri 7.30–9.30pm, Sat & Sun 7.30–10pm (exit the site by 11pm); €10). There's a small night-time entrance directly above the Tempio di Giunone, which is best reached from the main site entrance by shared taxi (€2 per person); there's no public transport to the Giunone entrance, and it's quite a walk. Note that the site is cleared before evening entry is allowed, so you cannot stay inside between 7pm and 7.30pm. Tickets for the evening session go on sale at the Giunone ticket office from 7.15pm, with a queue forming rapidly.

Hiring a **guide** can bring the history of the site to life and greatly enhance your visit. The talented and informed Michele Gallo (☎360 397 930, ⓦlavalledeitempli.it) is highly recommended. Tours start at €150 per half-day, plus entry fee, for a group of up to ten people.

In August and September, it's also worth looking out for posters advertising open-air **concerts** on the southeastern edge of the archeological zone at Piano San Gregorio, with tickets from €35, though the average price is nearer €50: call ☎0922 20 500 for details of the programme, or ask at the tourist office.

8

the almond trees blossom in January and February, and when it's carpeted with wild flowers in the spring.

A road winds down to the Valle dei Templi from Agrigento, passing the **Museo Regionale Archeologico**, a treasure-trove of magnificent artefacts recovered from the site. If you're intent upon doing the temples and museum in one go, you'll need to allow a full day, and arrive as the site opens. It makes sense to start with the **eastern zone**, home to the three major temples, then see the museum, and wind up in the **western zone**, with a restorative wander through the **Giardini della Kolymbetra**.

There are several basic places offering refreshments at the site entrances, and a few nearby restaurants mostly aimed at coach parties, but it's far more pleasant to buy a picnic in Agrigento before coming down to the site.

Brief history

In 581 BC, colonists from nearby Gela and Rhodes founded the city of **Akragas** between the rivers of Hypsas and Akragas. This was the concluding act of expansion that had seen Geloans spread west along the high points of their trade routes, subduing and Hellenizing the indigenous populations as they went. They surrounded the new city with a mighty wall, formed in part by a higher ridge where they placed the acropolis (and where, today, the modern town stands). The southern limit of the ancient city was a second, lower ridge, and it was here, in the so-called **Valle dei Templi** (Valley of the Temples), that the city architects erected their sacred buildings during the fifth century BC. They were – and are – stunning in their effect, reflecting the wealth and luxury of ancient Agrigento: "Athens with improvements", as Henry Adams had it in 1899.

The eastern zone

The **eastern zone** is the more popular, and is at its least crowded in the early morning, or when it's floodlit in striking amber light at night. From the eastern entrance, a path climbs up to the **Tempio di Giunone** (Juno, or Hera), an engaging structure, half in ruins, standing at the very edge of the spur on which the temples were built. A long altar has been reconstructed at the far end of the temple; the patches of red visible here and there on the masonry denote fire damage, probably from the sack of Akragas by the Carthaginians in 406 BC.

Tempio della Concordia

Following the line of the ancient city walls that hug the ridge, Via Sacra leads west to the **Tempio della Concordia** (Concord), dating from around 430 BC. Perfectly preserved and beautifully situated, with fine views to the city and the sea, the tawny stone lends the structure warmth and strength. It's the most complete of the temples, and has required less renovation than the others, mainly thanks to its conversion in the sixth century AD to a Christian church. Restored in the eighteenth century to its (more or less) original layout, the temple has kept its simple lines and slightly tapering columns, although sadly it's fenced off from the public. Circle the temple at least once to get a decent view, and stand well back to admire its elegant proportions.

Tempio di Ercole

From the Tempio della Concordia, Via Sacra continues past the site of the city's ancient necropolis and across what remains of a deep, wheel-rutted Greek street to the oldest of Akragas's temples, the **Tempio di Ercole** (Hercules). Probably begun in the last decades of the sixth century BC, it's a long structure, with nine of the original thirty-eight columns re-erected, and everything else scattered around like a half-finished jigsaw puzzle.

Tempio di Esculapio

No set hours • Free

The quickest way to reach the **Tempio di Esculapio** (Asclepius) is to climb over the wall to the side of the Tempio della Concordia and scramble down to the SS115, from which a track leads to the under-sized temple, which has solid walls instead of a colonnade.

The western zone

The **western zone** is less impressive than the eastern end of the site, though its vast tangle of stone and fallen masonry from an assortment of temples is still engaging. Most notable is the mammoth pile of rubble that was the **Tempio di Giove** (Jupiter, or Zeus). The largest Doric temple ever known, it was never completed, left in ruins by the Carthaginians and further damaged by earthquakes and the removal of stone to build the port of Porto Empedocle to the south. Still, the stereobate remains, unnaturally huge in scale, while on the ground, face to the sky, lies an eight-metre-high telamon: a supporting column sculpted as a male figure, arms raised and bent to bear the weight of the temple. As excavations continue, other scattered remains litter the area, not least piles of great column drums marked with a U-shaped groove, which enabled them to be lifted with ropes.

Tempio dei Dioscuri

Beyond the Tempio di Giove, behind the excavated gates and walls of the Greek city, is the earliest sacred site, the **Sanctuary of the Chthonic Deities**, dedicated to the gods of the underworld and marked by two altars (one square and fire-reddened, the other round), dating from the seventh century BC, before the official foundation of the colony. Considerably more romantic-looking are the ruins of the so-called **Tempio dei Dioscuri** (also known as Tempio di Castore e Polluce, or Castor and Pollux), assembled in 1832 from various columns and other random architectonic fragments discovered nearby.

Giardino della Kolymbetra

Daily: May, June & Sept 9.30am–6.30pm; July & Aug 9.30am–7.30pm; March, April & Oct 9.30am–5.30pm; Feb, Nov & Dec 10am–2pm; closed Jan • €5 (or with combined ticket, see page 281)

Behind the Temple dei Dioscuri is the entrance to the **Giardino della Kolymbetra**, for which you need a separate ticket. Part of the city's irrigation system in the fifth century BC, it's now an extensive sunken garden, lush and green amid the aridity of the rest of the archeological zone. There is nothing monumental here, but it makes a pleasant relief from temple-touring, the olive, almond and citrus groves overlooked by honey-toned calcareous cliff walls draped with cactus and pitted with caves. It also holds banana, pistachio and pomegranate trees, all meticulously labelled and explained, and a reedy stream.

Museo Regionale Archeologico

Tues–Sat 9am–1pm & 2–7pm, Mon & Sun 9am–1pm • €8, €13.50 includes the Valley of the Temples • Audioguide €5 • ☎ 0922 595 448

The road between town and the temples runs past the excellent **Museo Regionale Archeologico**. It holds an extraordinarily varied collection, devoted to finds from the temples, the ancient city and the surrounding area. There are brief notes in English throughout, and an informative audioguide.

Rooms 1–6

Unusually for an archeological museum, much of what's here holds artistic merit as well as historical interest. You could skip most of the initial local prehistoric and Bronze Age finds, though in **room 1** look out for the gold signet rings, engraved with animals. **Rooms 3 and 4** feature an outstanding vase collection: beguiling sixth- to third-century BC pieces, one of which depicts the burial of a warrior. The highlight is a stunningly detailed white-ground *krater* from 440 BC portraying a valiant Perseus freeing Andromeda. But it's the finds from the temples themselves that make this collection come alive: leaving room 4, you'll pass a series of sculpted lion's-head waterspouts, a common device for draining the water from the roofs of the city's temples, while **room 6** is given over to exhibits relating to the Tempio di Giove, with three enormous stone heads from the temples sitting in the recessed wall. Some useful wooden model reconstructions help to make sense of the disjointed wreckage on the ground, although the prime exhibit is a reassembled telamon stacked against one wall: all the weather damage can't hide the strength implicit in this huge sculpture.

Rooms 10–15

The finest statue in the museum is in **room 10**, where the Ephebus, a naked Greek youth, displays a nerveless strength and power that suggests that the model was probably a soldier. Rooms beyond hold coins, inscriptions and finds from local necropolises; typical is an alabaster child's sarcophagus in **room 11** showing poignant scenes from his life, which was cut short by illness. The last couple of rooms contain finds from the rest of the province, one of which, in **room 15**, is the equal of anything that's gone before, amply demonstrating the famed Geloan skill as masters of vase-ware: a fifth-century BC *krater* displays a graphic scene from Homer in which Achilles slays the queen of the Amazons at the moment when he falls in love with her.

San Nicola and the Hellenistic-Roman quarter

In the grounds of the Museo Regionale Archeologico, look out for the Gothic doorway of the adjacent church of **San Nicola**. From the terrace outside, you get an invigorating view over the temple valley, while just beyond is a small odeon (third century BC), used for public meetings, during which the participants stood rather than sat in the narrow rows. Nip over the road on the way out of the museum, too: the **Hellenistic-Roman quarter** opposite (daily 9am–1hr before sunset; free) contains rows of houses, inhabited (on and off) until the fifth century AD, many with mosaic designs still discernible.

San Biagio and the Santuario di Demetra

Via Demetra

Heading back up the road towards town from San Nicola and the Hellenistic-Roman quarter, you'll pass the Norman chapel of **San Biagio**, built over the visible remains of another ancient Greek temple. If you're fortunate, a custodian may appear and will lead you down the cliff behind the chapel to the eerie **Santuario di Demetra** (be prepared to tip), where a stone-built chambered shrine hides two dingy caves that stretch 20m into the hillside. The thin corridor between building and caves was a sort of vestibule with niches for water so that worshippers could wash themselves. The most ancient of Agrigento's sacred sites, it was once devoted to the cult of Demeter and Persephone, and in use even before Akragas was founded. A mysterious and evocative place, it's at its best as the sun sets, when shadows flit across the dark and silent caves.

ARRIVAL AND DEPARTURE

By bus Services operating from the bus terminal at Agrigento's central Piazza Rosselli include: Camilleri, Argento & Lattuca (☎ 0922 29 136, ✐ camilleriargentoelattuca.it) and Cuffaro (☎ 091 616 510, ✐ cuffaro.info) to Palermo; Lattuca (☎ 0922 36 125, ✐ autolineelattuca.it) to Sant'Angelo Muxaro; SAL (☎ 0922 401 360, ✐ autolineesal.it) to Palermo airport, Licata, Gela, Palma di Montechiaro and Porto Empedocle (for the Pelagie Islands); SAIS Trasporti (☎ 0922 29 324, ✐ saistrasporti.it) to Caltanissetta, Catania and Naro; Salvatore Lumia (☎ 0922 20 414, ✐ autolineelumia.it) to Castelvetrano, Cattolica Eraclea (for Eraclea Minoa, change at Montallegro), Marsala, Mazara, Sciacca and Trapani. There's a SAIS bus ticket/information office in the corner of the piazza. Otherwise, buy tickets on the bus. Timetables are posted in front of the various companies' stops.

Destinations Caltanissetta (roughly hourly Mon–Sat, 10 daily Sun; 1hr 35min); Catania airport/Catania (roughly hourly Mon–Sat, 10 daily Sun; 2hr 40min/2hr 50min); Cattolica Eraclea, for Eraclea Minoa (5 daily Mon–Sat; 1hr);

AGRIGENTO AND THE VALLE DEI TEMPLI

Licata (12 daily Mon–Sat; 1hr); Palermo (14 daily Mon–Sat, 5 daily Sun; 2hr); Palermo airport (2 daily Mon–Sat, 2hr 50min); Palma di Montechiaro (13 daily Mon–Sat; 30min); Porto Empedocle (1–2 hourly Mon–Sat, 6 daily Sun; 20min); Sant'Angelo Muxaro (2 daily Mon–Sat; 1hr 10min); Sciacca (8 daily Mon–Sat, 2 daily Sun; 1hr–1hr 40min); Trapani (3 daily Mon–Sat, 1 daily Sun; 3hr–3hr 20min); Trapani airport 3 daily Mon–Fri, 2 daily Sat, 1 daily Sun; 2hr 30min–3hr).

By train Trains pull in at the edge of the old town at Stazione Centrale, unusually fronted by a garden – don't make the mistake of getting out at Agrigento Bassa, which is 3km north of town.

Destinations Caltanissetta (6 daily Mon–Sat, 2 daily Sun; 1hr 20min–2hr 45min); Enna (4 daily Mon–Sat, 2 daily Sun; 2–3hr); Palermo (13 daily Mon–Sat, 6 daily Sun; 2hr).

By car The one-way system in Agrigento's old town is a nightmare. Some hotels are signposted, but you may well not be able to park anywhere near where you're staying (ask about *parcheggio* when you book).

GETTING AROUND

By bus From outside the train station on Piazza Marconi, city buses depart for the temples and the beach at San Leone; buy tickets prior to boarding from kiosks, *tabacchi* or the station bar (€1.20, or €3.40 for ticket valid all day); kiosks stand to either side of Piazza Marconi, though they're

not always open on Sundays. You can buy single tickets on board the bus for €1.70.

By taxi There are ranks at Piazzale Aldo Moro (☎ 0922 21 899) and outside the train station (☎ 0922 26 670).

INFORMATION

Tourist information The main office is inside the Prefettura building at the back of Piazzale Aldo Moro (Mon–Fri 9am–2pm & 2.30–7pm, Sat 9am–1pm; ☎ 0922 593

227 or ☎ 800 236 37. There's also an info desk at Stazione Centrale and a kiosk at the Valle dei Templi western zone car park.

ACCOMMODATION

SEE MAP PAGE 280

Finding **accommodation** in Agrigento itself is rarely a problem, although in peak season the nearby coastal resorts fill fast. All the budget choices, primarily small, family-run establishments, are in the old town above the temples, and there are several B&Bs signed on the main Via Atenea. Tour groups tend to stay in the grander hotels a few kilometres east of town at **Villaggio Mosè**, an unattractive traffic-

choked suburb on the coast road into Agrigento, though the hotels themselves – glossy, three- and four-star holiday palaces – are fine, and you may well find great deals online in one of them.

Arco Ubriaco Via Sferri 12 ☎ 335 745 6532, ✐ arco ubriaco.com. Three rooms in a warm, welcoming family home on the edge of Rabato, named for the tilting medieval arch leading off the living room. There's wi-fi, and all rooms have bathroom, a/c and a fridge. The motherly owner is adept at making all guests feel part of the family. €62

Camere a Sud Via Ficani 6 ⓣ349 638 4424, ⓦcamereasud.it. This bijou B&B in an alley off Via Atenea has charming hosts, three vividly coloured en-suite rooms with a/c, paintings by Catanese artist Antonio Recca and a roof terrace for breakfasts. €65

Fattoria Mosè Via M. Pascal 4, Villaggio Mosè ⓣ0922 606 115, ⓦfattoriamose.com. On an estate run by the same family for two hundred years, this *agriturismo*, midway between the sea and the temples (signposted from the SS115), offers a simple B&B option as well as self-catering apartments in a converted stable block. Rooms are simple but there's a huge garden and a small swimming pool. Breakfasts and meals (€10 for lunch, €28 for dinner) are mostly home-produced and organic, and the family also run cookery courses. There's free internet and a laundry service. Closed Nov–Feb. Rooms €130, apartments from €550 a week

Mille e Una Notte Via Garibaldi 46 ⓣ320 483 5856, ⓦmilleeunanottebeb.it. Sensitively run B&B on the fringe of the evocative Rabato quarter, with spick-and-span rooms including one sleeping four and one sleeping five, and a small apartment with cooking facilities. Doubles €88

★**Peppe e Romina Melisenda Giambertoni** Via Passeggiata Archeologica 29 ⓣ348 762 2790, ⓔcasinagiambertoni@gmail.com. There is simply no better place to stay in Agrigento than these three simple apartments on the ground floor of a nineteenth-century country villa set just between an olive grove and the Roman-Hellenistic area of the archeological zone, a short walk from the museum. They may not be luxurious, but you have everything you need, and the opportunity to sit outside your apartment at night, looking at the temples, is without a price. Weekly rates from €500

Le Scalette Salita Iacono 3 ⓣ335 745 6532, ⓦbeblescalette.com. Run by the same people as *Arco Ubriaco*, this house is higher up in town, close to Santo Spirito. There are four small, clean rooms, and a kitchen-dining room for the use of guests. €66

Terrazze di Montelusa Piazza Lena 6 ⓣ0922 28 556, ⓦterrazzedimontelusa.it. A smart, clean and airy second-floor B&B at the far western end of the old town, with large, fully equipped rooms and a charming, knowledgeable host who will offer useful tips for the area and even trot out a few tunes on the piano if you ask nicely. There are great views from the roof terraces, where a garden is being planned. Free internet. €90

8

EATING

SEE MAP PAGE 280

Agrigento has a fairly good choice of **restaurants**, many clustered around Via Atenea and offering some kind of *menu turistico*. Unsurprisingly, these tend to be a bit touristy, though prices are usually low. There are two distinct areas for **cafés** and **bars, via Atenea and Viale della Vittoria**. The town-centre *passeggiata* focuses on Via Atenea, and once the shops reopen in the late afternoon the whole street is packed. To watch the action, choose a seat at one of the little bars in Piazzale Aldo Moro, at the beginning of Via Atenea, a nice place to sit in the early evening, despite the occasional burst of organ music from a local crooner. For sunsets and views, stroll along the leafy Viale della Vittoria, where some lovely cafés and restaurants cater to a local family crowd.

Antica Panelleria Musicò Viale della Vittoria s/n. This little van parked at the beginning of Viale della Vittoria is an Agrigento institution, selling *pane e panelle* (chickpea-flour fritters in soft bread rolls) since 1954. Daily 8.30am–1pm & 5–8.30pm.

Caffeteria Nobel Viale della Vittoria 11 ⓣ0922 24 562. A relaxing spot for breakfast (amazing pastries), superior hot chocolate, an ice cream or a beer under the shady trees of the avenue. Daily 8am–late.

Capotavola Viale della Vittoria 15–17 ⓣ0922 21 484. Perfect for families – it even has a designated play area screened from the main restaurant by a glass window, so you can keep an eye on the kids while you eat in peace. There are pizzas (€5–8, with mini-pizzas at a euro less), including the crowd-pleasing *ricottina*, with mozzarella, ricotta, ham and parmesan, plus risotto with shellfish and *cedro lemon*, spaghetti with seafood and toasted breadcrumbs, and fish dishes featuring red prawns from Mazara, further up the coast. There are usually several fixed-price deals – the fish lunch consisting of an antipasto, pasta and water is a good deal at €14.90. Daily lunch & dinner.

Le Cuspidi Piazza Cavour 19 ⓣ0922 24 562. Come to this *gelateria* for the best ice creams in town – try the fresh ricotta, pistachio or almond. Daily 9am–late.

Per Bacco Vicolo Lo Presti ⓣ0922 553 369. Fish dominates the menu in this small, smart trattoria set in an atmospheric little alley. It's favoured by locals and run by lovely owners. There's a good selection of salads and risottos. Expect to pay around €30 for a full meal including wine. Tues–Sun dinner only.

★**Posata di Federico Secondo** Piazza Cavour 19 ⓣ0922 28 289. A lovely, elegant restaurant, with lots of atmosphere, just off tree-lined Viale della Vittoria. The food is strictly seasonal, with the menu divided according to the main ingredient (artichoke, veal etc) rather than the usual *primi* and *secondi*, so you may need a little help deciphering it. There's no pressure to order a four-course meal – try it for dinner, and you may well decide to come back for a light *antipasto* lunch or plate of pasta the next day. The signature dish is beef fillet with gorgonzola and honey – amazing. Expect to pay €40 for a full meal, but you could have a nice light lunch for under €20. Mon–Sat lunch & dinner.

Trattoria dei Templi Via Panoramica dei Templi 15 ☎ 0922 403 110. Fresh seafood in a traditional restaurant halfway between town and the Valle dei Templi. Among their ample pasta dishes, opt for *panzerotti della casa* (ravioli with seafood sauce; €8), or splash out on the *fettuccine all'aragosta*, served with a chunk of lobster (€15). Mon–Sat lunch & dinner; winter closed Fri & Sun.

DIRECTORY

Banks and exchange ATMs at banks on Via Atenea.
Hospital Ospedale Civile San Giovanni di Dio, Contrada Consolida, just outside town (☎ 0922 442 111).
Pharmacies Averna, Via Atenea 325 (☎ 0922 26 093); Maria Teresa Indelicato, Piazza Vittorio Emanuele 13 (☎ 0922 23 889); Minacori, Via Atenea 91 (☎ 0922 25 089). All are open Mon–Fri 9am–1pm & 4–8pm; the usual late- opening rota system is in operation, with details posted outside all pharmacies.
Police Call ☎ 112 or ☎ 113, or contact the Questura on Piazza Vittorio Emanuele (☎ 0922 483 111), or the Carabinieri at Piazzale Aldo Moro 2 (☎ 0922 499 000).
Post office Piazza Vittorio Emanuele (Mon–Fri 8.20am–7.05pm, Sat 8.20am–12.35pm).

Around Agrigento

The area around Agrigento has several places worth visiting that can be easily seen in day-trips from the town, and that are of interest in particular to fans of Sicilian literature – the highlights being **Caos**, birthplace of Luigi Pirandello, **Porto Empedocle**, birthplace of Montalbano creator Andrea Camilleri, and the ancestral seat of **Giuseppe Tomasi di Lampedusa**, author of *The Leopard*.

Caos

Southwest of Agrigento, at the end of the flyover leading out towards Porto Empedocle, the suburb of **CAOS** was the birthplace of writer **Luigi Pirandello** and the inspiration for the Taviani Brothers' film, *Kaos*, based on four of Pirandello's short stories. One of the greats of twentieth-century Italian literature, Pirandello is best-known for his dramatic works, such as *Six Characters in Search of an Author* and *Henry IV*, though his 1934 Nobel Prize was awarded as much for his novels and short stories. He had a tragic life: his wife was committed to an asylum, having lapsed into insanity following the ruin of her family and the birth of their third son, and for much of his life Pirandello was forced to write to supplement his frugal living as a teacher. His drama combines elements of tragedy and comedy with keenly observed dialogue, and the nature of identity and personality, reality, illusion and the absurd are all recurring themes. Pirandello's ideas – and innovations – formed the blueprint for much subsequent twentieth-century drama.

Casa Natale di Luigi Pirandello

Contrada Caos, just off the SS115 and past the Valle dei Templi • Daily 9am–7pm • €4, free on first Sun of month • ☎ 0922 511 826 • Bus #1/ runs here from Agrigento

Although he left Agrigento while still young, Pirandello spent time here every summer at the **Casa Natale di Luigi Pirandello**, where you can see the study in which he wrote, crammed with foreign editions of his works. As well as a couple of murals he painted, it holds stacks of photos, including one sent by George Bernard Shaw, and a fifth-century vase, depicting a bearded man attacking a young woman, that was formerly used as an urn for Pirandello's ashes. After seeing the house, with its bamboo and daub interior, you can wander down through the **grounds** to where the writer's ashes are interred, though the views he once enjoyed over the sea are now ruined by a patch of industrial horror.

Porto Empedocle

Six kilometres southwest of Agrigento, **PORTO EMPEDOCLE** is mainly of interest as the departure point for ferries to the Pelagie Islands (see page 294) – unless, that is, you happen to be a fan of **Andrea Camilleri**, who was born here. Porto Empedocle is Camilleri's Vigàta, the fictional home to many characters, including the beguiling **Inspector Montalbano** (see page 289), whom Camilleri based at the police station here, and who lived on the beach at nearby Marinella. Indeed, if you enter town from the south, you will pass a sign recently erected by the local council proclaiming "Vigàta (Porto Empedocle)".

Though it's an unprepossessing, functional port, much of it dominated by an enormous cement works, Porto Empedocle's workaday ambience has a certain appeal. If you're waiting for a ferry, you can enjoy a pleasant stroll along the town's spruced-up pedestrian walkway – very lively in the evenings – to check out the statue of Detective Montalbano on the main street (inspired by the books, not the TV series, with moustache and cigarette), or dine at inexpensive fish **restaurants** including (if you're lucky) the eccentric fish trattoria so beloved of Montalbano (see below).

ARRIVAL AND DEPARTURE   PORTO EMPEDOCLE

By bus SAL buses for Porto Empedocle leave once or twice hourly from Agrigento's bus and train stations, six times on Sunday (a 15–20min journey), dropping you in Piazza Italia, one block from the waterfront; the last bus from Agrigento leaves at 9pm (7pm on Sun). Note that adverse weather conditions will affect both hydrofoils and ferries, so it is wise to call before setting out to catch one. Ferries are operated by Caronte e Tourist (though the boats may still say something else on the side) (w carontetourist.it), hydrofoils by Liberty Lines (w libertylines.it).

By ferry and hydrofoil Services to Lampedusa and Linosa leave from the town's dock.
Ferry destinations Lampedusa (6 weekly; 8hr 15min); Linosa (6 weekly; 5hr 45min).
Hydrofoil destinations At the time of writing hydrofoil service timetables had not been confirmed. Expect daily services in July and August. For low season timings, check the website for updates.
By taxi A taxi from Agrigento will cost about €25. It's best to agree on a price before you leave.

EATING AND DRINKING

Bar La Spiaggetta SS115 ter 57, ☏ 0922 636397. Simple pizza joint on the beach below a stone tower that also makes appearances in the Montalbano books. No frills, no airs and graces, just damn good pizza and a party atmosphere – especially on weekend karaoke nights. Two pizza and beers for around €15. Open all day every day.
La Lampara Via F. Crispi 62 ☏ 339 490 6833. A rough and ready fish trattoria housed in what looks like a long wooden shed, a few minutes' walk from the port along the seafront, offering an abundant three-course meal plus good local wine for around €25. Open erratically for lunch & dinner.

Il Timone da Enzo Via Garibaldi 11 ☏ 334 342 7177. International literary fame has inspired Enzo's to smarten up the old shack with a battered boat on its roof that appears in the pages of Camilleri. It has a new mural, another boat inside and several caged birds. It often has the kind of dishes that would bring tears of joy and nostalgia to the eyes of Montalbano: polpette made of neonati (newborn fish), spaghetti al nivuru di siccia (with squid ink) and glistening fresh triglie (red mullet). Fixed menu at €25 per head, including carafes of the strong local plonk. Tues–Sun for lunch and dinner.

Scala dei Turchi

About 7km west of Porto Empedocle (follow signs for Realmonte), the stunning **Scala dei Turchi** beach lies at the bottom of furrowed and gleaming-white cliffs. Prone to landslides, the road above it collapsed in the winter of 2013, and was barricaded off to traffic at the time of writing (though you can still walk down to the beach). This only adds to the traffic congestion during the summer and on sunny weekends. If you want cliffs and sands without the crowds, continue on to Torre Salsa.

ARRIVAL AND DEPARTURE   SCALA DEI TURCHI

By car As there are no bus connections to Scala dei Turchi from Agrigento, the only way to get here is by car.

ACCOMMODATION AND EATING

Lido Scala dei Turchi Scala dei Turchi, Realmonte ☏ 0922 814 563. At the top of the steps leading down to Scala dei Turchi beach, this lido restaurant provides welcome sustenance in the form of delicious seafood meals for around €25 a head including wine. Daily July & Aug for lunch & dinner; Sept, Oct, May, June Tues–Sun for lunch and dinner.

Scala dei Turchi Via Grande 171, Realmonte ☎ 0922 816 238. A little B&B in the village of Realmonte – the main attraction being that it is close to the stunning white cliffs of Scala dei Turchi and the unspoilt beaches at Giallonardo, near Siciliana, and Torre Salsa, between Siciliana Marina and Eraclea Minoa. **€52**

Torre Salsa

Protected by a WWF nature reserve, and stretching for endless kilometres, the long, sandy beach of **Torre Salsa**, backed by cliffs of selenite crystal, has none of the crowds of Scala dei Turchi. For most of the year, underground springs make the dirt road to the beach inaccessible by car, though if you don't mind a muddy walk, you could park once the going gets too tough for your car, and continue to the beach on foot; just follow signs for the Ingresso Pantano. If you want to drive all the way to the beach you will need to enter via the Agriturismo Torre Salsa, which in high season charges for parking and beach access. Both entrances are well signposted from the SS115.

ARRIVAL AND DEPARTURE   **TORRE SALSA**

By car Torre Salsa is off the SS115 between Agrigento and Sciacca; turn off at the junction marked Montallegro/Bovo Marina/Torre Salsa.

ACCOMMODATION

Agriturismo Torre Salsa Torre Salsa ☎ 336 945 967, ⓦ torresalsa.it. An *agriturismo* with a double room, a triple suite and several apartments (from €130 a day for two people), all with terrace and sea view. The motto is "mente sana in corpo sano" ("a healthy mind in a healthy body"), and there's an emphasis on energetic healthy pursuits such as Nordic walking, bird-watching and mountain biking, with several marked trails. There is a restaurant, and organic, perma-culture raised vegetables are on sale for self-caterers. Rates include breakfast. Minimum stay 1 week Sat–Sat in Aug. Doubles **€110**

Palma di Montechiaro

Shabby **PALMA DI MONTECHIARO**, half an hour's drive southeast of Agrigento, was once the seat of the Lampedusa family, the last of whom – **Giuseppe Tomasi di Lampedusa** – wrote the acclaimed novel, *The Leopard*. He died in 1957 (*The Leopard* was published a year later), but the palace in Palma had lain derelict for a long time before that. Indeed, far more resonant for *Leopard* fans are the ruins in the western Sicilian town of Santa Margherita di Belice (see page 348). Today, the only echoes of the great feudal family recorded in the novel are to be found in Palma's imposing seventeenth-century **Chiesa Matrice**, built by one of Lampedusa's ancestors and approached by a wide flight of crumbling steps, and the ruined site of the **Castello di Palma**, a few kilometres west of town at the end of a small track.

Naro

The medieval hill-town of **NARO** makes a good destination for a scenic drive inland. The finest of the buildings are the Chiaramonte **castello** and the nearby ruins of the old cathedral; other churches in this walled and battlemented town are emphatically Baroque. Architecturally harmonious though Naro is, the real attraction is the drive itself from Palma, which is rewarded by extensive sweeping views down to the coast.

Licata

LICATA is a pleasant little port town some 50km down the coast from Agrigento, though there's certainly nothing left of ancient Phintias, the settlement founded here

THE MONTALBANO PHENOMENON

Inspector Salvo Montalbano is the most famous policeman in Italy, and his creator, the late **Andrea Camilleri**, was a chain-smoking, nonagenarian native of Porto Empedocle, and the country's most successful writer. The Montalbano books – twenty novels and four collections of short stories – have sold well over eleven million copies in Italy, while episodes of the Montalbano TV series regularly attract an astonishing nine million viewers here. Montalbano fever is fast becoming an international phenomenon, too. The TV series has been broadcast in fifty countries, including the UK and Australia, and intriguingly, Police HQ Scotland Yard in London recently requested copies of the entire TV series for use in "professional training courses".

A very human policeman, Montalbano lives on a beach, begins every morning with a swim, savours what he eats in silence with an almost religious passion, and suffers from bad digestion. Although the setting for the novels is contemporary, the core of Montalbano's world remains the provincial Sicily of Camilleri's youth, a fictional place in which elements of modern life, such as the mobile phone and computer, can at times seem anachronistic.

When it came to filming the TV series, however, director Alberto Sironi decided to re-create Camilleri's Sicily not in Agrigento, but in the province of Ragusa (see page 245), perhaps because Agrigento and Porto Empedocle were deemed a little too real for the tastes of TV viewers. Below are **locations** in Agrigento and Porto Empedocle that you could easily visit yourself, though keen Montalbano fans are unlikely to regret splashing out on a **guided tour** of the sites with Michele Gallo (☏ 360 397 930, ⊛ sicilytourguides.net); group prices start at €150 for a half-day tour.

MONTALBANO LOCATIONS

Questura The Police Headquarters (and base of the irascible Commissioner Bonetti Algheretti and his odious assistant Lattes) is in fact Agrigento's police station, on Piazza Municipio at the beginning of Via Atenea.

Rabato Semi-destroyed by a landslide, Agrigento's Arab quarter, just to the north of Via Garibaldi, serves as the home of Montelusa lowlifes, including the Tunisian prostitute mother of Montalbano's almost-adopted son.

La Mannara The car park and abandoned factory used as a base by Gigì and his prostitutes lie behind the ENI, at the edge of Porto Empedocle on the road to Agrigento.

The "dwarf skyscrapers" A frequently recurring cityscape detail of the TV shows, these occupy the ridge above the port at Porto Empedocle.

Montalbano's flat rock The place the inspector comes to digest both his lunches and the complexities of his current case lies at the end of the dock in Porto Empedocle.

Chiesa Madre This church on Via Roma, the main street of Porto Empedocle, provides the setting for several funerals, some of them Mafia affairs.

Via Granet This little street off Porto Empedocle's Via Roma serves as the site of former restaurant *San Calogero*, and the home of the observant Maestra Clementina and the melancholy violinist.

Bar Kenia, Marinella A favourite meeting place for Montalbano and his Swedish soul mate (and occasional lover) Ingrid, this bar is still functioning at the end of Marinella beach.

Scala dei Turchi Meeting place for Montalbano and his informer and ex-schoolmate, Gigì.

Da Enzo Montalbano's favourite restaurant is open for business in Porto Empedocle (see page 286).

8

in 280 BC by Greeks from Gela, whose own city had been destroyed in successive attacks. Instead, Licata's historic centre is largely Baroque, with a lower town split into two distinct halves. Pavement cafés line the two wide avenues – Corso Roma and Corso Umberto – that form an L-shape at the heart of town meeting at Piazza Progresso. Behind here, the narrow crisscrossed alleys of the old town reach back to the harbour. There's a lido and **beach** just up from the harbour, though as Licata is still a working port, full of maritime hardware, it's not exactly enticing. For a view over the harbour, climb to the top of the town from the main Corso Roma and then work your way around the hill to reach an imposing sixteenth-century **castello**. Other strolls can take in the lively old-town **market** (Mon–Sat from early morning till around 2pm), held in the cobbled square in front of the church, and some of Licata's elegant *palazzi*, the most prominent being the gargoyle-studded **Palazzo Canarelli** on Corso Roma. Housed in a sixteenth-century convent on Piazza Sant'Angelo, and reached by walking down Via Dante off Corso Umberto, the **Museo Archeologico Regionale della Badia** displays a good deal of local prehistoric and Greek material, as well as medieval art, now open after a lengthy renovation (Tues–Sat 9am–1pm, Thurs and Sat also 4–6pm; free).

ARRIVAL AND DEPARTURE

LICATA

By bus Buses pull up on Corso Roma, right in the centre; the bar at Corso Roma 36 posts timetables and sells tickets for the regular daily departures to Agrigento, Gela, Catania (and Catania airport) and Palermo. Main bus companies are Etnabus, Interbus, SAIS and SAL.

By train Licata is served by far fewer trains than buses; principal destinations are Caltanissetta and Gela. The train station is a 5min walk from the bus station.

ACCOMMODATION AND EATING

Antica Dimora San Girolamo Piazza San Girolamo ☎0922 875 010, ⍟dimorasangirolamo.it. This is a great little B&B in the heart of the old fishing quarter, La Marina, housed in an old building full of character on an atmospheric square, where, in fine weather, guests are served first-class breakfasts *al fresco*. **€60**

La Madia Corso Re Capriata 22, off Corso Serrovia ☎0922 771 443, ⍟ristorantelamadia.it. A pricey, critically acclaimed restaurant where world-class but distinctly Sicilian dishes can be sampled on tasting menus that kick off at €95 per person excluding wine. What is

fantastic about the place is the emphasis on simplicity and the highest-quality ingredients – no weird culinary pyrotechnics here. Summer Mon & Wed–Sat lunch & dinner, Sun dinner only; winter Mon & Wed–Sat lunch & dinner, Sun lunch only.

L'Oste e il Sacrestano Via Sant'Andrea 19 ☎0922 774 736. A small, smart but unpretentious *hostaria* and wine bar near the Duomo and Corso Vittorio Emanuele, where the tasting menu of five small courses (€50) is just lovely. Tues–Sun lunch & dinner.

North of Agrigento

The lively spa and port town of **Sciacca** and the lovely ancient site of **Eraclea Minoa** are the best-known destinations to the north of Agrigento, but if you have a car, Sciacca makes a good base for a day's circular drive, taking in a few minor inland towns, including the superbly sited village of **Caltabellotta**. Local buses also make certain simple excursions into the hinterland possible.

Sant'Angelo Muxaro

Some 30km north of Agrigento, in the steeply sloping Platani River valley, the small agricultural centre of **SANT'ANGELO MUXARO** boasts a number of local *tholos* (tombs) hollowed out of the rock in dome-shaped caves. The earliest date from the eleventh century BC, but most are from around the eighth to the fifth centuries BC, and recall Minoan and Mycenaean examples in design. You'll spot them as you approach the bare hillside on which the village stands: the road leads up past a ramshackle brick wall, beyond which a path heads along the sheer rock to the "beehive" caves. At the bottom, the largest is known locally as the **Tomba del Principe**: later converted into a Byzantine chapel, it's half-hidden by overhanging trees and you may have to backtrack to get inside. Like all the others, it's empty now, the finds scattered in various museums around Europe.

ARRIVAL AND DEPARTURE

SANT'ANGELO MUXARO

By bus From Agrigento, buses for Sant'Angelo run by Lattuca (☎0922 36 125, ⍟autolineelattuca.it) leave from Piazza Vittorio Emanuele.

By car Drivers should take the SS189 branching off westwards for Aragona and Sant'Angelo, or choose the more wriggly but faster SS118 via Raffadali.

THE ALBERGO DIFFUSO EXPERIENCE

Sant'Angelo boasts a great **accommodation** option which transforms the village from a day-trip destination into a place where you might well be tempted to stay a night or two. Run by the Val di Kam agency, who have a "reception" at Piazza Umberto I 31 (☎0922 919 670 or ☎339 530 5989, ⱳvaldikam.it), it's known as an **albergo diffuso** – a hotel that is "diffused" throughout the village, with en-suite rooms (€78 including breakfast) in a number of different houses – it's a formula that's becoming increasingly popular in Sicily, and it's proving to be a great way of reviving small rural centres. Breakfast is usually a grand affair with local delicacies, served in your room, and the agency can also arrange local dinners in private houses. In addition, Val di Kam organizes **hiking**, **caving** and **archeological trips** around Sant'Angelo (from around €50 per person), arranges pick-ups from Agrigento, and is a mine of useful information on the area.

Eraclea Minoa

Thirty-five kilometres along the coast northwest of Agrigento is the ancient Greek site of **ERACLEA MINOA**. According to the historian Diodorus, this was originally named Minoa after the Cretan king Minos, who chased Daedalus from Crete to Sicily and founded a city where he landed. The Greeks settled here in the sixth century BC, later adding the tag Heraklea. A buffer between the two great cities of Akragas, 40km to the east, and Selinus (Selinunte), 60km west, Eraclea was dragged into endless border disputes, but flourished nonetheless. Most of what's left dates from the fourth century BC, the city's most important period, three hundred years or so before it fell into decline.

While you're here, you'll be hard put to resist a trip down to the **beach**, one of the finest on Sicily's southern coast, backed by pine trees, chalky cliffs and a strip of holiday homes. Get here early in July and August to secure a parking spot.

8

The site

Daily 9am–1hr before sunset; may close Sun in winter if they are short of staff, or for safety reasons if there are storms at sea, as this stretch of coast is prone to erosion; call to check • €4 • ☎0922 846 005

The **site** sits on a ridge high above a beautiful arc of sand, with the mouth of the River Platani on the other side. Among the most attractive of all Greek sites in Sicily, it occupies a headland of which only around a third has so far been excavated. What there is to see is the fruit of successive excavations by foreign universities, who, together with the local *Comune*, have landscaped the remains to good effect. Don't stray too far off the paths, though, as snakes lurk in the undergrowth.

Apart from the city **walls**, once 6km long and with a good part still standing, the most impressive remains are of the sandstone **theatre**. Now restored to its former glory after years of deterioration of the seats (which are made of very soft stone), the theatre is protected from the worst of the elements by a plastic roof.

Above the theatre, excavations have also revealed tombs and traces of a Greco-Roman temple, while below stand the ruins of a grand house, with fragments of Roman mosaics, though these are covered and inaccessible. Many of the finds are displayed in a small on-site **museum**.

ARRIVAL AND DEPARTURE   ERACLEA MINOA

By bus You can get here between June and September by bus from Cattolica Eraclea, which has bus connections from Agrigento, but outside the summer months you're going to have to take any bus running between Agrigento and Sciacca and ask the driver to let you off at the turning on the SS115: from here, you'll have to walk the 3.5km to the site. To head onwards, walk back to the SS115, where you should be able to flag down any bus bound for Sciacca.

ACCOMMODATION

Eraclea Minoa Village ☎0922 846 023 (summer), ☎0922 29 101 (winter), ⱳeracleaminoavillage.it. A pine-shaded campsite, a few steps from the sea, which also has one- and two-bedroom bungalows and a bar, pizzeria, restaurant and disco. Camping/person including car and tent pitch €15, bungalows (including breakfast) from €60.

Sciacca

Just over 30km further up the coast from Eraclea Minoa, **SCIACCA** is a working fishing port that conceals a good-looking upper town, virtually untouched by tourism. A spa town for nearby Selinus in ancient times, it enjoyed great prosperity under the Arabs, from whom its modern name is thought to derive (the Arabic *xacca* meaning "from the water"). The town was at the centre of a feud between Catalan and Norman families that simmered on for a century, resulting in the deaths of a good half of the local population. Several notable buildings are scattered about, which infuse Sciacca's agreeable Mediterranean air with more than a passing historical interest and make for some pleasant strolling through the weaving streets.

The town is the main centre of **ceramic** production on Sicily's south coast, and you'll see colourful plates, vases and ornaments on sale everywhere. Its spa waters are still potent, and Sciacca remains a popular destination for Italians seeking all manner of cures, many of which are available on the state. There's also a decent arc of sandy **beach** 1km west of the centre at the end of Via Gaie di Garaffe.

The upper town

The still-walled upper town can be entered through any of the three grand gates remaining of the original seven. The westernmost, **Porta San Salvatore**, leads onto the **Chiesa del Carmine**, whose facade is lent a skew-whiff air by an off-centre Gothic rose window. Past the church, up Via P. Gerardi, the fifteenth-century **Palazzo Steripinto** is even more ungainly, its embossed exterior only partially offset by some slender arched windows.

From Palazzo Steripinto, the main **Corso Vittorio Emanuele** runs right the way down to the lovely **Piazza A. Scandaliato**, a large terrace with some good cafés, enhanced by wide views over the port and distant bays. The most enduring Arab legacy in town is the street layout and, back from the piazza, above the **Duomo**, a Moorish knot of passages and steep alleys leads up to the rather feeble remains of the fourteenth-century **Castello Conti Luna**, which belonged to one of the feuding families that disrupted medieval Sciacca. A little way down from here is the twelfth-century church of **San Nicolò**, a tiny construction with three apses and some elegant blind arcading.

The port

Steps from Piazza A. Scandaliato lead down the cliffside to the lower town and **port**, whose most distinctive feature is the hexagonally steepled modern church of **San Pietro**. Just north of the church you'll see further steps, each riser decorated with contemporary ceramic **tiles**, some depicting sea life, some just patterned, and each one different. Fishing vessels lie tied up at the quayside, lorries unload salt by the bucketful for anchovy- and sardine-processing, and repairmen, foundry workers and chandlers go about their business, breaking off work for a drink in some scruffy portside bar.

ARRIVAL AND INFORMATION
SCIACCA

By bus Buses pull up by the Villa Comunale (the town gardens) at the eastern end of Sciacca. Bus tickets are sold at the *Bar Giglio* on Viale della Vittoria for Lumia services to Agrigento, Caltabellotta, Castelvetrano and Trapani, and from the *Antico Chiosco* bar in the centre of Piazza Santa Friscia for Gallo services to Palermo.
Destinations Agrigento (8 daily Mon–Sat, 2 daily Sun; 1hr–1hr 40min); Caltabellotta (4–5 daily Mon–Sat; 45min); Castelvetrano (3 daily Mon–Sat, 1 daily Sun; 40–55min); Palermo (8 daily Mon–Sat, 5 daily Sun; 1hr 45min); Palermo airport (2 daily Mon–Sat; 1hr 50min); Trapani (3 daily Mon–Sat, 1 daily Sun; 2hr–2hr 20min), Trapani airport (3 daily Mon–Sat, 1 daily Sun; 1hr 40min–2hr).

ACCOMMODATION
SEE MAP PAGE 293

Aliai Via Gaie de Garaffe 60 ☎ 0925 905 388, ⬚ aliai. com. A pleasant B&B facing the sea in the lower town. The smartly renovated rooms boast antique touches, wood-beamed ceilings and one has its own terrace. **€70**

★ **Conte Luna** Vicolo Gino 1 ☎ 0925 993 396 or ☎ 348 120 3647, ⬚ contelunasciacca.com. Excellent value for money, this is a welcoming B&B in a lovely old *palazzo* in the heart of the upper town (off Via Licata), where the seven

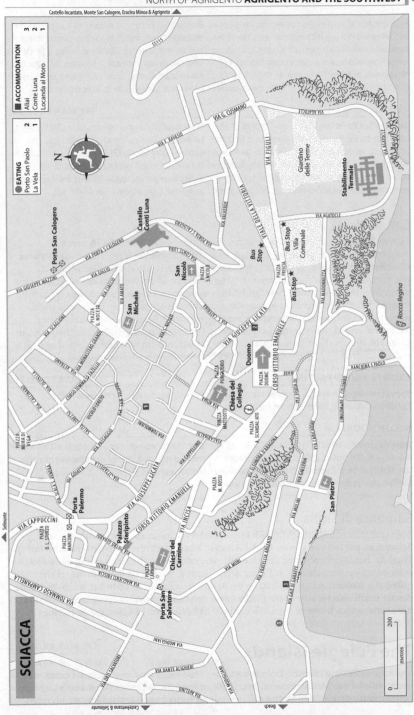

SCIACCA

■ ACCOMMODATION
Aliai	3
Conte Luna	2
Locanda al Moro	1

● EATING
| Porto San Paolo | 2 |
| La Vela | 1 |

8

en-suite rooms all have fridges and a/c. The top room is best, with a large balcony and panoramic views. There's also a spacious lounge and a terrace, and in summer, a minibus service is available to carry guests to nearby beaches. **€60**

★ **Locanda al Moro** Via Liguori 44 ☎ 0925 86 756, ⓦ almoro.com. Wonderfully set in a thirteenth-century Moorish tower in the heart of town, this is an excellent B&B, modern and clean, and run by a Sicilian-German couple. The only downsides are the difficulty in finding it by car (ask directions and don't attempt to negotiate the surrounding narrow lanes). Rooms – some small – have a/c, and there's free internet. Local wine tours can be organized. **€70**

EATING

SEE MAP PAGE 293

★ **Porto San Paolo** Largo San Paolo 1 ☎ 0925 27 982. Come here for the fine views over the harbour from the terrace, and delicious dishes such as seafood risotto and lobster fettuccine, as well as pizza in the evening. You'll pay around €40 for a full meal, including a glass or two of wine. Arrive early for the best tables, and in any case book ahead in summer. Daily lunch & dinner; closed Wed Sept–July.

La Vela Via Gaie de Garaffe 60 ☎ 0925 23 971. This quayside eatery serves a €25 set menu, which includes two first and two second courses plus dessert (drinks extra) – all very abundant and usually delicious. Booking advisable. Daily lunch & dinner; closed Wed Sept–July.

Caltabellotta

Twenty kilometres northeast of Sciacca, the village of **CALTABELLOTTA** perches magnificently on three jutting fangs of rock 950m above sea level. Tremendous **views** stretch out on all sides, apparently taking in 21 villages. On the highest pinnacle, you can pass through the solitary surviving entrance of the Norman **castello** (always open; free) that once stood here, and climb up steep, rock-cut steps to the very top, from which the village below appears as a patchwork of grey roofs. The castle itself, ruined by an earthquake, was where the Angevins and Aragonese signed the peace treaty that ended the Wars of the Vespers in 1302. Immediately below sit the Norman **Chiesa Madre** and the Gothic **Chiesa di San Salvatore**, both wonderfully sited against a rocky backdrop.

ARRIVAL AND DEPARTURE

CALTABELLOTTA

By bus Lumia buses run direct to Caltabellotta from Sciacca four times daily Mon–Fri, 3 times daily Sat, the last one back Mon–Fri leaving at 4pm, Sat leaving at 1.45pm.

ACCOMMODATION

Mulè Via Venezia 5 ☎ 0925 951 145 or ☎ 329 377 6740, ⓦ bbmule.it. The perfect B&B for anyone interested in staying right off the beaten track. It's set in a typical village dwelling, close to the entrance to the castle, and the plain rooms share a bathroom. You can also taste and buy local oil and other rural products, and view changing collections of local arts and crafts. **€50**

Sambuca di Sicilia

The Arab past of **SAMBUCA DI SICILIA**, around forty minutes' drive northwest of Sciacca, atop a hill to the west of the Arancio lake, is still discernible in the labyrinthine tangle of beautifully restored cobbled alleyways that form the heart of the old town. A sixteenth-century church in Piazza della Vittoria, the **Chiesa del Carmine**, is the home of a statue that's reputed to be by Antonello Gagini. In addition, a ten-kilometre detour north enables you to see the low-key excavations (always open; free) at **Monte Adranone**, a Greek city of the sixth century BC which fell to Carthage in the fourth.

The Pelagie Islands

The remote **Pelagie Islands** (Isole Pelagie) are little more than dry rocks set bang in the middle of the Mediterranean, over 200km from Sicily's south coast and lying even further south than Malta or Tunis. Throughout history they've been neglected, often

GETTING TO THE PELAGIE ISLANDS

The quickest way to Lampedusa is to **fly from Palermo or Catania** (current route operator is Danish Air Transport). Tickets cost from €60 one-way, and are cheapest booked online. Otherwise, there are ferries and hydrofoils **from Porto Empedocle** (6km southwest of Agrigento and connected to it by frequent buses). **Ferries** (Ⓦ carontetourist.it) leave Porto Empedocle year-round at midnight daily except Friday, calling at Linosa (5hr 45min) and Lampedusa (8hr 15min). You can buy tickets online. As a guide, one-way tickets to Lampedusa start at around €42 on the bridge, €46 with an assigned comfy seat, and €75 or so in a cabin, while cars cost around €120. Liberty Lines (Ⓦ libertylines.it) usually operates **hydrofoils** from May to October, departing from Porto Empedocle and arriving in Linosa three hours later and Lampedusa about four hours later; check the website for updates on timings; one-way tickets are around €45 to Linosa, €75 to Lampedusa.

abandoned or uninhabited, although the largest island, **Lampedusa**, now makes its living as a summer resort for an increasing number of Italians, who are attracted by its wonderfully clear waters and remote, end-of-the-line feel. Tiny, tranquil, volcanic **Linosa** is the perfect place most of the year for anyone wanting a few hours, days or weeks away from it all. B&Bs and restaurants are all seasonal, but there are always houses to rent for a song. The tiniest islet, **Lampione**, is uninhabited and mostly visited on dive and fishing trips.

In 1943 the Allies bombed Lampedusa prior to springing into Sicily, and Colonel Gaddafi of Libya nearly gave a repeat performance in 1987 when he retaliated against the American bombing of Tripoli by targeting missiles at the US base on Lampedusa. Italian troops were mobilized and Sicily was on a virtual war footing for three days, though in the event the missiles dropped into the sea short of the island. In recent years, the island has been the site of detention centres for enormous numbers of **immigrants** from Africa, either dumped here by unscrupulous people-traffickers, or intercepted at sea by naval vessels. Often they stay for months on end – kept firmly out of sight of tourists – until the legal processes for their repatriation or otherwise are completed.

8

Lampedusa

LAMPEDUSA is the largest of the Pelagie Islands (23 square kilometres), and is inhabited by around 5000 people, most based in the town of the same name. Many still earn a living from fishing, but most depend on the influx of tourists who swell the population to around 20,000 every August. This is a comparatively recent phenomenon, since Lampedusa has either been largely uninhabited or long neglected by Sicily's rulers. In 1667 it passed into the hands of the Tomasi family (as in Giuseppe Tomasi di Lampedusa, author of *The Leopard*), one of whose descendants attempted to sell the island to Queen Victoria in 1839, when it still had only twenty or so inhabitants. The queen lost out on the sale (at a cost of twelve million ducats) to Ferdinand II, the Neapolitan king, who was finally stirred into action at the prospect of losing such a scraggy but strategically important island.

Lampedusa is long, thin, flat and very dry, though the pristine waters offer some of the best **swimming**, **snorkelling** and **diving** in the Mediterranean. There are excellent **beaches**, almost all found on the south coast, and some fantastic swimming coves and grottoes. Dolphins are often seen, there's a sperm whale migration in March, and an offshore nature reserve where turtles come to lay their eggs. Bear in mind that it's a small, exposed island, so summer evenings are cooler than on the mainland. It's also not really somewhere you'd want to holiday in winter, when the wind whips across the barren landscape.

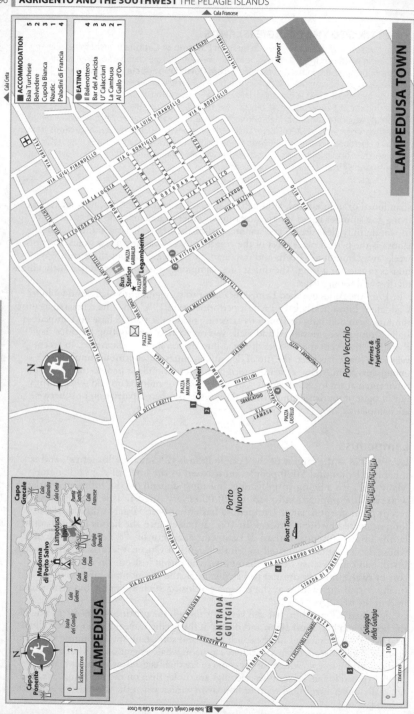

▲ Cala Francese

▲ Cala Creta

LAMPEDUSA TOWN

■ ACCOMMODATION
Baia Turchese 5
Belvedere 2
Cupola Bianca 3
Nautic 1
Paladini di Francia 4

● EATING
Il Balenottero 4
Bar del Amicizia 3
U' Calacciuni 5
La Cambusa 2
Al Gallo d'Oro 1

LAMPEDUSA

Capo Grecale

Cala Galandra
Cala Creta
Punta Sottile
Cala Francese

Cala Greca
Cala Croce
Guitgia (Beach)

Lampedusa Town

Madonna di Porto Salvo

Cala Galera

Isola dei Conigli

Capo Ponente

0   2
kilometres

Airport

VIA LUIGI PIRANDELLO
VIA G. BONFIGLIO
VIA LUIGI PIRANDELLO
VIA G. BONFIGLIO
VIA LA LOGGIA
VIA OBERDAN
VIA V. S. PELLICO
VIA ROMA
VIA G. MAZZINI
VIA CAVOUR
VIA ELEONORA DUSE
VIA ALGHERO
VIA GRECALE
VIA CAMERONI
VIA VITTORIO EMANUELE
VIA CROCE
VIA MANISTALERDE

Bus Station
PIAZZA GARIBALDI
PIAZZA BRIGNONE
Legambiente

PIAZZA PIAVE
VIA G. VERGA
VIA DELLE GROTTE
VIA PALIZZO
PIAZZA MARCONI
Carabinieri

VIA MACCAFERRI
VIA ENNA
VIA STAZZONE
VIA POLLINI
VIA SBARCATOIO
VIA SIRACUSA
VIA LAMASA
PIAZZA CASTELLO

VIA RISO
VIA CALA
VIA CALA PISANA

Porto Vecchio

Ferries & Hydrofoils

Porto Nuovo

Boat Tours

VIA ALESSANDRO VOLTA
STRADA DI PONENTE
VIA DEI DEPOSITI
VIA MADONNA
CONTRADA GUITGIA
STRADA DI PONENTE
VIA CRISTOFORO COLOMBO
VIA UDO AZZURRO
Spiaggia della Guitgia

VIA CAMERONI

N

0   100
metres

8

LAMPEDUSA'S FAUNA AND FLORA

When Lampedusa became a Bourbon colony in the 1840s, one of the first actions of the new settlers was to strip the land of its indigenous Mediterranean maquis, in order, it was thought, to render the island cultivable. The result was one of Europe's most extreme examples of **deforestation**, resulting in massive soil erosion that accounts for the arid state of the land today. However, a programme of conservation and reforestation is gradually having some effect and, while Lampedusa still appears devoid of greenery at first glance, a closer look reveals a wide range of **plant life**. Date palms are dotted along otherwise barren stretches, and, at Cala Galera in particular, look out for the Phoenician juniper, carob and wild olive trees, all survivors of the original maquis. Rare plants include the *Caralluma europaea*, a cactus-like plant with star-shaped flowers, and the *Centaurea acaulis*, from the centaury family, while during spring the flowering squills, irises, crocuses, orchids, echinops and thyme make up a vibrant display. Meanwhile, the nature reserve of Isola dei Conigli is the only habitat in Italy of the *Psammodromus algirus* **lizard** – a common species in North Africa – and Lampedusa and Linosa are among the few surviving nesting places in Italy of the **turtle** *Caretta caretta*. During summer evenings, the turtles deposit between 100 and 150 eggs in deep holes, from which the babies stagger out after sixty days. The nests are individually fenced off, but that doesn't help protect them from peregrine falcons. Injured turtles are cared for at the World Wildlife Fund's **Centro Recupero Tartarughe Marine** on the island's east coast at Cala Creta, before being released back into the sea.

Lampedusa Town

Its location – set back from two curving harbours – is the best thing about **LAMPEDUSA TOWN**, as otherwise it is nothing special to look at. Low concrete buildings hug a dusty grid of streets between airport and harbours, though things improve along the wide, main **Via Roma**, which is largely closed to traffic and lined from top to bottom with gift shops, pavement cafés and restaurants. On summer evenings, as the temperature drops, out come the wicker café chairs, souvenir stalls, jewellery hawkers and fruit-and-veg stands, and a real street-market atmosphere develops. Indeed, there are far more people on the street at 11pm than at 11am. You can buy the usual beach gear, postcards and T-shirts, but there's also a thriving trade in souvenirs like turtle carvings, sculpted beach rocks and hand-crocheted Arab caps. Enterprising local kids sell polished shells from the beach, while **island produce** – sun-dried tomatoes, mountain capers, wild oregano and fennel seeds, handmade cheese – is widely available from stalls and grocery stores.

A twenty-minute walk around the large **Porto Nuovo** harbour leads to the busy main beach, **Spiaggia della Guitgia**, backed by bars, hotels and restaurants. There's a stretch of fine sand, and good swimming in gently shelving water, though it's always packed here in summer; for a change of view try the next bay west, **Cala La Croce**. The other place you can explore from town is the smaller harbour, **Porto Vecchio**, where the ferries and hydrofoils dock, which also has a few bars and restaurants, and fishing boats coming and going during the day.

Isola dei Conigli and the south coast

Hourly buses for Isola dei Conigli depart from Lampedusa town bus station, off Via Roma

The best single beach destination on the island is at **Isola dei Conigli** (Rabbit Island), 5km to the west of Lampedusa town. From the clifftop road you clamber down the jagged path to a stretch of fine, white sand and gorgeous aquamarine waters. Just offshore is the little island itself, which you can reach either on foot or by swimming, depending on the tide. Conigli Island, and much of the rest of Lampedusa's **southern coast**, is protected as a nature reserve and there are various access places along the clifftop road to viewpoints and short signposted footpaths. With a bike or scooter you can find more windswept vantage points and hidden bays if you continue along the road past Isola dei Conigli, or you can turn inland opposite the Conigli parking area and loop back towards town high above the **north coast**. However, you can only swim on the north side of the island from a boat – it's mostly sheer cliffs, tiered like a wedding cake, and pierced by deep gorges and grottoes.

8

Cala Creta

Buses for Cala Creta depart from Lampedusa town bus station, off Via Roma; ask to get off at Cala Creta, and follow the signpost down a dusty track

Some 3km to the east of Lampedusa town, **Cala Creta** is a magnificent swimming cove, where steps lead from a tiny rock apron directly into stunning waters. It gets busy in summer, but it's a pretty spot with a sophisticated beach bar on the rocks – Cala Creta is a cut above the other island beaches, overlooked as it is by pristine *dammusi* houses and a holiday village.

ARRIVAL AND DEPARTURE

LAMPEDUSA

By plane Lampedusa's airport (☎ 0922 970 006) is on the edge of town, a 10min walk to Via Roma and the centre – most hotels have courtesy buses for guests. Taxis charge €10.

Destinations Catania (1 daily, 1hr); Palermo (2–4 daily; 1hr).

By ferry and hydrofoil Ferries and hydrofoils dock at Porto Vecchio; a bus meets arrivals in summer, or you can jump in a taxi. The ferry (ⓦ carontetourist.it) to Linosa/ Porto Empedocle departs daily (not Sat) at 10.15am. Liberty Lines hydrofoil (ⓦ libertylines.it) timings to Porto Empedocle change from year to year, so check the website for details.

Ferry destinations Linosa (1 daily Sun–Fri; 1hr 45min); Porto Empedocle (1 daily Sun–Fri; 7hr 45min).

GETTING AROUND

By bus The bus station is on Piazza Brignone in the centre of the town, off Via Roma. Timetables are posted, but basically there are buses every hour (roughly 8am–8pm) to Isola dei Conigli and the south coast, and to Cala Creta and the east coast.

By bike, scooter or quad It's much easier to see the whole island by renting some form of transport, either a bike (from €8 a day), scooter (from €80 per week) or a mini-moke (€40 a day) outside July and Aug. For the best deals, book in advance online from an agency like Servizi Mikael (ⓦ servizimikael.com) or Licciardi (ⓦ lampedusa-licciardi.it) – who offer a number of services, including villa rentals, boat trips and airport transfers. There are lots of rental agencies around town and harbour, or ask at your accommodation. Bike rental in particular is a great idea – you can easily do a complete circuit of the island in a day, and even in the hottest months a refreshing breeze blows constantly. You can also rent your own self-drive motorboat via Licciardi and various harbour agencies, for around €80 per day plus fuel.

INFORMATION AND TOURS

Tourist information There's online information (in Italian) at ⓦ lampedusa35.com and ⓦ lampedusa.it, while on the island you can call in at the environmental agency, Legambiente, Via Vittorio Emanuele 25 (highly erratic hours, and usually closed in winter; ☎ 0922 971 611). Some English is spoken here, and you can pick up an island sketch map and information about the nature reserve and hiking trails.

Tours Boat trips and cruises (from €30 per person for deals without lunch, from €50 per person with lunch) mostly depart from the Porto Nuovo, particularly the part of the harbour by the petrol station. Departures are usually around 10.30am, returning at 5.30pm, and options include round-island cruises with swimming stops and lunch included, or more specialist tours like dive trips to Lampione or night-fishing for squid.

Diving centres The larger hotels can all book you onto dive trips, or contact one of the operators direct; try Blue Dolphins (☎ 338 819 4489, ⓦ bluedolphins.it), Lo Verde Diving (☎ 329 178 6723, ⓦ loverdelampedusa.it), or Moby Diving Center (☎ 335 528 1984, ⓦ mobydiving.it). Single dives are €40, night dives €60, beginner scuba courses €70–90, open-water PADI dive courses €340 including equipment, and all places are open April–Nov.

ACCOMMODATION

SEE MAP PAGE 296

The season on Lampedusa runs from Easter to the end of October, and you'll generally have no problem finding a room; however in **August**, advance booking is essential and half or full board is often obligatory. There are several **hotels** in the town itself, another half a dozen within a stone's throw of the port and Spiaggia della Guitgia beach, and others just outside town and near Cala Creta.

Self-catering accommodation (usually by the week) is available either in apartments or in one of Lampedusa's stone-built *dammusi* – updated versions of the traditional dome-roofed, thick-walled shepherd's hut, typical of rural western Sicily and North Africa. *Dammusi* are found all over the island, some in village-style developments, and prices vary widely (some are very boutiquey in style) – there's

SCIACCA HARBOUR

more information from Servizi Mikael (⬚servizimikael. com), Licciardi (⬚lampedusa-licciardi.it) and Dammusi di Borgo Cala Creta (⬚calacreta.com).

Baia Turchese Via Lido Azzurro ☎0922 970 455, ⬚hotelbaiaturchese.it. This cheery four-star seaside hotel has the best location at Spiaggia della Guitgia beach, a skip across from the sands, which explains the high prices. **€180**

★**Belvedere** Piazza Marconi 4 ☎0922 970 188, ⬚lampedusahotelbelvedere.it. In town, rather than by the beach, this is a friendly, family-run place overlooking the harbour (rooms with a view cost extra), with a good panoramic dining room and terrace restaurant, to boot. It's pretty good value for most of the year. Closed Nov–Feb. **€130**

Cupola Bianca Via Madonna ☎0922 971 274, ⬚cupola biancaresort.it. A luxury outfit 2km out of town, with a North African feel and plush rooms as well as upmarket *dammusi*-style accommodation. There's a fabulous pool and terrace, plus a restaurant and all sorts of boat trips and excursions available. At least half board is required, as is the Bianca Card (€65) which includes airport transfers, beach towels and a boat trip with lunch. Closed Nov–April. Half-board doubles **€300**

Nautic Via delle Grotte ☎0922 971 531, ⬚lampedusa nautichotel.it. This chic little four-star hotel off Via Roma is the classiest town-centre choice, with only a dozen rooms and a light, stylish touch throughout. There's a decent restaurant too, with a corner terrace. **€110**

Paladini di Francia Via Alessandro Volta ☎0922 970 550, ⬚hotelpaladinidifrancia.com. A contemporary three-star resort hotel and restaurant on the harbour, close to the beach, with rooms set around bright, white courtyards, the four at the front with portside balconies. Closed Nov–Feb. **€110**

EATING

SEE MAP PAGE 296

There are lots of **restaurants** in Lampedusa town, and more around the harbours, and while prices are much higher than on most of the Sicilian mainland, the quality is largely excellent. In fact, you're unlikely to have a bad meal, given the abundance of fresh-off-the-boat fish and the exacting standards of Italian holiday-makers. Specialities available everywhere include fish couscous, grilled tuna and swordfish (often simply served with a garlic, olive oil, lemon and parsley salsa), and whole sea bream or bass baked with potatoes. At night, the whole of Via Roma is basically one long open-air **café**, with hundreds of chairs and tables spread out down the traffic-free road. Some places are more **bar** than café, with DJs and music, and it's a pretty lively scene until well into the small hours. Most cafés and restaurants close from mid-October to mid-May, but you'll find something open whenever you come.

★**Il Balenottero** Via Sbarcatoio 40 ☎0922 970 830. A lovely, genuine, family-run place near the old port that's nice and cool inside but also has an outdoor terrace. The menu is simple and the results delicious: seafood pasta, fish couscous and grilled fish, with squid, shrimp, clams, mussels, tuna, swordfish and bream depending on what the chef-fisherman, Battista, has caught that day, and most dishes are under €15. Daily lunch & dinner; closed Dec–Feb.

Bar del Amicizia Via Vittorio Emanuele 34. Not exactly a secret, but you have to know it's here to come this far down the street. Inside is a huge array of stuffed pastries, simply amazing ice cream and a dozen flavours of *granita* (from strawberry to watermelon), plus a large terrace that overlooks Lampedusa's back gardens to the sea beyond. Daily lunch & dinner; closed Nov–Easter.

★**U' Calacciuni** Spiaggia della Guitgia ☎339 435 0300. A summer-season beach-shack trattoria that's great for whiling away the hours over typical *lampedusani* dishes. There's no menu but you'll be offered pasta (say, with clams and mussels, or *con le sarde*, with sardines and wild fennel), followed by the day's catch, which might be a slab of grilled tuna with a breadcrumb and pistachio crust. You can eat a full meal with wine for around €35 a head. Daily lunch & dinner; closed Nov–April.

La Cambusa Piazza Municipio ☎0922 970 826. Down an alley just off Via Vittorio Emanuele, this cavernous underground restaurant serves good pizzas (€5–10) straight from the wood-fired oven. It's also a great place for fish (with daily dishes at dishes €10–17.50); try the pasta with scampi, tomato, garlic and parsley. Daily eves only; closed Nov–Easter.

★**Al Gallo d'Oro** Via Vittorio Emanuele 45 ☎0922 970 249. A cheerful trattoria, with seats inside and out, serving a fish and seafood menu that's a cut above most in town. Typical dishes are pasta tossed with fresh tuna, cherry tomatoes and parsley, followed by oven-roast bass with potatoes. Expect to pay €30 a head for a full meal à la carte, or go for the €25 tourist menu. Daily for lunch and dinner; closed 31 Oct–1 May.

DIRECTORY

Banks There are banks and ATMs on Via Roma.
Hospital Via Grecale, Lampedusa town (☎0922 970 604).
Pharmacy Dottore Inglisa, Via Vittorio Emanuele 35 (Mon–Sat 9am–12.45pm & 5–7.30pm, Sun 10am–noon & 6–7.30pm; ☎0922 970 195).

Police Carabinieri, Via Roma 37 (☎0922 970 001 or 112).
Post office Piazza Piave, Lampedusa town (Mon–Fri 8.20am–1pm, Sat 8.20am–12.35pm).

Linosa

Fifty kilometres north of Lampedusa, and easily visitable as a day-trip by hydrofoil, **Linosa** is basically the tip of a submerged **volcano**, with four extinct **craters** and some **lava beaches** to explore, and not much else in the way of actual sights. It's much smaller than Lampedusa (just five square kilometres), and the only **village** has just a few hundred inhabitants, rather fewer cars and a minimal road system. Some Italian families come here year after year, revelling in the peace and quiet. If you take the tracks that lead away from the brightly coloured houses on either side of the port, you can clamber around the cliffs and coves, and reach a couple of black-sand beaches with crystal-clear water. **Swimming** and **diving** here are, of course, fantastic, and there are all sorts of dive trips, courses and excursions on offer. Don't expect the island to be fully up and running until July, and be prepared for things to be winding down in September – arrive in May and you could easily be the only tourist.

ARRIVAL AND INFORMATION   LINOSA

By hydrofoil Linosa is only an hour from Lampedusa by Liberty Lines hydrofoil. Tickets cost about €19. The journey to Porto Empedocle takes 3 hours and tickets are about €44 one-way.

Ferry destinations Lampedusa (Sun–Fri 1 weekly; 1hr 45min); Porto Empedocle (1 daily Sun–Fri; 5hr 45min).

Diving Operators such as Linosa Blu Diving (☎333 965 4595, ⊛linosabludiving.it) and Terra Ferma (☎347 343 5027, ⊛terrafermadiving.it) offer all sorts of dive trips, courses and excursions.

ACCOMMODATION AND EATING

You might find **B&B rooms** offered on arrival in the summer, and restaurants and several locals let out rooms, apartments and houses. The local website ⊛linosa.biz has a few lovely little houses to rent, and there is a handful of options on Airbnb. There are half a dozen **trattorias** and bars, which open between June and September – only *Bar Dammuso* stays open all year.

Bar Dammuso Via V Alfieri 5 ☎0922 97 2195. The heart and soul of Linosa, this friendly bar is where locals gather all year round, happily joined by tourists in the summer. They have *cornetti* in the morning, and snacks such as cheese and ham or bruschetta to accompany drinks. Daily 8am–late.

Residence La Posta Vicolo Pisa 3 ☎320 601 0556 or ☎339 741 0705, ⊛linosaresidencelaposta.it. Linosa's only conventional hotel, with smartly furnished, air-conditioned rooms in the heart of the village. Closed Nov–May. **€160**

8

Trapani and the west

304 The Golfo di Castellammare

312 Segesta

313 Calatafimi

313 Trapani

318 Erice

322 North of Trapani

325 The Egadi Islands

332 Mozia and the saltpans

335 Marsala

338 Mazara del Vallo

341 Selinunte and Marinella di Selinunte

346 The interior

348 Pantelleria

ETTORE E INFERSA SALTPANS AND WINDMILLS

9 Trapani and the west

Closer to North Africa than the Italian mainland, Sicily's western reaches are traditionally poor and remote, the economy dependent on fishing and small-scale farming. Since the opening of the A29 autostrada in the 1970s, connecting it with Palermo, the region has become more integrated with the rest of Sicily, but even today, it remains very different from the rest of the island, more old-fashioned, with Mafia ways still deeply entrenched. Historically, the region has always been distinct, influenced by a strong Phoenician and Arab culture rather than the Greek and Norman traditions that prevail elsewhere in Sicily. The Arab influence can still be tasted in its food – couscous is a local favourite – and visually too, the flat land, dotted with white cubic houses, is strongly reminiscent of North Africa.

On the northern coast, the **Golfo di Castellammare** is only an hour by train or road from Palermo. Despite patches of industrial development along the gulf, it still manages to offer some empty beaches and a couple of unspoiled villages at its western end. Particularly appealing is the coastline between the old tuna-fishing village of **Scopello** and the resort of **San Vito Lo Capo**, which is part of the beautiful **Zingaro** nature reserve. The capital of the province that encompasses this entire area, **Trapani**, is a congenial port town within sight of the flat saltpans on which its wealth was based. It is also a departure point for the **Egadi Islands**, and makes a good base for visiting the mountain town of **Erice** – originally a centre of Punic influence, though diverging from the region's dominant trend in its uniform Norman and medieval character. The pattern re-establishes itself a little way down the coast at **Mozia**, Sicily's best-preserved Phoenician site, while further south the Moorish imprint is discernible in the secretive alleys and courtyards of **Marsala** and **Mazara del Vallo**.

Although the Greeks never wielded much influence in the area, the Hellenic remains at **Segesta** and **Selinunte** (Selinus) count among the island's most stunning. Between the two, the Valle del Belice delineates the region struck by an earthquake in 1968, which left a trail of destruction. This is still visible in at **Gibellina**, abandoned in its ruined state as a powerful reminder, and at the little town of **Santa Margherita di Belice**, whose once-proud palace and church were immortalized in that quintessential Sicilian novel, *The Leopard*. There could be no greater contrast to this disorder than the peaceful island of **Pantelleria**, a distant outpost just a short hop away from the African coast, mountainous and wind-blown, and adopted as a chic resort by a few high-profile glitterati.

GETTING AROUND — TRAPANI AND THE WEST

By public transport Getting around the coast is relatively straightforward, as frequent buses cover the short distances between all the towns and villages. Trains are useful for the main towns (Trapani, Marsala, Mazara del Vallo and Castelvetrano) and also for getting to Segesta. Inland, what interior bus services there are depart from Marsala or Castelvetrano.

By car Apart from the two arms of the A29 autostrada there are only two other main roads: the SS115 following the coast between Trapani and Castelvetrano, and the inland SS188 between Marsala and Salemi.

The Golfo di Castellammare

Backed by a forbidding wall of jagged mountains, the wide bowl of the **Golfo di Castellammare** is almost entirely made up of small holiday towns. Some are uncomfortably close to industrial plants, though these disappear as you progress west. The main train line from Palermo (and the SS187 road) skirts the bay from Trappeto to

THE CABLE CAR FROM TRAPANI UP TO ERICE

Highlights

❶ Riserva Naturale dello Zingaro Hike the footpaths or swim from isolated pebble coves in Sicily's loveliest nature reserve. See page 310

❷ Segesta The most romantic of all Greek sites on the island, the theatre and temple here are beautifully positioned amid rolling hills. See page 312

❸ Funierice cable car to Erice This stately ascent from Trapani to the hilltop town of Erice opens up a stunning panorama. See page 321

❹ Swimming at San Vito Lo Capo Hidden away on Sicily's northwestern tip, the idyllic beach at this appealing resort boasts a dramatic mountainous backdrop. See page 323

❺ Hiking on Marettimo Take some panoramic walks on the most remote of the Egadi Islands, and end the day with a fish supper overlooking the port. See page 331

❻ Pantelleria Though there's not a beach in sight, this craggy island en route to Tunisia still makes an enticing place to unwind. See page 348

HIGHLIGHTS ARE MARKED ON THE MAP ON PAGE 306

9

Castellammare del Golfo, but despite the ease of access and the consequent development, the resorts have not entirely shrugged off their original role as fishing villages – though they have completely lost the mean look they had when fishing was the only source of income. If you're after a beach, **Trappeto**, **Balestrate** or **Alcamo Marina** make a reasonable place to stop off, with popular summer pizzerias, fish restaurants and hotels, but there's no real reason to stay: in summer, it's just too busy, and in winter, too funereal. The train ride is stunning, hugging the coast at the base of massive wedges of rock, often of a raw red colour, echoed by smaller, weathered nuggets poking out of the sea.

Alcamo

Just inside the Trapani provincial boundary, **ALCAMO** was founded by Frederick II early in the thirteenth century. White wine of varying qualities is made from Alcamo grapes,

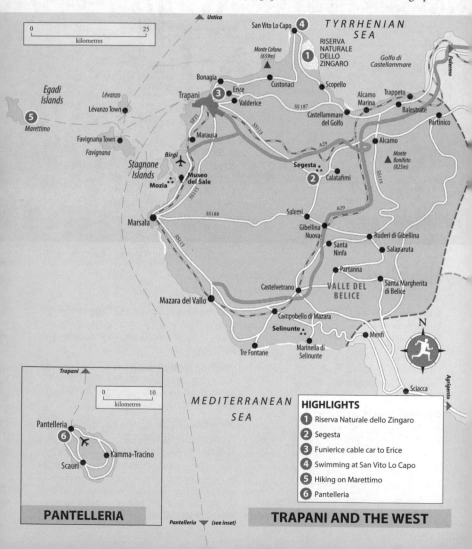

DANILO DOLCI: THE "SICILIAN GANDHI"

Today, the two villages of Trappeto and Balestrate, down on the coast northeast of Alcamo and just 5km apart (and both on the train line), display a tidy sense of well-being that's in sharp contrast to the poverty found by social reformer **Danilo Dolci** (1924–97) when he came to the region in 1952. Regarded in Sicily as something of a secular saint, Dolci was born near Trieste, and having first worked among the poor in Tuscany, he moved to Trappeto in 1952, determined to settle in "the poorest place I had ever known". His *Sicilian Lives* records his first impressions of Trappeto: "Coming from the North, I knew I was totally ignorant. Looking all around me, I saw no streets, just mud and dust. Not a single chemist – or sewer. The dialect didn't have a word for sewer." He **campaigned** tirelessly but non-violently (including by fasting and "reverse strikes") to draw attention to the local conditions, and to have a dam built outside nearby Partinico – something that was resisted at every turn by the Mafia and their political clients, who controlled the existing water supplies. Inevitably, Dolci stirred up the opposition not just of the Mafia, but of the police, the church, and – eventually – even local people, who accused him of publicity-seeking and ill-conceived campaigns, and though twice nominated for the Nobel Peace Prize, he spent the last twenty years of his life in obscurity. Today, the area presents a far more prosperous face, and the beaches on either side of Trappete and Balestrate, backed by orange groves, are regularly visited by Palermitan holiday-makers. However, this economic reversal is more a reflection of the general improvement in Sicilian standards of living during the late twentieth century than of Dolci's campaigning.

and the town, spread across a low hill with views towards the coast, has also become known thanks to the atmospheric descriptions in **Mary Taylor Simeti**'s classic memoir *On Persephone's Island* (1986), much of which is set hereabouts. Otherwise, Alcamo will mainly be of interest to fans of medieval castles: adjacent to the broad main Piazza della Repubblica, the fourteenth-century **Castello dei Conti di Modica** in Piazza Castello has a small collection of archeological scraps and farming items, as well as the headquarters of the regional wine association; the building has been closed for restoration for some time, but may have reopened by the time you read this. Alcamo also boasts some fine ecclesiastical architecture, its largely Baroque **churches** all found along and around the lengthy main street of the old town, Corso VI Aprile. The Chiesa Madre on the Corso is typical, with its bold frescoes and elaborate sculptures by members of the Gagini family.

If you have your own transport, it's worth driving up the well-signposted, corkscrew road to **Monte Bonifato** (825m), 5km south of Alcamo, for the panoramic views from the top.

ARRIVAL AND INFORMATION ALCAMO

By bus There are bus connections to Palermo with Segesta (www.segesta.it), which also operates a Trapani bus, though these are less frequent than you might hope, and they all leave before 9am. Russo Autoservizi buses (www.russoautoservizi.it) runs services to and from San Vito del Capo and Valderice.

By train The nearest train station is down on the coast at Castellammare del Golfo, from where a few buses run up to Alcamo daily.

Tourist information Alcamo's tourist office is at Via Martino Gaetano 21 (Mon–Fri 9am–1pm, with longer hours in summer, staffing permitting; ☎0924 22301).

EATING

Bar 900 Corso VI Aprile 105. Founded in 1937, this Alcamo institution has the best pastries in town – including a fabulous choice of miniature morsels – perfect for sampling everything that takes your fancy. There is also an excellent *tavola calda* at lunchtime, with a €12 set menu. The ice cream is great, as well. Mon & Wed–Sun 5am–9pm, much later in summer.

Locanda dei Matti Piazza della Repubblica 66 ☎333 233 2122. A great little place for steak, grilled meats and local, fennel-seed, spiked sausages – you choose your own steaks from the display fridge. Meats are served with little hand-written butcher labels so that you know what you are eating (or will do if you have a dictionary). As portions are huge, it's best to go straight for a main with a salad, and you can spend less than €25 a head with a dessert and house wine. Open Wed–Mon for dinner, Sun also for lunch.

9

Castellammare del Golfo

CASTELLAMMARE DEL GOLFO, on the coast about twenty minutes' drive northwest of Alcamo, is the biggest of the local fishing ports, entirely surrounded by high hills and built on and around a hefty rocky promontory that's guarded by a squat castle from which the town takes its name. Castellammare's incredible pedigree of bloodshed once gave it one of the worst reputations in Sicily for **Mafia** violence. The writer Gavin Maxwell, who lived locally during the 1950s, claimed that in that period eighty percent of the town's adult males had served prison sentences, and one in three had committed murder; coupled with this are the official statistics for the same period that classify one family in six as destitute. Needless to say, all of this is extremely hard to believe today: strolling down the sloping Corso Garibaldi towards the castle and harbour, past handsome *palazzi* interspersed with bars and shops selling beach gear, it seems a most benign place, ideal for a few days' relaxation. Originally Norman, but much remodelled in later centuries, the **castello** (Tues–Sat 9am–1pm & 3.30–7.30pm; free) contains well-presented collections dedicated to the history, archeology and maritime culture of the area.

Beneath the castle walls, on the harbourside, the row of cafés and restaurants that face the fishing boats is a nice place to kill time and eat lunch. There's a scrappy sand beach at the harbour, though you may prefer the fine sands 2km east of the centre, between the town and train station, while the coastline northwest of Castellammare is perhaps the most beautiful in the whole of Sicily, abounding in unspoiled coves and white-pebble beaches, connected by paths to the road above. The road passes **Baia di Guidaloca**, a small bay that some people believe to be the spot where Nausicaä found the naked, shipwrecked Odysseus and finally set him on the last leg of his journey home to Ithaca. Legends apart, it's a pretty beach with a stream running into the water and pleasant swimming. Away from the sea, the pinewood slopes of **Monte Inici**, accessed from the SS187 2km west of town, are a popular spot for picnics and views. They provide some relief from the summer heat, and there is a restaurant here.

ARRIVAL AND DEPARTURE
CASTELLAMMARE DEL GOLFO

By bus The bus station is in the upper part of the town on Via della Repubblica, just off Via Segesta. Regular services operated by Russo (w russoautoservizi.it) run from here to Scopello; summer services carry on to Lo Zingaro.
Destinations Alcamo (8 daily Mon–Sat; 25min); Calatafimi (5 daily Mon–Sat; 30min); Palermo (4–8 daily Mon–Sat, 1–2 daily Sun; 1hr 10min–1hr 40min); San Vito Lo Capo 1–4 daily Mon–Sat, 1–2 daily Sun; 1hr–1hr 30min);

Scopello (4–8 daily Mon–Sat, 4 daily Sun in summer only; 30min); Segesta (2 daily; 40min); Trapani (4 daily Mon–Sat; 1hr–1hr 20min).
By train The local train station is 4km east of town; a bus meets arrivals and shuttles you into Castellammare, passing the campsite on the way, and dropping off passengers at the bus station.

INFORMATION AND TOURS

Tourist information There is a little tourist office is inside the Municipio on Corso Bernardo Mattarella (Mon–Fri 9am–1pm & 4–8pm; ☎ 0924 592 111).

Tours Between June and September, there are boat tours up the coast to Zingaro and San Vito Lo Capo (€25 for full day, leaving at 10am, returning for 6.30pm; w penelopetour.it).

ACCOMMODATION

Cala Marina Via Don Leonardo Zangara 1 ☎ 0924 531 841, w hotelcalamarina.it. In a prime position right by the marina and beach, this smart, modern hotel provides a relaxed atmosphere. Ask for one of the three bright rooms with balconies and sea views (costing extra). **€90**
★ **Case d'Anna** Corso Garibaldi 120 ☎ 0924 31 101 or ☎ 320 060 6126, w casedanna.it. The large, clean rooms in this intimate, centrally located, family-run place are beautifully and meticulously decorated with Art Deco or

Victorian furnishings, and come with a/c, minibars and wi-fi. You'll pick up loads of helpful tips from the friendly host family, and breakfast includes home-made pastries. **€73**
Nonna Giò Via A. Mario 28 ☎ 334 594 1224, w sicilian elgolfo.it. Four en-suite and air-conditioned rooms are available, just up from Piazza Petrolo and the seafront. Breakfast is taken on the roof terrace. The owners also organise airport transfers, excursions by car to Segesta, boat trips, boat hire and diving (w nonnagiotranfer.it). **€75**

EATING AND DRINKING

Most of the **restaurants** around the centre of Castellammare or down by the harbour feature *cuscus a pesce* (fish couscous). The harbour is also the place for an evening stroll and **drink**, with a selection of late-opening bars.

La Cambusa Via Don Luigi Zangara 67 ☎ 0924 30 155. Very nice harbourside fish restaurant that does a lovely fish couscous, and makes all its own pasta. You can also choose your own fish (on display) to have cooked *al cartoccio* (dressed with herbs and baked in a parcel). First courses go for €8–14 and second courses €10–18. Arrive early or book for the best tables. Daily lunch & dinner.

★ **H 80 Fame** Via Marina di Petrolo 23 ☎ 0924 31629. The place in Castellammare to indulge in fish and seafood – indeed you may be tempted to make many return visits after your first lunch or dinner. Fish is super-fresh, and they really know how to cook it here – whether you opt for a classic like spaghetti with clams, or something more unusual such as local *busiate* pasta with sea urchin and pistachio. The mixed fish and seafood *antipasto* is a lunch in itself; even the simple grilled fish are superb. Primi €8–16. Daily for lunch and dinner.

Scopello

SCOPELLO, 10km northwest of Castellammare, is a tiny inland hamlet perched on a ridge a couple of hundred metres above the coastline where stands the old tuna fishery (*tonnara*) that the village once serviced. The village consists of little more than **Piazza Fontana** – a paved square and a fountain – and a couple of alleys running off it. On one side of the square sits the gateway and enclosed courtyard of the village's eighteenth-century **baglio**, or manor house, now the focus of local life. In here – centred on a huge eucalyptus tree – the courtyard buildings harbour a ceramicist's workshop, artist's studio, craft shop, a couple of bars and a pizzeria-restaurant. With the lights on and the wind rustling the leaves, it's a magical place at night, though in July and August – when every bar table is full and queues develop – you could be forgiven for wishing for more solitude. Outside high summer, traditional village life is more to the fore: men playing cards at the tables, people gossiping around the fountain and neighbours helping out in each other's fields.

Three kilometres south of Scopello, the lovely bay of **Cala Bianca** offers some great swimming; the bus from Castellammare stops here.

Tonnara di Scopello

Always open • €3 when there is a guard

Just before Scopello on the road from Castellammare, a right-hand fork will bring you after a few hundred metres down to the coast and the **Tonnara di Scopello**, set in its own tiny cove. This old tuna fishery and its associated outhouses was where the writer Gavin Maxwell lived and worked in the 1950s, basing his *Ten Pains of Death* on his experiences there. It's almost too picturesque to be true – not least the row of abandoned buildings on the quayside, fronted by lines of rusting anchors, and the ruined old watchtowers tottering on knobbly columns of rock above the sea. From the shore, it's still precisely as Maxwell described it more than fifty years ago: "a sea of purple and blue and peacock green, with a jagged cliff coastline and great *faraglioni* (rock towers) thrusting up out of the water as pinnacle islands, pale green with the growth of cactus at their heads".

The *tonnara* remained in intermittent use until the 1980s. Although it's still privately owned, the gate is always open (beverage machines inside the building) to allow visitors to wander around the quayside – provided, according to the notice, they don't bring with them a whole host of proscribed items (dogs, radios, chairs, umbrellas). An injunction like this is usually a red rag to a bull for your average Sicilian, and the place is regularly engulfed with all of the above on summer weekends – though more strictly enforced regulations may yet come into effect. Most visitors come to swim in the crystal-clear waters off the tiny shingle **beach** here. Whether or not you indulge in a dip, it's a thoroughly photogenic spot (and scenes from the film *Ocean's Twelve* were shot here).

ARRIVAL AND INFORMATION

By bus Outside July and August the bus from Castellammare drops you in Scopello's square; in the summer there are usually some buses that continue to the Zingaro entrance. Timings and frequency vary considerably from year to year, and are usually decided at the last minute, so it's best to check the website (☞ russoautoservizi.it).

Services You won't have to look far to find everything – there's an *alimentari*, a bakery, a butcher's shop and a post office, and an ATM inside the *baglio* courtyard.

ACCOMMODATION AND EATING

Scopello can be rather an exclusive retreat, given the building restrictions that limit the **accommodation** choices. Book well in advance if you want to stay here in summer, and be prepared to accept **half-board** terms in the *pensioni*. Out of season you'll be able to pick and choose, and the prices drop a little, too. All the official places to stay are within a thirty-second walk of the square – if everything is booked up, you might find **rooms to rent** by asking around in the bars and shops.

Il Baglio Baglio Isonzo 4 ☏ 0924 541 200. An extremely popular place for pizzas (€5.50–10), pastas (€10–16) and seafood dishes (€12–20), with attractive outdoor seating in the *baglio* courtyard. Eat early to avoid queues at weekends and in summer. Daily lunch & dinner; closed Nov–Feb.

La Tavernetta Via A Diaz 3 ☏ 0924 541 129, ☞ albergola tavernetta.it. Twelve very pleasant, freshly refurbished rooms, all with balconies, sea views and pretty stencilled furniture. The friendly, accommodating owners also run a restaurant (daily lunch & dinner; closed Nov–April), set in a huge garden of olives, prickly pears and citrus trees, specializing in local dishes like couscous (€10) and *spaghetti con le sarde* (€8). A hearty three-course meal with local wine runs to around €35, though you could eat for less. Half board in Aug. **€140**

La Tranchina Via A. Diaz 7 ☏ 0924 541 099, ☞ pensione tranchina.com. Simple en-suite rooms with a/c, and a friendly English-speaking owner: you'll eat well here, too, on fresh fish and interesting pasta dishes. **€100**, half board **€50–75** per person depending on season

Riserva Naturale dello Zingaro

Reserve Daily: April–Oct 9am–5pm; Nov–March 8am–4pm • €5, includes entrance to the museums • ☏ 800 116 616 or ☏ 0924 35 108, ☞ riservazingaro.it

Accessible from both Scopello and San Vito Lo Capo (see page 323), the **Riserva Naturale dello Zingaro** was the first nature reserve to be established in Sicily – in 1980 – following a successful protest to prevent a coast road being constructed from Scopello to San Vito Lo Capo. It comprises a completely unspoiled seven-kilometre-stretch of coastline backed by steep mountains, and is home to some six hundred species of **plant**. Around forty different bird species nest and mate here, including the rare Bonelli's Eagle. Apart from the wide variety of fauna and flora, there's great archeological interest in an area that supported some of Sicily's earliest prehistoric settlements.

If you are approaching the reserve from San Vito, via the **northern entrance** (**Ingresso Nord**), note that there are no shops, bars or restaurants along the road from town. There are none in the park itself either (just seasonal refreshments at the two entrances), and in summer, there is little shade, so come prepared. If you're coming from the other direction, the road from Scopello ends at **Ingresso Sud**, the **southern entrance** to the reserve, from where you can proceed on foot through pristine country and past some extremely beautiful coves and beaches. This is not exactly unknown territory, since hundreds of Palermitani descend on Scopello and its surroundings on summer weekends – but at other times – and especially out of season – it's one of the most tranquil places in Sicily. In addition, since the whole area is regulated by building restrictions that actually seem to be enforced, the water quality – and hence the swimming – is excellent. The easiest and best-maintained of the network of **paths** through the reserve keep close to the coast. Of the two main routes, the **Sentiero Alto** is best in spring for the vegetation and natural life, while the **Sentiero Basso**, hugging the shore, is best in summer if you want to stop for swims. The mid- and high-mountain routes are favoured by well-prepared walkers and ornithologists; refuges here can be used at night, so long as you book ahead through the park authority.

WALKING IN THE RISERVA ZINGARO

If you're heading off on Riserva Zingaro's coastal path, make sure you carry plenty of **water** – any water you see along the way may not be fit for drinking. There's a water fountain at the Ingresso Sud information hut and, in summer, a van selling ices and drinks. At the Ingresso Nord – the northern, San Vito Lo Capo, park entrance – you'll find another information hut, water and, in summer, refreshments. Before you decide to walk on to San Vito, 11km away, make sure you have water, as there are no facilities en route.

The Sentiero Basso

Following the **Sentiero Basso** from the southern entrance, it takes under twenty minutes to reach the first beach, **Cala Capreria**, which can be crowded at weekends and in July and August. When it's not, it's perfect: a tiny cove of white pebbles, azure water, shoals of little fish nibbling at the edge and baby squid darting in and out. A small **Museo Naturalistico** and visitor centre stand just above the beach. Further up the coast, another twenty minutes or so onwards, there's a museum above **Cala del Varo** dedicated to manna and the flowering manna-ash, examples of which grow hereabouts.

Stick with the coastal path (the *sentiero basso*) and it's 3km from the southern entrance to the successive coves of **Disa**, **Berretta** and **Marinella**, which should be a little more secluded. The next cove, **Cala dell'Uzzo**, holds a museum of rural life, while the **Cala Tonnarella dell'Uzzo**, 7km from the southern entrance, has a museum of fishing and other marine activity.

The northern entrance

The northern entrance to the reserve (Ingresso Nord) is accessible by car or on a boat trip from San Vito Le Capo. It also makes a fine, if lengthy, walk from from San Vito (11km); follow the road along the lungomare from San Vito and across the flat headland, before winding up into the mountains. The views are exhilarating, with the surrounding scenery almost alpine in character – fir trees, flowers edging the road, and the clank of bells from goats roaming the hillsides. Sadly, though, the road through this secluded and dramatic landscape offers few opportunities to descend to the alluringly deserted coves below.

The **access road** to the reserve is signposted just before the ruined Torre dell'Impiso. From the sign to the park entrance itself is about another 1km, following a gravel track and then a path, which runs down into the reserve, past the Tonnara dell'Uzzo. The beautiful little **cove-beach** below the entrance offers translucent water, with glorious peace and quiet all around – at least, whenever the first few little creeks here aren't inundated with bathers. Travel on for less crowded spots, or else take one of the higher paths for greater isolation. Scopello is a ten-kilometre walk south from the San Vito entrance.

ARRIVAL AND INFORMATION   RISERVA NATURALE DELLO ZINGARO

By bus Russo buses runs a summer-only service from Castellammare del Golfo to the southern entrance; timings and frequencies vary from year to year.

Tourist information There are information huts at the Ingresso Sud and Ingresso Nord entrances. You can pick up a simple map showing the trails through the reserve – though, as it's not entirely accurate, it should be treated with some scepticism.

Boat tours and diving The waters offshore of the reserve have some excellent dive sites, with wrecks and grottoes to explore; Cetaria, Via Marco Polo 3, Scopello (☎ 368 386 4808, ⓦ cetaria.it), offers dives to natural sites and WW2 shipwrecks, boat excursions and equipment rental.

ACCOMMODATION

★ **Baglio La Luna** Via del Secco 11 ☎ 335 836 2856, ⓦ bagliolaluna.com. Seven kilometres out of San Vito on the Zingaro road, making it ideal for forays into the reserve, this rural B&B boasts lofty views from its terrace and complete tranquillity. The airy, whitewashed interior with tiled floors has five simple rooms – some with sea views. You'll need your own transport to stay here, and there's a two-night minimum stay in Aug. Closed Nov–March. **€120**

9

Casale Corcella Contrada Scardina ☎ 368 365 4482, ⓦ casalecorcella.com Ideal for walkers, this friendly, family-run B&B is located 1km north of Scopello, within the Zingaro reserve. It has five simple, cheerful and spotlessly clean rooms. Closed Nov–March. **€68**

Segesta

Set amid deserted green countryside around 15km south of Castellammare del Golfo (and 30km east of Trapani), the remains of the ancient city of **Segesta** are among the most inspiring on the island. All that still stands is a Doric temple and a brilliantly sited **theatre**, relics of a city whose roots – like Erice's – lie back in the twelfth century BC. Unlike Erice, though, ancient Segesta was eventually Hellenized and spent most of the later period disputing its border with Selinus. The temple dates from a time of prosperous alliance with Athens, but it was never finished – work on it was abandoned when a new dispute broke out with Selinus in 416 BC.

Apart from the small café and shop at the site, the café-restaurant near the signposted turn-off is the only nearby place for **refreshments**. **Concerts and plays**, including **Greek tragedies and comedies,** are staged at Segesta's theatre between mid-July and early September (ⓦ calatafimisegestafestival.it). Tickets kick off at €23.

The site

Daily 9am–1hr before sunset; last entry 1hr before closing • €6 • Half-hourly shuttle buses (€1.50) run from the site entrance to the theatre • Parking €5 plus free shuttle to ticket office

The site is best seen early or late in the day, when visitors are fewer and the light less blanching in its effect. The **temple** itself, started in 424 BC, crowns a low hill beyond the café and car park. From a distance you could be forgiven for thinking that it's complete: the 36 regular stone columns, entablature and pediment are all intact, and all it lacks is a roof. However, get closer (and for once you're allowed to roam right inside) and you see just how unfinished the building really is: stone studs, always removed on completion, still line the stylobate, the tall columns are unfluted, and the cella walls are missing. In a way, this only adds to the natural grandeur of the site, and it's not too fanciful to imagine that the pitted and sun-bleached temple simply grew here – a feeling bolstered by the birds nesting in the unfinished capitals, the lizards scampering over the pale yellow stone, and, in spring, the riot of flowers underfoot.

From the main entrance, a road winds up through slopes of wild fennel to a small **theatre** on a higher hill beyond; if you don't relish the twenty-minute climb you can use the bus service. The view from the top is terrific, across green slopes and the plain to the sea, the deep blue of the bay a lovely contrast to the theatre's white stone – the panorama not much damaged by the motorway snaking away below.

Behind the theatre, **excavations** (explained by information boards) have revealed the foundations of a mosque and Arab-style houses. These were pulled down in the thirteenth century when a Norman castle was erected on the high ground – though this itself lasted fewer than a hundred years, as political forces on the island waxed and waned. There are also the remains of a late medieval church, built for local shepherds and landholders and used, in one form or another, until the nineteenth century. Thus it is a site of enormous significance and utility, spanning generations.

ARRIVAL AND DEPARTURE SEGESTA

By bus Tarantola buses run direct to Segesta from Piazza Malta in Trapani, usually leaving at 8am, 10am, noon & 2pm (Sun 10am only), returning at 12.50pm, 1.05pm, 4.05pm & 6.30pm (Sun 1.05pm only). There are also less frequent bus services from Castellammare del Golfo and Palermo.

By car If you're driving, it's easiest to see the site en route between Palermo and Trapani, since it lies just off the motorway.

Calatafimi

Defended by a castle (hence the Arabic *kalat* of its name), whose remnants top a wooded hill, **CALATAFIMI** gained fame as the site of the first of Garibaldi's victories against the Bourbon forces in 1860, which opened the way to Palermo and hence the rest of Sicily. The battle took place on the Salemi road, around 1km south of Calatafimi and then 3km up a hill, the summit marked by a white obelisk. It's signposted "Ossario di Pianto Romana", and named as such because the bones of the fallen from the battle are collected here. They used to be on display in cases for the edification of the local population; now they're hidden behind commemorative tablets underneath an Italian flag. The custodian might attempt an explanation of the history if your Italian is up to it – a tip wouldn't go amiss. The views outside, to Calatafimi itself, Erice and the Castellammare gulf, are magnificent.

ARRIVAL AND DEPARTURE   CALATAFIMI

By bus Calatafimi lies 4km south of its train station, so it's better to come by bus – there are four services daily from Trapani.

ACCOMMODATION AND EATING

Mille Pini Piazza F. Vivona 2 ✆ 0924 951 260, ⓦ hotel millepini.com. An old-fashioned hotel in a 1960s building which has ten basic rooms with balconies and valley views, and a restaurant where you can eat well for around €15 – overall, it's a very nice place for a quiet night in the sticks. **€50**

Trapani

Although predominantly modern, **TRAPANI**, the first of three major towns on Sicily's western edge, has an elegant old centre that's squeezed into a narrow arm of land pointing out to sea. Lent an end-of-the-line feel by its port, the town's inconspicuous monuments give no great impression of its long history. Nonetheless, Trapani flourished as a Phoenician **trading centre** and as the port for Eryx (modern Erice), profiting from its position looking out towards Africa. As an important stopover on the sea routes linking Tunis, Naples and Aragon, the town played an enduring role throughout the Middle Ages, when Europe's crowned heads virtually passed each other on the quayside. The Navarrese king Theobald died here of typhoid in 1270; two years later, Edward I of England touched down after a Crusade to learn he'd inherited the throne, while Peter of Aragon arrived in 1282 to claim the Sicilian throne, following the expulsion of the Angevin French. The city's growth over the last century has been founded on the development of salt, fishing and wine industries, though severe bombardment during World War II has given rise to an excess of dull postwar building around the outskirts.

Still, as a **base** for the rest of the west, Trapani can't be beaten. It offers a good few accommodation possibilities, mostly in the old-town area; regular trains south to nearby Marsala and Mazara del Vallo; buses to Erice, the resort of San Vito Lo Capo and the more distant site of Segesta; and the nearest of the Egadi Islands is only twenty minutes away by hydrofoil. The only time when you might find a room hard to come by is during the procession of the **Misteri** at Easter (see page 315).

The old town

Almost everything of interest in Trapani is found in the **old town**, west of the Villa Margherita gardens. Churches and palaces have been renovated in recent years, and a plethora of bars and restaurants has opened along stylish pedestrianized streets – notably Corso Vittorio Emanuele, Via Torrearsa and Via Garibaldi, and the northern seafront, above a long beach, has been considerably smartened up. However, away from here,

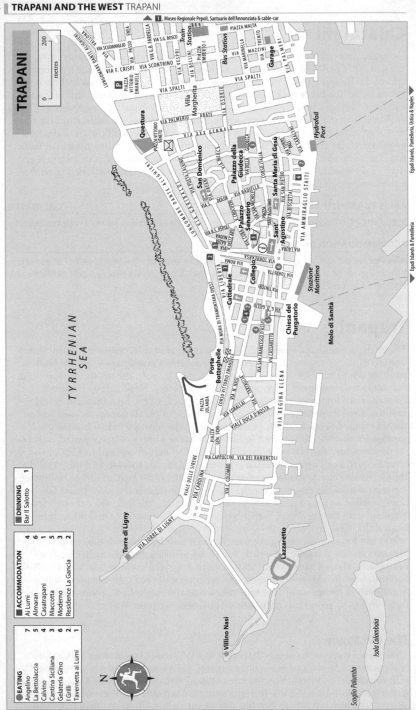

TRAPANI

▲ 1, Museo Regionale Pepoli, Santuario dell'Annunziata & cable-car

T Y R R H E N I A N   S E A

EATING
Angelino	7
La Bettolaccia	5
Calvino	4
Cantina Siciliana	3
Gelateria Gino	6
I Grilli	2
Tavernetta ai Lumi	1

ACCOMMODATION
Ai Lumi	4
Almaran	6
Casatrapani	1
Maccotta	5
Moderno	3
Residence La Gancia	2

DRINKING
Bar Il Salotto	1

Egadi Islands, Pantelleria, Ustica & Naples ▶

Egadi Islands & Pantelleria ▶

TRAPANI'S MISTERI

One of Sicily's most evocative religious processions, held since the seventeenth century, takes place in Trapani at Easter, when the **Misteri**, extraordinary life-sized wooden statues depicting scenes from the Passion, are carried shoulder-high through the streets on Good Friday. The procession through the town takes ten hours, starting at 2pm and finishing back at the **Chiesa del Purgatorio** at midnight. Sculpted from cypress wood and cork in the eighteenth century, each of the twenty groups of chocolate-brown figures is associated with one of the town's trades – fishermen, metalworkers, saltworkers, and so on – whose representatives undertake to maintain them and, draped in cowls and purple robes, annually parade them. The rest of the time the statues are kept in the **Chiesa del Purgatorio**, on Via Francesco d'Assisi, south of the main Corso. The church is usually locked, but when it's open, there should be a priest around to explain which of the trades is responsible for each of the sculpted groups, and what the particular figures represent – though most of the scenes are familiar enough. When it's closed, you can arrange admission at the Cattedrale office.

Note that this is a very popular time to visit Trapani, so be sure to **book accommodation** well in advance.

there's still a scruffy, salty-old-port air to much of Trapani, its stark cubic houses, dusty streets and wind- and sun-thrashed palms more redolent of North Africa than Italy.

Corso Vittorio Emanuele

The old town is most elegant along **Corso Vittorio Emanuele**, the pedestrianized main street, dominated at its eastern end by the pinkish marble front of the **Palazzo Senatorio**, the seventeenth-century town hall. With its twin clocks separated by an imperious eagle, it adds a touch of grandeur to the thin promenading strip, otherwise hemmed in by balconied *palazzi*, a couple of Baroque churches, and the **Cattedrale** on the right, with its Baroque portico, cupolas and vast interior. Dedicated to San Lorenzo, it has a *Crucifixion* inside, in the fourth chapel on the right, attributed to Van Dyck.

Changing its name along the way, the Corso runs almost to the end of the curving promontory from which the town took its Phoenician name of Drepanon (sickle). At its very tip is the **Torre di Ligny**, a squat Spanish fortification dating from 1671, now privately owned, but a good spot for a sit-down with a sandwich. On the way back into town, a walk down the north side of the promontory will show you what's left of the medieval city wall, the *bastione*, breached by the thirteenth-century **Porta Botteghelle**.

Via Torrearsa

Back at the eastern end of Corso Vittorio Emanuele, **Via Torrearsa** is one of the old town's main shopping streets. At its southern end, the church of **Sant'Agostino** on Piazzetta Saturno boasts a pretty fourteenth-century rose window of interlocking stone bands; the church is occasionally used as a concert hall (details of performances from the tourist office). Architecturally more appealing is the sixteenth-century church of **Santa Maria di Gesù**), just to the east of Via Torrearsa, on Via San Pietro, whose two doors display a diversity characteristic of the town, the right-hand one Gothic, the other defiantly Renaissance.

The Jewish quarter

There's little more to see in this part of town apart from a few unusual facades, one of them buried in the wedge of hairline streets and alleys north of Corso Italia, at Via della Giudecca 43, where the sixteenth-century **Palazzo della Giudecca** sports a plaque-studded front and some Spanish-style Plateresque windows. The building lies at the heart of Trapani's old **Jewish quarter**, an area dating from Trapani's medieval heyday at

9

the centre of Mediterranean trade. From here, it's not far to the **Villa Margherita**, the shady town gardens; concerts are staged here in summer (information available from the tourist office).

Santuario dell'Annunziata

Via Conte Agostino Pepoli 180 • Daily 8am–noon & 4–8pm, closes 7pm in winter • Free • ☎ 0923 55 3269

The main point of interest in Trapani's somewhat dull modern city is the lavishly decorated **Santuario dell'Annunziata**, a fourteenth-century convent and church, whose cloisters incorporate the town's main museum. The sanctuary was rebuilt in 1760 and only the facade, with its Gothic portal and magnificent rose window, is original. Inside you'll find a series of sumptuous chapels, two dedicated to Trapani's fishermen and seamen – one echoes the facade's shell motif around the sides of the room – and, best of all, the Cappella della Madonna, containing Trapani's sacred idol: the beautiful, smiling Madonna and Child, attributed to Nino Pisano in the fourteenth century. Responsible for a host of miracles, the statue is housed beneath a grandiose marble canopy sculpted by Antonello Gagini and surrounded by polychrome marble – as well, generally, as a crowd of hushed worshippers.

Museo Regionale Pepoli

Adjacent to the Santuario dell'Annunziata, entrance via the Villa Pepoli park • Tues–Sat 9am–5pm, Sun 9am–noon • €6

The wide-ranging collection at the **Museo Regionale Pepoli** takes in everything from exemplary Gagini statuary to seventeenth-century coral craftwork. Highlights downstairs include a little bronze **horse and rider** by Giacomo Serpotta and a sixteenth-century marble **doorway** by Berrettaro Bartolomeu, taken from the old church of San Giuliano, which, though badly worn in parts, displays a lively series of tableaux. Downstairs, too, bizarrely, is a grim wooden guillotine from 1789, with a basket for the head and a coffin at the ready. The museum houses a good **medieval art** section – including the powerful *Pietà* by Roberto Oderisio, and a couple of fine fifteenth-century triptychs by the anonymous *Maestro del Polittico di Trapani*. Other displays include a **coin collection**, with Greek, Roman, Arab and Italian examples; an eighteenth-century majolica-tiled scene of **La Mattanza** (tuna slaughter), with the fishermen depicted corralling the fish in their boats; a small **archeological section** with a few finds from Selinunte and Mozia, though nothing outstanding, and some intricate **coral work**, including crib scenes with alabaster and shell decoration.

ARRIVAL AND DEPARTURE

TRAPANI

By plane Trapani's airport, 15km south of the centre at Birgi, has flights to and from several Italian cities, and Lampedusa and Pantelleria (1–3 daily; 40min). Buses (run by Segesta and AST) call at Trapani port and Trapani station. If you're picking up the bus at the port, tickets need to be bought before boarding from the Egatour agency, across the road from the bus stop at Via Amm. Stati 13 (daily 5.30am–8pm; ☎ 0923 21 754, ⊕ egatourviaggi.it). Top Transfer (☎ 0923 27 899 or ☎ 337 896 010, ⊕ toptransfer.it) offers airport shuttles as well as longer-distance transfers.

By train Trains stop at the Stazione Centrale, just around the corner from the bus station and a short walk along Via Garibaldi from the old town.

Destinations Castelvetrano (13 daily Mon–Sat, 5 daily Sun; 1hr 10min); Marsala (13 daily Mon–Sat, 5 daily Sun; 30min); Mazara del Vallo (13 daily Mon–Sat, 5 daily Sun; 40min–1hr); Palermo (4 daily; 4hr–4hr30min).

By bus Most buses (including those to and from Erice) pull up at the terminal in Piazza Malta. If you're heading straight off to the Egadi Islands, note that the fast buses from the airport, Palermo, Palermo airport and Agrigento stop at the ferry and hydrofoil terminals, as well as the bus station.

Destinations from Trapani Agrigento (3 daily Mon–Sat, 1 daily Sun; 3hr 10min–3hr 40min); Alcamo (2–3 daily Mon–Sat; 1hr); Bonagia (7 daily Mon–Sat, 2 daily Sun in summer; 25min); Castellammare del Golfo (4 daily; 1hr–1hr 20min); Erice (7 daily Mon–Sat, 4 daily Sun; 45min); Marsala (3 daily Mon–Sat; 45min); Mazara del Vallo (3 daily Mon–Sat; 1hr 30min); Palermo (1–2 hourly Mon–Sat, 14 daily Sun; 2hr); Palermo airport (4 daily; 1hr); San Vito Lo Capo (8 daily Mon–Sat, 4 daily Sun in summer; 1hr 20min); Segesta (4 daily Mon–Sat, 1 daily Sun; 50min); Trapani airport (1–2 hourly; 20–40min).

Destinations from Trapani airport Agrigento (3 daily

BUS COMPANIES IN TRAPANI

S. Lumia ☎0922 20 414, ⓦautolineelumia.it. Departures from Piazza Malta and Trapani airport for Agrigento and Sciacca.
Segesta ☎091 342 525, ⓦsegesta.it. Departures from Piazza Garibaldi for Alcamo, Palermo and Palermo airport.

Salemi ☎0923 981 120, ⓦautoservizisalemi.it. Departures from Trapani airport for Marsala and Palermo.
Tarantola ☎0924 31 020. Departures from Piazza Malta for Segesta.

Mon–Sat, 1 daily Sun; 2hr 45min–3hr 20min); Marsala (1–4 daily Mon–Sat, 2 daily Sun; 15min); Palermo (6–8 daily; 2hr 10min); Trapani (1–2 hourly; 20–40min).
By ferry and hydrofoil Ferries for the Egadi Islands and Pantelleria dock at the Molo di Sanità, while hydrofoils for the Egadi Islands, Ustica and Naples dock to the east of the Molo, on Via A. Stati. The frequencies given below are year-round. Services are usually more frequent between June 20 and September 10.
Ferry and hydrofoil companies Caronte Tourist ferries (☎0923 031 911, ⓦcarontetourist.it) sail to the Egadi

Islands and Pantelleria; and Liberty Lines ones (☎347 873 4219, ⓦlibertylines.it) to the Egadi Islands, Pantelleria and (usually summer only) Ustica.
Ferry destinations Favignana (1–2 daily; 1hr–1hr 25min); Lévanzo (1–2 daily; 50min–1hr 40min); Marettimo (1 daily; 2hr 35min–2hr 50min); Pantelleria (6 weekly; 5hr 45min).
Hydrofoil destinations Favignana (roughly hourly; 15–40min); Lévanzo (11 daily; 20–40min); Marettimo (4 daily; 1hr); Naples (1 on Sat June–Sept; 7hr); Ustica (1 on Sat usually June–Sept; 2hr 30min).

GETTING AROUND

By bus Everything in the old town is easily reachable on foot, though you'll need to catch a city bus to visit Trapani's museum, in the new part of the city: most routes depart from Piazza Vittorio Emanuele. Tickets are available from *tabacchi*, and are valid for one hour.

By taxi During the day, taxis usually wait outside the train station – just make sure they switch on the meter, or you could be in for a nasty surprise. If you need to call a taxi, try ☎392 851 7798 (24hr).

TOURS

Tours Egatour, Via Amm. Stati 13 (daily 5.30am–8pm; ☎0923 21 754, ⓦegatourviaggi.it), runs boat tours to

Favignana and Lévanzo (€40) and to Zingaro (€25), as well as a fascinating bus tour of the nearby salt flats (€15).

ACCOMMODATION   SEE MAP PAGE 314

Ai Lumi Corso Vittorio Emanuele 71 ☎0923 540 922, ⓦailumi.it. Five small, but pristine, rooms entered through a flower-filled courtyard. In summer, street-facing rooms can be noisy. **€88**
Almaran Via San Cristoforo 8 ☎0923 549 847 or ☎349 611 0211, ⓦalmaran.it. A clean and pretty B&B close to the hydrofoil port; rooms have private bathrooms and a/c. The English-speaking owner is friendly and helpful, but breakfasts are basic. **€65**
Casatrapani Via Livio Bassi 196 ☎333 532 2010, ⓦcasatrapani.it. In the modern town, but just a 10min walk from the station, this friendly B&B offers great rates, a pick-up from the airport or station, clean, colour-themed en-suite rooms with a/c, and the use of a kitchen with a washing machine. They also have several small, self-contained apartments. Double room **€60**, apartments **€150**

Maccotta Via degli Argentieri 4 ☎0923 28 418, ⓦalbergomaccotta.it. A smart and friendly B&B behind the Palazzo Senatorio. The spacious, modern rooms have comfortable beds and a/c, but bathrooms are small, and it can be noisy. **€55**
Moderno Via Ten. Genovese 20 ☎0923 21 247, ⓦhotel moderno.trapani.it. As you might imagine, the *Moderno* is no such thing, though it does have more character than some, housed in an old *palazzo* with a courtyard where limited parking is available. The simple rooms have a/c and some have little balconies over the street. Breakfast €5. **€60**
Residence La Gancia Piazza Mercato del Pesce ☎0923 438 060, ⓦlagancia.com. Smart, if slightly sterile, contemporary rooms, a great roof terrace (where breakfast is served) and a superb position on the northern seafront right above the town beach at the head of Via Torrearsa. Doubles **€170**

EATING AND DRINKING   SEE MAP PAGE 314

Eating out in Trapani is a real treat – you can get fresh fish and couscous almost everywhere, while the local pasta speciality, *alla trapanese*, is terrific – either spaghetti or

home-made *busiate* (long, thick twists of pasta) served with a pesto of fresh tomato, basil, garlic and almonds. There are quite a few lively **bars** around, good for breakfast

9

and snacks, and bustling at night with people stopping off from the clamorous *passeggiata* that fills Via Torrearsa and the bottom end of Corso Vittorio Emanuele.

★**Angelino** Via Ammiraglio Staiti 87 ☎0923 26 922. Examine the mouthwatering displays in this no-frills *pasticceria/tavola calda*, take a ticket, order at the bar and grab a table in the conservatory. You're spoiled for choice – involtini of aubergine rolled around *spaghettini*, stuffed sardines, rosemary-roast potatoes, lasagne and focaccia, all at extremely reasonable prices. Wine by the glass and coffee and delicious *dolci* to follow, if you can manage it. You can eat very heartily for €15, including wine. Tues–Sun for lunch & dinner.

★**La Bettolaccia** Via Gen. Enrico Fardella 25 ☎0923 25932. Popular with locals, this informal but sophisticated *osteria* is known for its excellent pasta dishes – wonderful spaghetti with red prawns, cherry tomatoes and almonds, and *busiate alla trapanese* or with smoked cheese and sun-dried tomatoes are both lovely. Delicious desserts include *parfait al pistacchio*. Expect to pay €35–45 per head, including good local wine. Book, or arrive early. Mon–Fri lunch & dinner, Sat & Sun dinner only.

★**Calvino** Via N. Nasi 72 ☎0923 21 464. This backstreet pizzeria, with Moorish-style cubbyhole rooms, is a bit rough-and-ready, but well worth a visit. The tasty pizzas come in four sizes, from *Piccola* (€3.50–6) to *Tripla* (€14–17), cut into bite-sized pieces and served on squares of greaseproof paper. Try the *Rianata*, a local speciality made with fresh oregano, tomato, garlic, anchovies and pecorino cheese; or a hearty plate of sausages and potatoes roasted with onions in the pizza oven, best washed down with cold beer. Book for a table, or be prepared to take away or queue. Cash only. Wed–Mon 7pm–midnight.

Cantina Siciliana Via della Giudecca 32 ☎0923 28 673. This cosy restaurant with blue-tiled walls is a great spot for a romantic dinner, though service can be a bit slow. The menu features traditional Sicilian dishes, as well as fish couscous, and desserts include a sublime lemon ice cream with limoncello. You can eat well with a glass of house wine for €30. Daily lunch & dinner.

Gelateria Gino Piazza dalla Chiesa ☎0923 21 104. Make a beeline here for excellent ice cream and *frullati*, from kiwi to coconut, and grab a table in the piazza. Daily 9am–2.30pm & 3.30pm–late.

★**I Grilli** Corso Vittorio Emanuele 69 ☎0923 20 663, 🌐igrillibraceria.it. Several cuts above your average Trapani eatery, *I Grilli* focuses on simple, carefully sourced, high-quality grilled meats, along with an eclectic menu of French and Italian cheeses and hams, and over 150 wines. Even the mixed bruschetta is a gastronomic experience. Cheese and ham plates from €9, grilled meats €8–18, salads and grilled veg from €6. April–Oct daily for dinner only; Nov–March Mon–Tues & Thurs–Sun dinner only.

Tavernetta ai Lumi Corso Vittorio Emanuele 71–77 ☎0923 872 418. This long-established restaurant occupies the brick-vaulted stables of an old palace – and there's a shady outdoor terrace for summer dining. A typical meal from the regional menu might be home-made pasta with zucchini and shrimp, followed by a seafood stew or braised rabbit, and the wine list features good Sicilian wines. It's not cheap – you could easily spend €45 a head, including wine, but it is full of atmosphere. Mon & Wed–Sun lunch & dinner.

Bar Il Salotto Via Garibaldi 1, cnr Via Torrearsa ☎349 456 3480. This is a nice setting for an evening aperitivo, with seats outside on Via Garibaldi, but don't bother eating here. Daily 7am–4am; closes earlier in summer.

DIRECTORY

Banks There are banks with ATMs on Piazza Umberto I, Corso Italia, Via Garibaldi and at the Stazione Marittima.

Hospital Ospedale S. Antonio Abate, Via Cosenza (☎0923 809 111).

Pharmacies Marini, Corso Vittorio Emanuele 117; Occhipinti, Corso Italia 67 (both Mon–Sat 8.30am–1.30pm & 4.30–8pm).

Police Questura at Piazza Vittorio Veneto (☎0923 598 111); Carabinieri, Via Orlandini (☎0923 330 000).

Post office At Piazza Vittorio Veneto, at the bottom of Via Garibaldi. Mon–Fri 8.20am–7.05pm, Sat 8.20am–12.35pm.

Erice

Despite being just a brief hop from Trapani and the coast, **ERICE** couldn't be further away in spirit. It's a walled mountain town – around 750m above sea level – thoroughly medieval, with its creeping hillside alleys, grey-stone buildings and silent charm, but boasting a truly ancient lineage. Nowadays, it's a centre for scientific conferences, and you're likely to see numbers of foreigners with labels on their lapels among the milling tourists.

Though there are enough cobbled alleys and quiet spots to enable you to avoid the tour groups, the constant tourist presence in this small town can be wearisome – especially in

9

August, when the streets are busy until late at night, as trippers and sojourners negotiate the polished cobblestones. **Easter** is another popular time to visit Erice, when the **Misteri** sculptures representing the Stations of the Cross are paraded through the streets on Good Friday. But the greatest pleasure here is simply to wander around. You'll soon get lost in the town's winding alleys, but the most convoluted of routes is only going to take a couple of hours, and every aspect is delightful. Square and solid from the outside, the houses hide pretty courtyards, and while most of the churches are locked, there's usually something to admire – a carved door, a cupola or a belltower. The only modern blots in the town's otherwise homogeneous aspect are the pylons that tower above the grey walls. Beyond these, the views from Erice's terraces are superb, taking in Trapani, the Egadi Islands and even (allegedly) distant Cap Bon in Tunisia.

Brief history

Founded by Elymians, who claimed descent from the Trojans, the city was known to the ancient world as **Eryx**. A magnificent temple, dedicated to Aphrodite Erycina, Mediterranean goddess of fertility, once topped the mountain and was big enough to act as a landmark to sailors. According to legend, it was here that **Daedalus** landed, (unlike his son Icarus who flew too near the sun), after fleeing from Minos; he presented the temple with a honeycomb made of gold as his gift to the goddess. Even though the city was considered impregnable, Carthaginian, Roman, Arab and Norman armies all forced entry over the centuries, but all respected the town's sanctity, the Romans rebuilding the temple and setting two hundred soldiers to serve as guardians of the shrine. Later, the Arabs renamed the town Gebel-Hamed, "Mohammed's mountain", while Count Roger called it **Monte San Giuliano**, a name that stuck until Mussolini returned its ancient moniker in 1934.

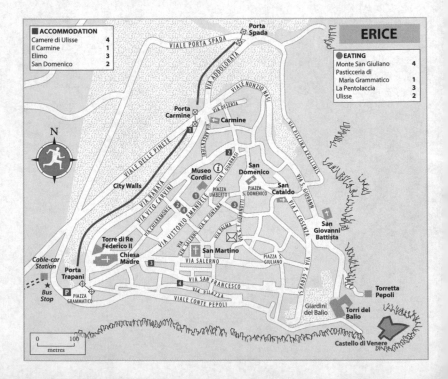

THE FUNIERICE CABLE CAR TO ERICE

Even if it weren't the quickest means to reach Erice – far more convenient than driving or catching a bus – the **Funierice cable car** (*funivia*) ride from Trapani would be worth the excursion. In fact the ascent, which takes about twelve minutes, constitutes one of the region's most memorable experiences, revealing a gradually expanding panorama that extends over the flat saltpans to the south, the mountainous coast north, and out over the narrow limb that holds the old city to the Egadi Islands and the blue sea beyond. By night, the scene is very different, with Trapani's lights sparkling under a starry sky.

From the Trapani terminal on Via Caserta, **departures** are continuous (Mon 1–8pm, Tues–Fri 8.10am–8pm, Sat 10am–9pm, Sun 10am–8pm; ⓦ funiviaerice.it), with tickets costing €5.50 one-way, €9 return. Note that the service may be cancelled if it's windy, in which case you'll have to take the AST bus from the stop on Via G.B. Fardella. Check whether the service is operating on ⓣ 0923 569 306.

Driving to the cable-car station on Via Caserta, at the extreme eastern end of the modern city, is not straightforward: from the old centre, follow Via G.B. Fardella east, bear left at Corso Mattarella, keep straight along this and its continuation Via Manzoni (following signs for Erice), and turn left at the end into Via Fratelli Aiuto, from which it's a right turn into Via Caserta and the large car park. It's simpler **by bus**: take #21 or #23 from Piazza Vittorio Emanuele (direction Ospedale S. Antonio Abbate) and get off at the stop before the hospital, from where the cable car station is a short walk.

Chiesa Madre

Daily: March 10am–4pm; April–June & Oct 10am–6pm; July & Aug 10am–8pm; Sept 10am–7pm; Nov–Feb 10am–12.30pm • Tower €5

Just inside the Norman **Porta Trapani**, at the southwestern edge of town, is the battered stone **Chiesa Madre**. It dates from around 1314, though the massive Gothic entrance was added a century later and much of the structure was rebuilt in the nineteenth century. The neo-Gothic interior preserves some exceptional lace-like **carving**.

The church's stout, battlemented campanile owes its name, **Torre di Re Federico II**, to its original role as a lookout tower for Frederick III of Aragon (Frederick II of Sicily), who made Erice his base during the Wars of the Vespers. Climb to the top for sublime views over village, mountains and sea.

Museo Cordici

April & May daily 10am–6pm; June to mid-July & mid-Sept to end Oct daily 10am–7pm; mid-July to mid-Sept daily 10am–8pm; Nov–March by appointment only Sat & Sun 10am–4pm (call ⓣ 346 577 3550) • €4

From Porta Trapani, the main Via Vittorio Emanuele climbs steeply past houses, shops and *pasticcerie* to the pretty **Piazza Umberto I**, where café tables are strewn adventurously across the sloping cobbles. The small **Museo Cordici** here boasts a good *Annunciation* by Antonello Gagini, and the pick of the local archeological finds. Further north, the medieval **Porta Carmine** marks the other end of town, from where the line of ancient **city walls** leads back to the Chiesa Madre.

Castello di Vénere

April–Oct daily 10am–1hr before sunset; Nov–March Sat & Sun 10am–4pm • €4

A natural start or finish to an exploration of Erice is the ivy-clad **Castello di Vénere** at the far end of town; the Norman castle was built on the site of the famed ancient temple, chunks of which are incorporated in the walls. When it's fine, the **views** from the terraces of Erice are phenomenal – over Trapani and the slumbering whales of the Egadi Islands.

9

Giardini del Balio and around

Below the Castello di Venere are the **Giardini del Balio** public gardens, in the middle of which sits a restored fifteenth-century tower, the **Torretta Pépoli**. From here, you can wind towards Piazza Umberto I, perhaps passing clifftop **San Giovanni Battista** and its distinctive dome before eventually negotiating the minuscule **Piazza San Domenico**, whose church and palace facade are among the town's most harmonious sights.

ARRIVAL AND INFORMATION   ERICE

By cable car The easiest way to get to Erice fom Trapani is the cable car (see box page 321).

By bus Buses from Trapani (5 daily Mon–Sat, 2 daily Sun; 45min) stop outside the Porta Trapani by the cable-car terminal.

By car From Trapani, it's a twisty half-hour's drive. Leave your car in the car park outside the Porta Trapani – don't even think of driving into the old town.

ACCOMMODATION   SEE MAP PAGE 320

Staying the night in Erice is relatively expensive, and in summer, or at Easter and Christmas, you'd do well to book in advance. If you stay in the old town it's best to park outside Porta Trapani and carry your luggage up. The other option is to stay in Valderice (see page 323), a 20min drive back down the mountain.

Camere di Ulisse Via S. Lucia 2 ☎0923 860 155 or ☎389 985 6089, ⓦsitodiulisse.it. Nicely furnished rooms dispersed over two buildings, with private bathrooms. The most evocative are grouped around a tranquil central courtyard. €65

Il Carmine Piazza del Carmine 23 ☎0923 869 089 or ☎0923 194 1532, ⓦilcarmine.com. Spacious, bright

rooms, with separate private bathrooms, in a former Carmelite convent in the heart of town. €84

Elimo Via Vittorio Emanuele 75 ☎0923 869 377, ⓦhotelelimo.it. Comfortable rooms in a beautifully restored hotel with a small courtyard garden – and if you book well in advance prices (as little as €65) can undercut anywhere else in town. €69

San Domenico Via Tommaso Guerrasi 26 ☎0923 860 128, ⓦhotel-sandomenico.it. An engaging, family-run hotel in a medieval house in the heart of Erice – with the owners' children's toys in evidence in the sitting room along with some robust rustic antiques. Two sets of connecting rooms, and a triple. Breakfast is in a tiny courtyard. €99

EATING   SEE MAP PAGE 320

Though **restaurant** prices are a good bit higher in Erice than elsewhere in the region, you can still eat out fairly reasonably if you stick to the set-price menus. Bring a picnic and you can sit in the shady Giardini del Balio, or get something from the *panineria* on Via Vittorio Emanuele.

Monte San Giuliano Vicolo San Rocco 7 ☎0923 869 595. Entering this backstreet restaurant is like visiting a castle: through a stone archway and up steps. There's a sort of courtyard, too, where tables are spread out amid plants with seaward views. First courses are from €10, mains are €14–20. Tues–Sun lunch & dinner; closed three weeks in Nov & Jan.

Pasticceria di Maria Grammatico Via Vittorio Emanuele 14. A famous speciality cake shop and café selling marzipan fruits, *amaretti* and the like; a popular tourist stop. Maria Grammatico learned her trade as a girl in a convent, and has co-written a recipe book with writer Mary Taylor Simeti. You can admire the view from

a minuscule balcony, and there's a more spacious garden with tables. Open daily all day in summer; closed Tues in winter.

La Pentolaccia Via G.F. Guarnotti 17 ☎0923 869 099. Atmospherically housed in an old monastery, this place serves excellent home-made pasta and couscous. Try ravioli stuffed with *cernia* (a sauce of cherry tomato, swordfish, mint and prawns; €12), *busiate alla trapanese* (pasta with tomato, basil, garlic and almonds; €9), or the more unusual *pasta nostromo*, dressed with the roe of a John Dory, Mazzara prawns, tomatoes and garlic (€16). Daily lunch & dinner; may close for one day a week in low season.

Ulisse Via Chiaramonte 45 ☎0923 869 333. Reached down the stepped Vico San Rocco, just off the main square, and with a pretty courtyard garden. The pizzas here (€5.50–10) are popular with locals (Sunday sees a queue form early). Gluten-free dishes are offered. Daily lunch & dinner; closed Thurs in winter.

North of Trapani

North of Trapani, the main attraction is the resort town of **San Vito Lo Capo**, though with a car you could explore the rugged **coastline** en route, the road weaving under some of the gigantic outcrops of rock that characterize Sicily's west. The most spectacular, **Monte Cofano** (659m), is protected as a nature reserve. Although none of the settlements is particularly beautiful, a couple of outstanding hotels might make you decide to base yourself near **Valderice** or **Bonagia**.

Valderice and Bonagia

Between Trapani and San Vito Lo Capo, 40km away, two wide gulfs – Bonagia and Cofano – are backed by holiday homes and small plantations, overlooked both by the heights of Erice and by its lower neighbour **VALDERICE**, a ribbon development occupying a prominent ridge. From Valderice, a minor road winds 5km down to the coast at **BONAGIA**, where the old tuna fishery has been converted into a hotel that's well worth considering for anyone travelling with children.

ACCOMMODATION   VALDERICE AND BONAGIA

★ **Baglio Santa Croce** SS187, Km 12.3 ☎ 0923 891 111, ⊛ bagliosantacroce.it. A glorious renovation of a seventeenth-century stone-built estate, some 1km outside Valderice, whose rooms have beamed ceilings, exposed walls, tiled floors and iron bedsteads (other rooms are in the modern annexe). There's a pool, a renowned restaurant and superb views to the coast. €70

Lido Valderice ☎ 0923 573 477 or ☎ 349 854 2190, ⊛ campinglidovalderice.it. Located close to the sea and a couple of good bars, this is a small, but clean and friendly, campsite. It's connected by up to six buses a day from

Trapani's bus terminal, a 30min ride, then a 5min walk from the bus stop. Closed Nov–Feb. Per person €6.90, plus per tent €7.40

Tonnara di Bonagia Piazza Tonnara di Bonagia, Valderice ☎ 0923 431 111, ⊛ tonnaradibonagia.it. Occupying the mellow buildings of an old tuna fishery, this is a perfect base for a pool-and-beach summer holiday. There is an excellent pool, and activities for children in summer. Paths lead to miniature rocky coves for those who prefer to swim in the sea. Accommodation is in either hotel rooms or self-catering apartments. Doubles €94

San Vito Lo Capo

With its dense ranks of trattorias, hotels and bars, **SAN VITO LO CAPO** is certainly geared to holiday consumers, but its comparative remoteness has helped to stave off the worst pressures of the tourist industry, even in high season. All the same, you'll have a lot more elbow room outside the peak months – the best time to appreciate the town's beach, one of Sicily's finest.

Running down to the beach, San Vito's long shop- and restaurant-lined main strip, the pedestrianized **Via Savoia**, is the focus of the evening *passeggiata*, with its shops staying open late in summer. It holds one sight worth a glance: the curious, square and fortified-looking **Santuario** (concerts are held outside in summer; check posters around town). A pleasant promenade backs the **beach**, which stretches east of town. Framed by the looming cliffs behind and overlooked by jagged slabs of rock, the wide, curving stretch of white sand is ideal for swimming and sunbathing, though it gets pretty congested in August. Deckchairs and parasols are available to rent.

West of the main beaches, a ten-minute walk past the harbour brings you to the point of **Capo San Vito** itself – a rocky and windswept plain on which a fenced-off lighthouse is perched. For views, you need to climb above the town (bear left on the way out to the lighthouse), up a steep road leading to the top of the high cliffs and looking down over the Golfo di Castellammare. The other local walk is east to the Riserva Naturale dello Zingaro, a nature reserve (see page 310).

ARRIVAL AND DEPARTURE   SAN VITO LO CAPO

By bus Regular daily AST buses run to San Vito from Trapani's bus terminal and Russo buses from Palermo's Piazza Marina; all stop on Via P.S. Mattarella, close to the seafront and three blocks up from Via Savoia.

Destinations Palermo (3–4 daily in summer, 1–2 daily in winter; 2–3hr); Trapani (8 Mon–Sat, 4 daily Sun in summer only; 1hr 20min).

Bus companies AST, for Trapani and Bonagia (☎ 0923 23 222, ⊛ aziendasicilianatrasporti.it); Russo, for Castellammare

9

del Golfo and Palermo (☏ 0924 31 364, ⌨ russoautoservizi.it). **By car** Parking is highly restricted during the summer months: your best bet is to head for the free Parcheggio Comunale Sud (Villaggio Azzurro) – for which take an early right turn onto Via La Piana as you enter town – which has a

free shuttle bus running to the centre in the summer months (8am–1am every 15min). Alternatively, you can park between the blue lines in a few more central areas (€1/hr Mon–Fri, €2/hr Sat & Sun; buy a scratch card from *tabacchi*).

GETTING AROUND

Car, bike and scooter rental Auto Vesco, Via Orazio di Bella 20 (☏ 388 140 8305, ⌨ autovesco.it), and Serse, Via Dogana 3 (☏ 0923 974 434, ⌨ autonoleggioserse.com),

have cars, motorbikes and scooters. Bikes can be rented May–Sept from various stalls behind the beach with especially good deals for rental by the day.

FESTIVALS AND TOURS

Festivals San Vito gets impossibly busy during the Cous Cous Fest (⌨ couscousfest.it), which takes place over six days in late September and includes free samplings of dozens of versions of the dish, as well as nightly concerts in Piazza Santuario and a fireworks extravaganza on the last night at midnight. In recent years, a Cous Cous Preview, a sort of mini-version of the main event, has been staged over three days in early June; and there are free concerts and more festivities around San Vito's day in mid-June.

Boat excursions Between May and September, boats

operated by several companies run daily to Zingaro, Scopello and Monte Cofano. Hippocampus (☏ 338 612 5140, ⌨ hippocampus-sanvito.it) is well organized, with space for just twelve people in its boats, and has both morning and afternoon departures (€35 per person per half-day).

Services There's a pharmacy at Via Regina Margherita 26 (Mon–Sat 9.30am–12.30pm & 4.30–8.30pm, reduced hours in winter), and a Post office at Via Savoia 58 (Mon–Fri 8am–1.30pm, Sat 8am–12.30pm).

ACCOMMODATION   SEE MAP PAGE 324

Accommodation in San Vito is plentiful and mostly central – as with all resorts, the nearer the sea, the more expensive the room. It's worth noting that in July and August and during the Cous Cous Fest of late September (see above), many places virtually double their prices and demand a minimum stay of three days or a week, often on

half-board terms. As ever, however, there are good deals if you book online six months at least in advance, and Airbnb has some nice places. In winter, you won't find many places open; ask around the bars in the centre if you get stuck. There are several **campsites** in the area and the "No camping" signs on the town beach should be heeded.

SAN VITO LO CAPO

● EATING	
Agorà	5
Caffè Pino	2
Delfino	3
Pocho	6
La Sirenetta	1
Thaam	4

■ ACCOMMODATION	
Capo San Vito	1
Halimeda	5
La Pineta	4
Pocho	6
Poseidon	2
Sigiuma	3

TYRRHENIAN SEA

Porto

Bus terminal

VIA FARO
V. DOGANA
V. CORTESE
V. PRINCIPE TOMMASO
V. ORAZIO DI BELLA
Santuario
VIA LITTORANEA LUNGOMARE
PIAZZA SANTUARIO
V. SANTUARIO
V. ANTONIO VENZA
PIAZZA MARINELLA
VIA REG. MARGHERITA
VIA PIER S. MATTARELLA
VIA DUCA DEGLI ABRUZZI
VIA MATTEO PERALTA
VIA SAVOIA
VIA TOMMASO ZABUT
DANTE ALIGHIERI
VIA NINO BIXIO
VIA GIARDINI
VIA VINCENZO CONSOLO
VIA CAMPOBELLO
VIA CAVOUR
VIA GEN. ARIMONDI
VIA A. AMODEI
VIA C. COLOMBO
VIA MULINO
VIA LITTORANEA LUNGOMARE
VIA DEL SECCO
VIA NUNZIO NASI
VIA ST. TRAVERSA D. SECCO
VIA STR. GIUSEPPE GARIBALDI
Riserva Zingaro

N

0   200
metres

6, 6 & Trapani   P (Parcheggio Comunale Sud)

Capo San Vito Via San Vito 1 ☎0923 972 122, ⓦwww. caposanvito.it. Right on the seafront, this top-of-the-range hotel has smart, modern rooms, those at the front (costing more) with balconies and sea views; those at the back can be noisy. There's a spa (not included in the price), meals are taken in the terrace restaurant, and a small garden gives on to the beach. Minimum stay six nights in high season. €360

Halimeda Via Generale Arimondi 100 ☎0923 972 399, ⓦhotelhalimeda.com. This small, modern hotel away from the sea has spacious, themed rooms – Arabic, Nordic, Oriental, etc – each with minibar, a/c and internet access, and there's a lovely Art Nouveau staircase. Breakfast on the terrace includes fresh *cornetti*, biscuits and local *dolci*. There's free parking, too – a useful bonus in San Vito. Normally a one-week minimum stay in Aug. Closed Nov–Feb. €170

La Pineta Via del Secco ☎0923 972 818, ⓦcamping lapineta.it. With a bar, pizzeria, a pool, and bungalows and rooms to rent, this is the best of San Vito's campsites, shady and efficiently run, located a 10min walk from town east along the seafront. Per person €4, plus per tent €6.50, bungalows €130

Pocho Contrada Macari ☎0923 972 525, ⓦpocho. it. Making the most of its coastal location, 4km south of town, this cliffside hotel-restaurant provides a stylish and soothing base for anyone with transport, with twelve quiet and elegant rooms with fridges and wi-fi (those with sea views cost extra). The food is terrific, too (see below), and there's access to the small, rocky beach below. Closed Oct–March. €180

Poseidon Via P.S. Mattarella 28 ☎0923 972 444, ⓦposeidonresidence.com. Good for families, these stylish one- and two-room apartments have a/c, kitchenette and shower, plus parking. Ground-floor apartments have garden access but no views; you get more light and a balcony higher up. Low-season rates are negotiable. Closed Dec–Feb. Two-person apartments per week from €600 in high season

Sigiuma Via Santuario 39 ☎0923 972 952 or ☎347 863 8967, ⓦsigiuma.it. A very central B&B offering spacious rooms in bright, summery colours with fridges and a/c, and there's a patio (where breakfast is served) and a tranquil garden. The welcoming hosts – two brothers – are ready with local info and good advice. Closed Dec–March. €90

EATING

SEE MAP PAGE 324

Via Savoia and the seafront are lined with **bars**, ice-cream parlours and pizzerias, and there's no shortage of fish **restaurants** either, most on the pricey side. It's always worth booking during San Vito's couscous festivals (see page 324), when restaurant queues are common.

Agorà Piazza Marinella 5 ☎0923 974 442. Always busy, this smart trattoria near the seafront has tables in the piazza, and serves pasta for €8–16, mains for €12–18, or fresh fish by weight. The house speciality is *cassatelle Agorà*, fresh pasta stuffed with zucchini, pistachio and basil, served with mussels and shrimps (€13.50). Daily for lunch and dinner; closed Wed in low season.

Caffè Pino Via Savoia 24 ☎392 358 0791. A nice choice for breakfast, with friendly service and delicious cakes and pastries. Try the *torrone* ice cream and the *cannoli*, but preferably not at the same time. Open all day daily, closed Thurs in winter.

★ **Delfino** Via Savoia 15 ☎0923 972 711. Pizzeria-trattoria on the main street, near the beach, with smoked-fish *antipasti*, fresh pasta, fish couscous and a short list of pizzas to eat in or take away. One of the cheaper places in town, it offers some reasonably priced tourist menus. Tues–Sun for lunch & dinner.

★ **Pocho** Contrada Macari ☎0923 972 525. Small and casually chic, and with an unparalleled location overlooking the rocky coast, 4km south of town, this place has tables inside – where there's a collection of Sicilian puppets – and on a lovely panoramic terrace. Inventive dishes are available on a six-course set menu (€38, including water and an aperitivo), and there is a children's menu for €20. The owner, Marilù, ends the evening with Sicilian songs. There are also vegetarian and gluten-free options if you inform them in advance. Mon–Sat dinner, Sun lunch.

La Sirenetta Via Savoia, cnr Via Faro. A *gelateria* overlooking the beach, with a summer shaded terrace and a choice of twenty ice creams. Specialities are *gelsomino* (jasmine flower, summer only), *torrone* and *caldofreddo* (ice cream with hot chocolate sauce). Daily 9am–late, closed Tues Nov–March.

Thaam Via Duca degli Abruzzi 32–36 ☎0923 972 836. An elaborately decorated restaurant with a Tunisian influence; *merguez*, kebabs and couscous (€12–15) feature alongside more mainstream Italian dishes. The outdoor tables beneath a tent-like canopy fill fast, so book or arrive early. Daily lunch & dinner.

The Egadi Islands

Moored off the western coast, the three **Egadi Islands** (Isole Egadi) are the easiest of Sicily's offshore islands to visit – which accounts for the summer crowds that swarm over Favignana. The other islands are much less affected, however, and if you come out of season things are noticeably quieter everywhere.

GETTING TO THE EGADI ISLANDS

Ferries operated by Caronte Tourist (ⓦcarontetourist.it) and **hydrofoils** operated by Liberty Lines (ⓦlibertylines.it) depart several times daily **from Trapani**. They're more frequent between June and September, and most frequent in July and August. They generally call at Favignana, Lévanzo and Marettimo, in that order, though Lévanzo is sometimes the first stop, and some services don't run as far as Marettimo.

Ferries depart from the Stazione Marittima in Trapani, and hydrofoils from further east along Via A. Staiti. Ferries are less frequent than hydrofoils and take at least twice as long, but they're cheaper. One-way hydrofoil tickets from Trapani to Favignana and Lévanzo cost around €10, and to Marettimo around €16.50; one-way ferry tickets are about half that.

Liberty Lines also operates a year-round hydrofoil service three times daily Sept 11–June 19 and four times daily June 20–Sept 10 to Favignana **from Marsala** (30min; about €10). In summer there is also one hydrofoil daily for Lévanzo, and two daily for Marettimo, and in winter there is one service daily to Lévanzo and Marettimo.

The largest of the Egadis and the nearest to the Sicilian mainland, **Favignana** is also the site of the main fishery. The Genovese link is most apparent in the island of **Lévanzo**, across the strait, which is named after a quarter in Genova and shelters the **Grotta del Genovese**, a cave in which a rich bounty of prehistoric cave paintings was discovered. These days, with the annual tourist influx, the greatest hope for peace and quiet lies in the furthest island, **Marettimo**, whose rugged coasts are indented with a succession of coves, ideal for clean and secluded swimming. The island also offers a choice of **hikes** across its interior and along the rocky coasts.

You could easily see any of the islands as a **day-trip** from Trapani; seeing two on the same day is also feasible. If you want to stay longer, be warned that **accommodation** is extremely limited, and in summer you should phone ahead to reserve a room. It's certainly worth staying over, though you should also bear in mind that, in general, **prices** for rooms and food are higher than on the mainland.

Brief history

Before the advent of tourism, the economic success of the Egadi Islands was largely based on a historical relationship with the northern Italian city of Genova, whose sailors plied the **trading routes** on which the Egadis stood throughout the Middle Ages. The link was formalized in the middle of the seventeenth century, when the Bourbon king Philip IV sold all the islands, in lieu of a debt, to Genoan businessmen. Then, as now, a major element in the local economy was the **tuna fish**, which congregate here to breed at the end of spring. Channelled through the Straits between the two main islands during their migrations around the Sicilian coast, they have traditionally been systematically slaughtered in an age-old rite known as **La Mattanza** – though in recent years the practice has been discontinued owing to falling stocks and the efficiency of the offshore "factory ships".

Favignana

Fifteen to forty minutes from Trapani by hydrofoil, **FAVIGNANA** has progressed over the years from tuna centre to prison and now tourist resort. Shaped like a lopsided butterfly, the island is almost split in two, its narrow "waist" holding the port, **Favignana town**, and most of the population. To the east lie the best swimming spots, accessible from a succession of rocks and inlets, while the western half of the island is only reachable along the southern coastal road, which tunnels through **Monte Santa Caterina** (300m).

Favignana town

FAVIGNANA TOWN is the focus of most of the tourist traffic. As the archipelago's only town, it holds the island's main services and best choice of accommodation and restaurants, but otherwise there's no particular reason to hang around. From the port, you can see the dome of the church: aim for that and you'll reach the main square, Piazza Madrice. Everything else is contained in the short streets between here and the nearby Piazza Europa.

The town's only distinctive feature is the imposing building near the port, the **Palazzo Florio**. Now part of the town hall, it was built by Ignazio Florio, an entrepreneur who took over the islands in 1874 and revitalized the fisheries; there's a statue of him in nearby Piazza Europa. His tuna fishery, **Stabilimento Florio**, is similarly impressive, its vaulted nineteenth-century buildings a solid counterpoint across the bay. It is currently open for visits (with a flexible timetable), and plans are afoot to open a marine and fishing museum here at some future date. Otherwise, all there is to do is window-shop in the many places selling "*prodotti tipici*" – traditional tuna products, of course, as well as *bottarga* (fish roe), oil, local dried herbs, wine and postcards of the bloody *la Mattanza*.

Monte Santa Caterina

The island's sole hill, **Monte Santa Caterina** is topped by an abandoned Norman **castello**, floodlit at night, and reached by a crazy-paved stairway from the west side of Favignana town. Alternatively, follow the lower path over the mountain to a crest with views to Marettimo. The path down the other side, however, is hard to follow and you may end up scrambling over walls and through fields to reach the road.

The rest of the island

Away from the town, Favignana is tidily cultivated, and pitted with square white houses built from **tufa** quarried from curious pits all over the island – an export that has historically provided the island with a second source of cash (after fishing). One of the old quarries, on the fringe of town by the decrepit chapel of Santa Anna, has been landscaped and turned into a quirky **sunken garden**.

You can swim at the beach near the town, but the sandy beach at **Lido Burrone**, on the island's south side, is better, with a friendly pizzeria-restaurant-bar that rents out parasols and sun-loungers. Otherwise, just follow the coast roads and plunge in off the rocks, or settle down on one of the tiny handkerchiefs of sand. Call in at **Cala Azzurra**, below the lighthouse at the island's eastern end, where there's a beautiful blue bay but little sand; or, just north, the spectacular **Cala Rossa**, where you can swim off rocks at the base of towering tufa cliffs. Its name – Red Cove – is said to derive from the blood washed ashore after the Roman defeat of the Carthaginians in a fierce sea battle in 241 BC. The road to Cala Rossa in particular is noted for its tufa quarries – just before the cove itself is a huge quarry where stacks of tufa and unexcavated pillars rise high from the gloomy depths. On the other side of the mountain, the best beach is at **Cala Rotonda**, where, local legend would have it, Odysseus washed up before being attacked by the Cyclops.

ARRIVAL AND DEPARTURE	FAVIGNANA

Ferry departures Lévanzo (2–3 daily; 35min); Marettimo (1 daily; 40min); Trapani (2–3 daily; 1hr 10min).
Hydrofoil departures Lévanzo (5 daily; 10–15min);

Marettimo (4 daily; 45min); Marsala (3 daily; 30min); Trapani (hourly; 20–40min).

GETTING AROUND

By bike The best way to get around the island is by bike, since the flat terrain and good road surfaces enable you to see the whole of Favignana in an afternoon. There are bike-rental shops all over town, including down at the port – look for the words "*noleggio bici*", or try Isidoro, at Via Mazzini 40 (☎ 347 323 3058), which rents bikes for €5 a day (€7 in high

season), and scooters for €30 a day (€35–45 in July & Aug).
By bus A bus service leaves from down by the port on three routes: #1 to Cala Azzurra, #2 to Punta Sottile, #3 to the turn-off for Cala Rossa. Departures are roughly hourly during the summer, much less frequent in winter; buy tickets on board (€1).

9

INFORMATION AND TOURS

Tourist information A useful website for Favignana and the whole archipelago is ⓦegadi.com.

Boat tours Trips to the island's offshore grottoes are offered down at the port, costing €35 per person for a full day (less for a 2hr or 3hr excursion) – there's always someone around in summer, but you may have to ask in town at other times.

Diving Progetto Atlantide (ⓣ347 517 8338, ⓦprogetto atlantide.com) offers courses and equipment rental.

ACCOMMODATION

Albergo Aegusa Via Garibaldi 11, Favignana town ⓣ0923 922 430, ⓦaegusahotel.it. A central, clean and quiet three-star hotel just off Via Roma. Rooms have a/c, minibar and safe; some are in an annexe, 100m away. It's worth taking half board here, as there's a good garden restaurant. Closed Nov–March. **€120**

B&B Favignana Via Roma 15, Favignana town ⓣ392 725 2398, ⓦbbfavignana.com. One of the cheapest choices on the island, this place has simple, colour-themed rooms with private bathrooms and a/c. It's a good choice if you want to stay centrally, just minutes away from the port. Prices almost halve in low season. No credit cards. Closed mid-Jan to mid-March. **€80**

Bouganville Via Cimabue 10, Favignana town ⓣ0923 922 033, ⓦalbergobouganville.it. This small, reasonably priced hotel has spacious rooms and a restaurant in the garden. It's near the beach on the southwestern edge of town: follow Via Diaz and Via Battisti from the centre, a 10min walk. Half board obligatory in summer; prices are much reduced for the rest of the year. Closed Dec–Easter. Half board **€120**

Camping Egad Contrada Arena ⓣ0923 921 555, ⓦcampingegad.com. A little over 1km east of town, and 500m from the beach at Lido Burrone, this has a range of accommodation, including rooms in wooden cabins, and igloo-type apartments with cooking facilities sleeping two to four. Facilities include bar, restaurant, store and scooter and bike rental, and there's transport to and from the port. Closed Nov–Easter. Camping/person **€7.20**, plus per tent **€7**, cabins **€60**, igloos **€120**

Cave Bianche Cala Azzurra ⓣ0923 925 451, ⓦcave bianchehotel.it. A boutique hotel within an abandoned quarry, with chic and minimalist rooms. There's a pool, hydro-massage and a great restaurant, and scooters and bikes are available to rent. It's about 10min from town by bike. Closed Nov–March. **€200**

Hotel delle Cave Contrada Torretta Strada, Vic. della Madonna ⓣ0923 925 423, ⓦhoteldellecave.it. This boutique hotel is built on the lip of an abandoned quarry a couple of kilometres east of town, in an area known locally as Zona Cavallo, with gardens, a hydro-massage pool and a restaurant inside the quarry itself. The structure is severely functional, but the rooms are full of designer features, and come with minibar, a/c and wi-fi. Excellent deals in low season. Closed Nov–Easter. **€170**

Villa Antonella Via Punta Marsala, Favignana town ⓣ0923 921 073, ⓦegadi.com/villaantonella. A family-run B&B, a couple of kilometres outside town, which also has self-catering mini-apartments sleeping 2–4 people. A good choice for families or those on a budget who want to be able to cook for themselves. It is walkable from town, but you might prefer to have your own transport. **€50**

EATING AND DRINKING

Piazza Madrice, Piazza Europa and the surrounding streets are where you'll find Favignana's **bars** and **restaurants**, but be warned: restaurant prices on the island tend to be high. Excellent slices of pizza, *schiacciata* and the like are sold at the bakery Costanza on Via Roma, just up from Piazza Madrice, or you may prefer to **picnic** on the town beach. For picnic provisions, carry on past Costanza to the Egadi **supermarket**, where the deli counter has local ricotta and a good range of cheeses and hams.

La Bettola Via Nicotera 47 ⓣ0923 921 988. With a terrace for eating *al fresco*, this popular spot serves up a memorable *couscous di pesce* (€20). As an *antipasto*, the *fritelle di gamberi* (prawn fritters) are also worth sampling. Prices are reasonable, with starters at €7–9, mains €10–15. Tues–Sun lunch & dinner.

Pizza Pazza Via Mazzini 16, off Piazza Madrice. You can pick up excellent and inexpensive pizzas here, cooked in a wood-fired oven. Don't miss the local pizza speciality, *rianata*, made with pecorino instead of mozzarella, and oregano instead of the usual basil, and picnic on them in the piazza. Daily 7–10.30pm; closed Tues in winter.

DIRECTORY

Banks The banks in Piazza Europa and Piazza Madrice both have ATMs.

Pharmacy Abramo, Piazza Europa; Barone, Piazza Madrice (both Mon–Fri 8.30am–1pm & 5–8.30pm). At other times see rota on the door.

Post office Via Marconi 2 (Mon–Sat 8.20am–12.35pm).

GETTING TO THE GROTTA DEL GENOVESE

All visits to the **Grotta del Genovese** (ⓦgrottadelgenovese.it) have to be arranged at least a day in advance through the official custodian, Signor Natale Castiglione: either telephone ☏ 0923 924 032 or ☏ 339 741 8800, or pass by at Via Calvario 11, above the quay. Tickets cost €23.50 each, either by jeep or by boat. **By boat**, the round trip will take nearly two hours, usually departing at 10.30am and (if there's enough demand) 3pm. Note that the smallest swell may be enough to make it impossible for the boat to pull into the narrow rocky disembarkation point. You can also extend the tour by opting for the round-island trip (€5 supplement), which takes up to three hours including a swimming stop.

By jeep, the two-hour round trip is roughly 10km, following an inland route through the valley in the centre of the island. The fairly difficult descent on foot to the grotto from where the jeep stops is not recommended for anyone infirm. You might negotiate a discount jeep fare if you feel like walking back. Booking for either route is essential. Winter tours only take place when the conditions are right – again, always telephone ahead.

Lévanzo

LÉVANZO, 4km north of Favignana, is the smallest of the three main Egadi Islands. Most of it is used to pasture sheep and goats, and, with its turquoise seas and white houses, it has very much the feel of a Greek island. Its population is concentrated in **LÉVANZO TOWN**, little more than a cluster of square houses and holiday homes around a tiny port, where you'll find the island's two hotel-restaurants and a couple of bars.

The **coastline** is rocky and largely inaccessible, but you can get around on foot by following the dirt paths along the shore and over the hills. Following the only road twenty minutes west of the port, you'll come to a rocky spire sticking out of the sea – the **Faraglione** – beyond which a rocky path leads north up the coast. This becomes a stone and dirt track once it reaches the upper part of the valley. If you stick to it, it takes around an hour to reach the lighthouse at **Capo Grosso** at the northeastern point of the island.

On your way to the cape, you can swim at the lovely white **Tramontana bay**: just before you reach an old metal gate, a track leads down the red-earth mountainside, ending in an acute concrete slope, which you can just about slither down, though scrambling back up is hard work. Tracing the coast eastwards from Lévanzo town, you can reach **Cala Minnola** in about fifteen minutes – a lovely rocky cove ideal for swimming.

Grotta del Genovese

On the island's northwest coast, on a slope overlooking the sea, the **Grotta del Genovese** is the main attraction for most visitors. The cave walls display some remarkable Paleolithic **incized drawings**, discovered in 1949, as well as later Neolithic pictures; they're mostly of animals, and are between six thousand and ten thousand years old. Despite their age, these evocative drawings retain their impact, drawn by prehistoric man in an attempt to harness and influence the power of nature: one lovely picture of a deer near the entrance dates from when the island was still connected to the Sicilian mainland. The later Neolithic sketches are easy to pick out, too: less well-drawn, more stylized representations of men and even of tuna fish and a dolphin.

ARRIVAL AND DEPARTURE   LÉVANZO

By ferry and hydrofoil The port is just below the island's only road, Via Calvario. Services are good enough throughout the year to make day-trips from Trapani and Favignana an easy prospect.

ACCOMMODATION

In summer, the island's hotel will usually require a week's minimum stay and will only accept guests on half-board terms, though as the only other options for food on Lévanzo are two bars, an *alimentari* and a bakery, this is no hardship.

9

If you're self-catering at the *Lisola Residence*, consider bringing supplies from the mainland, as the choice of food at the *alimentari* is a bit limited.

Lisola Residence ☎ 0923 194 1530 or ☎ 320 180 9090, ⓦ lisola.eu. Seven apartments 400m outside the port sleeping between two and four, occupying simple tufa cottages originally built by nineteenth-century tuna-canning magnate Florio for his workers. Extras include

a large pool with parasols and sun-loungers, and free transport to the port whenever you need it. Closed Nov–March. Two-person apartments **€100**

Paradiso ☎ 0923 924 080, ⓦ albergoparadiso.eu. Close to the port, next to the bar, this hotel has a terrace-restaurant and marvellous sea views from the en-suite, air-conditioned rooms, some of which are a bit cramped. Half-board doubles per person **€80**

Marettimo

The wildest of the islands, and the furthest out from Trapani, **MARETTIMO** was claimed by Samuel Butler, in his *The Authoress of the Odyssey*, as the original Ithaca, home of Odysseus. Even more far-fetched, Butler also thought that Homer himself was the princess Nausicaä of ancient Trapani. These theories aside, there are compelling reasons to come to Marettimo. Its spectacular fragmented coastline is pitted with rocky coves sheltering hideaway beaches, several of which – such as those at **Cala Sarde** and **Cala Nera** on the south coast, or at the **Saracen castle** at the northeastern point of the island – can be reached by footpath. Even in high season, you're likely to have much of Marettimo to yourself, as few tourists can be bothered to visit a place with limited accommodation and no more than half a dozen trattorias. That said, there are signs of heightened interest these days in the shape of a sprinkling of new holiday homes, while EU money has gone towards paving a couple of sections of track. However, such "improvements" are still fairly low-key and, at least for now, the island retains its air of being far off the beaten track.

Marettimo town

As you pull into port and explore its few streets, **MARETTIMO TOWN** appears almost North African in character, with its flat-roofed cube houses with blue shutters and painted tiles, and alleys full of tumbling bougainvillea. There's one main street, a little square and church, and a second harbour, the **fishing port**, just along from the main harbour. Two of the island's most popular **bathing** spots are conveniently close, one near the main harbour, one near the fishing harbour.

ARRIVAL AND INFORMATION   MARETTIMO

By ferry and hydrofoil Both ferries and hydrofoils run year-round from Trapani and Favignana to Marettimo, but there are far fewer services than to Favignana and Lévanzo. There is a skeleton low-season service, and boats are often cancelled owing to bad weather.

Tourist information There is plenty of useful information online at ⓦ marettimoweb.com.

Boat trips Various options are available via *Rosa dei Venti* (see page 331): around the island to Cala Bianca for swimming will cost around €20–25 per person; the same with a picnic (including home-cured fish and local cheeses

and wines) is around €30–35 per person. On either, you can be left at a cove to swim and be collected an hour or so later. Alternatively, you could take a three-hour boat tour of the island (a "*giro dell'isola*"), available from operators at the main harbour, which allows you to see Marettimo's entire rocky coastline and dive into otherwise inaccessible waters that are clean and clear and a joy for snorkellers.

Services Marettimo's main street, Corso Umberto I, is about a minute's walk from the harbour where the ferries and hydrofoils dock. It has a bank with an ATM, and ferry and hydrofoil ticket office.

ACCOMMODATION

Marettimo offers a better choice of **accommodation** than Lévanzo, with a couple of B&Bs and a few apartments and holiday residences for weekly rents. If these are full, ask around in the bars and restaurants for **rented rooms**, but it's always best to book before you come.

I Delfini Corso Umberto 34 ☎ 0923 923 137 or ☎ 339

239 9867, ⓦ idelfinimarettimo.it. A central B&B with great sea views on one side. Rooms are simple but clean and comfortable, with private bathrooms, and there's a roof terrace on which delicious breakfasts are served. Closed Nov–March. **€105**

Marettimo Residence Via Telégrafo 3 ☎ 0923 923

MARETTIMO HIKES

None of the walks detailed below is particularly onerous, though you might have to scramble at times. Always make sure you're carrying enough water with you.

TO THE CASE ROMANE

Marettimo's simplest walk takes you to some old Roman defensive works, the **Case Romane**, which are still in pretty good condition. Climb up the road to the side of *Caffè Tramontana* and, at the top, scout around to the left and then right to find the signpost for the start of the walk. The remains are half an hour on, sitting next to a small and dilapidated church that shows marked Arab characteristics but is thought to have been built by Byzantine monks in the twelfth century.

TO CALA SARDE AND CALA NERA

Follow the road south of Marettimo port, turning inland after about 1km where the path divides. There's a steep climb, with the town's cemetery below you, rising to about 300m. After about half an hour, you'll pass a pine forest and a small outhouse, looking out on views towards Tunisia; below is the **Cala Sarde**, a small bay reachable along a smaller path to the left in another half an hour.

Instead of descending to the bay, continue for about an hour on the main path along the island's rocky west coast. You'll pass a lighthouse and a route down to **Cala Nera**, where you can swim off the rocks in perfect isolation.

TO THE CASTLE AT PUNTA TROIA

This walk follows the footpath all the way to the **northeastern tip** of the island, a hike that should take you around three hours; you'll need a head for heights in certain stretches. Go past the fishing harbour with the sea on your right, and keep to the coast along the path for about ten minutes, until the terrace wall on your left stops. When a sign here ("Castello Punta Troia") points to the left, cut up to find the main path on a small spur above you. This stretches along the whole length of the island about 100m above the sea, ending at some concrete steps that descend to a lovely secluded beach and the foot of the **castle**, perched on an impregnable rocky crag. This precipitous fortification was originally built by the Saracens, enlarged by Roger II, and further extended by the Spanish in the seventeenth century, when it became a prison, and acquired a dire reputation for cruelty.

202, ⓦ marettimoresidence.it. A small, resort-like cluster of cottages above a stony beach south of the main port, available for B&B or weekly rental (upwards of €1000 per week in high season). Demand is high, but you'll find greater availability and much lower prices outside the summer period. B&B doubles €215

Rosa dei Venti Punta Simone 4 ☎ 0923 923 249 or ☎ 333 675 8893, ⓦ isoladimarettimo.it. As well as operating various other tourist activities, this outfit has rooms and self-catering apartments (prices on application) dispersed around the island, also available for short stays. Doubles €90

Sealife Corso Umberto and Via Tedesco ☎ 0923 923

288 or ☎ 347 542 9713, ⓦ sealifesnc.com. The two apartments are centrally located, accommodating two to five people usually by the week, though they'll let you have them for shorter periods if there are vacancies. One has a terrace, the other a small courtyard, and both are equipped with barbecues. €500 per week

★ **La Terrazza** Via G. Pepe 24 ☎ 0923 923 252 or ☎ 368 768 1571, ⓦ bedandbreakfastmarettimo.it. The best feature here is the wide, semi-shaded terrace, with terrific views over the castle and sea, where breakfast is served and which guests can use all day. The four rooms are simply and tastefully decorated. No credit cards. Closed mid-Oct to March. €92

EATING AND DRINKING

Marettimo offers a reasonable range of **eating** options, though prices are a little higher than on the mainland, given the cost of shipping in ingredients. Not all the places listed below stay open throughout the year, but there's always something open. There are two *alimentari* on Via Garibaldi, off the main drag, one of which has takeaway items.

Baia del Sole Piazza Umberto I 5 ☎ 346 106 5401. Located next to the Siremar office on the main road, this bar has a few tables and excellent ice cream and *granitas*. Daily 8am–8pm.

Caffè Tramontana Via Campi. On the road above the fishing harbour, people gather here all day for the superb

9

sea views. It's *the* place to come for breakfast, or for an aperitif with snacks at sunset. Summer daily 8am–late.

Il Pirata Via Scalo Vecchio ☎ 0923 923 027. *Pesce spada all'arancia* (swordfish with orange) and *pasta con le sarde* (pasta with sardines, fennel seeds, pine nuts and raisins) are among the specialities in this pleasant trattoria by the fishing harbour. First courses are around €12, mains €12–18. For a real feast, splash out on the *zuppa di aragosta*

– first you eat the flavoursome broth with pasta, then the lobster. Daily lunch & dinner.

Il Veliero Corso Umberto ☎ 0923 923 274. Owned by a fisherman, this trattoria has excellent fresh seafood and a summer terrace bedecked with fishing traps right by the harbour. First courses, such as pasta with squid ink or *bottarga* (tuna roe), cost €13; mains aren't much more. Daily lunch & dinner; closed Nov–Feb.

Mozia and the saltpans

Fifteen kilometres down the coast from Trapani, the uninhabited **Stagnone Islands** (Isole dello Stagnone) have been mostly given over to salt extraction since the fifteenth century. On the mainland opposite, several windmills still stand near the surviving **saltpans**, which form a crystalline patchwork between Trapani and Marsala. Offshore, the long, thin Isola Grande shelters the only one of the Stagnone group that you can visit, **San Pantaleo**, which is set in the middle of a shallow lagoon that's now the year-round scene of **windsurfing**, **kitesurfing** and **sailing**. You can rent the equipment from shacks on the coast road; some outlets also rent out **canoes** (€10 per half-day), allowing you to weave around the saltpans. San Pantaleo also holds the site of the ancient Phoenician settlement of Motya (**Mozia** in Italian); this is the big cultural attraction hereabouts, and the whole island is usually referred to as Mozia rather than San Pantaleo.

Mozia

April–Oct 9.30am–1.30pm & 2.30–6.30pm; Nov–March 9am–3pm • €9

Flat, cultivated and only 2.5km in circumference, **Mozia** is one of the most manageable of Sicily's ancient sites, with the unique Phoenician ruins spread across the whole island. You could circle the perimeter in an hour or so, but it's more enjoyable to make a day of it and bring a picnic (and there's a bar with basic snacks on the island).

Along with Palermo and Solus (Solunto), Mozia was one of the three main Phoenician bases in Sicily, settled some time during the eighth century BC and completely razed to the ground by Dionysius I in 397 BC. It's the only one of the three sites that wasn't subsequently built over, though it remained undiscovered until the seventeenth century, and wasn't properly excavated until **Joseph "Pip" Whitaker** (amateur archeologist and member of one of the marsala wine dynasties) bought the island in the late nineteenth century and started to dig it up.

You reach the island site and its archeological museum by a short **ferry** ride from the mainland. Although the linguistic link between the archipelago's name (Stagnone) and our "stagnant" is not entirely coincidental, that doesn't deter some visitors from wading into the lagoon on the mainland side and crossing to Mozia in beachwear – the island museum, at least, has had enough and won't allow entry to anyone who's not properly clothed.

Museo Whitaker

Daily same times as site • Included in Mozia entry ticket

Joseph Whitaker's house – once incongruously furnished in Edwardian style – now holds the **Museo Whitaker**, which displays finds from the site. Its cool rooms are packed with a beautiful collection of jewellery, arrowheads, terracotta figurines and domestic artefacts, with the earliest pieces dating from the eighth century BC. Pride of place goes to the magnificent fifth-century BC marble **sculpture** of a youth, *Il Giovinetto di*

FLORIO

FLORIO & C.

HOSPITAL SIZE

MARSALA
TONIC
S O M
CONTENTS 1 PT. - 5 FLD.OZ - OLCOHOL 18%

Florio & C.
Establisched 1833
SOCIETA' ANONIMA VINICOLA ITALIANA
MARSALA - ITALY

SANFI PRODUCTS CORP - NEW YORK
SOLE IMPORTERS FOR U.S.A. & CANADA
APPROVED BY U.S. TREASURY DEPT
Dose: A small glassfull twice a day

9

Mozia, sensual and self-assured in his pose. The identity of the subject is unknown, but he was likely to have been a high-ranking official, suggested by the subtle indentations round his head, indicating some kind of crown or elaborate headwear.

Outside stands an aristocratic bust of "Giuseppe" Whitaker, and there's a shaded picnic area under the trees nearby.

Casa dei Mosaici and the cothon

The remains of ancient Mozia start immediately outside the Museo Whitaker. In front and 100m to the left is the **Casa dei Mosaici**, two houses containing some faded black-and-white mosaics made from sea pebbles. One, probably belonging to a patrician, shows animal scenes; the other, thought to be a craftsman's, yielded numerous shards of pottery. Further along the path you come to the **cothon**, a small artificial boat dock built within the ancient town's walls and similar in style to a much larger one at Carthage itself.

The north gate

To the right of the Museo Whitaker, rough tracks that were once the city's main thoroughfares cut through flowering cacti and vine plantations. Most of the tracks end at the once-impenetrable **north gate**, now a ragged collection of steps and ruined walls, which stands at the head of a causeway built by the Phoenicians in the sixth century BC to connect the island with the mainland (and a necropolis) at Birgi, 7km to the north. The road is still there, although these days it's submerged under the water.

Tophet burial ground

Left along the shore from the north gate is the **Tophet burial ground**. Most of the information about day-to-day life in Motya has come from here, the sanctuary revealing a number of urns containing the ashes of animals sacrificed to the Phoenician gods (chiefly Baal Hammon) and of children, probably stillborn or who died of natural causes. A remarkable series of inscribed votive stele from the Tophet is on display in the museum.

Cappiddazzu

Just inland of the north gate, the **Cappiddazzu** site shows the foundations of a large building, probably a temple, while between gate and Cappiddazzu is a Punic **industrial zone** that was dedicated to the production of pottery and ceramics. This was where the famous marble sculpture was found, probably hidden by the city's inhabitants as the Greeks stormed the island.

ARRIVAL AND DEPARTURE   MOZIA

By bus From Marsala, take the local Linea D bus from Piazza del Popolo to the Mozia ferry landing. Return buses are on a similar schedule; a reduced service in either direction operates on a Sunday. From Trapani, you'll have to take the bus or the train to Marsala and connect from there.

By ferry Ferries out to the island are run by Arini & Pugliese (☎ 347 779 0218, ⓦ ariniepugliese.com) and Mozia Line (☎ 329 476 0294, ⓦ mozialine.com) from two separate spots. Arini & Pugliese boats leave from the ferry landing near the bus stop, Mozia Line from a dock about 1km away. A steady flow of visitors ensures that there's usually a ferry waiting during the hours when the museum is open; tickets for the 10min crossing cost €5 return. Parking is available near the two embarkation points.

EATING

Mamma Caura Mozia Lines Ferry Landing ☎ 0923 966 036. You can eat well here – try the fish couscous – but try to arrive early enough to watch the sun setting over the sea (they serve wine and nibbles, as well). There are also canoes to rent. Daily dinner only.

The saltpans

The series of **saltpans** glistening in the shallows between Trapani and Marsala has been worked since Phoenician times. Bare-chested men toil with shovels, carting full wheelbarrows across from the pans to a rising conveyor belt that dumps two-metre-high mounds of white salt along the banks. At different times of the day, as the light changes, there's a pink tint to the saltpans, while Marettimo rises in the distance through the haze.

Saline Ettore e Infersa and the Museo del Sale

April–Sept 9.30am–6.30pm; call ahead in winter, as hours vary • ☎ 0923 733 003

On the mainland, just opposite Mozia, one of three windmills has been turned into a showroom and museum, the **Saline Ettore e Infersa**, dedicated to the whole salt-making process. It's free to enter if you just want to browse the locally produced foods and crafts in the showroom, but the **Museo del Sale** (€6) is fascinating, especially if you take the instructive audioguided tour.

Marsala

When the island-city of Motya had been put to the sword by the Syracusans, the survivors founded Lilybaeum (modern **MARSALA**), 10km to the south. The main city of the Phoenicians in Sicily, and the only one to resist the Greek push westwards, Lilybaeum finally succumbed to Rome in 241 BC, and not long after was used as a springboard for an attack against the Carthaginian heartland itself. The town's position at Sicily's western tip later made it the main Saracenic base on the island, and it was renamed Marsah Ali, Arabic for the "port of Ali", son-in-law of the Prophet, from which its modern name derives.

The town scored a place in modern Italian history for its role in the saga of the **Risorgimento**, the struggle for Italian unity in the nineteenth century. It was here that

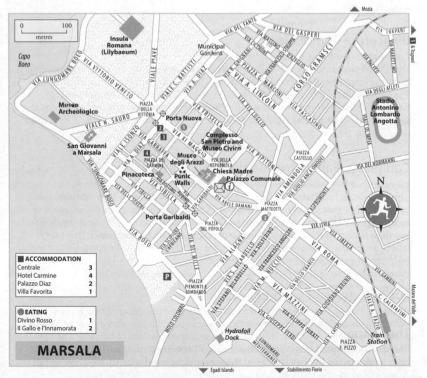

9

Garibaldi kicked off his campaign to drive out the Bourbons, in the company of his red-shirted "Thousand". Until a planned Garibaldi museum on Marsala's southwestern seafront (on Via Scipione l'Africano) gets round to opening, memorials to the swashbuckling freedom-fighter are confined to a few statues and street names, and the nearby Porta Garibaldi, at the end of Via Garibaldi, which recalls the hero's entry into the town. Local enthusiasts clad in red shirts parade through the gate each year on May 11, in commemoration of the exploits of the "Thousand".

Piazza della Repubblica

Marsala's town centre is a predominantly Baroque assortment of buildings, though there are hints of the older town's layout in the narrow, largely traffic-free streets around the central **Piazza della Repubblica**. The elegance of the square is due to its two eighteenth-century buildings: the arcaded **Palazzo Comunale**, and the **Chiesa Madre** – dedicated to San Tommaso di Canterbury, patron saint of Marsala – from which four statues peer loftily down. The church's large, but rather disappointing, interior has a few Gagini sculptures.

Museo degli Arazzi

Via Garraffa 57 • Tues–Sat 9.30am–1pm, Sun 9.30am—12.30pm • €4 • ☎ 0923 711 327

Behind the Chiesa Madre, the sole display at the **Museo degli Arazzi** is a series of eight enormous hand-stitched wool and silk **tapestries** depicting the capture of Jerusalem. Made in Brussels in the sixteenth century, they were the gift of the Spanish ambassador, who doubled as the archbishop of Messina, and are beautifully rich, in burnished red, gold and green.

Pinacoteca Comunale

Piazza del Carmine • Wed–Sat 9am–6.30pm, Tues & Sun 9am–1.30pm • €4

Past the Museo degli Arazzi, you can view the remains of **Punic walls** and pavements from the Greco-Roman period in Piazza San Girolamo. Still further, a left turn off Via Garraffa leads into Piazza del Carmine, where a fourteenth-century convent has been stylishly renovated to hold the **Pinacoteca Comunale**. Visitors can enjoy a good collection of art and regular exhibitions – mostly contemporary and with local connections.

Complesso San Pietro and the Museo Civico

Via Ludovico Anselmi Correale • Tues–Sun 9am–1pm & 4–8pm • Free • ☎ 0923 718 741

The **Complesso San Pietro** is a fifteenth-century monastery, now fully restored as a cultural centre that incorporates the **Museo Civico**, where you can see a selection of archeological items from the Punic, Greek and Roman eras and, more compellingly, rooms dedicated to Garibaldi's triumphant campaign in western Sicily, including letters, photos, arms and uniforms. The complex also contains the town library and a courtyard for occasional open-air performances.

Porta Nuova and Capo Boeo

At the far end of Via XI Maggio, through the eighteenth-century **Porta Nuova**, Piazza della Vittoria has a gate into the municipal gardens and a bar where you can sit and admire the austere Art Deco front of the Cine Impero, so out of keeping with the Baroque arch opposite. Beyond the piazza lies **Capo Boeo**, the westernmost point of Sicily that was the first settlement of the survivors of annihilated Motya. All the town's major antiquities are concentrated here, including the old **Insula Romana,** closed to the public at present, but normally accessible from Via Vittorio Veneto. The site contains all that's been excavated so far of the city of Lilybaeum, though most of it is third-century BC Roman, as you might guess from the presence of a vomitorium, lodged in the most complete section of the site – the **edificio termale,** or bathhouse. There's some good mosaic work here: a chained dog at the entrance and, much better, a richly coloured **hunting scene** in the atrium, showing a stag being savaged by a wild beast.

San Giovanni a Marsala

Viale N Sauro • Usually daily 9am–noon & 3–6pm

From Piazza della Vittoria, Viale N. Sauro leads to the church of **San Giovanni,** under which is a grotto reputed to have been inhabited by the sibyl Lilibetana, who was endowed with paranormal gifts. There's another slice of mosaic here, and a well whose water is meant to impart second sight. A pilgrimage takes place every June 24, the feast day of San Giovanni.

Museo Archeologico

Lungomare Boeo • Wed–Sat 9am–6.30pm, Tues & Sun 9am–1.30pm • €4 • ☎ 0923 952 535

One of the stone-vaulted warehouses that line the lungomare contains the **Museo Archeologico,** mostly dedicated to a very skeletal but still surprisingly well-preserved warship from the classical period. Displayed in a heat- and humidity-regulated environment, it ranks as the only extant *liburnian,* a specifically Phoenician or **Punic warship,** probably sunk during the First Punic War in the great sea battle off the Egadi Islands that ended Carthage's rule of the waves. It was discovered in 1971 and brought here after eight years of underwater surveying by a British team working under the archeologist Honor Frost. Originally 35m long, nearly 5m wide and rowed by 68 oarsmen, the vessel has been the source of much detailed information on the period, including what the crew ate and the stimulants they chewed to keep awake. Scattered about lie ranks of amphorae and anchors, and other items found in or around the ship, plus photographs and explanations (in Italian and English) of the ship's retrieval from the sea.

On the left-hand side of the building is displayed a medley of archeological finds from various sites hereabouts, both on land and sea. Prize exhibit is a marble torso

THE MAKING OF MARSALA WINE

The Baglio Anselmi, which houses Marsala's archeological museum, is one of a number of old **bagli,** or warehouses, conspicuous throughout this winemaking region. Many are still used in the making of the famous dessert wine that carries the town's name. It was an Englishman, John Woodhouse, who first exploited the commercial potential of **marsala wine,** when he visited the town in 1770. Woodhouse soon realized that, like port, the local wine could travel for long periods without going off, when fortified with alcohol. Others followed: Ingham, Whitaker, Hopps and many more whose names can still be seen on some of the warehouse doors. Interestingly, it was the English presence in Marsala that persuaded Garibaldi to launch his campaign here rather than in Sciacca (his first choice), judging that the Bourbon fleet wouldn't dare to interfere so close to Her Majesty's commercial concerns.

Marsala owes much of its current prosperity to the marketing of its wine, which is still a thriving industry, though no longer in British hands. You can visit some of the *bagli* and sample the stuff for free: try the **Cantine Montalto** (Mon–Fri 9am–1pm & 3–6pm, Sat 9am–1pm, other times can be booked at ☎ 0923 969.667) at Contrada Bérbaro, 3km along the road south towards Mazara del Vallo, reached along Lungomare Mediterraneo. Free guided tours and samplings are offered, and there's an **Enomuseum** where you can look over the old apparatus and techniques for winemaking. Otherwise, you'll find marsala or the sweeter *marsala all'uovo* (mixed with egg yolks) in every bar, enoteca and restaurant in town.

9

dredged up from the sea in 2005, the **Venus of Lilybaeum**: comparable in style to the more famous Venus Landolina in Siracusa, it's probably a Roman copy of a Hellenistic statue of the second century BC. Other items include more mundane ceramics from the Punic tophet ("sacrificial grounds") on Motya and other ancient necropolises in the neighbourhood, a good Roman mosaic, and some colourful examples of Italian and North African pottery.

ARRIVAL AND INFORMATION
MARSALA

By train Trains to Marsala, from Trapani in particular, are quicker and more frequent than buses. The train station is at the southeastern edge of town on Viale A. Fazio, a 15min walk from the centre.
Destinations Castelvetrano (13 daily Mon–Sat, 5 daily Sun; 40min); Mazara del Vallo (13 daily Mon–Sat, 5 daily Sun; 20min); Palermo (7 daily Mon–Sat, 4 daily Sun; 3hr 10min; may involve change); Trapani (13 daily Mon–Sat, 5 daily Sun; 30min).
By bus Buses arrive centrally at Piazza del Popolo (also known as Piazza Marconi), near Porta Garibaldi.
Destinations Agrigento (3–5 daily Mon–Sat, 1 daily Sun; 2hr 45min); Castelvetrano (7 daily Mon–Sat; 1hr 15min);

Mazara del Vallo (1–2 hourly Mon–Sat, 4 daily Sun; 30min); Palermo (about 1 hourly Mon–Sat, 7 daily Sun; 2hr 30min); Porto Empedocle (3 daily Mon–Sat, 1 daily Sun; 2hr 10min); Salemi (2 daily Mon–Sat, 1 daily Sun; 35min); Sciacca (3 daily Mon–Sat, 1 daily Sun; 1hr–1hr 30min); Trapani (4 daily Mon–Sat; 55min–1hr 15min); Trapani airport (1–4 daily Mon–Sat, 2 daily Sun; 15min).
By hydrofoil Hydrofoil services to and from the Egadi Islands are operated by Liberty Lines (☏ 348 357 9863) at the harbour, a 15min walk from the centre – you can buy tickets on the dockside. There is year-round service to Favignana (30min) and in recent years there has also been a summer-only service to Lévanzo and Marettimo.

ACCOMMODATION
SEE MAP PAGE 335

Centrale Via Salinisti 19 ☏ 0923 951 777, ⊚ hotel centralemarsala.it. Plain but spacious and comfortable en-suite rooms with a/c and minibar, arranged around a courtyard. The hotel has a quiet location in the old town, and there's off-street parking. Breakfast is in a nearby bar. €55

★ **Hotel Carmine** Piazza del Carmine 16 ☏ 0923 711 907, ⊚ hotelcarmine.it. Marsala's most stylish hotel is also very central. It has domed rooms, chic decor, antique trimmings and fabulous breakfasts. The spacious rooms have exposed brickwork and wood or tiled floors, some with balconies, some overlooking the internal garden. €109

Palazzo Diaz Via Salinisti 22 ☏ 348 019 0662 or ☏ 329 216 3780, ⊚ palazzodiaz.com. This B&B in a converted nineteenth-century *palazzo* has large, airy rooms with a/c and en-suite bathrooms, and there's a grand roof terrace where breakfast is served. €75
Villa Favorita Via Favorita 27 ☏ 0923 989 100, ⊚ villa favorita.com. This beautiful, secluded villa on the outskirts of town is set in its own gardens and has a pool, a tennis court and a restaurant, where the food and service alternate between superb and dire. Regular wedding receptions can disrupt the overall serenity of the place. It's signposted 2km northeast of the centre, off Via Trapani. €92

EATING
SEE MAP PAGE 335

In the centre of Marsala at least, **restaurants** can be hard to come by, but you'll eat well and relatively cheaply at the ones listed below. The couple of **bars** in Piazza della Repubblica are good for a cold beer, accompanied by earnest discussion of lottery numbers, otherwise try the places listed below. For general groceries, there's a lively daily **market** around the Porta Garibaldi, selling fresh fish, as well as fruit and vegetables.
Divino Rosso Largo di Girolamo ☏ 0923 711 770. A congenial pizzeria and wine bar where you can sit outside opposite a seventeenth-century *palazzo*. Snack on cheeses,

cold meats, panini and salads, or go for one of the tasty and inventive pizzas (around €7.50). There is also a fantastic range of wines. Daily dinner only.
★ **Il Gallo e l'Innamorata** Via S. Bilardello 18 ☏ 0923 195 4446. A small and friendly *osteria* with great food, including bruschetta with tuna, salami and tomato, grilled fish and a fine *busiate al pesto trapanese*. Prices are very reasonable for food of this quality – you can eat abundantly for €30 per head, including drinks. Tue–Sun lunch & dinner, Mon dinner only.

Mazara del Vallo

The North African element in Sicily's cultural melange is at its strongest in the major fishing port of **MAZARA DEL VALLO**, 22km down the coast from Marsala. Under the

Muslims, Mazara was one of Sicily's most prosperous towns and capital of the biggest of the three administrative districts, or *walis*, into which the island was divided – hence the "del Vallo" tag. The first Sicilian city to be taken by the Arabs, and the last they surrendered, Mazara's prosperity lasted for 250 years, coinciding with the height of Arab power in the Mediterranean. Count Roger's anxiety to establish a strong Norman presence in this Muslim powerbase ensured that Mazara's importance lasted long after his conquest of the city in 1087, and it didn't give up its rank as provincial capital until Trapani took over in 1817.

The Arab links have revived since the port became the prime Sicilian destination for **Tunisian immigrants** flocking across the sea to work in the vast fishing fleet – one of Italy's biggest. Indeed, wandering through Mazara's casbah-like backstreets, there are moments when you could imagine yourself to be in North Africa, passing Tunisian shops and a café plastered with pictures of the Tunisian president, and Arab music percolating through small doorways. For the visitor, the attraction of Mazara is its profusion of fine churches in a slowly reviving – though far from genteel – old town. The tree-shaded lungomare and seafront gardens add another facet to its character, and with a row of sea-view restaurants, Mazara is one of the few towns in the west to make the most of its coastal location.

The old town

Mazara's **old town** is where all the interest lies; it's bordered by the River Mazaro and sea on two sides and the main corsos – Umberto I and Vittorio Veneto – on the other two. At the southern end of Corso Umberto I, Piazza Mokarta holds the scant ruins of Count Roger's **castello**, magnificently floodlit at night, when the square is the focus of promenading crowds.

From Piazza Mokarta, Via Garibaldi leads up to Santa Veneranda, perhaps the most beautiful of Mazara's Baroque churches, its twin belltowers styled with a jaunty twist. Further west, at the edge of the old town, on a platform overlooking the Mazaro River,

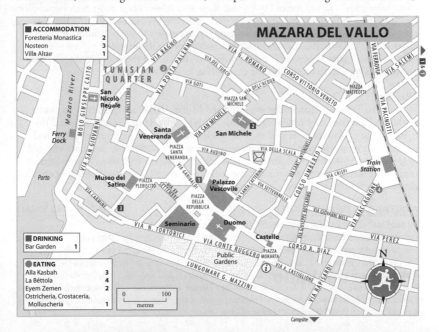

9

the church of **San Nicolò Regale** has a more restrained air. A restored Norman church, it has strong Arab elements, with a honey-toned, battlemented exterior and a simple interior rising to a single cupola.

The Duomo

Piazza della Repubblica • Daily 9am–6pm (7pm in summer) • Free

Mazara's **Duomo** was originally Norman but was completely remodelled in the late seventeenth century – though the relief over the main door showing a mounted Count Roger trampling a Saracen underfoot was carved in 1584. The light and airy **interior** reveals an almost indigestible profusion of stuccoed and sculptured ornamentation, including, behind the altar, a group of seven marble statues depicting the *Transfiguration*, carved by Antonello Gagini. To the right, a niche reveals a fragment of Byzantine fresco, dating from the end of the thirteenth century, while, through the marble doorway on the right side of the nave, you'll find some excellently chiselled Roman sarcophagi, with reliefs of a lively hunting scene and a battle, rich with confusion. Outside the Duomo, **Piazza della Repubblica** heralds a harmonious set of Baroque buildings: the square itself is flanked by the elegant, double-storey porticoed facade of the **Seminario** and the **Palazzo Vescovile**, both eighteenth century.

Museo del Satiro

Piazza del Plebiscito • Daily 9am–7pm • €6

The fifteenth-century church of Sant'Egido now houses the **Museo del Satiro**, named for its a rather risqué fourth-century-BC bronze satyr captured in the ecstatic throes of an orgiastic Dionysian dance. It was, quite literally, caught by a Mazara fishing boat in the waters between Pantelleria and Cap Bon, Tunisia, in 1998. Sadly, as the fishermen hauled the catch aboard, one of the arms broke off and has yet to be recovered. A 25-minute video with English subtitles relates the story.

The Tunisian quarter

Most of what remains of the old town was built after Mazara's teeming Arab population had dwindled to nothing, but it's here, especially in the Pilazza neighbourhood, that their descendants have returned, making up what is now a low-key **Tunisian quarter** centred on Via Porta Palermo and nearby Via Bagno. Stroll around the quiet alleys here and you'll pass authentic Tunisian cafés and shops, and the occasional social club resounding with Arab music and the clack of backgammon tables.

The port

West of the Tunisian quarter, the waters of the Mazaro River are hidden by the hulls of the two-hundred-odd trawlers that clog Mazara's **port**. Heavy overfishing and the use of illegal explosives (dropped into the sea to stun the fish) have greatly decreased the catch in recent years, but the rich waters above the continental shelf have ensured that there are enough fish left to make it worthwhile for the fishermen to pursue their trade worthwhile, that is, in terms of the reduced wages that the Tunisians are prepared to accept.

ARRIVAL AND INFORMATION · MAZARA DEL VALLO

By bus Buses stop at Via Salemi, either outside the train station or 200m up at Piazza Matteotti.

Destinations Agrigento (3 daily Mon–Sat, 1 daily Sun; 2hr–2hr 40min); Castelvetrano (3 daily Mon–Sat; 40min); Marsala (At least 1§ hourly Mon–Sat, 4 daily Sun; 30min); Palermo (8–12 daily Mon–Sat, 2–6 daily Sun; 2hr–2hr 35min); Trapani (4 daily Mon–Sat; 1hr 30min–1hr 45min).

By train Mazara's train station is centrally located off Corso Vittorio Veneto.

Destinations Castelvetrano (10 daily Mon–Sat, 5 daily Sun; 20min); Marsala (13 daily Mon–Sat, 5 daily Sun; 20min); Palermo (4–5 daily; 2hr 40min–3hr; may involve change); Trapani (13 daily Mon–Sat, 5 daily Sun; 50min).

Tourist information Lots of information on current events and things to do can be found on ⓦ mazaraonline. it (in Italian only).

ACCOMMODATION
SEE MAP PAGE 339

Foresteria Monastica Piazza San Michele Arcangelo 6 ☏ 0923 906 565 or ☏ 347 722 5069, ⓦ viaggispirituale. it. The rooms in this old-town convent annexed to San Michele church are very plain, but clean and quiet. You probably won't see any sign of the seven Benedictine nuns who are resident here, and who make the local pastries served at breakfast, which costs €5. Closed Nov–Feb. €50

Nosteon Via Plebiscito 9 ☏ 0923 651 619 or ☏ 347 571 8904, ⓦ nosteon.it. A great-value B&B off Piazza Plebiscito, with a double room and an apartment consisting of a double in the loft and a bunk downstairs, with a kitchen and bathroom. Breakfast is taken at a nearby bar. No credit cards. €60

★ **Villa Altair** Via Salemi 9 ☏ 0923 944 088 or ☏ 347 666 2963, ⓦ villaaltair.com. A couple of kilometres southeast of town (call for directions), this peaceful B&B occupies an old *baglio*, or farmhouse, in the middle of vineyards and olive groves. The five rooms have a/c and wi-fi connections, and there is a very welcome swimming pool. €80

EATING AND DRINKING
SEE MAP PAGE 339

Food in Mazara is good value, with restaurants aimed more at locals than tourists, making it a great destination for sampling couscous, Tunisian specialities and fantastic, raw, fresh fish.

Alla Kasbah Via Itria 10 ☏ 0923 906 126. Don't be fooled by the name: apart from a very acceptable fish couscous, the food here is modern Sicilian rather than North African. You can have an *antipasto*, couscous and house wine for less than €20; other fixed-price menus are €20–25. The ambience is relaxed and friendly. Daily lunch & dinner; closed Mon Sept–June.

Bar Garden Piazza della Repubblica 7 ☏ 0923 941 909. Facing the town's most harmonious buildings, this is a nice place for a breakfast or sit-down by day, and to soak up the weird, green illuminations in the evening. Tues–Sun 8am–8pm, open daily and till late in summer.

★ **La Béttola** Via Maccagnone 32 ☏ 0923 946 422. Near the train station, this simple place serves fantastic regional fish and seafood specialities. Try the catch of the day, sliced thin and marinated, or the lovely fish couscous. Choose carefully and you'll spend less than €20 with house wine. Daily lunch & dinner.

Eyem Zemen Via Porta Palermo 36 ☏ 347 386 9921. A tiny place, with three or four tables outside and authentic, cheap Tunisian snacks – *brik* (fried pastry parcels), oily aubergine salads and couscous. You can eat well for €15. Daily lunch & dinner; closed Tues in winter.

★ **Ostricheria, Crostaceria, Molluscheria** Contrada Pesca Strada Statale 115 ☏ 366 904 4937. If you have a car and like raw fish, don't miss this place, outside town on the SS115 (direction Marsala) just after the exit for the E90. It serves only oysters, crustaceans and molluscs, all raw, and all, naturally, spanking fresh, washed down with a nice, cold bottle of local white. €15 a head. Lunch & dinner Tues–Sat, lunch only Sun & Mon.

Selinunte and Marinella di Selinunte

SELINUNTE, the site of the Greek city of Selinus, lies around 30km east of Mazara del Vallo, stranded on a remote corner of the coast in splendid isolation, just west of the modern village of **Marinella di Selinunte**. Selinunte is a crucial sight if you're travelling through the west of Sicily, its series of mighty temples lying in great heaps, where they were felled by earthquakes.

Most westerly of the Hellenic colonies, **Selinus** reached its peak during the fifth century BC. A bitter rival of Segesta, whose lands lay adjacent to the north, the powerful city and its fertile plain attracted enemies hand over fist, and it was only a matter of time before Selinus caught the eye of Segesta's ally, Carthage. Geographically vulnerable, the city was sacked by Carthaginians, any attempts at recovery forestalled by earthquakes, which later razed it altogether. However, people continued to live here until 250 BC, when the population was finally transferred to Marsala before the Roman invasion. The Arabs did occupy the site briefly, but the last recorded settlement at Selinunte was in the thirteenth century, after which time it remained forgotten until rediscovered in the sixteenth century. Despite the destruction, the city ruins have exerted a romantic hold over people ever since.

Marinella di Selinunte

Although it can get a bit hectic in summer, **MARINELLA DI SELINUNTE** is an atmospheric place to spend a few hours. Its most appealing parts lie on and around the long, narrow

9

SELINUNTE AND MARINELLA DI SELINUNTE

**ANCIENT CITY
(UNEXCAVATED)**

North Gate

ACROPOLIS

Temple D

Temple C

Temple A

Temple B

Temple O

Castelvetrano & Campobello

SS115

**EAST
GROUP**

Temple G

Temple F

Temple E

Park
Entrance

VIA MEGARA HYBLEA

VIA CABOTO

Allmentari

★Bus Stop

VIA PIGAFETTA

VIA MARCO POLO

VIA DELLA CITTARELLA

VIA PIGAFETTA

PIAZZALE
EFEBO

VIA CASTELLO

Bank

Harbour

VIA PLATONE

VIA ARISTOTELE

VIA PISCINA

VIA PISANO

VIA CALIPSO

VIA ITALMARIO

VIA SAN GIORGIO

VIA CASSIOPEA

VIA CASTORE E POLLUCE

VIA NAUSICA

VIA PERSEPHONE

VIA VEGA

VIA SIRIO

VIA ARGONAUTI

MARINELLA

Supermarket

VIA ANTIGONE

& Mare Pineta

**MEDITERRANEAN
SEA**

N

& Antiquarium (600m)

Santuario Malophoros (400m)

0   100
metres

● EATING
La Pineta   1
Tukè   2

■ ACCOMMODATION
B&B Garzia   2
Il Pescatore   1

road that winds down to the small **harbour**, where fishing boats are hauled up onto the sands by pulleys.

Marinella is no longer the isolated place it used to be, with new buildings and streets in evidence everywhere, while the seafront has become top-heavy with trattorias, and shops selling Tunisian carpets, souvenirs and beachwear. But it remains an attractive place, of particular appeal if you're planning to use the fine sand **beach** that stretches west from the village to the ruins. The water isn't great to swim in, since it's often clogged with seaweed at the sand's edge, though this doesn't deter the kids. However, the **surfing** here can be okay, and you can rent equipment in the summer, as well as pedalos, chairs, shades and all the usual beach paraphernalia. Another beach, **Mare Pineta**, is located east of the village, backed by pine trees stretching into the distance; follow the road east of the port for ten minutes.

ARRIVAL AND GETTING AROUND

MARINELLA DI SELINUNTE

By bus Buses from Castelvetrano (4–8 daily; 30min) to Selinunte pass through Marinella, and continue to the site.

ACCOMMODATION

SEE MAP PAGE 342

B&B Garzia Via A. Pigafetta 2 ☏ 0924 46 024. This large, Arabic-themed hotel on the seafront road lacks charm, but it has a wide range of rooms (some with sea-facing balconies), friendly staff and its own patch of beach. **€75**

★ **Il Pescatore** Via Castore e Polluce 31 ☏ 0924 46 303.

With a roof terrace that enjoys views over to the temples and sea, this place offers eight good-sized rooms with private bathrooms and a/c or fans, breakfast (that includes fresh fruit) on the terrace, plus use of a kitchen. No credit cards. Doubles **€110**

EATING

SEE MAP PAGE 342

Most of the best eating and drinking places are on Via Marco Polo, the road above the west beach. If you want to take a picnic up to the temple, visit the *alimentari* on Via Caboto.

La Pineta Mare Pineta ☏ 0924 46 820. This trattoria on the beach east of the harbour is a real find, serving fresh seafood including sea urchins (*ricci*). It's the perfect spot for a lunch or leisurely evening meal just metres from the sea (€10–18 for most dishes). Call ahead to book in winter. Summer daily lunch & dinner; winter lunch only.

Tukè Piazza Empedocle ☏ 0924 1934 4048. Simple place right by the water, with its own little beach in the summer, where you can eat a truly excellent mixed seafood *antipasto* (€12) featuring perfectly battered anchovies and the tenderest of octopus salads. They also do a hearty *pasta con le sarde* (€12). Local *pane nero* (wholemeal bread) to accompany, and decent house white. Fri–Wed for lunch and dinner, open daily in summer.

CAVE DI CUSA

If you have your own transport, it's well worth calling in at the quarries where the stone for the building of Selinus was extracted in the fifth century BC. They lie 3.5km south of the scruffy town of **Campobello di Mazara**, deep in olive country. From Selinunte, a lovely 20km drive takes you along country roads lined with olive groves and vines. When you reach Campobello, take the road to Tre Fontane and follow the signs "Cave di Cusa", keeping your eyes peeled and fingers crossed.

At the site of the **Cave di Cusa** (daily 9am–1hr before sunset; free), a path leads into a bucolic setting that is more reminiscent of English Romanticism than of ancient Greece. In early summer, workers fork hay into piles in between the rock ledges and tended shrubs, while behind them stretch shaded groves of olives. Everywhere, you can see the massive column drums and stumps lying randomly about, quarried and chiselled into shape here before being dragged to the ancient city on wooden carts, where they formed part of the great temple complex. There are examples of all the various stages of the process, with unfinished pieces poignantly abandoned, the work interrupted when Selinus was devastated in 409 BC. The most impressive pieces are those stone drums and column sections that remain in place where they were being excavated. A couple are 6m high and 2m across, with a narrow groove dug all the way around in which the stonemasons had to work – the reflected heat must have been appalling. Other rock sections indicate clearly where drums have already been cut – parts of the site look as though someone has been through with a giant pastry-cutter.

9

The Selinus ruins

Daily 9am–1hr before sunset; last entry 1hr before closing • €6 • Navetta buggies cost €6 for the nearer temples, €12 for the complete circuit

The **ruins** of Selinus are back behind the main part of Marinella di Selinunte, split into two main sections, the **east group** and the **acropolis**, with individual temples known simply as "A", "B", etc. The two parts are enclosed within the same site, with the car park and **entrance** – lying through the landscaped earthbanks that preclude views of the east group of temples from the road. Selinus is claimed to be the biggest archeological site in Europe, so it can be quite a challenge if you want to see everything; you might make use of the buggy service, or **navetta**, for the remoter sites, or rent a bike. On foot, you could cover everything in two or three hours, but the total lack of shade makes for hard work in the full heat of summer.

The east group

Shrouded in the wild celery that gave the ancient city its name, the **east group** temples are in various stages of reconstructed ruin. The most complete is the one nearest the sea (**Temple E**), probably dedicated to Hera (Aphrodite) and re-erected in 1958. A Doric construction, almost 70m by 25m, it remains a gloriously impressive sight, its soaring columns gleaming bright against the sky, its ledges and capitals the resting place for flitting birds. **Temple F**, behind, is the oldest in this group, from around 550 BC, while the northernmost temple (**Temple G**) is an immense tangle of columned wreckage, 6m high in places and crisscrossed by rough footpaths. In Sicily, the only temple larger than this is the Tempio di Giove at Agrigento.

The acropolis

The road leads down from the east group, across the (now buried) site of the old harbour, to the second part of excavated Selinus, the **acropolis**, containing what remains of the other temples (five in all), as well as the well-preserved city streets and massive stepped **walls** that rise above the duned beach below. These huge walls were all constructed after 409 BC – when the city was sacked by the Carthaginians – in an attempt to protect a limited and easily defensible area of the old city.

Temple C stands on the highest point of the acropolis, giving glorious views out over the sparkling sea. Built early in the sixth century BC (and probably dedicated to Apollo), it originally held the finest of the metopes (decorative panels) that are now in Palermo's archeological museum. Its fourteen standing columns were re-erected in the 1920s: other fallen columns here, and at the surrounding temples, show how they were originally constructed – the drums lying in a line, with slots and protrusions on either side that fitted into each other. The buildings immediately behind **temples C and D** were shops, split into two rooms and with a courtyard each.

The rest of the site

At the end of the main street beyond stands the **north gate** to the city – the tall blocks of stone marking a gateway that was 7m high. Behind the north gate stood the rest of the ancient city, still largely unexcavated, though crisscrossed by little paths through the undergrowth. The **agora** was sited just north of here, and a necropolis further up, while to the west, across the Modione River, stood the **Santuario Malophoros**, part of a complex that marked the western boundary of the city. Animal sacrifices were performed at the small well in front of the structure. Beyond it, on the edge of the archeological zone, the **Antiquarium** holds statuettes and terracotta fragments, mostly excavated in the 1980s from a temple dedicated to Hera Matronale, south of the Malophoros.

9

The interior

The **interior** of Trapani province is intensely rural, its few small towns little changed by the coming of the A29 autostrada, which cuts across the region. The whole area is green and highly fertile, mainly given over to vine-growing; indeed, the wine around the **Salemi** district is among Sicily's best. But, hard though it is to believe, the entire region still hasn't recovered from the **earthquake** of January 15, 1968, which briefly spotlighted western Sicily, sadly, more for the authorities' inadequate response to it than for the actual loss of life. Four hundred died and a thousand were injured, no great number by Sicilian standards, but it was the 50,000 left homeless that had the most lingering impact on this already depressed part of the island, and the effects of the earthquake are still evident everywhere. Ruined buildings and ugly temporary dwellings still being used more than four decades later testify to the chronically dilatory response to the disaster, aggravated by private interests and particularly by the Mafia contractors who capitalized on the catastrophe. Even where rebuilding went ahead, such as in the new town of **Gibellina**, it's still possible to see the dread hand of inertia.

It goes without saying that this is a little-visited area of Sicily, but it's intriguing nonetheless. This is, after all, the part of the world known best to Giuseppe Tomasi di Lampedusa, whose classic novel, *The Leopard*, is partly set in the little town of **Santa Margherita di Belice** – also badly damaged in 1968, but emerging slowly from the doldrums, and an essential stop for anyone who's read the book.

GETTING AROUND   **THE INTERIOR**

By car Local buses run to all the towns in the region, but it's impossible to construct any kind of sightseeing itinerary using them – you have to have your own car, not least to avoid the possibility of getting stuck in backwaters with no accommodation.

Salemi

The town of **SALEMI**, 30km east of Marsala, enjoyed the privilege of being the first capital of a united Italy in 1860, albeit for only three days, as recorded by a plaque in front of its heavily restored thirteenth-century **castello** on Piazza Alicia, at the top of the town. Another plaque marks Garibaldi's declaration of a dictatorship, asserting that "in times of war, it's necessary for the civilian powers to be concentrated in the hands of one man" – namely Garibaldi himself, though King Vittorio Emanuele still gets a mention.

The Collegio dei Gesuiti museums

Via d'Aguirre • Tues–Sat 10am–1pm & 4–7pm • Combined ticket €5

On Via d'Aguirre, the former Collegio dei Gesuiti houses a quintet of museums. The **Museo del Risorgimento** holds assorted pieces of "Garibaldini" – letters, documents and arms connected with the town's finest hour; the **Museo Archeologico** contains finds from local excavations including Monte Polizzo; the **Museo dell'Arte Sacra** gathers treasures from various local churches, including the cathedral destroyed in the earthquake; and the **Museo del Paesaggio** explores aspects of the Sicilian landscape by means of videos. The **Museo della Mafia** brings together films, photographs, recordings of interviews, and paintings and sculptures by local artists of prominent figures in the Mafia's history – including representations of the two assassinated anti-Mafia judges Falcone and Borsellino, plus work by a *pentito*, or informer. It's a pretty disparate mix, and fairly indigestible if you attempt to take them all in, but the collections are definitely worth putting aside a couple of hours for.

INFORMATION   **SALEMI**

Tourist information The best source of information is ⓦ salemionline.it.

Gibellina Nuova

Salemi got off lightly in terms of earthquake damage, even though a third of the population had to abandon their shattered homes. Other towns, like Gibellina, were completely flattened, and the population moved en masse to **GIBELLINA NUOVA**, a modern town that was once a symbol of progress in the region, its wide, empty streets adorned with numerous weird constructions and abstract **sculptures** designed by a handful of iconoclastic architects with big budgets. A vast stainless-steel star straddles the motorway where you exit for Gibellina, while elsewhere the town holds huge white spheres, giant ploughs, snails and much besides – some fifty constructions in all, though many of them are crumbling already (one church collapsed in 1994), and many of the designs themselves are embarrassingly frozen in the image of what appeared futuristic in the 1970s. The town, meanwhile, bakes in the summer sun, since all the modern piazzas are vast concrete spaces with little shade.

You can get a taste of what Gibellina is all about by driving to the main square – **Piazza XV Gennaio 1968**, in case there was any doubt about what's to blame for all this – where the arcaded City Hall is fronted by some particularly abstract examples, and the tall **Torre Belice** clocktower chimes four times a day with taped human voices instead of bells, a reminder of the earthquake victims.

Baglio di Stefano

Museums Tues–Sun 9am–1pm & 3–6pm • €5 • ☏ 0924 67 844, ⓦ fondazioneorestiadi.it

The cultural centre, **Baglio di Stefano**, to the east of the centre, is home to a couple of museums, one containing **contemporary art** – mainly works by Italian painters, but the sculptor Arnaldo Pomodoro is also represented – the other dedicated to **Mediterranean culture**, from Spain to Turkey and from Corsica to Africa, taking in costumes, jewellery, ceramics, tapestries, calligraphy and carpets, all beautifully presented. A separate space here, the **Atelier**, has pieces donated by the various sculptors and designers who contributed to Gibellina Nuova's townscape.

The Baglio di Stefano complex also holds a **theatre**, which is the main venue for the **Orestiadi**, a series of classical and modern dramas, concerts and events performed almost nightly every July and August. As well as works by Euripides, Sophocles and others, there are modern interpretations by the likes of Jean Cocteau, Stravinsky and John Cage, plus a full programme of exhibitions, cinema and music.

EATING   GIBELLINA NUOVA

La Massara Viale dei Vespri Siciliani 41 ☏ 0924 67 601. This is an inexpensive trattoria, a 10min walk from the central piazza, where the very filling house pasta, the rather aptly named *busiate napoleonica* (€6.50), is made with aubergines, tomato and sausage. Tues–Sun lunch & dinner.

Ruderi di Gibellina

Eighteen kilometres east of Gibellina Nuova, overlooked by ranks of wind turbines, the old town of **RUDERI DI GIBELLINA** complements the new: a mountain of rubble from which smashed and mutilated houses poke out, strewn over a green hillside. It is not well cared for at all, often strewn with rubbish, so unless you are particularly interested, give it a miss. On the way into town, you'll pass what is ironically its best-preserved fragment: a shady **cemetery** stretching down the side of the valley, where the inhabitants of the new town return every year to remember the catastrophe. Further down, modernism has left its mark here too, in the form of a wide, grey-white mantle of concrete, **Il Cretto**, poured over one slope, and carved through by channels that recall the previous layout of streets. It's an arresting spectacle, not least for its sheer scale.

Everything else remains as it was after the earthquake struck: only a church has since been restored.

9

Santa Margherita di Belice

Often ranked among the finest of all historical novels, Giuseppe Tomasi di Lampedusa's *The Leopard* ("Il Gattopardo" in Italian) is a masterpiece of manners and morals, written by a Sicilian prince who only ever completed this one work. Set in 1860s Sicily, it draws heavily on Lampedusa's own experiences, not least the summers he used to spend in his grandmother's palace in **SANTA MARGHERITA DI BELICE**. This is the Donnafugata of the book – the fictional prince's summer home, a place cherished for the "sense it gave him of everlasting childhood". The 1968 earthquake, unfortunately, completely wrecked the seventeenth-century palace and church described so intensely in the novel, though fragments of the palace have been incorporated in a gleaming new **Municipio**. This, with its cool internal courtyards and lovely garden to the side, at least echoes the spirit of the original. More poignant is all that's left of the adjacent **Chiesa Madre** – an elaborately stuccoed and frescoed two-storey corner glassed in to create the wall of the **Museo della Memoria** (daily 10am–1pm & 4–7pm; €4) which retells the haunting story of the 1968 earthquake and its aftermath in photos.

Pantelleria

With an area of 83 square kilometres, and consisting of no fewer than fourteen spent or dormant volcanoes, **PANTELLERIA** is the largest of Sicily's offshore islands. Forty kilometres closer to Tunisia than to Sicily, it has been occupied since early times by whichever power controlled the central Mediterranean. The Phoenicians, who colonized it in the seventh century BC called it Hiranin, "island of the birds", after the

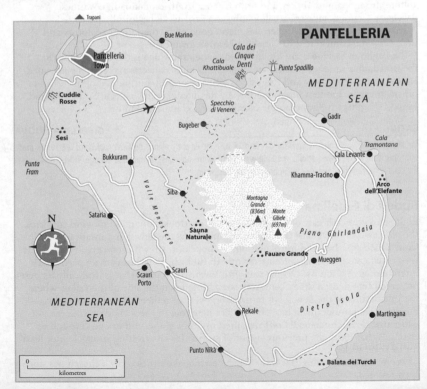

GETTING TO PANTELLERIA

You can **reach Pantelleria** by overnight ferry (year-round) or hydrofoil (summer only) from Trapani. Flights from Trapani or Palermo take under an hour and are convenient, if more expensive.

Ferries do the journey in 7 hours 30 min (June–Sept daily; Oct–May daily except Sat), leaving Trapani at 11pm, for a deck-class fare of about €30 one-way (slightly less in low season). There are ferries from Pantelleria back to the mainland (June–Sept daily; Oct–May Mon–Sat). For an extra €5.50 you can reserve a reclining chair (*poltrona*), an expense worth considering since the regular seats are difficult to sleep in; or there are couchette-cabins with WC for an extra €20 or so per person. Tickets are on sale online in advance or at the Stazione Marittima in Trapani (☎0923 24 968, 🌐siremar.it), right up until departure. **Liberty Lines** operates **hydrofoils** to Pantelleria from June to Sept only.

Pantelleria is just a forty-minute **flight** from Trapani (3 flights daily) or a fifty-minute flight from Palermo (2–3 flights daily). One-way tickets are €50–90, depending on availability and flexibility; it's worth booking some time in advance in summer.

birds that still stop over here on their migratory routes; for the Greeks, it was Kossyra, or "small". Its present name probably derives from the Arabic *hint ar-riah* ("daughter of the winds"), after the restless breezes that blow around the island's rugged shores.

Pantelleria is a dramatic, black island, its coastline thick with treacherous volcanic debris, the contours of its fertile volcanic hills traced with an intricate embroidery of dry-stone terraces, walls and walled gardens created over the centuries to make cultivation possible on this wind-lashed piece of earth where the only sources of water are thermal springs and rain. Agricultural practices unique to the island have developed too – most of Pantelleria's olive trees are barely knee-high, and the island technique of terraced bush vine growing has been recognized by UNESCO and included on its Intangible Heritage of Humanity list. Pantelleria's traditional houses (*dammusi*) are also intimately tied to their unique environment – sombre, dry-stone cubes with thick walls, minimal windows and shallow, domed roofs surrounded by a channel designed to collect every drop of rainwater. Some *dammusi* stand alone, some in clusters – it is perhaps testimony to the toughness of life that it is often impossible to tell the difference between a *dammuso* built as a dwelling and one built to shelter animals or act as storage.

The main port, known simply as **Pantelleria**, was bombed in World War II. It is shabby, charmless and full of concrete, and the only reasons to visit are to buy petrol or visit the bank machine. There are two other main settlements, both set slightly inland: **Khamma-Tracino**, strung along the road above the east coast, wins no prizes for aesthetics, but is an authentic rural town where home-brewed wine and home-cured capers are sold alongside the imported necessities of life. **Scauri**, on the west coast, is a little smarter – and its little port has the island's most welcoming restaurant bar.

Despite an **airport** which gives easy access to the mainland, tourism infrastructure on Pantelleria remains pretty undeveloped, apart from a scant strip of ugly hotels and functional cement holiday villas along the northwest coast. The east coast – where Armani has a villa – is the most enticing, with any number of rough asphalt and dirt tracks leading down to dramatic little volcanic coves. For an island of its size, there are not very many **places to stay** – nor even very many places to eat. The best option by far is to rent a *dammuso*, villa or part of a villa (see page 351) and to plan on mostly cooking at home. The **best times to visit** are May/June or September/October, before and after the crowds and scorching heat of summer.

Pantelleria town

From far away at sea, **PANTELLERIA TOWN** presents an undeniably romantic aura, revealing a spread of white-painted cubes. Only close up do these emerge as modern,

9

scruffy, concrete blocks. During World War II, the town had the misfortune to be one of the main German bases in the Mediterranean and was pulverized by Allied bombers.

Castello Barbacane

Via Castello • Aug daily 6pm–midnight; call to arrange a tour at other times • Free • ☎ 327 363 9284

The only building that predates the war is the morose, black Castello Barbacane, a legacy of the Spaniards. Its partly restored interior is destined to hold an archeological museum, but in the meantime it's the venue for changing exhibitions and has photos and videos showing aspects of island history and culture, from World War II bombing to carnival celebrations.

ARRIVAL AND DEPARTURE   PANTELLERIA TOWN

By plane The airport (☎ 0923 911 172, ⍵ pantelleriairport. it) is 5km southeast of town. A bus service makes the 12min run into town four times daily from a stop outside. Taxis into town charge €15; alternatively, it's a 45min downhill walk. If you don't have internet access and need airline tickets, try the La Cossira travel agency, Via Borgo Italia 77 (☎ 0923 911 078, daily 9am–1pm & 3–8pm).

Destinations Palermo (2–3 daily in summer; 50min); Trapani (3 daily in summer; 40min).

By ferry and hydrofoil Arriving by sea, you'll disembark

right in the centre of town, close to most of the bars, restaurants and hotels. In bad weather, you may be deposited instead at Scauri, a smaller port on the island's southwestern side, from where a bus takes foot passengers into town (remember to disembark promptly or it will leave without you). Siremar operates a ferry service to Trapani (see page 349); buy ferry tickets from Agenzia Rizzo, Via Borgo Italia 22 (☎ 0923 911 120) or online at ⍵ carontetourist.it). Liberty Lines hydrofoil tickets are available from Agenzia Minardi, Via Borgo Italia 15 (☎ 0923 911 502, ⍵ libertylines.it).

GETTING AROUND

You'll need a lot of patience – and a willingness to walk to the various coves and coastal spots – to get around the island by bus. Renting a car or moped is strongly recommended: if you're limited to public transport, you'll miss the best of the island – the remote coves and mountain trails. To visit the isolated coves of the southeastern Dietro

Isola, and other good swimming spots, you'll need to go by boat. There are notices in the agencies along the harbour, in every hotel, and on the boats themselves.

By bus Local buses make regular departures from Piazza Cavour to all the main villages on the island, with no services on Sundays. Buy tickets in advance from any

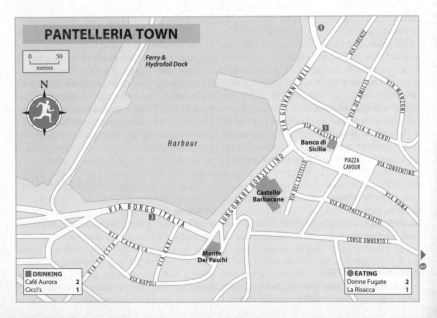

PANTELLERIA TOWN

0   50
metres

N

Ferry & Hydrofoil Dock

Harbour

VIA EBERLE
VIA GIOVANNI MELI
VIA DE AMICIS
VIA MANZONI
VIA CAGLIARI
VIA G. VERDI
Banco di Sicilia
PIAZZA CAVOUR
VIA CONVENTINO
LUNGOMARE BORSELLINO
VIA DEL CASTELLO
Castello Barbacane
VIA ARCIPRETE D'AIETTI
VIA ROMA
VIA BORGO ITALIA
CORSO UMBERTO I.
VIA TRIESTE
VIA CATANIA
VIA BARI
Monte Dei Paschi
VIA NAPOLI

■ DRINKING
Café Aurora   2
Cicci's   1

● EATING
Donne Fugate   2
La Risacca   1

PANTELLERIA ACCOMMODATION

Hotel accommodation on Pantelleria is generally expensive, though sites such as **Airbnb** have transformed the market, making it fairly easy to find a lovely, affordable **dammuso** in a good location – especially if you book well in advance. There are also several residences, offering hotel-like services, and accommodation in little ersatz *dammusi*. During July and August, many places impose a minimum stay of three days or even a week, but at other times of the year, there are no such constraints (indeed islanders are only too happy to have some out-of-season business), and prices drop considerably: be prepared to bargain. There's no campsite on the island, and camping rough is impractical given the terrain and lack of water.

If you are in search of luxury, check out ⊛ sicilyluxuryvillas.com, which has some gorgeous *dammusi* villas, including the one in which the movie *A Bigger Splash* was filmed. There are also several local sites specializing in *dammusi*, such as La Cossira (☎ 0923 911 078, ⊛ lacossirapantelleria.it), which has *dammusi* to suit all pockets. Expect to pay €300–1000 per week according to size and season (you may be able to book less than a week's rental in low season), and bear in mind that you'll inevitably need a car to get to and from them.

---

tabacchi or on the bus. Services are run by Marsala Travel bus (⊛ marsalatravelbus.it). There are no buses on Sunday. There are seven buses daily from Pantelleria town along the east coast to Tracino, with stops at Punta Karuscia, Kattibuale, and the junctions for Punta Spadillo and Gadir. There four buses daily from Pantelleria town to Bukkaram via the airport.

Destinations Bugeber (4 daily; 20min); Khamma (7 daily Mon–Sat; 25min); Rekale via Sesi (6 daily Mon–Sat; 20min); Scauri (6 daily Mon–Sat; 20min); Tracino (7 daily Mon– Sat; 30min).

By taxi Consolo, Piazza Castello (☎ 0923 912 716 or ☎ 339 715 7586).

Bike rental Viva Pantelleria, Vicolo Leopardi 5 (☎ 0923 911 078 or ☎ 349 619 9210), charges €12 for up to 2hr, €16 for half a day. Escorted bike tours and kayak rental are also available.

Car and scooter rental Autonoleggio Policardo is at Via Messina 31 (☎ 0923 912 844, ⊛ policardo.it) and at the airport. Expect to pay up to €65 per day for a Fiat 600, €50 per day for a scooter, much less in low season.

INFORMATION AND TOURS

Tourist Information There's no tourist office on Pantelleria, but the Italian-language websites ⊛ prolocopantelleria. it, ⊛ pantelleria.it and ⊛ tuttopantelleria.it are all useful, while, if you speak Italian, Tano Petrillo (☎ 339 742 0921) is a font of knowledge on all kinds of practical matters, including car rental.

Guided walking and boat tours Excursions by jeep, on foot and boat are organized by the Gira l'Isola agency at Vicolo Messina 21 (☎ 0923 913 254, ⊛ giralisola.com). Prices: €30 per person for a half-day trek including guide and transport; €20 for a half-day jeep tour; €35 per person

for a full-day boat tour. They also run archeological and gastronomic tours from €25 per person.

Diving There are several well respected diving schools on the island, offering diving excursions and courses. Green Divers (⊛ greendivers-sub.com, ☎ 349 646 6504) comes highly recommended. Expect to pay around €70 for a single scuba dive, with good deals for packages of five or ten dives, especially outside July and August. They also have a package that includes seven nights in a *dammuso* and five dives at €300 per person.

EATING

SEE MAP PAGE 350

There are several restaurants and trattorias in town. Many double as pizzerias.

Donne Fugate Corso Umberto I, 10 ☎ 334 760 3261. A small, rather unprepossessing-looking place where you can nevertheless indulge in an excellent selection of *antipasti* and first courses such as *spaghetti alla menta e gamberi* (spaghetti with mint and prawns). Fish couscous is a special every Thursday (worth booking for this). You'll pay around €40 for a full meal, drinks excluded. Mon, Tues & Thurs–

Sat dinner only.

La Risacca Via Errera 18 ☎ 0923 912 975. At the end of the harbour, this busy ristorante-pizzeria with a terrace has an array of grilled seafood and outdoor seating. Try the *ravioli con pomodoro, burro e salvia* (ravioli with tomato, butter and sage) for €12, or, in the evening, *couscous alla pantesca*, with fish, aubergine, peppers, courgette and tomato (€17). Tues–Sun lunch & dinner, open daily in July & Aug.

9

DRINKING

SEE MAP PAGE 350

The bars on the harbourfront are where the action is, starting at 6am (when they open their doors for the arriving ferry passengers) and finishing any time between 10pm and 2am, depending on the season and the manager's inclination.
Café Aurora Via Borgo Italia 43 ☎ 0923 911 313. With a seating area overlooking the port, this bar serves aperitifs with olives and other nibbles. Daily 10am–late; closed winter.
Cicci's Via Cagliari 7 ☎ 0923 913 696. Just off the main piazza, this place has a lively evening crowd, musical accompaniment, and snacks. Daily 6am–late; closed Sun in winter.

DIRECTORY

Banks ATMs at Banco di Sicilia, Piazza Cavour, Monte dei Paschi, Via Napoli 2, and Banco Nuova, Via Catania 5.
Hospital Ospedale B. Nagar, Piazzale Almanza (☎ 0923 910 111).
Pharmacy Farmacia Greco on Piazza Cavour (Mon–Fri 8.30am–1pm & 5–8.30pm; ☎ 0923 911 310). Pharmacies operate on a rota outside normal opening hours, noted on the door.
Police Carabinieri, Via Trieste 29 (☎ 0923 911 109).
Post office The island's main post office is off Piazza Cavour on Via de Amicis (Mon–Fri 8.20am–1pm, Sat 8.20am–12.30pm).

The east coast

Although not the most striking part of the northeast coast, **Bue Marino**, some 1km east of Pantelleria town, has reasonable swimming from the rocks, though there is better swimming a little further on, from the flat rocks at **Cala Khattibuale**, below the junction with the road to Bugeber and the Specchio di Venere. Scant patches of volcanic sand and natural, shallow pools make this a good choice if you have young kids, though the reef itself is rough, so you'll need swimming shoes.

East of here lies the **Cala dei Cinque Denti**, where fantastically shaped rocks jut out of the sea like monstrous black teeth – hence its name, "Bay of the Five Teeth" (though the rocks are really best seen from the sea). Just beyond, a minor road cuts away to the lighthouse at **Punta Spadillo**. There is parking here, outside the semi-abandoned volcanology museum (though it usually opens for a while in August). Straight ahead are an abandoned lighthouse and military gun emplacements. More enticing, a path/jeep-track has recently been cut across the eerie lava landscape, heading back north to Cinque Denti via the tiny bouldery bay of **Cala Ondine**; climb down on a calm day to swim below a fantastic formation of lava columns.

The Specchio di Venere and Bugeber

It is a short (signposted) drive from the *perimetrale* (the road that runs right around the island's perimeter) above Cala Khattabuale to the stunning **Specchio di Venere** (Venus's Mirror), eerily shimmering in a former crater. Though it glistens aquamarine in the middle, the lake has a muddy-brown edge, deposits of which you're supposed to apply to your body and allow to bake hard in the sun. Then you dive in and swim, washing

---

THE BEST PLACES TO SWIM AND WALK ON PANTELLERIA

There are no beaches of any kind on Pantelleria, its rough black coastline consisting mainly of jagged rocks, but wooden decking has been put down on the rocks in several little coastal villages, making sunbathing less of a torture than it used to be. In the more remote coves – which you will probably have to yourself outside July and August – fantastic volcanic rock formations compensate for the lack of comfort, although swimming shoes, and a thick mat make a world of difference. The most effortless **place to swim** – and consequently the biggest tourist attraction on the island – is the **Specchio di Venere**, an inland volcanic lake with thermal springs, pale mud-sand beaches and milky turquoise waters.

Inland, the largely mountainous country offers plenty of **rambling opportunities**, with landscapes varying from high meadows (carpeted with wild flowers in spring) to the ancient coniferous forests that cloak the highest mountain, **Montagna Grande**.

MAKING A LIVING ON PANTELLERIA

Most of Pantelleria's population of 8500 are **farmers** rather than fishermen. With a soil nourished by frequent past eruptions (the last offshore in 1891), the islanders traditionally preferred tilling to risking life and limb in a sea swarming with pirates on the prowl. Farming on Pantelleria does have its problems, however, not least the numerous chunks of lava and basalt in the earth that preclude mechanical ploughing, not to mention the incessant wind, scorching sun and almost complete lack of water. Over thousands of years, islanders have come up with such ingenious methods of minimizing these disadvantages, that their agricultural ways have earned them recognition by UNESCO. The prolific **zibbibo vines** are kept tiny and individually planted in little ridges designed to capture the precious rainwater; and the famous *giardini panteschi* – high walls of stone often built around a single orange or other fruit tree – afford protection from the wind. All over the island, home-grown produce is on sale from people's houses and gardens to visitors and locals – capers, wine, oregano, giant raisins, chilli, sundried tomatoes and honey – while the pioneering winemaker, Emanuela Bonomo (see page 356), may mark the way ahead, with her fantastic range of pestos, conserves and herbs, as well as her marvellous wines.

all the mud off in the pleasantly warm water. A path skirts the edge of the lake, around which horse races take place as part of the August *ferragosto* celebrations. If you prefer to walk – definitely worth it in low season – follow the signposted path that runs from the main road above Cala dei Cinque Denti.

Beyond the lake, the road climbs up for another 2km to the hamlet of **Bugeber**, set amid tumbling fields of vines and craggy boulders.

Gadir

At a fork in the road past Punta Spadillo, a steeply twisting asphalt road runs down into **Gadir**, one of the most perfect spots on Pantelleria. It's a small anchorage, with just a few houses hemmed in by volcanic pricks of rock, which – when the wind is up – can be battered and lashed by violent waves. At other times, people lie about on the wooden decking laid out on the harbourside, and dunk in the tiny thermal pools. There are three little stone pits on the harbourside (one of them 90° C, so watch out) and a larger pool around the headland.

Cala Levante and around

The *perimetrale* continues from the Gadir junction, following slopes that are terraced and corralled behind a patchwork of stone walls. Vines grow in profusion, with capers and blackberry bushes in the hedgerows. One of the loveliest places on the island is **Cala Levante**, a huddle of houses around two tiny fishing harbours. The first, Cala Tramontana, is idyllic, with a cluster of whitewashed *dammusi*, one of the island's coolest hotels, a few fishing boats, and wooden decking for sunbathing. The other side of the headland is Cala Levante, something of a suntrap in the afternoon, with good swimming and snorkelling and views of the Arco dell'Elefante, or "Elephant Arch", named after the lovely hooped formation of rock that resembles an elephant stooping to drink. You can follow a dirt road along the coast to see it from close-up. There is no beach, but it's a good place to snorkel.

Khamma-Tracino

Strung along a steep inland ridge high above the *perimetrale*, **Khamma-Tracino**, originally two villages, but now a continuous roadside strip, is the island's second-largest settlement. Beautiful it is not, but anyone looking for a genuine village – the kind of place where shopkeepers will send you down the road to their next-door neighbour's to buy wine and capers – need look no further. There is nowhere to stay here, but it's a great little place to do your grocery shopping. Afterwards you could stop for a drink at one of the two bars in the tiny piazza that marks the centre of Tracino.

9

EATING AND DRINKING ON PANTELLERIA

With its mix of Sicilian and North African elements, Pantelleria offers some unique gastronomic experiences. At some point, you ought to sample the locally produced ricotta-type cheese known as **tumma**, which is one of the ingredients of ravioli *con menta e ricotta*, a slightly bitter but fresh-tasting dish for which Pantelleria is famous. Pasta often comes served with **pesto pantesco**, a rough sauce of tomatoes, garlic and basil; while an *insalata pantesca* utilizes tomatoes, onions, cubes of boiled potato, herbs and local capers – the local capers are touted as the best in the Mediterranean.

The island's **wine** is well thought of too, made from the *zibbibo* grapes that grow well in this volcanic soil. The day-to-day drinking stuff – *vino pantesco* – is mostly white, with a nice fruity fragrance, while for something considerably stronger try the fortified **Moscato**, a sweet, amber-coloured dessert wine. Even better is the raisin wine, known generically as *passito*, which has a rich golden colour and a dry and heady flavour – the best-known variety is Tanit.

If you're **self-catering**, you'll find all you need in Pantelleria town's supermarkets, bakery and fruit and veg shops, though for a taste of traditional island life, buy fresh fish from the stalls on the road to the hospital and the lighthouse, on the far side of the harbour from the dock, and fruit and veg from the morning market (Tues & Fri) on Via San Leonardo. Most shops are open daily in summer, and close Wednesday afternoons and Sunday at other times.

From Tracino one road continues into the pretty **Piano Ghirlanda**. The road runs out the other side of Tracino and continues all the way down to meet the road on the south coast near Rekale.

Martingana

Back on the *perimetrale*, the next place worth exploring is the tiny coastal settlement of **Martingana**. A steep, narrow road twists down to a car park, the road lined with mimosa trees, passing a scattering of lava-stone and whitewashed *dammusi*, and meticulously tended vineyards and gardens perched right above the sea. From the car park it's a short walk to the bay, a tiny inlet where you can lie – comfortably, for Pantelleria – on the smoothly eroded tops of lava columns.

Balate dei Turchi

Continue along the *perimetrale*, and your next point of access to the coast is at **Balate dei Turchi**. A steep road, initially asphalted, and then a rough track (driveable, but it's a lovely walk) winds down, bordered with pines, lentisk, wild rosemary and lavender, with wonderful views across terraced vineyards back up the coast, where a series of lava buttresses slide into the sea like petrified crocodiles. Eventually, you arrive at a World War II gun emplacement, where the road forks. Follow the right branch for the Balata, where a dramatic polychromatic cliff, stained ochre, yellow and porcelain blue by volcanic minerals, soars above a protected bay. Nature has provided flat slabs of lava to lie on, a perfectly circular, ankle-deep pool for kids, and even a mini waterslide. The waters are as clear as you could wish, and the snorkelling fantastic.

Punto Nikà

Signposted from the main road (where there are a couple of parking spaces), a rough, lava track descends to **Punto Nikà**, with exciting swimming below another of Pantelleria's polychrome cliffs – this one green, rust, rose and white – in a little cove with fishermen's huts built into the rock. Bring swimming shoes, as the whipped-up lava is knife-sharp. In summer, there is usually someone renting out kayaks, which you can paddle out to a cluster of hot springs back up the coast.

It is also possible to reach the hot springs on foot, though the path is not marked. As you head down from the main road, instead of continuing to the cove, walk past the first house on your left (with metal gates), and look for a narrow path that begins 3m or 4m beyond it. The path leads to another entrance to the house, then plunges steeply downhill following a rope railing along the edge of the house's garden. As the garden ends, white arrows direct you to the bay. Note that the springs are offshore, so you need a calm day to swim out.

ACCOMMODATION AND EATING   **THE EAST COAST**

SPECCHIO DI VENERE

Venere House Via Notaio Policardo 10, Bugeber ☏ 366 6807317, ⓦ casavacanzelagodivenere.com. About five-minute's drive from the Specchio di Venere lie these three clean, simple, basically furnished self-contained apartments, with fantastic views from the terrace of the sea and lake. There is also a garden with barbecue. €75

CALA LEVANTE

Le Cale Cala Levante ☏ 347 797 5259. An unpretentious, family-run café-bar with a terrace overlooking Cala Levante. On offer are simple, local dishes, including *spaghetti alla cala* (spaghetti with sun-dried tomatoes, capers, toasted breadcrumbs, raisins and pine nuts; €12) and a fillet of locally caught fish for €15. Daily mid-May to mid-Oct.

KHAMMA-TRACINO

Pantelleria Dream Contrada da Tracino s/n ☏ 0923 915 670, ⓦ dreamhotelpantelleria.com. The individual lava-stone and whitewashed *dammusi* with traditional domed roofs may not be original, but they are comfy and beautifully styled, with white walls and Maghrebi textiles, and all have bamboo-shaded terraces. There's an infinity pool, chilled sounds in the bar, and lots of good, fresh, local produce in the restaurant. Great deals if you book in advance. €150

MARTINGANA

Appartamento Cristina Martingana ☏ 368 382 244, ⓔ crismartingana@gmail.com. A simple apartment on the upper floor of the family house, with two bedrooms, a cheerful yellow kitchen and spacious terraces with stupendous sea views, located on the upper edge of Martingana. Per person €30

Inland: Tracino to Rekale

It surprises many visitors to discover that, beautiful as the coastline is, it is Pantelleria's interior, with its beautiful meadows, volcanic outcrops and peaceful villages, that makes a lasting impression.

Piano Ghirlanda

One of the most beautiful drives on the island takes you from Tracino through the intricately terraced valley of **Piano Ghirlanda** – at its most lush and magical in spring, when it is carpeted with wild flowers – past the scores of lava-stone *dammusi* that make up the scattered settlement of **Mueggen**. A few have been restored as holiday homes, and some are little farmsteads, while most are still abandoned. A rough track (signposted) branches off to a small car park, from where you can follow a well-marked mule track to the **Favare Grande**, a cluster of rocks where sulphurous volcanic steam puffs through clefts. There are places to lie down above the steam – a perfect place to while away an hour or so doing nothing but gazing out across upland meadows carpeted with wild flowers. You could call it a day here, and settle down for a picnic, or continue along tracks north to Montagna Grande, or west to Fossa del Russo and the Grotta del Bagno Asciutto.

Siba and the Montagna Grande

The summit of Pantelleria's main volcano, the **Montagna Grande** (836m) is the island's most distinctive feature when seen from out at sea. The walk up to the top begins in the crumbly old village of **SIBA**, perched on a ridge below the volcano, with views over the terraced slopes and cultivated plains to the sea. Few of the ancient *dammusi* here are so much as whitewashed, let alone bristling with mod cons. Outside, large wooden water barrels sit on the mildewed, dry-stone volcanic walls, while the hamlet's only services are an *alimentari* and a *tabacchino*. If time hasn't exactly stood still here, it's in no great hurry to get on with things either. To find the trailhead, keep left at the telephone sign by the *tabacchino* here, and strike off the main road. The mountain's

9

slopes afford the best views on the island, and are pitted by numerous volcanic vents, the **Stufe de Khazen**, marked by escaping threads of vapour.

From Siba you could either head directly down to Scauri or take a leisurely drive into the interior, to the peaceful, crumbling village of Bukkuram.

Grotta del Bagno Asciutto

From Siba, another (signposted) path – on the left as you follow the road through the village – brings you in around twenty minutes to a natural sauna, **the Grotta del Bagno Asciutto**, where you can sweat it out for as long as you can stand. It's little more than a slit in the rock face, where you can crouch in absolute darkness, breaking out into a heavy sweat as soon as you enter. It's coolest at floor level; raising yourself up is like putting yourself into a pizza oven, while the ceiling is so hot it's impossible to keep the palm of your hand pressed flat against it. Ten minutes is the most you should attempt the first time – emerging into the midday sun is like being wafted by a cool breeze. Bring a towel.

Valle Monastero and Rekale

From the road that descends from Siba to Scauri and the coast, you can take a track off to the left that runs through the so-called **Valle Monastero**. This lovely route leads past the abandoned monastery which gives the valley its name. Make sure you carry enough water if you tackle this hike, which is best accomplished early in the day. The path meets the road midway between Scauri and **Rekale**. Rekale is a small agricultural village, worth a stop to buy home-grown fruit and veg (look out for the sign on the main road through the village) or to buy pestos, conserves and *passito* (see page 354) from the Emanuela Bonomo vineyard. Beyond here the **Dietro Isola**, the extensive southeastern segment of the island, curves round to **Punto Nikà** (see page 354).

SHOPPING   **INLAND: TRACINO TO REKALE**

Azienda Agricola Emanuela Bonomo Via Ziton di Rekale 45, Rekale ☎ 0923 916 331, ⓦ aziendabonomo pantelleria.it. Winemaker Emanuela Bonomo makes a fantastic *passito*, as well as a wonderful range of pestos and conserves – the tomato *ammoggiu* (a kind of tomato jam) and pesto of capers, almonds and wild fennel are superb. Emanuela and her husband will show you around the gardens – that include a walled *giardino pantesco* – and, if you call ahead, take you up to Monte Gibele where they grow capers. Daily 9am–1pm & 4–8pm.

Scauri and around

Sited on the west coast, looking out across the sea to Tunisia (which you can see on a clear day), **Scauri** is a likeable place. The village, set high above its harbour, consists of no more than a minuscule church perched on a shelf of land, surrounded by a cluster of houses. There's a well-stocked *alimentari* that does decent panini, a huge caper-salting factory, and couple of locals selling local produce from their homes. Scauri Porto (used by hydrofoils if the winds are in the wrong direction for docking at the main port) is a wonderful place to while away summer days, with good swimming in the harbour, and two tiny hot pools just along the coast (5min walk from La Vela). In summer there are kayaks and windsurfers to rent from below La Vela (ⓦ pantelleriawindsurf.it).

Sataria

At **Sataria**, north of Scauri, concrete steps lead down to a tiny square-cut **sea-pool**. In the cave behind are more pools where warm water, reputed to be good for curing rheumatism and skin diseases, bubbles through. It is all rather neglected, though, and feels more like a Montalbano crime scene than somewhere you would want to spend an afternoon. The local pensioners don't seem to mind, though.

The Sesi and Punta Fram
The Sesi are clearly marked and there is a car park • Free

As the *perimetrale* passes **Punta Fram**, you hit the most developed stretch of coast, lined with modest holiday villas and large concrete hotels, two of which, owned by the Gadaffi family, have been sequestered. Of more interest are the island's strange **Sesi**, massive black Neolithic funeral mounds of piled rock, with low passages leading inside. They're thought to be products of Pantelleria's first settlers, possibly from Tunisia. The main one is 6m high, a striking sight, completely at one with its lunar-like environment. Scores of these must once have dotted the island, satisfying some primeval fears and beliefs. That so few survive is not so hard to understand when you take a look around at the regular-shaped stones from which the *dammuso* houses are built – centuries of plunder have taken their toll.

EATING

La Nicchia Contrada Scauri Basso ☎ 0923 916 342. This is one of the island's most renowned restaurants, and is worth dressing up for. You can dine inside or in the garden, beneath the shade of an old orange tree, on such dishes as shrimps in a *zibbibo* sauce (see page 354) and the island speciality, mint- and *tumma*-stuffed ravioli bathed in sage butter (both €15). *Antipasti* run at €10–14, *secondi* are around €16. Daily dinner only; closed Wed in low season.

SCAURI AND AROUND

★**La Vela** Scauri Porto ☎ 0923 916 566. A very nice family-run bar-restaurant, with a terrace right on the portside, where you can eat a superlative aubergine parmigiana (€8), spaghetti with cherry tomatoes, zucchini and ricotta *salata* (€12) or grilled fish (€5 per 100g). It's a great place for a simple glass of wine with local olives, as well, especially at sunset. Open daily drinks, lunch & dinner from around 9.30am until everyone has left; closed Nov–Easter.

CAPPELLA PALATINA, PALERMO

Contexts

359 History

372 The Mafia in Sicily

377 Sicilian Baroque

381 Books

384 Films

385 Italian

History

Sicily has a richer and more eventful past than any other Mediterranean island. Its strategic importance made it the constant prey of conquerors, many of whom, while contributing a rich artistic heritage, also turned Sicily century after century into one of the most desolate war zones in Europe, transforming its ecology and heaping misery onto the vast majority of its inhabitants. As one of the most seismically active areas in Europe, natural disasters – earthquakes, volcanic eruptions and landslides – have also shaped the fate of the island.

Prehistoric Sicily

Numerous remains survive of the earliest human settlements in Sicily. The most interesting of these are the cave paintings in the Grotta del Genovese, on Lévanzo in the Egadi Islands, which give a graphic insight into late Ice Age **Paleolithic** culture between 20,000 and 10,000 BC.

During the later **Neolithic period**, between 4000 and 3000 BC, a wave of settlers arrived from the eastern Mediterranean, landing on Sicily's east coast and in the Aeolian Islands. Examples of their relatively advanced culture – incised and patterned pottery and simple tools – are displayed in the museum on the Aeolian island of Lipari. Agricultural advances, the use of ceramics and the domestication of animals, as well as the new techniques of metalworking imported by later waves of Aegean immigrants in the **Copper Age** (3000–2000 BC), permitted the establishment of fixed farms and villages. In turn, this caused an expansion of trade, and promoted greater contact with far-flung Mediterranean cultures. The presence of Mycenaean ware from the Greek mainland became more noticeable during the **Bronze Age** (2000–1000 BC), an era to which the sites of Capo Graziano and Punta Milazzese on the Aeolian Islands belong. In about 1250 BC, further population movements took place, this time originating from the Italian mainland: the **Ausonians** settled in the Aeolians and the **Sikels** in eastern Sicily, pushing the indigenous tribes inland. It was the Sikels, from whom Sicily takes its name, who are thought to have first dug the vast necropolis of Pantalica, near Siracusa. At about the same time, the **Sicans**, a people believed to have originated in North Africa, occupied the western half of the island, as did the **Elymians**, who claimed descent from Trojan refugees: their chief city, Segesta, was alleged to have been founded by Aeneas's companion, Acestes.

The Carthaginians and the Greeks

After about 900 BC, Mycenaean and Aegean trading contacts began to be replaced by **Carthaginian** ones from North Africa, particularly in the west of the island. The Carthaginians – originally Phoenicians from the eastern Mediterranean – first settled at Panormus (modern Palermo), Solus (Solunto) and Motya (Mozia) during the eighth

20,000–10,000 BC	4000–3000 BC	2000–1000 BC
Paleolithic Sicilians paint caves on the island of Lévanzo	Neolithic adventurers from the Eastern Mediterranean settle on the Aeolian Islands and Sicily's east coast	Trade between eastern Sicily and Mycenaean Greece flourishes. Ausonians and Sikels from mainland Italy settle in the east, and Sicans and Elymians from North Africa in the west

and seventh centuries BC. Their arrival coincided with the establishment of Aegean **Greek colonies** in the east of Sicily, which was driven by a shortage of cultivable land back home and began with the colonization of **Naxos** in 734 BC. The Chalcidinians and Naxians who founded this colony were quickly followed by Megarians at **Megara Hyblaea**, Corinthians at **Ortigia** (Siracusa), and Rhodians, Cnidians and Cretans in **Gela**. While continuing to have close links with their original homes, these cities became independent city-states and founded sub-colonies of their own, most important of which were **Selinus** (Selinunte) and **Akragas** (Agrigento). Along with the Greek colonies on the Italian mainland, these scattered communities came to be known as Magna Graecia, "Greater Greece".

The settlers found themselves with huge resources at their disposal, not least the island's **fertility**, which they quickly exploited through the widespread cultivation of corn – so much so that Demeter, the Greek goddess of grain and fecundity, became the chief deity on the island (the lake at Pergusa, near Enna, was claimed to be the site of the abduction of her daughter, Persephone). The olive and the vine were introduced from Greece, commercial activity across the Ionian Sea was intense and profitable, and the magnificence of the temples at Syracuse and Akragas often surpassed that of the major shrines in Greece. But the settlers also imported their native **rivalries**, and the history of Hellenic Sicily is one of almost uninterrupted warfare between the cities, even if they did generally join forces in the face of common foes such as the Carthaginians.

The Rise of Syracuse

It was the alliance against Carthage of Gela, Akragas and Syracuse, and the resulting Greek victory at **Himera** in 480 BC, that determined the ascendancy of **Syracuse** in Sicily for the next 270 years. The defeat, in about 450 BC, of a rebellion led by **Ducetius**, a Hellenized Sikel, extinguished the remnants of any native resistance to Greek hegemony, and the century which followed has been hailed as the "Golden Age" of Greek Sicily.

The accumulation of power by Syracusan **tyrants** attracted the attention of the mainland Greek states; Athens in particular was worried by the rapid spread of Corinthian influence in Sicily. In 415 BC, Athens dispatched the greatest armada ever to have sailed from its port. Later known as the **Great Expedition**, the effort was in response to a call for help from its ally, Segesta, while at war with Syracuse-supported Selinus. By 413 BC Syracuse itself was under siege, but the disorganization of the attacking forces, who were further hampered by disease, led to their total defeat, the execution of their generals and the imprisonment of 7000 soldiers in Syracuse's limestone quarries. This victory represented the apogee of Syracusan power. Civil wars continued throughout the rest of the island, attracting the attention of the Carthaginians, who responded to attacks on their territory by sacking in turn Selinus, Himera, Akragas and Gela. A massive counterattack was launched by the Syracusan tyrant **Dionysius I**, or "the Elder" (405–367 BC). That culminated in the complete destruction of the Phoenician base at **Motya**; its survivors founded a new centre at Lilybaeum, modern Marsala, on the western tip of the island.

The general devastation in Sicily caused by these wars was to some extent reversed by **Timoleon** (345–336 BC), who rebuilt many of the cities and re-established democratic institutions. But the carnage continued under the tyrant **Agathocles** (315–289 BC),

700–800 BC	734 BC	480 BC	450 BC
The Carthaginians arrive in Sicily and found Palermo	The Greeks establish their first Sicilian colony at Giardini Naxos	The battle of Himera sees the Greeks triumph over the Carthaginians	A Sikel rebellion led by Ducetius is defeated. Syracuse becomes the most important power in the Mediterranean

who was unrivalled in his sheer brutality. Battles were fought on the Italian mainland and North Africa, and the strife he engendered back in Sicily didn't end until **Hieron II** (265–215 BC) opted for a policy of peacekeeping, and even alliance, with the new power of the day, Rome.

The **First Punic War** – which broke out in 264 BC after the mercenary army in control of Messina, the **Mamertines**, appealed to Rome for help against their erstwhile Carthaginian protectors – left Syracuse itself untouched. It did, however, once again lead to the ruin of much of the island, before the final surrender of the Carthaginian base at Lilybaeum in 241. For Syracuse and its territories, though, this was a period of relative peace, and Hieron used the breathing space to construct some of the city's most impressive monuments.

Roman Sicily

Roman rule in Sicily can be said to have begun with **the fall of Syracuse**. That momentous event became inevitable when the city, whose territory was by now the only part of Sicily still independent of Rome, chose to side with Carthage in the **Second Punic War**, provoking a two-year siege that ended with the sacking of Syracuse in 211 BC. For the next seven hundred years, Sicily was a province of Rome, though in effect a subject colony, since few Sicilians were granted citizenship until the third century AD, when all inhabitants of the empire were classified as Romans. The island became Rome's granary or, as Cato had it, "the nurse at whose breast the Roman people is fed". As a key strategic province, Sicily suddenly became susceptible to age-old Roman political intrigue, notably during the **civil war** between Octavian, the future Emperor Augustus, and Sextus Pompey, who seized Sicily in 44 BC. For eight years the island's crucial grain exports were interrupted, and the final defeat of Sextus – in a sea battle off Mylae, or Milazzo – was followed by harsh retribution.

Once Octavian was installed as emperor, in 27 BC, Sicily entered a more peaceful period of Roman rule, with isolated instances of imperial splendour, notably the extravagant villa at Casale near Piazza Armerina. The island benefited especially from its important role in Mediterranean trade, and Syracuse, which handled much of the passing traffic, became a prominent centre of **early Christianity**, supposedly visited by Sts Peter and Paul on their way to Rome. Here, and further inland at Akrai, catacombs were burrowed from the third century AD onwards – and in caves throughout Sicily, Christian sanctuaries took their place alongside the shrines of the dozens of other cults prevalent on the island.

Barbarians, Byzantines and the arrival of the Arabs

Though Rome fell to the Visigoths in 410 AD, Sicily became prey to another Germanic tribe, the **Vandals**, who launched their invasion from the North African coast. The island was soon reunited with Italy under the Ostrogoth Theodoric, but the barbarian presence in Sicily was only a brief interlude, terminated in 535 AD when the **Byzantine** general Belisarius occupied the island. Although a part of the population had been Latinized, Greek remained the dominant culture and language of the majority, and the island willingly joined the Byzantine fold.

397 BC	265–215 BC	264 BC	212 BC
A force of 80,000 men from Syracuse destroys the Carthaginian base of Motya	Syracusan ruler Hieron II allies the city with Rome	The first Punic War between Rome and Carthage breaks out in Messina	In the Second Punic War, Syracuse sides with Carthage and is eventually sacked by Rome

Constantinople was never able to give much attention to Sicily, however. The island was perpetually harried by piratical attacks, particularly from North Africa, where the Moors had become the most dynamic force in the Mediterranean. In around 700, the island of **Pantelleria** was taken, and only discord among the Arabs prevented Sicily itself from being next. In the event, trading agreements were signed, Arab merchants settled in Sicilian ports, and a fully-fledged **Arab invasion** did not take place until 827, when a Byzantine admiral rebelled against the emperor and invited in the Aghlabid Emir of Tunisia. Ten thousand Arabs, Berbers and Spanish Muslims (known collectively as **Saracens**) landed at Mazara del Vallo, and Palermo fell four years later, though the invading forces only reached the Straits of Messina in 965. As with the Roman invasion, however, the turning point came with the fall of Syracuse in 878, when its population was massacred and the city plundered of its legendary wealth.

Arab Sicily

Palermo became the capital of the **Arabs in Sicily**, under whom it grew to become one of the world's greatest cities, wholly cosmopolitan in outlook, furnished with gardens, mosques (more than anywhere the traveller Ibn Hauqal had seen, barring Cordoba) and luxurious palaces. The Arabs brought great **benefits** to the rest of the island, too, renovating and extending irrigation works, breaking down many of the unwieldy *latifundia* (private estates) and introducing new crops, including citrus trees, sugar cane, flax, cotton, silk, melons and date palms. Mining was developed, the salt industry greatly expanded and commerce improved, with Sicily once more at the centre of a flourishing trade network. Many Sicilian place names testify to the extent of the Arab settlement of the island. Prefixes such as *calta* (castle) and *gibil* (mountain) are plentiful, while other terms still in use indicate their impact on fishing, such as the name of the swordfish boats prowling the Straits of Messina (*felucca*), or the tuna-fishing terminology of the Egadi Islands. Taxation was rationalized and reduced, and **religious tolerance** was greater than under the Byzantines (though non-Muslims were subject to a degree of social discrimination).

The Arabs were prone to divisive feuding, however, and when in the tenth century the Aghlabid dynasty was toppled in Tunisia and their Fatimid successors shifted their capital to Egypt, Sicily lost its central position in the Arab Mediterranean Empire and was left vulnerable to external attack. In 1038, the Byzantine general **George Maniakes** attempted to draw the island back under Byzantine sway, but he was unable to extend his occupation much beyond Syracuse. The real threat came from western Europe, particularly from the **Normans**, some of whom had accompanied Maniakes and seen for themselves the rewards to be gained. One of these, William "Bras de Fer" ("Iron Arm"), who had earned his nickname by his slaying of the Emir of Syracuse with one blow, was the eldest of the Hauteville brothers, whose exploits were soon to change the map of southern Europe.

The Normans

The **Hauteville brothers** had long been active in southern Italy by the time the youngest of them, **Roger**, seized Messina in 1061 in response to a call for help by one of the warring Arab factions. It took another thirty years to take control of the whole island,

38 BC	59 AD	410 AD	535 AD
Sextus Pompey is defeated by the future Emperor Augustus at the Battle of Mylae (modern-day Milazzo)	St Paul allegedly visits Syracuse. Christianity begins to gain followers	Rome falls to the Visigoths, and Sicily is attacked by tribes of Vandals	Sicily is occupied by Byzantines under General Belisarius

in a series of bloody and destructive campaigns that often involved the enlistment of Arabs on the Norman side. In 1072 Palermo was captured and adopted as the capital of **Norman Sicily**, and was subsequently adorned with palaces and churches that count among the most brilliant achievements of the era.

The most striking thing about the Norman period in Sicily is its brief span. In little more than a century, five kings bequeathed an enormous legacy of art and architecture that is still one of the most conspicuous features of the island. When compared with the surviving remains of the Byzantines, who reigned for three centuries, or the Arabs, whose occupation lasted roughly two, the Norman contribution stands out, principally due to its absorption of previous styles: the finest examples of Arab art to be seen in Sicily are elements incorporated into the great Norman churches. It was this fusion of talent that accounted for the great success of Norman Sicily, not just in the arts but in administration, justice and religious tolerance. The policy of **integration** was largely determined by force of circumstances: the Normans could not count on having adequate numbers of their own settlers, or bureaucrats to form a governmental class, and instead were compelled to rely on the existing framework. They did, however, gradually introduce a Latinized aristocracy and clerical hierarchy from northern Italy and France, so that the Arabic language was largely superseded by Italian and French by 1200.

The Hauteville dynasty

The first of the great Sicilian-Norman dynasty was **Count Roger**, or Roger I. He was a resolute and successful ruler, marrying his daughters into two of the most powerful European dynasties, one of them to the son of the western (or Holy Roman) Emperor Henry IV. Roger's death in 1101, followed soon after by the death of his eldest son, left Sicily governed by his widow Adelaide as regent for his younger son, who in 1130 was crowned **Roger II**. This first Norman king of Sicily was also one of medieval Europe's most gifted and charismatic rulers, who made the island a great melting pot of the most vigorous and creative elements in the Mediterranean world. He spoke Greek, kept a harem and surrounded himself with a medley of advisers, notably **George of Antioch**, his chief minister, or Emir of Emirs. Roger extended his kingdom to encompass all of southern Italy, Malta and parts of North Africa, and more enduringly drew up the first written code of law in the island.

His son, William I (1154–66) – "**William the Bad**" – dissipated these achievements by his enthusiasm for pleasure-seeking and his failure to control the barons, who exploited racial tensions to undermine the king's authority. During the regency that followed, the Englishman Walter of the Mill had himself elected archbishop of Palermo and dominated the scene for some twenty years, along with two other Englishmen, his brother Bartholomew and Bishop Palmer. This triumvirate preserved a degree of stability, but also encouraged the new king William II (1166–89), "**William the Good**", to establish a second archbishopric and construct a cathedral at **Monreale** to rival that of Palermo, just 10km away. The period saw a shift away from Muslim influence, though Arabs still constituted the bulk of the rural population and William himself resembled an oriental sultan in his style and habits, building a number of Arab-style palaces.

The death of William, aged only 36 and with no obvious successor, signalled a crisis in Norman Sicily. The barons were divided between **Tancred**, William's illegitimate

827 AD	902 AD	1038	1061
A North African army of 10,000 lands at Mazara del Vallo	Tauromenium (Taormina) is the last Sicilian city to fall to the Arabs, who then make Palermo their capital	Byzantine General Maniakes occupies Syracuse; and William Hauteville slays the Emir of Syracuse	Roger Hauteville seizes Messina

nephew, and **Constance**, Roger II's aunt, who had married the Hohenstaufen (or Swabian) Henry, later to become the Holy Roman Emperor Henry VI. Tancred's election by an assembly was the first sign of a serious erosion of the king's authority: others followed, notably a campaign in 1189 against Muslims living on the island, which caused many of them to flee; and a year later the sacking of **Messina** by the English Richard I, on his way to join the Third Crusade. Tancred's death in 1194 and the succession of his young son, **William III**, coincided with the arrival in the Straits of Messina of the Hohenstaufen fleet. Opposition was minimal, and on Christmas Day of the same year Henry crowned himself King of Sicily. William and his mother were imprisoned in the castle at Caltabellotta, never to be seen again.

Hohenstaufen and the Angevins

Inevitably, Henry's imperial concerns led him away from Sicily, which represented only a source of revenue for him on the very outer limits of his domain. A revolt broke out against his authoritarian rule, which he repressed with extreme severity, but in the middle of it he went down with dysentery, died, and the throne passed to his three-and-a-half-year-old son, who became the Emperor Frederick II, **Frederick I** of Sicily.

At first the running of the kingdom was entrusted to Frederick's mother Constance, but there was little stability, with the barons in revolt and a rash of race riots in 1197. Frederick's assumption of the government in 1220 marked a return to decisive leadership, with an immediate campaign to bring the barons to heel and eliminate a Muslim rebellion in Sicily's interior. The twin aims of Frederick's rule in Sicily were to restore the broad framework of the Norman state, and to impose a more imperial stamp on society, indicated by his fondness for classical Roman allusions in his promulgations and coinage. He allowed himself rights and privileges in Sicily that were impossible in his other possessions, emphasizing his own authority at the expense of the independence of the clergy and the autonomy of the cities. As elsewhere in southern Italy, strong **castles** were built, such as those at Milazzo, Catania, Siracusa and Augusta, to keep the municipalities in check.

A unified **legal system** was drawn up, embodied in his *Liber Augustales*, while his attempts to homogenize Sicilian society involved the harsh treatment of what had now become minority communities, such as the Muslims. He encouraged the arts, too, championing Sicilian vernacular poetry, whose pre-eminence was admitted by Petrarch and Dante. Frederick acquired the name "**Stupor Mundi**" ("Wonder of the World"), reflecting his promotion of science, law and medicine, and the peace that Sicily enjoyed during the half-century of his rule.

However, the balance of power Frederick achieved within Sicily laid the foundations for many of the island's future woes – for example, the weakening of the municipalities at a time when most European towns were increasing their autonomy. His centralized government worked as long as there was a powerful hand to guide it, but when Frederick died in 1255, decline set in, despite the efforts of his son **Manfred**, who strove to defend his crown from the encroachments of the barons and the acquisitiveness of foreign monarchs. New claimants to the throne were egged on by Sicily's nominal suzerain, the pope, anxious to deprive the Hohenstaufen of their southern possession, and he eventually auctioned it, selling it to the king of England, who accepted it on

1072	1166	1190
The Normans capture Palermo and make it their capital	William Hauteville dies. Norman barons elect his illegitimate nephew Tancred to replace him	English King Richard I sacks Messina on his way to join the Third Crusade

behalf of his 8-year-old son, Edmund of Lancaster. For ten years Edmund was styled "King of Sicily" despite the fact that the bill was never paid.

Charles of Anjou

French pope Urban IV deposed Edmund, who had never set foot in Sicily, and gave the title instead to **Charles of Anjou**, brother of the French king, on condition that he took over England's debt and paid the papacy a huge annual tribute. Backed by the papacy, Charles of Anjou embarked on a punitive campaign against the majority of the Sicilian population, who had supported the Hohenstaufen. He plundered land to give to his followers, and imposed a high level of taxation, though in the end it was a grassroots revolt that sparked off the **Sicilian Vespers**, an uprising against the French that began on Easter Monday 1282; it is traditionally held to have started after the bell for evening services, or Vespers, had rung at Palermo's church of Santo Spirito. The incident that sparked it all off was an insult to a woman by a French soldier, which led to a general slaughter in Palermo, soon growing into an island-wide rebellion against the French. This was the one moment in Sicilian history when the people rose up as one against foreign oppression – though in reality it was more an opportunity for horrific butchery and the settlement of old scores than a glorious expression of patriotic fervour.

The movement was given some direction when a group of nobles enlisted the support of **Peter of Aragon**, who landed at Trapani five months after the initial outbreak of hostilities and was acclaimed king at Palermo a few days later. The ensuing **Wars of the Vespers**, fought between Aragon and the Angevin forces based in Naples, lasted for another 21 years, mainly waged in Spain and at sea, while, in Aragonese Sicily, people settled down to over five centuries of Spanish domination.

The Spanish in Sicily

Sicily's new orientation towards **Spain**, and its severance from mainland Italy, meant that the island was largely excluded from all the great European developments of the fourteenth and fifteenth centuries. Large parts of Sicily were granted to the Spanish aristocracy, meaning a continuation of suffocating feudalism, and little impact was made by the Renaissance, while intellectual life on the island was stifled by the strictures of the Spanish Inquisition.

Although Peter of Aragon insisted that the two kingdoms of Aragon and Sicily should be ruled by separate kings after his death, his successor James reopened negotiations with the Angevins to sell the island back to them. His younger brother Frederick, appointed by James as Lieutenant of Palermo, convened a "parliament", which elected him king of an independent Sicily as **Frederick II** (1296–1337). Factions arose, growing out of the friction between Angevin and Aragonese supporters, and open warfare followed until 1372, when the independence of Sicily was guaranteed by Naples. Under the terms of the subsequent treaty the island became known as **Trinacria** ("three-cornered"), an ancient name revived to distinguish the island from the mainland Regnum Siciliae, ruled by the kingdom of Naples.

The constant feuding had laid waste to the countryside and the interior of Sicily became depopulated and unproductive, exacerbated by the effects of the Black Death. The feudal nobility lived mainly in the towns, building wealthy mansions in the

1194	1198	1220
Tancred dies. His son William III succeeds him but is defeated by Henry Hohenstaufen, who crowns himself King of Sicily	Henry Hohenstaufen's son Frederick becomes King of Sicily and Holy Roman Emperor at the age of three and a half. Sicily is ruled by his mother, Constance	Frederick takes the reins of power, initiating a period of strong rule

Chiaramonte or the later, richly ornate Catalan-Gothic styles. A tradition of artistic patronage grew up, though most of the artists operating in Sicily came from elsewhere – for example, Francesco Laurana and the Gagini family were originally from northern Italy. A notable exception was **Antonello da Messina** (1430–79), who soaked up the latest Flemish techniques on his continental travels. Following the closing off of the eastern Mediterranean by the Ottoman Turks in the fifteenth century, Sicily was isolated from everywhere except Spain – from which, after 1410, it was ruled directly. Sicily found itself on the very fringes of Europe, and the unification of Castile and Aragon in 1479, followed soon after by the reconquest of the whole Spanish peninsula from the Moors, meant that Sicily's importance to its Spanish monarchs declined even further. The island came under the rule of a succession of **viceroys**, who were to wield power for the next four hundred years. Few of these were Sicilian (none at all after the first fifty years), while the only Spanish king to visit the island during the entire viceregal period was Charles V, on his way back from a Tunisian crusade in 1535.

The island's political bond to Spain meant that its degeneration deepened in tandem with Spain's decline in the seventeenth and eighteenth centuries. There were occasional revolts against the excesses of the zealous Inquisition, but on the whole discontent manifested itself in a resort to **brigandage**, for which the forest and wild maquis of Sicily's interior provided an ideal environment. The mixed fear and respect that the brigand bands generated played a large part in the future formation of an organized criminal class in Sicily.

Already burdened by the ever-increasing taxes demanded by Spain to finance its remote religious conflicts (principally, the 1618–48 Thirty Years' War), the misery of the Sicilians was compounded at the end of the seventeenth century by two appalling natural disasters. The **eruption of Etna** in 1669 devastated a large part of the area around Catania, while the **earthquake** of 1693 – also in the east of the island – flattened whole cities, and killed around five percent of the island's population. With the death of Charles II of Spain in 1700 and the subsequent Wars of the Spanish Succession, the island once more took a back seat to mainland European interests. It was bartered in the **Treaty of Utrecht** that negotiated the peace, and given to the northern Italian House of Savoy, only to be swapped for Sardinia and given to Austria seven years later.

The Bourbons

The **Austrian government** of the island lasted only four years, cut short by the arrival of another Spaniard, **Charles of Bourbon**, who claimed the throne for himself. Although he never visited Sicily again after his first landing, **Charles III** (1734–59) brought a refreshingly constructive air to the island's administration, showing a more benevolent attitude towards his new subjects. But, with his succession to the Spanish throne in 1759 and the inheritance of the Neapolitan crown by his son, **Ferdinand IV**, it was back to the bad old days. Any meagre attempts at reform made by Ferdinand's viceroys were opposed at every turn by the reactionary local aristocracy, who were closing ranks in response to the progress of the Enlightenment and the ideas unleashed by the French Revolution. When the ensuing **Napoleonic Wars** wracked Europe, Sicily, along with Sardinia, was the only part of Italy not conquered by Napoleon, while the Neapolitan *ancien régime* was further buttressed by the decision of Ferdinand (brother-in-law of

1255	1261	1282	1410
Frederick dies and his son Manfred is crowned king	French Pope Urban IV gives Sicily's throne to Charles of Anjou	The Sicilian Vespers uprising. Peter of Aragon is declared king, and the War of the Vespers begins	Spain wins the War of the Vespers, and Sicily falls under direct Spanish rule

Marie Antoinette) to wage war against the revolutionary French. He was supported in this by the British, who sustained the Bourbon state, so that when Ferdinand and his court were forced to flee Naples in 1799, it was **Nelson's** flagship they sailed in, accompanied by the British ambassador to Naples, Sir William Hamilton, and his wife Lady Emma. Nelson was rewarded for his services by the endowment of a large estate at Bronte, just west of Etna.

The arrival of the British

Four years later, Ferdinand was able to return to Naples, though he had to escape again in 1806 when Napoleon gave the Neapolitan crown to his brother Joseph. This time he had to stay longer, remaining in Palermo until after the defeat of Napoleon in 1815 – a stay that was accompanied by a larger contingent of British troops and a heavy involvement of British capital and commerce. **Liberalism** became a banner of revolt against the king's continuing tax demands, and Ferdinand's autocratic reaction provoked the British commander **William Bentinck** to intervene. Manoeuvring himself into a position where he was the virtual governor of Sicily, Bentinck persuaded the king to summon a new parliament and adopt a **constitution** whereby the independence of Sicily was guaranteed and feudalism abolished.

Although this represented a drastic break with the past, the reforms had little direct effect on the peasantry, and, following the departure of the British, the constitution was dropped and Ferdinand (now styling himself Ferdinand I, King of the Two Sicilies) repealed all the reforms previously introduced. Renewed talk of independence in Sicily spilled over into action in 1820, when a rebellion was put down with the help of Austrian mercenaries. The **repression** intensified after Ferdinand I's death in 1825, and the island's fortunes reached a new low under Ferdinand II (1830–59), nicknamed "Re Bomba" for his five-day **bombardment of Messina** following major insurrections there and in Palermo in 1848–49. Another uprising in Palermo in 1860 proved a spur for Giuseppe Garibaldi to pick Sicily as the starting point for his unification of Italy.

Unification

On May 11, 1860, **Giuseppe Garibaldi** landed at Marsala with a thousand men. A professional soldier and one of the leading lights of **Il Risorgimento**, the movement for Italian unification, Garibaldi intended to liberate the island from Bourbon rule, in the name of the Piedmont House of Savoy. His skill in guerrilla warfare, backed by an increasingly cooperative peasantry, ensured that the campaign progressed with astonishing speed. Four days after disembarking, he defeated 15,000 Bourbon troops at **Calatafimi**, closely followed by an almost effortless occupation of Palermo. A battle at **Milazzo** in July decided the issue: apart from Messina (which held out for another year), Sicily was free of Spain for the first time since Peter of Aragon acquired the crown in 1282.

A **plebiscite** was held in October, which returned a 99.5 percent majority in favour of union with the new **kingdom of Italy** under Vittorio Emanuele II. The result, greeted by general euphoria, marked the official **annexation** of the island to the Kingdom of Savoy. Later, however, many began to question whether anything had been achieved

1693	1700	1713	1735
An earthquake devastates southeast Sicily and kills around five percent of the population	Charles II dies childless, prompting the War of the Spanish Succession	Sicily is handed to the royal Italian House of Savoy at the Treaty of Utrecht	The Spanish King Charles of Bourbon claims the throne of Sicily, initiating a brief period of enlightened rule

by this change of ruler. The new **parliamentary system**, in which only one percent of the island's population was eligible to vote, made few improvements for the majority of people. Attempts at opposition were met with ruthless force, sanctioned by a distant and misinformed government convinced that the island's problems were fundamentally those of law and order. Sicilians responded with their traditional defence of *omertà*, or silent non-cooperation, along with a growing **resentment** of the new Turin government (transferred to Rome in 1870) that was even stronger than their distrust of the more familiar Spanish Bourbons.

The "southern problem"

A series of reports made in response to criticism of the Italian government's failure to solve what was becoming known as the "**southern problem**" found that the lot of the Sicilian peasant was, if anything, worse after Unification than it had been under the Bourbons. Power had shifted away from the landed gentry to the *gabellotti*, the middlemen to whom they leased the land. These men became increasingly linked with the **Mafia**, a shadowy, loose-knit criminal association that found it easy to manipulate voting procedures, while simultaneously posing as defenders of the people. At the end of the nineteenth century a new, more organized opposition appeared on the scene in the form of **fasci** – embryonic trade-union groups demanding legislation to protect peasants' interests. Violence erupted and the Italian prime minister, **Francesco Crispi** – a native Sicilian who had been one of the pioneers of the Risorgimento – dispatched a fleet and 30,000 soldiers to put down the "revolt", while also closing newspapers, censoring postal services and detaining suspects without trial.

Although there were later signs of progress, in the formation of worker cooperatives and in the enlightened land-reform programmes of individuals such as **Don Sturzo**, mayor of Caltagirone, the overwhelming despair of the peasantry was expressed in **mass emigration**. One and a half million Sicilians decided to leave in the years leading up to 1914, most going to North and South America. Many had been left homeless in the wake of the great **Messina earthquake** of 1908, in which upwards of 80,000 lost their lives. Though the high rate of emigration was a crushing indictment of the state of affairs on the island, it had many positive effects for those left behind, who benefited not only from huge remittances sent back from abroad but from the wage increases that resulted from labour shortages.

The world wars

The Italian **conquest of Libya** in 1912 was closely followed by **World War I**, and both were heavy blows to the Sicilian economy. In 1922 **Mussolini** gained power in Rome and dispatched **Cesare Mori** to solve "the southern problem" by putting an end to the Mafia. Free of constitutional and legal restrictions, Mori was able to imprison thousands of suspected *mafiosi*. The effect was merely to drive the criminal class deeper underground, while the alliance he forged with the landed classes to help bring this about dissolved all the gains that had been made against the ruling elite, setting back the cause of agrarian reform. In the **1930s** Mussolini's African concerns and his drive for economic and agricultural self-sufficiency gave Sicily a new importance for Fascist Italy, the island now vaunted as "the geographic centre of

1848	May 1860	October 1860	1893
Insurrections against Bourbon autocracy are put down at Messina and Palermo	Garibaldi and 1000 followers land at Marsala, and defeat 15,000 Bourbon troops at Calatafimi. Sicily is freed from Spanish rule	Sicilians vote to join the Kingdom of Italy	Italian Prime Minister Francesco Crispi sends an army of 30,000 into rural Sicily to quash those demanding rights for peasants

the empire". In the much-publicized **"Battle for Grain"**, wheat production increased, though at the cost of the diversity of crops that Sicily required, resulting in soil exhaustion and erosion. Mussolini's popularity on the island is best illustrated by his order, in 1941, that all Sicilian-born officials be transferred to the mainland, on account of their possible disloyalty.

During **World War II**, Sicily became the first part of Europe to be **invaded** by the Allies when, in July 1943, Patton's American Seventh Army landed at Gela, and Montgomery's British Eighth Army came ashore between Pachino and Pozzallo further east. This combined army of 160,000 men was the largest ever seen in Sicily, but the campaign was longer and harder than had been anticipated, with the Germans mainly concerned with delaying the advance until they had moved most of their men and equipment across the Straits of Messina. Few Sicilian towns escaped **aerial bombardment**, and Messina itself was the most heavily bombed of all Italian cities before it was taken on August 18.

Postwar Sicily

The aftermath of the war saw the most radical changes in Sicily since Unification. With anarchy and hunger widespread, a wave of banditry and crime was unleashed, while the Mafia were reinstated in their behind-the-scenes role as adjudicators and power brokers, now allied to the landowners in the face of large-scale land occupations by a desperate peasantry. **Separatism** became a potent rallying cry for protesters of all persuasions, who believed that Sicily's ills could best be solved by cutting its links with the mainland. A Separatist army was formed, financed by some of the gentry, but it lacked the organization or resources to make any great impact. It was largely in response to this call for independence that, in 1946, Sicily was granted **regional autonomy**, with its own assembly and president. The same year saw the declaration of a republic in Italy, the result of a popular mandate.

Autonomy failed to heal the island's divisions, however, and brute force was used by the Mafia and the old gentry against what they perceived as the major threat to their position – **communism**. The most famous bandit of the time, **Salvatore Giuliano**, who had previously been associated with the Separatists, was enlisted in the anti-communist cause. He organized a campaign of bombings and assassinations, most notoriously at the 1947 May Day celebrations at Portella della Ginestra. Giuliano's betrayal and murder in 1950 was widely rumoured to have been carried out to prevent him revealing who his paymasters were, though it all helped to glorify his reputation in the popular imagination.

By the 1950s, many saw the **Christian Democrat** party, Democrazia Cristiana, as the best hope to defend their interests. Along with the emotional hold it exerted by virtue of its close association with the Church, the DC could draw on many of the Sicilians' deepest fears of change; the party was also too closely involved with business and the land-owning classes to have any real enthusiasm for genuine reform. All attempts at enterprise were channelled through the DC's offices, and favours were bought or bartered. Cutting across party lines, political patronage, or **clientelismo**, grew to be stronger than ever. It still affects people's lives on every level today, especially in the field of work – from finding a job to landing a contract. The favours system was also

1908	1908–15	1914	1943
An earthquake devastates Messina, killing 80,000	With the island racked by poverty, one and a half million Sicilians emigrate	World War I breaks out, severely damaging the Sicilian economy	160,000 English and American troops land in Sicily. Messina becomes the most heavily bombed city in Italy

THE MIGRANT CRISIS

The **migrant crisis** – which saw more than one million displaced people entering Europe in 2015 – has hit Sicily hard: the closure of the Turkish border in March 2016 has led to even greater numbers attempting the hazardous journey across the Mediterranean sea to Sicily and Italy. In the first six months of 2016 almost 50,000 refugees had arrived – mostly on the island of Lampedusa and along Sicily's southeastern coast.

The crossing from North Africa to Italy can take days, even weeks, by which time the migrants often run out of food and water and fuel. The boats are often poor quality and crammed beyond capacity, and many boats founder and cannot be saved. Between January 1 and May 29, 2016, 2061 people died on the central Mediterranean route from North Africa to Sicily.

When the refugees arrive in Sicily they are handed over to medics, police and immigration services as well as large NGOs and small volunteer organizations. The migrants are put into temporary accommodation in Sicily or taken to camps in mainland Italy. If they can prove that they were persecuted or at risk in their home country then they can apply for asylum. Other migrants who do not have a history of political persecution are classified as "irregular migrants" and are held in detention centres. The asylum process is long. Many of the migrants hope to move on to northern European countries, but the system is slow and there are still many obstacles for them to overcome in their journey to a better life there.

evident in the workings of Sicily's sluggish **bureaucracy**, so that the smallest reforms often took years to effect. The essential problem is unchanged today, with the elaborate machinery of the civil service often exploited to accumulate and dispense personal power.

One area that managed to avoid bureaucratic control or planning of any sort was **construction** – one of Sicily's greatest growth industries, the physical evidence of which is among the visitor's most enduring impressions of the island. The building boom was inextricably connected with the Mafia's involvement in land speculation, and boosted by the phenomenal rate of urban growth all over Sicily. But in both the towns and rural areas, minimum safety standards were rarely met, as highlighted by the **1968 earthquake**, in which 50,000 were made homeless along the Valle di Belice in the west of the island. **Industry**, too, has been subject to mismanagement and, apart from isolated cases, has rarely fulfilled the potential it promised after the discovery of oil near Ragusa and Gela in the 1950s, and the development of refineries and petrochemical plants along the Golfo di Augusta.

Substantial subsidies have been channelled into many ventures, largely from the **European Union**, which Italy joined in 1958. However, it's still the great urban centres in the north that flaunt their prosperity, while the south of Italy, known as Il Mezzogiorno, is left far behind. Conversely, the huge financial concessions made to Sicily have provoked resentment from Italy's more self-sufficient regions, who point to massive corruption and incompetence on the island. Few Sicilians would wholly deny this; a longer view, however, argues that Sicily's disadvantages are derived principally from the past misuse of resources, coupled with a culture and mentality that have never given much credence to collectivist ideals. There is more awareness, too, on the part of the state that the fight against **organized crime** requires more than moralistic speeches. Indeed, in 1992, following the murders of anti-Mafia investigators Falcone

1946	1950	1968
Sicily is granted regional autonomy	The conservative (and Mafia-backed) Christian Democrat party dominates Sicilian politics	An earthquake at Belice leaves 50,000 people homeless

and Borsellino, the chief of police of Palermo was sacked, while 7000 troops were sent to the island to patrol prisons and search towns with a known Mafia presence. There have been significant breakthroughs, though these are mostly connected with a change in the public attitude towards criminality, resulting in part from a campaign to reform Sicily's dilapidated **education** system. In the 1990s, a campaign of anti-Mafia education began in Sicilian schools, aiming to cut the secondary-school drop-out rate by encouraging children away from the path of corruption and crime.

Sicily today

Despite superficial improvements, the deep problems that have always bedevilled Sicily remain. Unemployment is still high, especially among the young, many of whom head to the UK and other Northern European cities in search of work. In the long run, perhaps the greatest hope for Sicily lies in **tourism** and related services. Visitor numbers are growing, and many towns and resorts (Ortigia, Ragusa, and the Aeolian islands for example) have a positively fashionable air, while more and more Italians are throwing off their distrust of the south and discovering Sicily's potential, especially its outdoor attractions, wildlife and crystal-clear seas. The creation of **regional parks** in Etna and the Nebrodi and Madonie ranges, and the **marine reserves** around Ustica and the Egadi and Pelagie islands, are a reflection of this, and an encouraging pointer for the future.

late 1990s–present day

Political and economic immigrants – mostly from North Africa – arrive in Sicily. In Italian parliament, right-wing Lega leader Matteo Salvini begins to rise to power, on an anti-immigration ticket. In 2019, former PM Matteo Renzi moves in to challenge the ruling coalition

The Mafia in Sicily

In Sicily, there is "*mafiosità*" and there is "the Mafia". *Mafiosità* refers to a mentality, the Mafia to a specific criminal organization. In Sicily, a man can act like a *mafioso*, meaning he has the aura – or stench – of criminality, power and corruption about him, even though he has no explicit connection to the crime syndicate. And, while notions of family solidarity and the moral stature of the outlaw mean that *mafiosità* may never be completely expunged from Sicilian society, the Mafia is an entity whose members can be eliminated and its power emasculated.

What has always prevented this is the shadowy nature of the organization, protected by the long-standing **code of silence**, or *omertà*, that invariably led to accusations being retracted at the last moment, or to crucial witnesses being found dead with a stone, cork or a wad of banknotes stuffed into their mouths, or else simply disappearing off the face of the earth. As a result, many have doubted the very existence of the Mafia, claiming that it's nothing more than the creation of pulp-thriller writers, the invention of a sensationalist press and the fabrication of an Italian government embarrassed by its inability to control an unusually high level of crime in Sicily.

The background

In 1982, however, proof of the innermost workings of the Mafia's organization emerged when a high-ranking member, **Tommaso Buscetta**, was arrested in Brazil, and – after a failed suicide attempt – agreed to prise open the can of worms. His reason for daring this sacrilege, he claimed, was to destroy the Mafia. In its stampede to grab huge drug profits, the "Honoured Society" (La Società Onorata) had abandoned its original ideals: "It's necessary to destroy this band of criminals", he declared, "who have perverted the principles of Cosa Nostra and dragged them through the mud." He was doubtlessly motivated by revenge: all of those he incriminated – Michele Greco, Pippo Calò, Benedetto Santapaola, Salvatore Riina and many others – were leaders of, or allied to, the powerful Corleone family who had recently embarked on a campaign of terror to monopolize the drugs industry, in the process eliminating seven of Buscetta's closest relatives in the space of four months, including his two sons.

Buscetta's statements to Giovanni Falcone, head of Sicily's anti-Mafia "pool" of judges, and later to the Federal Court in Manhattan, provided crucial revelations about the structure of Cosa Nostra. Mafia "families" are centred on areas, he revealed: villages or quarters of cities from which they take their name. The boss (*capo*) of each group is chosen by election, and appoints a lieutenant (*sottocapo*) and one or more *consiglieri*, or counsellors. Above the families is the *cupola*, or **Commission**, a governing body that includes representatives from all the major groupings. Democracy and collective interest, Buscetta claimed, had been replaced in the Commission by the greed and self-interest of the individuals who had gained control. Trials of strength alone now decided the leadership, often in the form of bitter feuds between rival factions, or *cosche* (literally, "artichokes", their form symbolizing solidarity).

The existence of the Commission sets the Mafia apart from the normal run of underworld gangs, for without a high level of organization the international trafficking in heroin in which they engage would be inconceivable. The route is circuitous, starting in the Middle and Far East, moving on to the processing plants in Sicily, and ending up in New York, where American Mafia channels are said to control sixty percent of the heroin market. This multimillion-dollar racket – known in the US as the "**Pizza**

Connection", because Sicilian pizza parlours were used as covers for the operation – was blown apart chiefly as a result of Buscetta's evidence, and led to the trial and conviction of the leading members of New York's Mafia Commission in September 1986.

The history

The Mafia has certainly come a long way since its rustic beginnings in **feudal Sicily**. Although Buscetta denied that the word "Mafia" is used to describe the organization – the term preferred by its members is "Cosa Nostra" – the word has been in currency for centuries, and is thought to derive from the Arabic, **mu'afah**, meaning "protection". In 1863, a play entitled *Mafiusi della Vicaria*, based on life in a Palermo prison, was a roaring success among the high society of the island's capital, and gave the word its first extensive usage. When the city rose against its new Italian rulers three years later, the British consul described a situation where secret societies were all-powerful: "*Camorre* and *maffie*, self-elected juntas, share the earnings of the workmen, keep up intercourse with outcasts, and take malefactors under their wing and protection." Until then, *mafiosi* had been able to pose as defenders of the poor against the tyranny of Sicily's rulers, but in the years immediately following the toppling of the Bourbon state in Italy *mafiosi* were able to entrench themselves in Sicily's new power structure, acting as intermediaries in the gradual redistribution of land and establishing a modus vivendi with the new democratic representatives.

There is little documentary proof of the rise to power of the "Honoured Society", but most writers agree that between the 1890s and the 1920s its undisputed boss was **Don Vito Cascio Ferro**, who had close links with the American "Black Hand", a Mafia-type association of southern Italian emigrants. Ferro's career ended with Mussolini's anti-Mafia purges, instigated to clear the ground for the establishment of a vigorous Fascist structure in Sicily. **Cesare Mori**, the Duce's newly appointed Prefect of Palermo, arrived in the city in 1925 with the declared aim of "clearing the ground of the nightmares, threats and dangers which are paralysing, perverting and corrupting every kind of social activity". This might have worked, but the clean sweep that Mori made of the Mafia leaders (in all, 11,000 cattle rustlers, thieves and "conspirators" were jailed during this period, often on the basis of flimsy hearsay) was annulled after World War II when the prisons were opened and Mafia leaders, seen as unjustly jailed by the Fascist regime, returned to their regular operations. In the confusion that reigned during Italy's reconstruction, crime flourished throughout the south, and criminal leagues regrouped in Naples (the Camorra) and Calabria ('ndrangheta). In Sicily, men such as **Don Calogero Vizzini** were the new leaders, confirmed in their power by the brief Anglo-American postwar administration, in return for their contribution towards the smooth progress of the Allied landings. One of them, **Lucky Luciano**, a founder member of the American Commission, was even flown out from prison in America to facilitate the invasion. Later he was alleged to be responsible for setting up the Sicilian-American narcotics empire, which was taken over at his death in 1962 by **Luciano Leggio**, who subsequently manoeuvred himself into the leadership of the Corleone family.

The new Mafia

The cycle was by now complete: the Mafia had lost its original role as a predominantly rural organization, and had transferred its operations to the cities, moving into entrepreneurial activities such as construction, real estate and, ultimately, drug smuggling. The growth of the heroin industry raised the stakes immensely, as shown by the vicious feuds fought over the division of the spoils, and the struggle for control of narcotics trafficking played a key role in the consolidation of power within the Mafia. The Italian state responded with an **anti-Mafia Parliamentary Commission** that sat from 1963 to 1976, and posed enough of a threat to provoke a change of tactics by the

Mafia, who began to target important state officials in a sustained campaign of terror. In 1971, Palermo's chief public prosecutor, Pietro Scaglione, became the first in a long line of "**illustrious corpses**" – *cadaveri eccellenti* – which have included journalists, judges, lawyers, police chiefs and left-wing politicians. A new peak of violence was reached in 1982 with the murder in Palermo's city centre of **Pio La Torre**, regional secretary of the Communist Party in Sicily, who had proposed a special government dispensation to allow lawyers access to private bank accounts.

Among the mourners at La Torre's funeral was the new Sicilian prefect of police, **General Dalla Chiesa**, a veteran in the state's fight against the anarchist/terrorist Red Brigades. The prefect began to investigate Sicily's lucrative construction industry, and his scrutiny of public records and business dealings threatened to expose one of the most enigmatic issues in the Mafia's organization: the extent of corruption and protection in high-ranking political circles, the so-called "**Third Level**". However, exactly 100 days after La Torre's death, Dalla Chiesa himself was gunned down, together with his wife, in Palermo's Via Carini. The whole country was shocked, and the murder revived questions about the depth of government commitment to the fight. In his engagement with the Mafia, Dalla Chiesa had received next to no support from Rome, to the extent that Dalla Chiesa's son had accused the mandarins of the Christian Democrat party – former prime minister Andreotti among them – of isolating his father. Nando Dalla Chiesa refused to allow many local officials to his father's funeral, including Vito Ciancimino, former mayor of Palermo and a Christian Democrat. Later, Ciancimino was accused, not just of handling huge sums of drug money, but of actually being a sworn-in member of the Corleone family. Those who were present at the funeral included the Italian president and senior cabinet ministers, all of them jeered at by an angry Sicilian crowd.

To ward off accusations of government inertia or complicity, the law that La Torre had demanded was rushed through Parliament soon afterwards, and was used in the **super-trials**, or *maxiprocessi*, that arose from the confessions of Buscetta and the other *pentiti* (penitents) who had followed his lead. The biggest of these trials, lasting eighteen months, started in February 1986, when five hundred *mafiosi* appeared in a specially built maximum-security bunker adjoining Palermo's Ucciardone prison. The insecurity felt by the Mafia was reflected in continuing bloodshed in Sicily throughout the proceedings, but the worst was to come after the trial closed in December 1986, starting right on the steps of the courthouse with the murder of one of the accused *mafiosi* – many of whom were freed after they had squealed on their accomplices. Of those who were convicted, 19 received life sentences, and 338 others had sentences totalling 2065 years.

The fightback in the 1990s

The violence reached a new level of ferocity during the 1990s, starting in 1992 with a wave of assassinations of high-profile figures. In March, **Salvatore Lima**, a former mayor of Palermo who later became a Euro MP, was shot dead outside his villa in Mondello. Lima didn't have police bodyguards because he didn't believe he needed them; he had, in fact, been in the Mafia's pocket throughout his political career. His "crime" was his failure to fix the Supreme Court, which had gone ahead and confirmed the convictions of scores of *mafiosi* who had been incriminated in the super-trials of the 1980s.

This murder was followed by two more atrocities in quick succession: in May, the best-known of Sicily's anti-Mafia crusaders, **Giovanni Falcone**, was blown up by half a tonne of TNT on his way into Palermo from the airport, together with his wife and three bodyguards, while two months later his colleague, **Paolo Borsellino** (with five of his police guards), was the victim of a car bomb outside his mother's house, also in Palermo. As ever, public opinion was divided over what it all meant. There were those who claimed that these murders were public gestures, while others saw in them increasing evidence of the panic percolating through the Mafia's ranks in the face of the growing number of defections of former members who were turning *pentiti*.

The carnage certainly propelled the state into action, and a dramatic breakthrough came shortly afterwards. In January 1993, **Salvatore Riina**, the so-called "Boss of all the Bosses", and the man held ultimately responsible for the murder of the anti-Mafia judges, was arrested. **Leoluca Bagarella**, Riina's successor and brother-in-law, and the convicted killer of the chief of the Palermo Flying Squad in 1979, was captured in 1995 (Bagarella's hideout turned out to be a luxury apartment overlooking the heavily guarded home of two of the judges who had helped catch him). Another of the Corleone clan, **Giovanni Brusca**, was arrested in 1996 – a particularly gratifying coup for the anti-Mafia forces, as Brusca was one of the organization's most ruthless hitmen, the mastermind behind Falcone's assassination and believed to have been responsible for the strangling of an informant's 11-year-old son, whose body was then disposed of in a vat of acid. Elsewhere, **Natale D'Emanuele**, alleged to be the financial wizard behind the Mafia in Catania, was arrested and charged with trafficking arms throughout Italy, using hearses and coffins to transport them, in a throwback to 1930s Chicago.

On the political front, **Leoluca Orlando**, the mayor of Palermo who was forced out of office by his own Christian Democrat party in 1990, established an independent power base on an anti-Mafia ticket, at the head of his Rete (Network) party. Meanwhile, the confessions of Tommaso Buscetta began to provide evidence for the first time of the postwar alliance between Italy's former leading party and organized crime. Allegations inexorably focused on the very highest levels of government, and specifically on the relationship of Mafia stooge Salvatore Lima to his protector, **Giulio Andreotti**, the Christian Democrat leader and Italy's most successful postwar politician. Formerly considered untouchable, Andreotti finally bowed to increasing pressure to relinquish his parliamentary immunity and, in September 1995, aged 75, went on trial in Palermo for complicity and criminal association. Much fuss was made of the famous *bacio*, a kiss he was reported to have symbolically exchanged with Riina, according to *pentiti* revelations in 1994. However, the fact that most of the charges levelled against Andreotti were based on the testimony of Mafia informers (and therefore unreliable witnesses) led to Andreotti's complete acquittal in 1999. Many saw the result as simply further evidence of the famous cunning and survival skills of this political stalwart, which have given him the nickname *la volpe* ("the fox").

Statements by *pentiti* and others accused of Mafia associations were also at the bottom of investigations into the business dealings of the then-prime minister **Silvio Berlusconi**. This time they were considered serious enough to warrant a raid on Berlusconi's Milan headquarters by an elite anti-Mafia police unit in July 1998, and a hasty dash to Sicily by Berlusconi to defend himself against charges of money-laundering for Cosa Nostra. Despite these high-profile events, though, the very concept of Mafia involvement was becoming increasingly irrelevant to most Italians, as reports of political and business corruption began to dominate public life throughout the 1990s. As the mayor of Venice remarked, in response to whispers of Mafia involvement in the fire that destroyed La Fenice opera house in 1996, "claiming it was burnt by the Mafia is about as useful as saying it was attacked by alien spacecraft."

The 21st Century

Since the turn of the millennium, the violence has for the most part calmed down. While killings still occur, few political figureheads are targeted these days, perhaps because fewer are willing to take the visible risks that sealed the fate of crusaders like Falcone and Borsellino. More Mafia bosses have been jailed – **Bernardo Provenzano**, for thirteen years *capo dei capi*, was captured in 2006, quickly followed by 52 arrest warrants against the top echelons of Cosa Nostra in Palermo. Perhaps more significantly, is the of billions of euros in assets held by *mafiosi*, largely from the real estate and construction industries.

The most important development, however, has been the growth of a new open attitude towards the Mafia, in contrast to the previous denial and *omertà*. Sicilians themselves are now bolder than ever in their public demonstrations of disgust at the killings and intimidation, and the movement against paying **pizzo**, or protection money, has gathered force throughout the island. Anti-mafia education is now standard in all schools, beginning at primary level, and few Sicilians now hold any illusions about the true nature of the Mafia. Most crucially of all, the myth of the Mafia's invincibility has been irreparably dented.

Sicilian Baroque

Most of the church and civic architecture that you'll come across in Sicily, certainly in the east of the island, is Baroque in style. More particularly, it's of a type known as Sicilian Baroque. What follows is a brief introduction to the subject, designed to serve as a handy reference for some of the more important aspects of the style mentioned in the Guide.

Origins

To some extent, the qualities that attract art historians to the Sicilian Baroque – its "warmth and ebullience", "gaiety", "energy", "freedom and fantasy" – typify all **Baroque** architecture. The style grew out of the excesses of Mannerism, a distorted sixteenth-century mode of painting and architecture that had flourished in Italy in reaction to the restraint of the Renaissance. The development of a full-blown, ornate Baroque style followed in the late sixteenth century, again originating in Italy, and it quickly found a niche in other countries touched by the Counter Reformation. The Jesuits saw in Baroque art and architecture an expression of a revitalized Catholicism, its theatrical forms involving the congregation by portraying spiritual ecstasy in terms of physical passion. The origin of the word "Baroque" itself is uncertain: the two most popular theories are that it comes either from the seventeenth-century Portuguese *barroco*, meaning a misshapen pearl, or the term *barocco*, used by philosophers in the Middle Ages to mean a contorted idea. Whatever its origins, it was used by contemporary critics in a derogatory sense, implying odd or extravagant shapes, as opposed to the much-vaunted classical forms of the Renaissance.

Although Baroque was born in Rome, the vogue quickly spread throughout Europe. Everywhere, the emphasis was firmly on elaborate **ornamentation** and **spectacle**, something that reflected the growing power of the aristocracy, who had begun to challenge the established wealth and tradition of the Church. The primary motivating force behind the decoration of the buildings was the need to impress the neighbouring gentry; building to the glory of God came a poor second.

Some of the finest examples of Baroque architecture are to be found in Sicily, although there's some debate as to the specific origins of the **Sicilian Baroque** style. During the eighteenth century alone, Sicily was conquered and ruled in turn by the Spanish Habsburgs, the Spanish Bourbons, the House of Savoy, the Austrian Habsburgs, and the Bourbons from Naples, lending a particularly exuberant flavour to its Baroque creations – which some say was borrowed from Spain. Others argue that the dominant influence was Italian: Sicilian architects tended to train and to travel in Italy, rather than Spain, and brought home what they learned on the mainland, adapting prevalent Roman Baroque ideas to complement peculiarly Sicilian architectural traditions. Both theories contain an element of the truth, though perhaps more pertinent is Sicily's unique long-term history: two and a half millennia of invasion and domination have produced a very distinct culture and society – one that is bound to have influenced, or even produced, an equally distinct architectural form.

Baroque towns

Sicily's seismic instability has profoundly affected its architectural history. The huge **earthquake of 1693** that almost flattened Catania, and completely destroyed Noto, Ragusa, Avola and Modica, provided a fantastic opportunity for local architects, who began massive rebuilding programmes in the southeast corner of Sicily. To them, a **Baroque town** aspired to be, and should be seen to be, a centre of taste and sophistication. They designed their new towns to delight their citizens, to encourage the participation of passers-by and to impress outsiders, with long vistas contriving to focus on the facade of a church or a palace, or an unexpected view of the sea. To enhance the visual effect even more, a building was designed to offer multiple, changing views from different angles of approach. This way, a completed plan might include all the buildings in a square or series of squares, and the experience of walking from place to place through varied but harmonious spaces was considered as important as the need to arrive at a destination. Moreover, as much of eighteenth-century Sicilian town-life took place outside, the **facade** of a building became synonymous with the wealth and standing of its occupant. External features became increasingly elaborate and specialized, and some parts of buildings – windows and staircases, for example – were often merely there for show. Invariably, what seem to be regular stone facades have been cosmetically touched up with plaster to conceal an asymmetry or an angle of less than ninety degrees: a self-conscious approach to town planning that can sometimes give the impression of walking around a stage set. Interestingly, this approach remained confined to the south and east of Sicily; outside the earthquake zone, in the west of the island, local architectural traditions continued to dominate in towns that hadn't had the dubious benefit of being levelled and left for the planners.

The "ideal city"

Ideally, where there was scope for large-scale planning, an entire city could be constructed as an aesthetic whole. As early as 1615 the Venetian architect and theorist **Vincenzo Scamozzi** published a treatise, *Dell'Idea dell'architettura universale*, in which he stated that the architectural harmony of the "**ideal city**" should reflect the perfect relationship between the prince, the judiciary, the Church, the marketplace and the populace.

Noto is an almost perfect example of Scamozzi's ideal. After the 1693 earthquake, the old town was so devastated that it was decided to move its site and rebuild from scratch, and the plan that was eventually accepted was almost an exact replica of Scamozzi's. Noto is constructed on a grid plan, traversed from east to west by a wide corso crossing a main piazza, which is itself balanced by four smaller piazzas. The buildings along the corso show remarkable balance and grace, while the attention of the Baroque planners to every harmonious detail is illustrated by the use of a warm, golden stone for the churches and *palazzi*.

Neighbouring towns in the southeast were also destroyed by the earthquake and rebuilt along similar lines. Both **Avola** and **Grammichele** were moved from their hilltop positions to the coastal plain, and their polygonal plans were similarly influenced by Scamozzi. Grammichele, particularly, retains an extraordinary hexagonal layout, unique in Sicily. **Ragusa** is more complex, surviving today as two towns: the medieval Ragusa Ibla, which the inhabitants rebuilt after the earthquake, and the Baroque upper town of Ragusa, which is built on a sloping grid plan, rather similar to Noto. Although Ibla isn't built to any kind of Baroque pattern, it does lay claim to one of the most spectacular of Sicilian Baroque churches.

Catania was not completely destroyed by the earthquake, but was instead rebuilt over its old site. Broad streets were built to link existing monuments and to facilitate rescue operations in case of another earthquake. The city is divided into four quarters by wide streets that meet in Piazza del Duomo, and wherever possible these spaces are used to maximize the visual impact of a facade or monument. The main Piazza del Duomo was conceived as a uniform set piece, while the main street, Via Etnea, cuts a swath due north from here, always drawing the eyes to Mount Etna, smoking in the distance.

On the other side of the island, Baroque **Palermo** evolved without the impetus of natural disaster. There's no comparable city plan, Palermo's intricate central layout owing more to the Arabs than to seventeenth- and eighteenth-century designers; what Baroque character the city possesses has almost entirely to do with its highly individual churches and palaces. These were constructed in a climate of apparent opulence but encroaching bankruptcy; as the Sicilian aristocrats were attracted to Palermo to pay court to the Spanish viceroy, they left the management of their lands to pragmatic agents, whose short-sighted policies allowed the estates to fall into neglect. This ate away at the wealth of the gentry, who responded by mortgaging their lands in order to maintain their living standards. The grandiose palaces and churches they built in the city still stand, but following the damage caused during World War II many are in a state of terrible neglect and near collapse; wild flowers grow out of the facades, and chunks of masonry frequently fall into the street below.

Specific features

Eighteenth-century aristocrats in Palermo escaped the heat by going to **summer villas** outside the city, and many of these still survive around **Bagheria**. The villas tend to be simply designed, but are bedecked with balconies and terraces for afternoon strolling, and were approached by long, impressive driveways. Above all, they are notable for their **external staircases**, leading to the main entrance on the first floor (the ground floor usually contained the kitchen and servants' quarters). It's typical of the Baroque era that an external feature should take on such significance in a building – and that they should show such a remarkable diversity, each reflecting the wealth of the individual owners. Beyond the fact that they were nearly always double staircases, symmetrical to the middle axis of the facade, each was completely different.

While **balconies** had always been a prominent feature of Sicilian domestic architecture, during the eighteenth century they became prolific. The balcony supports, or buttresses, were elaborately carved: manic heads, griffins, horses, monsters and mythical figures all featured as decoration, fine examples of which survive at Noto's **Palazzo Villadorata**, as well as in Modica and Scicli. The wrought-iron balustrades curved outwards, almost like theatre boxes, to allow room for women's billowing skirts.

Church building, too, flourished during this period. Baroque architects could let their imaginations run wild: the facade of the **Duomo** at Siracusa was begun in 1728, based on designs by Andrea Palma of Palermo, and the result is highly sophisticated and exciting. Other designs adapted and modified accepted forms for church architecture, as well as inventing new ones. In Palermo especially, typically Sicilian elements – like central circular windows – were used to great effect.

It was in the **church interiors**, however, that Sicilian Baroque came into its own, with tomb sculpture ever more ostentatious and stucco decoration abundant. Inlaid marble, a technique introduced from Naples at the start of the seventeenth century, became de rigueur and reached its prime during the second half of the century, when entire walls or chapels would be decorated in this way. Palermo fields some of the best examples of all these techniques, at their most impressive in the church of **San Giuseppe dei Teatini**, designed by Giacomo Besio, a Genovese who lived most of his life in Sicily. For real over-the-top detail, though, see the churches of **Santa Caterina** and **Il Gesù**, also in Palermo, both of which conceal a riot of inlaid marble decoration.

Architects and sculptors

Rosario Gagliardi was responsible for much of the rebuilding of Noto and Ragusa, and became known as one of the most important architects in southeast Sicily. Born in Siracusa in 1698, he worked in Noto as a carpenter from the age of 10, and was first acknowledged as an architect in 1726. Between 1760 and 1784 he was chief architect for the city of Noto, and during this time also worked on many different projects in Ragusa and Modica. As far as is known, he never travelled outside Sicily, let alone to Rome, yet he absorbed contemporary architectural trends from the study of books and treatises, and reproduced the ideas with some flair.

Gagliardi's prime interest was in facades, and his work achieved a sophisticated fusion of Renaissance poise, Baroque grandeur and local Sicilian ornamentation. He had no interest, however, in spatial relationships or structural innovation, and the interiors of his buildings are disappointing when compared to the elaborate nature of their exteriors. Perhaps his most significant contribution was his development of the **belfry** as a feature. Sicilian churches traditionally didn't have a separate belltower, but incorporated the bells into the main facade, revealed through a series of two or three arches – an idea handed down from Byzantine building. Gagliardi extended the central bay of the facade into a tower, a highly original compromise satisfying both the local style and the more conventional notions of design from the mainland. The belfry on the church of **San Giorgio** in Ragusa Ibla, Gagliardi's masterpiece, is an excellent example of this.

The principal architect on the design and rebuilding of Catania after the 1693 earthquake, **Giovanni Battista Vaccarini**, was born in Palermo in 1702. He trained in Rome and embraced the current idiom, working with such illustrious figures as Alessandro Specchi (who built the papal stables) and Francesco de Sanctis (designer of the Spanish Steps). In 1730 he arrived in Catania, having been appointed as city architect by the Senate, and at once began work on finishing the Municipio. Outside he placed a fountain, whose main feature is an obelisk supported by an elephant, the symbol of Catania – reminiscent of Bernini's elephant fountain in Rome.

Giacomo Serpotta, master of the Palermitan oratories, was born in Palermo in 1656. He cashed in on the opulence of the Church and specialized in decorating oratories with moulded plasterwork in ornamental frames. He would include life-sized figures of Saints and Virtues, surrounded by plaster draperies, trophies, swags of fruit, bouquets of flowers and other extravagances much beloved of the Baroque. Among his most remarkable works is the Oratory of the Rosary in the church of **Santa Zita**, where the end wall is a reconstruction of the Battle of Lépanto. Three-dimensional representation is taken to an extreme here, and actual wires are used as rigging.

Other Baroque architects are less well known, but are influential in Sicily all the same. **Giacomo Amato** (1643–1732) was a monk, sent to Rome in 1671 to represent his Order, where he came into contact with the works of Bernini and Borromini. Dazzled by what he'd seen, he neglected his religious duties after his return to Palermo in order to design some of the city's most characteristic churches, **Sant'Ignazio all'Olivella** and **San Domenico** among them. **Vincenzo Sinatra** had a more traditional career, starting as a stonecutter before working with Gagliardi in the 1730s as his foreman. In 1745 he married Gagliardi's niece, a move which did him no harm at all, since by 1761, when Gagliardi had a stroke, Sinatra was managing all his affairs. For ten years he directed the construction of Noto's Municipio, and during the rest of his life Sinatra worked in collaboration with the other city architects on a variety of projects. More important was **Giovanni Vermexio**, who was active in Siracusa at around the same time. His work graces the city's Piazza del Duomo, notably the **Palazzo Arcivescovile**, while he gets a couple of ornate-interior credits, too, in the shape of one of the Duomo's chapels, and the octagonal **Cappella di San Sepolcro** in the church of Santa Lucia in the Achradina quarter of Siracusa.

Books

Although only a few modern writers have travelled in and written about Sicily, the island has provided the inspiration for some great literature, by both Sicilians and foreign visitors. Translations of Italian and Sicilian classics are also often available at bookshops in major towns and resorts in Sicily. The best books in this selection are marked by a ★ symbol.

TRAVEL AND GENERAL

★ **Vincent Cronin** *The Golden Honeycomb*. Disguised as a quest for the mythical golden honeycomb of Daedalus, this classic, erudite travelogue is a searching account of a sojourn in Sicily in the 1950s.

Duncan Fallowell *To Noto*. Follows the author's trip from London to Baroque Noto in an old Ford – a witty tale, complete with pithy observations on Sicily and the Sicilians.

Matthew Fort *Sweet Honey, Bitter Lemons*. Cheery food-writer Fort returns to the island he first visited in the 1970s, only this time he comes on a Vespa and eats his way around, from ice cream to anchovies.

★ **Norman Lewis** *In Sicily*. A sweeping portrait of the island which Lewis came to know well through his wife and her family. Subjects range from reflections on Palermo's ruined *palazzi* to the impact of immigration, and there's plenty on the Mafia.

Daphne Phelps *A House in Sicily*. An Englishwoman inherits a house in Taormina in the late 1940s, and turns it into a guesthouse to make ends meet. Cue the usual cultural misunderstandings while she learns to love the locals,

leavened by vignettes of her eminent guests – including Bertrand Russell, Tennessee Williams and Roald Dahl.

Gaia Servadio *Motya*. On one level, an account of Phoenician history and culture as they relate to the excavated ruins of Motya – but in truth, so much more than that, as Servadio explores the fabric of Sicily and its people in uncompromising, enlightening detail.

★ **Mary Taylor Simeti** *On Persephone's Island: A Sicilian Journal*. Sympathetic record of a typical year in Sicily by an American who married a Sicilian professor and has lived in the west of the island since the early 1960s. It's full of keenly observed detail about flora and fauna, customs, the harvests, festivals and – above all – the Sicilians themselves.

Elio Vittorini *Conversations in Sicily*. A Sicilian emigrant returns from the north of Italy after fifteen years to see his mother on her birthday. The conversations of the title are with the people he meets on the way, and reveal a prewar Sicily that, while affectionately drawn, is ridden with poverty and disease.

HISTORY, POLITICS AND ARCHEOLOGY

David Abulafia *Frederick II: A Medieval Emperor*. Definitive account of the Hohenstaufen king, greatest of the medieval European rulers, with much on his reign in Sicily. It's a reinterpretation of the received view of Frederick, revealing a less formidable king than the omnipotent and supreme ruler usually portrayed. Also see the same author's *Italy, Sicily and the Mediterranean, 1100–1400*.

★ **Sandra Benjamin** *Sicily: Three Thousand Years of Human History*. An instantly engaging book that brings the history of Sicily vividly to life. If you buy only one book on Sicily, make it this one.

Samuel Butler *The Authoress of the Odyssey*. Eccentric book, by the author of dystopian novel *Erewhon*, which presents the argument that *The Odyssey* was written by a Sicilian woman, and was set around Trapani and in the Egadi Islands.

Brian Caven *Dionysius I: Warlord of Sicily*. The life of Dionysius I, by a historian who sees him not as a vicious

tyrant but as a valiant Crusader against the Carthaginians.

Christopher Hibbert *Garibaldi and His Enemies*. A popular treatment of the life and revolutionary works of Giuseppe Garibaldi, thrillingly detailing the exploits of "The Thousand" in their lightning campaign from Marsala to Milazzo.

R. Ross Holloway *The Archaeology of Ancient Sicily*. The standard work on the ancient monuments and archeological discoveries of Sicily, from the Paleolithic to the later Roman period.

★ **John Julius Norwich** *The Normans in Sicily*. Published together under one title, J.J. Norwich's *The Normans in the South* and *Kingdom in the Sun* tell the story of the Normans' explosive entry into the south of Italy, and their creation in Sicily of one of the most brilliant medieval European civilizations.

Steven Runciman *The Sicilian Vespers*. The classic account of Sicily's large-scale popular uprising in the thirteenth century. Runciman's *A History of the Crusades: 1, 2 & 3*, meanwhile, covers the Norman kings of Sicily, as well as the crusading Frederick II.

CRIME AND SOCIETY

John Dickie *Cosa Nostra*. Dickie, a professor of Italian Studies at University College London, is an expert on the

Mafia and its role in Sicilian society, and offers an in-depth look at the secret workings of the organization, from its early days in the mid-1800s to its current manifestation.

David Lane *Into the Heart of the Mafia*. This look at life in the Italian south offers a contemporary journey through corruption from Naples to Sicily, an essential counterpoint to any number of expat-life-in-a-vineyard experiences.

Norman Lewis *The Honoured Society*. Written in the 1960s, this is a classic account of the Mafia, its origins, personalities and customs, and is still the most accessible introduction available to the subject.

Clare Longrigg *Boss of Bosses*. One of the Mafia's most notorious *capo dei capi* (Boss of Bosses), Bernardo Provenzano, was arrested in Sicily in 2006 after four decades spent evading the law. Longrigg's careful unravelling of his successful shifting of criminal enterprise into mainstream business explains the subtitle: *How One Man Saved the Sicilian Mafia*.

★ **Gavin Maxwell** *The Ten Pains of Death*. Maxwell lived in Scopello during the 1950s, and recorded the lives of his neighbours in their own words. There's much on Sicilian small-town life and poverty, and sympathetic portraits of traditional festivals and characters. His *God Protect Me*

from My Friends is a sympathetic biography of the notorious bandit Salvatore Giuliano, ripe with intrigue and double-dealing.

★ **Peter Robb** *Midnight in Sicily*. The Australian Robb spent fifteen years in the Italian south tracing the contorted relations between organized crime and politics. Here, he focuses on the structure of the Mafia, the trials of the bosses in the 1980s, the high-profile assassinations that ensued, and the trial of Andreotti, providing deep insights into the dynamics of Sicilian society.

★ **Roberto Saviano** *Gomorrah*. Saviano's exposé of the Neapolitan Camorra is the first to have dished the dirt on the most violent grouping of Italy's various organized criminal gangs, and he is currently in hiding because of it. At its heart, the book is a passionate protest against a problem which only seems to get worse, and it has also been made into a highly regarded film.

Alexander Stille *Excellent Cadavers*. An important book tracing the modern fight against the Mafia as led by Giovanni Falcone and Paolo Borsellino, whose assassinations in 1992 finally sparked the Italian state into action.

NOVELS ABOUT SICILY

Michael Dibdin *Blood Rain*. Dibdin's Venetian detective, Aurelio Zen, is an idiosyncratic loner, always up against the Italian state and society in an unequalled series of crime novels. Here, Dibdin sends him to Sicily, with dark consequences for all concerned.

Simonetta Agnello Hornby *The Marchesa; The Almond*

Picker. From aristocratic nineteenth-century Palermo to 1960s' village life, Hornby's bestselling Sicily novels are full of subtle intrigue, voluptuous imagery and period detail.

Norman Lewis *The March of the Long Shadows*. An affectionate novel set in postwar Sicily, dealing with the Separatist movement, the bandit Giuliano and a whole

---

SICILIAN CUISINE AND COOKBOOKS

There are Sicilian recipes in all the major Italian cookbooks, starting with **Elizabeth David**'s classic *Italian Food* (published 1954), the book that introduced Mediterranean flavours and ingredients to Britain. (Olive oil, famously, was previously something you could only buy at the chemist.) **Antonio Carluccio**, Britain's avuncular Italian master, is good on Sicilian fish and snacks in his *Southern Italian Feast* – his *arancini* recipe is definitive – while *Southern Italian Cooking* by **Valentina Harris** has an excellent chapter on Sicilian cooking. **Viana La Plante**'s *Verdura*, although not explicitly Sicilian, is packed with seasonal Sicilian recipes. If you are self-catering, this is the book to bring – it is the perfect companion to Sicilian market shopping, while **Ruth Rogers** and **Rose Grey**'s *River Café* cookbooks have a wealth of recipes using ingredients such as wild fennel and fresh ricotta, and **Jamie Oliver**'s *Jamie's Italy*, has some good recipes from Palermo and from the island of Marettimo.

Specifically Sicilian cookbooks include ★ *Sicilian Food* by **Mary Taylor Simeti**, the kind of book you can read cover to cover, and which combines recipes with fascinating detail about life and traditions on the island. Simeti also co-authored *Bitter Almonds: Recollections and Recipes from a Sicilian Girlhood*, alongside **Maria Grammatico**, who was raised in a convent where she learned the pastry-cooking skills that she employs in her outlets in Erice. For an anecdotal trawl through the classics and the lesser-known dishes, including several from out-of-the-way places like Pantelleria and Stromboli, consult *The Flavors of Sicily* by **Anna Tasca Lanza**, the respected owner of a cooking school established at her family estate on the island – hence also her *Heart of Sicily: Recipes and Reminiscences of Regaleali, a Country Estate*. At the other end of the social scale, *Pani Caliatu*, by Susan Lord and Danilo Baroncino, explores the austere cuisine of the Aeolian Islands in a fascinating and beautifully designed book that combines social history, interviews, recipes and photographs.

cast of endearing characters. *The Sicilian Specialist* is Lewis's Mafia thriller, which flits from Sicily to the US to Cuba on the trail of a Mob assassin.

★ **Dacia Maraini** *The Silent Duchess*. The tale of a noble eighteenth-century family seen through the eyes of a mute duchess – beautifully written and dripping with authentic detail. *Bagheria*, meanwhile, is a disturbing – on several levels – account of Maraini's relationship with the town of the title, and how it fell into the grip of the Mafia.

Lily Prior *La Cucina*. Subtitled a "novel of rapture", this chronicles the romance between a spinster librarian from Castiglione and an enigmatic English chef. Drawn into the plot are the Mafia, copious recipes and the convolutions of Sicilian family life.

★ **Mario Puzo** *The Godfather*. The New York Godfather – Don Corleone – was born in Sicily and this majestic book (a great read, even if you've seen the films) touches on all things Sicilian.

SICILIAN LITERATURE

Gesualdo Bufalino *The Plague Spreader's Tale, Blind Argus, The Keeper of Ruins* and *Night's Lies*. Bufalino arrived late on the literary scene, publishing his first novel, *The Plague Sower*, in his 60s. Subsequent publications enhanced the reputation made by this remarkable debut, notably *Night's Lies*, which won Italy's most respected literary award, the Strega Prize, in 1988. Bufalino himself – seeking to explain the Sicilian character – commented, "Don't forget that even our most obscene vices nearly always bear the seal of sullen greatness".

★ **Andrea Camilleri** *Inspector Montalbano Mysteries*. Born in Agrigento, Camilleri is one of Italy's favourite modern authors, though he writes in Sicilian dialect that not all Italians can understand. His intelligent – and often vulgar and graphic – crime novels have subsequently become hugely popular all over Europe, masterfully translated into English by the New York poet, Stephen Sartorelli. Inspector Montalbano delves deep into the folds of Sicilian culture in an ongoing series, starting with *The Shape of Water*. More than a dozen of the books have been translated into English, including *The Terracotta Dog, The Voice of the Violin* and *August Heat*.

★ **Giuseppe Tomasi di Lampedusa** *The Leopard*. The most famous Sicilian novel was written after World War II, but recounts the dramatic nineteenth-century years of transition from Bourbon to Piedmontese rule from an aristocrat's point of view. David Gilmour's *The Last Leopard: A Life of Giuseppe Tomasi di Lampedusa*, is the first biography in English of Lampedusa, a readable account of the life of an otherwise rather dull man.

Luigi Pirandello *Six Characters in Search of an Author, Henry IV, The Late Mattia Pascal, Short Stories*. His most famous and accomplished work, *Six Characters...*, written in 1921, and his *Henry IV*, written a year later, contain many of the themes that preoccupied Pirandello throughout his writing career – the idea of a multiple personality and the quality of reality. *The Late Mattia Pascal* is an entertaining early novel (1904), though the collection of abrasive short stories is perhaps the best introduction to Pirandello's work.

★ **Leonardo Sciascia** *Sicilian Uncles, The Wine-Dark Sea, Candido, The Knight and Death, Death of an Inquisitor, The Day of the Owl, Equal Danger*. Sciascia's short stories and novellas are packed with incisive insights into the island's quirky ways, and infused with the author's humane and sympathetic view of its people. The first to describe the Mafia in Italian literature, he wrote metaphysical thrillers in which the detectives often turn out to be the hunted; the best known is *The Day of the Owl*.

Giovanni Verga *Short Sicilian Novels, Cavalleria Rusticana, Maestro Don Gesualdo, I Malavoglia* or *The House by the Medlar Tree, A Mortal Sin, La Lupa* and *Sparrow*. Born in the nineteenth century in Catania, Verga spent several years in various European salons before coming home to write his best work. Much of it is a reaction against the pseudo-sophistication of society circles, stressing the simple lives of ordinary people, with much emotion, wounded honour and feuds to the death. D.H. Lawrence's translations are suitably vibrant, with excellent introductions.

Films

Though Sicily doesn't have its own motion picture industry, the island's stunning scenery has served as a backdrop to a number of very successful films. The Aeolian and Pelagie islands, in particular, have proved popular settings for some interesting films, a few of them now classics of Italian cinema.

Michelangelo Antonioni *L'Avventura* (1960). Shot on the barren rocks of Panarea's Lisca Bianca, this film notes the beginning of a marked change in postwar Italian social mores. When a group of friends get together for a day out in the islands, one gets lost, and the relationships between those remaining begin to fracture. Here, Antonioni focuses ingeniously on the internal responses of those affected.

Emanuele Crispalese *Terraferma* (2011). Heart-warmer set on the island of Linosa, with the local fishermen coming to the rescue of shipwrecked migrants. Crispalese's earlier film, *Il Respiro* (2002), filmed on the southern island of Lampedusa, is a timeless, well-constructed look at how an eccentric mother is misunderstood by other islanders. Crispalese addresses the overwhelming patriarchy of Italian families and the sexual tension latent between family members.

Francis Ford Coppola *The Godfather* (1971). Mario Puzo's brilliant screenplay tells the story of how Don Vito Corleone, *capo* of the New York Sicilian Mafia, tries to maintain his hold on the family business and his old-world values, in the face of escalating violence and inter-family feuds. Since the town of Corleone itself was far too developed for the period filming, much of it was shot in Savoca and Forza d'Agro, outside Taormina.

Pietro Germi *Divorzio alla Siciliana* (1961). Proof that not all Sicilian films need be deep or cinematic, this is a hilarious and pointed satire of Italian marital conventions. Marcello Mastroianni plays a Sicilian nobleman trying to prove his wife unfaithful so he can kill her and marry his younger cousin. Known as *Divorce Italian Style* in English, it was filmed in Ispica near Ragusa, and on Isola Bella near Taormina, and got Germi nominated for a Best Director Oscar.

Luca Guadagnino *A Bigger Splash* (2016). Getting away from it all on Pantelleria are Tilda Swinton, playing a Bowie-esque international rock star who has lost her voice, and Matthias Schoenaerts, her photographer boyfriend, a recovering alcoholic. Then her ex-lover Ralph Fiennes turns up, with a young woman who appears to be his daughter. Jealousy, intrigue, anguish, passion and a swimming pool.

Nanni Moretti *Dear Diary* (1994). Moretti plays himself as he tours Rome on a Vespa, before visiting all the Aeolian Islands, showing how the inhabitants of each differ in mentality and lifestyle. Mostly comic, but more sombre at the end.

Michael Radford *Il Postino* (1994). An international favourite, featuring a postman on a small island who learns to love poetry after befriending the exiled poet Pablo Neruda. The film was shot in the town of Pollara on Salina, leading to a dramatic increase in tourism to the island.

Gianfranco Rosi *Fire at Sea* (2016). A haunting documentary film paralleling the lives of islanders on Lampedusa with the plight of refugees.

Roberto Rossellini *Stromboli: Terra di Dio* (1949). Starring Ingrid Bergman as a tormented young refugee who marries an Italian to escape the war, this is a sad story of solitude and cynicism, which received little praise in its home country. The real star, however, is the volcano itself, whose brooding presence undermines the illusion of an idyllic, happy island.

Giuseppe Tornatore *Cinema Paradiso* (1988). Though derided by critics for its saccharine storyline, this Oscar-winning film by Sicilian director Tornatore received popular acclaim the world over. Shot around Cefalù, it follows the friendship between a young boy and the local cinema projectionist, and is in many ways a homage to cinema itself.

Italian

The ability to speak English confers enormous prestige in Sicily, and plenty of locals are willing to show off their knowledge. As a consequence, your attempts to speak Italian may be met with responses in equally halting (or worse) English. The best technique is to say, firmly and politely, in Italian of course, that you have come to Sicily to practice your Italian, and if they take no notice (not unusual) to persist in speaking Italian.

Although Italian is a complex language (the finer points of grammar elude many Italians, including several politicians and journalists) getting a basic grasp is quite easy, especially if you already have a smattering of French or Spanish. Easiest of all is the **pronunciation**, since every word is spoken exactly as it's written, and usually enunciated with exaggerated, open-mouthed clarity. The only difficulties you're likely to encounter are the few **consonants** that are different from English:

c before **e** or **i** is pronounced as in chur**ch**, while **ch** before the same vowels is hard, as in **cat**.

g is soft before **e** and **i**, as in **gentle**; hard when followed by **h**, as in **garlic**.

gn has the **ni** sound of our o**ni**on.

gl in Italian is softened to something like **li** in English, as in vermi**li**on.

h is not aspirated, as in **hour**.

schi and **sche** are pronounced as in **ski**ttle and **ske**tch respectively

sci or **sce** are pronounced as in **she**et and **she**lter respectively.

When **speaking** to strangers, the third person is the polite form (ie *Lei* instead of *Tu* for "you"); using the second person is a mark of disrespect or stupidity. It's also worth remembering that Italians don't use "please" and "thank you" half as much as we do: it's all implied in the tone, though if you're in doubt, err on the polite side.

The majority of Italian words are **stressed** on the penultimate syllable, although there are loads of exceptions. Note that the ending **-ia** or **-ie** counts as two syllables, hence *trattoria* is stressed on the i.

None of this will help very much if you're confronted with the **Sicilian dialect**, which virtually qualifies as a separate language (see box). However, most Sicilians can communicate in something approximating standard Italian.

USEFUL WORDS AND PHRASES

BASICS

Good morning Buongiorno
Good afternoon/evening Buonasera
Goodnight Buonanotte
Hello/goodbye Ciao (informal; when speaking to strangers use the phrases above)
Goodbye Arrivederci (formal)
Goodbye Arrivederla (more formal)
Yes Sì
No No
Please Per favore
Thank you (very much) Grazie (molte/millegrazie)
You're welcome/after you Prego
Alright/that's OK Va bene
How are you? Come stai/sta? (informal/formal)

I'm fine Bene
Do you speak English? Parla inglese?
I don't speak Italian Non parlo italiano
I don't understand Non capisco
I haven't understood Non ho capito
I don't know Non lo so
Excuse me/sorry Scusa (informal)
Excuse me/sorry Mi scusi (formal)
Excuse me Permesso (in a crowd)
I'm sorry Mi dispiace
I'm here on holiday Sono qui in vacanza
I live in... Abito a...
I'm English Sono inglese
I'm Welsh Sono gallese
I'm Scottish Sono scozzese

THE SICILIAN LANGUAGE

For political reasons, all regional languages in Italy are considered **dialects** of Italian. In reality, however, each has its own history and influences, and the majority of them are, linguistically speaking, separate languages. During the 600-year-long Roman occupation of Sicily, Vulgar Latin became the lingua franca for the entire island, though it was highly influenced by close contacts with Arabic, Norman and Spanish languages. The grammar, lexicon and phonology of Sicilian thus differs immensely from modern standard Italian – so much so that during the American Mafia trials of the 1980s, the FBI had to enlist special agents fluent in Sicilian to translate the conversations of *mafiosi* based in New York. The **Sicilian language** even has its own regional dialects (*parrati*), though in general these are understood by all Sicilians.

Today, nearly all Sicilians speak and understand standard Italian, though, unlike numerous other dialects spoken throughout Europe, the language is in no danger of extinction: in most towns, the younger generation prefers Sicilian to Italian, and almost everyone speaks Sicilian at home. While Sicilians are well known for using their hands and arms as much as their vocal cords to communicate, their language is rich in idioms and sayings. Below are some favourites.

SICILIAN PROVERBS

Si vo' passari la vita cuntenti, statti luntanu di li parenti.
If you want a quiet life, stay away from relatives.
Sciarri di maritu e mugghieri duranu finu a lu lettu.
Quarrels between wives and husbands always end in the bed.
Cu'arrobba pri manciari nun fa piccatu.
He who steals to eat is no sinner.
Cu'asini caccia e fimmini cridi, faccia di paradisu nun ni vidi.
He who seeks girls and asses will never reach heaven.
Camina chi pantofuli finnu a quannu non hai i scarpi.
Walk with your slippers until you find your shoes (ie make the best of a bad situation).
Cu' va a Palermu e nun va a Murriali, si nni parti sceccu e torna maiali.
He who visits Palermo and not Monreale arrives an ass and returns a pig.

I'm Irish Sono irlandese
I'm American Sono americano/a (masculine/feminine)
I'm Australian Sono australiano/a (masculine/feminine)
I'm Canadian Sono canadese
I'm from New Zealand Sono neozelandese
I'm South African Sono sudafricano/a (masculine/feminine)
Today Oggi
Tomorrow Domani
Day after tomorrow Dopodomani
Yesterday Ieri
Now Adesso
Later Più tardi
Wait a minute! Aspetta!
In the morning Di mattina
In the afternoon Nel pomeriggio
In the evening Di sera
Tonight Stasera
Here/there Qui/là

Good/bad Buono/cattivo
Big/small Grande/piccolo
Cheap/expensive Economico/caro
Early/late Presto/ritardo
Hot/cold Caldo/freddo
Near/far Vicino/lontano
Vacant/occupied Libero/occupato
Quickly/slowly Velocemente/lentamente
Slowly/quietly Piano
With/without Con/senza
More/less Più/meno
Enough/no more Basta
Mr... Signor...
Mrs... Signora...
Miss... Signorina... (il signore, la signora, la signorina when speaking about someone else)
First name Primo nome
Surname Cognome

ACCOMMODATION

Hotel Albergo
Is there a hotel nearby? C'è un albergo qui vicino?
Do you have a room... Ha una camera...
for one/two/three people per una persona, due/tre persone

for one/two/three nights per una notte, due/tre notti
for one/two weeks per una settimana, due settimane
with a double bed con letto matrimoniale
with a shower/bath con doccia/bagno
with a balcony con terrazza

hot/cold water acqua calda/fredda
How much is it? Quanto costa?
It's too expensive È troppo caro
Is breakfast included? È compresa la prima colazione?
Do you have anything cheaper? Ha niente che costa di meno?
Full/half board Pensione completa/mezza pensione
Can I see the room? Posso vedere la camera?
I'll take it La prendo

What is the wi-fi password? Cos'è il password di wi-fi (pronounced wiffy)
I'd like to book a room Vorrei prenotare una camera
I have a booking Ho una prenotazione
Can we camp here? Possiamo fare il campeggio qui?
Is there a campsite nearby? C'è un camping qui?
Tent Tenda
Cabin Cabina
Hostel/ Youth hostel Ostello/Ostello per la gioventù

QUESTIONS AND DIRECTIONS

Where? (Where is/are...?) Dove? (Dov'è/Dove sono?)
When? Quando?
What? (What is it?) Cosa? (Cos'è?)
How much/many? Quanto/Quanti?
Why? Perché?
It is/There is (Is it/Is there...?) È/C'è (È/C'è...?)
What time is it? Che ora è?/Che ore sono?
How do I get to...? Come arrivo a...?
How far is it to...? Quant'è lontano a...?
Can you give me a lift to...? Mi può dare un passaggio a...?

Can you tell me when to get off? Può dirmi quando devo scendere?
What time does it open? A che ora apre?
What time does it close? A che ora chiude?
How much does it cost?/do they cost? Quanto costa?/Quanto costano?
What's it called in Italian? Come si chiama in italiano?
Left/right Sinistra/destra
Go straight ahead Sempre diritto
Turn to the right/left Gira a destra/sinistra

GETTING AROUND

Aeroplane Aereo
Bus Autobus/Pullman
Train Treno
Car Macchina
Taxi Taxi
Bicycle Bicicletta
Ferry Traghetto
Ship Nave
Hydrofoil Aliscafo
Hitch-hiking Autostop
On foot A piedi
Bus terminal Capolinea
Bus station Autostazione
Train station Stazione ferroviaria
Ferry terminal Stazione marittima
Port Porto

A ticket to... Un biglietto a...
One way/return Solo andata/andatae ritorno
Can I book a seat? Posso prenotare un posto?
What time does it leave? A che ora parte?
When is the next bus/train/ferry to...? Quando parte il prossimo pullman/treno/traghetto per...?
Where does it leave from? Da dove parte?
Which platform does it leave from? Da quale binario parte?
Do I have to change? Devo cambiare?
How many kilometres is it? Quanti chilometri sono?
How long does it take? Quanto ci vuole?
What number bus is it to...? Che numero di autobus per...?
Where's the road to...? Dov'è la strada a...?
Next stop, please La prossima fermata, per favore

SIGNS

Entrance/exit Entrata/uscita
Free entrance Ingresso libero
Gentlemen/ladies Signori/signore
WC/bathroom Gabinetto/bagno
Vacant/engaged Libero/occupato
Open/closed Aperto/chiuso
Arrivals/departures Arrivi/partenze
Closed for restoration Chiuso per restauro
Closed for holidays Chiuso per ferie
Pull/push Tirare/spingere
Out of order Guasto
Drinking water Acqua potabile
Not for drinking Non potabile

To let Affitasi
Platform Binario
Cash desk Cassa
Go/walk Avanti
Stop/halt Alt
Customs Dogana
Do not touch Non toccare
Danger Pericolo
Beware Attenzione
First aid Pronto soccorso
Ring the bell Suonare il campanello
No smoking Vietato fumare

DRIVING

Parking Parcheggio	**Road closed** Strada chiusa
No parking Divieto di sosta/Sosta vietata	**No through road** Vietato il transito
One-way street Senso unico	**No overtaking** Vietato il sorpasso
Both sides of the street Ambo i lati	**Crossroads** Incrocio
No entry Senso vietato	**Speed limit** Limite di velocità
Slow down Rallentare	**Traffic light** Semaforo

NUMBERS AND DAYS OF THE WEEK

1 Uno	**20** Venti
2 Due	**25** Venticinque
3 Tre	**30** Trenta
4 Quattro	**40** Quaranta
5 Cinque	**50** Cinquanta
6 Sei	**60** Sessanta
7 Sette	**70** Settanta
8 Otto	**80** Ottanta
9 Nove	**90** Novanta
10 Dieci	**100** Cento
11 Undici	**1000** Mille
12 Dodici	**Monday** Lunedì
13 Trédici	**Tuesday** Martedì
14 Quattordici	**Wednesday** Mercoledì
15 Quindici	**Thursday** Giovedì
16 Sédici	**Friday** Venerdì
17 Diciassette	**Saturday** Sabato
18 Diciotto	**Sunday** Domenica
19 Diciannove	

FOOD AND DRINK

USEFUL PHRASES

I'm vegetarian/vegan Sono vegetarian/a/vegano/a
I'm coeliac Sono celiaco/a
Gluten free Senza glutine
Lactose free Senza lattosio

BASICS AND SNACKS

Aceto Vinegar
Aglio Garlic
Biscotti Biscuits
Burro Butter
Caramelle Sweets
Cioccolato Chocolate
Formaggio Cheese
Frittata Omelette
Gelato Ice cream
Grissini Bread sticks
Maionese Mayonnaise
Marmellata Jam
Olio Oil
Olive Olives
Pane Bread
Pane integrale Wholemeal bread

Panino Bread roll
Patatine Crisps/potato chips
Patatine fritte Chips/French fries
Pepe Pepper
Pizzetta Small pizza
Riso Rice
Sale Salt
Uova Eggs
Yoghurt Yoghurt
Zucchero Sugar
Zuppa Soup

ANTIPASTI AND STARTERS

Antipasto misto Usually mixed cold cuts, salamis and cheese (sometimes accompanied by olives, sun-dried tomatoes or tasters of other dishes in this list)
Caponata Mixed aubergine, olives and tomatoes
Caprese Tomato and mozzarella cheese salad
Insalata di mare Seafood salad
Insalata di riso Rice salad
Insalata russa "Russian salad": diced vegetables in mayonnaise

Melanzane alla parmigiana Fried aubergine baked in tomato sauce with parmesan cheese

Mortadella Salami-type cured meat with nuggets of fat, often with pistachios

Pancetta Italian bacon

Peperonata Grilled green, red or yellow peppers stewed in olive oil

Pomodori ripieni Stuffed tomatoes

Prosciutto cotto Ham (cooked, usually boiled, sometimes roast)

Prosciutto crudo Parma ham

Salame Salami

Salmone/tonno/pesce spada/affumicato Smoked salmon/tuna/swordfish

PIZZAS

Biancaneve "Snow white": mozzarella only, popular with kids

Calzone Folded pizza with cheese, ham and tomato

Capricciosa "Capricious": topped with whatever they've got in the kitchen, usually including baby arti choke, ham and egg

Cardinale Ham and olives

Diavolo "Devil": spicy, with hot salami or Italian sausage

Funghi Mushroom: tinned, sliced button mushrooms unless it specifies fresh mushrooms, either funghi freschi or porcini

Frutti di mare Seafood: usually mussels, prawns, squid and clams

Margherita Cheese and tomato

Marinara Tomato and garlic

Napoli/Napoletana Tomato, anchovy and olive oil (often mozzarella too)

Norma Tomato, grilled or fried aubergine and grated ricotta (either salted, *salata*, or baked, *infornata*)

Quattro formaggi "Four cheeses": usually mozzarella, fontina, Gorgonzola and Gruyère

Quattro stagioni "Four seasons": the toppings split into four separate sections, usually including ham, peppers, onion, mushrooms, artichokes, olives, egg etc

Palermitana Tomato, anchovies, breadcrumbs

Rianata Fresh tomato, pecorino, oregano, garlic and anchovy; a western Sicilian speciality

Romana Anchovy and olives

THE FIRST COURSE (IL PRIMO)

PASTA

Busiate long, thick twists of pasta

Cannelloni Large tubes of pasta, stuffed

Farfalle Literally "bow"-shaped pasta; the word also means "butterflies"

Fettuccine Narrow pasta ribbons

Gnocchi Small potato and dough dumplings

Lasagne Lasagne

Maccheroni Macaroni (tubular pasta)

Pappardelle Pasta ribbons

Pasta al forno Oven-baked pasta, usually with minced meat, eggs, tomato and 0cheese

Penne Smaller version of rigatoni

Ravioli Ravioli (stuffed, square- shaped pasta)

Rigatoni Large, grooved, tubular pasta

Risotto Cooked rice dish, with sauce

Spaccatelle Long, open pasta curls

Spaghetti Spaghetti

Spaghettini Thin spaghetti

Tagliatelle Pasta ribbons, another word for fettuccine

Tortellini Small rings of pasta, stuffed with meat or cheese

Vermicelli Very thin spaghetti (literally "little worms")

PASTA SAUCES (SALSA)

Aglio e olio (e peperoncino) Tossed in garlic and olive oil (and hot chillies)

Amatriciana Cubed pork and tomato sauce, with onions and hot chillies (originally from Rome)

Arrabbiata Spicy tomato sauce, with chillies

Bolognese Meat sauce

Burro e salvia Butter and sage

Carbonara Cream, ham and beaten egg

Frutta di mare Seafood

Funghi Mushroom

Panna Cream

Parmigiano Parmesan cheese

Pesto Ground basil, pine nut, garlic and pecorino

Pomodoro Tomato sauce

Puttanesca Tomato, anchovy, olive oil and oregano sauce (literally "whorish")

Ragù Meat sauce

Trapanese Cold puréed tomato, garlic and basil

Vongole (veraci) Clam and tomato sauce (fresh clams in shells, usually served with oil and herbs)

THE SECOND COURSE (IL SECONDO)

MEAT (CARNE)

Agnello Lamb

Bistecca Steak

Cervello Brain

Cinghiale Wild boar

Coniglio Rabbit

Costolette/cotolette Cutlets/chops

Fegatini Chicken livers

Fégato Liver

Involtini Steak slices, rolled and stuffed

Lepre Hare

Lingua Tongue

Maiale Pork
Manzo Beef
Ossobuco Shin of veal
Pollo Chicken
Polpette Meatballs
Rognoni Kidneys
Salsiccia Sausage
Saltimbocca Veal with ham
Scaloppina Escalope (of veal)
Spezzatino Stew
Tacchino Turkey
Trippa Tripe
Vitello Veal

FISH (PESCE) AND SHELLFISH (CROSTACEI)

Note that *surgelato* or *congelato* written on the menu
next to a dish means "frozen" – it often applies to
squid and prawns.

Acciughe Anchovies
Anguilla Eel
Aragosta Lobster
Baccalà Dried salted cod
Bottarga Fish roe
Calamari Squid
Cappone/Lampuga Mahi Mahi
Céfalo Grey mullet
Cernia Grouper
Cozze Mussels
Dattile Razor clams
Déntice Dentex (like sea bass)
Gamberetti Shrimps
Gamberi Prawns
Granchio Crab
Merluzzo Cod
Nasello Hake
Orata Gilthead bream
Ostriche Oysters
Pesce spada Swordfish
Polpo/polipo Octopus
Ricci di mare Sea urchins
Ricciola Amberjack
Rospo Monkfish
Sampiero John Dory
Sarago White bream
Sarde Sardines
Séppie Cuttlefish
Sgombro Mackerel
Sogliola Sole
Spigola Sea bass
Tonno Tuna
Totani Species of squid
Triglie Red mullet
Trota Trout
Vongole Clams

VEGETABLES (CONTORNI) AND SALAD (INSALATA)

Asparagi Asparagus
Basilico Basil
Broccoli Broccoli
Capperi Capers
Carciofi Artichokes
Carciofini Artichoke hearts
Carotte Carrots
Cavolfiori Cauliflower
Cavolo Cabbage
Ceci Chickpeas
Cetriolo Cucumber
Cipolla Onion
Fagioli Beans
Fagiolini Green beans
Finocchio Fennel
Funghi Mushrooms
Insalata verde/mista Green salad/mixed salad
Melanzane Aubergine/eggplant
Origano Oregano
Patate Potatoes
Peperoni Peppers
Piselli Peas
Pomodori Tomatoes
Radicchio Red chicory
Spinaci Spinach
Zucca Pumpkin
Zucchini Courgettes

DESSERTS (DOLCI)

Amaretti Macaroons
Cassata Ice-cream cake with candied fruit
Gelato Ice cream
Macedonia Fruit salad
Torta Cake, tart
Zabaglione Dessert made with eggs, sugar and
marsala wine
Zuppa Inglese Trifle

CHEESE

Caciocavallo A type of dried, mature mozzarella
Fontina Northern Italian cheese used in cooking
Gorgonzola Soft, strong, blue-veined cheese
Mozzarella Soft white cheese, traditionally made from
buffalo's milk
Parmigiano Parmesan cheese
Pecorino Strong-tasting, hard sheep's cheese
Provolone Cheese with grooved rind, either mild or
slightly piquant
Ricotta Soft white cheese made from ewe's milk, used
in sweet or savoury dishes
Ricotta Salata Ricotta which has been salted to
preserve it; can be grated

Ricotta Infornata Oven-baked ricotta, with a sweet caramelized crust

Vastedda Similar to caciocavallo, but tastes slightly more acidic

FRUIT AND NUTS

Albicocca Apricot
Ananas Pineapple
Anguria/coccomero Watermelon
Arancia Orange
Banana Banana
Cacco Persimmon
Chicco d'uva/uva A grape/grapes
Ciliegia Cherry
Fico Fig
Fico d'India Prickly pear
Fragola Strawberry
Lemone Lemon
Mandorla Almond
Mela Apple
Melone Melon
Néspola Medlar
Pera Pear
Pesca Peach
Pinolo Pine nut
Pistacchio Pistachio nut
Smerge/Sberge Cross between a plum and a peach with a hint of vanilla

COOKING TERMS

Affumicato Smoked
Arrosto Roast
Ben cotto Well done
Bollito/lesso Boiled
Alla brace Barbecued
Brasato Cooked in wine
Cotto Cooked (not raw)
Crudo Raw
Al dente Firm, not overcooked
Ferri Grilled without oil
Al forno Baked
Fritto Fried
Grattugiato Grated
Alla griglia Grilled
Al marsala Cooked with marsala wine
Milanese Fried in egg and breadcrumbs
Pizzaiola Cooked with tomato sauce
Ripieno Stuffed
Sangue Rare
Allo spiedo On the spit
Stracotto Braised, stewed
Surgelati Frozen
In umido Stewed
Al vapore Steamed

SICILIAN SPECIALITIES

STARTERS AND PASTA

Arancini "Little oranges": deep-fried rice balls with minced meat, cheese and peas (*al ragù*) or cheese, ham and bechamel (*al burro*). Also made with spinach, pistachio, or aubergine

Caponata Sautéed aubergine, with olives, peppers, almonds and tomatoes; served cold

Cozze alla marinara Mussels in a rich wine-based soup

Cozze pepata Mussels in spicy tomato stock

Crocchè di patate Potato croquettes

Insalata di arance Orange salad, dressed with oil and parsley, and sometimes with fennel

Maccu Fava-bean soup flavoured with wild fennel

Panelle Chickpea fritters

Pasta con i broccoli arriminati Pasta cooked with broccoli, anchovy paste, pine nuts and saffron

Pasta con la mollica Pasta with oil and toasted breadcrumbs

Pasta con le sarde Macaroni with fresh sardines, fennel, raisins and pine kernels; a speciality of Palermo

Penne all'arrabbiata Short tubular pasta with spicy tomato sauce made with chillies (*arrabbiata* means "angry")

Peperonata Peppers (capsicum) sautéed in olive oil until soft and sweet, either served as antipasto or as a vegetable

Spaghetti alla carrettiera "Carter's spaghetti", cooked with garlic, oil, pecorino and salt and pepper; common in Catania province

Spaghetti alla Norma Spaghetti with tomato sauce topped with fried aubergine and parmesan or pecorino cheese; a speciality of Catania, named after one of Bellini's operas

Spaghetti alla Trapanese Spaghetti tossed with cold puréed tomatoes, basil and garlic; a pungent dish from Trapani

Uova/funghi in tegame Eggs/mushrooms fried in olive oil, served at the table in a little metal pan

Zuppa di San Giuseppe A kind of *maccu* made from pulses and a mixture of short or broken pasta, usually spiked with chilli and wild fennel.

MAIN COURSES

Cuscus Couscous, usually served with fish and vegetable sauce, sometimes meat; a common dish in western Sicily and on the islands of Lampedusa and Pantelleria

Fritto misto A standard seafood dish; deep-fried prawns and squid rings in batter

Fritto di pesce As above but also with other fried fish, like sardines and whitebait

Involtini di pesce spada Slices of swordfish, stuffed, rolled and fried

esce spada alla Ghiotta Swordfish cooked in spicy tomato sauce with capers and olives; from Messina province

Sarde a beccafico Sardines stuffed with breadcrumbs, nuts, dried fruit and anchovies; a Palermitan speciality

Scaloppine di maiale al Marsala Escalopes of pork cooked in marsala wine; the most common way of cooking meat with this Sicilian wine

Stocca alla Messinese Dried cod stewed with potatoes, olives, tomatoes, capers and celery; a speciality of Messina, although there are other regional variations

Zuppa di cozze/vongole A big dish of mussels/clams in rich wine-based soup

Zuppa di pesce As above but usually with pieces of cod, squid and prawns, and served with fried bread

FESTIVAL FOOD

Cannoli Fried pastry stuffed with sweet ricotta and candied peel; a Carnevale speciality

Crispelle di riso Sweet rice fritters

Frutti di Martorana Marzipan-based confection shaped and coloured to look like fruit, vegetables, and even fish

Ossa dei morti Literally "dead men's bones", a clove-flavoured, sugared pastry handed out to children on All Hallows' Eve (October 31), and almost identical to *Agnellini pasquali* (Easter lambs)

Sfinci Fried pastry stuffed with ricotta; served at the festival of St Joseph (San Giuseppe)

Torrone di mandorle Crystallized almonds and sugar, sold at markets around All Saints' Day

Zeppole Deep-fried bread dough, stuffed with ricotta and anchovies, or nutella

DRINKS

Acqua minerale Mineral water
Aranciata Orangeade
Bicchiere Glass
Birra Beer
Bottiglia Bottle
Caffè Coffee
Cioccolata calda Hot chocolate
Ghiaccio Ice
Granita Iced coffee/fruit drink
Latte Milk
Limonata Lemonade
Selz Soda water
Spremuta Fresh fruit juice
Spumante Sparkling wine
Succo di frutta Concentrated fruit juice with sugar
Tè Tea
Tonico Tonic water
Vino Wine
Rosso Red
Bianco White
Rosato Rosé
Secco Dry
Dolce Sweet
Litro Litre
Mezzo Half-litre
Quarto Quarter-litre
Salute! Cheers!

GLOSSARIES

ARTISTIC AND ARCHITECTURAL TERMS

Agora Square or marketplace in an ancient Greek city
Apse Domed recess at the altar-end of a church
Architrave The lowest part of the entablature
Atrium Forecourt, usually of a Roman house
Bothros A pit that contains votive offerings
Campanile Belltower
Capital Top of a column
Catalan-Gothic Hybrid form of architecture, mixing -elements from fifteenth-century Spanish and -northern European building styles
Cavea The seating section in a theatre
Cella Sanctuary of a temple
Cupola A dome
Decumanus The main street in a Roman town
Entablature The part of the building above the capital on a classical building
Ex-voto A thanksgiving or offering to a saint – sometimes a plaque, often a silver or pewter body part

Hellenistic period 323–30 BC (Alexander the Great to Augustus)
Hypogeum Underground vault, often used as an early Christian church
Kouros Standing male figure of the Archaic period (700 BC to early fifth century BC)
Krater Ancient conical bowl with round base
Loggia Roofed gallery or balcony
Metope A panel on the frieze of a temple
Naumachia Mock naval combat, or the deep trench in a theatre in which it took place
Nave Central space in a church, usually flanked by aisles
Odeon Small theatre, usually roofed, for recitals
Orchestra Section of the main floor of a theatre, where the chorus danced
Pantocrator Usually refers to Christ, portrayed with outstretched arms
Pediment The triangular front part of a building, -usually surmounting a portico of columns

Polyptych Painting or carving on several joined wooden panels

Portico The covered entrance to a building

Punic Carthaginian/Phoenician

Scene-building Structure holding scenery in Greek/Roman theatre

Stelae Inscribed stone slabs

Stereobate Visible base of any building, usually a temple

Stoa A detached roofed porch, or portico

Stylobate Raised base of a columned building, usually a temple

Telamon A supporting column in the shape of a male figure

Thermae Baths, usually elaborate buildings in Roman villas

Triptych Painting or carving on three joined wooden panels

ITALIAN WORDS

Aliscafo Hydrofoil

Anfiteatro Amphitheatre

Autostazione Bus station

Autostrada Motorway

Belvedere A lookout point

Cappella Chapel

Castello Castle

Cattedrale Cathedral

Centro Centre

Chiesa Church (main "mother" church, Chiesa Matrice/Madre)

Comune An administrative area; also, the local council or the town hall

Corso Avenue/boulevard

Duomo Cathedral

Entrata Entrance

Faraglione Obelisk-shaped deposits of volcanic rock rising out of the sea

Festa Festival, carnival

Fiume River

Fumarola Volcanic vapour emission from the ground

Golfo Gulf

Lago Lake

Largo Place (like piazza)

Lungomare Seafront promenade or road

Mare Sea

Mercato Market

Mongibello Sicilian name for Mount Etna

Municipio Town hall

Palazzo Palace, mansion or block (of flats)

Parco Park

Passeggiata The customary early-evening walk

Pedaggio Toll

Piano Plain (also "slowly", "gently")

Piazza Square

Pineta Pinewood

Pro Loco Local office, usually funded by the *Comune*, overseeing cultural events and providing tourist information

Santuario Sanctuary

Sottopassaggio Subway

Spiaggia Beach

Stazione Station (train station is *stazione ferroviaria*; bus station is *autostazione*; ferry terminal is *stazione marittima*)

Strada Road/street

Teatro Theatre

Tempio Temple

Torre Tower

Traghetto Ferry

Uscita Exit

Vicolo/Vico Alley

Via Road (always used with name, as in Via Roma)

Zona Zone

ACRONYMS

ACI Italian Automobile Club

FS Ferrovie Statali (Italian State Railways)

IVA Imposta Valore Aggiunto (VAT)

RAI The Italian state TV and radio network

SP Strada Provinciale; a minor road, eg SP116

SC Strada Comunale, a road maintained by the local council

SS Strada Statale; a main highway, eg SS120

ZTL Zona di Trafico Limitato – limited access area (eg for residents only)

Small print and index

395 Small print

397 Index

402 Map symbols

A ROUGH GUIDE TO ROUGH GUIDES

Published in 1982, the first Rough Guide – to Greece – was a student scheme that became a publishing phenomenon. Mark Ellingham, a recent graduate in English from Bristol University, had been travelling in Greece the previous summer and couldn't find the right guidebook. With a small group of friends he wrote his own guide, combining a contemporary, journalistic style with a thoroughly practical approach to travellers' needs.

The immediate success of the book spawned a series that rapidly covered dozens of destinations. And, in addition to impecunious backpackers, Rough Guides soon acquired a much broader readership that relished the guides' wit and inquisitiveness as much as their enthusiastic, critical approach and value-for-money ethos. These days, Rough Guides include recommendations from budget to luxury and cover more than 120 destinations around the globe, from Amsterdam to Zanzibar, all regularly updated by our team of roaming writers.

Browse all our latest guides, read inspirational features and book your trip at **roughguides.com**.

Rough Guide credits

Editor: Carine Tracanelli
Cartography: Carte
Managing editor: Rachel Lawrence
Picture editor and cover photo research: Aude Vauconsant

Senior DTP coordinator: Dan May
Head of DTP and Pre-Press: Rebeka Davies
Layout: Ruth Bradley

Publishing information

Eleventh edition 2020

Distribution

UK, Ireland and Europe
Apa Publications (UK) Ltd; sales@roughguides.com
United States and Canada
Ingram Publisher Services; ips@ingramcontent.com
Australia and New Zealand
Woodslane; info@woodslane.com.au
Southeast Asia
Apa Publications (SN) Pte; sales@roughguides.com
Worldwide
Apa Publications (UK) Ltd; sales@roughguides.com
Special Sales, Content Licensing and CoPublishing
Rough Guides can be purchased in bulk quantities at discounted prices. We can create special editions, personalised jackets and corporate imprints tailored to your needs. sales@roughguides.com.
roughguides.com

Printed in Poland by Interak
All rights reserved
© 2020 Apa Digital (CH) AG
License edition © Apa Publications Ltd UK
All rights reserved. No part of this publication may be reproduced, stored in or introduced into a retrieval system, or transmitted in any form, or by any means (electronic, mechanical, photocopying, recording or otherwise) without the prior written permission of the copyright owner.
A catalogue record for this book is available from the British Library
The publishers and authors have done their best to ensure the accuracy and currency of all the information in **The Rough Guide to Sicily**, however, they can accept no responsibility for any loss, injury, or inconvenience sustained by any traveller as a result of information or advice contained in the guide.

Help us update

We've gone to a lot of effort to ensure that this edition of **The Rough Guide to Sicily** is accurate and up-to-date. However, things change – places get "discovered", opening hours are notoriously fickle, restaurants and rooms raise prices or lower standards. If you feel we've got it wrong or left something out, we'd like to know, and if you can remember the address, the price, the hours, the phone number, so much the better.

Please send your comments with the subject line "**Rough Guide Sicily Update**" to mail@uk.roughguides.com. We'll credit all contributions and send a copy of the next edition (or any other Rough Guide if you prefer) for the very best emails.

Readers' updates

Thanks to all the readers who have taken the time to write in with comments and suggestions (and apologies if we've inadvertently omitted or misspelt anyone's name):
Edwina Currie, Erica Owden

ABOUT THE AUTHOR

Ros Belford co-authored the first edition of this guide, and has since written and broadcasted extensively about Italy and the Mediterranean. She lives in Cambridge and spends as much time as she can in Ortigia and on the Aeolian island of Salina.

Photo credits

(Key: T-top; C-centre; B-bottom; L-left; R-right)

Index

A

accommodation 28, 29
  rural 30
  unusual places to stay 30
Aci Castello 196
Acireale 196
Acireale Carnevale 197
Aci Trezza 196
Aeolian Islands 116
Aeschylus 211
Agrigento 9, 276
Aidone 268
airports 23
Akrai 230
  Santoni 231
  Teatro Greco 231
albergo diffuso 291
Alcamo 306
Alcantara gorge 178
Alcantara valley 177
Alicudi 149
Amato, Giacomo 380
Andreotti, Giulio 375
apartments 29
Arab Sicily 362
Archimedes 211
architecture 377
Avola 378

B

Bagarella, Leoluca 375
Bagheria 76, 379
Bagni di Cefalà 81
Balate dei Turchi 354
Baroque architecture 377
bars 33
beaches 39
bed and breakfasts 29
beer 33
Bentinck, William 367
Bergman, Ingrid 143
Berlusconi, Silvio 375
birreria 34
boat rentals 146
boat trips 125, 140, 143, 223
  Siracusa 224
body-rafting 178
Bonagia 323
books 381
Borsellino, Paolo 374
breakfast 31

British in Sicily 367
Bronte 205
Brusca, Giovanni 375
Bugeber 352
Buscemi 232
Buscetta, Tommaso 372
buses
  in Sicily 26
  to Sicily 24

C

cable cars
  Funivia dell'Etna (Mount Etna) 201
  to Erice 321
Caccamo 96
cafés 33
Cala Creta 298
Cala Junco 141
Cala Levante 353
Calatafimi 313, 367
Caltabellotta 294
Caltagirone 270
Caltanissetta 260
camping 30, 196
Campobianco 129
Canneto 129
Caos 286
Capo d'Orlando 107
Capo Graziano 148
Capo Milazzo 111
Caravaggio 215, 222
Carnevale 35
car rental 27
Carthaginians Sicily 359
Casalvecchio Siculo 165
Castelbuono 97
Castel di Lucio 105
Castel di Tusa 104
Castellammare del Golfo 308
Castelmola 176
Castiglione di Sicilia 178
catacombs 9
Catania 182, 378
  accommodation 193
  airport 190
  Anfiteatro Romano 189
  arrival and departure 190
  bars 195
  B&Bs 193
  beach resorts 196
  buses 192, 196
  bus terminal 190

car rental 192
Castello Ursino 188
Ciminiere 190
drinking 195
driving 192
Duomo 185
eating 194
entertainment 195
Fera o Luni market 189
ferries 192
Festa di Sant'Agata 185
history 185
hospital 195
hotels 193
information 193
metro 192
Museo Belliniano 188
Museo Civico 188
Museo del Cinema 190
Museo Diocesano 187
Museo Storico dello Sbarco in Sicilia
  1943 190
nightlife 195
parking 192
Pescheria 187
pharmacies 195
Piazza del Duomo 185
police 195
post office 195
restaurants 194
San Nicolò 189
Sant'Agata al Carcere 189
shopping 194
street food 193
taxis 192
Teatro Romano 188
Terme Achilliane 187
tourist office 193
tours 192
train station 190
transport 192
Via Crociferi 188
Via Etnea 189
Via Vittorio Emanuele II 187
Villa Bellini 190
Zo 190
Cava d'Ispica 239
Cava Grande del Fiume Cassibile
  238
Cave Caolina 130
Cave di Cusa 343
caves 9
Cefalù 88
ceramics 272, 292

Cesarò 260
Charles III 366
Charles of Anjou 365
Charles of Bourbon 366
Chiaramonte Gulfi 249
Chiesa, General Dalla 374
children, travelling with 38
chocolate 242
CIDMA 81
Circumetnea railway 204
climate 10
coffee 32
Comiso airport 249
Corleone 80, 81
costs 39
crime 40, 370
Crispi, Francesco 368
culture 38

D

D'Emanuele, Natale 375
Dionysius II 211
Dionysius the Elder 211
disabilities, travellers with 43
diving
    Aeolian Islands 126, 140
    Lampedusa 298
    Linosa 301
    Ustica 84
doctors 40
Dolci, Danilo 307
Drauto 141
driving
    in Sicily 26, 27, 28, 121
    to Sicily 24

E

earthquakes 6, 157, 208, 211,
    366, 368, 370
Easter 10, 35
economy 6
Egadi Islands 325, 326
electricity 40
Eloro 236
embassies, Italian 23
emergency phone numbers 40
Enna 252
entertainment 37
entry requirements 23
Epipolae 222
Eraclea Minoa 291
Erice 318
etiquette 38
Etna 6, 198
Etna Adventure 203
Etna Nord 200

Etna Sud 201
European Union 370

F

fact file 6
Falcone Borsellino airport 66
Falcone, Giovanni 374
fanghi 132
Favignana 326
Ferdinand IV 366
Ferragosto 36, 163
ferries
    Aeolian Islands 119, 120
    in Sicily 28
    Straits of Messina 162
    to Sicily 24
Ferro, Don Vito Cascio 373
Ferrovia Circumetnea 200
festivals 10, 35, 106, 163, 174,
    197, 231
Ficuzza 80
Filicudi 145
Filicudi Porto 147
films 384
Fiumara d'Arte 105
Fiume Ciane 223
flights
    from Australia and New Zealand 24
    from the UK and Ireland 23
    from the US and Canada 23
    in Sicily 28
Fontanarossa airport 190
food and drink 31, 127, 187
    cookbooks 382
    Sicilian cuisine 32
Forza d'Agrò 166
Forza, Parco Archeologico della
    240
Francavilla di Sicilia 177
Frederick I 364
Frederick II 365
Frutta di Martorana 55
Funivia dell'Etna cable car 201

G

Gadir 353
Gagliardi, Rosario 379
Gangi 102
Ganzirri 164
Garibaldi, Giuseppe 367
Gelso 133
Geraci Siculo 99
Giardini-Naxos 176
Gibellina Nuova 347
Ginostra 144
Giuliano, Salvatore 79, 369

glossaries 392
    trains and buses 26
Godfather, The 164
Gole dell'Alcantara 178
Gole di Tiberio 99
Golfo di Castellammare 304
Grammichele 273, 378
Gran Cratere, the 132
granita 31
Greek mythology in Sicily 269
Greek Sicily 359
Grotta del Bagno Asciutto 356
Grotta del Genovese 329
Gruppo di Scicli 244

H

Halaesa 105
health 40
Hieron I 211
Hieron II 211
hiking 37. See also volcano
    climbing
    Aeolian Islands 135, 147, 148, 150
    Marettimo 331
Himera 95
history 359
history timeline 359
horseriding 38
hostels 30
hotels 29
hydrofoils 28
    Aeolian Islands 120, 121

I

ice cream 8, 31
Iditella 140
industry 370
insurance 40, 41
internet 41
Isola dei Conigli 297
Ispica 239
itineraries 20

K

Khamma-Tracino 353

L

Lago di Pergusa 255
Lampedusa 295, 297
Lampedusa, Giuseppe Tomasi
    di 288
Lampedusa Town 297

language 385
Lawrence. D.H. 171
legends, Aeolian 120
Leggio, Luciano 80, 373
Leni 138
Lentini 197
Leonforte 258
Leontinoi 197
Lercara Friddi 81
Lévanzo 329
LGBTQ travellers 41
Licata 288
Lima, Salvatore 374
Lingua 135
Linosa 301
Lipari 122
literature 383
living in Sicily 41
Luciano, Lucky 373

M

Mafia, the 4, 308, 368, 372
    books about 381
    CIDMA (Corleone) 81
    in Corleone 80, 81
    in Palermo 49, 63
    Museo della Mafia (Salemi) 346
magazines 34
mail 42
Malfa 136
Manfred 364
manna 100
maps 42
    Agrigento 280
    Agrigento and the southwest 278
    Alicudi 149
    Caltagirone 271
    Caltanissetta 261
    Catania 186
    Catania, Etna and around 184
    Cefalù 92
    Cefalù and the Monti Madonie 90
    Central Palermo 52
    Enna 256
    Enna and the interior 254
    Erice 320
    Filicudi 146
    Itineraries 21
    Lampedusa Town 296
    Lipari 122
    Lipari Town 124
    Marsala 335
    Mazara del Vallo 339
    Messina 158
    Messina, Taormina and the
        northeast 156
    Milazzo 111
    Neapolis 221

Noto 233
Ortigia 214
Palazzolo Acreide 230
Palermo 50
Palermo and around 48
Panarea 139
Pantelleria 348
Pantelleria Town 350
Piazza Armerina 263
Ragusa 246
Salina 133
San Vito Lo Capo 324
Sciacca 293
Selinunte and Marinella di
    Selinunte 342
Sicily 5
Siracusa 212
Siracusa and the southeast 210
Stromboli Town 142
Taormina 168
The Aeolian Islands 118
Tindari (Tyndaris) 108
Trapani 314
Trapani and the west 306
Ustica 82
Villa Romana del Casale 266
Vulcano 131
Marettimo 330
Marina di Ragusa 249
Marinella di Selinunte 341
markets 31
    in Catania 187, 189
    in Palermo 54, 58, 62, 71, 73
    in Siracusa 213
Marsala 335
marsala wine 337
Martingana 354
Marzamemi 239
Mazara del Vallo 338
Mazzarò 176
media 34
Messina 156, 368
Messina, Antonello da 366
migrant crisis 370
Milazzo 110, 367
Milò 203
mini-mokes 27
Misteri 315
Mistretta 106
Modica 240, 242
mokes 27
Molino ad Acqua 240
Mondello 74
money 42
Monreale 74
Montagna Grande 355
Montalbano country 245, 287,
    289
Monte Bonifato 307
Monte Inici 308

Monte Pellegrino 64
Monte Pilato 129
Monte Soro 106
Monti Madonie 88
Monti Nebrodi 106
Morgantina 268, 269
Mori, Cesare 368, 373
Motta d'Affermo 105
mountain huts 30
Mount Etna 6, 38, 198, 366
    eruptions 204
Mozia 332
mud baths 132
Mulino ad Acqua Santa Lucia
    231
Mussolini 368

N

Napoleonic Wars 366
Naro 288
Nelson, Horatio 367
newspapers 34
Nicolosi 202
Nicosia 259
Norman Sicily 362
Noto 233, 378
Noto Antica 235
Noto Marina 236
Novara di Sicilia 110

O

Ognina 196
Olympieion 223
opening hours 33, 42
Orlando, Leoluca 375
outdoor activities 37

P

Palazzolo Acreide 229
Palermo 46, 378
    accommodation 68
    Albergheria 54
    arrival and departure 66
    bike rental 68
    buses 66, 67
    bus terminal 67
    cafés 71
    car rental 68
    Catacombe dei Cappuccini 65
    Cattedrale 56
    Convento dei Cappuccini 9
    drinking 72
    driving 67
    eating 70

entertainment 73
Falcone Borsellino airport 66
ferries 67
Festa di Santa Rosalia, La 65
Galleria d'Arte Moderna (GAM) 60
Galleria Regionale della Sicilia 61
horse-drawn carriages 68
hospitals 73
hydrofoils 67
Il Capo 58
Il Gesù 54
information 68
Kalsa, La 61
La Martorana 51
listings information 68
live music venues 73
Magione, La 61
markets 73
Monte Pellegrino 64
Museo Archeologico Regionale 63
Museo d'Arte Contemporanea della
    Sicilia 49
Museo delle Marionette 58
Museo Diocesano 56
Oratorio del Rosario di San
    Domenico 62
Oratorio del Rosario di Santa Zita 62
Oratorio di San Lorenzo 59
orientation 51
Palazzo Abatellis 61
Palazzo Branciforte 59
Palazzo dei Normanni 55
Palazzo Mirto 60
Parco della Favorita 64
parking 67
pharmacies 73
Piaggio Apes 68
Piazza Ballarò market 54
Piazza Bellini 49
Piazza Croce dei Vespri 59
Piazza Marina 60
Piazza Pretoria 49
Piazza XIII Vittime 63
Porta Nuova 56
post office 73
Quattro Canti 48
restaurants 72
San Cataldo 51
San Domenico 62
San Giovanni degli Eremiti 55
San Giuseppe dei Teatini 49
San Nicolò 54
Santa Caterina 50
Sant'Agostino 58
Santa Maria dello Spasimo 61
scooter rental 68
street food 71
taxis 68
Teatro Massimo 64
theatres 73

tourist office 68
tours 68
train station 67
trams 68
Ucciardone Prison 63
Via Garibaldi 58
Via Paternostro 59
Via Roma 58
Vucciria, La 62
waterfront 60
Zisa, La 65
Palma di Montechiaro 288
Panarea 139
Pantalica 9, 228
Pantelleria 348, 349
Parcallario 231
Parco Archeologico della Forza
    240
Parco Avventura 101
Parco Naturale dei Nebrodi 106
Parco Regionale delle Madonie
    97, 98
Patti 107
Pecorini Mare 148
Pelagie Islands 294, 295
Petralia Soprana 100
Petralia Sottana 100
Pettineo 105
pharmacies 40
phones 42
Piana degli Albanesi 79
Piano Battaglia 100
Piano Ghirlanda 355
Piano Zucchi 100
Piazza Armerina 262
Pindar 211
Pirandello, Luigi 279, 286
pistachios 205
pizza 31
Plato 211
police 40
politics 6, 369
Polizzi Generosa 101
Pollara 137
pony-trekking 38
Portella della Ginestra massacre
    79
Porticello 78, 129
Porto di Levante 130
Porto di Ponente 132
Porto Empedocle 286
Portopalo di Capo Passero 239
prawns 187
prehistoric sites 141, 148
Prizzi 81
Provenzano, Bernardo 80, 375
public holidays 36
pubs 34
Punta del Faro 164

Punta Fram 357
Punto Nikà 354
puppet theatre 37
    Acireale 197
    in Palermo 58
    in Siracusa 228

Q

quad bikes 26, 27
Quattrocchi 129

R

radio 34
Ragusa 244, 378
rainfall 10
Rekale 356
restaurants 32, 33
Rifugio Sapienza 201
Riina, Salvatore 80, 375
Rinella 138
Riserva Naturale dello Zingaro
    310, 311
Riserva Naturale di Vendicari 238
Risorgimento, Il 367
river-trekking 178
Rizzoto, Placido 80
Rocche Ciauli 148
Roger I 363
Roger II 363
Roman Sicily 361
Rossellini, Roberto 119
Ruderi di Gibellina 347

S

safety 40
Salemi 346
Salina 133
saltpans 334
Sambuca di Sicilia 294
Sampieri 249
San Calogero 129
San Fratello 106
San Pietro 140
Sant'Agata di Militello 106
Santa Lucia 216
Santa Maria la Scala 196
Santa Marina Salina 133
Sant'Angelo Muxaro 290
Santo Stefano di Camastra 105
San Vito Lo Capo 323
Sataria 356
Savoca 165
Scala dei Turchi 287
Scamozzi, Vincenzo 378

Scauri 356
Sciacca 292
Scicli 243
Scogli dei Ciclopi 195
scooters 26, 27
Scopello 309
Segesta 312
Selinunte 341
Serpotta, Giacomo 380
Sesi, the 357
sexual harassment 38
shopping 39
Siba 355
Sicilian Vespers 365
Simeti, Mary Taylor 307
Sinatra, Vincenzo 380
Siracusa 9, 208
  accommodation 224
  arrival and departure 223
  bars 227
  Basilica di San Giovanni catacombs
    220
  Basilica di Santa Lucia 219
  B&Bs 225
  boat trips 224
  buses 224
  bus terminal 223
  cafés 225
  campsite 225
  Caravaggio 215
  Castello Eurialo 222
  Castello Maniace 218
  drinking 227
  Duomo 215
  eating 225
  entertainment 228
  Fonte Aretusa 216
  Galleria Regionale di Palazzo
    Bellomo 218
  history 210
  hospital 228
  hostels 225
  hotels 225
  information 224
  Ipogeo di Piazza Duomo 215
  Latomia del Paradiso 222
  Latomie dei Cappuccini 222
  mainland 219
  Museo Archeologico Paolo Orsi 219
  Museo del Papiro 218
  Orecchio di Dionisio 222
  Ortigia 213
  Ortigia market 213
  Parco Archeologico della Neapolis
    220
  parking 224
  pharmacies 228
  Piazza Archimede 213

Piazza del Duomo 213
  police 228
  Porto Marina 218
  post office 228
  restaurants 226
  San Martino 218
  Santa Lucia alla Badia 215
  shopping 228
  swimming 219
  taxis 224
  Tempio di Apollo 213
  tours 224
  train station 223
  transport 224
  tunnels 215
  wi-fi 228
skiing 38, 202
snacks 31
Solus 78
souvenirs 39
Spanish Sicily 365
Specchio di Venere 352
Sperlinga 104
spirits 33
Spisone 176
sports 37
Stagnone Islands 332
Straits of Messina 162
Stromboli 38, 142
Stromboli village 143
Sturzo, Don 368

T

Taormina 166
tax 29
taxis 27
tea 32
Tellaro, Villa Romana del 239
temperatures 10
Tiberio, Gole de 99
time 43
Timoleon 211
Tindari 108
Tonnara di Scopello 309
Torre Salsa 288
tourism 6
tourist information 43
tourist offices 43
tour operators 25
trains
  in Sicily 25, 200
  to Sicily 24
transport 23
Trapani 304, 313, 315
Trecastagni 202
Trinacria 365

Troina 259, 260
TV 34

U

UNESCO geopark 88
Ustica 82

V

Vaccarini, Giovanni Battista 380
Valderice 323
Valdichiesa 138
Valle dei Templi 276, 280, 281
Valle Monastero 356
Vendicari, Riserva Naturale di
  238
Vermexio, Giovanni 380
Villaggio Preistorico 141
Villa Romana del Casale 264
Villa Romana del Tellaro 239
villas 29
vineyards 203
Vizzini, Don Calogero 373
volcano climbing
  Etna 198, 202
  Stromboli 145
volcanoes 123, 130, 142, 198
Von Gloeden, Wilhelm 171
Vulcano 130

W

watersports 37
websites 43
Whitaker, Joseph (Pip) 332
Wilde, Oscar 171
William I 363
William II 363
William III 364
wine 33, 34, 203, 337
women travellers 38
words and phrases 385
working in Sicily 41
World War I 368
World War II 369

Z

Zafferana Etnea 202
Zimmari beach 141
Zingaro, Riserva Naturale dello
  310, 311
Zucco Grande 147

Map symbols

The symbols below are used on maps throughout the book

– – –	Chapter boundary	(i)	Tourist information		Petrol station		Museum
	Motorway	⊠	Post office	≂	Pass		Monastery
	Road	⊞	Hospital		Mountain range		Church (regional maps)
	Steps	⊞	Pharmacy	▲	Mountain peak		Church (town maps)
– – – –	Path	P	Parking		Rocks		Building
	Railway	✈	Airport		Gorge		Market
●– – –●	Cable car	★	Bus stop	�	Viewpoint	◯	Stadium
	Ferry/hydrofoil route		Boat tours		Cave		Cemetery
	Wall		Ruins		Campsite		Park
	Point of interest		Fountain		Lighthouse		Beach
@	Internet access	⊠–⊠	Gate/entrance		Tower		

Listings key

■	Accommodation
●	Eating
■	Drinking/nightlife
●	Shopping

YOUR TAILOR-MADE TRIP
STARTS HERE

Tailor-made trips and unique adventures crafted by local experts

Rough Guides has been inspiring travellers with lively and thought-provoking guidebooks for more than 35 years. Now we're linking you up with selected local experts to craft your dream trip. They will put together your perfect itinerary and book it at local rates.

Don't follow the crowd – find your own path.

HOW ROUGHGUIDES.COM/TRIPS WORKS

STEP 1

Pick your dream destination, tell us what you want and submit an enquiry.

STEP 2

Fill in a short form to tell your local expert about your dream trip and preferences.

STEP 3

Our local expert will craft your tailor-made itinerary. You'll be able to tweak and refine it until you're completely satisfied.

STEP 4

Book online with ease, pack your bags and enjoy the trip! Our local expert will be on hand 24/7 while you're on the road.

BENEFITS OF PLANNING AND BOOKING AT ROUGHGUIDES.COM/TRIPS

PLAN YOUR ADVENTURE WITH LOCAL EXPERTS
Rough Guides' English-speaking local experts are hand-picked, based on their experience in the travel industry and their impeccable standards of customer service.

SAVE TIME AND GET ACCESS TO LOCAL KNOWLEDGE
When a local expert plans your trip, you save time and money when you book, even during high season. You won't be charged for using a credit card either.

MAKE TRAVEL A BREEZE: BOOK WITH PIECE OF MIND
Enjoy stress-free travel when you use Rough Guides' secure online booking platform. All bookings come witha money-back guarantee.

WHAT DO OTHER TRAVELLERS THINK ABOUT ROUGH GUIDES TRIPS?

Trip to Spain

This Spain tour company did a fantastic job to make our dream trip perfect. We gave them our travel budget, told them where we would like to go, and they did all of the planning. Our drivers and tour guides were always on time and very knowledgable. The hotel accommodations were better than we would have found on our own. Only one time did we end up in a location that we had not intended to be in. We called the 24 hour phone number, and they immediately fixed the situation.

Don A, USA ★★★★★

Trip to Morocco

Our trip was fantastic! Transportation, accommodations, guides - all were well chosen! The hotels were well situated, well appointed and had helpful, friendly staff. All of the guides we had were very knowledgeable, patient, and flexible with our varied interests in the different sites. We particularly enjoyed the side trip to Tangier! Well done! The itinerary you arranged for us allowed maximum coverage of the country with time in each city for seeing the important places.

Sharon, USA ★★★★★

PLAN AND BOOK YOUR TRIP AT ROUGHGUIDES.COM/TRIPS